Documentary Series

1 *Sherwood Anderson, Willa Cather, John Dos Passos, Theodore Dreiser, F. Scott Fitzgerald, Ernest Hemingway, Sinclair Lewis,* edited by Margaret A. Van Antwerp (1982)

2 *James Gould Cozzens, James T. Farrell, William Faulkner, John O'Hara, John Steinbeck, Thomas Wolfe, Richard Wright,* edited by Margaret A. Van Antwerp (1982)

3 *Saul Bellow, Jack Kerouac, Norman Mailer, Vladimir Nabokov, John Updike, Kurt Vonnegut,* edited by Mary Bruccoli (1983)

4 *Tennessee Williams,* edited by Margaret A. Van Antwerp and Sally Johns (1984)

5 *American Transcendentalists,* edited by Joel Myerson (1988)

6 *Hardboiled Mystery Writers: Raymond Chandler, Dashiell Hammett, Ross Macdonald,* edited by Matthew J. Bruccoli and Richard Layman (1989)

7 *Modern American Poets: James Dickey, Robert Frost, Marianne Moore,* edited by Karen L. Rood (1989)

8 *The Black Aesthetic Movement,* edited by Jeffrey Louis Decker (1991)

9 *American Writers of the Vietnam War: W. D. Ehrhart, Larry Heinemann, Tim O'Brien, Walter McDonald, John M. Del Vecchio,* edited by Ronald Baughman (1991)

10 *The Bloomsbury Group,* edited by Edward L. Bishop (1992)

11 *American Proletarian Culture: The Twenties and The Thirties,* edited by Jon Christian Suggs (1993)

12 *Southern Women Writers: Flannery O'Connor, Katherine Anne Porter, Eudora Welty,* edited by Mary Ann Wimsatt and Karen L. Rood (1994)

13 *The House of Scribner, 1846-1904,* edited by John Delaney (1996)

14 *Four Women Writers for Children, 1868-1918,* edited by Caroline C. Hunt (1996)

15 *American Expatriate Writers: Paris in the Twenties,* edited by Matthew J. Bruccoli and Robert W. Trogdon (1997)

16 *The House of Scribner, 1905-1930,* edited by John Delaney (1997)

17 *The House of Scribner, 1931-1984,* edited by John Delaney (1998)

18 *British Poets of The Great War: Sassoon, Graves, Owen,* edited by Patrick Quinn (1999)

19 *James Dickey,* edited by Judith S. Baughman (1999)

See also DLB 210, 216, 219, 222, 224

Yearbooks

1980 edited by Karen L. Rood, Jean W. Ross, and Richard Ziegfeld (1981)

1981 edited by Karen L. Rood, Jean W. Ross, and Richard Ziegfeld (1982)

1982 edited by Richard Ziegfeld; associate editors: Jean W. Ross and Lynne C. Zeigler (1983)

1983 edited by Mary Bruccoli and Jean W. Ross; associate editor Richard Ziegfeld (1984)

1984 edited by Jean W. Ross (1985)

1985 edited by Jean W. Ross (1986)

1986 edited by J. M. Brook (1987)

1987 edited by J. M. Brook (1988)

1988 edited by J. M. Brook (1989)

1989 edited by J. M. Brook (1990)

1990 edited by James W. Hipp (1991)

1991 edited by James W. Hipp (1992)

1992 edited by James W. Hipp (1993)

1993 edited by James W. Hipp, contributing editor George Garrett (1994)

1994 edited by James W. Hipp, contributing editor George Garrett (1995)

1995 edited by James W. Hipp, contributing editor George Garrett (1996)

1996 edited by Samuel W. Bruce and L. Kay Webster, contributing editor George Garrett (1997)

1997 edited by Matthew J. Bruccoli and George Garrett, with the assistance of L. Kay Webster (1998)

1998 edited by Matthew J. Bruccoli, contributing editor George Garrett, with the assistance of D. W. Thomas (1999)

1999 edited by Matthew J. Bruccoli, contributing editor George Garrett, with the assistance of D. W. Thomas (2000)

Concise Series

Concise Dictionary of American Literary Biography, 7 volumes (1988-1999): *The New Consciousness, 1941-1968; Colonization to the American Renaissance, 1640-1865; Realism, Naturalism, and Local Color, 1865-1917; The Twenties, 1917-1929; The Age of Maturity, 1929-1941; Broadening Views, 1968-1988; Supplement: Modern Writers, 1900-1998.*

Concise Dictionary of British Literary Biography, 8 volumes (1991-1992): *Writers of the Middle Ages and Renaissance Before 1660; Writers of the Restoration and Eighteenth Century, 1660-1789; Writers of the Romantic Period, 1789-1832; Victorian Writers, 1832-1890; Late-Victorian and Edwardian Writers, 1890-1914; Modern Writers, 1914-1945; Writers After World War II, 1945-1960; Contemporary Writers, 1960 to Present.*

Concise Dictionary of World Literary Biography, 20 volumes projected (1999-   ): *Ancient Greek and Roman Writers; German Writers; African, Carribbean, and Latin-American Writers.*

Dictionary of Literary Biography® • Volume Two Hundred Twenty-Eight

Twentieth-Century American Dramatists
Second Series

Twentieth-Century American Dramatists
Second Series

Edited by
Christopher J. Wheatley
The Catholic University of America

A Bruccoli Clark Layman Book
The Gale Group
Detroit • San Francisco • London • Boston • Woodbridge, Conn.

Printed in the United States of America

The paper used in this publication meets the minimum requirements
of American National Standard for Information Sciences–Permanence
Paper for Printed Library Materials, ANSI Z39.48-1984. ∞™

ISBN 0-7876-3137-X

10 9 8 7 6 5 4 3 2 1

For Barbara, because she insisted

Contents

Plan of the Series

. . . Almost the most prodigious asset of a country, and perhaps its most precious possession, is its native literary product—when that product is fine and noble and enduring.

Mark Twain*

The advisory board, the editors, and the publisher of the *Dictionary of Literary Biography* are joined in endorsing Mark Twain's declaration. The literature of a nation provides an inexhaustible resource of permanent worth. We intend to make literature and its creators better understood and more accessible to students and the reading public, while satisfying the standards of teachers and scholars.

To meet these requirements, *literary biography* has been construed in terms of the author's achievement. The most important thing about a writer is his writing. Accordingly, the entries in *DLB* are career biographies, tracing the development of the author's canon and the evolution of his reputation.

The purpose of *DLB* is not only to provide reliable information in a convenient format but also to place the figures in the larger perspective of literary history and to offer appraisals of their accomplishments by qualified scholars.

The publication plan for *DLB* resulted from two years of preparation. The project was proposed to Bruccoli Clark by Frederick G. Ruffner, president of the Gale Research Company, in November 1975. After specimen entries were prepared and typeset, an advisory board was formed to refine the entry format and develop the series rationale. In meetings held during 1976, the publisher, series editors, and advisory board approved the scheme for a comprehensive biographical dictionary of persons who contributed to North American literature. Editorial work on the first volume began in January 1977, and it was published in 1978. In order to make *DLB* more than a reference tool and to compile volumes that individually have claim to status as literary history, it was decided to organize volumes by

From an unpublished section of Mark Twain's autobiography, copyright by the Mark Twain Company

topic, period, or genre. Each of these freestanding volumes provides a biographical-bibliographical guide and overview for a particular area of literature. We are convinced that this organization—as opposed to a single alphabet method—constitutes a valuable innovation in the presentation of reference material. The volume plan necessarily requires many decisions for the placement and treatment of authors who might properly be included in two or three volumes. In some instances a major figure will be included in separate volumes, but with different entries emphasizing the aspect of his career appropriate to each volume. Ernest Hemingway, for example, is represented in *American Writers in Paris, 1920–1939* by an entry focusing on his expatriate apprenticeship; he is also in *American Novelists, 1910–1945* with an entry surveying his entire career, as well as in *American Short-Story Writers, 1910–1945, Second Series* with an entry concentrating on his short stories. Each volume includes a cumulative index of the subject authors and articles. Comprehensive indexes to the entire series are planned.

Since 1981 the series has been further augmented by the *DLB Yearbooks,* which update published entries and add new entries to keep the *DLB* current with contemporary activity. There have also been *DLB Documentary Series* volumes which provide biographical and critical source materials for figures whose work is judged to have particular interest for students. One of these companion volumes is devoted entirely to Tennessee Williams.

We define literature as the *intellectual commerce of a nation:* not merely as belles lettres but as that ample and complex process by which ideas are generated, shaped, and transmitted. *DLB* entries are not limited to "creative writers" but extend to other figures who in their time and in their way influenced the mind of a people. Thus the series encompasses historians, journalists, publishers, book collectors, and screenwriters. By this means readers of *DLB* may be aided to perceive literature not as cult scripture in the keeping of intellectual high priests but firmly positioned at the center of a nation's life.

DLB includes the major writers appropriate to each volume and those standing in the ranks behind them. Scholarly and critical counsel has been sought in deciding which minor figures to include and how full their entries should be. Wherever possible, useful references are made to figures who do not warrant separate entries.

Each *DLB* volume has an expert volume editor responsible for planning the volume, selecting the figures for inclusion, and assigning the entries. Volume editors are also responsible for preparing, where appropriate, appendices surveying the major periodicals and literary and intellectual movements for their volumes, as well as lists of further readings. Work on the series as a whole is coordinated at the Bruccoli Clark Layman editorial center in Columbia, South Carolina, where the editorial staff is responsible for accuracy and utility of the published volumes.

One feature that distinguishes *DLB* is the illustration policy—its concern with the iconography of literature. Just as an author is influenced by his surroundings, so is the reader's understanding of the author enhanced by a knowledge of his environment. Therefore *DLB* volumes include not only drawings, paintings, and photographs of authors, often depicting them at various stages in their careers, but also illustrations of their families and places where they lived. Title pages are regularly reproduced in facsimile along with dust jackets for modern authors. The dust jackets are a special feature of *DLB* because they often document better than anything else the way in which an author's work was perceived in its own time. Specimens of the writers' manuscripts and letters are included when feasible.

Samuel Johnson rightly decreed that "The chief glory of every people arises from its authors." The purpose of the *Dictionary of Literary Biography* is to compile literary history in the surest way available to us—by accurate and comprehensive treatment of the lives and work of those who contributed to it.

The *DLB* Advisory Board

Introduction

While there was socially and financially significant theatrical activity in the United States during the nineteenth century, few American plays from prior to 1900 were remembered—and still fewer staged—by the end of the twentieth century. In fact, there is little drama in English from most of the eighteenth and nineteenth centuries that is still considered producible, or readable, whatever its country of origin. For every Oliver Goldsmith or Richard Brinsley Sheridan, there are many forgotten playwrights from these centuries who were successful in their own day and are now consigned to oblivion.

Few playwrights find a lasting place in the dramatic canon unless they are wildly popular, superlatively gifted, or consistently innovative, and some cultural factors militated against theatrical innovation by nineteenth-century playwrights. The star system, for instance, curbed actors' and audiences' desire for new plays, because actors were significantly more important to the public than the parts they performed. The partisanship that fans showed stars in the mid nineteenth century has been unequaled in any other historical period. In 1849 the admirers of American actor Edwin Forrest, who was feuding with English actor W. C. Macready, rioted in Astor Place in New York City. The militia called in to quell the riot killed 31 and wounded 150. In the late nineteenth and early twentieth centuries James O'Neill (the father of Eugene O'Neill) was associated with the role of Edmond Dantès in *The Count of Monte Cristo*. A sure moneymaker, it became an artistic trap because audiences seemed not to want him to play any other. Even widely admired stars such as Edwin Booth (1833–1893) and Charlotte Cushman (1816–1876), who had a large and varied repertory, repeated some roles regularly, because the audience expected certain signature pieces. Other actors performed only in roles that they felt suited them, limiting the playwrights to certain "lines": leading man or lady, ingenue, soubrette. The twentieth-century parallel is the Hollywood star system of the midcentury; Jimmy Cagney once complained that if William Shakespeare were alive, Hollywood producers would require him to write a scene in which Cagney came through the door with a gun in his hand.

An increasing ability to stage spectacle also shifted the focus of nineteenth-century drama from dialogue to visual effects. The theater of that period could stage showstoppers such as a steamboat embarking, bursting into flames, and sinking. The elevator at the Madison Square Theatre in 1880 allowed the changing of an entire set in forty seconds. Even when audiences demand new plays—as they did at the end of the nineteenth century and the beginning of the twentieth century—the conservative preference of producers and stars has always been for plays that conform to existing types. It is cheaper and less risky to stage an established play than a new work.

It is clearly not the case that nineteenth-century playwrights are forgotten because of poor theatrical craftsmanship. Audiences do not throw their money away on badly constructed drama, nor did their plays avoid serious themes. Slavery, immigration, oppression of Native Americans, economic hardship—all of the tensions of a growing society—were dramatized on the nineteenth-century American stage. Nevertheless, the chief theatrical styles of the period make the plays seem dated. Serious drama was largely confined to melodrama, which assumes a clear demarcation between good and evil, while comedy presented characters who were natively good in opposition to figures who were vicious only insofar as they were corrupted by false (that is, European) sophistication.

The only two American playwrights of the nineteenth century whose plays are still performed with any regularity exemplify the skills of their contemporaries and limitations of their plays. The Irish-American playwright Dion Boucicault's plays show the strengths and weaknesses of melodrama. *The Octoroon* (1859) was successful in the North and the South on the eve of the Civil War, because to a northern audience it showed the hardships of slavery, while a southern audience saw the relationship between slave and master as essentially familial and the hardship within the system as a consequence of individual vice rather than systemic evil. Anna Cora Ogden Mowatt's *Fashion* (1845) is a witty comedy of manners in which rugged American virtues triumph over the affectations of the newly rich. The plays of Boucicault and Mowatt are still theatrically effective, but the closest imitations of them are found on television.

In both serious and comic drama, plays were shaped, consciously or not, by the conventions of the well-made play—a translation of the French *pièce bien faite* and associated with the French playwrights Eugène Scribe (1791–1861) and Victorien Sardou (1831–1908), among others. Such plays begin with detailed exposition and add further complications leading to crises, with each act closing on a climactic curtain. All strands of the plot are neatly tied up at the end.

The rise of realism in the nineteenth century, first associated with the novel, reinvigorated European drama. The conventions of realism in drama include nondeclamatory dialogue, middle- and lower-class characters in plausible crises, an avoidance of coincidence in plots, and an invisible fourth wall, through which the audience watches a slice of life. Improved lighting in the theater made it possible, and to some extent necessary, for set designers to create drawing rooms and tenement flats that closely resembled the places in which the audience lived. Writers committed themselves to showing that the upper classes were not the only source of theatrical interest and that ordinary lives could be rich in dramatic incident. Of course, even in realist drama people do not talk as they do off the stage, nor does the plot mirror the daily boredom of most lives. Yet, the conventions of realism reflect a shift in assumptions about human nature.

In particular Norwegian playwright Henrik Ibsen (1828–1906) and Russian playwright Anton Chekhov (1860–1904) introduced middle- and lower-class characters struggling with social expectations, economic constraints, and, at times, inherited traits. For example, in James A. Herne's *Margaret Fleming* (1890), usually regarded as the beginning of American realist drama, a character who never appears onstage, Lena Schmidt, dies while having an illegitimate child, and Doctor Larkin stresses, "She's a product of her environment. Under present social conditions. She'd probably have gone wrong anyhow." Several factors extrinsic to drama led to the rise of realism. Karl Marx explained human behavior in economic terms; Emile Durkheim called it a function of social conditioning; Sigmund Freud said it was shaped by psychological conflicts engendered in childhood; and, although Charles Darwin was hesitant, evolutionists who followed him explained it from the perspective of biological inheritance. If actions are determined rather than freely chosen, the moral standings of individuals become ambiguous because they cease to bear responsibility for their actions, however necessary it may be for society to assign blame.

In Aristotle's *Poetics* tragedy is defined as an imitation of an action of magnitude. The protagonist commits *hamartia,* a term from archery that means "to miss the mark." Because Aristotle uses *hubris,* an action committed from overweening pride, as an example, *hamartia* came to be seen as a tragic flaw rather than the tragic mistake that Aristotle may have intended. Well before the twentieth century, tragedy involved a flawed protagonist—above most men in status and ability—who violates divine and natural order and is punished for it. Fate determines the outcome, but the character is nevertheless responsible for his actions. Macbeth may be duped by the weird sisters, but he is still not supposed to kill his king. Tragedy becomes problematic in realism, not only because the protagonist lacks stature but because he is as much a victim as he is a perpetrator. Willie Loman, in Arthur Miller's *The Death of a Salesman* (1949), is unfaithful to his wife and tries to force his sons into the same kind of life that eventually leads him to suicide. He is like King Lear, more sinned against than sinning, but Lear acts against the advice of his fool and Kent, while Willie is incapable of seeing his error because he is the product of American capitalism. The cause of the catastrophe in Miller's play is American consumerism and contempt for manual labor; the only enlightenment is Biff's realization that people like him and his father are a dime a dozen.

The conventions of comedy as a dramatic genre survived realism: happy endings and weddings continued to mark the restoration of social order. But even in comedy, realism shifted the source of humor. American critic Kenneth Burke wrote that in the comic universe, problems occur because people make mistakes, but in the tragic universe things go wrong because of fate. That is, in comedy things ultimately turn out well because the universe is moving toward the end that God has designed for it; after all, Dante called his epic, which begins in hell and ends in paradise, the *Commedia.* As Travis Bogard has pointed out, Thornton Wilder may have been the last important American playwright to believe in just such a teleological universe. Granted the realist view by which character is the product of environment and the fact that belief in a divine plan is difficult for some to sustain, genre boundaries become blurred. Chekhov regarded his plays as comedies, while Konstantin Stanislavsky (1863–1938), founder of what Americans call "method acting," regarded the same plays as tragedies.

For many writers of realist comic drama the protagonist is nearly as much a victim of larger forces as the doomed characters in the tragic plays of Arthur Miller and Tennessee Williams. Only the effects of environmental forces are less catastrophic. In Neil Simon's comedy *The Odd Couple* (1965) Oscar is as incapable as Brick in Tennessee Williams's *A Cat on a Hot Tin Roof* (1955) of having a meaningful relationship with a woman. Brick is tragic because Maggie suffers from his indifference and because ultimately the "no neck monsters" will inherit and control enormous wealth, a guarantee that crassness and cruelty will continue to dominate the Delta. *The Odd Couple* is a comedy not only because Simon supplies his usual number of funny gag lines but also because Oscar's wife is much better off without him and because he is only dimly aware that his existence is a stereotype of male insensitivity.

Whether in comedy or tragedy, character ceases to be transparent in realist drama. That is, in melodrama the motivations of characters, good or bad, are perfectly clear. The hero may be motivated by love or altruism, but the motivation is not problematic. The villain is greedy, and that greed is a character flaw, not a consequence of a deprived childhood or faulty socialization. In realism, however, characters' avowed motivations must be analyzed by the audience, not necessarily because the characters are lying, but because the characters are themselves unaware of why they act as they do. In Eugene O'Neill's *The Iceman Cometh* (1946) the characters make their lives bearable through whisky and "pipe dreams," the illusions that they can resume normal lives. Each character can see through the other characters' self-deceptions, but not through his or her own. The central character, Hickey, begins a process of stripping away the illusions of the characters so that all may be at peace with their utter lack of any future, but he also hides from himself the central truth that he murdered his wife out of hate rather than love. The realist dramatist reveals the forces that shape personality and the extraordinary difficulty of changing behavior.

It is important to stress, however, that realism allows room for agency. The character is shaped by his environment but not entirely determined by it. Where behavior is entirely determined by environment, realism blends into naturalism. In naturalism characters are buffeted by forces in a hostile universe, with only the illusion of free will. In realism characters interact with their environment, are produced by it, but remain capable of changing it as well. Elmer Rice's *Street Scene* (1929) is an example of how difficult it is to draw a line between realism and naturalism. In a "mean quarter" of New York, various characters from the working poor talk on the front stoop of their tenement. They represent a variety of ethnic stereotypes, from socialist Jew to opera-loving Italian ice-cream vendor. The culmination of the action occurs when Frank Maurrant, a jealous and violent Irishman, in a drunken rage, murders his unfaithful wife and her lover. As the police take him away, he tells his daughter not to let his son grow up like him. For his daughter, Rose, the choice seems clear; she and her brother, Willie, must leave the hostile streets of New York. But Willie is already showing signs of his father's violence and misogyny; Rose has no money and little education; and she has only her determination to oppose a world that has no interest in her fate.

In the United States the primary subject of realist drama has been the family. While American realist drama does examine social and political issues, it usually does so through their effect on a family. In the United States the family is a more important organizational unit than it is in most European countries. The influence of the state in twentieth-century Europe is much more pervasive than in the United States. Historically, Americans distrust the state. The American family does not merely reflect the strains of the larger society but is regarded as the basis of the larger society.

While there were more than two thousand professional theater companies scattered around the United States in the nineteenth century, by the early twentieth century New York City had achieved significant control of original drama, as The Syndicate (run by Charles Frohman) and the Shubert Organization controlled booking rights at hundreds of theaters from coast to coast. The rest of the country saw touring companies from New York and amateur productions. Competition from the movies, which had much lower ticket prices, and radio caused a further decline in the number of non-movie theaters between 1920 and 1930, from around 1,500 to 500. Gerald M. Berkowitz points out that the dominance of New York was connected to the centrality of realism as the chief dramatic idiom of American theater. The characters in drama came from the same world as their audience: the urban middle class, stretching from blue-collar workers to middle managers. There are, of course, many exceptions, from historical subjects in the plays of Maxwell Anderson to the country settings employed by many playwrights.

But the New York monopoly underscores the creative tension between commerce and artistic aspiration that makes even the greatest achievements of American drama suspect with some critics. As in England (and unlike countries such as France and Germany, where patronage, first by the court and then by the state, subsidized the production of plays), the American theater is primarily profit driven, although patronage played a significant role in early-nineteenth-century American drama and public funding was important to regional theater in the second half of the twentieth century. The linkage of art and economics does not necessarily work against aesthetic achievement. Shakespeare's company was also motivated by profits, and every major American playwright has been a commercial as well as an artistic success. Nevertheless, Broadway producers who risk their own money in hopes of a long run look for plays that resemble previous successes. This desire for sure hits aided the dominance of realism. Even the Playwrights' Company, formed by Maxwell Anderson, S. N. Behrman, Sidney Howard, Elmer Rice, and Robert E. Sherwood in 1938, was largely motivated by the reduced production opportunities caused by the Great Depression. Although they produced many good plays, the Playwrights' Company attempted to write and sought from other playwrights plays that would have long runs in large theaters.

Yet, neither in Europe nor America did realism monopolize the stage. In fact many playwrights who are now regarded as realists did not regard themselves as such. Tennessee Williams repeatedly wrote that realism was too narrow as a dramatic genre. Before winning his Nobel Prize in 1936, Eugene O'Neill wrote plays that are relentlessly experimental. His beginnings as a playwright illustrate the ways in which an original vision in American drama is incorporated into the mainstream theater, becomes widely known, and influences subsequent playwrights. Among the European movements that reacted against theatrical realism was Expressionism. It is usually associated with German playwrights Georg Kaiser (1878–1945) and Ernst Toller (1893–1939), although both wrote in other styles as well. In Expressionism the narrative does not emphasize causality, as it does in realism, and the action and set reveal the emotional and spiritual experience of a central character. Thematically the genre attacks the dehumanizing aspects of capitalism.

O'Neill began his career with the amateur but theatrically high-minded Provincetown Players, who started producing their own plays, first on Cape Cod and then in Greenwich Village. The chief playwrights in the group quickly became O'Neill and Susan Glaspell. O'Neill's first plays, drawing on his experiences as a sailor, feature a dreamlike atmosphere alien to realism. Plays such as *The Emperor Jones* (1920) and *The Hairy Ape* (1922) are expressionist works. The former is a journey into the subconscious of an erstwhile porter who has become dictator of his own island. The latter, which uses masks, follows the destruction of a physically powerful but barely articulate stoker by an indifferent society. Critics recognized from the beginning that O'Neill was a powerful and original voice who had little in common with most of his contemporaries. The commercial theater has always had a genius for incorporating new movements. O'Neill's plays were successful enough that he was soon writing for the Broadway stage, an arrangement that was not merely more lucrative than his work for the Provincetown Players but also brought his works to the attention of a wider audience.

The Theatre Guild began as the Washington Square Players. After World War I the group produced German Expressionist plays and premiered plays by George Bernard Shaw (1856–1950). A realist, Shaw managed to write commercially successful drama that also explicitly dealt with complex ideas. As such he appealed to the desire of the Theatre Guild for intellectually challenging drama. Soon the group was introducing the most interesting, and, in the long run, important playwrights on Broadway. By the 1930s the Theatre Guild was successful and establishment, and theatrical revolutionaries felt the need to move on. The Group Theatre was founded in 1931 by Harold Clurman and Lee Strasberg (former members of the Theatre Guild) to produce politically conscious drama by an actors' collective, avoiding bourgeois drama and star-centered acting. Although remarkably short-lived, the Group Theatre is notable for featuring an acting style (The Method, based on Stanislavsky's ideas) that remains important in American actor training. Several actors, notably John Garfield and Franchot Tone, were discovered in Group Theatre productions and moved to Hollywood. Elia Kazan, who was perhaps the most important American director in the American theater of the mid twentieth century, was an alumnus of the Group Theatre. John Howard Lawson, a Group Theatre playwright, went on to some success in the commercial theater and Hollywood. Clifford Odets, who also went on to Hollywood, began with the Group Theatre and is still regarded as one of the most significant American playwrights.

The political nature of the Group Theatre and its disruption of the conventions of the fourth wall—for instance, in Odets's *Waiting for Lefty* (1935) the audience is drawn into the play to chant "Strike!" at the end—shows the influence of Bertolt Brecht (1898–1956). In Epic Theatre nonrealistic staging practices or alienation effects emphasize the artificial nature of the theater rather than appealing to theatrical illusion and force the audience to judge the characters rather than identify with them. Moreover, the political and economic structure is shown not to be natural but, like a play, a construction designed to maintain the status quo. Of course, theatrical experimentation was perfectly possible without any ulterior political purpose, and indeed the Modernist credo "Make it new" required attempts at theatrical innovation. Gertrude Stein's plays are formal experiments similar to those in the poetry of T. S. Eliot or the paintings of Pablo Picasso.

The authorial progression from small experimental theater rejecting the large-scale commercial drama of Broadway, to public recognition, to writing for Broadway became a common occurrence in the course of the twentieth century. (Although it was possible for a playwright to go straight to Broadway and become an overnight success, as was the case with Elmer Rice, who made it big with his first play, *On Trial,* in 1914). While the large stages of New York dominated American theater for the first half of the twentieth century, in Ireland the Abbey Theatre had shown that great drama could be produced in a small house on a limited budget. The Little Theatre Movement, which featured amateur performers in serious drama, grew steadily after the Irish Players toured the United States in 1911. Chicago (1912), Fargo (1912), Madison (1911), and Providence (1909) founded community theaters. By 1920 there were fifty such groups, and by World War II more than one hundred. The Barter Theatre in Abingdon, Virginia, has managed to remain open since 1933. Ethnic groups, colleges and universities, and labor or women's rights organizations also staged plays, providing venues for aspiring playwrights. There were also theaters for the immigrant communities in cities such as New York and Chicago, where non-English-language drama was regularly presented.

In the 1950s and 1960s there was an explosion of professional theater groups in the United States. In New York, Off-Broadway, Off-Off-Broadway, and the Shakespeare Festival provided venues for plays that were too experimental for the large commercial houses. Regional theaters were founded, including Arena Stage in Washington, D.C., Actors Workshop in San Francisco, Seattle Repertory, the Guthrie Theater in Minneapolis, Steppenwolf in Chicago, and Yale Repertory Theater. Edward Albee and Sam Shepard are just two of the playwrights who broke through to critical and popular acclaim from the avant-garde stages of New York, while David Mamet, Marsha Norman, and August Wilson are among the many playwrights whose works were first produced at regional theaters.

Regional theaters frequently lack the typical proscenium-arch structure that has dominated the English and American theater from the middle of the eighteenth century. The proscenium arch was conducive to realist drama because it created the invisible fourth wall through which the audience observed the action. The thrust stages (where the audience partially surrounds the action, as in Shakespeare's Globe) and arena staging (where the audience completely surrounds the acting space) encourage more audience and production interaction, partially because the audience can see other audience members beyond the actors. Moreover, the elaborate sets of realism are impractical on these stages because large stage properties would interfere with sight lines.

The rise of regional and Off-Broadway theaters corresponds with the rise of what William Demastes has called the New Realism, in which the causal explanations of realism are problematic. In Edward Albee's *Zoo Story* (1959), when the mysterious Jerry tells the upper-middle-class Peter that he walked up from Washington Square, Peter says "Oh: you live in the Village," and the stage directions say, "This seems to enlighten Peter." Jerry responds, "What were you trying to do? Make sense out of things? Bring order? The old pigeonhole bit?" Peter explains Jerry to himself in terms of Jerry's environment, the bohemian life of Greenwich Village, while Jerry's response denies the adequacy of such an explanation. Unlike the Absurdist drama of Samuel Beckett (1906–1989), in which characters exist on a stage divorced from any social context or divine or natural order, there are plenty of reasons for why Jerry is a threatening and alienated loner: his mother's desertion, his father's early death, and his own confused sexuality in a homophobic society. Nevertheless, there remains a gap between cause and effect, a gap subsequently emphasized by Shepard, Norman, and Mamet. Alternately, in Beth Henley's *Crimes of the Heart* (1979) the behavior of the sisters is overdetermined. There are too many reasons for Babe to shoot her husband and try to kill herself, and the revelation of underlying causes is frankly comic.

To some extent a New York production still implies critical validation, and the large theaters in New York are more profitable for a playwright than any regional house can be. Nevertheless, since around 1960 the majority of important new American plays have come from the regional theaters. The cost of putting on a new play in New York is astronomical: the price of tickets is high; competition from other forms of entertainment intense; and, consequently, the chance of expensive failure great. Producers tend to gravitate toward musicals that cost millions, because they may actually return millions. Regional theaters provide the most sensible alternative for the development of serious drama because they have lower costs and rarely attempt to turn a profit. The National Endowment for the Humanities, private foundations, and community contributions all help in the production of plays that would not be viable in a two-thousand-seat theater. For example, Robert Schenkkan's *The Kentucky Cycle* (1991) began with workshop production at the Mark Taper Forum in Los Angeles, premiered full-length as nine related one-act plays at Seattle's Intiman Theatre, and returned to the Mark Taper Forum; it was awarded the Pulitzer Prize for drama in 1992. In New York the cycle was turned into a two-night performance and bombed. Though New York reviewers had several other criticisms of the play, the length was clearly a problem. The comparatively small size of regional theaters allows for diversity in presentation if only because fewer bodies are necessary to fill the seats, but a large house in New York—such as the Royale Theatre, which seats 1,100— must be close to full night after night for the run to be successful. Yet, the success or failure in New York of a play such as *The Kentucky Cycle* is largely irrelevant to the long-term reputation of the play.

While women playwrights such as Mary Chase and Anne Nichols have long been among the most successful playwrights on Broadway, the regional theaters established since the 1960s have increased the voices of previously marginalized groups in the theater. African American, Asian American, Latino, and gay playwrights have achieved wider audiences than was possible in the first half of the century. In a sense the increasing recognition of the heterogeneity of American society is mirrored in the overt politicization of drama made possible by small, nonprofit theaters.

Above all, as the following biographical essays demonstrate, any generalizations about American drama must be carefully qualified, for in the last one hundred years almost any kind of drama one could imagine has appeared on a stage somewhere in the United States, from the frankly sentimental and patriotic comedies of George M. Cohan to the Happenings of the 1960s. Perhaps the best sentimental comedy in American drama, *Ah Wilderness!* (1933), was written by the most unlikely of authors, the chronically depressed and unrepentantly alcoholic Eugene O'Neill. Musicals alone run the gamut of forms from vaudeville to realism to farce. Whether one thinks of morality plays or courtroom dramas, commedia dell'arte or the theater of blood, virtually any genre of drama in world history has received new form in the work of some American dramatist. The purpose of this series of entries on American dramatists is partially to make available in a convenient form biographical information on the playwrights and partially to remind readers and the theater community of playwrights who are forgotten. There is a lengthy tradition in the United States of prophesying the death of the theater. Somehow "the Splendid Invalid" continues to limp along. In the twenty-first century new playwrights will doubtless come along and achieve critical and public success. Then most will fade from the stage, while a few will write plays that will continue to be performed into the twenty-second century. At that time some critics will still be predicting the death of the theater.

—Christopher J. Wheatley

Acknowledgments

This book was produced by Bruccoli Clark Layman, Inc. Karen L. Rood is senior editor. Tracy Simmons Bitonti was the in-house editor.

Production manager is Philip B. Dematteis.

Administrative support was provided by Ann M. Cheschi, Dawnca T. Williams, and Mary A. Womble.

Accountant is Kathy Weston. Accounting assistant is Amber L. Coker.

Copyediting supervisor is Phyllis A. Avant. Senior copyeditor is Thom Harman. The copyediting staff includes Brenda Carol Blanton, James Denton, Melissa D. Hinton, William Tobias Mathes, Jennifer S. Reid, and Nancy E. Smith. Freelance copy editor is Rebecca Mayo.

Editorial associates are Margo Dowling and Richard K. Galloway.

Layout and graphics supervisor is Janet E. Hill. The graphics staff includes Karla Corley Brown and Zoe R. Cook.

Office manager is Kathy Lawler Merlette.

Photography editors are Charles Mims, Scott Nemzek, and Paul Talbot.

Digital photography supervisor is Joseph M. Bruccoli. Digital photographic copy work was performed by Zoe R. Cook and Abraham R. Layman.

SGML supervisor is Cory McNair. The SGML staff includes Tim Bedford, Linda Drake, Frank Graham, and Alex Snead.

Systems manager is Marie L. Parker.

Typesetting supervisor is Kathleen M. Flanagan. The typesetting staff includes Kimberly Kelly Brantley, Mark J. McEwan, Patricia Flanagan Salisbury, and Alison Smith. Freelance typesetters are Wanda Adams and Delores Plastow.

Walter W. Ross did library research. He was assisted by Steven Gross and the following librarians at the Thomas Cooper Library of the University of South Carolina: circulation department head Tucker Taylor; reference department head Virginia W. Weathers; Brette Barclay, Marilee Birchfield, Paul Cammarata, Gary Geer, Michael Macan, Tom Marcil, Rose Marshall, and Sharon Verba; interlibrary loan department head John Brunswick; and Robert Arndt, Jo Cottingham, Hayden Battle, Barry Bull, Marna Hostetler, Nelson Rivera, Marieum McClary, and Erika Peake, interlibrary loan staff.

Twentieth-Century American Dramatists
Second Series

Dictionary of Literary Biography

Maxwell Anderson

(15 December 1888 – 28 February 1959)

Barbara Lee Horn
St. John's University

See also the Anderson entry in *DLB 7: Twentieth-Century American Dramatists.*

PLAY PRODUCTIONS: *White Desert,* New York, Princess Theatre, 18 October 1923;

What Price Glory, by Anderson and Laurence Stallings, New York, Plymouth Theatre, 5 September 1924;

Outside Looking In, adapted from Jim Tully's novel *Beggars of Life,* New York, Greenwich Village Theatre, 7 September 1925;

First Flight, by Anderson and Stallings, New York, Plymouth Theatre, 17 September 1925;

The Buccaneer, by Anderson and Stallings, New York, Plymouth Theatre, 2 October 1925;

Saturday's Children, New York, Booth Theatre, 26 January 1927;

Gods of the Lightning, by Anderson and Harold Hickerson, New York, Little Theatre, 24 October 1928;

Gypsy, New York, Klaw Theatre, 7 September 1927;

Elizabeth the Queen, New York, Guild Theatre, 3 November 1930;

Night Over Taos, New York, Forty-eighth Street Theatre, 9 March 1932;

Sea-Wife, Minneapolis, University of Minnesota, 6 December 1932;

Both Your Houses, New York, Royale Theatre, 6 March 1933;

Mary of Scotland, New York, Alvin Theatre, 27 November 1933;

Valley Forge, New York, Guild Theatre, 10 December 1934;

Winterset, New York, Martin Beck Theatre, 25 September 1935;

Maxwell Anderson

The Wingless Victory, Washington, D.C., National Theatre, 24 November 1936; New York, Empire Theatre, 23 December 1936;

High Tor, New York, Martin Beck Theatre, 9 January 1937;

The Masque of Kings, New York, Shubert Theatre, 8 February 1937;

The Star-Wagon, New York, Empire Theatre, 29 September 1937;

Knickerbocker Holiday, score by Kurt Weill, New York, Ethel Barrymore Theatre, 19 October 1938;

Key Largo, New York, Ethel Barrymore Theatre, 27 November 1939;

Journey to Jerusalem, New York, National Theatre, 5 October 1940;

Candle in the Wind, New York, Shubert Theatre, 22 October 1941;

The Eve of St. Mark, New York, Cort Theatre, 7 October 1942;

Storm Operation, New York, Belasco Theatre, 11 January 1944;

Truckline Cafe, New York, Belasco Theatre, 27 February 1946;

Joan of Lorraine, New York, Alvin Theatre, 18 November 1946;

Anne of the Thousand Days, New York, Shubert Theatre, 8 December 1948;

Lost in the Stars, adapted from Alan Paton's *Cry, the Beloved Country,* score by Weill, New York, Music Box Theatre, 30 October 1949;

Barefoot in Athens, New York, Martin Beck Theatre, 31 October 1951;

The Bad Seed, adapted from William March's novel, New York, Forty-sixth Street Theatre, 8 December 1954;

The Day the Money Stopped, adapted from Brendan Gill's novel, New York, Belasco Theatre, 20 February 1958;

The Golden Six, New York, York Playhouse, 25 October 1958.

BOOKS: *You Who Have Dreams* (New York: Simon & Schuster, 1925);

Three American Plays, by Anderson and Laurence Stallings (New York: Harcourt, Brace, 1926)—comprises *What Price Glory, First Flight,* and *The Buccaneer;*

Saturday's Children (New York, London, Toronto, Bombay, Calcutta & Madras: Longmans, Green, 1927);

Gods of the Lightning, by Anderson and Harold Hickerson, and *Outside Looking In* (London, New York & Toronto: Longmans, Green, 1928);

Elizabeth the Queen (London, New York & Toronto: Longmans, Green, 1930; New York: French, 1934);

Night Over Taos (New York, Los Angeles & London: French, 1932);

Both Your Houses (New York, Los Angeles & London: French, 1933);

Mary of Scotland (Washington, D.C.: Anderson House, 1933);

Valley Forge (Washington, D.C.: Anderson House, 1934);

Winterset (Washington, D.C.: Anderson House, 1935; London: John Lane, 1938);

The Masque of Kings (Washington, D.C.: Anderson House, 1936; revised edition, London: John Lane, 1938);

The Wingless Victory (Washington, D.C.: Anderson House, 1936);

High Tor (Washington, D.C.: Anderson House, 1937);

The Star-Wagon (Washington, D.C.: Anderson House, 1937);

The Feast of Ortolans (New York: Dramatists Play Service, 1938);

Knickerbocker Holiday, by Anderson and Kurt Weill (Washington, D.C.: Anderson House, 1938);

Key Largo (Washington, D.C.: Anderson House, 1939);

The Essence of Tragedy and Other Footnotes and Papers (Washington, D.C.: Anderson House, 1939);

Journey to Jerusalem (Washington, D.C.: Anderson House, 1940);

Second Overture (New York: Dramatists Play Service, 1940);

Candle in the Wind (Washington, D.C.: Anderson House, 1941);

The Eve of St. Mark (Washington, D.C.: Anderson House, 1942; revised, 1943; London: John Lane, 1943);

Storm Operation (Washington, D.C.: Anderson House, 1944);

Joan of Lorraine (Washington, D.C.: Anderson House, 1946; London: Bodley Head, 1950);

Off Broadway: Essays About the Theatre (New York: Sloane, 1947);

Joan of Arc (New York: Sloane, 1948);

Anne of the Thousand Days (New York: Sloane, 1948);

Lost in the Stars, by Anderson and Weill (New York: Sloane, 1949; London: Cape/Bodley Head, 1951);

Barefoot in Athens (New York: Sloane, 1951);

Morning, Winter, and Night, as John Nairne Michaelson (New York: Sloane, 1952);

The Bad Seed (New York: Dodd, Mead, 1955);

The Golden Six (New York: Dramatists Play Service, 1961);

Notes on a Dream (Austin: University of Texas Press, 1971).

Editions and Collections: *Eleven Verse Plays, 1929–1939* (New York: Harcourt, Brace, 1940)—comprises *Elizabeth the Queen, Night Over Taos, Mary of Scotland, Valley Forge, Winterset, The Wingless Victory, High Tor, The Masque of Kings, The Feast of Ortolans, Second Overture,* and *Key Largo;*

Four Verse Plays (New York: Harcourt, Brace, 1959)—
comprises *Elizabeth the Queen, Mary of Scotland, High
Tor,* and *Winterset.*

PRODUCED SCRIPTS: *All Quiet on the Western Front,*
motion picture, adapted from Erich Maria
Remarque's novel, Universal, 1930;
Rain, motion picture, adapted from John Colton and
Clemence Randolph's adaptation of Somerset
Maugham's story "Miss Thompson," Feature
Productions, 1932;
Washington Merry-Go-Round, by Anderson and Joe Swer-
ling, motion picture, Columbia, 1932;
Death Takes a Holiday, by Anderson and Gladys Lehman,
motion picture, adapted from Alberto Casella's
play, Paramount, 1934;
We Live Again, by Anderson, Leonard Praskins, and
Preston Sturges, motion picture, adapted from
Leo Tolstoy's novel *Resurrection,* Samuel Goldwyn,
1934;
So Red the Rose, by Anderson, Laurence Stallings, and
Edwin Justus Mayer, motion picture, adapted
from Stark Young's novel, Paramount, 1935;
The Feast of Ortolans, radio play, NBC, 20 September
1937;
John Keats and America, radio play, NBC, 7 April 1941;
The Miracle of the Danube, radio play, National Broadcast-
ing System, 27 April 1941;
Joan of Arc, by Anderson and Andrew P. Solt, motion
picture, adapted from Anderson's play *Joan of Lor-
raine,* Sierra Pictures, 1948;
The Christmas Carol, television, adapted from Charles
Dickens's novel, CBS, 23 December 1954;
The Wrong Man, by Anderson and Angus MacPhail,
motion picture, Warner Bros., 1956;
Never Steal Anything Small, motion picture, Universal,
1959.

OTHER: *Measure,* edited by Anderson, 1921–1926;
Gypsy, abridged version, in *Best Plays of 1928–29,* edited
by Burns Mantle (New York: Dodd, Mead, 1929),
pp. 283–315;
The Miracle of the Danube, in *The Free Company Presents,*
compiled by James Boyd (New York: Dodd,
Mead, 1941), pp. 239–267;
Your Navy, with music by Kurt Weill, in *This Is War: A
Collection of Plays about America on the March,* edited
by Norman Corman (New York: Dodd, Mead,
1942), pp. 47–68;
Letter to Jackie, in *The Best One-Act Plays of 1943,* edited
by Margaret G. Mayorga (New York: Dodd, Mead,
1944), pp. 5–7;
The Masque of Pedagogues, North Dakota Quarterly, 25
(Spring 1957): 33–48.

A teacher, journalist, and poet, Maxwell Anderson brought to the theater of the twentieth century an
awareness of contemporary events as well as a poet's
depth of feeling and sense of language. Though skilled
in writing for the theater of realism, he believed that
poetic tragedy alone was the proper aim of American
dramatists. A romantic at heart, Anderson had a penchant for the historical past and universal themes, treating Elizabethan subjects in an archaic dramatic form.
Yet, as scholar Donald Heiney observes, Anderson realistically converted "his historical figures into modern
personalities with modern psychologies, and his political liberalism and cutting irony mark him as a typical
American writer of his generation." Anderson came to
prominence in the 1930s, writing *Both Your Houses*
(1933), for which he won a Pulitzer Prize; *Winterset*
(1935), winner of the newly established New York
Drama Critics Circle Award; *High Tor* (1937), which
also won a Drama Critics Circle Award; and other
important works, such as *Elizabeth the Queen* (1930). His
most significant accomplishment was *Winterset,* a contemporary drama set in verse.

Anderson looked upon the theater as a religious
institution devoted entirely to the exaltation of the spirit
of man. At its best, he wrote in *Off Broadway: Essays
About the Theatre* (1947), "the theatre is the central artistic symbol of the struggle of good and evil within men.
The teaching is that the struggle is eternal and unremit-
ting, that the forces which tend to drag men down are
always present, always ready to attack, that the forces
which make for good cannot sleep through a night
without danger." While he wrote only for the Broadway stage, he viewed the theater above and beyond
entertainment in terms of its function in society, which
was to point out and celebrate the good in people's confused and often desperate lives. A champion of democracy, he made many of his heroes represent ideas of
liberty and justice.

Maxwell Anderson was born on 15 December
1888 on the farm of his maternal grandmother, near
Atlantic, Pennsylvania. His father, William Lincoln
Anderson, was a Baptist minister who moved every
year or two to parishes about Pennsylvania and the
states of the Middle West. His father was harsh, domineering, and uncompromising, as the gentle Anderson
recalled. As for his mother, Charlotta Perrimela
Anderson (née Stephenson), she was quiet and modest—traits that seem to have been passed along to her
son. Childhood was not easy for Anderson, because
of six moves, new schools, and not enough time to cul-
tivate lasting friendships. He grew up with a sense of
loneliness and insecurity; yet, as biographer Alfred S.
Shivers records, "he adored his mother and always
had plenty of music and books as well as his brothers

Prologue.

Mike & Mary enter

Mike — This is the place

Mary — Michael, are you sure

M — This is the track all right —

Mary — I am not sure you're right

M — Don't you worry, I am right enough this time.

Mary — Michael, are you sure this is the earth —

M — Oh say now —

Mary — No really, Michael, I think this is the moon and that's the earth out there —

M — Now, dear, you'll spoil my homecoming if you don't spoil that fooling.

Mary — It shines like the moon but it's really the earth — and this is the moon with its

Page from the first version of White Desert, *Anderson's first produced play, which opened on Broadway in 1923 (The Maxwell Anderson Collection, Harry Ransom Humanities Research Center, University of Texas at Austin)*

and sisters to play with." He had seven siblings, and they were all forced to attend church activities several times a week and to be mannerly and soft-spoken. Having listened to too many of his father's fire-and-brimstone sermons, Max developed a distrust of rhetoric, however, and turned from religion. Music was the only part of church that he enjoyed.

The family was Scotch and Irish, mostly Scotch. They were poor, but they had a library and were all avid readers. When Anderson was nine, he had a severe mastoid infection and missed so much school that he had to repeat a grade; he used the time to read. The following year, after the family had moved to Harrisburg, Pennsylvania, most of them were ill at one time or another with measles, earaches, sore throats, and even malaria. To cheer them Reverend Anderson bought used books, odds and ends that included the works of Charles Dickens, the works of the main American poets, and histories of France and England. In addition to the library, they had a piano and an organ, which Anderson learned to play.

Before finishing eighth grade, Anderson had read most of the well-known novelists, including Dickens, Robert Louis Stevenson, Sir Walter Scott, and James Fenimore Cooper, but his favorites remained the poets. When he went to high school, after the family had moved to New Hampton, Iowa, he discovered John Keats, Percy Bysshe Shelley, and William Shakespeare. This reading inspired him to write poetry of his own, though his father thought it a "sissy" activity. Anderson also developed, as Shivers observes, "a love for the poems of Matthew Arnold, who voiced a melancholy skepticism and classical restraint that seem peculiarly congenial to Max's own temperament."

Anderson completed his last year of high school in Jamestown, North Dakota, and then began undergraduate studies at the State University of North Dakota at Grand Forks. He was almost twenty years old at the time. While at the university, he joined the dramatic society and edited the school yearbook, in which he published several of his own poems. He also wrote two musical comedies: "Lost Labor's Love" when he was a freshman and *The Masque of Pedagogues* in his third and last year (1911) for graduation exercises. The latter play, published in 1957, affectionately satirized college life, faculty, and administrators. The use of Elizabethan techniques of verse dialogue and songs foreshadowed his mature plays about Queen Elizabeth, Mary of Scotland, and Anne Boleyn.

Shortly after graduation, Anderson married college classmate Margaret Haskett; the couple had three sons. In the fall of 1911 he took a position in Minnewaukan, North Dakota, as a high-school principal and teacher of English. In 1913 he moved with his family to California, where he pursued a master's degree in English from Stanford University. His master's thesis was titled "Immortality in the Plays and Sonnets of Shakespeare." For the next three years he taught high-school English in San Francisco and wrote editorials for the *San Francisco Evening Bulletin*. In 1917 he went to Whittier College, a Quaker school, as professor and head of the English Department. Though Quakers are reputed to advocate nonviolence, he was dismissed from the college at the end of the spring term in 1918 for expressing pacifist views on campus and in editorials that opposed American involvement in World War I. At that time the college was controlled by a conservative board, and the Quaker trustees were divided over support for the war and subject to community pressure. The incident left a lingering distaste that surfaced in the plays of the 1930s. In *Valley Forge* (1934), Shivers points out, a starving soldier in the Washington camp "is scornful that Quakers would prefer to sell their hogs to the British forces rather than deliver them up to the cause of freedom (Act I, Scene I); in *Knickerbocker Holiday* (1938), Councilman Tienhoven considers it more festive to hang a Quaker than a Baptist because the former takes a longer time to die (Act I)."

Anderson abandoned his teaching career after the Whittier incident. He was too much of an individualist and a rebel to submit to school administrators; he had also already become disenchanted with the students, who showed little love of writing and literature. After working for a few months on two San Francisco newspapers, he moved to New York in December 1918 to join the editorial staff of the *New Republic*. The editors had been impressed with the poems and essay that he had submitted, but they explained that his position was dependent on his ability to moderate his opinions. He was lured away by the *New York Evening Globe* and then in 1921 by the *New York World*, perhaps the leading American newspaper of the day and haven of many writers who later achieved literary distinction. During that time he founded and was the editor of the poetry magazine *Measure* (published from 1921 to 1926), noted for discovering and publishing the works of young poets such as Wallace Stevens, Robert Frost, Elinor Wylie, Langston Hughes, John Crowe Ransom, and Conrad Aiken, who happened to be Anderson's favorite. In 1925 *You Who Have Dreams,* a volume of his own youthful poems, was published by Simon and Schuster. Anderson showed a growing mastery of poetry and a particular interest in sonnet forms, as revealed by "Rain-Fugue," for example. While Anderson used traditional forms in his early poetry, his themes frequently suggest a spiritual wasteland, a world deprived of religious faith and/or meaningful social action, wherein love is all-important, but transient.

The Playwrights' Company: Robert E. Sherwood, S. N. Behrman, Sidney Howard, Elmer Rice, and Maxwell Anderson, 1938
(Billy Rose Theatre Collection, New York Public Library for the Performing Arts, Astor, Lenox and Tilden Foundations)

Anderson began his playwriting career by chance. A neighbor, John Howard Lawson, invited him to a reading of a first play for which he had received an impressive advance of $500. Anderson decided, "If that's a play, I can write one." Thus, he began writing *White Desert*, which was professionally produced on Broadway in 1923. Set in North Dakota, where he had been raised, the work is a gloomy tragedy in verse about obsessive jealousy. The action concerns the experiences of a young homesteading couple during the latter half of the nineteenth century. The young wife seduces a neighbor when her husband goes to town for two days. When she tells her husband and decides to leave him, he kills her in a jealous rage. Critics encouragingly noted the playwright's sense of form and his way with words, yet found that all too often his poetry had marred the emotional power of the play. The play failed after

only twelve performances, and Anderson decided to set aside verse for the time being.

His next attempt was *What Price Glory* (1924), a collaboration with Laurence Stallings, a fellow literary editor at the *New York World*. Written in prose, the work was based on the bitter World War I experiences of Stallings, who had lost his leg as a marine in France. The play made theatrical history as one of the first works to treat the war in an antiromantic manner; it shocked opening-night audiences with an unflattering picture of military life and language filled with marine expletives.

Some critics thought that Stallings wrote the entire second act, which differs in naturalist treatment from the other two, which are essentially comic; however, scholars have confirmed that he only made revisions to the weak second act that Anderson had written, adding the marine vernacular. The play was modeled after Shakespeare's *Henry IV,* part 1 (circa 1597). The end result was a clever blend of tragic theme with Rabelaisian humor that depicted the marine as he really was. Although the ugly aspects of the war were exposed, including the marines' disillusionment about their fighting for democracy, the work is more of a realistic account of the curse-flinging friendship between a captain and a sergeant, two professional marines who revile each other while off duty but hold fast to one another in battle.

Set in a French farmhouse, act 1 depicts a U.S. Marine company awaiting orders, while bringing together career military men Captain Flagg and Sergeant Quirt to renew rivalries begun elsewhere. Quirt steals Flagg's French girlfriend when Flagg goes to Paris. Flagg is about to get even, but the company is summoned to the front line. After a skirmish with the Germans in act 2, the wounded are brought to a dugout for care and morphine. A lieutenant breaks down at the sight of the men, his sobs echoing the theme of disillusionment:

> And since six o'clock there's been a wounded sniper in the tree by that orchard angel crying *"!Kameradei"* Just like a big crippled whippoorwill. What price glory now? Why in God's name can't we all go home? Who gives a damn for this lousy stinking little town but the poor French bastards who live here. God damn it! You talk about courage, and all night long you hear a man who's bleeding to death on a tree calling you *"Kamerad"* and asking you to save him.

At the end of act 2, Quirt is wounded and sent back to the French village of the first act, where he takes up with the fickle French girlfriend. In act 3 the company follows, as the battle has been a standoff. Flagg catches up with Quirt. They fight over the girl, but romance is once again put on hold as the company is called to the front line.

Later critics praised the description of the senselessness of war, yet faulted the authors' tendency to romanticize professional soldiering and their failure to probe causes and consequences. The play said, in effect, that modern war was a life-and-death brawl for a worthless prize, a game without rules played by soldiers who are happy only when they are brawling. This thesis can be seen in the rivalry between Flagg and Quirt, neither of whom has any life outside the war-brawl business. Flagg marks the first in a long series of rebel-heroes (with a heart of gold that defies externals) whose contempt for authority is their most compelling trait. The play also foreshadows Anderson's habit of ignoring questions implied in the socially significant materials that he chooses. "What are we fighting for?" the soldiers would like to know.

"There's something rotten about this profession of arms," says Flagg, "some kind of damned religion connected with it that you can't shake. When they tell you to die, you have to do it, even if you're a better man than they are." Thus, Anderson shelves the answer in the inscrutable realm of religion.

The show was a phenomenal box-office success, running for 299 performances. Capitalized at $10,000, it made a huge profit of almost $10,000 a week, enabling Anderson, at age thirty-five, to quit his newspaper job and spend full time writing for the theater. What followed was a period of collaboration and apprenticeship as he mastered his new trade.

During the 1920s Anderson wrote two historical plays in collaboration with Stallings: *First Flight* (1925), a swashbuckling romance that deals with the young General Andrew Jackson on the frontier in the days when the Constitution was widely believed to be a threat against liberty; and *The Buccaneer* (1925), a cloak-and-dagger romance about Sir Henry Morgan, the pirate, and his contempt for restraint of piracy laws and naval regulations. Both plays are inferior to *What Price Glory,* neither commanding the attention of serious theater study.

A series of comedies and dramas followed. The most successful was *Saturday's Children* (1927), written in prose, a sentimental comedy about the domestic problems of a young married couple, with the theme that marriage destroys romance. The work was inspired by Henrik Ibsen's *Love's Comedy,* (1862). *Gypsy* (1927) told the contemporary tale of an unstable woman who took her own life. Critics decried the play as an artistic failure, and it was never published. Anderson's first wife died in 1931; sometime before her death, he began living with Gertrude (Mab) Maynard, with whom he had one daughter. Like the protagonist of *Gypsy,* Mab was neurotic and unfaithful, and she committed suicide in 1953. Anderson married Gilda Oakleaf in 1954.

Between 1930 and 1938 Anderson wrote the poetic tragedies for which he is best remembered, beginning with *Elizabeth the Queen,* a blend of poetry, tragedy, romance, and history; it opened on Broadway on 3 November 1930. Anderson became interested in writing the play after reading Lytton Strachey's bestseller *Elizabeth and Essex: A Tragic History* (1928), choosing to make his work a human-interest story rather than primarily a tragedy. In the writing, he used an imitative Shakespearean pattern, though the cadence of Anderson's blank verse was more like Alfred Tennyson's in quality. He also applied modern psychological concepts. The literary and historical associations seem to have prepared audiences to accept what is considered the first successful drama of the modern theater to have been written in verse.

Viewpoints that underscore much of Anderson's later work are evident. Critic John Gassner points to Anderson's "distrust of government and of power politics, his conviction that men of good will are apt to be destroyed while 'the rats inherit the earth,' and his belief that the pageant of human desire and suffering is nevertheless awe-inspiring and magnificent." The play makes use of Anderson's theory of tragedy, which he formulated after rereading Aristotle's *Poetics* to assure himself of more than accidental success with his playwriting. He set forth these principles in published essays years later in *The Essence of Tragedy and Other Footnotes and Papers* (1939) and *Off Broadway: Essays About the Theatre*.

In the play Elizabeth and Essex are two strong and exceptional characters, destroyed by a tragic flaw, yet capable of asserting splendor in error and defeat. The plot moves into and away from the crisis and includes a scene of recognition, which Anderson deemed most important. Elizabeth is in love with Essex, who wants to share the throne. She is also a superior ruler who has difficulties surrendering power to love. Essex is in love with the older queen, yet he is an ambitious individualist who is incapable of self-control or compromise. Elizabeth believes at the beginning of the play that she can and will integrate love and power, but she comes to recognize that this union can never be. In a climax at the end of act 2, Essex defiantly returns from an expedition, after rival members of the court have tricked the lovers into a misunderstanding. He captures the palace with the support of his loyal army, leading Elizabeth to believe that his interest lies only in the throne. She tricks him into dismissing his guard by promising to let him rule equally, then orders him to the Tower of London, where they discuss their differences. In the last moments of act 3, she weakens, telling him to take her kingdom, but he pretends not to hear. "I know now how it will be without you," she tells him. "The sun / Will be empty and circle round an empty earth . . . / And I will be queen of emptiness and death . . . / Why could you not have loved me enough to give me / Your love and let me keep as I was?" At the end of the play, the audience is left with the image of the pitifully broken queen sitting alone on her throne.

Anderson set the play in iambic pentameter, which he felt combined the maximum of intensity and elevation of poetry with the minimum of artificiality in the theater. Though the verse was not consistently original, critics agreed that it had been adapted to an agreeable stage spectacle. The play had a successful run of 147 performances and is considered the cornerstone of Anderson's work.

During the 1930s Anderson had twelve professional productions on Broadway, eleven after *Elizabeth the Queen*. Most of his great plays were written during this period, his most productive. *Night Over Taos* (1932) was inspired by a series of articles by Harvey Fergusson on the Rio Grande Valley (*American Mercury,* May–October 1931). The play takes as its subject the American occupation of Taos, New Mexico, and explores the violent overthrow of an outdated social order–specifically the defeat of patriarchal society by capitalist democracy. The conflict between the invading American ideas and the Spanish way of life is portrayed chiefly in the family of the Montoyas, a father and his two sons. One son loves the girl who is betrothed to his father; the other son betrays Taos. At the conclusion the father takes his own life after killing the treacherous son. Anderson's central figure, Pablo Montoya, is sympathetically portrayed as a man of nobility, a spokesman for the old ways of Spanish Taos, while the Americans are portrayed as mercenaries; Montoya's death symbolizes the end of a feudal civilization and a hierarchy based on land, blood, and privilege.

Although the play touched on a neglected and rich period of American history, the subject matter seemed remote in time and place. Anderson sympathized with the conquistadores, despite their exploitation of the peasants, further confusing audiences with a blurring romantic and idealistic sentiments in act 3. To complicate matters, the production took on a cloistral and contemplative tone, which was not what the play called for; and thus the production failed, lasting only thirteen performances. Later scholars believe the play is more interesting than its failure suggests, arguing that a faulty production and inaccurate published texts have contributed to its neglect.

Soon after came *Both Your Houses* (1933), a political satire written during the Herbert Hoover administration, when public dissatisfaction with government was strong. The piece was intended as an attack upon political corruption and apathy. In the play, freshman Congressman Alan McClean of Nevada discovers that the Nevada Dam Appropriation Bill has been framed with several costly items, representing special interests and private graft, otherwise known as "pork." Chairman Simeon Gray has proposed a penitentiary in Culver that would save his shaky bank in that town; Representative Sol Fitzmaurice has asked for money to anchor the entire Atlantic Fleet near his private resort; and the list goes on. McClean, who is young and idealistic as his name implies, sets out to beat his seasoned colleagues at their own game. His contribution to the bill is graft so patently corrupt that he thinks the measure will either be killed on the floor or face a presidential veto, but neither outcome takes place. Instead, his colleagues add one preposterous rider after another until the cost of the bill skyrockets from $40 million to $465 million–and the bill gets passed. In the meantime,

Anderson (center) visiting Fort Bragg, North Carolina, a trip that inspired his 1942 play, The Eve of St. Mark *(U.S. Army)*

has been just like the ghosts of the Dutchmen in his clinging to the mountain and to the past. He sells the mountain and heads west with his girlfriend, preparing a grave site for the Indian before he leaves. Anderson gives the last words to the Indian: "Nothing is made by men / but makes, in the end, good ruins."

Critics praised the clever mixture of fantasy, comedy, and verse, despite various ambiguities of plot and a weak third act. Some thought the hero sold out, that his actions were blind and spurious; others thought he acted justifiably, preserving the High Tor of his mind and soul. Later critics commended the satire.

At the beginning of a new season, *The Star-Wagon* (September 1937) made its debut on Broadway. The play ran against unfavorable reviews to become one of Anderson's longest-running shows (223 performances). Critics faulted the hackneyed structure and the pretentious writing, yet praised the absorbing characters. Later critics singled out its sentimental charm. The play is a fantasy in prose "grounded in the assumption that past and present time co-exist and the belief that few people would go back

in time if the opportunity arose." It borrows from H. G. Wells's *The Time Machine: An Invention* (1895) for its plot and from J. M. Barrie's *Dear Brutus* (1917) to tell the story of a poor scientist who, with his loyal assistant, invents the Star-Wagon–a time machine that carries him back to the day on which he decided to marry his wife. Much of the play appeals to nostalgia for the past and to clichés about true love and marriage, and there are several elements from Anderson's personal experience. In a church in act 2, for instance, there is an organ similar to the one that Anderson played in his father's church. In the choir is a young girl named Hallie, modeled after Anderson's childhood sweetheart. And when Stephen, the inventor, plays "Jerusalem the Golden" on the organ, both he and the singer, Martha, who is to become his wife, are drawn together by the music that profoundly affects them.

Anderson's next experiment was *Knickerbocker Holiday* (1938), a musical play that he wrote because he was pressed for money. *Winterset* and *High Tor* had been artistic successes, but neither ran long enough to make a lot of money. This time he wanted the finan-

Marlon Brando in the 1946 Broadway production of
Truckline Cafe *(photograph by Fred Fehl)*

cial gains of a commercial success. The play was produced by the Playwrights' Company, which Anderson had organized in association with four other playwrights (Robert E. Sherwood, Elmer Rice, Sidney Howard, and S. N. Behrman) and attorney John F. Wharton because of their dislike of the power that producers had to choose or reject plays. The organization also ensured artistic and financial control of productions. The group presented their own plays and prospered until 1960; Anderson's plays made the most consistently successful contributions.

Knickerbocker Holiday is a collaboration with Kurt Weill, who wrote the music. Anderson wrote the entire libretto, modeling it after W. S. Gilbert's *The Mikado, or the Town of Titipu* (1885) and borrowing from Washington Irving's *A History of New York, from the Beginning of the World to the End of the Dutch Dynasty* (1809) to satirize President Franklin Delano Roosevelt and his New Deal policies of social reform. The preface to the play has an antifascist ring, warning against increased government

control and defending democracy as mankind's hope. The theme of totalitarianism is personified by the conflict between Peter Stuyvesant, the autocratic governor of New Amsterdam, who has qualities of Roosevelt and Adolf Hitler, and Brom Broeck, the freedom-loving "first American" who opposes government interventions. The main events take place during Stuyvesant's difficult reign as governor. They are embellished with a love story: Broeck and Tina are in love, but the girl's father orders her to marry the old peg-legged governor. Stuyvesant is attracted to the girl but vocalizes his anxieties about getting old in "September Song."

President Roosevelt found the musical amusing. He saw the show during its Washington tryouts, and newspapers and magazines ran the story, which generated much publicity but not enough. The show lost money during its twenty-one-week run. The reviews were mixed. Critics complained that Anderson knew nothing about writing a musical (the book was heavy-handed), yet praised the music, the witty lyrics, and Walter Huston's portrayal of Peter Stuyvesant. Huston sang "September Song," which became a standard, and after Bing Crosby recorded it for Decca in 1943 the sale of records, sheet music, and other royalties from sources eventually made *Knickerbocker Holiday* Anderson's most profitable show. Later considerations were less than favorable, concluding that the musical satire was a minor work. The play marks the end of Anderson's greatest period of creativity.

A series of spiritual plays followed, coinciding with World War II, a period of history in which man's inhumanity to man seemed to negate the code of individualism for which Anderson stood. The works of this period can also be understood as a mirroring of the playwright's own quest for the spiritual certitude that he had lost as a child. First came *Key Largo,* a poetic tragedy, which opened on 27 November 1939 (105 performances). The title and the plot had come from an unidentified incident that took place while Anderson was driving to Key Largo, Florida.

The story concerns a young American, King McCloud, who deserted his friends and the Loyalist cause in 1937 during the Spanish Civil War. His friends were all killed, while he fell in with the Franco forces, and in the aftermath he has been driven half-crazy with guilt. After the war he makes his way to the family of his best friend in Key West, where he falls in love with the friend's sister, philosophizes with his blind father, and confronts the gangsters who are hiding out at the family's tourist home. McCloud is thus led through a series of experiences to a climactic moment in which he goes from weakness to self-realization before acting to restore his honor in death, adhering strictly to the principles of tragedy that Anderson prescribed.

Intended as a parable of the need to resist fascism in Europe, the play can be seen as a dramatization of moral values and cosmic concepts, a working out of Anderson's existential essay "Whatever We Hope" (in *The Essence of Tragedy and Other Footnotes and Papers*), which posits that man lives in a world devoid of meaning save for the occasional glimmer of hope offered by art, science, religion, or the idealism of the young. The alienated McCloud is the personification of absolute pessimism. The blind father, who speaks for the playwright, tells McCloud that man must keep the faith, for it is all he has; someday man will be able to "face even the stars without despair, / and think without going mad." Because of its literary verse, the play reads better than it played on stage. Despite the rigorous application of Anderson's dramatic theory, critics faulted long-winded speeches as well as over-simplification of character and the melodramatic development of the gangsters' activities.

Produced in 1940, *Journey to Jerusalem* is based on a passage in the Gospel according to St. Luke (2:41–52), the account of the twelve-year-old Jesus speaking with the elders in the temple, but this part of the story was not the only element that interested the playwright. As Anderson explained in the preface, while studying the Sermon on the Mount in its relation to the old prophets and its own time, he realized that Jesus had come "from the ancient Jewish culture, out of a profound study of the great voice of His race, at a time when despair and unfaith had gripped His own people, when the Roman Empire, ruled by sensualists and materialists, hung over a world of doubting and cynical slave-states." The time seemed much like the present, and Anderson hoped that through his play modern men and women would "grasp the problem of unfaith as it presented itself to Jesus when He pondered the Old Testament in His youth." The preface suggests a parallel between the persecution of the Jews in the Judea of Jesus' time and their persecution in the Hitlerian Europe of the day, stressing the importance of faith.

The action of the play concerns the child Jesus and His spiritual awakening, initially to the knowledge that He is the Messiah and then to the terrifying realization that His mission will not be accomplished in heroic fashion by leading battalions of angels with flaming swords against the oppressors of His people, but rather by walking a harsh and lonely path and by dying an ignominious death. Critics found the play an earnest and reverent work, poetic in text, yet static in terms of drama, the writing never equal to the theme. One reviewer thought the play should be read since its beauty was dependent upon the sensitive imagination.

This critical disappointment was followed by another, *Candle in the Wind* (1941, 95 performances),

which tells the story of a famous American actress in Paris after the invasion as she plots to free her lover, a French officer, from the Nazi oppressors. Critics noted effective moments of melodrama resulting from the terror of the Nazis (and a stellar performance by Helen Hayes), yet criticized Anderson's inability to dramatize the depth and significance of the theme. Worth noting, nonetheless, is the preface to the play, which reflects Anderson's preoccupation with the war and the threat of fascism to the free world. It marks a change from his pacifist position to that of activist. The essay concludes with a description of Anderson's theory of theater as the central artistic symbol of the struggle of good and evil in men.

The Eve of St. Mark, produced in 1942, was one of Anderson's best and one of the most successful dramas about America at war, running for 307 performances. Based on Anderson's visit to Fort Bragg, North Carolina, in 1942, the play depicts a shy young man, Private Quizz West, who goes gallantly to his death on an island in the Philippines. The play is dedicated to the memory of Anderson's nephew, an army pilot shot down in the Mediterranean during the war. Later critics found the scenes of American soldiers facing the Japanese on a Pacific island sentimental and romantically superficial; the malaria-induced dream sequences, in which West talks to his mother and girlfriend, were considered improbable in their use of spiritual communication; and the ending, in which his two younger brothers enlist and appear in uniforms, was deemed patriotically overdone. Whatever the flaws, the work remains among the most appealing portraits of the World War II soldier.

Produced in 1944, *Storm Operation* added to the list of critical disappointments. By special permission of the War Department, Anderson had gone to North Africa during the invasion, interviewing General Dwight D. Eisenhower as part of his investigation for the play, which he intended as an exciting and timely piece; yet, it turned out to be too propagandist to be interesting drama. The play showed much of the same straightforward realism and romantic camaraderie as *What Price Glory,* but censorship by the War Department resulted in a toning down of issues that might have offended the Allies. The effectiveness of the play was compromised, and it ran only briefly.

Truckline Cafe, produced in 1946, was the fourth in Anderson's series of World War II vehicles. A study of the postwar era, *Truckline Cafe* took as its theme the ethical and emotional problems that former servicemen and their families experienced after the war, making its focal point situations that occur when couples are separated, such as adulterous wives and husbands who father illegitimate children. The play ends, how-

Ingrid Bergman in the title role of the 1946 Broadway production of Joan of Lorraine *(photograph by Vandamm)*

and the acting and directing talent available. Anderson states how important, but difficult, it is to keep the essential integrity of the play intact. By way of illustration, the action of *Joan of Lorraine* takes place during the rehearsals of a production of *Joan of Arc* that depicts the compromises that the Maid is forced to make with local politicians. The rehearsal scenes are followed by interludes in which the director, Masters, and leading lady, Mary, comment and disagree on the action and/or on the character portrayal. Act 1 takes Mary to important character discoveries regarding the Maid's faith. She disagrees with the author's script revisions, which suggest tolerance of dishonesty in order to get things done, but Masters draws analogies to the business part of the theater, "ice" at the box office, black-market materials for the set, cash from sponsors. Sounding much like Anderson, he says, "The human race is a mass of corruption tempered with high ideals." As act 2 begins, the director philosophizes on faith, extolling his belief that the theater is a temple of democracy, while Mary gains greater understanding of her character as the stage action takes Joan through various compromises with evil during the coronation and trial scenes. Although Joan made concessions on the little issues, Mary realizes that Joan has never compromised her faith.

The play became the outstanding hit of the season, with the help of Ingrid Bergman in the lead; it ran for 201 performances, though it did not please the contemporary critics. Later scholars found George Bernard Shaw's Joan more interesting, suggesting that Anderson's production might have benefited from fuller historical trappings and the continuity of uninterrupted action. (In the screenplay, which he wrote, Anderson abandoned the backstage interludes. The movie version was titled *Joan of Arc* and starred Ingrid Bergman and José Ferrer.)

Anderson returned to Elizabethan times for his next play, *Anne of the Thousand Days* (produced in 1948). The verse tragedy explores the Anne Boleyn – Henry VIII relationship, in which the royal adulterer charges his mistress-turned-wife with adultery and sends her to the Tower to be beheaded. The play completes Anderson's Tudor verse trilogy, the first though written last, while illustrating an increasing concern with the commanding role that gender takes in human behavior.

In a new form of experiment, Anderson places the action in Anne's reverie. A prisoner in the Tower, she awaits her execution, recalling in flashbacks the series of events in her life with the king. Henry divorced Catherine to marry her, but now he wants her to nullify the marriage and live in exile with their daughter, Elizabeth, because he is attracted to Jane Seymour. But Anne is strong-willed and chooses not to compromise her daughter's succession. In the last scene

ever, on a note of forgiveness, suggesting that the past, along with the horrors of war, should be forgiven. Members of the Playwrights' Company had tried unsuccessfully to discourage Anderson from staging the piece because they considered it overwritten and cluttered with too many characters. It opened to uniformly bad press and closed after only thirteen performances. In response to the negative opinions, Anderson blasted the critics, taking an ad in the *New York Herald Tribune* that insulted their competency.

Joan of Lorraine, produced at the end of 1946, concluded the war era by successfully dramatizing the message set forth in his essay "Compromise and Keeping the Faith" (in *Off Broadway,* 1947), written shortly after the publication of the play. The essay describes the concessions that playwrights make in order to get a play produced, the compromise between the original script

Nancy Kelly and Patty McCormack in the 1954 Broadway production of The Bad Seed *(photograph by Fred Fehl)*

Anne appears as a ghost, a ring of blood around her neck. Though Henry is free to marry Jane Seymour, Anne triumphs in death.

Joyce Redden and Rex Harrison were cast in the leading roles, and their presence partially accounted for the substantial advance sale that ensured the success of the production (286 performances). Notwithstanding self-conscious and bewildering verse, critics found the characters as alive and convincing as any historical personages in any American play, with Anne perfectly illustrating Anderson's theory of tragedy.

Next came the musical *Lost in the Stars* (1949, 273 performances), an adaptation of Alan Paton's novel *Cry, the Beloved Country* (1948). Anderson wrote the book and lyrics; Kurt Weill, the music. The story takes place in South Africa and concerns Arthur Jarvis, a wealthy British planter and staunch believer in apartheid, and Stephen Kumalo, a humble Zulu-Anglican preacher—two fathers who discover a common bond in the deaths of their sons. In a bungled robbery attempt, the

preacher's son kills Jarvis's son, an attorney and crusader for black equality. At the end of the play the two fathers become friends. Jarvis forgives and promises to help the preacher and his parishioners, as did his son, signaling the hopefulness of a new day. Anderson emphasized the theme of brotherhood, and the powerful reconciliation was his invention, an embellishment of the novel. In recognition thereof, Anderson was honored by the National Conference of Christians and Jews with its Brotherhood Award. Weill died unexpectedly during the lengthy run of the play.

Anderson read Xenophon's *Memorabilia* and Plato's *Dialogues* before writing his next play, *Barefoot in Athens* (1951), revising the story of the final months in the life of Socrates after also reading Karl R. Popper's *The Open Society and Its Enemies* (1945), an anti-Plato study. The final product was a talkfest for democracy that did not sit well with the critics. Although the trial scene was effective, Socrates' conviction by the so-called democratic jury seemed to weaken the message, as did the humanizing depiction of Socrates in the death scene, where he was portrayed as a loving father and loyal Athenian rather than as a compelling philosopher espousing a discourse on the immortality of the soul. The play was written during the period of the House Un-American Activities Committee hearings and the Joseph McCarthy witch hunts. Anderson identified the Spartans with Communists, making Socrates his mouthpiece of democracy.

When the production received an unfavorable critical reception, Anderson, then sixty-two, vowed never again to write for the theater. It seemed that audiences no longer wanted the kind of plays that he wrote, as *Barefoot in Athens* ran for only thirty performances. They only wanted entertainment that shocked and titillated, and empty musicals. However, he owed a huge tax debt on the profits from *The Eve of St. Mark,* so he did not retire from the stage. Instead he wrote three plays that he considered potboilers, plays designed strictly to make money: *The Bad Seed* (1954), *The Day the Money Stopped* (1958), and *The Golden Six* (1958).

The Bad Seed was based on a 1954 novel of the same title by William March about a psychotic little girl who was responsible for several murders. The novel, which Anderson had read while recuperating from a heart attack, was skillfully adapted into a shocking thriller that pleased the critics and the crowd, bringing with it the commercial success that he had counted on (332 performances). The one-act melodrama *The Day the Money Stopped,* based on Brendan Gill's 1957 novel of the same name, failed after four performances because it was dull and excessively talky. *The Golden Six,* an historical mystery based on the life of Roman emperor Claudius, also failed after fifteen performances, notwithstanding several well-written sequences and some excellent character portrayals.

Anderson died on 28 February 1959 following a stroke at his home in Stamford, Connecticut. At the time of his death, he was involved in the arrangements of a new play, "Madonna and Child." He was also in the early stages of writing the book for a musical, "Art of Love," based on Ovid's poems. During a career that spanned three decades, he had produced thirty-three plays, contributing to both the realistic and poetic traditions of American playwriting. His insistence upon spiritual values accounted for his abiding interest in verse drama. As he wrote in an essay titled "A Prelude to Poetry in the Theatre," his introduction to *Winterset:* "I have a strong and chronic hope that the theatre of this country will outgrow the phase of journalistic social comment and reach occasionally into the upper air of poetic tragedy. I believe with Goethe that dramatic poetry is man's greatest achievement on this earth so far, and I believe with the early Bernard Shaw

that the theatre is essentially a cathedral of the spirit, devoted to the exaltation of men." Though his successes and failures were not always uniform, nor were his successes always complete, his plays are known for their craftsmanship and dramatic effectiveness. As critic John Mason Brown wrote in his consideration of *Winterset,* "Mr. Anderson has tried to do matters much more than what he may or may not have succeeded in doing. His is the kind of play, although by no means the actual play, upon which the hope and glory of the future theatre rest."

Letters:

Dramatist in America: Letters of Maxwell Anderson, 1912–1958, edited by Laurence G. Avery (Chapel Hill: University of North Carolina Press, 1977).

Bibliographies:

Martha Cox, *Maxwell Anderson Bibliography* (Charlottesville: Bibliographical Society, University of Virginia, 1958);

William R. Klink, *Maxwell Anderson and S. N. Behrman: A Reference Guide* (Boston: G. K. Hall, 1977), pp. 1–54;

J. F. S. Smeal, "Additions to the Maxwell Anderson Bibliography," *North Dakota Quarterly* (Summer 1980): 61–63;

Klink, "Maxwell Anderson and S. N. Behrman: A Reference Guide Updated," *Resources for American Literary Study* (Autumn 1982): 195–214;

Alfred S. Shivers, *Maxwell Anderson: An Annotated Bibliography of Primary and Secondary Works* (Metuchen, N.J.: Scarecrow Press, 1985);

Barbara Lee Horn, *Maxwell Anderson: A Research and Production Sourcebook* (Westport, Conn.: Greenwood Press, 1996).

Biography:

Alfred S. Shivers, *The Life of Maxwell Anderson* (Briarcliff Manor, N.Y.: Stein & Day, 1983).

References:

Laurence G. Avery, *A Catalogue of the Maxwell Anderson Collection at the University of Texas* (Austin: University of Texas Humanities Research Center, 1968);

Avery, "The Maxwell Anderson Papers," *Library Chronicle of the University of Texas* (Spring 1965): 21–33;

Mabel Driscoll Bailey, *Maxwell Anderson, the Playwright as Prophet* (London & New York: Abelard-Schuman, 1957);

S. N. Behrman, *Tribulations and Laughter: A Memoir* (London: Hamilton, 1972), pp. 212–228;

John Mason Brown, "Two on the Aisle: *Winterset,*" *New York Evening Post,* 26 October 1935; republished in his *Two on the Aisle* (New York: Norton, 1938), pp. 148–150;

Barrett H. Clark, *Maxwell Anderson: The Man and His Plays* (New York: French, 1933);

Clark, "Stallings and Anderson," in his *An Hour of American Drama* (Philadelphia: Lippincott, 1930), pp. 89–95;

Nancy J. Doran and Kenneth Krauss, eds., *Maxwell Anderson and the New York Stage* (Monroe, N.Y.: Library Research Associates, 1991);

Bernard F. Dukore, "Maxwell Anderson," in his *American Dramatists 1918–1945 excluding O'Neill* (London: Macmillan, 1984), pp. 77–100;

Walter Prichard Eaton, "He Put the Poetry Back on the Stage," *New York Herald Tribune,* 28 January 1934, VII: 21;

John Gassner, *A Treasure of the Theatre,* revised edition (New York: Simon & Schuster, 1951), I: 837–838, 864–865;

Donald Heiney, "Maxwell Anderson," in his *Recent American Literature* (Great Neck, N.Y.: Barron's Educational Series, 1958), pp. 369–376;

Joseph Wood Krutch, *The American Drama Since 1918* (New York: Random House, 1939), pp. 286–318;

Jordan Y. Miller, "Maxwell Anderson: Gifted Technician," in *The Thirties: Fiction, Poetry, Drama,* edited by Warren G. French (De Land, Fla.: Everett/Edwards, 1967), pp. 183–192;

Miller and Winifred L. Frazer, "Maxwell Anderson: Man of Many Muses," in their *American Drama between the Wars: A Critical History* (Boston: Twayne, 1991), pp. 122–133;

North Dakota Quarterly, special Anderson issues, 25 (Spring 1957); 38 (Winter 1970);

Elmer Rice, *Minority Report: An Autobiography* (New York: Simon & Schuster, 1963), pp. 374–456;

Alfred S. Shivers, *Maxwell Anderson* (Boston: Twayne, 1976);

William E. Taylor, "Maxwell Anderson: Traditionalist in a Theatre of Change," in *Modern American Drama: Essays in Criticism,* edited by Taylor (De Land, Fla.: Everett/Edwards, 1968), pp. 47–57;

John F. Wharton, *Life Among the Playwrights, Being Mostly the Story of the Playwrights' Producing Company, Inc.* (New York: Quadrangle/New York Times Book Company, 1974).

Papers:

The major archive of Maxwell Anderson's correspondence, diaries, biographical documents, and manuscripts is the Maxwell Anderson Collection at the Hoblitzelle Theatre Arts Library, Harry Ransom Humanities Research Center, University of Texas at Austin. Other significant collections include: the Manuscript Division of the Library of Congress, Washington, D.C. (play manuscripts and correspondence); the Billy Rose Collection of the New York Public Library and the Theatre Collection, Library and Museum of the Performing Arts, New York Public Library at Lincoln Center (production scripts); the Beinecke Rare Book and Manuscript Library, Yale University (play manuscript and correspondence); the Maxwell Anderson Collection, Chester Fritz Library, University of North Dakota (diaries and play manuscripts); and the Playwrights' Company Collection, Wisconsin Center for Film and Theater Research, University of Wisconsin (correspondence).

Philip Barry

(18 June 1896 – 3 December 1949)

Kurt Eisen
Tennessee Technological University

See also the Barry entry in *DLB 7: Twentieth-Century American Dramatists.*

PLAY PRODUCTIONS: *Autonomy,* New Haven, Yale Dramatic Club, 1919;

A Punch for Judy, Cambridge, Harvard Workshop, 1921; New York, Morosco Theatre, 18 April 1921;

You and I, New York, Belmont Theatre, 19 February 1923;

The Youngest, New York, Gaiety Theatre, 22 December 1924;

In a Garden, New York, Plymouth Theatre, 16 November 1925;

White Wings, New York, Booth Theatre, 15 October 1926;

John, New York, Klaw Theatre, 4 November 1927;

Paris Bound, New York, Music Box Theatre, 27 December 1927;

Cock Robin, by Barry and Elmer Rice, New York, Forty-eighth Street Theatre, 12 January 1928;

Holiday, New York, Plymouth Theatre, 26 November 1928;

Hotel Universe, New York, Martin Beck Theatre, 14 April 1930;

Tomorrow and Tomorrow, New York, Henry Miller's Theatre, 13 January 1931;

The Animal Kingdom, New York, Broadhurst Theatre, 12 January 1932;

The Joyous Season, New York, Belasco Theatre, 29 January 1934;

Bright Star, New York, Empire Theatre, 15 October 1935;

Spring Dance, adapted from Eleanor Golden and Eloise Barrangon's play, New York, Empire Theatre, 25 August 1936;

Here Come the Clowns, New York, Booth Theatre, 7 December 1938;

The Philadelphia Story, New York, Shubert Theatre, 28 March 1939;

Philip Barry

Liberty Jones, New York, Shubert Theatre, 5 February 1941;

Without Love, New York, Saint James Theatre, 10 November 1942;

Foolish Notion, New York, Martin Beck Theatre, 13 March 1945;

My Name is Aquilon, adapted from Jean Pierre Aumont's play, New York, Lyceum Theatre, 9 February 1949;

Second Threshold, revised by Robert E. Sherwood, New York, Morosco Theatre, 2 January 1951.

BOOKS: *You and I* (New York: Brentano's, 1923);
The Youngest (New York: French, 1925);
In a Garden (New York: Doran, 1926);
The Dramatist and the Amateur Public (New York: French, 1927);
White Wings (New York: Boni & Liveright, 1927);
John (New York, Los Angeles & London: French, 1929);
Paris Bound (New York, Los Angeles & London: French, 1929);
Cock Robin, by Barry and Elmer Rice (New York, Los Angeles & London: French, 1929);
Holiday (New York, Los Angeles & London: French, 1929);
Hotel Universe (New York, Los Angeles & London: French, 1930);
Tomorrow and Tomorrow (New York, Los Angeles & London: French, 1931);
The Animal Kingdom (New York: French, 1932);
The Joyous Season (New York, Los Angeles & London: French, 1934);
Spring Dance (New York, Los Angeles & London: French, 1936);
War in Heaven (New York: Coward-McCann, 1938);
Here Come the Clowns (New York: Coward-McCann, 1939);
The Philadelphia Story (New York: Coward-McCann, 1939);
Liberty Jones: A Play with Music for City Children (New York: Coward-McCann, 1941);
Without Love (New York: Coward-McCann, 1943);
Second Threshold, revised by Robert E. Sherwood (New York: Harper, 1951).
Collection: *States of Grace: Eight Plays,* edited by Brendan Gill (New York: Harcourt Brace Jovanovich, 1975)—comprises *You and I, White Wings, Holiday, Hotel Universe, The Animal Kingdom, Here Come the Clowns, The Philadelphia Story,* and *Second Threshold.*

In the four-month period from December 1938 to March 1939, at a time when his stature as a mainstay of the American drama between the two world wars was in serious decline, Philip Barry brought two important new plays to Broadway. One, *Here Come the Clowns,* drew a respectful if baffled reaction from critics and audiences; the other, *The Philadelphia Story,* became a major hit on both stage and screen. Together these plays epitomize Barry's long, seemingly conflicting but in fact complementary pursuits of worldly fulfillment and spiritual truth. *Here Come the Clowns* marks perhaps his most comprehensive attempt to probe the ultimate meanings of life but fell short of the one-hundred-performance

threshold that signifies commercial success on Broadway. Six weeks later, *The Philadelphia Story* began its run of 417 shows and reaffirmed Barry as the master of the romantic "high comedy" for which he is best remembered—not least because of several durable Hollywood screen adaptations of his plays. If Barry seems archaic from the perspective of a drama dominated by social realism, diverse ethnic communities, and avant-garde experimentation, his obsessively dualistic search connects him nonetheless to a post-1945 American culture that has continued to raise self-critical questions about the value of its own success.

Philip James Quinn Barry was born on 18 June 1896, the youngest of four children in a prosperous Irish Catholic family in Rochester, New York. He grew up on the cusp between wealth and failure: his father, James Corbett Barry, died from appendicitis the year after Philip's birth, and the family's financial condition, on the verge of affluence from James Barry's marble and tile business, quickly began to worsen. The oldest son, Edmund, then sixteen, left school to help their mother, Mary Agnes Quinn Barry, assume management of the family business while also becoming a surrogate father to Philip. The loss of his father meant the loss of his chance to grow up socially and financially among the elite families of Rochester and suggests in part why Barry became obsessed with the lives of the moneyed classes despite his persistent sense that wealth—especially its pursuit—can dull the spirit. As Barry progressed through Catholic grammar school, public high school, and then Yale and Harvard Universities, he strove for social acceptance even as his skeptical stance toward the values of that world began to find expression in fiction, poetry, and drama.

One of the decisive early episodes in Barry's life—one that also supplied the plot for *The Youngest* (1924), his second Broadway play—followed the discovery that through a quirk in the inheritance laws of New York State, Barry was entitled to the entire family estate (diminished though it was), when his mother had to sell off some property and discovered the anomaly in 1910. Though he claimed later that he never intended to keep the money, in 1919, having earned his B.A. at Yale and put in some clerical service in London during World War I, Barry exploited his advantage. Before signing over the estate, he compelled his mother and two elder brothers, who felt that he should remain with the family in Rochester, to let him enroll in George Pierce Baker's renowned Workshop 47 playwriting course at Harvard.

By 1919 Barry's commitment to drama was settled. His first taste of literary glory had come at the age of nine when a Rochester newspaper published his story "Tab the Cat." Four years later he tried his hand at drama with the three-act "No Thoroughfare" (also the title of his first mature attempt in 1918, neither of which was produced), but he turned to poetry and short fiction during his years at the *Yale Literary Magazine*. Then in 1919, after his return from London, the Yale Dramatic Club mounted the first production of a Barry play, the one-act *Autonomy*. By the time he enrolled in Baker's workshop at Harvard later that year, Barry had turned his efforts entirely to writing plays; even during a stint writing copy for a New York advertising agency in 1920 and 1921, Barry sketched scenarios for new plays and oversaw—from a distance—the rehearsals of his first play for Baker, *A Punch for Judy,* in Cambridge during the spring of 1921. Though not a professional production, this comedy-farce had two performances at the Morosco Theatre in New York—also the venue of Barry's final New York premiere, the posthumously staged *Second Threshold,* in 1951. The Harvard workshop took the show on a brief tour to Worcester, Utica, Buffalo, Cleveland, and Columbus, but the play failed to interest a New York producer. It did, however, bring Barry to the attention of critic Robert Benchley and fellow aspiring playwright Robert E. Sherwood. Both men, despite their dubious first impression of what Sherwood called an "exasperating young twirp," became Barry's personal friends and professional colleagues—especially Sherwood, who completed *Second Threshold* after Barry's death.

By the time he quit his advertising job and returned to Harvard in 1921, Barry was engaged to Ellen Semple but determined to make his mark as a professional dramatist before he settled down to married life. Semple remained in New York while Barry moved back to Cambridge, and in a play titled "The Jilts" he took up the question then most crucial in his own life—how marital obligations might thwart an artistic career. "The Jilts," originally titled "The Thing He Wanted to Do," won the 1922 Herndon Prize as the best play written in Baker's workshop; on 15 July of that year he and Semple were married. Ultimately renamed *You and I,* Barry's pensive comedy opened on Broadway early in 1923 to popular and critical approval and was the first of nine Barry plays to be included in Burns Mantle's annual *Best Plays* series.

Barry's portrait of Maitland White—once an aspiring painter but now an executive for G. T. Warren, a beauty products manufacturer—establishes many of the issues that defined his own dramatic vision. "Matey" White's compromises have caused him acute suffering and a sense of "flouted destiny" that even his happy marriage and financial prosperity cannot erase. Though Matey occasionally rails against the demands of family responsibility and bourgeois decorum, his financial and domestic comfort is never seriously threatened. His wife, Nancy, staunchly supports him regardless of whether Matey wants to continue as a highly compensated corporate slave or break out, as he has always wished, to become an independent artist with his own studio and schedule. Bohemia is never an option; Matey's new life will be supported by the proceeds of his stock portfolio along with Nancy's thrifty household management—for example, having two servants instead of five.

Matey's more serious dilemma lies in how to support his son Ricky's pursuit of a career in architecture—here presented as essentially an artistic calling—after relinquishing his corporate salary. This dilemma is Barry's basic "you and I" paradigm, the competing claims of individual fulfillment and responsibility to others. But as in virtually all of Barry's subsequent work, pursuing one's destiny is primarily a male issue, with women sorted into those who help and those who hinder. Likewise, the middle class is an economic level to which one dips only for brief reality checks; the ideal is to have enough money to be free of financial worry but not so much that it obscures the nobler ends of life. In addition to a prosperous father and doting mother, Ricky is blessed with a fiancée, Ronny, who will not only "lie down and die for him" but also brings to the marriage a modest annual income and a house from her father. Eventually, Matey returns to his former position with Warren, who seems to him "uncannily like God," but first extracts a promise of a shortened work week so he may continue to pursue painting as a hobby. This restored income will also allow him to support Ricky's dream of architectural study abroad, meaning that Ricky, unlike his father, can both get married and pursue his art seriously.

By embracing his amateur status, Maitland also eschews the life of the "commercial artist," which he regards as a great compromise, something akin to the situation of his friend Geoff Nichols, a popular novelist who aspires to nothing loftier than healthy sales and a life of hobnobbing in Europe with more famous writers. For Barry, at the start of his own career, Maitland and Nichols represented the Scylla and Charybdis of artistic vocation, the noble amateur and the prosperous hack. Perhaps Ricky can become both noble and prosperous as a master architect, but even so his art will be driven less by an unfettered personal vision than by the needs of two spheres that remained crucial in many of Barry's most important subsequent plays: the home and the world of commerce. Barry's lifelong quest was to discover a clear vision of both these spheres but also of something outside them, a responsibility to self that could not be entirely subsumed in familial or professional relations.

You and I gave a career-launching boost to the newly married playwright. Noting its pedigree as a "47

Workshop" play, Mantle classified it as "society comedy" in a pleasingly epigrammatic style. Its 170 performances at the Belmont Theatre in New York were followed by a successful tour and many productions in college and regional theaters. Barry also had new family duties to occupy him when Philip Semple Barry was born in 1923. This beginning was certainly promising in every respect, but starting with the somewhat briefer run of 104 performances of *The Youngest* late in 1924, Barry experienced a four-play, three-year period of decreasing popular success, ending with the eleven-performance run of *John* in 1927. Yet, in important ways Barry was extending his artistic reach, as if to demonstrate that commercial acceptance was crucial only as a means to the freedom he needed to pursue questions that concerned him.

Like most New York critics, Barry himself found *The Youngest* less worthy than *You and I*, its autobiographical origins notwithstanding, perhaps because it capitalized on a good idea for a play rather than addressing an issue he was truly grappling with at the time. Certainly it takes on what Walter J. Meserve has called the "single idea" behind all of Barry's plays: "man's need for freedom." Yet, the plot depends so heavily on the same peculiar New York state inheritance law that had left Barry in control of the family estate at fourteen that the issue of achieving "freedom" seems reduced to pressing one's mostly circumstantial advantage. Even so, Barry introduces a theme he confronted to greater effect in subsequent plays as a kind of corollary to the individual's search for freedom and fulfillment: the danger of manipulating others as part of this quest, confusing freedom with control.

Richard Winslow, the young hero of this play, like Ricky White of *You and I*, is a budding artist who must choose between a career in business and his true calling. Richard has been preparing himself diligently to be a professional writer, but unlike Ricky's family, the Winslows neither respect nor encourage his ambitions. His mother and older siblings insist that the twenty-two-year-old Richard drop his literary study and take up his duties in the pin-manufacturing business that his late father left them. With some help from outside the immediate family—chiefly his lawyer brother-in-law and his sister's socialite friend Nancy Blake—Richard manages to extract both the personal respect and the financial support he needs to fashion an independent life.

The changing relationship between Nancy and Richard, not surprisingly, emerges as the central focus of the play. Richard's initial impression of her as a "sap-headed little social celebrity" gives way to awareness of a supremely confident young woman with a better conscience and more generous impulses than any of the Winslows. Even when she learns of Richard's legal advantage over his family, Nancy resolves to build Richard up through "kindness and understanding" first, before telling him about it. She sees Richard as a sensitive young man "on the brink of a great transition," one that she takes it upon herself to help him through. Nancy is thus a manipulator with a good heart, as well as an example of the enabling woman that Barry places close to his artist-heroes. She inspires Richard to a new level of rebellion, a stronger sense of destiny, convincing him that "a man's greatest victory is over his own family." The plot cannot be resolved, however, until the precise relationship between Richard's destiny and Nancy's help is articulated. When he discovers that Nancy acted initially on a bet with his sister Muff, Richard uses his new self-confidence to bring Nancy down a peg or two. They will marry, but only after declaring themselves "equals."

The themes and characters of *The Youngest* are clear and engaging, if not especially compelling. With his clipped speech and peevish manner, Richard is never entirely sympathetic. Given the various autobiographical elements in the play, he is probably a self-parody, the artist-as-young-twirp that Sherwood and Benchley encountered in 1921. The play was begun in Baker's workshop but revised in 1923 during the first of many summers that Barry and his wife spent at Cannes in the villa that Ellen's father had bought for them. The problem of distinguishing freedom from control is treated in rudimentary terms in *The Youngest*, but it received more sophisticated treatment in Barry's next play, *In a Garden* (1925); its distinct air of modernity may have accounted for its disappointing seventy-four-show run but made it the earliest of Barry's plays to sustain the interest of theater scholars.

If *In a Garden* established "the Barry stereotype and the Barry label" in the comedy-of-manners genre, as Joseph Patrick Roppolo has noted, it also served as a prototype of the Barry play in which a gracious tone seems at odds with the often disturbing implications. The metatheatrical themes, especially that of characters conscious of themselves as characters, recall the work of Luigi Pirandello; the concluding scene, in which Lissa Terry walks out of the world her husband has created for her, bears a strong resemblance to Nora Helmer's departure at the end of Henrik Ibsen's *A Doll's House* (1879). But Barry's emphasis on the ethics of playwriting, particularly its capacity to put the author in the position of a god who creates and orders his world according to a great plan of his own, seems ultimately the most characteristic aspect of the play, one that links it directly to such later works as *Hotel Universe* (1930) and *Here Come the Clowns*, which have seemed worthier to later scholars than to contemporary reviewers.

Through his playwright-protagonist Adrian Terry, Barry moves beyond the problem of art as a means of personal fulfillment to explore the implications of art itself. Adrian is neither a fledgling writer like Richard Winslow nor an artist who missed his great chance like Maitland White, but rather an accomplished professional in early middle age who has decided to suspend his career so he might experience life itself more fully and directly. In effect he applies his dramatic imagination to his marriage, testing the thesis offered by his self-described "hack novelist" friend Roger Compton that "every wife is at heart another man's mistress"— that no woman truly gets over her first lover. Adrian takes great pains to devise a setting in his library, using stage properties and lighting, that precisely re-creates the garden in which his wife, Lissa, many years before, had dallied with one Norrie Bliss, an old friend who happens to be staying with the Terrys in New York on his way to Maine. Updating Hamlet's "mouse trap" device with explicit references to Freudian unconscious motives and phallic symbolism, Adrian hopes this private theatrical will reveal the truth about his wife's hidden sexual passions and thus "kill the memory— painlessly, and with taste."

As Barry makes clear at several points in the play, Adrian is guilty of confusing life and theater, particularly the different ethics of control and freedom that apply to the two spheres. Adrian's theory that life should be realized with the vitality of "high comedy" makes him want to control other people as if they were characters in one of his plays: "We can apply to life," he tells Lissa, "what we've learned in the theatre." Lissa, even before her staged garden reunion with Norrie Bliss, warns her husband, "Plays are plays, my dear— and life's life. Don't try to mix them. People are too unexpected." These themes left many reviewers baffled, but scholars such as W. David Sievers and David C. Gild have touted *In a Garden* as an innovative "psycho-drama" that enacts therapeutic Freudian techniques in a theatrical context, a method they also find in such later plays as *Hotel Universe* and *Here Come the Clowns*.

Yet, Adrian Terry's vision of a world transformed by a guiding idea with unlimited range and nothing left to chance also fills Lissa with dread, as if her husband's inverted artistry makes her sense the thin line between creating an exquisite stage play and envisioning a totalitarian political state. When Lissa finally leaves Adrian and forces him to admit, "I know no one!", the implication is that art must be a process of discovery that respects the lives of others rather than imposing master plans on them. This issue, however, moved neither audiences nor critics, even with Laurette Taylor in the role of Lissa and Arthur Hopkins as producer-director. Barry was clearly a playwright determined to explore questions important to him personally; though not as directly autobiographical as his previous play, *In a Garden* seems closer to his deeper artistic preoccupations.

Barry's defiance of audience expectations continued in 1926 with an even less popular offering, the whimsically symbolic *White Wings*. He knew it "would probably ruin the man who produced it" because of its calculated departures from Broadway formulas. In certain respects anticipating Thornton Wilder's *The Skin of Our Teeth* (1942), this play about a proud guild of street cleaners at the turn of the twentieth century departs from the domestic settings of his previous plays to take on one of the great themes in modern drama: the increasing mechanization of life. The young hero, Archie Inch, is caught between the traditional world of his father's "white wings," the men who clean up after horse-drawn carriages, and the emerging dominance of the automobile, championed by his sweetheart, Mary Todd, who idolizes her father and the vehicles he has designed. Horses stand for tradition; motorcars for progress. Fighting change to the end is Archie's grandfather, Major Philip Inch, a hero of the Civil War battle of Antietam who now battles the "fiendish engines for return to the great God-given means of conveyance, Holy Horse." Ultimately, progress—in the form of a romantic-comic resolution—carries the day. Archie forsakes the Inch family tradition (as well as a vow to his dying mother), lets Mary teach him to drive a motorized taxi, and thus joins the modern mechanized world.

Barry characteristically avoids the harder expressionist edges of other 1920s plays that examine this theme—those of German playwrights Ernst Toller and Georg Kaiser, Eugene O'Neill's *The Hairy Ape* (1922) and *Dynamo* (1929), or even Elmer Rice's *The Adding Machine* (1923). Barry's modernism in *White Wings* never casts a cold eye on tradition; rather, it casts a fond if melancholy gaze on a past irretrievably but perhaps fortunately left behind. In the comic resolution of the play the representative of progress, Mary Todd, prevails by affirming the old ways, personified by the Inch family, within the new order.

Despite its sometimes confusing negotiations of tradition, innovation, and overall tone, *White Wings* had begun to gain an audience in its third week; but another play had been scheduled to open at the Booth Theatre, so Barry and producer Winthrop Ames had to absorb the losses of a twenty-seven-performance run. Barry now found himself and his career in a precarious spot. His second son, Jonathan Peter, had been born in 1926, but Barry's popularity on Broadway had been tarnished by diminishing audiences and critical dissatisfaction.

In early 1927 Barry returned to France and began work on two new plays that reached the stage later that year. On the strength of its 234-performance run, *Paris Bound* became Barry's first major hit and established him in the top rank of American dramatists. The other play, *John,* did not finish out its second week. Anticipating his experience eleven years later with *Here Come the Clowns* and *The Philadelphia Story,* Barry was writing both his most "serious" play to date as well as his most successful to date. Simultaneously, to express his increasing dismay with audiences, Barry was concocting a deliberately crowd-pleasing piece called *Cock Robin* (1928) with fellow playwright Rice, whom he had encountered on board the RMS *Tuscania* en route to Cannes. No time in Barry's career better supports Brendan Gill's charge that he "wrote too much," but one might also argue that Barry's failures were as integral as his successes in a long process of restless philosophical searching affirmed by periods of popular and critical approval.

The critics found *John* an unwieldy mix of the grandiose and the mundane, especially its language, usually a reliable strength even in Barry's lesser works. The casting of the play came particularly under fire, especially the pairing of Yiddish actor Jacob Ben-Ami as John and British actress Constance Collier as Herodias. Some reviewers, however, did acknowledge the playwright's "noble" and "brave" effort to treat weighty religious themes. Barry's portrait of John the Baptist as a leader caught between two moral orders—Judaic law and Christian mercy—is the most compelling aspect of the play. John is a militant leader with political ambitions for his people, though he also knows that someone else, a Messiah, is destined to be their true leader. He cannot ally himself with the corrupt Antipas and Herodias, whom he condemns as incestuous adulterers; nor can he fully accept the new precepts of forgiveness and submission espoused by Jesus, whom Herodias describes as a young "idealist, more poet than politician." Gerald Weales notes aptly that Herodias is actually much like John, since both of them envision "an avenging political Messiah" quite different from the nonviolent Jesus. John's in-between position is, like Archie Inch's, the kind that Barry found fascinating, but as a "tragic" figure John's stature seems undermined by the overall comic structure of the Christian teleology—the simple fact that John's submissive death is presented as a providential fulfillment rather than the disturbing if cathartic outcome of an impossible predicament.

The wildly successful *Paris Bound* opened in New York during the final week of 1927, exactly six weeks after the final performance of *John. Paris Bound* may be seen as a far more appealing version of a similar debate between a strict moral code and the higher virtues of love and forgiveness that Barry explored in *John.* Reviewers praised its mature treatment of infidelity and

divorce, and commentators on its moral implications have generally agreed with the publicity notes in the Samuel French edition proclaiming Barry's thesis "that the family is more important than the pride of the 'injured' party."

This principle is given voice in the play by James Hutton Sr., father of the newlywed Jim Hutton. On Jim's wedding day, James reproves his former wife, Helen, for her implacable and unwise decision to divorce him because of his meaningless dalliance with another woman. "I may have committed adultery," James tells Helen, "but I never committed divorce." For their part, Jim and his new wife, Mary, vow to be "nice and sensible and modern" about marriage, not to insulate themselves from other men and women and even to respect each other's need to be alone. They succeed until Mary finds out several years later that Jim, during one of his annual solo holidays in Europe, has been seen with Noel Farley, the woman he left behind still desperately in love with him. Jim's father counsels Mary to keep her discovery quiet, to see Jim's lapse within the larger perspective of their otherwise supremely happy marriage, and especially not to surrender to the kind of "vain and selfish" moralism for which his own wife had divorced him many years earlier.

Mary knows this attitude makes sense in theory, but she cannot overcome her hurt feelings until her own sexual fidelity is tested by Richard Parrish, a friend and composer whose ballet she has been helping to transcribe during Jim's European holiday. Late in the play, when Richard declares his passion, Mary begins to feel "something raging inside," an alien, amoral self that responds to Richard's urgings. A self-consciously avant-garde artist, Richard is able to explain Mary's unexpected passion in terms closer to modern psychological concepts of the divided subject: "We're four people, you and he [Jim] and you and I. *His* you can't ever in this world be mine, any more than *my* you can be his." Mary realizes finally that she has powerful sexual desires like all women—indeed like all men, including her husband, whose infidelities she begins to see with great understanding and empathy. Still, she is rescued from a liaison with Richard only when Jim comes home early from Europe and sweeps her up into a plan to fetch their children home for a family-style celebration of their sixth wedding anniversary.

Mary's decision to keep silent and stay with Jim has impressed commentators as a mature alternative to concluding the play with either an indignant, self-righteous sermon on fidelity or a sentimental act of forgiveness. No one seemed bothered that the husband's sexual freedom is condoned while a plot contrivance relieves the wife of having to determine her own sexual

Frank Fenton, Joseph Cotton, Katharine Hepburn, and Van Heflin in the 1939 Broadway production of The Philadelphia Story

freedom. Joseph Wood Krutch praised *Paris Bound* as a "true comedy" that presented the "triumph of the critical faculties over emotional impulses," and Emmet Lavery, writing a decade after Barry's death, judged *Paris Bound* his strongest affirmation that "the marriage bond is exalted and protected," while noting that audiences were nonetheless shocked by the departure from conventional stage morality.

The unreliable response of audiences was virtually the only theme of substance in *Cock Robin,* the play that Barry and Rice had crafted deliberately as an exercise in audience pleasing. Though *Paris Bound* continued to hold the stage far longer than any of his previous works, Barry, like Rice, had recently suffered through a string of box-office failures. Because these had been the works closest to his heart, his confidence in audiences was shaken. *Cock Robin* was a

way for Barry and Rice to restore confidence in their power to reach playgoers while enjoying an elaborate joke at the audience's expense. Ostensibly a murder mystery, the play features a group of amateurs directed by a seasoned and cynical theatrical trooper named McAuliffe. When one of the actors is killed onstage, the other actors' motives for murder are brought out one by one until McAuliffe admits that he killed "Cock Robin" to avenge a wronged woman. Though the other actors tacitly agree to cover up his guilt, McAuliffe knows that they, like the spectators who saw the murder from the other side of the proscenium, are not reliable witnesses to the truths that unfold right in front of them. The play concludes with the police at the door and McAuliffe "laughing silently to himself," just as Barry and Rice must have been amused by the one-hundred-performance run of *Cock Robin* in early 1928, a nominal success on Broadway and little more.

After this flurry of stage production in New York, Barry returned to Cannes to write his next play; the working title, "The Dollar," was dropped in favor of *Holiday* (1928), a title perhaps more familiar to theater and movie audiences than the name Philip Barry. With 230 performances, it enjoyed a success on Broadway equal to that of *Paris Bound,* then reached the screen in two movie adaptations (1930 and 1938). In *Holiday* Barry returns to his earlier critique of American business but manages an even more delicate balance in the character of Johnny Case, a shrewd yet romantic young up- and-comer whose vision of the "self-made man" differs sharply from that of his fiancée, Julia Seton, and his prospective father-in-law, Edward Seton. Johnny is not a frustrated artist like Maitland White or Richard Winslow but rather a man of commerce whose driving ambition is to amass just enough money to support a life based on freedom and self-fulfillment. By contrast, the official Seton family line is strict emulation of Julia's late grandfather, the Seton patriarch who began with nothing and left his heirs laden with wealth and obsessed with the work that enlarges it. Edward declares Johnny's ambition "un-American," as if any pause in the great pursuit would undermine the national character.

But there are serious cracks in the Seton armor, notably the free spirit of Julia's sister, Linda, and the alcoholism and nihilism of their brother, Ned. Whatever vitality and vision drove Grandfather Seton to make a better life has become a narrow and insular existence for his grandchildren. Both Ned and Linda feel themselves already trapped in a rigid set of roles and expectations that Linda calls "the sickness." Johnny, at the last minute, manages to avoid a stifling marriage only when Edward lays out in rhapsodic detail the life he can expect to lead with Julia. Linda makes her escape as well when she leaves New York in pursuit of Johnny; however, Ned, completely unable to make a life for himself, seems doomed to drink himself to death bearing the onus of his family's empty affluence. In light of the imminent 1929 stock-market crash and the Great Depression that followed, Barry's critique of American finance as a mindless juggernaut seems especially prescient. Though Johnny has made his liberating personal fortune in the stock market, his demonstrated knack is for struggling through hard times while never confusing work and life. In the end, Johnny and Linda emerge as the true descendants of Grandfather Seton, who "wasn't satisfied with the life he was born into, so he made one for himself," according to Linda's close friend Nick.

The world that seemed to be opening up for Linda, Johnny, and anyone else with enough imagination not to worship money was shaken after 1929 as economic hardship called into question their cherished individual freedom. Rather than examining this downward plunge as explicitly as he had featured the perils of rising fortunes in *Holiday,* in his next play Barry chose instead to create a world virtually disassociated from economic realities, a world created almost entirely out of language and memory. As Roppolo observes, *Hotel Universe* picks up where *Holiday* leaves off, in essence following through to see what happens when people value freedom over self-knowledge. Reviewers were generally confused by its mood and symbolism, lamenting Barry's departure from the pleasing idiom of *Paris Bound* and *Holiday,* but as usual Barry was compelled to question the implications of his own successes, especially when he found them at odds with the more general malaise of the world as he saw it in 1930.

Certainly, Barry took pains to abstract his audience from familiar contours of locale and time. Played with no intermission, *Hotel Universe* is set in a villa in southern France with a terrace "like a wedge into space." Gathered there are six unhappy characters in search of meaning if not an author, though in effect they find one in Stephen Field, the aging invalid whose lonely daughter, Ann, they have all come to cheer up. By the time Stephen appears more than halfway through the play, "a figure in white, watching them," we have learned that most of them are suffering from suicidal disillusionment and unresolved pasts. Pat Farley, for example, had once left Ann to marry an English girl, whose father refused to allow the marriage, leading to the girl's suicide and Pat's own decision to kill himself. Each visitor begins to act out roles based on past traumas, involving each other in complicated psychodramas similar to those developed for clinical use in the 1920s by Jacob L. Moreno, as Gild and Sievers have explained.

This dimension would not have been evident to Barry's Theatre Guild audience in 1930, nor was Barry himself directly familiar with Moreno's writings. But Barry had always been fascinated with drama as a means of self-revelation and self-fashioning, and with father-characters who either foster the dreams of youth (Maitland White in *You and I*) or try to stymie them (Edward Seton in *Holiday*). In this play Stephen Field takes on the role of confessor-therapist whose mission is to reshape the general ennui into more manageable, individual, and hopeful terms. His theory of the "three estates" of life, comprising the mundane world, the imagination, and "the life past death, which in itself contains the others," is generally taken to be the playwright's own metaphysics, with the goal of seeing life "whole, present and past together in one living instant." By the time Stephen dies, a restored faith in beginnings and possibilities prevails as all the characters, free of illusion and empowered by their inward discoveries, prepare to face life without Stephen's help.

Hotel Universe closed after just eighty-one performances, adding to the financial woes of the Theatre Guild and displeasing early commentators such as Eleanor Flexner, who deemed its philosophizing "little more than a jaunt to a Never-Never land." Krutch was even harsher, condemning it as vulgar and pretentious, its Freudian modernism a mangled assemblage of "New Thought" given voice as "the most appalling mystical chitchat." This Freudianism is precisely what impressed Sievers, who in 1955 called *Hotel Universe* "one of the truly original masterpieces of the modern American drama." In any case, Barry clearly saw the early 1930s as an era in need of self-analysis, and his next play, *Tomorrow and Tomorrow* (1931), revisited the theme of adultery that fascinated audiences in *Paris Bound* with a psychobiological edge that has led critics to compare it favorably to O'Neill's more imposing *Strange Interlude* (1928).

Barry based his plot on II Kings 4:8–37, the story of the childless Shunammite woman who is rewarded with a son for feeding the prophet Elisha. In Barry's play the woman, Eve Redman, is the childless young wife of a businessman whose grandfather founded the college in the Indiana town where they live. The prophet's role is taken by a visiting young psychologist, Dr. Nicholas Hay, whose world-weariness is matched only by his conviction that his work (its specific nature is left vague) will transform "the whole system of education, of literature and art" and indeed "may be the future of the human race." Dr. Hay's lectures at the college are also an important step toward making education there open to women, an opportunity Eve seizes. While he educates her in the "science of the emotions," she for her part renovates his emotional outlook; they fall in love and eventually produce the child that Eve has always longed for but which her husband, Gail, apparently cannot give her (though Gail believes the child is his). As a mother, Eve finds the focus that makes her one of the "artists outside the arts," as Hay describes, who "must do something about life, with it, to it." When their son, Christian, later becomes ill, Hays diagnoses the symptoms as psychopathological, an emotional blockage that Eve eventually cures in semimiraculous fashion that parallels the recovery of the Shunammite woman's child. Ultimately, Eve decides that her destiny lies not with Hays but with her husband, who remains unaware of his son's true paternity.

Eve's rejection of life with Hays allows Barry to affirm conventional marriage vows while allowing Eve to pursue fulfillment by extramarital means. By linking motherhood and art, Barry brings together such previous wives as Nancy White in *You and I* and Mary Hutton in *Paris Bound,* making Eve a mother-artist whose adultery serves the larger moral good of creating a family. Hays, on the other hand, belongs to the line of Barry characters who attempt to control life by means of theory, like Adrian Terry of *In a Garden.* His grandiose vision of transforming the world makes him an even more potentially ominous figure, especially given his doctrine of emotion over reason: this method is precisely what European fascists were using to crush the intellectual elite and consolidate their power over "the people" in the 1930s. By rejecting Hays, whom she still loves, Eve shows that she has a mind and will of her own; though not quite a feminist, Eve has charted a new course toward a traditional end: "Not changed," she says of herself at the curtain, "Complete."

Tomorrow and Tomorrow is generally ranked below Barry's other examinations of marriage, but its 206-performance run restored him once more as a bankable playwright, and it became one of five Barry plays to be adapted for the screen between 1929 and 1932. His next play, *The Animal Kingdom,* with a run of 171 performances, crowned the most productive and successful period in Barry's three-decade career: six plays in just over four years, with an average run of 170 performances each. Leslie Howard wished to produce and star in Barry's new play, which also tackled the themes of marriage, adultery, and divorce. As leading lady Barry wanted to cast Katharine Hepburn, a young actress who had impressed him while understudying as Linda Seton in *Holiday* in 1928 (later to immortalize the character on-screen opposite Cary Grant in 1938), but Howard did not work well with her, and she was replaced in the role of Daisy Sage by Frances Fuller.

In certain respects *The Animal Kingdom* is the male-centered counterpart of *Tomorrow and Tomorrow,* with a husband forced to choose between a spouse who fulfills social convention and a lover who makes him feel alive. Howard's character, Tom Collier, is a young book publisher whose wealthy father sees him as squandering his life in idle pursuits. As if to counter this opinion, Tom marries the well-bred and beautiful Cecelia and relinquishes his attachment to Daisy, a working artist with whom Tom has been living out of wedlock for the past three years. Predictably, Cecelia drains all the bohemian spirit out of Tom; moreover, she contrives to link money and sexuality by favoring Tom's advances only when he shows a willingness to boost profits at his once-selective publishing house, the Bantam Press, which becomes increasingly a best-seller factory. Meanwhile, Daisy, a free spirit reminiscent of Linda Seton, devotes herself to serious painting instead of the magazine illustrations that had previously supported her. In a provocative concluding scene in which Tom appears to be seducing Cecelia, he departs decisively to join the woman he now sees as his true wife and soul mate, Daisy.

Though a success with critics and audiences, as well as a major motion picture in 1932 again starring Howard along with Ann Harding and Myrna Loy (remade in 1946 as *One More Tomorrow* with Ann Sheridan), *The Animal Kingdom* in retrospect seems more an amalgam of Barry's previous plays. The title echoes a speech in *Paris Bound* when James Hutton Sr. scolds his former wife Helen for her unwillingness to see his infidelity as merely "a physical impulse" shared "with the rest of the animal kingdom." Tom's predicament also resembles the situation that Johnny Case in *Holiday* resolves never to fall into: selling out his personal freedom for success in business. A passing reference to hard times in the 1930s may account in part for Tom's greater susceptibility to commercial seduction; in fact, the play includes one of Barry's most conspicuous working-class characters, the bumptious butler Regan, whom Tom later finds sick and jobless after leaving his service. Nonetheless, Tom's decision to leave his wife contrasts directly to Eve Redman's choice in *Tomorrow and Tomorrow*, as if Barry wants to suggest once more that wives find their highest fulfillment in self-sacrificing union while husbands should devote themselves only to marriages that do not thwart their freedom—here symbolized in the rooster that gives its name to Tom's publishing house.

After *The Animal Kingdom* Barry suffered through his worst stretch as a playwright as well as what may have been his worst personal loss. His next three plays—*The Joyous Season* (1934), *Bright Star* (performed in 1935), and *Spring Dance* (1936)—managed a combined total of only forty-seven performances (sixteen, seven, and twenty-four, respectively), far less than even the shortest-lived of his previous six, *Hotel Universe*. Yet, all three featured actors went on to have fame in movies or had already achieved it, most notably Lillian Gish in *The Joyous Season*. Barry's productivity also dropped sharply, down to three premieres in the almost seven years between early 1932 and late 1938. On the personal side, late in 1933 Ellen Barry gave birth to a daughter, their third child, who died in infancy. In his preface to *Second Threshold* Sherwood remarks how deeply this loss hurt the Barrys and suggests further that the strong daughters in *The Philadelphia Story* and *Second Threshold* represent the playwright's vision of how his own daughter might have grown up. Even in *Paris Bound* there are traces of Barry's esteem for daughters when Jim Hutton's father laments that his broken marriage denied him the daughter he always wanted.

Though he started writing *The Joyous Season* well before Ellen's latest pregnancy, Barry endowed its main character, Christina Farley, with healing, conciliatory powers that he no doubt associated with daughters. A nun, Christina is reunited with her siblings at Christmas in the country home the family had left behind when they moved to join the Beacon Hill elite in Boston. Each of her brothers and sisters is beset with problems and controversies that include marital distress, unemployment, alcoholism, and radical politics. Christina's spiritual influence puts most of the Farleys back on paths that may lead to happiness, not unlike the effect Stephen Fields has on the lost worldlings of *Hotel Universe* though in a more explicitly family-centered, Roman Catholic mode. Most reviewers objected to Christina's near-miraculous influence on her family, though later commentators such as Roppolo and Meserve have noted that Barry actually stresses her sacrificial love and clear vision rather than her miraculous powers. Indeed, in the final moment of the play, as her youngest brother, Hugh, inveighs against her, Christina is crying rather than triumphant.

With the Depression and the political situation in Europe worsening, along with his own personal and professional distresses, Barry had little reason to think any individual capable of filling the role of savior. The hero of his next play, *Bright Star*, seems the secular male counterpart of Christina Farley, an idealist named Quin Hanna; but his ethical ruthlessness and the hopeless demise of his plans for reform suggest Barry's darkening vision in the mid 1930s. Not even two out-of-town tryouts and the casting of such in-demand movie stars as Julie Haydon and Lee Tracy in the lead roles could keep *Bright Star* on a New York stage longer than one week, the briefest run of Barry's career. In 1936 he was finally induced, perhaps by recent failures, to bring out *Spring Dance*, his adaptation of a play originally written by two Smith College undergraduates. This story of college girls plotting to corral a "dark, silent, contemptuous" Yale fellow into marriage fared only slightly better than *Bright Star*, though it spawned another movie and featured such rising young performers as Mary Wickes, Imogene Coca, Tom Neal, and José Ferrer. The play had charm but no edge or purpose. By the end of 1936 Barry found himself at an artistic dead end.

For the next two years Barry struggled with his growing despair by writing his only novel, *War in Heaven* (1938), which he revised for the stage as *Here Come the Clowns*, one of his most daring and important plays. In *War in Heaven* Barry works out the terms of the cosmic allegory in which the world is beset by illusion and by a continuous battle between good and evil. Departing from his usual upper-class milieu, Barry sets the action in a barroom frequented by vaudeville performers, a move comparable in his work perhaps only to the street setting of *White Wings,* which features a somewhat similar grotesque charm. The narrator of the novel is John Dickinson, who offers his story in the hope that "it may mean something in a world in which so little does." The relationship between Dickinson and the main character of the novel, the disabled and ill-starred stagehand Dan Clancy, is developed with much greater complexity in the novel than it is in the stage version. Dickinson is a sardonic commentator but not the restless pilgrim searching for truth that Clancy is; Dickinson also utters the words that Barry used for the title of the play but left out of the play itself: "Daddy—look! Here come the clowns!"

The central conflict involves Clancy and an illusionist named Max Pabst, whom Monroe Lippman has identified as Barry's personification of the fascist spirit. Clancy's rejection of Pabst's gospel of illusion, based on the disturbing premise that evil may actually have defeated goodness in the war in heaven that appears in Revelations, emphasizes mankind's free will as the true source of the ills of the world and therefore the possible source of its redemption. The Easter weekend setting of the novel further brings out this theme of rebirth. As Pabst descends through a trap door, Clancy climbs the stairway marked "private" to carry on his search for truth, and Dickinson expresses hope that others will follow Clancy's example.

Here Come the Clowns retains most elements of the novel, though Clancy dies at the curtain after taking a bullet to save Pabst from Dickinson's avenging gun. Eddie Dowling, who also produced the play, was ideal as Clancy because his own career had been a kind of quest, moving from the easy successes of vaudeville to the challenges of serious drama. Clancy's martyrdom is even more pronounced on stage than in the novel, as are the larger moral implications of life presented as a stage performance, an illusion contrived by the Great Director who is either God or Satan. When the benevolent, almost deific owner of the Globe Theater, Mr. Concannon, is revealed to be none other than Pabst enacting one of his illusions, Dickinson blurts out that "the Devil is God and we do his will!" But finally Clancy's dauntless faith in human will carries the play past cynicism and into faith. Pabst is a sinister instance of the controlling impulse that emerged most strongly in *In a Garden* with Adrian Terry's metatheatrical manipulations; in this play, with the Globe Theater and adjoining barroom full of social outcasts ranging from lesbians to midgets, the human race is offered in microcosm, with all its diversity, imperfection, and delusions, as something worth saving.

Critical approval of the play, though not unanimous, was strong enough to restore much of Barry's prestige on Broadway. The financial losses of its mere eighty-eight-performance run, moreover, were almost immediately wiped out by the stunning triumph of his next play, *The Philadelphia Story,* which at 417 performances ran nearly twice as long in New York as his greatest previous success. It was quickly adapted into an enduring major motion picture (1940) and helped to rescue the Theatre Guild from financial peril. It is tempting in retrospect to judge one of Barry's noble failures his greatest work of art and to see *The Philadelphia Story* as a mere cash cow. However, none of his other plays so completely realizes Barry's gift for conveying serious themes in sharp but disarmingly witty dialogue. After the more overtly symbolic allegorizing of *Here Come the Clowns,* Barry offers a vision of American society at early mid-century that encompasses issues of class, gender, filial devotion, family, marriage, money, business, art, politics, the media, personal ethics, and historical change; *The Philadelphia Story* thus serves as a culmination of his playwriting career.

Shifting back to his accustomed setting of wealth and privilege, Barry nonetheless tasks his privileged characters with proving themselves worthy amid the "fading elegance" of their world. Tracy Lord, portrayed indelibly by Katharine Hepburn on stage and screen, "sets exceptionally high standards for herself," according to her mother, "and although she always lives up to them, other people aren't always quite able to." She is spirited but priggish, vital but aloof, a strong and independent woman whom the men closest to her regard as a kind of "virgin goddess," in the words of former husband C. K. Dexter Haven, her only socioeconomic peer among the three men who pursue Tracy romantically during the course of the play. The other two, writer Macaulay (Mike) O'Connor and rising coal magnate George Kitteredge, embody Barry's critiques respectively of art oppressed by commerce and commerce unleavened by generosity. Mike begins his assignment to report on Tracy's wedding for *Destiny* magazine full of contempt for the rich, but soon comes to idolize Tracy as "the golden girl . . . full of love and warmth and delight." The climactic scene in which Tracy breaks her engagement with George, declines Mike's impetuous proposal, and then eagerly accepts Dexter's proposal of remarriage demonstrates not only how fully she has achieved her goal of becoming "like a human being" at last but also how elegiac Barry's view of the American beau monde—and by implication his own portrait of it—had become.

The reunion of Dexter Haven and Tracy Lord seems a redemption of Barry's peculiarly upscale view of life valued for its own sake rather than as a quest for perfection in art or commerce. Marriage to Mike O'Connor would mean perpetuating her exalted but aloof persona, and marriage to the self-made "man of the people"

George Kitteredge would serve to make them an exemplary couple in an American capitalist mode dangerously parallel to the cultural exemplars of fascist Germany. Tracy herself seems vaguely aware of some imminent cultural "revolution" in the world around her, but when George storms offstage condemning Tracy, Dexter, and their "whole rotten class" as doomed, Barry does not try to counter this view so much as devise a kind of "haven" of good breeding and toleration in which Dexter and Tracy may live out their lives as the world is transformed, or rather disfigured, around them.

As the ugly consequences of European totalitarianism became fully evident during World War II, Barry's work took an allegorical turn. *Liberty Jones,* his musical fantasy for the 1941 season, features the title character on the edge of death along with the three others—the everyman troika of Tom, Dick, and Harry—who can save her from the evil machinations of the Three Shirts, who clearly symbolize Nazism, Communism, and Fascism in Europe and America. Lippman has called *Liberty Jones* Barry's only "protest play" as such, but reviewers were united in finding the intentionally childlike style, including music by Paul Bowles, too far out of step with its grim themes and context. Audiences likewise found Liberty not nearly as appealing or credible as Tracy Lord, and the play closed after just twenty-two performances.

Toward the end of the war, Barry brought out another fantasy-allegory inspired by wartime events, *Foolish Notion* (performed in 1945), in which various characters build personal fantasies that speculate on the return of a soldier reported missing in action. As in the earlier psychodramas, the people here are ultimately freed of their "foolish notions" and brought to confront a reality with unclear terms. Unlike *Liberty Jones, Foolish Notion* enjoyed a mildly successful run of 104 performances, attributed by most critics to the casting of Tallulah Bankhead; like *Bright Star* and his final completed work, *My Name is Aquilon*—with its notably short-lived run of just thirty-one performances—it remains unpublished. Barry had adapted *Aquilon* from a work by French playwright Jean Pierre Aumont, and its failure in early 1949, the year of his fatal heart attack in New York at age fifty-three, reaffirmed that Barry wrote best when impelled by the need to work out a personal problem or vision in theatrical terms.

The star-driven success of *Foolish Notion* notwithstanding, Barry's only two achievements of any substance after 1940 were *Without Love,* the 1942 play he wrote for Hepburn, and *Second Threshold,* completed by Sherwood after Barry's death and brought to the Morosco Theatre in early 1951. Neither rivaled the theatrical impact of earlier hits, but both revealed Barry's skill in a new light: one as an entertaining convergence of romantic and political themes; the other as a kind of self-reflexive backward glance at his life and career.

Set in Washington, D.C., on the eve of American involvement in World War II, *Without Love* reprises many aspects of *The Philadelphia Story,* including the casting of Hepburn as Jamie Rowan, a rich young woman with more money than warmth or purpose. In fact, she is first described as "pale and rather dim looking . . . an object, rather than a person," a less lustrous version of Tracy Lord. The play addresses a pressing wartime question in the person of Pat Jamison, an Irish American economist who has just returned from Europe in search of a government post that will help him convince Ireland to come to England's aid despite long-standing hostilities between them. Just as Jamie suggests that she and Pat should marry even "without love" so neither will be alone in the midst of global cataclysm, the play itself proposes that an Ireland-England alliance also makes good sense. Later, as Pat laments the general lack of "any real love of country, any real love of liberty," a revitalized Jamie notes the parallel between this apathy and their own officially loveless marriage. By this time they acknowledge they really are in love, and, in the hopeful thematic parallel, Pat is assigned to Dublin as a special U.S. attaché to play matchmaker between Ireland and England.

Without Love surpassed the crucial 100-performance measure with 110, but when it was adapted by Hollywood in 1945 (with Hepburn and Spencer Tracy in their second movie together) the urgent setting of wartime diplomacy had been changed, in effect, to a Cold War situation in which Tracy plays a scientist at work on high-altitude oxygen technology for the military. This screenplay, written by Barry's friend Donald Ogden Stewart, eliminated much of the mingling of love and politics that made the play compelling for wartime audiences, replaced instead by the powerful on-screen chemistry of Hepburn and Tracy.

The posthumous staging of *Second Threshold* in 1951 clarified Barry's legacy to American playwriting. In his preface to the completed version of the script Sherwood explains his own role as one of "carpentry rather than creation," and his motive as "a sense of professional obligation." He notes that in writing *Second Threshold* Barry had at last discovered that "bright comedy and dark tragedy must blend," but this same blending is evident throughout Barry's career, though not often quite so dark. Its run of 126 performances, while far from rivaling his greatest triumphs, made *Second Threshold* a satisfactory conclusion to three decades of new Barry plays on Broadway.

Sherwood's revisions consisted largely of tightening the structure of the play, including the time frame, which he shortened from three days to twenty-four hours; he also abridged Barry's often lavish set directions and curtailed some of the stage business. The dialogue also is much sparer. Sherwood clearly focuses on the emotional relationship between Josiah Bolton and his daughter, Miranda. Josiah is a middle-aged government lawyer who, though respected and accomplished, finds himself emotionally detached and isolated, a witty but sardonic, self-critical, and (as his repeated "accidents" indicate) chronically suicidal man. A key player behind the scenes during World War II, Josiah seems at a loss in the postwar era. Miranda, who has recently graduated from Bennington, is engaged to one of her father's wartime associates, despite Josiah's objections. She feels acutely alienated from her father, as does her brother, Jock, a law-school dropout who has taken instead to show business. Miranda resolves "to face it out" with their father, to get to the root of his malaise and convince him that others still love and need him. Though Josiah sees himself on a "second threshold" leading to death, Miranda and a young physician named Toby Wells, with whom she falls in love, finally make Josiah view this threshold as a gateway to life rather than death.

It is difficult not to see shades of William Shakespeare's *The Tempest* (circa 1611) in the regeneration of Miranda's father, especially given the valedictory mood that pervades the play. In a late speech Josiah uncovers the key reason for his despair: his own fulfilled ambitions have marooned him on an emotional island, and he believes he has put Miranda on a similar path by trying to create her in his own image—his "god complex," in Jock's phrase. But just prior to this revelation he has invoked an old friend, a great World War I fighter pilot who killed himself because life after the Armistice made no sense to him. "One must belong to his times," Josiah remarks, "live them, write them, paint them, be of them." Likewise Josiah has reached a similar impasse in which his successes seem tragically beside the point, in which the prospect of death seems logical and comforting. Josiah ultimately chooses life because his daughter affirms his value and "doesn't want her father to die." He calls for a carpenter to fix the steps to the garden so no further "accidents" will occur and bids some unnamed presence—perhaps death itself—to be gone at last.

Second Threshold, the final work of Barry's career, became a kind of bridge between the vision of his earlier plays and the future path of American drama. Barry's persistent understanding in such plays as *Here Come the Clowns, Hotel Universe,* and *You and I,* as well as *White Wings*

and *Paris Bound,* is that the very mixing of achievement and failure that makes life absurd is the only possible basis of its meaning. Though few of his plays except those better-known as movies—*Holiday* and *The Philadelphia Story*—have enjoyed major stage revivals since 1960, Barry's witty and inventive critiques of character, society, and values have left a mark on American drama that is still present if not always acknowledged.

References:

Alan Downer, *Fifty Years of American Drama* (Chicago: Regnery, 1951), pp. 70–73, 147–150;

Eleanor Flexner, *American Playwrights: 1918–1938: The Theatre Retreats from Reality* (New York: Simon & Schuster, 1938), pp. 249–271;

John Gassner, "Philip Barry: A Civilized Playwright," in his *The Theatre in Our Times: A Survey of the Men, Materials, and Movements in the Modern Theatre* (New York: Crown, 1954), pp. 322–328;

David C. Gild, "Psychodrama on Broadway: Three Plays of Psychodrama by Philip Barry," *Markham Reviews* (1970): 65–74;

Jean Gould, *Modern American Playwrights* (New York: Dodd, Mead, 1966), pp. 78–98;

Joseph Wood Krutch, *The American Drama Since 1918* (New York: Random House, 1939), pp. 163–180;

Emmet Lavery, "The World of Philip Barry," *Drama Critique,* 3 (1960): 98–107;

Monroe Lippman, "Philip Barry and His Socio-Political Attitudes," *Quarterly Journal of Speech,* 42 (1956): 151–156;

Walter J. Meserve, "Philip Barry: A Dramatist's Search," *Modern Drama,* 13 (1970): 93–99;

Joseph Patrick Roppolo, *Philip Barry* (New York: Twayne, 1965);

James M. Salem, "Phillip Barry and the Spirituality of Love," *Renascence,* 19 (1966): 101–109;

W. David Sievers, "The Psychodramas of Philip Barry," in his *Freud on Broadway: A History of Psychoanalysis and the American Drama* (New York: Hermitage House, 1955), pp. 187–211;

Gerald Weales, "The Very High Comedy of Philip Barry," *Commonweal* (27 August 1976): 564–566.

Papers:
Collections of Philip Barry's papers are housed at the Beinecke Library, Yale University, and the Lauinger Library, Georgetown University.

Marita Bonner

(16 June 1899 – 6 December 1971)

Jude R. Meche
Texas A&M University

BOOK: *Frye Street and Environs: The Collected Works of Marita Bonner,* edited by Joyce Flynn and Joyce Occomy Stricklin (Boston: Beacon, 1987).

SELECTED PERIODICAL PUBLICATIONS: *The Pot Maker: A Play to Be Read, Opportunity,* 5 (1927): 43–46;
The Purple Flower, Crisis, 35 (1928): 9–11, 28–29;
Exit, An Illusion, Crisis, 36 (1929): 335–336, 352.

Marita Bonner is perhaps the most unorthodox playwright of the early part of the century to turn her attention toward the concerns of the African American community. Yet, despite an unusual, nonrealistic approach to her subject, Bonner won a great deal of praise for her dramatic work—as well as for her short fiction—in the black magazines *Crisis* and *Opportunity.* Her three one-act plays—*The Pot Maker: A Play to Be Read* (1927), *The Purple Flower* (1928), and *Exit, An Illusion* (1929)—remained unstaged during her lifetime, probably because of the nationwide economic difficulties following 1929 and the subsequent neglect and dismissal of her work as that of a minor author; but each play nevertheless offers a compelling glimpse into the realities of being an African American during the first half of the twentieth century. Beyond merely presenting a portrait of black life in America, as she does in her short stories and essays, Bonner seemed to envision the dramatic space as one of more freedom and possibility than the fictional sphere in which she most often worked.

While Bonner's short stories almost inevitably have a tragic outcome, and while race and class always play a contributing role in these conclusions, her plays—particularly her best-known work, *The Purple Flower*—offer a possibility of change for her protagonists. And while strife among the generations is inevitable in Bonner's fiction, *The Purple Flower* shows cooperation between young and old. Perhaps most significantly, Bonner's use of questions directly addressed to her predominantly black audience suggests that the potential for change lies with them rather than with those who

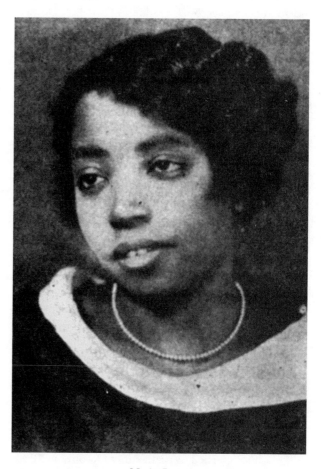

Marita Bonner

would oppress them. However, despite such hints of promise, these plays are not fantasies; they are grounded in the African American's actual situation in the American landscape, and they guarantee neither salvation nor freedom but merely the possibility of both. In the end, this mixture of unfriendly reality and potential future redemption makes her plays compelling and still worthy of attention.

Bonner's birthdate is a subject of debate; while the date is generally held to be 16 June 1899, scholars

Lorraine Elena Roses and Ruth Elizabeth Randolph assert that her actual birthdate was 16 June of the previous year. Bonner was the third of four children born to Joseph Andrew and Mary Anne Noel Bonner. She was educated in Brookline, Massachusetts, where she attended the Cabot School until third grade. After the Cabot School, she attended the Edward Devotion School and Brookline High School, from which she graduated in 1918. In high school Bonner contributed to the student magazine, *The Sagamore,* and gained the attention of its faculty sponsor, Alice Howard Spaulding, who urged Bonner to apply to Radcliffe. Bonner did so and was accepted, graduating in 1922. Despite regulations prohibiting blacks from residing on campus, Bonner was active in the university community, joining several musical clubs (she was an accomplished pianist) and founding the Radcliffe chapter of the black sorority Delta Sigma Theta. She majored in English and comparative literature and studied creative writing in Charles Townsend Copeland's exclusive writing seminar. Bonner also continued her study of German, which she had begun in high school. Toward the end of her career at Radcliffe, Bonner began teaching at the nearby Cambridge High School, perhaps for financial reasons.

In 1924 Bonner's mother died of a brain hemorrhage. Her father died two years later. After her graduation and during these years of hardship, Bonner again obtained teaching positions to support herself. She taught at the Bluefield Colored Institute in Bluefield, Virginia, from 1922 until 1924 and at the Armstrong High School in Washington, D.C., from 1924 until 1930. During her time in Washington, Bonner joined "The Round Table," Georgia Douglas Johnson's literary salon; she also began to seriously pursue writing and publishing her work. Her first published story, "The Hands," appeared in 1925 in *Opportunity.* In the same year, she published her essay "On Being Young—A Woman—and Colored" in *Crisis.*

Bonner married William Almy Occomy in 1930. Occomy was a graduate of Brown University and held an M.B.A. from Boston University. Following their marriage, the couple moved to Chicago, where they raised three children: William Almy Jr., Warwick Gale Noel, and Marita Joyce. In 1941, the same year in which she ceased publishing her work, Bonner and Occomy joined the First Church of Christ Scientist. Around the same time, Bonner also decided to return to teaching and, after satisfying Board of Education questions concerning her qualifications, taught at Philips High School from 1944 until 1949. From 1950 until 1963 Bonner taught at the Dolittle School, working with mentally handicapped students.

Prior to 1941, however, Bonner's move to Chicago had a momentous impact upon her writing, because there she found and developed the microcosm of Frye Street. This fictional location became the setting for much of her subsequent fiction and became, for Bonner, a universal landscape representing all the varieties of life for the urban-living African American as well as for the other ethnic minorities of the city. She describes the street, in a foreword to "A Possible Triad on Black Notes," in the following terms:

> *Now, walking along Frye Street, you sniff first the rusty tangy odor that comes from a river too near a city; walk aside so Jewish babies will not trip you up; you pause to flatten your nose against discreet windows of Chinese merchants; marvel at the beauty and tragic old age in the faces of the young Italian women; puzzle whether the muscular blond people are Swedes or Danes or both; pronounce odd consonant names in Greek characters on shops; wonder whether Russians are Jews, or Jews, Russians—and finally you will wonder how the Negroes there manage to look like all men of every other race and then have something left over for their own distinctive black-browns. . . .*
>
> *All the World is there.*

Frye Street challenges the then-current idea of the American "melting pot" in which all races merge into a single identity. The Frye Street of Bonner's fiction, rather, serves as a refuge for those who are unable to achieve the ideal homogeneity of the American, and it is a place where the residents' race, ethnicity, and otherness are never to be forgotten.

Bonner's plays have frequently been labeled allegories, but though there is some truth to this labeling—each play contains at least a few allegorical elements—Bonner's works function in ways entirely different from the medieval morality plays to which they have been compared. Unlike these earlier works that each carry a specific, clear didactic message, Bonner's plays allow an ambiguity to enter into their allegoric structures. The final actions of each play do not ring with the unswerving optimism of a work such as *Everyman,* and even allegorical characters such as the White Devils in *The Purple Flower* do not perform only acts of deviltry; in addition to their trickery, Bonner attributes to them a grace, an "adroitness," and an artfulness that are not essentially negative. Through this ambivalence, Bonner seems intent not upon forcing a view upon her audience but upon forcing her audience to arrive at a decision of their own.

Bonner's use of second-person narration in her stage directions and descriptions of sets and characters further emphasizes the necessity for audience participation in any effort to extract a meaning from her plays. Particularly, Bonner's use of queries directed to her audience makes clear the viewer's need to answer fundamental questions before any understanding can be gained. Additionally, Esther Beth Sullivan observes that the use of second-person narration implicates the viewer in those social issues that Bonner presents through her plays, further compelling her audience to work toward their own understandings of the actions on the stage since—finally—those actions are inextricably related to their own actions offstage.

In her first play, *The Pot Maker,* Bonner begins with her characteristic use of the second-person point of view to draw her audience into the setting and then the action of the play. The setting is a room in which Elias Jackson, who has been "called of God," is preparing to rehearse his first sermon before his father and mother; his wife, Lucinda; and her lover, Lew Fox. Bonner offers descriptions of each person, calling for the audience to recognize each of them for what they are: Lew as a ridiculous, foolish, facetious swaggerer; Lucinda as the "base fool" who is the only one capable of loving him; the mother as guardian of the family's pride and propriety; the father as quietly proud; and Elias as "ruggedly ugly" though "You want to give both hands to him." Elias's calling has not allowed him time to go to a theological school: "God summoned him on Monday. This is Wednesday. He is going to preach at the meeting-house on Sunday."

As the curtain rises, Elias busily seats his audience so that they simulate the audience he expects for his first sermon. Immediately after, he attempts to begin his sermon only to be cut off by his mother's objection that his opening, "Brothers and sisters," has been overused. Beginning again, he attempts to launch into his parable of a pot maker and his pots only to be interrupted by Lucinda and then again by his mother. Throughout Elias's attempts to launch into his sermon, Lucinda and Lew are exchanging amorous glances while Elias's mother casts venomous looks toward her daughter-in-law.

After these repeated false starts, Elias is finally able to relate his parable of a pot maker who promises his pots that if they are able to stand through the long night and hold all of their contents, they will then be transformed from earthenware into a higher metal: "Tin pots, iron pots, brass pots, silver pots. Even gold." After he offers this promise, one pot cries out that it is cracked, and the pot maker bends over it and seals it. The pot maker then leaves, and several of the pots tip over from fear of the dark or of noises. When the pot maker returns, he points to those pots that are still standing, and they realize that they have turned into gold. Those pots that "kinder had hung their heads but was still settin' up" were transformed into silver, and those pots on the ground that "snuk up and tried to stand up and hol' up their heads" were turned

to brass. Those that simply lay on the ground turned to tin. Elias then points to his congregation and tells them that if they are able to hold the truth as the pot maker's pots held their contents that they would then be transformed by God, and he urges any member of his congregation with a crack to call out, as did the pot, and be healed by God.

Elias's sermon has little impact on his listeners, all of whom are too preoccupied with the actions of the others. In fact, the only member of Elias's audience who reacts favorably to the sermon is his father. Lew makes a quick exit after the sermon, and Lucinda escorts him under the ruse of getting him a drink of water. When she returns, she decides to go out "where folks got some sense" and fights with Elias's mother over a good pair of shoes, eventually giving them up to their rightful owner. Elias's mother and father then leave, and Elias confronts Lucinda. Lucinda accuses Elias of being unmanly since he is unable to provide her with a home of her own and since they must live with his parents. While she berates Elias, they hear Lew whistle. Lucinda tries to join Lew, but Elias holds her back. Then Lew, stumbling around in the dark outside the house, falls into the well. Lucinda breaks free from Elias, and she too falls in the well. As their struggles are heard offstage, Elias berates both as "tin," but then he cries out "*God, God, I got a crack in me too!*" and runs out to the well only to fall in as he tries to rescue his wife. The play ends with Bonner's stage directions: "*A crack has been healed. A pot has spilled over on the ground. Some wisps have twisted out.*"

This ending, comprised of both a healing and a falling over, offers little in the way of clear meaning for Bonner's audience and allows the play to move beyond the didacticism of the morality play from which it borrows many elements. Indeed, while the son who is "called of God" is clearly suggestive of Christ, his death in the well is not the kind of sacrifice for the sins of others that one might expect from a Christ figure. Bonner does suggest that Elias's death might be redemptive with the observation that a crack was healed, but her final stage directions simultaneously suggest that even he is unable to hold God's truth.

The Pot Maker also offers interesting commentary on the role that the African American community plays in the formation of both the Christian leader and—since Elias is also involved in the fashioning of a story—of the artist. In the presence of both, the family becomes more of an obstruction than an aid. Elias's mother attempts to shape both Elias's Christianity and his artistic production through her criticism of his unorthodox parable. Similarly, Lew and Lucinda draw the attention of Elias and the rest of his small congregation away from his message and art and down to their own base level.

Finally, Lucinda's attacks upon Elias's manhood, implying that his new, nonpaying vocation is less manly than his previous employment in the cornfields, suggest that religious and artistic inclinations are incompatible with the community's vision of masculinity.

Bonner's next play, *The Purple Flower,* also examines the role of community in the progress of a people toward a goal. In this play, perhaps Bonner's most allegorical, the protagonists, the Us's, are prevented by the White Devils from climbing the hill to reach the purple Flower-of-Life-at-Its-Fullest. Bonner describes the White Devils as thoroughly artful creatures and ones who are skilled at deceit. She gives no definite requirements for the Us's color or appearance.

The play is set during the Middle-of-Things-as-They-Are and focuses on a group of Us's discussing their fate in the valley at the foot of the White Devils' hill. This valley lies between Nowhere and Somewhere. Bonner also divides the set horizontally, with an upper stage where the action takes place and an underlit lower stage. She notes that the division between upper and lower stages is The Skin-of-Civilization—a boundary so thin that a thought "can drop you through it."

As the curtain rises, the Us's bemoan their situation. Some of the Us's describe the way that they have worked for the White Devils all day, only to be pushed off the hill at nightfall. Most of the Us's agree that work is not a viable means of winning the White Devils' respect or of reaching the Flower. Next, an Old Man among the Us's calls for a Young Man who has been reading books to tell them what he has learned about getting up the hill. The Young Man, however, throws his books down in disgust. These books, written by the White Devils, have no information of use to the Us's. The Us's then turn to another Us, who carries bags of money, and they question him about his unhappiness. This Us replies in turn that his money does him no good in reaching the top of the hill. Meanwhile, during the course of this conversation, a young Us named Sweet comes running onstage crying because a White Devil hiding in the bushes pinched her as she walked by.

Finally, one Old Lady tells the others of her dream in which "I saw a White Devil cut in pieces—head here *(pointing)*, body here—one leg here—one there—an arm here—an arm there." Upon hearing this, an Old Man proclaims that "It's time then!" and calls for an iron pot. He then calls for a handful of dust, one from "the depths of the things you have made," to put into the pot. The Old Man then asks for books, which the Young Man supplies, and gold, which the Us with money readily provides. Only the Old Man's call for blood makes the other Us's pause. They deliberate over whose blood should be taken, objecting to the offer by

an Us named Finest Blood to use his own blood. Other Us's suggest that they ambush the White Devil hiding in the bushes, but the Old Man tells them "An Old Us will never tell you to play White Devil's games!" Instead, the Old Man instructs Finest Blood to lure the White Devil out of the bushes and then issue a challenge, saying to him:

> White Devil, God is using me for His instrument. . . . He says it is almost day, White Devil. The night is far gone. A New Man must be born for the New Day. Blood is needed for birth. Blood is needed for the birth. Come out, White Devil. It may be your blood—it may be mine—but blood must be taken during the night to be given at the birth. . . . You have taken blood. You must give blood. Come out. Give it.

After receiving these instructions, Finest Blood asks if there is another way, but the Old Man tells him that there is none. The play ends as the Us's listen to Finest Blood's voice offstage as he issues the challenge to the White Devil. Bonner calls for the curtain to close "*leaving all the Us, the White Devils . . . listening, listening. Is it time?*"

With this final question directed toward her audience, Bonner again prevents her work from slipping into the didacticism of a medieval morality play and also underscores the importance of the events in her play to those who are witnessing these actions. The play is clearly a call to violent resistance and leaves little question about what actions Bonner advocates as a means of achieving equality between whites and blacks, but this final question does place the responsibility for choosing the appropriate time for this violence squarely upon the viewer. Indeed, the action that Bonner advocates must be one agreed upon by the entire community just as, for the Us's, the formation of the New Man required contributions from all members of the Us community.

Bonner's final play steps away from race relations to examine the effects of racism within the black community. Particularly, *Exit, An Illusion* focuses upon the ways in which racial concerns interfere in the relationship between protagonists Dot and Buddy. Dot is of mixed blood and is the victim of rumors that she is trying to pass for white. The play opens with stage directions that immediately bring the main issue to the forefront: "*The room you are in is mixed. It is mixed.*" This statement refers not only to gender but also to racial mixing, as Dot is described as almost as "pale as the sheets" while Buddy is "blackly brown," and the emphasis on passing and mixing continues as Dot applies white powder to her face through much of the play.

When the curtain rises, Dot is sprawled in bed, and Buddy lies asleep on the floor beside the bed. Dot awakens with a start, waking Buddy in the process, and begins rushing around in preparation for a date. Buddy objects to her plans to go out, because she is clearly ill. However, as he questions Dot about her upcoming date, he finds even more reason to object. Dot admits that she has "been knowing the guy all my life" and tells Buddy that her date's name is Exit Mann. Buddy mocks the name but grows suspicious as he sees Dot applying heavy amounts of powder to her face.

His questions about whether she plans to go out passing are quickly dismissed by Dot, but Buddy becomes increasingly suspicious and begins to connect this date to the white man that rumor has linked to her name. Despite Dot's protests, Buddy becomes increasingly certain that Exit Mann is that white man, and he vows that he will kill both Dot and her date. Dot tells Buddy that, if he loves her, her date will not be able to come; however, Buddy is so enraged that he denies his love for Dot. When Exit suddenly appears behind Buddy, Dot begins to panic and begs Buddy to tell her that he loves her before it is too late. Buddy instead commands Dot to join her lover; when she does, she falls limp, and Buddy realizes that Exit Mann is, in reality, Death.

At this moment, suddenly, the lights flare, and the room and its occupants again appear as they did at the opening curtain. Dot cries for Buddy to say he loves her before she goes, but he does not hear her. The stage directions note, however, that "*You think you hear the rattling*" of her throat. Immediately after Dot's cries cease, Buddy awakens, still shouting that he does not love her. Upon realizing that he was dreaming, he turns to Dot, touches her, "*begins to cry like a small boy*" and finally admits, "Oh Dot! I love you! I love you!" As the curtain falls, it is by no means certain that Dot hears Buddy's declarations of his love for her. What is clear, though, is that Buddy's concerns with race obscure all else from his view. Indeed, he cannot associate Dot's paleness with anything other than whiteness and does not realize until too late that her skin color is no longer a signifier of race but of declining physical health.

Exit, An Illusion is Bonner's least ambiguous play. Unlike *The Pot Maker* or *The Purple Flower,* Bonner's final play does not leave a great deal for the audience to interpret for themselves. She offers no question for her viewers to ponder as they leave the theater. In fact, this play—though not the most allegorical of her dramatic pieces—is her most didactic work. In her fiction Bonner also criticizes black prejudices against other blacks because of skin color, opposing this behavior in no uncertain terms.

Bonner died on 6 December 1971 from smoke inhalation after a lamp in her apartment caught fire. After trying to smother the flames, Bonner barricaded herself in a bathroom, where she was found by firefighters. She was rushed to the hospital, where she later died. Her literary output consisted, finally, of twenty short stories, three plays, and two essays.

Despite her tendency toward a more didactic drama in *Exit, An Illusion,* Bonner's willingness to initiate racial and political discussions dominates her dramatic style. And though there is no evidence—nor even the suggestion—that Bonner's style was influenced by her German contemporary, Bertolt Brecht, her drama shares with Brecht's the intent of reforming humankind. Certainly Bonner merits comparison with Brecht, despite her relative anonymity and her geographical distance from the German playwright. Both were adept at forcing social issues into the consciences of their audiences. And like Brecht—and her other contemporaries in the Harlem Renaissance—Bonner was undoubtedly aware of the discussions of class inspired by Karl Marx's treatises on the bourgeoisie's abuses of the proletariat. Bonner's drama took up this reformist spirit and turned the viewer's attention to the problems of the African American.

References:

Errol Hill, "The Revolutionary Tradition in Black Drama," *Theatre Journal,* 38 (1986): 408–426;

Lorraine Elena Roses and Ruth Elizabeth Randolph, "Marita Bonner: In Search of Other Mothers' Gardens," *Black American Literature Forum,* 21, no. 1–2 (1987): 165–183;

Esther Beth Sullivan, Introduction to *The Purple Flower,* in *Modern Drama by Women, 1880s–1930s: An International Anthology,* edited by Katherine E. Kelly (London & New York: Routledge, 1996), pp. 309–311.

Papers:

Marita Bonner's letters and manuscripts are located in the Arthur and Elizabeth Schlesinger Library, Radcliffe College, Harvard University, Cambridge, Massachusetts.

Mary Coyle Chase

(25 February 1907 – 20 October 1981)

Kathleen M. Gough
University of Maryland, College Park

PLAY PRODUCTIONS: *Me, Third,* Denver, WPA Theater, 1936; revised as *Now You've Done It,* New York, Henry Miller's Theatre, 5 March 1937;

Sorority House, Denver, University Civic Theater, University of Denver, 1938;

Too Much Business, Denver, University Civic Theater, University of Denver, 1940;

A Slip of a Girl, Camp Hall, Colorado, U.S.O., 1941;

Harvey, New York, Forty-eighth Street Theatre, 1 November 1944;

The Next Half Hour, New York, Empire Theatre, 29 October 1945;

Mrs. McThing, New York, Martin Beck Theatre, 20 February 1952;

Bernardine, New York, The Playhouse, 16 October 1952;

Lolita, Abingdon, Virginia, Barter Theatre, 30 August 1954; revised as *Mickey,* Denver, Changing Scene Theater, 12 December 1968;

The Prize Play, Denver, University Civic Theater, University of Denver, 30 October 1959;

Midgie Purvis, New York, Martin Beck Theatre, 1 February 1961;

The Dog Sitters, Phoenix, Arizona, Phoenix Playhouse, 1966;

Cocktails with Mimi, Abingdon, Virginia, Barter Theatre, 3 July 1973.

Mary Coyle Chase

BOOKS: *Sorority House* (New York, Los Angeles & London: French, 1939);

Too Much Business (New York, Los Angeles & London: French, 1940);

Harvey (New York: Dramatists Play Service, 1944; London: English Theatre Guild, 1952);

Mrs. McThing (New York: Oxford University Press, 1952);

Bernardine (New York: Oxford University Press, 1953);

Loretta Mason Potts (Philadelphia: Lippincott, 1958);

The Prize Play (New York: Dramatists Play Service, 1961);

Midgie Purvis (New York: Dramatists Play Service, 1963);

The Dog Sitters (New York: Dramatists Play Service, 1963);

The Wicked Pigeon Ladies in the Garden (New York: Knopf, 1968);

Mickey (New York: Dramatists Play Service, 1969);

Cocktails with Mimi (New York: Dramatists Play Service, 1974).

PRODUCED SCRIPT: *Harvey,* motion picture, by Chase and Oscar Brodney, Universal-International Pictures, 1950.

Mary Coyle Chase was the fourth woman to win the Pulitzer Prize in drama after the establishment of the award in 1918. She is perhaps best known for her play *Harvey* (1944), which won the 1944–1945 Pulitzer (over such contenders as Tennessee Williams's *The Glass Menagerie,* 1944) and became one of the ten longest-running shows in Broadway history. Although Chase had a total of six plays that appeared on Broadway from 1937 to 1961, as well as eight plays that were produced at both the regional and university levels, none of her other works came close to rivaling the success of *Harvey.* This singular triumph may be one reason why her work has received such limited critical attention.

Like many dramatists writing in the aftermath of World War II, Chase used her work in order to "champion the necessity of dreams, and the powerful life of the human imagination," as scholar Albert Wertheim describes. Although some critics have performed a cursory examination of Chase's works in relation to Eugene O'Neill, Williams, Henrik Ibsen, Luigi Pirandello, and even John Millington Synge, her predominant use of comedy, farce, and fantasy have left many critics apprehensive of finding in her plays an avenue for scholarly inquiry. Evaluation is further complicated by the fact that her dramatic career falls into two camps. Plays such as *Too Much Business* (1940), *The Prize Play* (1959), *The Dog Sitters* (published in 1963), and *Mickey* (1968) contribute to her frequent categorization as a writer of children's plays. But she was also a writer of comedies, which she used as a means of critiquing social norms and political systems, exploring relationships across generations or between parents and children, and, of course, challenging the norms of polite society and the prescribed duties of the individual. However, in some respects the construction of these categories, children's writer versus comic writer, is quite arbitrary, since Chase's use of fantasy and the supernatural pervades almost all of her dramatic writing. Both *Mrs. McThing* (1952) and *Bernardine* (1952), for instance, resisted classification as purely children's theater and helped to pave the way for other cross-pollinated productions to reach the Broadway stage.

Mary Coyle was born on 25 February 1907 in West Denver, Colorado, to Frank Bernard and Mary McDonough Coyle. In a profile of the author, Wallis M. Reef noted that "her birthplace was not quite on the wrong side of the tracks, but the noise from the trains reached it." Both of her parents came from Ireland to the American West at an early age in hopes of attaining part of the American dream. Frank Coyle had tried his luck, although unsuccessfully, in the Oklahoma land rush before deciding to settle in Denver. Chase's mother came from Ulster at sixteen in order to attend to her four brothers, who had also been unsuccessful in the Colorado gold camps during the 1880s and 1890s. From her Irish uncles and her mother, Chase received much of her early knowledge of Irish legend and folk culture, including the stories of banshees, leprechauns, and *pookas* (spirits that take animal form) that emerge in some of her most notable plays.

In 1922, at the age of fifteen, she graduated from West Denver High School and immediately began attending the University of Denver, where she studied Greek. She stayed at the University of Denver for two and a half years before leaving to attend the University of Colorado at Boulder from 1924 to 1925. She continued her study of the classics there for one year before leaving school at age eighteen to accept a position as a newspaper reporter for *The Rocky Mountain News.* As a young "stunt girl" reporter, Chase covered stories of mine explosions, murders, and love nests—all of which fit quite well into what she called her "exhibitionist tendencies." During this time she became engaged to Robert Lamont Chase, a reporter and later managing editor for *The Rocky Mountain News;* they were married on 7 June 1928. She continued to work at the paper for three more years before leaving in 1931 to devote her time to raising their three sons—Michael, Colin, and Jerry. During these years her time was also occupied by reading and writing plays, working as a freelance correspondent for the International News Service and the United Press (from 1932 to 1936), and lobbying for various causes.

Her first play, *Me, Third* (1936), was completed at about the same time her third son was born. The title of the play comes from the campaign slogan used by Harlan Hazlett, the protagonist, to depict (quite ironically) his humble and self-deprecating character: "God first, the other guy second, and me third." It was originally produced by the WPA Theater in Denver, and the critics and audiences loved it. However, when it opened on Broadway on 5 March 1937 as *Now You've Done It,* under the direction of Brock Pemberton, it was a dismal failure, lasting only forty-three performances.

Like all Chase's plays, *Me, Third* is set simply in "a city in the western United States," and the time is "the present." The almost negligible importance of geographic location allows for the development of character to take precedence in her works and, in turn, allows the audience to easily accept the fluidity between reality, farce, and fantasy that she creates. The action of the play surrounds Harlan Hazlett, a self-centered and unscrupulous political candidate who wishes to be elected to office at any cost. The unlikely heroine is his wife, Stella, who was Harlan's secretary before they were married and who is still treated like hired help by Harlan and his mother and sisters, Etta and Janet. The complicated and comedic plot begins when Grace Dosher, a parolee from a girls' reformatory and former cashier at a genteel bor-

Chase and her husband, Robert, in 1946 (photograph © Hulton-Deutsch Collection/CORBIS)

dello, is hired by Etta and Janet to be the Hazletts' maid. Chase fashioned Grace's character from her own experience: after the birth of one of her sons, while on a tight budget, she hired a maid from a home for delinquent girls to help her with the household chores.

When Etta introduces Grace to Harlan, it becomes apparent that because of Harlan's past indiscretions at this same bordello, he and Grace have no need for introduction. This confrontation, however, initiates a series of comic gags and devices that evoke elements of the Restoration comedy of manners: secret identities, witty repartee, love triangles, and sexual innuendo. These elements are evident not only in Grace's ability to blackmail Harlan but also in her power to blackmail his would-be political supporters—and frequent companions to the bordello—into financially backing his campaign. Moreover, while Etta and Janet are busy making Grace into the proper maid, Grace is charming them with her beauty and exercise tips, which transform them into images of proper prostitutes.

The story comes to its climax when Stella, who has been used and cast aside by Harlan throughout the play,

is discovered in the arms of another man. She is believed to be kissing the hired lawn man (a friend of Grace and her boyfriend, Mugsy), but it is actually Ainsworth Emory, a St. Louis millionaire. Although Harlan makes a great show of his disgust for Stella's actions, he quickly begins to praise her infidelities when he realizes the true status of their unsuspecting houseguest. After finally seeing her husband as the self-serving hypocrite that he has always been, Stella leaves him, while Emory promises to wait for her until she is divorced.

The play was composed as both farce and satire; it pokes fun at the foibles and self-righteousness found in political leaders, while it also employs stock stereotypes of the hidden convict and reformed prostitute who, by not hiding behind false pretense, become the moral center of the play. However, what has rarely been discussed is the problematic role of Stella. Her inability to evoke the audience's sympathy could be one reason for the failure of the play. In an unpublished dissertation, the only full-length biographical and critical study of Chase's life and art, Marice Berger stated that the play, by "either conscious design or subconscious inclination, was patterned after a classic fantasy, *Cinderella*." However, unlike the dreams Cinderella has of meeting a prince and being swept away, Stella's dreams are focused on her husband, who the audience knows is a weak man; therefore, Stella's dreams inspire little empathy. Furthermore, in order for Stella to win her real Prince Charming, Ainsworth Emory, she must divorce her husband. Although justified, divorce was certainly a morally ambiguous act in the 1930s. Interestingly, *Me, Third* is one of only two plays Chase wrote that center around a married heroine. The rest of her plays focus on women who are widowed or divorced, just as it is clear Stella will be. Whatever the reasons, the play failed. As Chase told Berger, "the reviews were brutal. They were not mixed, they were a unanimous panning of the play." The reviewer for *The New York Times* (6 March 1937) called it "hackneyed in theme and laboriously written and staged"; however, the review also mentioned that theatergoers were "laughing their heads off."

Chase's next play, *Sorority House,* did not appear on Broadway but was produced at the University Civic Theater at the University of Denver in 1938 under the direction of Edwin Levy. It was the beginning of a long, mutually beneficial relationship between Chase and the university. Two more of her plays were produced at this theater, and she also taught playwriting and was awarded an honorary doctorate from the university in 1947, after she won the Pulitzer Prize for *Harvey.*

Sorority House is certainly the most autobiographical of Chase's plays. It is not a simple comedy as much as it is a scathing satire on the Greek-letter system and sorority life at co-educational institutions—a system Chase was all too familiar with from her own days at the University of Denver. The play centers around Alice, an eighteen-year-old woman whose college experiences bear a striking resemblance to those of Chase, who also came from limited financial means and struggled to afford college while living on $4 a week and wearing secondhand clothes. Alice enters college after taking a year off to work and save money for school. It is clear from the beginning that she is pursuing a college degree out of her desires for an education and to have more financial security than her parents. Although Alice's parents, Lew and Nell Wyckoff, are young, good-hearted people, they have always lived on shaky financial ground. While moving into her dormitory a week before classes start, Alice is caught up in the excitement of Rush Week and begins dating Bud Loomis, football hero and president of the student body. After coaxing from her new boyfriend and college friends, she decides to rush one of the most popular and elite of the sororities: Omicron Chi. Because she has little money and no "background" to speak of, she is made a pawn in an arrangement between Bud and the president of the sorority: if Bud can get two wealthy freshmen to pledge Omicron Chi, then Alice will be allowed to join; otherwise, the deal is off.

During one of the secret pledge ceremonies, with only hours to go before being inducted into the sorority, Alice receives a surprise visit from her father, Lew. The unexpected appearance of her father—a flashy young working-class type—completely humiliates Alice, and she tries to pass him off as an old friend. However, the sorority members mistake Lew for Alice's thug boyfriend and withdraw their offer to let her join. It is clear that the outward embarrassment that Alice shows over the appearance of her father crushes him.

The lessons that Alice and Lew learn are twofold. Alice realizes her place in the social hierarchy of college, and more importantly, she recognizes her father not as a figure who is greater than life, but as a man who, although capable of great acts of love, is also merely human. This realization, in turn, allows Alice's entrance into adulthood, while also freeing Lew from the unattainable role of the omnipotent, archetypal father figure. They begin to rebuild their relationship on more realistic ground. Although the play ostensibly ends on a happy note, it still paints a dark picture of sorority life. It is not clear, even in the final resolution of the play, if one can assimilate to college without joining the Greek-letter system.

As with the opening of *Me, Third* in Denver, *Sorority House* received strong reviews from the local press. The critic for the *Denver Post* called it "a tense and entertaining little drama with plenty of comic relief, well concealed plot and natural progressive action, strengthened by the author's complete familiarity with her subject." Although it never received any national attention as a play, it was sold to RKO Productions for $2,500 to be made into a movie (which was released in 1939). The sum was not enormous, but Chase wanted to ensure a profit after accruing a sizeable financial loss with the New York production of *Now You've Done It.*

After the local success of *Sorority House* at the Civic Theater, Chase decided to return to the university to premiere her first one-act play, *Too Much Business,* in 1940. This play is important for several reasons. Not only is it a precursor to her later children's plays, as it illuminates a world seen through the eyes of children, but it also requires the participation and faith of the audience members, who are asked to take the roles of children in this metatheatrical production.

As the play begins, the director (both as character and director) steps before the closed curtain and briefly explains to the audience the design of the play in which they are about to participate. His speech is both a preface to the play and part of the scripted text:

This play tonight is different. You act in this one. I will give you your part. You are to assume that this is the Palace Motion Picture Theater in any American City. The time is late Saturday afternoon. You are school boys and girls who want to see the stage show again. . . . The management has hundreds of adult patrons waiting outside. They want to get in and see the show. But they can't because you won't leave.

Throughout this long introduction the audience is asked to negotiate their roles as school children, in which they are told to insult the assistant manager of the theater, while "during the backstage scenes" they are asked to "be quiet." After much noisy, insulting banter from the audience yelling "we want the stage show," and frenzied brainstorming by the management on how to get the children out of the theater, the kids are tempted with food. There is a mass exodus to the diner next door, and the play ends.

Years later, with the success of *Mrs. McThing* in 1952, Chase told Berger her views about the efficacy of children's theater in America. These views are clearly evident in *Too Much Business*. Chase believed that the young adults of her time had lost their capacity to use their imaginations fully because as children they were moviegoers. Establishing a viable children's theater, she reasoned, would in time provide the "ultimate adult audience." Clearly, issues of children's imaginative laziness caused by passive cinematic experiences, as well as her beliefs in creating a generation of adults interested in the theatrical performance, are set forth in *Too Much Business*.

In 1941, while serving as the publicity director for the National Youth Administration in Denver, Chase wrote a short comedy titled *A Slip of a Girl*. The play was performed at army camps around Denver until the Federal Theater closed. Although it was never published and was not reviewed, Chase told Berger that it entertained audiences throughout its duration.

Although *A Slip of a Girl* was not a big stepping-stone for Chase as a playwright, its performance at army camps around Denver sets the context for the most famous and successful play of her career: *Harvey*. Chase wanted to use her talents as a playwright to make people laugh in spite of the devastation, loss, and chaos wrought in America during World War II. Chase said that the idea for *Harvey* came when she was looking out her window one morning in 1942 and saw a neighbor, a middle-aged woman, walking slowly toward the bus stop. As she told Eleanor Harris in 1954, "I was not acquainted with this woman, nor she with me. I am not to this day, but I heard her story. She was a widow who had worked for years to send her only son through college. The day I looked at her, her boy had been dead about two months, killed in action in the Pacific. I asked myself this question: could I ever possibly write anything that might make this woman laugh again?"

For three months, during which time she was also writing a weekly radio program for the Teamsters Union (which she did from 1942 to 1944), Chase searched for material for her new comedy. She turned to the memories of her childhood, when her Irish mother told her marvelously inventive stories of her native country; she recalled to Harris that her mother "told us of the Irish fairies—pookas and banshees and leprechauns. And she gave us advice I'd always remember: never make fun of those whom others consider crazy, for they often have a wisdom of their own." She had almost lost hope of finding the right catalyst for her play when she woke up one morning and remembered her mother's story about the pooka, a large, benign creature that was visible only to those who believed in it. Chase immediately started to write a play about a six-foot one and a half inch tall white rabbit who appears to an amiable drunk. She continued work on *Harvey* (originally titled "The White Rabbit") for two years. Then, in the summer of 1944, when she had finished writing the comedy, she mailed the manuscript to Pemberton in New York. He called a few days later, told her that he was putting it into immediate production, and wired her $500 to come East.

Harvey begins in the library of the Dowd family mansion, where Veta Louis Simmons (played by Josephine Hull in the original Broadway production) and her daughter, Myrtle Mae, are giving a tea and reception for members of the Wednesday Forum. This gathering is, ostensibly, to honor Veta's mother, the late Marcella Pinney Dowd, who was a pioneer cultural leader and founder of the forum. However, it is also a way to introduce Myrtle Mae into the proper social circles and thus to ensure her accessibility to proper suitors and, in turn, a proper husband. Yet, the women's attempts are foiled when Veta's brother, Elwood P. Dowd (played by Frank Fay, who continued in the role for 1,351 straight performances), unexpectedly arrives and proceeds to introduce his invisible friend, Harvey, the pooka, to the members of the Wednesday Forum. With this introduction, the women quickly begin to take leave of the party.

Wertheim notes that from the outset of the play, Chase has reversed the usual procedure of comedy, in which audiences laugh at the illusions of the central characters until they are restored to the "level-headed, normative thinking of society." Instead, in this play "we find ourselves identifying positively with the benign fantasy world of Elwood P. Dowd and his pooka, and rejecting the everyday world of social norm and social forms." Yet, because of Elwood's inability or unwillingness to assimilate the role set for him by polite society (compounded by the fact that he is the rightful heir of his late mother's estate), Veta feels that she needs to have him committed to a sanatorium in order to cure him of his disorder, while at the same time securing a "proper" life for her daughter.

Scene 2 begins at Chumley's Rest, a home for mental patients. Chase uses the location of the sanatorium to frame her comic critique of how society has come to understand normalcy. Veta's frustrated efforts to relay her brother's problems to the psychiatrist, Dr. Sanderson, result in his questioning her sanity: "Doctor—do I have to keep repeating myself? My brother insists that his closest friend is this big white rabbit. The rabbit is named Harvey. Harvey lives at our house. Don't you understand? He and Elwood go every place together. . . . Doctor, I'm going to tell you something I've never told anyone in the world before. Every once in a while I see that big white rabbit myself. Now isn't that terrible?" After her outburst Dr. Sanderson mistakenly believes that Veta is the one who needs to be committed and goes to her "normal" brother to explain his diagnosis. Elwood says he will discuss the arrangement with Veta, and then he takes leave to have a drink at Charlie's Bar. After the psychiatric staff is chastised by Dr. Chumley for their inability to recognize the "difference between those who are reasonable, and those who merely talk and act reasonably," they take off on a wild-goose chase to find him.

When Elwood later resurfaces at the sanatorium to escort Dr. Sanderson and Nurse Kelly to Charlie's for a drink, Dr. Sanderson tries to talk some reason into Elwood by announcing that "we all have to face reality, Dowd—sooner or later." Elwood replies, "Doctor, I wrestled with reality for forty years, and I'm happy to state that I finally won out over it." By illuminating the difficulty in coming to a consensus over what constitutes individual realities, Elwood has summed up the overriding message of the play.

At the beginning of act 3, while the staff at Chumley's Rest focus their efforts on committing Elwood, it seems that Elwood has already made a convert out of the head psychologist, Dr. Chumley, who now wishes Harvey to stay and live with him. He is quite taken with Elwood's description of Harvey's powers: although "Einstein has overcome time and space," Elwood explains, "Harvey has not only overcome time and space—but any objection." As Chumley reflects on Harvey's wonder, Dr. Sanderson is preparing formula 977, an injection that will make Harvey disappear and allow Elwood to return to his "duties and responsibilities." However, at the moment before the treatment, a cab driver steps into the lobby of the sanatorium and forces Veta to question whether she really wants Harvey to disappear and Elwood to change. "Lady," the cabby yells, "after this, he'll be a perfectly normal human being and you know what bastards they are!" With that, Veta frantically calls Elwood out of the doctor's office, and she, Myrtle Mae, Elwood, and Harvey return home.

Critics have often said that the overwhelming success of *Harvey* was because its escapist theme appealed

James Stewart as Elwood P. Dowd in Chase and Oscar Brodney's 1950 movie version of Harvey, *Chase's 1944 Pulitzer Prize–winning play*

to audiences trying to take leave of the harsh realities of the world (if only for the length of the performance) during World War II. However, the fact that *Harvey* continues to be performed at both the amateur and professional levels in America and abroad suggests that its appeal to the sanctity of the human imagination and individualism is more enduring.

When the show opened on Broadway, under the direction of Antoinette Perry, on 1 November 1944 at the Forty-eighth Street Theatre, it was a critical as well as popular success. In a review for *The New York Times* (2 November 1944) critic Lewis Nichols called it "one of the treats of the fall theater." Josephine Hull's performance as Veta was lauded as a "masterpiece," and Nichols was quick to note that "when Mr. Fay is on the stage quietly explaining his relationship with Harvey, the theater could ask for little more." In an 11 November *New York Times* article Nichols again exclaimed: "Obviously *Harvey* will defy classification, although on this sunny side of history the play does not lack category. *Harvey* quite simply is one of the delights of the season."

The play ran on Broadway for four and a half years, totaling 1,775 performances, making it one of the ten longest-running shows in Broadway history. This distinction was just the beginning of many honors and awards that Chase received for her work on *Harvey*. In 1944 she was the recipient of the William MacLeod Raine Award, presented by the Colorado Author's League. Then, on 7 May 1945, Chase was awarded the Pulitzer Prize for the best drama during the 1944–1945 season. She stood in the company of Aaron Copland, who was awarded the Pulitzer Prize in music for *Appalachian Springs* (a ballet written for and presented by Martha Graham), and John Hersey, who received the Pulitzer Prize for best novel with his *A Bell for Adano* (1944).

During this period of award ceremonies and the long-term engagement on the New York stage, *Harvey* also traveled abroad to captivate many European audiences. It received favorable reviews in both London and Vienna (but bad reviews in the French press). One foreign news correspondent for the *Times News Magazine* (25 April 1949) noted that "even the Polish Minister seemed to have fallen sway to the rabbit's charm. At a dinner at the legislation recently, he called [Oscar] Karlwies [who played Elwood in Vienna] for a vodka. He poured two glasses. 'One for you,' he told Vienna's Elwood, 'and one for Charrryey' [Harvey]."

While the Pulitzer Prize and the world success of *Harvey* secured for Chase a position as an accomplished playwright, Universal-International ensured her financial well-being. On 30 June 1947 *The New York Times* confirmed reports that the movie rights to *Harvey* had been sold to Universal-International for $1 million. This price was said to have topped any previous amount paid for any stage play or book. Chase was brought to Hollywood to write the movie version with Oscar Brodney; it was completed in 1950. The movie was so successful that Josephine Hull won an Academy Award for her portrayal of Veta, and James Stewart as Elwood received a nomination for best actor.

For Chase, the success of *Harvey* was overwhelming. Although she reaped the benefits of the critical acclaim and financial security, success brought a dark cloud of envy and jealousy from her friends and colleagues. Chase, an extroverted, sociable woman, quickly began to retreat from the public eye. Reflecting on this period in her life, she recalled to Harris, "I found lies everywhere. I was still the same person I had always been, yet everyone had changed in their attitude toward me."

This disillusionment over her newly found fame was compounded by the utter failure of her next Broadway show—a melodrama titled *The Next Half Hour* (1945). The play was produced by Max Gordon with Fay Bainter in the lead role as Margaret Brennan. Just less than a year after the debut of *Harvey,* on 29 October 1945, *The Next*

Half Hour premiered at the Empire Theatre. It closed after eight performances.

The play takes place in 1913 in the home of an Irish American family. It opens with the figure of Margaret, a widowed mother of three, who is characterized as both deeply religious and superstitious. After finding a piece of black crepe from her husband's funeral and running into Aunt Bridget—a relative she has not seen since the last funeral in the family—Margaret is convinced something horrible is going to happen to her oldest son, Pat. He has been having an affair with a married woman, Jessie Shoemaker, whose husband, a night-working railroad repairman, is rumored to be hot-tempered. Margaret's steadfast belief that she can both predict and single-handedly alter the future of her family members becomes the basis for the dramatic action.

After Margaret makes an unsuccessful attempt to break up the relationship between Pat and Jessie, Margaret's brother, Peter (an old-world Irishman living with her family), warns her of the dangers of trying to control fate: "The next half hour belongs to God, and you'd better let Him have it." Margaret refuses to heed his advice and, in one of many superstitious acts, takes out a deck of cards to try to see the future. She pulls the ace of spades, "the death card." At this point she arranges to meet Jessie's husband, Dutch, to try and persuade him not to hurt her son.

The second act takes place in the next half hour and begins with a heavy-handed attempt to juxtapose the character of Margaret's younger son, Barney—the promising student who never causes a moment of trouble—with that of Pat. It is clear that Chase wishes to turn the audience's attention to Barney in order to indicate the possibility that he might be the one who is actually in danger. Some critics suggest that if Chase's point were brought to stage in a more subtle manner, the ultimate irony of the climax would not be thrown away so early and would thus give the audience more to sustain their attention. The growing sense of foreboding rapidly increases after Barney exits the stage and Margaret is left alone. She is suddenly filled with terror as she hears the scream of the banshee, which signifies the imminent death of a loved one (just as Harvey is invisible, Margaret is the only one who hears the banshee's scream). She quickly sends Barney to find Pat and bring him home. When Barney arrives at the Shoemakers' residence, Pat has already left. Jessie's husband mistakes Barney for Pat and kills him. Act 3 culminates in the arrival of the police to tell the family of the murder. Margaret, dazed and confused, refuses to believe the officer and leaves the house to find her son.

Although the play has several weaknesses, its biggest failure, noted by Nichols in *The New York Times* (30 October 1945), was that where there should be dramatic action, there is only plodding monologue with scant relation to the overarching story line. Nichols reported: "*The Next Half Hour* is a long and quite tedious piece of business, relieved only intermittently by bursts of good acting." Furthermore, he noted, "long before death takes his victim, it is obvious who he is to be—and how. The Irish tell stories with suspense, which Mrs. Chase does not."

However, a later article by Nichols (4 November 1945) illuminates another explanation for the failure of the play: *The Next Half Hour* "was found to be just an earlier play." Chase had written it before *Harvey* and titled it "The Banshee," but Pemberton had advised her to put off producing it until after the war. Nichols suggested that "in it were suggestions of some things, which, with later authority, make *Harvey* what it is, the touches of characterization, the liking for humanity which is not strictly earth-bound." He added that "between *The Next Half Hour* and *Harvey*, Mrs. Chase learned the power of concentration." His observations touched upon some of the difficulties that Chase had in several of her lesser-known plays, as well as some unproduced works. As dramatic works they are laboriously written, with little attention paid to the theatrical qualities needed to make the works translate from script to stage. They might have succeeded as novels where they failed as drama.

A few years after Chase's Broadway failure, she decided to return to writing plays. This time, however, she was determined to write for children and never to return her work to the Broadway stage. The impetus for this decision was twofold: she no longer wished to write for an audience that could hurt her, and while she also wanted to concentrate her efforts on creating a viable theater for children, one that would in turn create the "ultimate adult audience." Her first play to emerge from this new effort was *Mrs. McThing*.

Once Chase had tried out her play using the neighborhood children as her "small fry" audience and was satisfied with its reception, she mailed it to New York agent Harold Freedman. Chase sent strict instructions that she "would like it to have one semiprofessional performance as a Christmas play for children," but under no circumstances was it to be produced on Broadway. Although Freedman was unsuccessful in convincing Chase to do otherwise, Robert Whitehead, managing director of the ANTA play series, flew to Denver a year later to persuade her to try a two-week Broadway production of *Mrs. McThing* instead of the one semiprofessional performance she had specified. Mary acquiesced to Whitehead's offer, and again returned to New York. *Mrs. McThing* premiered at the Martin Beck Theatre on 20 February 1952. Instead of the agreed-upon two-week run, the play stayed at the theater for one year and ran for 350 performances.

Chase told Harris that the idea for *Mrs. McThing* came from a childhood memory in which she recalled a friend of her mother's who said: "Last week we buried that whining, querulous old harridan we called our mother, but we all knew she wasn't *really* our mother. Mother was a happy, pretty woman who was taken twelve years ago. They left this stick in her place, and it was the stick we buried." This "stick myth," as it is called, is based on an old Irish legend of the changeling. According to the legend, it was possible for a witch to kidnap a real person and leave in his place a stick, or simulacrum, whose outward appearance would be that of the missing person in every respect but whose behavior would be quite different.

Mrs. McThing begins in the sitting room of Mrs. Howard V. Larue, an affluent widow (played by Helen Hayes in the Broadway production) who is busy entertaining three longtime friends. Although the women do bear striking resemblance to the members of the Wednesday Forum at the beginning of *Harvey*, the setting and costumes indicate that *Mrs. McThing* is a complete fantasy. During the visit, Mrs. Larue's son, Howay—a poor little rich boy—begins exhibiting signs of abnormal behavior. Earlier his mother forbade him to play with a girl named Mimi (daughter to the infamous witch, Mrs. McThing). Although he would normally be angry at such an order, he is in every way polite and generous to both his mother and the guests. Mrs. Larue's growing suspicion of Howay's fastidious and unnerving manner reaches its peak when she receives a call from a boy claiming to be her seven-year-old son, who is now working as a dishwasher on lower Seventh Street. Not knowing what to believe, Mrs. Larue takes off to find him.

The next setting is the Shantyland Pool Hall Lunchroom, where Mrs. Larue finds both Howay and Mimi amid a cast of comic, stereotypical mobsters. She chastises Mimi and tells her that she is never to come near her son again. At this command Mimi threatens to put a curse on her as well, and she promptly leaves. When Mrs. Larue calls home and finds that she, too, has been replaced by a stick woman, she is left with no option but to stay in the pool hall and wash dishes with her son.

Finally, a plan is made to return things to their rightful order. Mimi will go against her mother's wishes and banish the stick family, while the mobsters, lead by Poison Eddie Schellenbach, agree to break into the house and cause a diversion under the condition that they receive cash and property. After a few slapstick scenes between the mobsters and the police, everything returns to normal in the Larue family. This order, however, is not without a cost.

By using the magic her mother has taught her, Mimi goes against the wishes of Mrs. McThing and sides with her human counterparts. It is now time for Mimi to leave her supernatural mother and to live in the world beyond the forest. Unlike the pooka in *Harvey* or the banshee in *The Next Half Hour*, Mrs. McThing

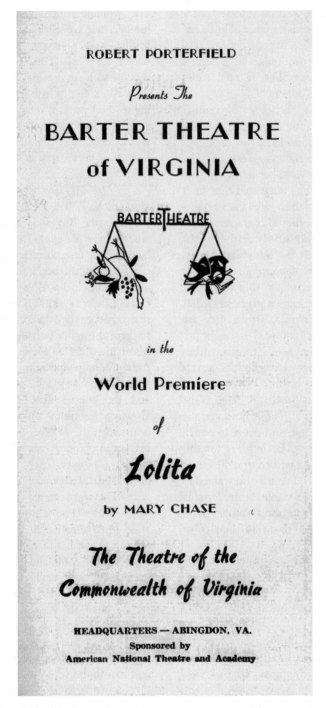

ROBERT PORTERFIELD

Presents The

BARTER THEATRE
of VIRGINIA

BARTER THEATRE

in the

World Premiere

of

Lolita

by MARY CHASE

The Theatre of the
Commonwealth of Virginia

HEADQUARTERS — ABINGDON, VA.
Sponsored by
American National Theatre and Academy

Program for the premiere of Chase's 1954 play based on her children's book Loretta Mason Potts

actually takes human form at the end of act 2: she first appears as an ugly hag; then, before leaving Mimi for good, she appears as a beautiful witch. When Howay asks Mimi "who was the ugly one? Who was she?" Mimi replies that they were both her mother: "Sometimes when my mother is helping me, she has to look ugly." With this explanation Mrs. Larue is able to understand that Mrs. McThing appeared as a hag to

incite her maternal instincts and get her to realize that children, with all of their boisterous energy, are infinitely more desirable than a refined stick simulacrum. The play ends in the living room of Larue Towers, with Mrs. McThing resolving to give Mimi to Mrs. Larue to raise as her daughter.

Mrs. McThing was the first American play written for children ever to be produced on Broadway for a successful commercial run. Although Chase was leery of staging this show for a Broadway audience, it received favorable reviews from critics, who praised its originality and its appeal to both children and adults. On 21 February 1952 a reviewer for *The New York Times* described *Mrs. McThing* as "a fairy story that manages to combine *Alice in Wonderland* with Superman and Hopalong Cassidy." Another *Times* critic, Brooks Atkinson (25 February 1952), pointed to "Leste Polakov's story-book settings and Lucinda Ballard's comically imposing costumes" that "portray the world of fable" as further reason for the success of the play.

In the fall of 1952, while *Mrs. McThing* was still being successfully performed at the Martin Beck Theatre, Chase brought another play to Broadway. This time it was *Bernardine,* a play inspired by watching her teenage sons and their friends. "I wrote the play about them and for them," she told Harris. Later that year, on 7 December, *The New York Herald Tribune* announced that "Mary Chase had 2 hits on one block." In fact, the plays were so successful that for a short time the city of New York renamed Schubert Alley "Mary Chase Alley" and posted signs directing passersby to the theaters where *Mrs. McThing* and *Bernardine* were playing. *Bernardine* opened at the Playhouse Theater on 16 October 1952 and ran for 157 performances.

The story of *Bernardine* focuses on a group of teenage boys living with one foot in the world of their parents and one in their own insular world where adults are not allowed. They hang out at "the Shamrock," listen to music, and dream of an imaginary girl named Bernardine Crud. "She's through with school. She's lived. She's a little older . . . beat up looking, but not too much." Bernardine is said to live in a town in Idaho called "Sneaky Falls," on the "Itching River," and the whole range of her vocabulary is the word "*yes.*"

Although the cast includes a large gang of boys, the action focuses on a girl-crazy teenager named Beauford "Wormy" Weldy, who must constantly negotiate between the world of his friends and that of his mother. Ruth Weldy is a single, divorced mother who blames Wormy's friends for his behavior and does not understand that they are a crucial support network or that they know more about her son than she does.

On a dare from the gang, Wormy goes to the ritzy Barclay Hotel, where he poses as a young sailor about to be shipped out the following day in order to pick up an older woman, who is a physical manifestation of the boys' mythical Bernardine. Much to everyone's surprise (including his own), the plan works. At the beginning of act 2, Enid Lacey, the older woman, takes Wormy to her apartment. When she does not refuse his advances, however, he is left completely baffled as to how to react. By stepping out of the social codes set forth by the adult world, Enid acts as a liminal figure who stands at the threshold to Wormy's passage into adulthood and allows him to feel that his emotions are valid. Although Enid does finally refuse him, she offers him sound advice: "Beauford, you must not approach older women. . . . She could learn to adore you . . . no matter what your name might be. She could steal away your youth. Make it pass like a dream." Of course, not knowing the implications of this statement, Wormy thinks that is exactly what he wants.

The character of Enid is used to articulate Chase's own thoughts about the dangers of rushing through one's youth. As she told a *New York Herald Tribune* writer (7 December 1952), teenage boys "are in that no-man's land when they are not quite of the earth yet, when there is a kind of bewilderment, a kind of joy in life. They aren't the same after they are twenty." When Wormy finally stands up to his mother, she begins to realize the positive impact his friends have made on his life and apologizes for her own lack of faith. In the end Wormy begins to date a nice girl whom he admires, and he appears to have found a way to bridge that gap between his two worlds. Hence, the "battle between generations" comes to an end.

Critic Brook Atkinson, writing for *The New York Times* (17 October 1952), discussed various "shortcomings in stagecraft" and stated that "the play and the performances are very uneven–mixing the trivial with the pertinent." Similarly, in a later article for *The New York Times* (9 November 1952), Atkinson declared that "Mrs. Chase's random, floundering craftsmanship is a serious defect in a most ingratiating play." These reviews, however, are not a complete panning of the play. Atkinson also declared that the audiences' appreciation was because of Chase's "artless and fresh material" and stated that "Mrs. Chase writes like a woman who goes straight to life for her information on adolescents." 20th Century-Fox made *Bernardine* into a movie in 1957.

From the experience of having two simultaneous and successful shows on Broadway, Chase regained some of the confidence she felt before *Harvey.* As she told Harris, she understood that despite bad reviews or theatrical failures, "work is the solution: it stays with you when all else is gone." Chase continued to write and have plays produced for the next twenty years.

When her next play, *Lolita* (1954), had its world premiere, it was not produced on Broadway or in her home state of Colorado, but at Robert Porterfield's Barter Theatre in Abingdon, Virginia, the oldest active regional theater in the United States. Chase was given a vast amount of creative freedom there and played an integral part in the directing and staging of her work. Years earlier, during a workshop production of *Harvey* at the Barter before it moved to Broadway, Chase had

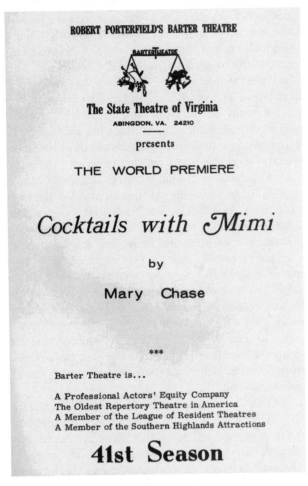

ROBERT PORTERFIELD'S BARTER THEATRE

The State Theatre of Virginia
ABINGDON, VA. 24210

presents

THE WORLD PREMIERE

Cocktails with Mimi

by

Mary Chase

***

Barter Theatre is...

A Professional Actors' Equity Company
The Oldest Repertory Theatre in America
A Member of the League of Resident Theatres
A Member of the Southern Highlands Attractions

41st Season

Program for the last of Chase's produced plays (1973)

established a great professional relationship with director Owen Phillips. He continued to direct many of her plays at this theater for the next twenty years.

Lolita opened at the Barter Theatre on 30 August 1954. It was never published or produced under the same name again, and there are no known copies of this version of the play. Originally based on her children's novel *Loretta Mason Potts* (written in 1953 and published in 1958), the play had several titles during the course of its revision—including "Loretta" and "Loretta and the Little People"—before it was revised again as *Mickey* in 1968. Although *Lolita* did not excite professional interest, six producers who attended the Barter Theatre production were so taken with the character of Mrs. Purvis that they persuaded Chase to write a play that focused on this character. That play became *Midgie Purvis,* which premiered on Broadway in 1961.

Between *Lolita* and *Midgie Purvis* Chase decided to write a short farcical skit titled *The Prize Play* (1959). Just like *Too Much Business* and *Sorority House,* it was produced at the University Civic Theater at the University of

Denver under the direction of Levy. It premiered on 30 October 1959. It was intended as pure farce, and because of the witty dialogue and physical humor, the fast-paced skit has been a frequently produced revue piece since its publication.

Early in 1961 Chase had finished work on *Midgie Purvis,* which opened at the Martin Beck Theatre on 1 February 1961 with Tallulah Bankhead in the title role. Bankhead appears to have been cast because the producers hoped that placing a well-known actress in the role would bring in money at the box office. They made a tactical error. *Midgie Purvis* received negative reviews. It lasted twenty-one performances before closing, and it was Chase's last play produced on Broadway.

The play opens in the living room of Raw Foods tycoon Edwin Gilroy Purvis and his wife, Midgie, who is in the middle of a dress fitting for the wedding of their son, Colin. The maid, Mrs. Durkee, enters and changes into her work clothes. After the dressmaker makes a side comment to Midgie about the maid's appearance, Midgie responds: "Listen to her singing! She may be a lot happier than we are. Did you see the article in *LIFE* magazine this week? About those people in India. At middle life—having fulfilled the body—and raised their families—they put off their silken robes—take up a staff and begging bowl and go forth on a search for spiritual adventure. Don't you wonder what they find?" Although this idea is masked in the comic sequences of the play, it is the driving philosophy underlying Midgie's own archetypal journey in which she revisits the splendors of childhood in order to come to terms with her own passage from middle age into old age.

Like Chase herself, Midgie is something of a practical joker. She intends to surprise Colin and his well-to-do fiancée by greeting them in the maid's clothes; but before she can do so, Colin leaves and several of Midgie's haughty friends are ushered into the room. Midgie runs out of the back of the house to avoid them, just as a teenager's car pulls in to pick up Mrs. Durkee for her babysitting job. Midgie, not knowing what to do, pretends she is the maid and jumps into the car.

The rest of the play focuses on the crazy adventures of Midgie, who, after meeting the children she is to babysit, takes up residence in the back of a candy store, dresses like an older woman, and becomes the children's full-time babysitter. As an old woman, stripped of worldly status, she is able to enjoy the things not available to her in the upper echelons of polite society: she sits on park benches, watches passersby, and creates wonderfully imaginative adventures for the kids—all without the watchful eye of her society friends. She has stepped out of her role as upper-class wife and mother, as well as her role as a fading "glamour girl," to live a life without constraints.

By casting off the costume of the old woman at the end of the play, Midgie has arrived at her metaphorical death and is now ready to return to her family with a qualitatively different understanding of her role. In preparing for her son's wedding she had, in a sense, become displaced, not knowing how Colin's new status as husband would alter her role as mother. She returns to her family with a concrete sense of self.

The poignancy of this dramatic message was lost on critics and audience members who were preoccupied with more technical matters. One critic for *The New York Times* (12 February 1961) stated that "through most of the play she [Bankhead] shuttles between character and caricature, masquerading as an old woman, she persists in double takes of movement and voice. A few of these sudden shifts from creaking old age to boisterous vitality win easy laughs, but undermine Midgie as a human being." Likewise it was noted that most of the characters "are stereotypes in a farce . . . they rant and run but do not amuse. They are slapdash hurly-burly that had drained the imagination of a fresh idea."

Whether because Bankhead was miscast as Midgie or because the production lacked good direction, the play was horribly received. Nonetheless, *Midgie Purvis* is a noteworthy piece of dramatic literature that, through the use of comedy, conveys the struggle of a woman coming to terms with her own mortality.

After *Midgie Purvis* Chase began to work almost solely in the fields of children's literature and children's theater. In 1966 her play *The Dog Sitters* premiered at the Phoenix Playhouse in Phoenix, Arizona. She dedicated this work to "The Children's Theater Conference, a group of American educators organized in 1934 for the purpose of promoting a higher standard of live theater for the children in this country, which, for years has been a source of encouragement to me in my playwriting in this field." The play takes place in the Barbizon Mansion at Versailles Kennels, which is home to an eccentric dog lover named Mrs. Barbizon. *The Dog Sitters* is primarily a didactic comedy, which, by examining the relationships between children and their pets, teaches patience, sharing, and greater compassion. The play was not successful but was still published in 1968.

In the same year that *The Dog Sitters* premiered, Chase also completed an unproduced one-act play titled "Punish Willie." In 1968 she published her second children's novel, *The Wicked Pigeon Ladies in the Garden,* which earned her a nomination for the Dorothy Canfield Fisher Award for children's literature. By this time Chase had also finished revising her earlier play *Lolita,* which she now titled *Mickey.* She refashioned the play to utilize both puppets and live actors. This version premiered at the Changing Scene Theater in Denver on 12 December 1968. It received marvelous

reviews in her hometown paper, *The Rocky Mountain News,* and it continues to be produced by amateur groups and schools around the country.

The story is really an extended metaphor that explores some of the inherent dangers that arise when a child loses touch with reality and takes flight into the nether regions of the imagination. *Mickey* is the story of a little girl named Mickey Mason who, at the age of five, disappears behind the home of Farmer Potts and discovers a world of little people replete with a countess, a general, a knight, and a footman. When she later resurfaces, she refuses to move with her family to the city and demands to stay with Farmer Potts and his wife so she can continue to visit the tiny kingdom. Seven years later, when the Pottses sell their farm, she is forced to move in with her real family in the city. When she returns home, she begins to have a strange influence over her brother and sister, and it is soon discovered that they have all been sneaking though a tunnel in Mickey's closet to visit her small friends. The story makes clear that Mickey finds in her imaginary world the kind of solace and companionship that she is missing in the reality of her adolescence. In order to fight for her children's return to reality, Mickey's mother enters the kingdom to collect her children, who are literally being held hostage. Mickey, now realizing the dangers in this kind of flight from reality, returns to the world with the knowledge of her mother's love.

In 1973, at the age of sixty-six, Chase returned to the Barter Theatre to premiere *Cocktails with Mimi.* At this time she told a reporter for the *Roanoke Times* (1 July 1973) that she had "finally adjusted to the likelihood that she would never write another hit play like *Harvey.*" *Cocktails with Mimi* was not only poorly received by the critics, it was also the last produced play of Chase's life.

Cocktails with Mimi, like *Midgie Purvis,* appears to have all of the necessary elements to constitute a successful comedy. The play, which opened on 3 July 1973, takes place in the home of Mimi Ralston during one of her infamous cocktail parties. Mimi is a rich, eccentric divorcée with a penchant for practical jokes. At this particular party, unbeknownst to her guests, Mimi has hired an actor to play a rude, clumsy waiter to insult the future in-laws of her daughter, Edith. After meeting Paul, the actor-waiter, Mimi believes that he would be perfect for her daughter. Mimi abhors Edith's current beau, Lew Calthorpe, a pretentious graduate student in psychology who insists on offering his psychoanalytic services to Mimi. By inviting Judge and Mrs. Leland Calthorpe to her cocktail party, Mimi hopes to thoroughly humiliate them so that they will refuse to accept her daughter into their family.

Knowing her mother's flair for the dramatic, Edith also hires a set of benevolent, middle-aged actors to play the part of the Calthorpes at Mimi's party. Edith's plan is flawlessly executed. In fact, Mimi is so taken with the couple that she reverses her previous judgment about the family and allows Edith early access to her trust fund so that she can marry without financial worry. However, when the real Calthorpes unexpectedly appear, all goes wild. In an effort to try and conceal their presence from her mother, Edith continues to switch the roles of the actors until finally a kind of dementia sets in. The actors begin to lose track of their alleged identities until the whole plan unravels and the truth is revealed.

At the end of act 2, frustrated and humiliated by her mother, Edith leaves with the Calthorpes. Yet, the constant reversal of roles throughout the party allows Edith to realize that the real Calthorpes, as well as Lew, are not the people she thought they were. Edith finally understands that Mimi, despite her erratic nature, really was looking out for Edith's best interests. The play ends with Edith going to find Paul, the actor-waiter, and it is suggested that all will end happily.

Chase summarized the play as simply "a practical joke, at a cocktail party, and the joke misfires. It has no relevance—or what they call relevance." She hoped that it would prove to be pure entertainment. Even with established actress Ann Buckles returning to her home state to play the role of Mimi, the play did not attract positive critical attention, though it still succeeded in captivating the audience. Just as with Chase's first comedy, *Me, Third,* the audience was exceptionally receptive, and the performance received a standing ovation. This acclaim was not, however, the view of several critics. A reviewer for the *Kingsport Times-News* observed that "what the audience found funniest—they laughed frequently and warmly—were today's trite terms." Another critic for *The National Observer* (14 July 1973) went so far as to say that "this is a depressing play because it suggests that a playwright of demonstrated comic gifts has simply lost her comic ear." It is not clear whether Chase had finally had enough of the negative criticism that had plagued her throughout her career as a playwright, but she did not write another play after *Cocktails with Mimi.*

Although critics and scholars have often pointed to the fact that Chase's plays lack both the dramatic structure and technical organization needed to sustain their appearance and importance in the American theater, the heart of Chase's vision and her goal were beyond the question of critical worthiness. Though audience response is not always the best litmus test for predicting longevity, Chase believed in writing for her audience. She often said that she did not write for

money, while sarcastically pointing out that before *Harvey,* money was always something she owed, not something she had. Her only desire was to make people laugh. She endeared herself to the American public by tapping into the human desire to believe in what is pure and good in spite of ourselves. Her philosophy lives on in Elwood P. Dowd as he recounts, "my mother used to say to me 'In this world Elwood, you must be oh, so smart or oh, so pleasant.' For years I was smart. I recommend pleasant. You can quote me."

Bibliography:
Andrew L. Erdman, "Mary Coyle Chase: A Bibliography of Critical and Biographical Sources," *Bulletin of Bibliography,* 53 (December 1995): 307–310.

Biography:
Marice Berger, "Mary Chase: Her Battlefield of Illusion," dissertation, University of Denver, 1970.

References:
Andrew L. Erdman, "From Frank Fay to Jimmy Stewart: Broadway, Hollywood, and the Construction of Creativity," *Theater Studies,* 53 (1996): 13–28;
Eleanor Harris, "Success Almost Ruined Her," *Cosmopolitan* (February 1954): 98–104;
George Jean Nathan, *The Theater in the Fifties* (New York: Knopf, 1953);
Wallis M. Reef, "She Didn't Write it for the Money, She Says," in *More Post Biographies,* edited by John E. Drewry (Athens: University of Georgia Press, 1947), pp. 98–104;
Wieder David Sievers, "New Freudian Blood," in his *Freud on Broadway: A History of Psychoanalysis and American Drama* (New York: Hermitage House, 1955), pp. 347–369;
Albert Wertheim, "The Comic Muse of Mary Chase," in *Women in American Theater,* edited by Helen Krich Chinoy and Linda Walsh Jenkins (New York: Crown, 1981), pp. 163–170.

Papers:
The two major archives of Mary Coyle Chase's papers are at the Penrose Library, University of Denver, which has several manuscripts, including the original manuscript of *Harvey,* and at the Library of Special Collections, University of Oregon, Eugene, which houses Chase's papers from 1947 to 1968, comprising personal correspondence and manuscripts, including early versions and revisions of *Bernardine* and *Harvey* and the screen treatment of *Harvey.*

Pearl Cleage

(7 December 1948 –   )

Marta J. Effinger
Northwestern University

PLAY PRODUCTIONS: *Hymn for the Rebels,* Washington, D.C., Howard University, 1968;

Duet for Three Voices, Washington, D.C., Howard University, 1969;

The Sale, Atlanta, Spelman College, 1971;

The Jean Harris Reading, Atlanta, Georgia, 1981;

The Pearl and the Brood of Vipers, Indianapolis, independently produced by Michelle Smith, 1981;

Puppetplay, Atlanta, Georgia, Just Us Theatre, 1981;

Nothin' but a Movie, Atlanta, Georgia, independently produced by Cleage, 1982;

Hospice, New York, Colonnades Theatre Lab/New Federal Theatre, 1983;

Good News, Atlanta, Georgia, Just Us Theatre, February 1984;

Essentials, Atlanta, Georgia, Just Us Theatre, 1984;

Porch Songs, Indianapolis, Phoenix Theatre, August 1985;

Flyin' West, Atlanta, Georgia, Alliance Theatre Company, November 1992;

Blues for an Alabama Sky, Atlanta, Georgia, Alliance Theatre Company, July 1995;

Bourbon at the Border, Atlanta, Georgia, Alliance Theatre Company, 30 April 1997.

BOOKS: *We Don't Need the Music* (Detroit, Mich.: Broadside Press, 1972);

Mad at Miles: A Blackwoman's Guide to Truth (Southfield, Mich.: Cleage Group, 1990);

The Brass Bed and Other Stories (Chicago: Third World Press, 1991);

Deals with the Devil: And Other Reasons to Riot (New York: Ballantine, 1993);

Flyin' West (New York: Dramatists Play Service, 1995);

What Looks Like Crazy on an Ordinary Day– (New York: Avon Books, 1997);

Blues for an Alabama Sky (New York: Dramatists Play Service, 1999);

Flyin' West and Other Plays (New York: Theatre Communications Group, 1999)–comprises *Flyin'*

Pearl Cleage *(photograph by Barry Forbus; from the dust jacket of* What Looks Like Crazy on an Ordinary Day–, *1997)*

West, Blues for an Alabama Sky, Bourbon at the Border, Late Bus to Mecca, and *Chain.*

PRODUCED SCRIPT: *Banana Bread,* television, *Playhouse 30,* PBS (Atlanta, Georgia), 1985.

RECORDING: "Hairpeace," read by Cleage, *A Nation of Poets,* Atlanta, Georgia, National Black Arts Festival, 1990.

OTHER: Contributions by Cleage, in *Dear Dark Faces: Portraits of a People,* edited by the Bookers (Detroit: Lotus Press, 1980);

"Lesson," in *Double Stitch: Black Women Write About Mothers and Daughters*, edited by Patricia Bell-Scott (Boston: Beacon, 1991), pp. 71–73;

Hospice, in *The Woman That I Am: The Literature and Culture of Contemporary Women of Color*, edited by D. Soyini Madison (New York: St. Martin's Press, 1994).

SELECTED PERIODICAL PUBLICATIONS—
UNCOLLECTED: "Hairpeace," *African American Review*, 27 (Spring 1993): 37;

"When the Music Doesn't Play," *Ms.*, 4 (September–October 1993): 27;

"Saving Our Sons: Raising Black Children in a Turbulent World," *Ms.*, 5 (January–February 1995): 70;

"Daddy," *SAGE: A Scholarly Journal on Black Women*, 9 (Spring 1995): 48;

"Breaking the Rules," *Essence* (May 1995): 207;

"Built for Comfort," *Essence* (September 1995): 54;

"The Second Time Around," *Ms.*, 6 (January–February 1996): 92;

"Not Just Race, Not Just Gender: Black Feminist Readings," *Ms.*, 9 (September–October 1998): 89.

"I will always write about Black people and our efforts to build a community where we can live safely. . . . These will always be my themes, regardless of the forum," claimed Pearl Cleage in a 4 February 1998 *Washington Informer* interview. Throughout Cleage's career, the Atlanta-based playwright, journalist, poet, and novelist has used the written word to explore blacks' experiences on the American landscape. Self-described as a third-generation black nationalist feminist, Cleage uses her writing to examine the relationships and the impacts of racism and sexism.

Pearl Cleage was born in Springfield, Massachusetts on 7 December 1948, but she was raised in Detroit, Michigan. Her father, the Reverend Albert B. Cleage Jr. (also known as Jaramogi Abebe Agyman), was founder and leader of the Shrine of the Black Madonna; her mother, Doris Graham Cleage, was a schoolteacher. Her stepfather, Henry W. Cleage, was a lawyer and philosopher. In her father's Detroit congregation, Cleage was exposed to the voices of activists such as Malcolm X and Martin Luther King Jr. After finishing high school, Cleage left Detroit for college during the height of the Civil Rights Movement in the 1960s. She attended Howard University in Washington, D.C., for three years before transferring to Spelman College in Atlanta in 1969. She graduated from Spelman in 1971 with a B.A. in drama.

Cleage married former mayoral candidate and Fulton County commissioner Michael Lomax in Atlanta on 30 October 1969. Though this union ended in divorce, the couple had one daughter, Deignan. Cleage's second husband, Zaron Burnett Jr., whom she married on 23 March 1994, is a writer and producing director of Just Us Theatre Company.

Cleage's writing is accessible, yet provocative. She has been a contributor for such publications as *Ms., Essence,* and the black-owned newspaper *The Atlanta Tribune,* where her column "Stop Making Sense" appeared for almost a decade. Cleage's collections of critical essays *Mad at Miles: A Blackwoman's Guide to Truth* (1990) and *Deals with the Devil: And Other Reasons to Riot* (1993) are concerned with topics as varied as the Rodney King beating and criticism of the 1990 film *Driving Miss Daisy.* Cleage is also cofounder and editor of the literary magazine *Catalyst,* and her work has appeared in several anthologies.

Cleage served as the first playwright in residence at Just Us Theatre Company and premiered several new plays there. She assumed the role of artistic director in 1992 and wrote several performance pieces with Burnett. These pieces were presented in the "Club Zebra" environment, a speakeasy set created by Burnett. Just Us presented shows in the Club Zebra format at the National Black Arts Festivals in 1988, 1990, and 1992. The Alliance Theatre in Atlanta has premiered three of Cleage's plays. However, her voice as a playwright was not nationally recognized until *Flyin' West* (1992) and *Blues for an Alabama Sky* (1995). She is one of the most progressive and insightful contemporary dramatists exploring issues involving women of color.

In Cleage's play *Hospice* (1983), Alice, a poet and expatriate who is dying of cancer, has returned to her childhood home, where she unexpectedly finds her pregnant daughter, Jenny, whom she has not seen for several years. In this one-act drama, a daughter is in desperate pursuit of words of wisdom and life lessons from a "stranger" who is just discovering her own right to be afraid. After a successful run at the Colonnades Theatre Lab in New York City, *Hospice,* which was directed by acclaimed actress Frances Foster and produced by Woodie King Jr.'s New Federal Theatre, received five Audelco Recognition Awards, including best drama of 1983.

Cleage's 1992 one-act drama *Late Bus to Mecca* (published in 1999) is also simply staged. Set in a Detroit bus station in 1970, Cleage juxtaposes the silence of a battered homeless woman with the spirited chatter of a prostitute to delineate the painful, yet triumphant, pilgrimage of these two different women.

The power to disappear or to take flight to escape the brutality of their masters was often associated with the Angolan slaves of the Gullah Islands, who were thought to possess supernatural powers. Similarly, the

Cover for Cleage's second collection of essays (1993)

title of Cleage's play *Flyin' West* also speaks of a people taking flight in order to find a safer space to land. Cleage is among a small group of African American dramatists who place African Americans, particularly black women, on the Western frontier. Cleage extends the narrative of the flying Africans to black female migrants who, at the end of the nineteenth century, searched for refuge in Western states. In Cleage's title the word "flyin'" connotes agency for the characters who participate in an emigration, an escape, a mapping, and a crossover.

Flyin' West premiered in November 1992. Cleage's work was finally shared with audiences throughout the United States as the play was produced at the Indiana Repertory Theatre, Crossroads Theatre Company, New WORLD Theater, St. Louis Repertory Theatre, Long Wharf Theatre, the Majestic Theatre at the Brooklyn Academy of Music, Intiman Theatre Company, San Diego Repertory Theatre, and the Kennedy Center. *Flyin' West* is a domestic melo-

drama that takes place on the Kansas prairie just outside the all-black town of Nicodemus. When the play begins, Sophie Washington, a former slave, and Fannie Dove are awaiting the return home of their youngest sister, Minnie Dove Charles, and her husband, Frank Charles, who have been living in Europe.

Sophie and Fannie, after nearly twenty years of arduous labor, are now wheat farmers and rising leaders in their community. They are fearful that white speculators will buy up Kansas property and resell it to whites, thereby disrupting the economic, social, and political autonomy they sought in this all-black community. Like thousands of blacks who left Tennessee, Mississippi, and Kentucky for what they considered to be a modern Canaan, the sisters headed West during the "Kansas Exodus of 1879." They were captivated by the "free land" being given out by the U.S. government. Cleage says of her characters that by flying West "they were no longer the creature of another's will."

The adopted older sister, Sophie, is the most aggressive in her attempts to organize the Nicodemus community to pass a rule that stipulates no one can sell to outsiders without the consent of the entire community. Though Nicodemus is not depicted onstage, Cleage uses the language of the characters to dramatize the freedom that the physical Western space possibly offers. In act 1, scene 1, Sophie proclaims:

> We could have so much here if these colored folks would step lively. We could own this whole prairie. Nothing but colored folks farms and colored folks wheat fields and colored folks cattle. . . . They look at Nicodemus and all they see is a bunch of scuffling people trying to get ready for the winter instead of something free and fine and all our own. Most of them don't even know what we're doing here!

The Kansas landscape serves as a metaphor for home, where black residents can experience a newly defined freedom. Through their ownership of "colored folks farms" and "colored folks wheat fields" the sisters reclaim ownership over themselves. In particular, Sophie's drive to make Nicodemus a place that is devoid of white rule is also a result of the confinement she experienced in Memphis, Tennessee, during and after Emancipation. Sophie declares that blacks who remained behind in Memphis were puzzled by the sisters' departure for the "wilderness." She notes, "I kept trying to tell them it does not matter. Anyplace is better than there." *Flyin' West* is as much about how the characters remember the brutality of the South as it is about how they imagine the West.

The sisters' freedom is threatened, however, when Frank, excluded from his white father's inheritance, plans to take the deed to Minnie's land and sell it to speculators. When the older sisters learn Frank has been physically abusing their sister and plans to sell their land to outsiders, their focus shifts from the external adversary to the enemy within. Unlike Sophie, who is also of mixed parentage, Frank is tormented by his inner conflicts. He is in love with the thing that hates him (whiteness—represented by his father, male privilege), yet he hates the thing that loves him (blackness—represented by his wife, the poetry of Paul Laurence Dunbar). In Frank, Cleage, who is fair-skinned, has created a poignant and complex examination of the impact of color.

The plot is resolved when Miss Leah, the old woman who was the first to migrate to Kansas and is now a de facto grandmother to the family, bakes a poison apple pie from the recipe of an African cook on the plantation where she was enslaved. Frank dies; the land is saved; the women are safe; and Minnie's baby is born healthy. In the final moments of the play, Miss Leah tells the baby stories of her ancestors while Sophie slowly turns in a full circle to see the land that belongs to her family.

Cleage says of her playwriting: "My work is deeply rooted in, and consciously reflective of, African-American history and culture since I believe that it is by accurately expressing our very specific and highly individual realities that we discover our common humanity." *Blues for an Alabama Sky* is further evidence of the playwright's obsession with history. This play, set in a Harlem apartment building during the summer of 1930, is less melodramatic than *Flyin' West*. It premiered in July 1995 at the Alliance Theatre, but it has also been staged at the Arena Stage (Washington, D.C.) and the Goodman Theatre (Chicago). In contrast to *Flyin' West,* the lives of black men and women in *Blues for an Alabama Sky* are dramatized as a struggle to gain access to the sparse opportunities in the early years of the Great Depression. The characters include Angel Allen, a thirty-four-year-old former backup singer at the Cotton Club; her roommate, Guy Jacobs, a gay costume designer who dreams of going to Paris; and their neighbor Delia Patterson, a young social worker at the Margaret Sanger Family Planning Clinic. Sam Thomas, a doctor at Harlem Hospital, and Leland Cunningham, Angel's young suitor, are also critical to the dramatic narrative.

In her short essay "The Motion of Herstory: Three Plays by Pearl Cleage" Freda Scott Giles refers to Delia as merely an "idealistic social worker." Though the young woman has a naive outlook on black life during the Depression, she is a critical voice for a black feminist discourse. Margaret Sanger is considered the national voice of reproductive rights in America during the 1920s and 1930s, but Delia is the one who transfers information and who attempts to mobilize the mostly poor black community in Cleage's play. Delia faces opposition from the Reverend Adam Clayton Powell Sr. and the congregation at Abyssinian Baptist Church as they respond to a family-planning clinic in Harlem. Cleage places Delia among a community of characters who challenge her to construct a discourse that does not attack or blame Harlem residents for their conditions. In particular, Delia's lover, Sam, provides her with suggestions for more realistic and more progressive ways of reaching black families at Powell's church:

> **SAM**: (*Gently*): I deliver babies everyday to exhausted women and stone-broke men, but they never ask me about birth control. They ask me about jobs.
> **DELIA**: What does that mean?
> **SAM**: It means we still see our best hope in the faces of our children and it's going to take more than some

Phylicia Rashad and Deidrie Henry in the 1995 Atlanta production of Blues for an Alabama Sky

rich white woman playing missionary in Harlem to convince these Negroes otherwise.

Sam shows her that in order for the congregation to hear her, Delia must understand more carefully the ways in which blacks in the Harlem church view birth control. Some see birth control as genocide and a hindrance to racial progress and the woman's role in her family, while others feel that discourse on birth control is inappropriate in a black sacred space.

Cleage's access to the black intelligentsia as a young girl appears to have informed her writing of *Blues for an Alabama Sky*. In a 15 March 1998 *Chicago Sun-Times* interview she remarked, "And my father, an activist minister, was always working to define, build and strengthen our community in Detroit, and to understand what it is that can destroy that sense of community as well." Though Cleage refers to well-known figures from the era, such as Powell, Langston Hughes, Josephine Baker, and Bruce Nugent, it is clear that the

play examines what happened to ordinary people when the Harlem Renaissance ended.

Unlike Delia, Angel does not triumph. She makes choices that destroy any possible opportunities. At the end of the play Angel is sitting alone in her apartment with the blues. Cleage claims that *Blues for an Alabama Sky* is the first play in which one of her black female characters did not overcome obstacles: "When I got to the end of this play, I realized I was trying to make Angel do something that had not been justified by the characters and by their story. . . . I had to come to terms with what it meant for me to create a character who doesn't triumph."

Cleage was only fifteen when civil rights activists launched the black voter registration drive in Mississippi in 1964. In her 1997 play, *Bourbon at the Border,* a contemporary couple is haunted by the memory of that Freedom Summer. The Alliance Theatre first produced *Bourbon at the Border* for an extended run from 30 April through 15 June 1997.

This production was billed as Cleage's "third successful artistic collaboration" with Kenny Leon's Alliance Theatre. This collaboration, in part, was credited for helping attract larger audiences to the theater. *Bourbon at the Border* received mixed reviews from critics. For instance, after seeing a production at the Charles H. Wright Museum of African American History in Detroit, one reviewer for *The Detroit News* (10 November 1998) argued Cleage "takes too long" to get to her key moments, "and the real deaths going on offstage (and only talked of) seem like red herrings rather than signposts leading us on to a dawning, emotional awareness." However, most critics agree that Cleage has a gift for creating well-defined characters and for shaping a scene.

Cleage's first novel, *What Looks Like Crazy on an Ordinary Day—,* also appeared in 1997. It focuses on the challenges facing a black woman living with HIV. Cleage argues, "I think that a lot of Black women are still very much in denial about AIDS. They act as if it is somebody else's disease when, in actuality, Black women are the fastest growing group of persons infected." After the novel became a featured selection of talk-show host Oprah Winfrey's Book of the Month Club, sales exploded, allowing her to reach a much larger audience. The novel remained on *The New York Times* best-seller list for nearly ten weeks in 1998.

Cleage is working on her next play, "Ernesto's Eyes." She was playwright-in-residence at Spelman College, where she also taught drama and creative writing. Cleage came of age in an era that placed protest and resistance at the center of her consciousness. As a teacher and writer, she continues to provide inspiration and a framework for the next generation of black nationalist feminists.

Interviews:

Annette Gilliam, "Romance, AIDS Explored in Pearl Cleage's New Novel," *Washington Informer,* 34 (4 February 1998): 16;

Hedy Weiss, "Lifelong Interest Inspires Playwright," *Chicago Sun-Times,* 15 March 1998, p. 13;

Weiss, "Blues for an Alabama Sky," *Chicago Sun-Times,* 17 March 1998, p. 30.

References:

Tom Creamer and Susan V. Booth, eds., *Onstage,* 3 (Chicago: Goodman Theatre Series 1997–1998), p. 4;

Freda Scott Giles, "Bourbon at the Border," *African American Review,* 31 (Winter 1997): 725–726;

Giles, "The Motion of Herstory: Three Plays by Pearl Cleage," *African American Review,* 31 (Winter 1997): 709–712;

Larry A. Greene, "Harlem, The Depression Years: Leadership and Social Conditions," *Afro-Americans in New York Life and History,* 2 (July 1993): 36–47;

Virginia Hamilton, *The People Could Fly: American Black Folktales* (New York: Knopf, 1985), p. 171;

Jessie M. Rodrique, "The Black Community and the Birth Control Movement," in *"We Specialize in the Wholly Impossible": A Reader in Black Women's History,* edited by Darlene Clark Hine and Wilma King (Brooklyn, N.Y.: Carlson Publishing, 1995), pp. 505–520;

Jon Michael Spencer, "The Black Church and the Harlem Renaissance," *African American Review,* 30 (Fall 1996): 453–460;

Esther Beth Sullivan, "The Dimensions of Flyin' West," *Theater Topics,* 7, no. 1 (1997): 11–22;

William L. Van Deburg, *New Day in Babylon: The Black Power Movement and American Culture, 1965–1975* (Chicago: University of Chicago Press, 1992).

Laura Farabough

(24 July 1949 –)

Phaedra D. Bell
Stanford University

PLAY PRODUCTIONS: *The Wildman,* Agoura, a hillside, 1972;

The Rat Story, San Francisco, Produce Market Warehouse, 1973;

Beauty and the Beast, San Francisco, San Francisco Museum of Modern Art, 1974;

The Creation and Destruction of the World in 5 Acts, San Francisco, Intersection for the Arts, 1974;

The Bone Show/Calaveras, San Francisco, Capp Street Theater, 1975;

Jaja Man, San Francisco, Golden Gate Park, 1975;

The Hunger Show, San Francisco, Golden Gate Park, 1975;

The Fool Asleep, San Francisco, Waller Street Theater, 1975;

Eye of Darkness, San Francisco, Goodman Theater, 1975;

Como el Perro de las dos Tortas, San Francisco, Lone Mountain College, 1976;

La Mujer Afligada, San Francisco, Lone Mountain College, 1976;

Dead Play, Sausalito, Snake House, 1976;

Somewhere in the Pacific, Sausalito, Cronkhite Beach, 1977;

Her Building, Sausalito, City Hall, 1977;

24th Hour Café, San Francisco, Tenderloin Theater, 1977;

Sub-division, San Francisco, New Performance Gallery, 1978;

Auto, Sausalito, Mohawk Gas Station, 1979;

Femme Fatale: The Invention of Personality, San Francisco, Victoria Theater, 1981; rewritten as an opera, Minneapolis, Minneapolis Opera Company, 1986;

Surface Tension, Mill Valley, California, Bay Area Playwrights Festival, 1981;

Locker Room, Mill Valley, Tamalpais High School Girls' Locker Room, 1982;

Obedience School, San Francisco, Magic Theater, 1982;

Sea of Heartbreak, Sausalito, Smitty's Saloon, 1983;

Battle of the Brides, Mexico City, Coyoacan Plaza, 1983;

Beauty Science, Sausalito, Dorlane's Hair Design, 1983;

Liquid Distance/Timed Approach, Los Angeles, Beverly Hills High School swimming pool, 1984;

Under Construction, San Francisco, Pier 3, Fort Mason Center, 1985;

Baseball Zombie, San Francisco, Video Free America, 1985;

Bodily Concessions, San Francisco, Life on the Water, 1987;

Private Property, San Francisco, Climate Gallery, 1989;

Socrates' Lie, Mill Valley, Redwood High School, 1990;

Real Original Thinker, Stanford, Nitery Theatre, 1995;

M1, Stanford, Stanford University, 3 April 1997;

M2, San Francisco, The Lab, 10 May 1998.

PRODUCED SCRIPTS: *Twelve Stations of the Latrine,* video, 1986;

Investigation Through a Window, video, 1987;

M2, CD-ROM, 1999;

M3, CD-ROM, 1999.

OTHER: Selections from *Surface Tension,* in *West Coast Plays* (Berkeley: California Theater Council, 1982) pp. 167–180.

SELECTED PERIODICAL PUBLICATIONS–UNCOLLECTED: "Al Warsha In Cairo," *TheatreForum,* 1, no. 1 (1992): 4–11;

Bodily Concessions, TheatreForum, 3 (1993): 25–35;

Real Original Thinker, TheatreForum, 8 (1996): 75–88;

"*Nur Du (Only You)* A Piece by Pina Bausch," *TheatreForum,* 10 (1997): 60–66.

Laura Farabough is a pioneer in site-specific theater and in the use of video onstage. A central figure in the San Francisco alternative theater scene of the 1970s and 1980s, Farabough wrote and directed landmark pieces such as *Somewhere in the Pacific* (1977) for Cronkhite Beach, just north of San Francisco, and *Surface Tension* (1981), a play written to be performed in swimming pools. She began writing plays for performers and video in 1977; her theatrical application of video preceded that of many renowned video-savvy theater practitioners such as the Wooster Group and John Jesserun. Theater historians and critics who remember to take West Coast artists into account consistently recognize the importance of her contributions to contemporary American theater.

Until the 1990s, critics consistently treated Farabough as a theater practitioner despite the fact that she writes all the plays she produces, designs, directs, and sometimes performs. The striking visual content of her work leads critics not only to emphasize the stage portion of Farabough's work but also to draw attention even further away from any literary aspects by comparing her work with other plastic arts. Theodore Shank, for example, wrote of Farabough and her collaborators in 1982, "They think of puppets and live performers as moving sculptures, and of the performance as a painting animated by movement." Although accurate, these assessments ignore the literary element of Farabough's work.

Critic Jim Carmody began to argue for treating Farabough as the creator of literary as well as theatrical work. In 1991 Carmody described Farabough's plays as part of a movement in contemporary dramatic writing he calls "post-literary": "Post-literary writing for the theatre employs a hybrid dramaturgy influenced by visual art, media and music that is rich in recognizable detail as well as surreal transformations of what the traditional theatre represents as 'real.'" Perhaps Carmody's assessment will inspire literary critics to examine Farabough's playwriting. However, Farabough's plays have yet to receive subsequent performances, and their literary value remains to be appraised.

Laura Farabough was born in Santa Clara, California, on 24 July 1949. Farabough and her brother, John Ross, were raised by their father, Dr. Wayland Bruner Ross Jr., and their mother, Virginia Dumas Farabough Ross. Farabough's formal education was suspended before completion of secondary school and resumed in 1993 when she entered the doctoral program in drama at Stanford University. Primarily self-taught, Farabough also emphasizes the educational guidance she received from mentors throughout her life, including David and Jane Rosen, Alice Choates, Patricia Long, Kay Hardman Enell, David Shickele, Candra Day, and Douglas Martin. She married James Michael Cortesos in Arizona in 1967 and divorced shortly thereafter. She had a long-term relationship with her collaborator, Chris Hardman, from 1972 to 1979.

Farabough's career consists of four distinct periods that correspond to her four different companies: her work with Hardman in Beggar's Theatre; their re-invention of themselves as Snake Theatre; her work with her own company, Nightfire; and her work with

the ensemble known as "sponge." She founded her first company, Beggar's Theatre, with Hardman in Los Angeles in 1972. During her earliest years in the theater, Farabough and Hardman addressed primarily mythological themes. Hardman's previous work with Peter Schumann's Bread and Puppet Theatre influenced his input as they joined other theater practitioners of the time in mounting pieces that endeavored to revive the ritual function of theater through the use of puppetry and masks.

Beggar's Theatre organized their early work around the development of a play cycle. Their first performance took the form of a festival that Farabough refers to alternately as "Beelzebub" or "Lord of the Flies." This series of pageants and parades culminated in the burning of an enormous wooden structure representing the eponymous figure. This piece formed the summer segment of the cycle. Their first "play" in the traditional sense of the word premiered later in 1972 when the Los Angeles–based Renaissance Faire commissioned *The Wildman*. It featured archetypal figures in a struggle between the Church and Nature and formed the spring component of the play cycle. In 1973 Farabough and Hardman moved to San Francisco, where they developed *The Rat Story,* the winter play, first commissioned by the San Francisco Dickens Fair, and *The Bone Show/Calaveras,* the autumn Day of the Dead play developed over time with Galeria de la Raza.

In January of 1974 Farabough and Hardman moved to Sausalito, a town just over the Golden Gate Bridge from San Francisco. They lived in a building near "the waterfront," a community of artists and others living mostly in houseboats moored in the Sausalito marinas. As they slowly discovered the Sausalito waterfront community, Farabough and Hardman wrote, produced, and directed an average of three plays a year in the mid 1970s. From its new base, Beggar's Theatre produced *Beauty and the Beast* (1974) at the San Francisco Museum of Modern Art and *The Creation and Destruction of the World in 5 Acts* (1974) at a San Francisco nonprofit organization called Intersection for the Arts. In 1975 they created two outdoor plays, *Jaja Man* and *The Hunger Show,* for a San Francisco city parks tour. Beggar's Theatre also produced *The Fool Asleep* and *Eye of Darkness* at small San Francisco theaters that same year.

In 1976 Farabough and Hardman took Beggar's Theatre on tour to Mexico with two plays, *Como el Perro de las dos Tortas* (Like the Dog with Two Cakes) and *La Mujer Afligada* (The Afflicted Woman). The former, comic piece featured two dogs, Flacco and Gordo, fighting over a sandwich. The latter, more serious piece functioned as an alternative for the spring component of their play cycle. In an unpublished October 1998 interview Farabough claimed that she and Hardman idealized Mexican culture and saw their tour as a pilgrimage to their source of inspiration. They found not further inspiration but rather a revelation. Having attended several local rituals, Farabough and Hardman realized that the power of these rituals came precisely from the specificity of the shared history and knowledge of their respective communities and that ultimately, as outsiders, she and Hardman could never access the deepest meanings. Concurrently, the playwrights also noticed a culturally based discord between what Beggar's Theatre was trying to communicate and what their Mexican audiences understood. This experience instilled in Farabough an appreciation for specificity and for the importance of place in the theater.

Returning from their transformative Mexican tour in 1977, Farabough and Hardman joined forces with another waterfront couple–Larry Graber, a musician and composer, and Evie Lewis, a dancer and choreographer. First calling themselves the Ouroboros Mask Society, they renamed themselves Snake Theatre. This group abandoned the Beggar's Theatre interest in the mythological and focused instead on local, contemporary situations. Snake Theatre maintained, however, part of the aesthetic of their previous incarnation. Farabough and Hardman continued using masks and puppets for some time. These properties as well as new elements imbued the commonplace themes of their plays with what Shank called "epic dimensions." Farabough generally cowrote, codesigned, and directed Snake Theatre productions; Hardman cowrote, codesigned, and built the masks, props, and sets; Graber composed the scores and performed the music; and Lewis choreographed, performed, and organized logistical elements. Under pressure, however, all four worked on every aspect of their productions.

Part of Farabough's newfound interest in place manifested itself in site-specific work. Snake Theatre's environmental theater pieces brought them international notoriety and acclaim. The group's first production, Somewhere in the Pacific, attracted enormous critical attention. Farabough and Hardman wrote this piece for Cronkhite Beach, a fairly isolated area not far from the Sausalito side of the Golden Gate Bridge. Audiences gathered at the beach about an hour before sunset to find Carol, a giant female figure on a distant cliff facing the ocean. The figure would reach out to the horizon. A group of sailors on a concrete bunker chanted words that subsequently appeared one by one on placards that another set of sailors exhumed from the sand. Once revealed, these words composed a letter to Carol written by her now-deceased boyfriend, Ryan, a sailor during World War II whom the audience watched writing at the edge of the water.

Like many of Farabough's plays, Somewhere in the Pacific featured a simple dramatic situation that she complicated through what Carmody called "a principle of multiplicity." Repetition of carefully selected images gave multiple meanings to their simple romance. The figures of General and Mrs. MacArthur also watched the revelation of Carol and Ryan's story along with the audience. According to Shank, at first the sailors' chanted words had only musical value. As they appeared in the sand, they took on narrative value and then irony as they related differently to Carol, Ryan, and the MacArthurs. The chants then brought the words back into abstraction, although, now imbued with narrative, the abstractions carried emotional connotations of yearning and loss.

Farabough and Hardman wrote the second Snake Theatre play, Her Building, for Sausalito City Hall later in 1977. They extended their "dramaturgy of multiplicity" beyond the repetition of simple actions and images found in Somewhere in the Pacific. Farabough also duplicated the characters in Her Building by assigning two performers to play each role. Each character's two manifestations would perform simultaneously but not in unison. One would perform one set of actions in one part of the stage space while the other would perform another set elsewhere. Sometimes one would "catch up" with the other and "pass off" a set of actions to the other performer as though in a relay race. The action of the play also focused on duplication. "The building" calls upon Mrs. Stone to assist it in reproducing itself. The audience sat outside City Hall and watched the performers' actions in front of the building. The scenes that took place "inside" the building played on video monitors placed on stands scattered throughout the audience. Her Building was the first play Farabough and Hardman wrote for performers and video.

Snake Theatre created indoor shows for traditional stage spaces as well. Even these pieces went to great length to establish specificity of place. 24th Hour Café (1978), for example, took place in a desert truck stop, with large sculptures of cacti and customers creating the space. The Waitress seeks escape from her mundane existence through liaisons with the Truck Driver and the Lizard Man. Neither one takes her anywhere other than into the cacti for sex. As in Somewhere in the Pacific and Her Building, none of the performers spoke. Rather, Farabough delivered some of the dialogue and narration for them from the orchestra pit, and the rest appeared in slide projections.

Sub-division (1978), not unlike 24th Hour Café, featured a triangle of two males and one female: the former husband, the date, and the woman. In this play the woman's child, who misses the father, adds a fourth, exogenous element. Sub-division was Farabough's first cham-

Scene from the 1977 performance of Somewhere in the Pacific *on Cronkhite Beach in Sausalito*

ber piece for performers and video. The video featured realist images such as the interior of the house, the telephone on which the former husband and the date call, and the date's car driving through town. Onstage, two of the most renowned modern dancers in San Francisco, Larry McQueen of the Margie Jenkens company and Karen Attix of Merce Cunningham's company, performed the action of the play. Meanwhile, Graber played his score of piano and pre-recorded piano, and the recorded dialogue played on tape. Farabough describes this piece as one of the riskiest pieces Snake Theatre had created with respect to the uncertainty of the conceptual connections.

Auto (1979) was also a risky piece, but the risk was physical rather than conceptual. Full of fast cars, fireworks, and combustible materials, this play placed the performers and the spectators in considerable danger. Farabough wrote this piece for an abandoned Mohawk gas station in Sausalito. *Auto* featured a struggle between an upper-middle-class couple and a set of mystic mechanics. Farabough divided the play into "gears" rather than scenes that advanced the fragmented plot. Between each "gear" the God Auto sang

a "shift," a passage from a manual about automatic transmission. According to Shank, "The automatic transmission which conveys power from engine to wheels is a metaphor for other kinds of power transfers. . . . The play is not anti-automatic, but it does imply a widening gap between the abstract ideas of intellectuals and the concrete reality of the machines for which they are responsible."

Later that year Farabough and Hardman ended their romantic relationship. Snake Theatre had developed into a sophisticated nonprofit organization over the previous three years. They and their board of directors had made commitments to create more pieces for another California tour and for their first European tour. Graber and Lewis encouraged Farabough and Hardman to join them in continuing to function as a theater company despite the change in their relationship. The company devised a method of working that would require less interaction between the former lovers: Hardman would write one show that Farabough would direct, and then Farabough would write one show that Hardman would direct. They planned to alternate roles in that fashion while

Graber and Lewis continued in their functions as composer and choreographer/logistician. The first product of this new arrangement was *Ride Hard/Die Fast* (1980). For the first time, Farabough directed a play that she did not cowrite. It featured a conflict between drivers of cars, led by Henry Ford, and motorcyclists, led by Adolf Hitler. She disliked the play but enjoyed working on the production on her own, without any interference from Hardman.

In 1980, while Farabough was still touring with *Ride Hard/Die Fast* in California, Graber was diagnosed with an advanced case of acute leukemia. Graber and Lewis convinced Farabough to go on the first leg of the European tour on her own. *Ride Hard/Die Fast* was well received abroad, and Farabough was interviewed as one of the three important women theater practitioners on the festival circuit, with Pina Bausch and Arianne Mnouchkine. However, news soon reached Farabough that Graber had died just one month after his diagnosis. His death marked the end of Snake Theatre as a group. Farabough broke away from Hardman altogether and established her own company, Nightfire, while Hardman founded his own company, Antenna Theatre. The two companies operated as separate branches of Snake Theatre, the nonprofit organization through which they shared the same board of directors and some administrative staff for some time.

The first Nightfire production, *Femme Fatale: The Invention of Personality,* appeared in the spring of 1981. *Femme Fatale* examines the impact of men on the formation of two women's personalities. The enormously complicated story juxtaposes the biographies of Mata Hari and Greta Garbo. Farabough created the theatrical equivalent of a split-screen effect for this piece. Both narratives unraveled simultaneously, one on each side of the stage. Five years later Farabough worked with Opera America and the Minnesota Opera Company to develop an operatic version of *Femme Fatale*. The collaboration did not succeed, and ultimately only six songs were performed at the Minnesota Opera Company.

As artist in residence at the Bay Area Playwrights Festival for the 1981–1982 season, Farabough developed Nightfire's first location piece, *Surface Tension.* Unlike the site-specific work of Snake Theatre, this show could tour. It did not appear in theaters, but rather in competition-sized swimming and diving pools around California. As in her Snake Theatre productions and in *Femme Fatale,* the dialogue in *Surface Tension* was entirely prerecorded and played on tape during the performance. The Young Guy and The Woman flirt at a swimming pool. It is unclear whether or not one figure is simply imagining the presence of the other figure, or which character might be imagining the other, or if indeed the encounter occurs at all. *Surface Tension* con-

forms to Carmody's description of Farabough's technique of blending "a complex visual and verbal score to investigate human behavior at the level of idea and fantasy, collapsing the habitual distinction between these twin poles of mental activity." This production featured Farabough's first return to performance since her work with Hardman in Beggar's Theatre.

In 1982 Farabough developed the next Nightfire production, *Obedience School.* This piece featured three characters: The Model, The Pilot, and The Attendant. The Model and the Pilot are live-in lovers. She models the highest fashions, while he tests military planes; both must achieve perfection to perform their jobs. *Obedience School* was Farabough's most ambitious use of video yet, and she drew clear parallels between the perfect timing required of the actors and the perfection demanded of the main characters. When Farabough toured with *Obedience School* to the Wooster Group's Performing Garage in New York in 1983, her hosts and other local alternative-theater people were still practicing a form of theater descended from the "ecstatic political theater" of the 1960s that privileged the unmediated presence of the performer. These artists, who later became known for their use of video, reacted to Farabough's work with hostility. They were scandalized by her introduction of recorded action into the theatrical temple of live performance.

Farabough wrote *Beauty Science* (1983) for her twelve-year-old neighbor, Maude Bradley. It first ran at a Sausalito beauty salon, Dorlane's Hair Design. She originally wrote it for three women: Maude, a woman in her twenties (played by Farabough), and an older woman. She meant to address these three women's relationships to their sexuality. Two different older actors tried but ultimately refused to play the role of the older woman. In retrospect Farabough speculates that the role she wrote was oversimplified, insensitive, and naive about mature sexuality. To solve the problem, Farabough rewrote the piece for Maude and two women in their twenties, converting the piece into a Cinderella story of wicked older sisters, envious of the budding sexuality of the adolescent.

During her New York tour with *Obedience School* Farabough had been commissioned to create a piece for the Arts Festival of the 1984 Olympic Games in Los Angeles. Meanwhile, out of greater concern for their obligations to their sponsors than for artistic integrity, Nightfire's administrative director insisted on a second run of *Beauty Science* as a traditional stage play in San Francisco. Grants and awards from organizations such as the National Endowment for the Arts, the California Arts Council, the San Francisco Foundation, the Rockefeller Foundation, and the Hewlett Foundation sustained Nightfire. Farabough has referred to living in

Scene from the 1977 San Francisco production of 24th Hour Café

"non-profit prison" during these years. The rhythm of
the grants dictated the rhythm of production. The second run of *Beauty Science* left Farabough with only two
months to write and direct the piece for the Olympic
Arts Festival. That piece, her second swimming pool
play, *Liquid Distance/Timed Approach,* ran at the Beverly
Hills High School swimming pool. A critic for *High Performance* magazine (no. 27, 1984) gave this show about
the dangers and fantasies of swimming a positive
review. However, Farabough disliked the play and felt
she had made too many compromises under the pressure of her grant-driven production schedule.

Farabough also attributed her dislike of *Liquid
Distance* in part to concessions she made to the people
who were working for little or no compensation to create the show, such as the performers and the technicians. Like many directors, Farabough motivated their
participation by making them feel that the play was as
much their show as it was hers, but ultimately their
input undermined her vision. The production schedule
for *Liquid Distance* emphasized a problem that had
always haunted her work: the tension between auteurism and collectivity.

Under Construction (1985) addresses the ethical
dilemma, "the lie" (as Farabough describes it) that she
had to tell the people who worked to create her shows.

Farabough created this work for Pier 3, a gigantic
former army pier at Fort Mason Center in San Francisco. It incorporated both recorded and live video
taken during the production. In this piece an architect
who has reached the zenith of his career finds himself
free to build any building he desires. Blocked, he prays
for inspiration. Cleopatra responds to his prayer and
directs him to build a monument to his wife, who is his
muse. The performers build the monument over the
course of the play using a forklift, a crane, and a
one-ton truck. The architect cannot construct the building alone: he needs his wife, a master builder, and
workers. Ultimately, however, he locks his wife in the
pyramid he built for her. In a 1987 interview Farabough
explained, "The piece is really about the artist who
seduces the technician with his vision in order to get the
technician to make his vision come true."

Farabough's themes of doubling and repetition
become more sophisticated in this self-reflexive piece.
The architect uses his wife, the master builder, the con-
tractors, and the construction workers to create what he
ultimately claims as his. Simultaneously, Farabough
used these performers and technicians (many of whom
were longshoremen from her neighborhood who
received no compensation for their labors) to create a
play that she ultimately claims as hers. Farabough dis-

tinguishes herself from her main character only in her consciousness of the auteur's monstrosity. In unpublished 1998 interviews she described *Under Construction* as a way of addressing but not resolving the tension between auteurism and collectivity.

In stark contrast to the enormity of *Under Construction*, Farabough's next piece, *Baseball Zombie* (1985), featured just one performer and a wall of video monitors. In this first work for a solo performer, Bob Looker, a shy, isolated long-distance telephone operator with few friends, exorcises his familial demons through his infiltration of a televised baseball game. Farabough used a combination of live and recorded video in this piece as well as what she calls "holding patterns," recurring video images (of telephones, for example) that fill the screens when they are not displaying specific live or recorded sequences.

After *Baseball Zombie* Farabough turned her attentions away from the stage altogether to develop two video installations. She developed the first one, *Twelve Stations of the Latrine* (1986), for the Headlands Center for the Arts in Sausalito. The Headlands Center is located in a half-renovated military installation on the Main Headlands, not far from Cronkhite Beach, the location for *Somewhere in the Pacific*. She filmed and installed this video, which features a woman's gang-rape fantasy, in the rostrum of the center during an international conference for artists. Farabough developed the second video, *Investigation Through a Window* (1987), on commission from the Japan/United States Friendship organization. She installed it in the Sob Department Store in Tokyo. Later that year she integrated both videos into one of her most intricate combinations of live performance and recorded video, *Bodily Concessions*.

Farabough designed *Bodily Concessions* for a small stage, approximately twenty feet by fifteen feet. She placed a twelve-by-nine-feet video projection screen upstage and suspended a video projector overhead to project onto the screen. A television monitor was placed downstage left. Farabough wrote the play for what she deems three characters: monitor (The Woman on the monitor), video (The Woman on the video screen), and performer (The Woman on stage). Each "Woman" was portrayed by the same performer, however—in the original production, by Farabough herself. By first introducing the woman through her image on the monitor, Farabough tries to establish the monitor as more intimate, full, and convincing than either the video screen or the live performer.

The woman has discovered that she has been sleepwalking. Deeply troubled by what she learns of her unconscious behavior in what is called "a state of being abnormally awake," the monitor woman explains that she finds she must distinguish herself from her sleepwalking self by referring to the latter in the third person. Despite the monitor woman's adamant insistence on this grammatical distinction that jams a linguistic and psychological

wedge between her and her sleepwalking identity, she ardently wishes to make contact with this sleepwalking other self. Through references in her opening monologue, the monitor woman establishes herself as the conscious ("normally awake") self; the performer as "her," the sleepwalking self; and the screen as the dream-image itself.

Farabough developed *Real Original Thinker,* a "brother play" to *Bodily Concessions,* from 1991 to 1995. *Real Original Thinker* used the identical construct of performer, upstage screen, and downstage left monitor. It consisted of three parts: the opening monologue, the story of a man's murder of his mother, and an art history and criticism lesson. The opening monologue parodies the now-standard autobiographical solo performance. The man goes through five different incarnations of himself, which he marks with numbers written on a pad hanging around his neck. Each incarnation claims to be "the real me." The second section complicates theatrical illusion through the mechanism of the unreliable narrator. The same character who has demonstrated his penchant for instability and lies explains how he murdered his mother. He at once seems crazy enough to have done it and too crazy to be believed. Furthermore, throughout this segment someone on the monitor comments on the man's performance, urging the audience not to believe him and questioning the man directly about the veracity of his statements. The third section resumes the parody, this time targeting the self-absorbed intellectual. In 1993 Farabough entered the doctoral program in drama at Stanford University; her experiences during that enterprise may have influenced the portrayal of the man in the third section of *Real Original Thinker.*

In 1997 Farabough joined forces with colleagues Sha Xinwei and Chris Salter to form a collaborative artistic company they named sponge. It now includes artists and researchers in Paris, Brussels, Amsterdam, and Berlin as well as San Francisco. Through sponge Farabough continues to create art that straddles boundaries between media. Sponge's first production, *M1, Merge No End Of Or To; At the Edge of Visibility* (1997), sought to find the line between performing and not performing. Each member performed the same simple set of mundane actions twice in a row at the same time each week in a popular lunch spot on the Stanford University campus. The second piece, *M2* (1998), explored the communicative possibilities of peripheral vision through the creation of an algorithmic installation of video and performance in four rooms through which spectators moved. Sponge documented *M2* not with a final script for publication, but rather with a CD-ROM. In 1999 sponge began developing *M3* and published another CD-ROM that poses the three research questions of the piece in digital video form: "how do we play?" "how do we experience the word?" and "how do we shape the world?" They developed two parts of the larger *M3*

Scene from the 1979 production of Auto, *staged at the Mohawk Gas Station in Sausalito*

project: *Sauna,* a media environment for the San Francisco Electronic Music Festival, and a prose piece for EC/Arts, the French government art and technology publication. Farabough's later work is perhaps farther away than ever from that of the traditional dramatist.

Farabough has contributed greatly to twentieth-century American alternative theater. Her work in site-specific and video-intensive theater has always extended and sharpened the theatrical cutting edge. Critics are still forging the terminology to discuss the literary value of her plays. Carmody's notion of the "post-literary" may invite further analysis of her published works and perhaps inspire the publication of other scripts that document Farabough's craft.

Interviews:

"Laura Farabough," in *Interviews with Contemporary Women Playwrights,* edited by Kathleen Betsko and Rachel Koenig (New York: Beech Tree Books, 1987), pp. 139–153;

Theodore Shank, Interview with Laura Farabough, *California Performance,* 1 (1989): 118–155.

References:

Jim Carmody, "Laura Farabough: Director, Scenographer, Writer," *TheatreForum,* 3 (1993): 23–24;

Carmody, "Poets of Bohemia and Suburbia: The Post-Literary Dramaturgies of Farabough, Harrington, and Shank," in *Contemporary American Theatre,* edited by Bruce King (New York: St. Martin's Press, 1991), pp. 245–261;

Theodore Shank, *American Alternative Theatre* (New York: Grove, 1982), pp. 113–122;

Shank, "Laura Farabough and Chris Hardman: Background," *California Performance,* 1 (1989): 106–111;

Shank, "Laura Farabough: Story, Characters, and Ideas Nightfire Theatre," *California Performance,* 1 (1989): 112–155;

Shank, "Vu de San Francisco: performance en Californie," *Alternatives théâtrales,* 9 (1981): 34–43.

Rose Franken

(28 December 1895 – 22 June 1988)

Glenda Frank

See also the Franken entry in *DLB Yearbook 1984.*

PLAY PRODUCTIONS: *Another Language,* New York,
    Booth Theatre, 25 April 1932; London, Lyric
    Theatre, 1 December 1932;

Claudia, New York, Booth Theatre, 12 February 1941;
    London, St. Martin's Theatre, 17 September
    1942;

Outrageous Fortune, New York, Forty-eighth Street The-
    atre, 3 November 1943;

Doctors Disagree, New York, Bijou Theatre, 28 Decem-
    ber 1943;

Soldier's Wife, New York, John Golden Theatre, 4 Octo-
    ber 1944; London, Duchess Theatre, 27 August
    1946;

The Hallams, New York, Booth Theatre, 4 March 1948.

BOOKS: *Pattern* (New York: Scribners, 1925);

Another Language: A Comedy Drama in Three Acts (New
    York, Los Angeles & London: French, 1932; Lon-
    don: Rich & Cowan, 1933);

Mr. Dooley Jr.: A Comedy for Children, by Franken and
    Jane Lewin (New York & Los Angeles: French,
    1932);

Twice Born (New York: Scribners, 1935; revised edition,
    London: W. H. Allen, 1969);

Call Back Love, as Margaret Grant (New York & Toronto:
    Farrar & Rinehart, 1937);

Of Great Riches (New York & Toronto: Longmans,
    Green, 1937); republished as *Gold Pennies: The
    Story of a Marriage* (London: Constable, 1938);

Claudia: The Story of a Marriage (New York & Toronto:
    Farrar & Rinehart, 1939; London: W. H. Allen,
    1946);

Strange Victory, by Franken and William Brown Meloney,
    as Franken Meloney (New York & Toronto: Far-
    rar & Rinehart, 1939);

Claudia and David (New York & Toronto: Farrar & Rine-
    hart, 1940; London: W. H. Allen, 1946);

Rose Franken

When Doctors Disagree, by Franken and Meloney, as Fran-
    ken Meloney (New York & Toronto: Farrar &
    Rinehart, 1940);

American Bred, by Franken and Meloney, as Franken
    Meloney (New York & Toronto: Farrar & Rine-
    hart, 1941);

Claudia: A Comedy Drama in Three Acts (New York & Tor-
    onto: Farrar & Rinehart, 1941; London: S.
    French, 1942);

Another Claudia (New York & Toronto: Farrar & Rine-
    hart, 1943; London: W. H. Allen, 1946);

Outrageous Fortune: A Drama in Three Acts (New York & Los Angeles: S. French, 1944);

Soldier's Wife: A Comedy in Three Acts (New York & Los Angeles: French, 1945);

Young Claudia (New York & Toronto: Rinehart, 1946; London: W. H. Allen, 1947);

The Marriage of Claudia (New York: Rinehart, 1948; London: W. H. Allen, 1948);

The Hallams: A Play in Three Acts (New York: S. French, 1948);

From Claudia to David (London: W. H. Allen, 1949; New York: Harper, 1950);

Claudia: The Story of a Marriage (Garden City, N.Y.: Doubleday, 1951); republished as *The Book of Claudia: The Story of a Marriage* (London: W. H. Allen, 1951)—comprises the first six Claudia novels, revised;

The Fragile Years (Garden City, N.Y.: Doubleday, 1952); republished as *Those Fragile Years* (London: W. H. Allen, 1952);

The Quiet Heart (London: W. H. Allen, 1954);

Rendezvous (Garden City, N.Y.: Doubleday, 1954);

Intimate Story (Garden City, N.Y.: Doubleday, 1955; London: W. H. Allen, 1955);

Return of Claudia (London: W. H. Allen, 1957);

The Antic Years (Garden City, N.Y.: Doubleday, 1958);

The New Book of Claudia (London: W. H. Allen, 1958); republished as *Claudia Omnibus* (Garden City, N.Y.: Doubleday, 1958)—comprises the first seven Claudia novels, revised;

When All Is Said and Done (London: W. H. Allen, 1962; Garden City, N.Y.: Doubleday, 1963);

The Complete Book of Claudia (London: W. H. Allen, 1962; Garden City, N.Y.: Doubleday, 1963)—comprises all eight Claudia novels, revised;

You're Well Out of a Hospital (New York: Doubleday, 1966; London: W. H. Allen, 1966).

PRODUCED SCRIPTS: *Say Goodbye Again,* motion picture, Universal, 1934;

Beloved Enemy, by Franken, John L. Balderston, and William Brown Meloney, motion picture, United Artists, 1936;

Claudia and David, by Franken, Meloney, and Vera Caspary, motion picture, 20th Century-Fox, 1946;

The Secret Heart, by Franken and Meloney, motion picture, M-G-M, 1946.

Rose Franken was a celebrated Broadway playwright and director, a Hollywood screenwriter, and a popular novelist whose fiction touched a sympathetic chord in American women. After two of her plays that offered social commentary earned adverse criticism and low box office receipts, she elected to return to her winning formula for commercial success in other genres. She later said that the character of Claudia, her most famous creation, had overshadowed her. The sentimental prose that made her name a household word, however, has taken second place in her critical reputation to the plays.

She was born Rosebud Dougherty Lewin on 28 December 1895 in Gainesville, Texas. Shortly after her birth, her parents, Hannah (née Younker) and Michael Lewin, a businessman, separated. She and her older siblings (two brothers and one sister) were raised by her mother in the Younker family brownstone in Harlem, New York City. After leaving the Ethical Culture School, instead of enrolling at Barnard College she married Sigmund Walter Anthony Franken, an oral surgeon, on 1 September 1913. They spent the first ten months of their marriage at the Trudeau Sanitarium at Saranac Lake, New York, while Dr. Franken's tuberculosis went into remission. Fear of a recurrence inculcated a passionate love of family that shaped not only Franken's personal priorities but also her characters' values.

A misdelivered typewriter spurred her long, productive writing career. She discovered it on her doorstep and wrote her first short story that day. Her husband became an ardent supporter, reading her daily work each evening. Despite lifelong disclaimers, her dedication to writing was immediately apparent in her disciplined work habits and her persistent, systematic search for a publishing house for her first novel, *Pattern* (1925). Refusing to undertake major revisions without a contract and amused that one editor insisted that the beginning needed emendation while another said the same thing about the second half, she collected rejection slips until Maxwell Perkins at Scribners accepted the novel. This acceptance began a lifelong friendship. *Good Housekeeping* turned down her first story, which she offered free; years later, the magazine paid $5,000 for it. She continued to create fiction while raising her three sons, Paul (born in 1920), John (born in 1925), and Peter (born in 1928).

Franken was a self-taught playwright who was influenced by the domestic dramas of Sidney Howard and who learned dramatic construction from textbooks. Her first play, "Fortnight," was optioned but never produced. Her second play, *Mr. Dooley Jr.,* a work for children, was written with her aunt, Jane Lewin, and published by Samuel French in 1932. *Another Language,* her third play, which was originally titled "Hallam Wives," opened at the Booth Theatre in New York on 25 April 1932 and continued for 453 performances. She claimed she wrote it in three days. The central conflict in the play is between an iconoclastic wife, Stella, and the satirically rendered family of her husband, Victor.

*Herbert Duffy, Wyrley Birch, Margaret Wycherly, Maude Allen, Glenn Anders, Dorothy Stickney, and Margaret Hamilton in the
1932 Broadway production of* Another Language

Mother Hallam is the prototypical matriarch (with the "uncertain step of age" but an "indomitable will"); the sisters-in-law are postmarital versions of Cinderella's stepsisters—unattractive, catty, and stingy; and the materialistic sons enjoy a complacent rigidity.

When the play opens, Stella is recuperating from a miscarriage. She has already outraged the conservative family by studying sculpture and has considered taking a job instead of spending her time homemaking. Once romantic, Victor is becoming more like his older brothers. Seven years into the marriage, he talks about how he "threw way five bucks . . . without batting an eye-lash" on a gift for Stella when he was courting her. The plot heats up when Stella meets Jerry, her husband's bohemian nephew, who has completed three years of college. He has been drafted into the family business even though he dreams of studying architecture in Paris. The attraction between Stella and Jerry escalates in the face of family misunderstanding. They speak "another language."

In act 2 the Hallams have gathered at Stella's home. Victor is critical of his wife, while Jerry, who is infatuated, has brought her a present. The family members, a little intoxicated, dance to amuse themselves and insist that Jerry and Stella, the younger people, take a turn, although Stella resists. The chemistry between them is unmistakable. When the others tease them, Jerry exits. Stella confronts the clan about Jerry's distress over being forced to work at the factory, and Mrs. Hallam feigns illness. After demanding

that Stella apologize, Victor departs to take his mother home. Jerry returns.

Ostensibly, Stella's marriage to Victor is at stake, but the more engaging question is how these two people will reshape their lives. The adultery is so delicately handled that there is latitude to believe in Stella's innocence. She rejects Jerry's entreaties to leave her husband, dismissing his affection as the misdirected passion of a young man for the woman he will someday marry. In a tense, dramatic scene, Jerry and Stella confess to the family; but Victor, weighing his affections, reconciles with his wife and insists upon believing in her fidelity. There is no guarantee that the marriage will survive, but the air has been cleared for discourse.

As she did in later novels and plays, Franken achieved psychological depth and social perspective through the conflict between an inflexible moral standard and a revivifying but anarchic sexual latitude. *Another Language* also established her signature theme: the importance of maintaining family relationships. The leitmotiv of feminist independence is subsumed by the comedy to effect a marital reconciliation. Franken's satirical edge sharpens the dialogue, although typically the substance remains restricted to domestic annoyances, as in an exchange between the matriarch and the eldest sister-in-law:

Mrs. Hallam: The girl is out. – Her aunt is dying again.

Helen: Well, you got to believe her in a big house like this.

Arthur J. Beckhard produced and directed the play, with sets by Cleon Throckmorton. The cast included Margaret Wycherly (Mrs. Hallam), Margaret Hamilton (Helen), Glenn Anders (Victor), Dorothy Stickney (Stella), and John Beal (Jerry). The London production at the Lyric Theatre opened on 1 December 1932 and starred Herbert Marshall and Edna Best. On 8 May 1933 the play reopened at the Waldorf Theatre, New York. Helen Hayes starred in the 1933 movie version.

After her husband's death from tuberculosis in December 1933, Franken relocated to Hollywood and began the second phase of her writing career. Her success on the stage and her popularity as a writer of fiction made her a sought-after screenwriter; she began at $750 a week but was soon earning $2,000. She was a compulsive worker, completing assignments in weeks instead of the months allocated. During the next five years she wrote scripts (including *Say Goodbye Again* [1934], and *Beloved Enemy,* with John L. Balderston and William Brown Meloney [1936]), novels (*Twice Born* [1935], and *Of Great Riches* [1937]), and short stories, which were published primarily by *Redbook*. Her name often appeared on the magazine cover. On 27 April 1937 she married Meloney, a lawyer, journalist, and writer. They relocated to Longmeadow, a farm in Lyme, Connecticut, where they published individually and continued their collaboration on movie scripts and serial fiction, usually under the pseudonym "Franken Meloney." Their novels include *Strange Victory* (1939), *When Doctors Disagree* (1940), and *American Bred* (1941). Franken also published *Call Back Love* (1937) as Margaret Grant.

The war years inspired her to try new directions in theater. After an absence of nine years from the stage, Franken returned in 1941 with *Claudia,* her fourth play, a dramatization of the first of eight novels about her best-known character. This story of a young woman's adjustment to marriage ran for 722 performances. Dissatisfied with the casting choices, Franken took over the direction and auditioned nearly two hundred actresses for the title role, selecting twenty-three-year-old Dorothy McGuire as the lead and Phyllis Thaxter as the understudy, and discovering Jennifer Jones (Phyllis Walker at the time, later Mrs. David O. Selznick)—all unknowns and all chosen against the advice of John Golden, her producer, who recommended established actresses to ensure box office success. The play opened at the Booth Theatre in New York on 12 February 1941 and in London at St. Martin's Theatre on 17 September 1942, returning to the St. James Theatre in New York on 24 May 1942. Three additional road shows were cast, and there were tours of the United States, Australia, and England, as well as a radio series. Burns Mantle included *Claudia* in *The Best Plays of 1940–1941*. The script was sold to 20th Century-Fox for $187,000, an impressive sum at the time; the 1943 movie starred McGuire and Robert Young. The actors were paired again in *Claudia and David,* a 1946 movie sequel based on another Franken novel (1940) about the same heroine.

Still experimenting, Franken directed two more plays on Broadway in the 1943–1944 season: *Outrageous Fortune* and *Doctors Disagree.* Both were produced by Meloney when the initial producers backed out. *Outrageous Fortune* (1943), Franken's most daring play, takes a hard look at anti-Semitism and homosexuality. Despite considerable wealth and talent, many of the characters are hiding, living in conformity to the dominant culture. The text is overburdened by its several issues, but it includes some of Franken's most dynamic exchanges and dramatic shifts and explores problems that were rarely even whispered about at that time.

The setting is a weekend gathering at the country home of Madeleine and Bert Harris. Barry Hamilton, a tall, handsome violinist in his twenties, is the romantic center of the play. His sexual orientation is ambiguous; he is described by the playwright as exuding "a kind of inherent fragrance. In a male it must be marked against him as an extreme fastidiousness, and a sensitivity easily mistaken for a lack of virility." He is accompanied by Crystal Grainger, a beautiful woman of a certain age who is famous for being talked about. Although seriously ill, she is attracted to Barry. The interpersonal dynamic grows when the two are greeted by Madeleine, who is in love with Barry and envious of Crystal.

Bert's younger brother, Julian, who is enjoying a promising stage career as a composer, has entered into an engagement of convenience with Kitty Field, a bright, wealthy young woman who chaffs at his emotional indifference. She recognizes that his relationship with his friend Russell Train is more than professional: "From the conspicuous absence of the word 'love,' I gather I'd better make up a nice single bed and be prepared to lie on it most of the time," she snaps. He retorts, "It's not too late to back out." He also finds himself attracted to Barry, but when he makes advances that are repelled, Julian, frightened, shifts the blame to Barry, slandering the violinist's reputation. Like Kitty, Julian is a complex, self-centered character struggling unsuccessfully to find happiness. Madeleine, too, is unhappy, trying to use her infatuation with Barry to respark her marriage, but her husband lives within a blinkered moral code and will not acknowledge the presence of deeper or forbidden passions among his friends until Madeleine confronts him.

The theme of anti-Semitism is introduced by Dr. Andrew Goldsmith, a family friend who "invites immediate confidence as a physician." He was sure he would be named attending physician at his hospital but received "a package of neat regrets tied up in blue ribbon." The family indignation leads to a heightened sensitivity. The maids are fired for criticizing the mother's Jewish cooking–although the word "Jewish" is never spoken within that context. Mrs. Harris's herring in cream sauce becomes a metaphor for ethnic identity. Dr. Goldsmith asked for a jar, and when Crystal discovers the fish, she is ecstatic, revealing either her hidden Jewish roots or sympathies. Dismayed, Madeleine offers everyone canapés, the assimilated food of the upper middle class. Bert challenges her, accusing her of being ashamed of her ethnicity. "Not ashamed," she confesses, "no. But not proud of it either, the way you are, carrying your pride around like a challenge–like an eternal chip on your shoulder! That's what wrong with us, every last one of us. We can't act normal, we can't act natural. We either cringe or we strut–."

There are no resolutions. Kitty breaks her engagement and attempts suicide; there are hints she and Barry may become close friends. Julian escapes with Russell Train, and Crystal's medication fails. The play closes with a black spiritual sung by Cynthia, Crystal's maid. The only peace is "beyond the furthest star," which was the original title of the drama.

In an interview with Helen Ormsbee for *The New York Herald Tribune* on 28 November 1943, Franken said that *Outrageous Fortune* "has more of my own thinking and feeling in it than anything I've done in years." She called it "a gamble in its contrapuntal form and taboo in its subject matter." Franken's character descriptions indicate ethnic and gender stereotypes; yet, the stage directions specify that "no one is to be cast with racial typing, nor is any personality to play upon racial idiom or humour." This contradiction was further complicated by Franken's casting, in which the young Jewish woman had a turned-up nose, the Catholic wife had a turned-down nose, and a former prizefighter played Barry. The casting was meant to double the shock of discrimination, but it probably strained audience expectations, shifting attention from the unfolding drama to the question of whether someone looked the type.

The play met with mixed reactions. George Jean Nathan praised Meloney for stepping in, when Gilbert Miller withdrew his sponsorship, to produce "the best play of the season." The critic for the *Boston Monitor* judged it "a brilliant, subtle, moving drama, leagues beyond *Claudia* and *Another Language*." Other critics, such as Louis Kronenberger, however, advised her to return to a "more housefrauish direction; when, for example, she talks about food, she

Franken and William Brown Meloney, her second husband and frequent collaborator

makes sense" (*PM*, 4 November 1943). At this point, Franken canceled her clipping service. Even the public's reaction to the play was ambiguous. The drama received poor notices in the Boston tryout; opened at the Forty-eighth Street Theatre on Broadway to sell-out houses, earning $9,000; and then ran for only seventy-seven performances.

In *Doctors Disagree* Dr. Margaret Ferris finds herself challenged as both a surgeon and a woman when she attempts to combine marriage and career. Her test comes when she risks her reputation to save a boy whose case was declared hopeless by a powerful, established doctor. The physician who triaged the child is also the mother's lover. Dr. Ferris proves victorious, and her fiancé, who has insisted that she retire if they marry, withdraws his demand. The role of the woman surgeon might have been inspired by Franken's pediatrician. Critics panned the play as sentimental, citing contemporary dramas that also introduced successful career women to illustrate that the novelty was stale. There were rumors, which Franken denied, that the play was based on *Women in White*, a serial written by Franken and Meloney that appeared in the *Ladies' Home Journal* and was published in novel form as *When Doctors Disagree* (1940). The play ran for twenty-eight performances, and the script was never published.

Franken was accustomed to immediate success, both critical and financial, and the two theatrical failures forced her to reconsider her goals. In 1944 she retreated to the popular formula with *Soldier's Wife,* starring Martha Scott, and scored a hit that ran 253 performances. This story of domestic readjustment after World War II was timely. Kate Rogers is a young wife and mother whose husband, recently made a captain, has just received a medical discharge from the military. The war has taught her to be self-reliant. She makes household repairs and has recently published as a book the letters she wrote to her husband. She has become an overnight celebrity, with a $500 advance, a movie offer, and a newspaper column. Sandy Craig, who visits for an interview, begins a flirtation with Kate, while Peter Gray, the editor of the women's section, transforms her into a marketable commodity. In the end, however, Kate resists Craig's advances and chooses family over fame.

Franken's last play, *The Hallams,* which opened 4 March 1948 at the Booth Theatre, New York, is a sequel to *Another Language.* Jerry is now suffering from tuberculosis and is married to a strong-willed woman, Kendrick, reminiscent of Stella. When family tensions precipitate Jerry's death, Grandfather Hallam and Victor, now a widower, take a stand against the iron-willed matriarch, championing Kendrick. The play lacks a sense of vitality, however, and when it closed after twelve performances, Franken returned to fiction.

Franken's fiction was always popular, especially her eight Claudia books. They were frequently republished, sometimes with variant titles; collected in several omnibus editions, all of which sold well; and translated into several languages. As Beatrice Sherman wrote about *Another Claudia,* the third book, the novels were "like meeting old friends again," especially the "amusing and appealing child-wife" (*The New York Times Book Review,* 18 April 1943). The plots are replete with minor disasters, enough to keep the reader or viewer hooked, and in the end love conquers all. *Claudia and David,* for example, covers a séance, an appendectomy, Claudia's forgotten birthday, and her son's skating accident. In *The Fragile Years* (1952), the seventh novel, Pearl Harbor has been attacked; David enlists; and their eldest son dies, which is the first tragedy of Claudia's life.

The other novels were similar to the Claudia material. In *Intimate Story* (1955), a Book-of-the-Month-Club selection, Mrs. Gerry, a widow, must adjust to life alone in her large house, to her son-in-law and her daughter's pregnancy, and to a new love whom she meets on a tour of Europe. Franken spiced the pedestrian narrative with a critical social eye and perspective: for example, Mrs. Gerry's neighbor is a famous actress living quietly with her lesbian lover. During the course of the novel, the lover deserts her for a man. The focus never shifts, however, from the minor tribulations of the bright, outspoken widow.

Franken published her autobiography, *When All Is Said and Done,* in 1962. After Meloney died on 4 May 1971, Franken relocated from New York to Tucson, Arizona, where she died on 22 June 1988.

Franken's literary style and her diverting, off-beat humor were distinctive. Once she established a sentimental tone, she would deflate it, playing against expectations. Her hints of icy rationality behind a middle-class sensibility created depth in her often cardboard creations. Rapid literary construction, a denial of any revisions (which is not borne out by her manuscripts), and an emphasis on her featherbrained helplessness and domesticity became characteristics of Franken's public persona; but her plays reveal a serious, thoughtful writer.

Papers:

Rose Franken's papers can be found at the Rare Book and Manuscript Collection, Butler Library, Columbia University, New York City. There is also a clipping file in the Theatre Collection at the New York City Public Library for the Performing Arts at Lincoln Center.

Zona Gale

(26 August 1874 – 27 December 1938)

Leslie Goddard
Northwestern University

See also the Gale entries in *DLB 9: American Novelists, 1910–1945,* and *DLB 78: American Short-Story Writers, 1880–1910.*

PLAY PRODUCTIONS: *The Neighbours,* New York, Comedy Theatre, 3 December 1916;
Miss Lulu Bett, New York, Belmont Theatre, 27 December 1920;
Mister Pitt, New York, Thirty-ninth Street Theatre, 22 January 1924.

BOOKS: *Romance Island* (Indianapolis: Bobbs-Merrill, 1906);
The Loves of Pelleas and Etarre (New York & London: Macmillan, 1907);
Friendship Village (New York: Macmillan, 1908);
Friendship Village Love Stories (New York: Macmillan, 1909);
Mothers to Men (New York: Macmillan, 1911);
Christmas (New York: Macmillan, 1912);
When I Was a Little Girl (New York: Macmillan, 1913);
Civic Improvement in the Little Towns (Washington, D.C.: American Civic Association, 1913);
Neighborhood Stories (New York: Macmillan, 1914);
The Neighbours (Boston: Baker, 1914);
Heart's Kindred (New York: Macmillan, 1915);
A Daughter of the Morning (Indianapolis: Bobbs-Merrill, 1917);
Birth (New York: Macmillan, 1918);
Peace in Friendship Village (New York: Macmillan, 1919);
Miss Lulu Bett [novel] (New York & London: Appleton, 1920);
Miss Lulu Bett: An American Comedy of Manners [play] (New York: Appleton, 1921);
The Secret Way (New York: Macmillan, 1921);
Uncle Jimmy (Boston: Baker, 1922);
What Women Won in Wisconsin (Washington, D.C.: National Woman's Party, 1922);
Faint Perfume [novel] (New York: Appleton, 1923);
Mister Pitt (New York & London: Appleton, 1925);
Preface to a Life (New York & London: Appleton, 1926);

Zona Gale (photograph by Arnold Genthe)

Yellow Gentians and Blue (New York & London: Appleton, 1927);
Portage, Wisconsin and Other Essays (New York: Knopf, 1928);
Borgia (New York: Knopf, 1929);
Bridal Pond (New York: Knopf, 1930);
Evening Clothes (Boston: Baker, 1932);
The Clouds (New York: S. French, 1932);
Papa La Fleur (New York & London: Appleton, 1933);

Old-Fashioned Tales (New York & London: Appleton-Century, 1933);

Faint Perfume: A Play with a Prologue and Three Acts (New York & Los Angeles: S. French, 1934);

Light Woman (New York & London: Appleton-Century, 1937);

Frank Miller of Mission Inn (New York & London: Appleton-Century, 1938);

Magna (New York & London: Appleton-Century, 1939).

SELECTED PERIODICAL PUBLICATIONS–UNCOLLECTED: "The Appreciators: A Wooing," *Smart Set,* 14 (November 1904): 105–107;

"New Art for Old: A Review of Continental Stagecraft," *Theatre Arts Monthly,* 7 (April 1923): 158–164;

"The Dream of All Producers," *Theatre Magazine,* 46 (September 1927): 11–12.

In 1921 Zona Gale became the first woman to win the Pulitzer Prize in drama. For many, this event constitutes her primary claim to lasting significance as a dramatist, especially considering that her output as a novelist and short-story writer far exceeds the handful of plays she wrote and adapted. Only three of her seven plays received professional productions, and only one, *Miss Lulu Bett* (first performed in 1920), was considered a hit. Gale, however, deserves a place in theater history not only for her Pulitzer but also for the complex, sometimes conflicting ways in which her plays, like her fiction, capture the shifting currents of her times. Just as her own life balanced contradictions (she was both an educated professional and an obedient daughter, an outspoken social progressive and a small-town spinster), her writings also present complexities, mingling old-fashioned sentimentalism with thoroughly modern characterizations and situations.

Zona Gale was born on 26 August 1874 in Portage, Wisconsin. She retained throughout her life a deep attachment to her hometown, which appears frequently in various guises as the setting for her novels and plays. As an only child, she also had a strong bond with her parents, Charles Franklin and Eliza (Beers) Gale.

Gale's passion for writing manifested itself early, in a stream of romantic poems and stories produced during her years attending public schools in Portage and later the University of Wisconsin, where she wrote her first unpublished novel. After graduating with a degree in literature in 1895, she worked for several years as a reporter in Milwaukee. Although modest and retiring, she displayed a flair for newspaper work, covering society events and women's club meetings, reviewing plays, and interviewing such notables as Ellen Terry and Sir Henry Irving. At the same time, she pursued a master's degree in literature from the University of Wisconsin, which she received in 1899. After she moved to New York in 1901, her persistence secured her a position as a reporter with the *Evening World,* but she found the work kept her from creative writing. After just eighteen months she resigned in order to freelance and concentrate on creative work. Her first magazine story sold in 1903, and before long her sentimental stories were regular features in American magazines.

Gale's parents continued to exert a possessive influence on her during these years. Eliza Gale discouraged her daughter from marrying and was relieved when an intense romance with poet Ridgely Torrence ultimately ended in 1904. Visiting her parents in Portage inspired Gale to begin a series of short stories that won her first widespread popularity as a writer. The stories, set in the fictional town of "Friendship Village," revolve around the kindly, wise figure of Calliope Marsh (modeled on Gale's mother). Gale published four volumes of these stories, starting with *Friendship Village* (1908) and ending with *Peace in Friendship Village* (1919). Optimistic and idealistic, the Friendship Village stories secured for Gale both popularity and steady income.

Gale's flair for drama manifested itself more gradually. She reportedly wrote her first play in high school and completed several more while working in Milwaukee. In New York she wrote six plays and submitted them to producers. When Keene Sumner asked in a 1921 interview about her first play, Gale replied, "It seems to me I've always been writing a play," but few of her early efforts survived. A chambermaid accidentally destroyed one almost-completed effort, a play titled "A Garret in Gotham," by tossing it into the rubbish. The earliest surviving drama, therefore, is a brief one-act published in 1904 titled "The Appreciators: A Wooing." The play follows two couples, one youthful and the other mature, as they pursue romantic love. Simple and lightly comical, the play humorously points out the dissimilar paths love takes for the young and the old.

Since there is no evidence that "The Appreciators: A Wooing" was ever produced, and since it differs significantly in its poetic style from her later dramas, Gale's playwriting career is usually dated to 1910, when she was approached by Thomas Dickinson, a professor at the University of Wisconsin and organizer of the Wisconsin Dramatic Society (later known as the Wisconsin Players). Eager to promote the emergent little theater movement in America, Dickinson requested from Gale a one-act play "beating with one human emotion taken from the simple life of a village . . . with just a little tear and smile in it." Gale supported the group with a gift of $500, articles for their magazine,

Gale as a child

and a one-act play, *The Neighbours* (1914), similar to her popular Friendship Village stories.

The Neighbours focuses on a group of small-town women—"just folks"—whose repetitious chores are interrupted by the news that a neighbor is going to raise the son of a sister who died. The women set aside their mundane tasks and petty complaints to organize a party for the little boy, gathering food and clothing, only to learn that another relative will raise the boy. As in her short stories, Gale reveals a sharp ear for commonplace dialect and a strong sense of folkways, as well as a deeply romantic attitude toward small-town virtues and the triumph of friendship. The emptiness of women's lives and the disappointment of everyone's hopes are balanced by joy, as the community unites for the common good and a young couple (who just might need that baby clothing someday) finally comes together.

Critics admired the Wisconsin Dramatic Society production of *The Neighbours* for its charm and quiet sentimentality. In October 1917 the group took it to the Neighborhood Playhouse, where New Yorkers also welcomed the play; two months later it appeared on a bill of one-acts produced by the Washington Square Play-

ers. In keeping with her commitment to small-town values and community unity, Gale arranged for *The Neighbours* to be available, royalty-free, to the Wisconsin Players, as well as to any theater group that would plant a tree in the community. As a result *The Neighbours* became the most popular play in the repertoire of the Wisconsin Dramatic Society, and it enjoyed great popularity with college and community groups.

Despite her support for little theater, however, Gale's primary attention focused on fiction. In 1911 she won a $2,000 short-fiction competition, which allowed her to return permanently to her beloved Portage, where she concentrated on short stories and novels, publishing a volume almost annually. While retaining her characteristic keen observations of small-town life, her work during this period matured, gradually moving away from idealistic romanticism toward a more complex, harsher realism.

Gale's turn to realism was the result, in part, of the continuing development of her strong social conscience. A longtime friend of Jane Addams and a tireless supporter of Senator Robert M. LaFollette, she committed herself to such progressive causes as pacifism, labor rights, woman suffrage, and education. Beginning in the 1920s, Gale's expanding interest in social and political issues manifested itself in her writing in a heightened concern with issues of social justice.

Gale's short novel, *Miss Lulu Bett* (1920), displayed her emergent flair for realism and interest in women's rights. When it became a best-seller, at least one critic noted its obvious dramatic potential, and producer Brock Pemberton approached her about the possibility of a stage adaptation. No professional playwrights expressed interest in adapting the story, so Gale dramatized it herself; despite having virtually no professional theater experience, she finished the script in a mere ten days. Her only special request to Pemberton was that the Wisconsin Players be permitted to stage an amateur production of the show before the New York opening. After that production, and a one-night preview at Sing Sing prison, the Broadway production opened at the Belmont Theater in New York on 27 December 1920.

The character of Lulu Bett did not start out as the heroine of a play or a novel. Instead, she was a minor character in Gale's novel *Birth* (1918) who was excised when that book ran too long. In the play, as in the novel, Lulu is a spinster who toils in her sister's house until she is accidentally married to a family relative, Ninian Deacon, during a light-hearted family entertainment. The two choose to let the marriage stand, but Lulu soon returns home alone, with the news that Ninian was married previously to a woman who might still be alive. Lulu's transformation from a meek household drudge into an independent woman sets the stage for the final dramatic action, in which the family must choose whether to make the news of the previous wife known to the town or pretend her husband tired of her.

The appeal of the story for Pemberton—a first-year producer with only one other Broadway show to his credit—seems clear. Compressed and tightly constructed, the novel has a simple storyline and is full of memorable characters and witty dialogue, much of which Gale lifted intact from the novel into the script. Small touches proved charmingly effective onstage, such as opening two consecutive scenes with identical dialogue and action, and comic relief was provided by the silly daughter Monona and the endlessly confused but fundamentally wise grandmother. The minute observances of small-town American life, combined with a satirically biting but sympathetic family portrait, appealed to Americans feeling both fiercely nationalistic and morally jaded after World War I.

As expected, critics and audiences, for the most part, received the play warmly. A reviewer for *The Nation* (2 February 1921) declared it "the most genuine achievement of the American stage since Eugene O'Neill's 'Beyond the Horizon.'" Several critics singled out the "superbly real dialogue" and clever, Dickensian characterizations. Still, most reviewers stopped short of deeming it a great play. Some denigrated the weak plot, with its contrived timing and tedious passages with little action, while others, such as Robert Benchley in *Life* (13 January 1921), argued that the ordinariness of the language and "pitiless fidelity to every-day people and every-day life" made the play not so much realistic as dull. In *The New York Times* (28 December 1920) Alexander Woollcott, while admitting the play pleased its audience, declared that their enjoyment stemmed entirely from delight at seeing a beloved novel come to life, and not from the play itself, which was "rather dull and flabby" and "somewhat sleazily put together by a playwright who has but slight sense of dramatic values and no instinct at all for the idiom of the theater."

The major controversy, however, concerned the ending. In translating her story into a play, Gale altered Lulu's fate. While the novel ends with Lulu agreeing to marriage with a local piano-shop owner, the play instead sends Lulu off in search of work, with just the possibility of a future marriage to the shop owner. In the *Literary Review* (19 February 1921) Gale justified her decision to remove Lulu's marriage to another man by saying that two marriages in two hours would have strained any audience's credulity. Several critics declared the revised ending "weightier and severer," and compared it favorably with Henrik Ibsen's *A Doll's House* (1879). Later scholars have also agreed; Harold P. Simonson notes that "the unromantic ending creates a more artful ambiguity" by refusing to answer the questions of whether or not Lulu is truly free and what her chances really are, with no marriage and no immediate job prospects.

Nonetheless, while the ambiguous ending might have pleased some progressive critics, it apparently did not please audiences. Pemberton and Gale allegedly received hundreds of letters from disappointed playgoers who wanted Lulu to get her man. So, in a remarkable move, Gale altered the conclusion of the play after the first two weeks, this time bestowing on Lulu a conventional happy ending. Ninian returns with the news that his first wife indeed is dead, and he and Lulu are reconciled. Those critics who had previously approved Gale's depiction of women's independence now railed against her for giving in to popular, conventional tastes. One critic for *The New York Tribune* (6 February 1921) felt that the demand for a traditional happy ending was about as sensible as demanding feathers on mountain lions.

In a *New York Tribune* article (21 January 1921) Gale defended her revised ending, arguing not only that happy endings sometimes do occur in life, but that the play is just the story of one woman—one like many others she knew—"overshadowed, browbeaten women, wives or Lulus enslaved by duty, dead duty." Whatever the disappointment of some critics, audiences appeared pleased with the revision, and the production ran for 201 performances, followed by a tour with the original cast to Chicago and then Madison. A silent movie starring Lois Wilson soon appeared, and years later the Radio Theatre Guild presented it with Jean Arthur.

Later that year, *Miss Lulu Bett* again surprised critics when it received the 1921 Pulitzer Prize for drama (only the third such prize ever awarded). Critics protested that the selection wrongly overlooked Eugene O'Neill's *Emperor Jones* (1920), although that play was notably handicapped not only because it was not considered a full-length play but also because O'Neill had won the prize the previous year. Still, the fact that Gale's friend and supporter Hamlin Garland sat on the Pulitzer committee that year undoubtedly improved her chances. But Garland was not the only reason the play won. Like O'Neill's *Beyond the Horizon* (1920), the previous Pulitzer winner, *Miss Lulu Bett* shrewdly balanced techniques characteristic of conventional Broadway formula plays (such as contrived entrances and a tantalizing, unopened letter sitting in full view of the audience) with startlingly realistic techniques (everyday dialogue and a topic of contemporary social concern).

Lulu Bett is a study in complexity—similar to conventional melodramatic heroines in her initial meekness and desire to be rescued by a Prince Charming and strikingly modern in her transformation into an assertive, self-knowledgeable woman. Few other heroines in drama could be convincingly compared, as Lulu was by different critics at different times, to both Cinderella and Ibsen's Nora. Like O'Neill, Gale tapped into the division emerging at that historical moment between the early-twentieth-century profit-driven American theater of ready-made plays and melodramas and the modern American drama of contemporary social issues that matured in the 1920s.

Despite the success of *Miss Lulu Bett* onstage, Gale continued to see herself primarily as a novelist. The regional realism of such novels as *Birth* and *Faint Perfume* (1923) earned her a growing reputation as one of the leading contemporary American novelists. Plans for a full-length play based on the Friendship Village stories never materialized, but she did complete a short one-act. *Uncle Jimmy* (1922) focuses on the grandfatherly man who runs "urrants" for the women of Friendship Village while insisting he wants nothing more than to leave. When his chance finally comes, he finds he cannot go.

Uncle Jimmy, even more than *The Neighbours,* capitalized on audiences' familiarity with the Friendship Village stories. Many characters, especially Calliope

William Llywelyn Breese, whom Gale married in 1928

Marsh and her neighbors, Mis' Toplady and Mis' Sykes, were lifted straight from the stories, as were the flower-filled backyard setting and the pervasive warmhearted community spirit. Gale drew on the quaint local expressions and Midwestern regionalisms familiar to her readers, such as Mis' Toplady's frequent exclamation, "For the good land sakes alive!" Although lacking the weighty drama of *Miss Lulu Bett,* the play captured well the charm and poignancy of the Friendship Village stories. It proved successful enough among amateurs to be published in *The Ladies' Home Journal,* in the anthology *Short Plays for Modern Players* (1931) and as a book.

Still, with the stage success of *Miss Lulu Bett,* Pemberton encouraged Gale to dramatize another of her heavier, realistic novels. She chose *Birth,* the novel she and many others considered, even in later years, her best work of fiction. In one sense it was a logical choice. One of her few novels to that point written in the realistic style that had proved so favorable for stage adaptation, *Birth* similarly displayed Gale's masterful approach to dialogue and photographic observation of small-town mores. On the other hand, whereas *Miss Lulu Bett* features a relatively simple plot, easily transferable to compressed stage action, *Birth* is a sprawling novel, Gale's longest, encompassing more than twenty years of action. Whereas *Miss Lulu Bett* was easily altered to fit

The Breeses' house in Portage, Wisconsin. Gale's study is on the right.

within one or two set changes, the dramatization of *Birth* ultimately demanded ten distinct settings.

The end result, retitled *Mister Pitt* (1925), tells the story of Marshall Pitt, an inarticulate door-to-door salesman who arrives in the small town of Burage and proceeds to rescue the debt-ridden Barbara Ellsworth by marrying her. Despite the birth of a son and Pitt's successful payment of her debts, Barbara cannot stand living with her socially inept husband and ultimately runs off. In the third act Pitt returns from a twenty-year sojourn in Alaska to reconcile with his son, but Jeffrey Pitt is embarrassed and disappointed by his father, who eventually announces he is going back to Alaska.

Compressing the novel into a play required Gale to eliminate characters and dramatically alter crucial plot developments. Even with drastic changes, the play still required thirteen scenes, many of them short and choppy, and the resultant frequent set changes necessitated long waits between scenes. The reviewer for *The New York Tribune* (23 January 1924) described opening night as "more or less chaos," with too many short scenes, too many long waits, and an insufficient amount of rehearsal. More problematically, much of

the subtlety and complexity of the novel had been sacrificed in the interest of theatrical time and space. Whereas the novel reveals two characters—a kindly neighbor and then Jeffrey—gradually awakening to Pitt's underlying commendable qualities of integrity and noble-heartedness, the play provides little space for such subtle denouements. As a result, most critics of the play found Pitt simply an unmitigated bore; the *Tribune* reviewer admitted there were moments when he "felt homicidal toward him, he was such a monotonous simpleton." George Jean Nathan argued in the *American Mercury* (March 1924) that "Her Pitt is not a character so much as a characteristic: a single idiosyncrasy in trousers." As they had with *Miss Lulu Bett,* critics were quick to declare Gale far more capable as a novelist than as a dramatist.

Still, most critics found something positive to say about the play, especially in terms of the original central theme and Gale's attention to the commonplace nuances of everyday language. Also highly praised was Walter Huston, the virtually unknown young actor recruited from vaudeville to play Pitt. Huston accomplished, in the opinion of the *New York Times* reviewer (6

January 1924), the remarkable feat of seldom letting his audience lose interest, despite the evident weakness in the character he played.

In their understandable focus on the title character and the actor playing him, few critics noticed the understated feminist message in Gale's play. Heywood Broun alone, writing for the *New York World* (28 January 1924), noted that the recurrent appearance of a chorus of gossiping women between major scenes functions like interludes in a Greek play. More than just a means of filling in crucial plot developments, the women comment on the primary action and shape the audience's reaction along the lines of small-minded small-town hypocrisies, revealing in the process their own limitations. Unlike most critics who saw *Mister Pitt* as a play about an inarticulate man, Broun described it as the story of a woman. Comparing Barbara to Ibsen's Nora (just as earlier critics had with Lulu Bett), he argued that the play was about the psychology of incompatibility, with the end result being "the most subtle and the most thrilling piece of playwriting I have seen all season." Ultimately, however, most audiences and critics failed to discern the subtle power Broun did, and the play ran for a disappointing six weeks, with even that brief run largely attributed to the appeal of Huston.

After the lukewarm response to *Mister Pitt,* Gale turned her attention almost wholly back to fiction. In the next few years her continuing interest in drama manifested itself only in a few magazine articles, including a favorable 1923 review of Kenneth Macgowan and Robert Edmond Jones's *Continental Stagecraft* (1922), and a contribution to a 1927 series in *Theatre Magazine* on what constitutes the "perfect" drama.

If Gale's work as a playwright declined in these years, her output as a writer remained high. She produced several volumes of short stories, a book of essays, and several novels, of which *Preface to a Life* (1926) is generally considered the best. The latter displayed a marked turn away from regional realism toward mysticism, a strain apparent in all her later works.

Gale's productive writing in these years was matched by her equally productive participation in public affairs. She campaigned vigorously for LaFollette, supported a variety of causes from prohibition to international peace, and enjoyed high demand as a lecturer. She helped write the 1923 Wisconsin Equal Rights Law and served as the Wisconsin representative to the International Congress of Women in Chicago in 1933. She also established a series of scholarships at the University of Wisconsin for students in the creative arts, and from 1923 to 1929 she served on the University of Wisconsin Board of Regents. Now a prominent figure in Wisconsin literary circles, she received honorary doctorates from three universities. On 28 June 1928, at the age of fifty-three, she married William Breese, a wealthy manufacturer and banker from Portage whom she had admired since childhood. The two adopted a daughter, Leslyn, whom Gale had begun to support in 1927.

While *Mister Pitt* was the last of her plays to be produced on the professional stage, it did not mark the end of Gale's playwrighting career. In the 1930s she returned to playwrighting, publishing three more plays: *Evening Clothes* (1932), *The Clouds* (1932), and *Faint Perfume* (1934). All three include many of the ingredients by then familiar to Gale's readers: a blending of domestic realism with an optimistic faith in the power of goodness and an understated concern with the fate of women, especially unmarried women. *Evening Clothes* marks Gale's final foray into Friendship Village, more than ten years after she abandoned the town in her fiction writing. The plot revolves around the discovery of a chest of old-fashioned, colorful women's gowns, which the ladies of the town don to celebrate an unexpected wedding. The simple symbolism of the play, in which the older women learn that personal vivacity can be achieved as easily as putting on colorful clothes, reflects Gale's continuing interest in the fundamental goodness of humans and the links between generations. The same simplicity and optimism appears in *The Clouds,* in which the Misses Amy, Elsa, and Lily Cloud receive a visit from a purported lost relative who eventually reveals her duplicity but is nevertheless welcomed into the warm family. *Faint Perfume,* a dramatization of her 1923 novel of the same name, came at the end of Gale's literary career. While comedic and lighthearted, the play fits more easily with Gale's sentimental works than with her later realism. The heroine, Leda Perrin, is an intellectual but financially destitute young woman who falls in love with her wealthy cousin's former husband while he is fighting for custody of his young son. The play not only bestows on Leda a drastically altered happy ending, it also flattens and simplifies the complex characters and tragic theme that make the novel one of Gale's best works.

Faint Perfume was Gale's final play to be published. Several critics noted that her late novel *Light Woman* (1937) appeared clearly written for the stage, and Gale reportedly did prepare a dramatization. But no production ever materialized, in part because of the altered tastes of theatergoers by the 1930s, and the play version has not survived. In 1938 Gale gave up her customary two-month winter sojourn in New York because of ill health. Later that year she died of pneumonia in a Chicago hospital and was buried in Portage.

Gale's reputation as a playwright never equaled her status as a novelist and short-story writer, and she never considered the theater her primary literary arena. Still, she earned a distinctive place in theatrical history with just a handful of noteworthy plays. Gale is remembered primarily as the first woman to win the Pulitzer Prize for drama, but her more significant contribution lies in her commitment to the promotion of dramatic realism. Her use of commonplace language, her keen observations of everyday life, and her ability to capture characters sharply with the utmost brevity all mark her as an outstanding contributor to the rise of modern American realism.

Her intense devotion to her home state and promotion of amateur theater in Wisconsin mark her also as a primary exponent of early twentieth-century regionalism and the emergent little theater movement. After her death the people of Wisconsin expressed their gratitude for her encouragement of theater in their state. The University of Wisconsin Library founded the Zona Gale Memorial Dramatic Collection.

In the wake of increasing interest in productions of plays by American women, *Miss Lulu Bett* enjoyed several revivals and adaptations. A 1984 production at the Berkshire Theater Festival starring Carol Kane sold out continually and received critical acclaim. Productions at the Horizons Theater in Washington, D.C., in 1985 and the Center Theater in Chicago in 1988 earned praise for the characters and action. Contemporary critics note the appeal of the early feminist message of the play as well as the sharpness of its insights into small-town middle-class life in the early part of the twentieth century. Most modern productions retain the original ambiguous ending, although Horizons included both endings, to encourage spectators to consider which is the "happy" ending and to offer a glimpse at the playwright's creative process.

Interview:

Keene Sumner, "The Everlasting Persistence of This Western Girl," *American Magazine,* 91 (June 1921): 34–35, 137–141.

Biography:

August Derleth, *Still Small Voice: The Biography of Zona Gale* (New York: Appleton-Century, 1940).

References:

Henry James Forman, "Zona Gale: A Touch of Greatness," *Wisconsin Magazine of History,* 46 (Autumn 1962): 32–37;

Robert Gard, *Grassroots Theater: A Search for Regional Arts in America* (Madison: University of Wisconsin Press, 1955);

Ima Honaker Herron, *The Small Town in American Drama* (Dallas: Southern Methodist University Press, 1969);

William Maxwell, "Zona Gale," *Yale Review,* 76 (Winter 1987): 221–225;

Yvonne Shafer, "Zona Gale," in her *American Women Playwrights: 1900–1950* (New York: Peter Lang, 1995), pp. 216–228;

Harold P. Simonson, *Zona Gale* (New York: Twayne, 1962);

Simonson, "Zona Gale," *American Literary Realism,* 3 (1961): 14–17;

Bertha W. Smith, "Contemporary Authors: IV–Zona Gale," *Writer,* 39 (March 1927): 95–96;

June Sochen, *Movers and Shakers* (New York: Quadrangle, 1973).

Papers:

The Theatre Collection of the New York Public Library Performing Arts Research Center has a clippings file dealing with Zona Gale's theatrical career. Her letters to Ridgely Torrence are held in the Princeton University Library. Gale's typescripts and papers are located at the State Historical Society of Wisconsin in Madison.

Jack Gelber

(12 April 1932 –)

Robert E. Brooks
Eastern Illinois University

See also the Gelber entry in *DLB 7: Twentieth-Century American Dramatists.*

PLAY PRODUCTIONS: *The Connection,* New York, Living Theatre, 15 July 1959;
The Apple, New York, Living Theatre, 7 December 1961;
Square in the Eye, New York, Theatre de Lys, 19 May 1965;
The Cuban Thing, New York, Henry Miller's Theatre, 24 September 1968;
Sleep, New York, American Place Theatre, 10 February 1972;
Barbary Shore, adapted from Norman Mailer's novel, New York, New York Public Theatre / Anspacher Theatre, 18 December 1974;
Farmyard, translated by Gelber and Michael Roloff from Franz Xaver Kroetz's play, New Haven, Yale Theatre, 22 January 1975;
Jack Gelber's New Play: Rehearsal, New York, American Place Theatre, 8 October 1976;
Starters, New Haven, Yale Theatre, 1980;
Big Shot, New Rochelle, New York, East Coast Arts, 1988.

BOOKS: *The Connection* (New York: Grove, 1960; London: Evergreen Books, 1960);
The Apple (New York: Grove, 1961);
On Ice (New York: Macmillan, 1964; London: Deutsch, 1965);
Square in the Eye (New York: Grove, 1966);
The Cuban Thing (New York: Grove, 1969);
Sleep (New York: Hill & Wang, 1972);
The Apple & Square in the Eye (New York: Viking, 1974).

PRODUCED SCRIPT: *The Connection,* motion picture, Clarke/Allen, 1962.

TRANSLATION: Franz Xaver Kroetz, *Farmyard,* translated by Gelber and Michael Roloff, in *Farmyard, & Four Other Plays,* translated by Gelber,

Jack Gelber

Roloff, Peter Sander, and Carl Weber (New York: Urizen, 1976).

SELECTED PERIODICAL PUBLICATIONS–
UNCOLLECTED: "Julian Beck (1925–1985)," *Drama Review,* 30 (Spring 1986): 11;
"Julian Beck, Businessman," *Drama Review,* 30 (Summer 1986): 6–29.

Jack Gelber was one of the leading voices of a movement in American playwriting in the 1960s that challenged the commercialism of Broadway and attempted to fill the literary void left by the fading careers of figures such as Arthur Miller, Tennessee Williams, and William Inge. Remembered primarily for the Living Theatre production of his play *The Connection* in

1959, Gelber was an active participant in the experimental theater scene of the 1960s and 1970s in New York. Along with playwrights such as Edward Albee, Jack Richardson, Arthur Kopit, and Amiri Baraka, Gelber challenged the form of conventional American drama, thus providing a significant body of plays that helped bring credibility to Off-Broadway and Off-Off-Broadway theater.

Jack Gelber was born on 12 April 1932 in Chicago, where he lived as a child. He attended the University of Illinois, receiving a bachelor's degree in journalism in 1953. In 1957 he married Carol Westenberg; they have two children, Jed and Amy. Gelber, by his own admission in a 1996 interview with David Sedevie, had no formal training in the theater when he began to write plays. His attraction to the theater seems to have been inspired by his association with a small theater company in New York that let him use their space to hold jazz concerts in 1957. Gelber stated to Sedevie that he helped the company by painting sets and was introduced to the idea of an intimate theater for the first time. In 1957 Gelber wrote his first play, *The Connection*.

Structurally, *The Connection* is a play within a play. Two characters, Jim and Jaybird (author and producer), have assembled a group of heroin addicts to improvise dialogue before a live audience. Jaybird has outlined themes around which the spontaneous dialogue is meant to revolve, but the junkies, of course, stray from the intended topics. The improvised play is set in the apartment belonging to Leach, one of the addicts. Four of the eight addicts are jazz musicians who perform "approximately thirty minutes of jazz in each act." All of the addicts are waiting for a heroin dealer named Cowboy, their "connection," so that they may obtain their next "fix." Finally, the performance is being filmed by two cameramen hired by Jim so that he may turn the play into a motion picture.

The innovative aspects of this play involved the complex relationship between the performers and the spectators and the blurring of the lines between fiction and reality called for by the text. The audience participates in the drama, for even as they observe the performance of *The Connection,* they are also playing the role of audience for Jim and Jaybird's play of the same name. Jim and Jaybird serve as intermediaries between the audience and the junkies; the two cameramen exist on this level as well. The drug addicts operate within the innermost layer of fiction, speaking the lines written for them by Gelber, even though these lines are considered improvisation by Jaybird and Jim.

All three of these levels are blurred by the interactions between the worlds. The world of the overall play intrudes upon the inner play through the camera-men's remarks concerning the stage action; one cameraman, for example, repeatedly comments upon the addicts' dialogue, stating: "That's the way it really is." Jim and Jaybird directly interrupt the action whenever they feel that the improvisation has strayed from their initial vision. Certainly the most disturbing interaction between the two levels of reality within the overall play involves the addicts' use of the heroin that Cowboy procures during his absence in the first act. Until Cowboy arrives in the second act, there has been some question about whether or not the junkies will be paid with real narcotics; at one point, Jim tells the audience that real drugs will not be used, yet he continues to assure the addicts that they will receive their fix. In the second act, Cowboy leads the junkies, one by one, into the restroom offstage to administer the drugs; he even initiates Jaybird and one of the cameramen into the circle of users, thus significantly breaking the "illusion" of the improvised play by firmly establishing the reality of the heroin. The climax occurs when Leach, whose tolerance for the drug has reached such a level that he can no longer get high from normal doses, injects himself with an overdose in full view of the audience and nearly dies.

The sight of the needle entering Leach's arm brought such a heightened level of reality to the production that it consistently caused audience members to faint. In fact, so many spectators fainted ("hundreds," according to Gelber) during this climactic moment that the theater had to hire a nurse to stand by during the first run of the play. Such extreme audience participation is more directly encouraged through several other instances of interaction (or at least the illusion of interaction) between the worlds of the addicts and the spectators. For example, the script calls for the addicts to mingle with the audience and panhandle during the act break. One actor, who has been planted in the audience, rises during the second act and demands a story from one of the addicts to whom he claims to have paid five dollars for this purpose during the intermission. The script, therefore, calls for the employment of the entire theater as a performance space, including the panhandling in the aisles and lobby, the seating of actors in the audience, and Jim and Jaybird's use of the audience space for entrances and exits. The boundaries between the real and the fictional are also blurred through the jazz musicians' use of their real-life names, rather than character names, and the deliberate lighting miscues written into the text near the beginning of the play.

The apparent lighting mistakes, the delivery of lines by actors placed in the audience, the panhandling, and the junkies' inability to follow Jaybird's guidelines for the improvised play all contribute to an overall feeling of spontaneity that pervades the entire production. Gelber explained to Sedevie that he drew his inspiration for writing the play from an interest in improvisation, related to his love of jazz music and the "kind of anarchistic, surreal energy" associated with "the Allen Ginsbergs and the certain kind of freewheeling dada events that were happening at art galleries and various other spaces in San Francisco." From a theatrical point of view, one of the issues that concerned Gelber as he wrote the play involved how to keep the performance fresh each night; he attempted to solve this problem through the employment of what he refers to as "studied improvisation," the idea that carefully crafted dialogue and staged events may provide the illusion of an extemporaneous performance. The success of this technique may be confirmed by the length of the first run, which was highly unusual for an Off-Broadway production of its time: 722 performances from 1959 to 1963.

Despite its eventual success, positive critical response to *The Connection* grew only gradually after it first opened on 15 July 1959. Gelber recalled to Sedevie that the initial daily newspaper reviews were extremely negative, referring to the production as a "farrago of dirt" and calling for the author to leave town. Gelber stated that by the first of August he had given up the play as a failure. A small cult of fans had developed around the production, however, and were spreading its reputation by word of mouth. When *The New Yorker* critic Kenneth Tynan first attended the production in August, he was not allowed by contract to review Off-Broadway plays, but he nevertheless continued to spread the word-of-mouth praise and sent several of his friends to performances. Tynan ultimately wrote the introduction to the published play. Finally, in September and October of 1959, positive reviews appeared in *The New Yorker,* the *Saturday Review,* and *The New Republic.* Gelber often credits these critics and John Gassner for supporting his productions and encouraging his career as a playwright. The popularity of the production increased significantly after the positive reviews, to the extent that it became "a cultural must," in the words of Tynan. The play won the Obie and Vernon Rice Awards for Gelber in 1960. He was also named the most promising playwright of 1960 by the New York Drama Critics Poll.

The critics who have praised *The Connection* consistently compare the play to Maksim Gorky's *Na dne* (The Lower Depths, 1902) for its harsh naturalism, Samuel Beckett's *En attendant Godot* (1952; translated as *Waiting for Godot,* 1954) for its theme of waiting and lack of narrative plot, and Michael V. Gazzo's *A Hatful of Rain* (1956) for its treatment of drug abuse. Although all three of the comparisons ring true on some level, they also fail on other levels. For example, the comparisons

with *Na dne* and *A Hatful of Rain* collapse because of Gelber's frequent disruptions of the dramatic illusion and his refusal to provide a sentimental treatment of the junkies. In the case of *Waiting for Godot,* Gelber told Sedevie that he had "never even heard of Samuel Beckett at that time." Rather, he was merely presenting what he "saw going on at the time–people waiting for the next thing to happen."

Critics and audiences alike seem to respond most to what Robert Brustein referred to as a "Spartan honesty" in the play. This honesty allows individuals to see the junkies on some level as a metaphor for their own lives. The character Sam makes this connection when he states: "I used to think that the people who walk the streets, the people who work every day, the people who worry so much about the next dollar, the next new coat, the chlorophyll addicts, the aspirin addicts, the vitamin addicts, those people are hooked worse than me." Sam, unsure about the meaning of what he has just said, finds his words clarified by Solly, the most intellectual of the junkies: "You are fed up with everything for the moment. And like the rest of us you are a little hungry for a little hope. So you wait and worry. A fix of hope. A fix to forget. A fix to remember, to be sad, to be happy, to be, to be." Gelber achieves a fusion of naturalistic truth and heightened poeticism in this exchange. Tynan described this successful combination as "the kind of truth that goes beyond verisimilitude and achieves, at times, the robust, amoral candour of folk-poetry."

Certainly, the brutal honesty and poeticism of the play, combined with the socially oriented nature of its difficult subject matter, influenced Julian Beck and Judith Malina's decision to perform *The Connection* as only the second production in the new space for the Living Theatre: a converted department store downtown at Sixth Avenue and Fourteenth Street. Gelber's association with the Living Theatre began with this production, which arguably made the reputations of both parties. Before the Living Theatre agreed to produce the play, Gelber had received minimal interest from the other theaters that he had approached. One multiracial theater turned down the play because, in their opinion, it presented a "ghettoized" depiction of African Americans, even though Gelber believed that the play could be cast without regard to race. Beck and Malina, on the other hand, identified more directly with the subject matter; they had met many drug addicts during the time they spent in jail for refusing to participate in the mandatory bomb drills of the 1950s. In the program Malina even dedicated the production to a woman she had met in prison who subsequently died of an overdose of heroin. Furthermore, the Living Theatre was at that time producing the poetic dramas of figures such as

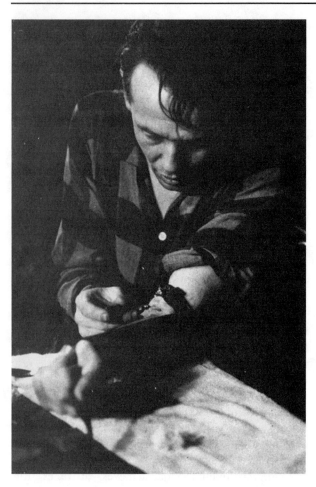

Warren Finnerty in the scene in the 1959 Broadway production of The
Connection *which caused some audience members to faint*

T. S. Eliot, W. H. Auden, Ezra Pound, William Carlos
Williams, Gertrude Stein, and Jean Cocteau; they therefore had the motivation and experience to handle a
work such as Gelber's effectively.

The Living Theatre also produced Gelber's sec-
ond play, *The Apple,* in 1961. *The Apple* is set in a coffee
shop or restaurant; in the Living Theatre production,
the audience space, as well as the stage, was set up as
the coffee shop, with some of the actors serving drinks
to the spectators before the performance. Like its predecessor, *The Apple* is also a play within a play. The characters are an acting troupe that is putting on a
performance in the coffee shop. Gelber, therefore, once
again clearly attempts to blur the relationship between
the performers and the spectators. For example, in a
note following the list of characters, Gelber states that
the actors should use their real names in production
rather than the character names provided in the script,
repeating a technique he employed with the jazz musicians in *The Connection.* However, the clearest example of
performer/spectator ambiguity lies in the opening stage

directions, in which Gelber calls for one of the characters—Tom in the script—to mill about in the lobby before
the play begins, offering audience members sips from
his pint bottle and behaving in a generally obnoxious,
drunken manner. Tom then emerges from the audience
during the first act and disrupts the performance, asking for a drink and spouting racist and sexist slurs
against the other characters. This episode resembles the
interjection of the actor that Gelber plants in the audience in *The Connection,* but Tom's interruption proves to
be much more than a temporary distraction.

The entire structure of *The Apple,* in fact,
revolves around the disruptive and clearly mad character Tom. The play opens with Ace, an African
American male (played by James Earl Jones in the Living Theatre production) who is clearly the leader of
the troupe, announcing: "Sorry, no more drinks. Show
about to begin." The other characters include Jabez, a
Jewish man whom Gelber lists as a "Con Man"; Anna,
an "Oriental-American"; Ajax, a "Nihilist"; Mr. Stark,
a "Spastic"; and Iris, a "Hustler." Ajax, who is about
to leave the troupe, introduces Mr. Stark as his
replacement when they arrive. The remaining characters, except for Tom, are already members of the
troupe. Tom's arrival in the first act disrupts a dentist's
office sketch that the performers have just started; at
the end of the act, Tom and Mr. Stark engage in a
physical confrontation and Tom is killed. Tom's death
is not without ambiguity, however, as he arises once
the other characters have left the stage, while a
voice-over reconfirms his death.

The second act consists of several short scenes
told from Tom's point of view. Because Tom is dead,
the scenes are presented as the disconnected, surrealistic
nightmares of a dead man—or, at least, of a man dreaming of his own death. Gelber stated that this act was
inspired by his readings of the *Egyptian Book of the Dead*
and the *Tibetan Book of the Dead.* There is a sense in this
act that the other characters are goading Tom, which is
probably a manifestation of his own paranoia. The act
ends with Tom proclaiming: "I can't bear this any
longer. I want to go back to living."

The final act returns to the realm of the awake
and living, opening with the statement that Tom is, in
fact, alive; he is further revealed to have been an actor
that played extras in silent movies. Likewise, Mr. Stark
reveals himself to be an actor as well; when asked why
he feigned the spastic routine, he replies: "You've
never wanted to play a spastic? It was an incredible
opportunity." As the act progresses, Tom's madness
intensifies until it endangers the other characters and
even the audience. Mr. Stark, in fact, is drawn from
his spastic role by this real threat and even voluntarily
takes Tom to a hospital at the end of the play. After

they leave, the remaining characters gradually go their separate ways, leaving Ace to close up the coffee house as the lights fade.

Gelber recalled in a 1978 interview with Albert Bermel that *The Apple* was inspired by events that occurred during the previews of *The Connection*. The actor playing Cowboy suddenly "went stark raving mad." Gelber, Beck, and Malina hurried backstage to find him holding a light pole and threatening to kill anyone who approached. They were able to get him back on stage with the help of sleeping pills, but were later forced to have him committed. As Gelber stated, "For the Becks to take anyone to Bellevue was a defeat of no small measure. That they should succumb to a tactic of putting someone in an institution was contrary to every principle that they stood for." In *The Apple,* therefore, Gelber was wrestling with the question of when an individual's behavior or even morality (Tom's incessant racist and sexist insults) becomes so dangerous that it threatens others to the point of requiring the individual's removal from society.

The initial critical response to *The Apple* was ambivalent and lukewarm at best. The consensus of the daily reviews may perhaps be best summed up by critic Walter Kerr, who stated in the *New York Herald Tribune* (8 December 1961) that he did not "admire" the production, but also "did not hate" it. But as with *The Connection,* enthusiasm for the production and the play grew with time. Critics and scholars seem to have focused primarily on the symbolism of the title: the many apples eaten, passed, and thrown throughout the performance; the mixed races and types of characters in the play serving as a microcosm of New York City–the "Big Apple"; and the biblical "original sin" references that arise repeatedly in the dream scenes of the second act and the wandering dialogue of the play as a whole (as when Jabez says, "Start from the beginning. Do the Adam and Eve bullshit"). Gelber stated that, although many who appreciated the social realism of *The Connection* did not enjoy *The Apple,* he gained the interest of new fans and critics who were attracted more to the surrealism of the second act.

Gelber parted ways with the Living Theatre after *The Apple* closed in 1962. According to Gelber, there were no arguments between them at the time of their separation; rather, Beck and Malina had become involved with political activities that were taking up more of their time than they were devoting to the theater. Gelber began writing his next play, *Square in the Eye* (1965), while on a Guggenheim Fellowship that he was awarded in 1963. In the meantime, he completed the screenplay for the 1962 movie version of *The Connection,* which drew media controversy over censorship issues. His first and only novel, *On Ice,* was published in 1964.

Square in the Eye was written as an experiment in multimedia, with two screens, one on either side of the stage, that displayed filmed sequences and slides as a supplement to the action. The play involves a failed artist and high-school teacher, Ed, who would rather be painting full time. When his wife, Sandy, dies suddenly of peritonitis, he remarries quickly; his new wife has the wealth to support his art. In addition to the use of multimedia, Gelber also experimented with dramatic form by placing the scenes out of order. The first act chronologically depicts Ed and Sandy before her illness, Sandy's death and funeral, and Ed's remarriage. The second act goes back in time to show Ed shortly after the funeral and concludes with Ed and Sandy in her hospital room just before her death. Gelber explained to Bermel his thoughts on formulating the play: "I'd do a first act with a happy ending to a disastrous event. In the second act I'd show what really happened." Critically, the play was a failure, viewed as an essentially conventional and even sentimental story veiled by the use of multimedia and the misordering of the scenes. Gelber admitted that the multimedia experiment failed for lack of experts to handle the technical aspects effectively.

From 1965 to 1966 Gelber served as writer in residence at the City College of New York, thus beginning an academic career that spanned more than thirty years. In 1966 he was awarded his second Guggenheim Fellowship before being hired as adjunct professor of drama at Columbia University in 1967, where he remained until 1972. His fourth play, *The Cuban Thing,* opened on Broadway in 1968 to the most significant degree of attention and controversy that Gelber had received since the closing of *The Connection.* In *The Cuban Thing* Gelber attempted to examine the effects of the Cuban Revolution on the middle class. Gelber told Bermel that the themes dealt with the tendency of the revolution "toward the diminution of (the middle class') material wealth and the acquisition of their soul." The play, however, was viewed by many as pro–Fidel Castro propaganda. A tear-gas bomb was set off during previews, and although five men were arrested, the bomb threats continued. After opening-night reviews that included extreme attacks on Gelber's personal abilities as a writer–some say for political reasons more than literary–the production closed with only one performance. Gelber, however, lists the play among his personal favorites and blames both extremes of the political spectrum for its failure, stating that even the pro-Castro activists disliked the play for its frank depiction of the treatment of homosexuals during the revolution.

The failed production of *The Cuban Thing* was also the first time Gelber attempted to direct one of his own works. It was not, however, his first attempt at directing; in 1966 he had directed a production of Arnold Wesker's *The Kitchen* (1959). Furthermore, in 1968 he directed the world premiere of Arthur Kopit's *Indians* for the Royal Shakespeare Company at the Aldwych Theatre in London. Certainly, this production established his reputation as a director, and he directed two more productions before his next play, *Sleep,* opened in 1972, accompanied by a Rockefeller Foundation playwright-in-residence grant at the American Place Theatre.

Sleep is set in a sleep research laboratory and involves the interactions between Gil, the volunteer subject, and the two researchers, Merck and Morphy, as well as the interactions between Gil and the figures in his dreams, which are depicted onstage. The action frequently oscillates between the laboratory and dream realities, as a significant component of the experiment demands that the researchers wake Gil often to ask him questions. According to Gelber, the play was a departure from his previous works, deriving from inward explorations of the individual mind and the self rather than outward explorations of society. Critically, the play was a success, drawing the most favorable overall response since *The Connection.* Commercially, the production was not successful, however, running for only thirty-two performances. Much to Gelber's disappointment, scholars and producers alike have tended to ignore *Sleep* since its initial production (and its subsequent run at the Edinburgh Fringe Festival in 1972).

After the production of *Sleep* Gelber began teaching full time at Brooklyn College in 1972. In 1973 Gelber's directorial efforts were rewarded for the first time with an Obie Award for his production of Robert Coover's *The Kid* (1972). Gelber received a National Endowment for the Arts grant in 1974, as well as a CBS Fellowship at Yale University. He also directed his own adaptation of Norman Mailer's 1951 novel, *Barbary Shore,* at the New York Public Theatre in 1974, as well as *Farmyard,* his translation (with Michael Roloff) of Franz Xaver Kroetz's 1971 play *Stallerhof,* in 1975 at the Yale Theatre.

In 1976 *Jack Gelber's New Play: Rehearsal* opened at the American Place Theatre under the direction of the author. With this work Gelber returned to the play-within-a-play format of *The Connection* and *The Apple,* focusing this time on a play written and rehearsed by former convicts, only to be ultimately canceled. By this point in his career, Gelber admitted to Bermel, he was having difficulties getting his plays produced: "I virtually had to bludgeon Handman (Artistic Director of the American Place Theatre) into doing it." *Rehearsal* was the last new play by Gelber that has received a significant New York production.

Gelber's career in the theater did not fade after *Rehearsal,* however, as he won his second Obie for directing and the third of his career for his production of Sam Shepard's *Seduced* (1978) in 1979. His unpublished play *Starters,* about a 1950s–1960s liberal activist dealing with aging, was produced by the Yale Theatre in 1980. Since then he has written *Big Shot* (1988); *Magic Valley* (written in 1990); and *Rio Preserved* (written in 1993), an adaptation of Thomas Otway's play *Venice Preserved* (1682). Despite his relatively long playwriting career and successes as a director, Jack Gelber's significance to the American theater lies primarily in his association with the Living Theatre, and most particularly in their production of *The Connection.* Through the attention he received from this play and the controversy surrounding the production and those that followed, Gelber became a leading figure in the reaction against convention that is associated with the Off- and Off-Off-Broadway theater of the 1960s.

Interviews:

Albert Bermel, "Jack Gelber Talks about Surviving in the Theater," *Theater,* 9 (Spring 1978): 46–58;

David Sedevie, "Jack Gelber," in *Speaking on Stage: Interviews with Contemporary American Playwrights,* edited by Philip C. Kolin and Colby H. Kullman (Tuscaloosa: University of Alabama Press, 1996), pp. 115–124.

Bibliography:

Steven H. Gale, "Jack Gelber: An Annotated Bibliography," *Bulletin of Bibliography,* 44 (June 1987): 102–110.

References:

C. W. E. Bigsby, "The Living Theatre," in his *Confrontation and Commitment: A Study of Contemporary American Drama, 1959–66* (Columbia: University of Missouri Press, 1968), pp. 50–70;

Pierre Biner, *The Living Theatre* (New York: Avon, 1972), pp. 46–49;

Robert Brustein, *Seasons of Discontent* (New York: Simon & Schuster, 1965), pp. 23–26;

Bernard Dukore, "The New Dramatists, 5: Jack Gelber," *Drama Survey,* 2 (Fall 1962): 146–157;

Steven H. Gale, "Jack Gelber," in *Critical Survey of Drama,* edited by Walton Beacham (Pasadena, Cal.: Salem, 1984), II, pp. 737–746;

Jerry Talmer, "Applejack," *Evergreen Review,* 6 (May–June 1962): 95–106;

Gerald Weales, "Front Runners, Some Fading," in his *The Jumping-Off Place: American Drama in the 1960's* (New York: Macmillan, 1969), pp. 54–62.

Susan Glaspell

(1 July 1876 – 27 July 1948)

Mary E. Papke
University of Tennessee, Knoxville

See also the Glaspell entries in *DLB 7: Twentieth-Century American Dramatists; DLB 9: American Novelists, 1910–1945;* and *DLB 78: American Short-Story Writers, 1880–1910.*

PLAY PRODUCTIONS: *Suppressed Desires,* by Glaspell and George Cram Cook, Provincetown, Massachusetts, Wharf Theatre, 1 August 1915;

Trifles, Provincetown, Massachusetts, Wharf Theatre, 8 August 1916;

The People, New York, Provincetown Playhouse, 9 March 1917;

Close the Book, New York, Provincetown Playhouse, 2 November 1917;

The Outside, New York, Provincetown Playhouse, 28 December 1917;

Woman's Honor, New York, Provincetown Playhouse, 26 April 1918;

Tickless Time, by Glaspell and Cook, New York, Provincetown Playhouse, 20 December 1918;

Bernice, New York, Provincetown Playhouse, 21 March 1919;

Inheritors, New York, Provincetown Playhouse, 21 March 1921;

The Verge, New York, Provincetown Playhouse, 14 November 1921;

Chains of Dew, New York, Provincetown Playhouse, 27 April 1922;

The Comic Artist, by Glaspell and Norman Matson, London, The Strand, 24 June 1928; New York, Morosco Theatre, 19 April 1933;

Alison's House, New York, Civic Repertory Theatre, 1 December 1930.

BOOKS: *The Glory of the Conquered: The Story of a Great Love* (New York: Stokes, 1909; London: Pitman, 1909);

The Visioning: A Novel (New York: Stokes, 1911; London: Murray, 1912);

Lifted Masks: Stories (New York: Stokes, 1912);

Fidelity: A Novel (Boston: Small, Maynard, 1915; London: Jarrolds, 1924);

Susan Glaspell

Trifles (New York: Shay/The Washington Square Players, 1916; London & New York: S. French, 1932);

Suppressed Desires, by Glaspell and George Cram Cook (New York: Shay, 1917);

The People, and Close the Book: Two One Act Plays (New York: Shay, 1918);

Inheritors: A Play in Three Acts (Boston: Small, Maynard, 1921; London: Benn, 1924);

The Verge: A Play in Three Acts (Boston: Small, Maynard, 1922; London: Benn, 1924);

Bernice (London: Benn, 1924);

Tickless Time: A Comedy in One Act, by Glaspell and Cook (Boston: Baker, 1925);

The Road to the Temple (London: Benn, 1926; New York: Stokes, 1927);

The Comic Artist: A Play in Three Acts, by Glaspell and Norman Matson (New York: Stokes, 1927; London: Benn, 1927);

A Jury of Her Peers (London: Benn, 1927);

Brook Evans (New York: Stokes, 1928; London: Gollancz, 1928);

Fugitive's Return (New York: Stokes, 1929; London: Gollancz, 1929);

Alison's House (New York & London: S. French, 1930);

Ambrose Holt and Family (New York: Stokes, 1931; London: Gollancz, 1931);

Cherished and Shared of Old (New York: Messner, 1940);

The Morning Is Near Us: A Novel (New York: Stokes, 1940; London: Gollancz, 1940);

Norma Ashe: A Novel (Philadelphia: Lippincott, 1942; London: Gollancz, 1943);

Judd Rankin's Daughter (Philadelphia: Lippincott, 1945); republished as *Prodigal Giver* (London: Gollancz, 1946).

Editions and Collections: *Plays* (Boston: Small, Maynard, 1920)—comprises *Trifles, The People, Close the Book, The Outside, Woman's Honor, Bernice, Suppressed Desires,* and *Tickless Time;*

Three Plays (London: Benn, 1924);

Trifles and Six Other Short Plays, by Glaspell and George Cram Cook (London: Benn, 1926)—comprises *Trifles, The People, Close the Book, The Outside, Woman's Honor, Suppressed Desires,* and *Tickless Time;*

Plays, edited by C. W. E. Bigsby (Cambridge & New York: Cambridge University Press, 1987)—comprises *Trifles, The Outside, The Verge,* and *Inheritors;*

Lifted Masks, and Other Works, edited by Eric S. Rabkin (Ann Arbor: University of Michigan Press, 1993).

SELECTED PERIODICAL PUBLICATIONS—
UNCOLLECTED: Reports on the Hossack murder case, *Des Moines Daily News,* 3 December 1900 – 13 April 1901;

"Dwellers on Parnassos," *New Republic,* 33 (17 January 1923): 198–200.

Susan Glaspell was one of the founding figures of modern American drama and, along with Eugene O'Neill, one of the most prominent playwrights of the little theater movement in the 1910s and 1920s. The value of her contribution to American drama rests largely upon her evocative portrayals of women's psychological oppression. Her work is also important as drama that interrogates what it means to be an American and what in particular constitutes an American idealism worth preserving.

Susan Keating Glaspell was born on 1 July 1876 in Davenport, Iowa, the second of three children and the only daughter of Elmer S. and Alice Keating Glaspell. (She routinely gave her birthdate as 1882, but census and school records verify the earlier date as correct.) Proud to be the daughter of pioneers, Glaspell later drew on her Midwestern heritage for material for her plays and fiction.

After graduating from public schools, Glaspell briefly worked as a reporter for the *Davenport Morning Republican.* From 1895 to 1899 she attended Drake University, acting as literary editor for the college newspaper and publishing stories in *The Delphic.* In 1896 she also served as the society editor for the *Davenport Weekly Outlook,* in which she published her first short story, "Tom and Towser." Upon her graduation she was hired as a statehouse and legislative reporter for the *Des Moines Daily News* and also wrote the "News Girl" column for that paper. While successful as a newspaper writer, she made a decisive move from journalism to freelance fiction writing in 1901. Thereafter she continued to publish frequently in various popular magazines and journals.

Glaspell briefly attended the University of Chicago in 1903 but curtailed graduate work to return to Davenport. There she led an active social life as a member of the elite Tuesday Club, a woman's association, and of the Monist Society, a socialist group through which she met the most important influence on her life, George Cram Cook, the well-born classics scholar who had by then resigned from university teaching to return to his family's country estate. Even though Cook was engaged to the woman who became his second wife, he and Glaspell became involved and remained so throughout his second marriage.

Despite her complicated love life, Glaspell was most productive as a writer during this period. Her first novel and best-seller, *The Glory of the Conquered: The Story of a Great Love,* the melodramatic subject of which is evident in its subtitle, appeared to strong reviews in 1909. Her second, the more realistic but less popular *The Visioning,* followed in 1911. She also proved successful as a short-story writer, perhaps because her stories blended sentimental realism and moral didacticism with political critique to suit popular tastes. A collection of her best short works was published in 1912. Separated from Cook for much of this time, she reunited with him after his divorce, and they were married on 14 April 1913; they lived thereafter in Provincetown, Massachusetts, during the summers and in Greenwich Village the remainder of the year until their final move to Greece in 1922.

George Cram Cook, whom Glaspell married in 1913

While Glaspell determined early on to live as a writer, she claimed in her later account of this time, *The Road to the Temple* (1926), to have had no interest in drama until her husband pressured her to write a play. Certainly Cook was the primary stimulus for her shift from fiction to drama, but Glaspell may also have been trying to buoy up Cook's artistic reputation by making him out to be the party responsible for her subsequent success, one that he was never able to equal through his own work. Their mutual interest in the development of an American drama was inspired by their involvement in various liberal and socialist groups in New York as well as the emergent little theater movement. The Washington Square Players, for instance, had recently formed to stage experimental works dismissed by the commercial theater. In 1915 Cook and Glaspell collaborated on the one-act *Suppressed Desires,* a satire on the new craze for Freudian psychoanalysis, and they submitted it to this group only to see it rejected as having

too specialized a subject (the group later staged it after Glaspell became famous).

That summer in Provincetown, the couple and several friends decided to mount an informal production of their play along with Neith Boyce's *Constancy,* a one-act illustrating the disparity between male and female definitions of fidelity. These Provincetown artists, under the charismatic leadership of Cook, then later restaged the two plays in the Wharf Theatre, Mary Heaton Vorse's refitted fish house, together with Cook's own *Change Your Style,* a satire on the conflicts between artistic freedom and commercial demands, and Wilbur Daniel Steele's *Contemporaries,* which suggests that Christ was one of the earliest anarchists. In that same year, Glaspell published *Fidelity* (1915), her third novel, generally considered one of her better ones, although it was not particularly well-received at the time because of its subject—an adulterous relationship—and its sympathetic portrayal of an emancipated woman.

In the search for more new American plays to stage the following summer, Glaspell invited the then-unknown Eugene O'Neill to join their group. Cook encouraged Glaspell to write another play, and she drew upon her experience reporting on a Des Moines murder case to write *Trifles* (1916), her best-known work. Frequently cited as a sterling example of the well-made one-act, the play dramatizes the investigation of the murder of a taciturn farmer, John Wright, by his wife, Minnie, a character who never appears onstage. The county attorney, assisted by the sheriff and a neighboring farmer, seeks proof of a clear motive for Minnie's act, but because of their utter dismissal of women's work and concerns as trifles, the men fail to recognize the clues the women accompanying them find. Through the slow process of retracing Minnie's last days, the women come to acknowledge their complicity in the crime because of their neglect of her, and so they elect to conceal the most damning evidence against Minnie: the pet canary murdered by the husband. The play is striking in the moral complexity of its story and its focus on gender difference and strife. The play quickly became a standard repertory piece for several little theater and amateur companies; both the play and the short-story version, the 1917 "A Jury of Her Peers," have been included in many drama and literature anthologies and have become standard texts for many introductory college English courses.

Encouraged by the interest shown in the Provincetown group's work, Cook decided to move the company to New York City, where they created a distinctive venue for new American drama. After formally incorporating the group as the Provincetown Players in September 1916, Cook secured an empty brownstone in Greenwich Village and with the help of his group transformed it into the Playwright's Theatre, more generally known as the Provincetown Playhouse (the group later moved down the street to a similar site). The Provincetown theaters, though extremely modest in the facilities offered, housed some of the most innovative drama to be staged in New York.

The Provincetown Players were notable not only for their determination to support new American playwrights but also for the communal nature of their venture. That is, a playwright would also be called upon to act, direct, build sets, take subscriptions, or do whatever else was necessary for staging productions. Glaspell proved proficient in all capacities, acting in the earliest of her plays, directing several others, and helping to oversee the daily operations of the Playwright's Theatre. She also continued to hone her stagecraft in important ways through her close relationship with O'Neill, and their early works are profitably read together for shared concerns and similar dramatic effects. While

Glaspell and O'Neill quickly emerged as the major talents in the Provincetown Players, other notable members of the group included Edna St. Vincent Millay, Alfred Kreymborg, Djuna Barnes, Edna Ferber, Floyd Dell, and Michael Gold.

The positive response to *Trifles,* described by New York critics as a small tragedy of intense pathos, must have convinced Glaspell of her dramatic promise, for she then wrote in quick succession several more one-act plays: *The People* (1917), *Close the Book* (1917), *The Outside* (1917), *Woman's Honor* (1918), and, with Cook, *Tickless Time* (1918). None has the utter control of *Trifles,* but each foregrounds concerns that became central in her full-length works.

The People takes place in the office of a radical journal about to close because of near bankruptcy and because the editor no longer believes in its philosophy. After a series of debates with The Woman from Idaho and supportive remarks by The Boy from Georgia and The Man from the Cape, the very people to whom the messianic social vision of the journal is addressed, the editor rediscovers his belief in the truth of America's promise. Since Glaspell's reputation had by then been established by well-received restagings of *Suppressed Desires* and *Trifles,* reviewers were kind, overlooking the sometimes too-poetic rhetoric and the reliance on caricature rather than characterization, focusing instead on the wit, complicated structure, and heartfelt idealism of the play.

Close the Book, a comedy, is also radical in content. Peyton Root, son of American revolutionary bluebloods, has brought home his fiancée to meet his family. Jhansi believes herself to be the illegitimate child of gypsies and urges Peyton to leave his sterile, bourgeois life for the nonconformist path of free love and radical politics. Genealogy records reveal, however, that Jhansi is the daughter of a highly respectable Baptist couple and a relative of a state senator, a revelation that appalls her since it robs her of social difference. She then discovers that some of her ancestors were lawbreakers and that the Root history is also not morally faultless. At the end of the play, Peyton is about to discover further family secrets in the records when his grandmother commands him to close the book. While some reviewers found the generational and moral gap entertaining, others faulted the work for being too dependent on talk and therefore not particularly dramatic, a typical dismissal of the drama of ideas that arose in response to virtually every Glaspell play.

A sharp departure from these two light pieces, Glaspell's next work, *The Outside,* was her first serious drama of ideas and her most experimental work up to that time. *The Outside* takes place on the dunes of Cape Cod in an abandoned lifeguard station, now the home of the embittered Mrs. Patrick, an abandoned wife, and her servant, Allie Mayo, a widow whose intense grief has rendered her nearly mute for the last twenty years. Rescuers have brought a drowned man to the station and attempt to resuscitate him there. Mrs. Patrick is infuriated that men intrude upon her solitude; but the lifesavers' efforts, although they are futile, reawaken Allie to feeling life. In turn, she argues at length with Mrs. Patrick about the need to abjure reclusiveness in the Outside, a death-in-life, in favor of alliance with others. Allie's vision of life fighting impossibly against death revives Mrs. Patrick in the final moments of the play. The drama is notable for its starkness in setting and action, its heavy philosophical content, and the abstruse, tortured language between the women, a further development of the halting speech of the two women in *Trifles*. In the premiere Provincetown productions, Glaspell was featured in *Trifles*, acted as The Woman from Idaho in *The People*, and appeared as Allie in *The Outside;* in each case, she played the defender of the life force battling against gender, social, or self-oppression.

Glaspell followed this serious piece with two more comedies, both concerning social conventions that inhibit self-expression. *Woman's Honor* involves, as did *Trifles*, another accusation of murder. In this case the suspect refuses to present his alibi since to do so would besmirch a woman's honor. Several women, each representing a particular attitude about woman's honor, enter the scene, taking over the stage; in turn they either claim to be the suspect's alibi or argue against his chauvinistic protection of women (and one simply seeks employment). These women, recalling the regional figures in *The People*, are nameless types (Glaspell played The Cheated One), and together mount so concerted an attack on patriarchal ideology that the prisoner finally admits his guilt, perhaps because his male construct of woman's honor has been proven bankrupt.

Tickless Time, her second one-act written with Cook, attacks another form of tyranny–that of time and its demands for self-regulation. A couple, the Joyces, decide to throw off conventional time, measured by clocks, for true time, measured by the sun. After burying all their clocks, they discover how difficult it is to live in a standardized world according to radical principles; further, they must admit to the relativity even of true time. By the end of this witty one-act, the Joyces and their friends have decided to live each by his or her own time. The play, along with *Suppressed Desires* (which it resembles in its satirical treatment of bohemian ideals), was taken up in the repertory of many little theater companies and was highly popular with amateur and school groups as well.

Theater at 133 Macdougal Street that was the second New York base of the Provincetown Players, established by Glaspell and Cook

Glaspell's second play of the 1918–1919 season was her first full-length attempt, *Bernice* (1919), and its effect depends greatly upon a device Glaspell had introduced in *Trifles:* the absence onstage of the central character. Bernice lies dead offstage throughout, but her spirit is ever-present on the stage through her influence on her family, particularly her writer husband, Craig, and her best friend, Margaret, neither of whom was with her when she died. Craig, in fact, was in New York with his latest lover. The action consists of a series of revelations and consequences: even though Bernice was a tremendously loving but independent woman, she committed suicide, according to her servant, Abbie (played by Glaspell in the premiere); Craig takes that assertion as a sign that she did love him passionately and so he did possess her completely. Abbie later tells Margaret that she has lied about the suicide at Bernice's request (Bernice realized she was dying from her ulcer-related illness), and both Abbie and Margaret see this request as the act of a vengeful woman, which destroys their idealistic vision of Bernice. Finally, Margaret and Abbie come to see Bernice's act as one of selfless love:

through the lie, she returns to Craig his sense of superiority and, thus, self-worth. By the end of the play, all agree that Bernice was the ideal embodiment of the life spirit, and they celebrate her immense love for them.

The play received strong reviews citing its powerful psychological realism, its poetic language, and its penetrating analysis of male vanity. While the *Nation* critic noted in a 3 May 1919 overview of the little theater season in New York that *Bernice* was "too subtle, too slow, too real" for the commercial stage, he called the play the best of the Provincetown season. The reviewer for *The New York Times* (30 March 1919) averred that Glaspell's exquisitely sensitive plays alone justified the existence of the Playwright's Theatre.

Although their theater and Glaspell's works had by this time achieved international recognition, Cook and Glaspell decided to take a sabbatical year in Davenport to devote themselves to writing. Upon their return in 1920, Glaspell had completed the two plays that many consider her best: *Inheritors* (1921) and *The Verge* (1921). *Inheritors* again develops, in serious fashion, issues Glaspell had already introduced–primarily those of the right of all in America to free speech, the public university as the necessary defender of democratic ideals, and the evils of racial prejudice and isolationism. Glaspell also returned to her roots in *Inheritors,* setting the play in Iowa and drawing her main characters from the pioneer stock from which she came.

The play opens on the Fourth of July in 1879 in the farmhouse of the Mortons, some of the earliest settlers of Iowa. Patriarch Silas Morton decides to bequeath part of his land for the founding of a college, both because he is ashamed of his family's treatment of the Indians who once lived there and because he has been inspired by his friend Felix Fejevary, an emigré Hungarian revolutionary, to believe in one's inalienable right to education and freedom. The remainder of the play takes place in 1920–first at Morton College, where Madeline Fejevary Morton, the descendant of both radical dreamers, fights futilely to uphold their ideals, and then in Silas's farmhouse, where Madeline's deranged father, an embittered recluse, pursues his obsession with raising perfect corn and keeping its pollen from neighboring fields. At the end of the play Madeline faces trial and an almost certain jail sentence for her support of Hindus protesting British rule. Refusing compromise, Madeline passionately takes a stand for the revolutionary democratic ideals her ancestors fought for in the Hungarian uprising of 1848 and the American Civil War.

While several critics found the special pleading tiresome, others saw the play as a powerful attack on the compromise of national ideals, on America's turn to materialism and isolationism. In the *New York Call* (27 March 1921) one reviewer praised the play highly, noting that it "has remained for a woman dramatist to tell the truth about the stifling of truth today in the United States." The opening-night performance of Eva Le Gallienne's 1927 revival of the play at her Civic Repertory Theatre was repeatedly interrupted by bursts of applause, and at its end Glaspell was lifted out of her seat and carried to the stage in triumph. Jasper Deeter, director of the Provincetown premiere, found its message of such urgency that he mounted productions of the play with his Hedgerow Theatre every year from 1923 to 1948, except the war years, and in 1954. A critic for the *Nation* (6 April 1921) said of the premiere that *Inheritors* was the first American play to evince "strong intellect and a ripe artistic nature" in the presentation of "the central tradition and most burning problem of our nationality."

The Verge shares the same philosophical belief in the necessity of individual revolt against the corruption of ideals, but does so in a profoundly nonrealistic fashion. Glaspell's most ambitious and experimental undertaking, *The Verge* depends for its effect not only upon dialogue and characterization but also on settings, symbolic objects and gestures, and the sometimes anguished deconstruction of language, and so it is difficult to summarize.

Claire Archer, the central character, seeks to create in her greenhouse new life in utterly new forms, to break through to "outness" and "otherness." She is, at the opening of the play, on the verge of her greatest success and is surrounded by her former lover, her current lover, and her husband, provocatively named Tom, Dick, and Harry. Her husband first dismisses the importance of her experiments, then comes to think her increasingly "queer" after she extols World War I for its great destruction, isolates herself in her tower (a structure both strangely phallic and womblike), violently rejects her daughter, plays one man off another, and grows increasingly incomprehensible in her diatribes about her desire for liminality and "by-myself-ness."

Claire feels trapped by her relationships with men and the various expectations they have of her, by her gender and the limitations it imposes, and by social conventions that require conformity to what she sees as a herd mentality. Like her creation the Edge Vine, Claire is both "repellent and significant." She demands utter loyalty but gives little in return to her companions; she considers herself vastly superior to virtually everyone with whom she comes into contact; and she promotes a radical lifestyle that would seemingly preclude responsibility to others and, therefore, community. At the same time, she has "the fire within," which draws all to her for the heat of life. Like Bernice but far less sympathetic, Claire is not only the center of her own world but of everyone else's, even though they find her overly sensitive, maliciously hateful, and strangely seductive. Claire, herself "the flower of New England," succeeds in creating the Breath of Life, a flower of unearthly beauty, but her inability to alter in any significant way the pattern of her relationship to the others, especially Tom, drives her to strangle him. At the conclusion, she slowly intones "Nearer My God To Thee," a mark both of her divine aspirations and final insane transcendence.

A reviewer for *The Greenwich Villager* (16 November 1921) suggested that *The Verge* would be "the most significant dramatic event in the city, bar none," and it was certainly one of the most controversial productions of the season. Many critics denounced the play as execrable; others were simply bewildered by its neurotic melodramatics; still others celebrated the immense challenge of its anarcho-feminist philosophy. The play was quickly taken up by the women's group Heterodoxy and other feminist sympathizers who regarded it with reverence for its portrayal of a Nietzschean superwoman. Glaspell was compared favorably by several critics to August Strindberg and Anton Chekhov, considered equal or even superior to George Bernard Shaw, and lauded by others as the foremost American dramatist.

The reception of *The Verge* was without doubt the high point of Glaspell's dramatic career. However, Cook chose shortly thereafter to sojourn in Greece with Glaspell for an indefinite time. In addition, the Provincetown Players decided in February 1922 to suspend activities for one year. Cook was dismayed by both the failure of his own work to garner favorable critical attention and the increasing professionalization of the company. The group's most noted productions were now limited to those by Glaspell and O'Neill, and the move to Broadway of O'Neill's *The Emperor Jones* in 1920 had convinced Cook that the group had abandoned its original charter. Cook and Glaspell sailed for Greece in March 1922 and so missed the run of her final play for the Provincetown group, *Chains of Dew*, the last production mounted by the original Players before the theater closed.

Chains of Dew, which premiered in April 1922, is the only one of Glaspell's produced plays extant only in typescript copy. Earlier plays were published shortly after production, and interest in her work was great enough by 1920 to warrant an edition collecting her five one-acts, two collaborations with Cook, and the full-length *Bernice*. *Chains of Dew* was not a success on the stage, perhaps because both its writing and presentation were rushed, the latter taking place after Glaspell had left for Greece. Focusing on another artist, the poet Seymore Standish, the plot recalls that of *Bernice*: a wife is

again called upon to sacrifice her own self-integrity in order to make her husband feel superior. In the first scene Seymore bemoans his regular, nonartistic life—that of a rich Midwestern businessman—to his radical New York friends. Nora Powers, a vocal promoter of the birth control movement, follows him to the Midwest to ruin his respectability and thus save his soul. Upon her arrival, she becomes more interested in saving his wife, Diantha, whom Seymore calls Dotty and treats as a woman of trivial pursuits and intelligence. Under Nora's influence, Diantha takes up the cause of birth control, proving to be more open to radical action than is her husband. It then becomes evident that Seymore needs to feel he suffers being trapped in a parochial, bourgeois life and that Diantha must surrender her newfound sense of self—become Dotty once more—if Seymore is to retain his romantic vision of himself as "trapped revolutionist." He cannot "see more," cannot write poetry, unless his women cater to his every need and efface their own desires.

Glaspell intended *Chains of Dew* to be a comedy, and the enthusiasm with which Dotty and Seymore's mother takes up radical activism is amusing. However, the smug self-centeredness of Seymore and the sacrifice he implicitly exacts from his wife made the play seem to some a grim comedy at best. Glaspell later reworked the theme and plot in her 1931 novel, *Ambrose Holt and Family*, suggesting that the material was more suited to narrative rather than dramatic form. *Chains of Dew* did not reflect well the talent revealed earlier in her best works, and her removal from the dramatic world hurt her reputation and future in immeasurable ways.

Glaspell lived in Greece until Cook's sudden death in 1924 from a rare disease contracted from their dog. During the two years abroad, except for a visit home after her father's death to assist her ailing mother, Glaspell devoted herself to Cook's projects and the care of his two children. After her return to Provincetown, Glaspell edited a collection of Cook's poetry and wrote *The Road to the Temple*, her adulatory biography of Cook, often misread as a factual account of the Provincetown Player years. She also became involved with novelist and playwright Norman Matson, with whom she lived for eight years but never formally married (though she told her mother they were married, and biographical and encyclopedic materials published after 1924 list her as Mrs. Norman Matson). In 1927 Glaspell and Matson collaborated on *The Comic Artist*, a play that was generously reviewed in London, where it premiered in 1928 and where Glaspell's reputation had been strong from the start of her career. It was not, however, successful on Broadway when it premiered there in 1933.

The Comic Artist again visits the theme of the artist and his demands. Karl Rolf, the successful creator

Clark Branyon, Glaspell, Ida Rauh, Justus Sheffield, three unidentified women, and Norma Millay in the 1918 Provincetown
Players production of Woman's Honor *(Fales Library, Elmer Holmes Bobst Library, New York University)*

of the Muggs comic-strip character, brings his wife, Nina, to meet his brother, Stephen, a painter, and Stephen's wife, Eleanor, a centered but emotionally aloof woman. In a series of shattering scenes, Nina belittles Karl's art and manhood; plays up to her former lover, Stephen; and is caught making love to Stephen by Eleanor and Karl. Eleanor acts decisively to save her marriage after Stephen admits he is powerless without her love, recalling the central relationship in *Bernice.* Nina threatens to kill herself, but Karl is the one who ultimately dies in the sea, attempting to save Nina, who is not there. As in the Muggs comic strip, acts of giving lead only to abuse.

Glaspell and Matson revised the play several times in an attempt to correct its weaknesses, most dramatically in the case of a happy ending for the Broadway production, in which Karl does not die but is reunited with Nina. No version overcame what many critics faulted as the too-precious language and monotonous bleakness of the play. While several reviewers praised the intellectual demands it made on the audience, the play lasted for only twenty-one performances in its Broadway run and was not a strong finale to Glaspell's career as a dramatist.

Alison's House (1930), written after *The Comic Artist* but produced in America before that play, also did not do full justice to Glaspell's talent, though it is the play that earned her the 1931 Pulitzer Prize. Inspired by

Genevieve Taggard's 1930 biography of Emily Dickinson, Glaspell invented the poet Alison Stanhope of Iowa after the Dickinson estate refused her the right to use Dickinson's name or poems. The events of the play occur on 31 December 1899 in the Stanhope home as Alison's family meets to close the house before its sale. As in *Trifles* and *Bernice,* the central character, in this case Alison, never appears, since she is long dead, but she controls all of the ultimate actions of the characters. The plot concerns Alison's secret, that of her love for a married man, detailed in a series of poems hidden in the house. Alison, it transpires, sacrificed her own needs for the love of her family. Her love poems are discovered, fought over, and finally given to her niece Elsa, heretofore shunned by her family because of her own attachment to a married man, for preservation and eventual publication. The play explores the interrelationship of an artist's private and public lives, the need of the artist to suffer in order to produce, and the making of humanist art that defends love in even its thwarted manifestations as the life force.

What limited success the play did achieve was no doubt primarily because of the superb production mounted by Le Gallienne's Civic Repertory Theatre, starring Le Gallienne as Elsa. Reviews were not particularly strong, however, though some critics continued to champion Glaspell's case. The play was nevertheless awarded the Pulitzer Prize, the announcement of which occasioned a concerted assault on the credibility and expertise of the Pulitzer jury and on the play itself. *Alison's House* was criticized as too derivative of Chekhov, "a narrative of suppressions," according to the *Variety* critic (3 December 1930), lacking in sufficient action and burdened with too-rarefied language and a thin plot. Drama, most critics now agreed, had simply not proven to be Glaspell's strongest medium.

Glaspell did continue to contribute to American dramaturgy in her role as the director of the Midwest Play Bureau of the Federal Theater Project from 1936 to 1938, and she attempted at least one more play, "Springs Eternal," written in 1945 and submitted for consideration to her friend Lawrence Langner, the founder of the Washington Square Players and later the Theatre Guild. He rejected the play as too tired and incoherent a work for his company. Glaspell's dramatic career peaked, then, in the early 1920s. While she attempted to capitalize on that early fame upon her return from Greece, her later works could not equal the achievement of her Provincetown period, and her dramatic career was effectively over by the mid 1930s. The major accomplishment in the last part of her life was her novels, notably *The Morning Is Near Us* (1940), *Norma Ashe* (1942), and *Judd Rankin's Daughter* (1945). Glaspell died of pulmonary embolism and viral pneumonia on 27 July 1948.

Glaspell created and promoted some of the best native dramas of ideas produced on the modern American stage. Uncompromising in her efforts to challenge audiences intellectually and to foreground the desire of women for self-expression and fulfillment, Glaspell created striking dramatic experiments in content and form. Often criticized for her abstractness and polemicism, she provoked careful reconsideration of the American spirit and the legacy of democratic idealism.

Bibliographies:

Gerhard Bach, "Susan Glaspell (1876–1948): A Bibliography of Dramatic Criticism," *Great Lakes Review,* 3, no. 2 (Winter 1977): 1–34;

Mary E. Papke, *Susan Glaspell: A Research and Production Sourcebook* (Westport, Conn.: Greenwood Press, 1993).

Biography:

Marcia Noe, *Susan Glaspell: Voice from the Heartland* (Macomb: Western Illinois University, 1983).

References:

Gerhard Bach, *Susan Glaspell und die Provincetown Players: Die Aufänge des modernen amerikanischen Dramas und Theaters* (Frankfurt am Main: Peter Lang, 1979);

Linda Ben-Zvi, "'Murder, She Wrote': The Genesis of Susan Glaspell's *Trifles*," *Theatre Journal,* 44, no. 2 (May 1992): 141–162;

Ben-Zvi, ed., *Susan Glaspell: Essays on Her Theater and Fiction* (Ann Arbor: University of Michigan, 1995);

Helen Deutsch and Stella Hanau, *The Provincetown: A Story of the Theatre* (New York: Farrar & Rinehart, 1931);

Isaac Goldberg, *The Drama of Transition: Native and Exotic Playcraft* (Cincinnati: Stewart Kidd, 1922);

Ludwig Lewisohn, *Expression in America* (New York: Harper, 1932);

Veronica Makowsky, *Susan Glaspell's Century of American Women: A Critical Interpretation of Her Work* (New York: Oxford University Press, 1993);

Robert Károly Sarlós, *Jig Cook and the Provincetown Players: Theatre in Ferment* (Amherst: University of Massachusetts Press, 1982);

Arthur E. Waterman, *Susan Glaspell* (New York: Twayne, 1966).

Papers:

The majority of Susan Glaspell's papers are housed in the Henry W. Berg and Albert A. Berg Collection of English and American Literature in the New York Public Library. Also of interest are the Provincetown Players Theater Collection, office files, and clippings scrapbook housed in the Billy Rose Theatre Collection of the Library and Museum of the Performing Arts at Lincoln Center; the Provincetown Players File at the Museum of the City of New York; the Susan Glaspell Papers in the Clifton Waller Barrett Library at the University of Virginia; and the Susan Glaspell Collection of the St. Ambrose College Library in Davenport, Iowa.

Lillian Hellman
(20 June 1906 – 30 June 1984)

Pamela Monaco

See also the Hellman entries in *DLB 7: Twentieth-Century American Dramatists,* and *DLB Yearbook 1984.*

PLAY PRODUCTIONS: *The Children's Hour,* New York, Maxine Elliott's Theatre, 20 November 1934;

Days to Come, New York, Vanderbilt Theatre, 15 December 1936;

The Little Foxes, New York, National Theatre, 15 February 1939;

Watch on the Rhine, New York, Martin Beck Theatre, 1 April 1941;

The Searching Wind, New York, Fulton Theatre, 12 April 1944;

Another Part of the Forest, New York, Fulton Theatre, 20 November 1946;

Monteserrat, adapted from Emmanuel Roblès's play, New York, Fulton Theatre, 29 October 1949;

The Autumn Garden, New York, Coronet Theatre, 7 March 1951;

The Lark, adapted from Jean Anouilh's play *L'Alouette,* New York, Longacre Theatre, 17 November 1955;

Candide, adapted from Voltaire's novel, book by Hellman, score by Leonard Bernstein, lyrics by Richard Wilbur, John Latouche, and Dorothy Parker, New York, Martin Beck Theatre, 1 December 1956;

Toys in the Attic, New York, Hudson Theatre, 25 February 1960;

My Mother, My Father and Me, adapted from Burt Blechman's novel *How Much?,* New York, Plymouth Theatre, 12 March 1963.

BOOKS: *The Children's Hour* (New York: Knopf, 1934; London: Hamilton, 1937);

Days to Come (New York & London: Knopf, 1936);

The Little Foxes: A Play in Three Acts (New York: Random House, 1939; London: Hamilton, 1939);

Lillian Hellman

Watch on the Rhine: A Play in Three Acts (New York: Random House, 1941; London: English Theatre Guild, 1946);

The North Star: A Motion Picture about Some Russian People (New York: Viking, 1943);

The Searching Wind: A Play in Two Acts (New York: Viking, 1944);

Another Part of the Forest: A Play in Three Acts (New York: Viking, 1947);

Montserrat: Play in Two Acts, adapted from Emmanuel Roblès's play (New York: Dramatists Play Service, 1950);

The Autumn Garden: A Play in Three Acts (Boston: Little, Brown, 1951; revised acting edition, New York: Dramatists Play Service, 1952);

The Lark, adapted from Jean Anouilh's *L'Alouette* (New York: Random House, 1956);

Candide: A Comic Operetta Based On Voltaire's Satire, book by Hellman, score by Leonard Bernstein, lyrics by Richard Wilbur, John Latouche, and Dorothy Parker (New York: Random House, 1957);

Toys in the Attic (New York: Random House, 1960);

My Mother, My Father and Me, adapted from Burt Blechman's novel *How Much?* (New York: Random House, 1963);

An Unfinished Woman: A Memoir (Boston: Little, Brown, 1969; London: Macmillan, 1969);

Pentimento: A Book of Portraits (Boston: Little, Brown, 1973; London: Macmillan, 1974);

Scoundrel Time (Boston: Little, Brown, 1976; London: Macmillan, 1976);

Maybe: A Story (Boston: Little, Brown, 1980; London: Macmillan, 1980);

Eating Together: Recipes and Recollections, by Hellman and Peter S. Feibleman (Boston: Little, Brown, 1984).

Editions and Collections: *Four Plays by Lillian Hellman* (New York: Modern Library, 1942);

Six Plays by Lillian Hellman (New York: Modern Library, 1960);

The Collected Plays (Boston: Little, Brown, 1972; London: Macmillan, 1972);

Three (Boston: Little, Brown, 1979; London: Macmillan, 1979)—comprises *An Unfinished Woman, Pentimento,* and *Scoundrel Time.*

PRODUCED SCRIPTS: *The Dark Angel,* by Hellman and Mordaunt Shairp, based on Guy Bolton's play, motion picture, United Artists, 1935;

These Three, adapted from *The Children's Hour,* motion picture, United Artists, 1936;

Dead End, adapted from Sidney Kingsley's play, motion picture, United Artists, 1937;

The Little Foxes, by Hellman, Alan Campbell, Arthur Kober, and Dorothy Parker, motion picture, RKO, 1941;

The Watch on the Rhine, screenplay by Dashiell Hammett with additional dialogue by Hellman, motion picture, Warner Bros., 1943;

The North Star, motion picture, RKO, 1943;

The Searching Wind, motion picture, Paramount, 1946;

The Chase, adapted from Horton Foote's novel, motion picture, Columbia, 1966.

OTHER: *The Selected Letters of Anton Chekhov,* translated by Sidonie K. Lederer, edited by Hellman (New York: Farrar, Straus, 1955; London: Hamilton, 1955);

Dashiell Hammett, *The Big Knockover: Selected Stories and Short Novels,* edited by Hellman (New York: Random House, 1966); republished as *The Dashiell Hammett Story Omnibus* (London: Cassell, 1966).

SELECTED PERIODICAL PUBLICATIONS–
UNCOLLECTED: "Perberty in Los Angeles," *American Spectator,* 2 (January 1934): 4;

"A Day in Spain," *New Republic,* 95 (13 April 1938): 297–298;

"Back of Those Foxes," *New York Times,* 26 February 1939, section 10, pp. 1–2;

"I Meet the Front Line Russians," *Collier's,* 115 (31 March 1945): 11, 68–71;

"Author Jabs the Critics," *New York Times,* 15 December 1946, section 2, pp. 3–4;

"Scotch on the Rocks," *New York Review of Books,* 17 October 1963, p. 6;

"Sophronia's Grandson Goes to Washington," *Ladies Home Journal,* 80 (March 1964): 78–80, 82;

"Lillian Hellman Asks a Little Respect for Her Agony, An Eminent Playwright Hallucinates after a Fall Brought on by a Current Dramatic Hit," *Show,* 55 (May 1964): 12–13;

"The Time of the Foxes," *New York Times,* 22 October 1967, section D, pp. 1, 5.

At Lillian Hellman's funeral, John Hersey, referring to the title of Hellman's 1969 volume of memoirs, *An Unfinished Woman,* declared that Hellman was at last a finished woman. Just as some of her plays enjoy periodic revivals, however, Hellman's reputation, dramatic writings, and memoirs continue to be reexamined and reevaluated. The classification of her plays as "well-made" and "melodramas" has been challenged by many who believe her plays cannot be easily categorized. The veracity of Hellman's memoirs continues to be questioned. Since her death Hellman has been the subject of two plays, a television movie, a documentary, and several biographies; interest in her life at times seems to eclipse interest in her drama. Yet, her contributions to the American stage cannot be ignored. Her unflinching examination of individuals' actions and their consequences, her fully realized characters speaking realistic dialogue, and her ability to bring her characters to a climactic confrontation epitomize Hellman's dramaturgy.

Lillian Florence Hellman, an only child, was born in New Orleans, Louisiana, on 20 June 1906 to Max Hellman and Julia Newhouse Hellman. Both parents

Robert Keith, Anne Revere, Florence McGee, Katherine Emery, and Katherine Emmet in the 1934 New York production of
The Children's Hour *(Theatre Collection, Museum of the City of New York)*

were descendants of German Jews who immigrated to the United States during the 1840s. The Newhouse side of the family was wealthy and successful, and through his marriage Max Hellman acquired enough money to open the Hellman Shoe Company. Sophie Marx Newhouse, Lillian's maternal grandmother, ruled the family. Sophie and her brother, Jake, became the models for Regina and Ben in *The Little Foxes* (1939). In her memoir, Hellman recalls meals with the Newhouse family as tense, unpleasant affairs where talk about money and possessions dominated, and reminders of her father's lower-class background and business failures were frequent. Hellman did not truly appreciate her mother until after the latter's death; instead, Hellman remembered her as refined, quiet, eccentric, and overly religious. Traces of her mother later appeared in Birdie of *The Little Foxes.* Although Hellman idolized her father, this feeling diminished as she learned of her father's infidelities.

At the age of six, Hellman moved with her family to New York City, where the Newhouses had relocated.

After his shoe business failed, Max Hellman became a traveling salesman, and for the next eleven years the family divided their time between New York and New Orleans. The two worlds could not have been more different. When in New York, Hellman lived with her mother's wealthy relatives on West Ninety-fifth Street; when in New Orleans, she lived in a boardinghouse full of eccentric roomers and run by her father's sisters. These two unmarried aunts, Jenny and Hannah, were favorites of Hellman. The rooming house later served as the model for the Tuckerman home in Hellman's 1951 play, *The Autumn Garden,* and the situation of two sisters devoted to their married brother appeared, with violence and intrigue unknown to the Hellman sisters, in *Toys in the Attic* (1960).

This disruptive lifestyle had several consequences. Hellman's schooling became erratic with the shuttling between two divergent school systems; she was never a stellar student, and her brief college career at New York University and Columbia University was pursued without great enthusiasm or diligence. The constant moving, a frequently absent father, and life as an only child also bred in Hellman lifelong character traits of independence and rebellion. One of the few constants in her childhood was her black nurse, Sophronia Mason, whom Hellman describes in her memoirs as "the first and most certain love of my life." The number of black characters in Hellman's plays, many of whom serve as moral compasses, has been attributed in part to the positive influence of this woman. Sophronia Mason was the only person from Hellman's childhood who escaped criticism in her writings.

Leaving college at the age of nineteen, Hellman took a job as a manuscript reader for Horace Liveright, owner of the prestigious publishing firm of Boni and Liveright. During the heyday of the firm, it published works by such authors as Sherwood Anderson, Hart Crane, T. S. Eliot, William Faulkner, Ernest Hemingway, and Eugene O'Neill. The excitement of the discovery of new writers was matched by the glamour of the after-hours party life. Hellman's vocation and lifestyle were undoubtedly influenced by this early professional experience.

In December 1925 Hellman married press agent Arthur Kober, later known for his plays *"Having Wonderful Time"* (1937) and *Wish You Were Here* (1952) and his thirty movies. Hellman quit working for Boni and Liveright but held several jobs during this period. She did publicity for *Bunk of 1926,* an unsuccessful show, and for a Rochester, New York, stock company. Her first published work was a book review for the *New York Herald Tribune.* During her marriage to Kober, Hellman also became a play reader for Anne Nichols, author of *Abie's Irish Rose* (1927). Hellman's great "discovery" was Vicki Baum's play *Grand Hotel* (1930), which had a long Broadway run.

In 1926 Hellman and Kober left for Paris after Kober was offered a position as editor of the *Paris Comet,* a new English-language literary periodical. Hellman's first two works of fiction, short stories she described as "lady-writer" tales, were published by the *Paris Comet.* Hellman traveled frequently during this period and decided in 1929 to study at the university in Bonn, Germany. Through the boardinghouse in which she lived, Hellman was recruited by a Nazi student group and briefly considered joining, mistakenly thinking it was a socialist organization. When she discovered the nature of the organization, she promptly left Germany, recalling in her memoirs that "for the first time in my life I thought about being a Jew." This experience later influenced the writing of two plays, *Watch on the Rhine* (1941) and *The Searching Wind* (1944).

In 1930 Hellman and Kober moved to Hollywood, where Kober had been offered a scriptwriter position with Paramount. Through Kober's connec-

tions Hellman acquired a job writing synopses of potential material for M-G-M, a position that was terminated because of her militant support for the nascent Screen Writers' Guild. Her marriage also ended, on amicable terms, in 1932. By this time she had begun what became a lifelong relationship with Dashiell Hammett, the former Pinkerton agent and best-selling detective writer, whom she met in November 1930. Hammett proved to be her most devoted mentor, companion, and critic.

Biographer William Wright perhaps articulates the relationship best when he writes that Hammett's "collaboration" with Hellman was not as much in the development of her plays as it was in the development of Hellman herself. From Hammett she learned the importance of research and revision, habits she continued to develop throughout her lifetime.

Shortly after her return to New York, Hellman published two short stories in the *American Spectator,* a literary journal recently begun by Theodore Dreiser and others. "I Call Her Mama Now" (1933) and "Perberty in Los Angeles" (1934) are narrated by precocious preteenage girls who are encouraged by bohemian adults to give up their bookish ways and embrace the "brave new world." Both are funny stories that satirize those enamored with sexual liberation. Hellman first attempted playwriting in 1932 with Louis Kronenberger on a collaborative effort called "The Dear Queen," a comedy about a royal family that attempts to become commoners, finds middle-class morality too stifling, and returns to the life of royalty. Although they offered the play to several producers, there was no interest, and "The Dear Queen" was neither published nor produced. Hellman later wrote that they knew it was pretty bad but they had great fun writing it.

During this time Hellman worked as a script reader for Herman Shumlin (who later produced and directed her first four plays) but was known primarily as "Hammett's girl." In 1933 Hammett completed his last novel, *The Thin Man* (published in 1934, the same year as Hellman's first playwriting success), modeling the character of Nora, he said, on Hellman. In his reading for new ideas, he found a book by William Roughead called *Bad Companions* (1931), about British court cases. One chapter in particular, "Closed Doors, or The Great Drumsheugh Case," struck Hammett as good material for a play, and he suggested it to Hellman. The true story about two women who ran a boarding school for girls in Scotland and were ruined after a student falsely accused them of a lesbian relationship appealed to Hellman. Hammett supervised the writing and extensive rewriting of the resulting play, *The Children's Hour.* Opening at Maxine Elliott's Theatre in Manhattan on 20 November 1934 for 691 perfor-

*Producer-director Herman Shumlin, Hellman, and Tallulah Bankhead during rehearsals for the
1939 New York production of* The Little Foxes

mances, it became Hellman's longest-running production and one of her most popular plays.

The play focuses on Karen Wright and Martha Dobie, who own and operate a private boarding school and have finally reached a point when financial stability and success seem possible. The women's dreams are destroyed when Mary Tilford, an evil pupil trying to avoid punishment at school, tells her wealthy grandmother, Mrs. Tilford, the social pillar of society, that Karen and Martha are involved in an unnatural sexual relationship. Despite the fact that Mrs. Tilford's nephew, Dr. Joe Cardin, is engaged to Karen, Mrs. Tilford believes Mary and convinces the other parents to withdraw their daughters from the school. The headmistresses sue for libel but lose the case because Martha's aunt fails to appear in court to help clear their names. Karen breaks her engagement, and Martha—who realizes that she does have feelings for Karen—commits suicide. Mrs. Tilford learns too late that her granddaughter has lied and comes to Karen to make amends. Karen replies: "You've come to the wrong place for help. . . . A public apology and money paid, and you can sleep again and eat again. That's done and there'll be peace for you. . . . But what of me? It's a whole life for me. A whole God-damned life." The play ends with

Karen agreeing to let Mrs. Tilford try to help as they talk about the weather.

Because Hellman was provided with a story, she was able to devote her attention to dialogue, character development, and structure. *The Children's Hour* reveals the elements that helped categorize her as a writer of melodrama or of the well-made play, such as the blackmail device and use of the "significant" phone call. The sensationalism of the lesbian issue, rare on the stage in 1934, drew attention away from Hellman's primary concern, an issue that appeared in almost all of her plays: the damage that a single lie can do to multiple lives. For Hellman, the interest is not in who tells the lie or why, but in examining the consequences.

Most of the reviews were positive. A critic for *The New York Times* (21 November 1934) complained, however, of the overwriting of act 3, saying, "In the last ten or fifteen minutes of the final act she tries desperately to discover a mettlesome dramatic conclusion. Having lured *The Children's Hour* away from the theatre into the sphere of human life, she pushes it back among the Ibsenic dolls and baubles by refusing to stop talking." Hellman agreed with this assessment, writing in her introduction to *Four Plays by Lillian Hellman* (1942) that the play should have concluded with Martha's suicide but that she could not prevent herself from a final summation.

Despite the occasional criticism, the play met with success and some notoriety. *The Children's Hour* was banned in London, Boston, and Chicago, although it was performed privately in London at the Gate Theatre in November 1936 to enthusiastic audiences but tepid reviews. The play earned Hellman $125,000, but it did not win any major awards. Many people felt it should have won the Pulitzer Prize, bestowed instead on Zoë Akins's *Old Maid* (1935), a play lacking a controversial theme. Indignant theater critics joined together to form the Drama Critics' Circle with the intention of awarding its own annual prize for drama.

The play created other interest as well. In 1935 Samuel Goldwyn hired Hellman as a screenwriter for $2,500 a week. Her first screenplay was an adaptation of Guy Bolton's play *The Dark Angel* (1925). The movie, released in 1935 with Merle Oberon and Fredric March, did well, but Hellman later characterized it as "silly." Goldwyn was pleased and allowed Hellman to choose her next project. According to Hellman biographer Wright, Goldwyn acquired the movie rights to *The Children's Hour* for $50,000, and Hellman had her next project: turn the play into a movie that would pass the censors. She felt this task would be easy, for she always maintained that the play was not about lesbianism but about slander. *These Three* (1936), the finished product, utilized a heterosexual love triangle instead (which also made it easier for Goldwyn to find actresses to accept the roles) to dramatize the damage of lies. In this version Mary tells her aunt that Joe and Martha are having an affair; a slander suit is brought and dismissed; and Martha confesses her love for Joe, but he and Karen find happiness in the end. Although it bears little resemblance to the play, the movie received good reviews. In 1962–after a revision of the Production Code that made homosexuality a permissible topic for movies– William Wyler released another movie version, calling it *The Children's Hour* and adhering more closely to the play. Despite a strong cast, including Audrey Hepburn and Shirley MacLaine, this movie was less successful.

Hellman's next play, *Days to Come,* which opened at the Vanderbilt Theatre on 15 December 1936, was a failure, lasting for only seven Broadway performances. The action is set in a small town in Ohio, home of the Rodman Brush Company. Arthur Rodman, owner of the once-profitable company, has been forced to cut wages in order to keep the factory going. A union leader, Leo Whalen, has incited the workers to go on strike, and after several weeks Rodman, with the help of his attorney, brings in Sam Wilkie and his band of strikebreakers. Problems intensify when one of the strikebreaking agitators knifes another in a card game,

and Wilkie decides to dump the dead body outside Whalen's office in an effort to frame him. When Whalen is arrested, a riot breaks out between the workers and strikebreakers, during which the foreman's young daughter is killed. Rodman's wife, Julie, who had been having an affair with her husband's attorney and best friend and had attempted to seduce Whalen, provides an alibi and confesses her indiscretions. The strike comes to an end, but not without losses on every side. The disdain and disappointments of each family member have been revealed, and the trusting relationship between factory owners and workers has been forever destroyed.

One of Hellman's political plays, *Days to Come* suffers from too many plots. None of the characters is fully developed, and the last act suffers because too many conflicts have to be resolved. Hellman clearly delineates the good, the bad, and the bystander characters; however, because there are too many characters and conflicts, the evil characters are mere stereotypes, and the others lack the requisite depth for audiences to care about them. Critics trounced the play. A reviewer for *The New York Times* (16 December 1936) complained of an "elliptical style of writing" that left one uncertain whether the play was about crime, neurotic females, or labor troubles. Hellman admitted weaknesses but liked the play overall: "It is crowded and overwrought, but it is a good report of rich liberals in the 1930's, of a labor leader who saw through them, of a modern lost lady, and has in it a correct prediction of how conservative the American labor movement was to become."

Hellman recalled the feelings of failure following the poor reception of this play: "The failure of a second work is, I think, more damaging to a writer than failure ever will be again. It is then that the success of the first work seems an accident. . . . You go into the second work with confidence you will never have again if you have any sense." Two years passed before Hellman started another play.

During her hiatus from playwriting, Hellman returned to screenwriting, this time to write the 1937 screenplay adaptation of Sidney Kingsley's play *Dead End* (1935). After completing that project, she left for Europe. During her visit to Paris, she met Hemingway and the American expatriates through her friend Dorothy Parker. She also went to Russia and to Spain. With Hammett, Archibald MacLeish, and Margaret DaSilva, she became a member of a group called Contemporary Historians, which financed *The Spanish Earth,* an early antifascist movie directed by Joris Ivens and narrated by Hemingway. (John Dos Passos was originally to collaborate but withdrew over political differences.)

In 1939 Hellman's next play, *The Little Foxes,* was produced. The prodigious research she did for this play into turn-of-the-century America, particularly the American South and American business practice and development, filled notebooks. Hellman rewrote the play nine times and said it was the most difficult play to write, in part because of her experiences with *Days to Come:* Hellman assumed guilt for the failure of that play, and guilt became "an excuse for not thinking." The play may also have been challenging to write because of the connections to her own family: the characters of Birdie, Regina, and Addie were inspired in part by Hellman's mother, grandmother, and Sophronia Mason, and Hellman said she also meant to mock herself in youth through the character of Alexandra. Parker supplied the title, taken from the Song of Solomon 2:15: "Take us the foxes, the little foxes, that spoil the vines, for our vines have tender grapes." The Hubbard family demonstrates the cunning, destructive greed suggested by the biblical reference.

The play is set in the elegant home of Regina and Horace Giddens in an unidentified Southern town in Alabama in 1900. Regina, with her two brothers, Oscar and Ben Hubbard, have persuaded a Chicago businessman, William Marshall, to build a cotton mill, to be controlled by the Hubbard siblings if they can raise the required investment of 51 percent into the company. One-third of the money will have to come from Horace, who has been in a Baltimore hospital with a heart condition. When Horace fails to respond to his wife's letters, Regina sends their daughter, Alexandra, to bring him home. Once apprised of the situation, Horace recognizes that the success of the factory depends on capitalist corruption and refuses to invest in the plan. Ben, the eldest brother, is delighted, for he had hoped his domineering sister would be shut out of the deal. Oscar, the weaker brother, also sees that this financial obstacle could work to his advantage and consents to his son Leo's suggestion that Leo "borrow" $88,000 in bonds from Horace's safety-deposit box. Regina cannot believe that her plans are being thwarted, and the second act ends with her raging at Horace and wishing he were dead.

In the next act Horace learns of the theft and sees it as an opportunity to permanently prevent Regina from partaking of the deal. He tells Regina he will loan his brothers-in-law the money rather than press charges of theft, but before he can tell them his decision, Horace has a heart attack. Regina denies Horace his lifesaving medicine; in desperation Horace stumbles out of his wheelchair and tries to climb the stairs. Regina turns her back. When Horace dies shortly thereafter, Regina gives her brothers a choice: they can go to jail, or they can give her a 75 percent share of the mill. This blackmail threat brings Regina her desired money and the opportunity to move to Chicago. Although defeated,

Ben nonetheless admires his sister's cunning. Regina's victory, however, comes with a price. Alexandra has listened and learned from her father, her aunt Birdie (Oscar's wife), and the maid, Addie, who have warned her about the viciousness of the Hubbard siblings. She vows to leave home: "I want to leave here. As I never wanted anything in my life before. Because now I understand what Papa was trying to tell me." Regina is alone onstage as the curtain descends.

Critics have studied *The Little Foxes* from multiple perspectives. Many praise the play as an examination of the rape of the agrarian South by the industrialized North. Horace explains that Northern companies come to the South because of cheap labor, and he sees how race relations can further deteriorate. More metaphorically, the values of the Old South, as represented by Horace, Birdie, and Addie, are destroyed by the new industrialists, such as Regina, Ben, and Oscar. In this context the play demonstrates the role American society plays in shaping individuals. Consequently, some saw the play as a warning to a nation coming out of the Depression. Some, of course, believed Hellman was attacking America's capitalistic system. Hellman discounted these interpretations, saying she was not intending to make a statement about capitalism or the changing South. What draws audiences to this play are the characters whose motivation is a greedy lust for power. Particularly intriguing is Hellman's development of the evil characters. As in her previous two plays, the "good" and "bad" characters are clearly marked, and as in *The Children's Hour,* evil succeeds because decent people do not try to prevent it.

The theme of evil triumphing because of well-intentioned but impotent people pervades Hellman's works and is most forcibly articulated in this play by Addie: "Well, there are some people who eat the earth and eat all the people on it. . . . Then there are people who stand around and watch them eat it. Sometimes I think it ain't right to stand and watch them do it." Implicit in Addie's remarks is the thrust of Hellman's theme: abdicating one's social responsibility can be costly for everyone.

Hellman had not intended people to take the play as seriously as they did. She felt the play had humor in it, and she expected people to see themselves: "I had meant the audience to recognize some part of themselves in the money-dominated Hubbards; I had not meant people to think of them as villains to whom they had no connections." Only recently have critics begun to see the mixture of humor and seriousness as a strength rather than a weakness. John Gassner commented that the mix of tragedy and comedy has roots in William Shakespeare, and Katherine Lederer noted the use of irony.

The play opened at the National Theatre in New York on 15 February 1939 and ran for 410 performances. Most reviews were fairly good. Many commented, once again, on Hellman's debt to Ibsen, her skill with dialogue, and her tendency to write melodrama rather than tragedy. The most common complaint was that the plot seemed too contrived. Much praise was given for the performances, particularly that of Tallulah Bankhead as Regina. *The Little Foxes* held its own in a rich theatrical season: William Saroyan's *The Time of Your Life,* Philip Barry's *Philadelphia Story,* George S. Kaufman and Moss Hart's *The Man Who Came to Dinner,* and Howard Lindsay and Russel Crouse's *Life with Father* were running at the same time. In 1941 a movie version of *The Little Foxes* opened with Bette Davis in the lead, and in 1949 a musical version, *Regina,* with music by Marc Blitzstein, opened on Broadway. Hallmark Hall of Fame produced a version for television with Greer Garson as Regina. Despite the occasional negative review, *The Little Foxes* continues to be Hellman's most revived play. One of the most notable revivals was a 1981 production with Elizabeth Taylor making her stage debut as Regina. This production was so popular that it went on an international tour. A 1997 production at Lincoln Center with Blythe Danner as Regina was panned, partly because it attempted to make Regina more sympathetic and less vicious. *The Little Foxes* has been produced in French, Spanish, and English; it has also been performed in Moscow and Belgrade.

By her early thirties, Hellman was an established playwright. She had made considerable money from her first play but had squandered her earnings; however, in 1939 she and Hammett made an investment that brought great pleasure to both of them. Hardscrabble Farm, a 130-acre property in New York, remained her primary residence until she was forced to sell it to pay legal bills and taxes thirteen years later. She and Hammett hosted a steady stream of visitors who would stay in the various outbuildings, one of which also became her studio. When she was not writing, she devoted herself to gardening, raising ducks, and becoming a gourmet chef. Hellman and Hammett spent some of their happiest times at Hardscrabble Farm.

Watch on the Rhine, Hellman's next play, responds to the political climate of the day. The play is set in 1940 in the Washington, D.C., mansion of Fanny Farrelly, the widow of an American diplomat. As the play opens, Fanny is awaiting the arrival of her daughter, Sara, whom she has not seen in twenty years. Arriving with Sara will be her German husband, Kurt Müller, and her three children, none of whom Fanny has met. Sara and her family have been living abroad for the past twenty years as Kurt has worked with the anti-Nazi underground movement. (Kurt was based on Otto Katz, a communist organizer and friend of Hellman's.) Living with Fanny are her son, David; Marthe, the daughter of a family friend; and Teck de Brancovis, Marthe's husband, a Romanian count and former diplomat. Teck, penniless, has survived by taking advantage of the hospitality of others and keeping his connections with the German embassy, where he goes for gambling and gossip. Teck immediately suspects Kurt's political affiliations and confirms his suspicions by going through Kurt's belongings. Teck threatens to expose Kurt unless Kurt pays him $10,000, money that Kurt plans to use to ransom his friends in Europe. Fanny decides to get the money to help protect Kurt, but before that is possible, Kurt kills the count, and the family conspires to dispose of the body. At the conclusion of the play, Kurt flees to help his friends and to avoid arrest. Kurt tells his children that he has done something wrong and must leave, but he is going to make the world a safer place: "In all over the world, in every place and every town, there are men who . . . want what I want: a childhood for every child." Sara and the children remain with Fanny, who recognizes that they, too, will face trouble. Fanny is, as she says, "shaken out of the magnolias," but she is "happy to learn" how to manage and survive.

Opening on 1 April 1941 at the Martin Beck Theatre in New York, eight months before Pearl Harbor, *Watch on the Rhine* responded to the continuing debate on American neutrality. Hellman did not need to introduce American audiences to World War II, nor did she need to convince anyone of the evils of Nazism. Instead, by placing the antifascist message within a domestic situation, she implicated all Americans through the theme that those who chose to ignore the international crisis were helping to perpetuate it and that no one can count himself or herself free of danger. Most critics hailed the play as Hellman's best to date; some called it the best war play of its time. In calling the play a melodrama, critics this time used the term as one of praise, saying that the form fit the action. Hellman had always been praised for her characterizations, and the character of Kurt was particularly praised for being a modern hero. Overall, Hellman created more likable characters, and even her villain, Teck, is more pathetic than evil. The play ran for 378 performances and won the Drama Critics' Circle Award. Hammett wrote the screenplay for the movie version, cited as one of the best movies of 1943. Paul Lukas reprised his Broadway role of Kurt Müller, for which he won the Academy Award for best actor. Although the Hayes Commission initially balked at the ending because no one was punished for the killing, the movie retained the original outcome. In 1942 the play had the distinction of being chosen by President Franklin Delano Roosevelt to be performed at a

Hellman sitting on the sofa used in the 1939 New York production of The Little Foxes

benefit for infantile paralysis, an event the president attended.

During the 1940s Hellman's political activism continued to develop. When Hammett left for the Aleutian Islands after enlisting as a private in 1942, Hellman returned to Hollywood and screenplay writing. She was hired by Goldwyn to write the screenplay for a quasi-documentary movie set in a Russian village during a Nazi invasion. The idea was to foster better feelings toward the Russians. The filming of *The North Star* proved disastrous, however, and when the movie became more fiction and less documentary, Hellman pulled out. She was able to buy out her contract for $30,000, and her association with Goldwyn came to an end.

During this period Hellman began work on her next play, *The Searching Wind,* which opened in 1944 at the Fulton Theatre and ran for 326 performances. Once

again Hellman set a political theme within a domestic situation, and again the message was that when decent people ignore their political responsibilities, fascism spreads. For the first time Hellman experimented with structure, using a rambling, flashback approach to take the action through three decades and four settings.

The play begins in Washington, D.C., in 1944 in the home of Alex and Emily Hazen as they await a visit from Cassie Bowman, Emily's childhood friend whom she has not seen in twenty years. Emily is the daughter of a liberal newspaper owner, and Cassie is a college professor and Alex's mistress. The Hazens' son, Sam, who was wounded in the war, and his grandfather, Moses, are also at home. The next scene flashes back to Rome in 1922 with Benito Mussolini marching on the city. Cassie and Alex are in love despite their divergent political views. Cassie is an ardent antifascist, but Alex, a young career diplomat and an appeaser, believes

America cannot take sides and fails to see the implications of Mussolini's rise to power. Later, in Berlin in 1923, Alex has married Emily, an apolitical socialite, on the rebound. The scene is set in a restaurant, outside of which a mob chases Jews. Alex sits by, still believing that noninvolvement is the correct position. From there the play moves to Paris in 1938, where Alex, now an ambassador, has come to believe that Adolf Hitler's demand for Sudetenland will not be his last; however, Alex's policy of appeasement and nonintervention continues. He declares that ambassadors are men with little power who cannot effect change. The final scene is set in the Hazens' home. The evasions that have worked for the Hazens to date will not work anymore. The triangle is made to face the consequences of their actions, political and personal. Sam becomes the spokesman for moral outrage, railing against his father's passivist politics, his mother's carefree lifestyle, and his grandfather's inactivity. The world has had to pay the price of their frivolity through the rise of fascism, and he has had to bear the personal price through the amputation of his leg.

The Searching Wind, Hellman's most political play, fell one vote short of the majority needed to win the Drama Critics' Circle Award (none was given that year). Those who praised it did so for the ideas and the writing, but the structural flaws are clear. The repetitive flashback technique that shifts the action among four countries and three decades results in tedium. The yoking of the personal and the international sacrifices Hellman's usually strong characterization. The relationship between the women, and the development of the grandson and grandfather, are particularly vague. At times the attention to the love triangle seems disproportionate to the larger picture, resulting in characters who seem dehumanized. Hellman also wrote the screenplay for the 1946 movie adaptation, which starred Robert Young, Sylvia Sidney, and Ann Richards.

In 1944 Hellman left for a second trip to Russia at the invitation of the Russian government. At the time of her visit, productions of *The Little Foxes* and *Watch on the Rhine* were being mounted there. The trip is described in detail in *An Unfinished Woman.* She had the opportunity to meet with the movie director Sergei Eisenstein and to visit a recently liberated Polish concentration camp, but the highlight of the trip seems to have been the two weeks she spent on the Warsaw front with the Russian army.

Back home, Hellman began work on her sixth play, *Another Part of the Forest* (1946), a prequel to *The Little Foxes* and part of a planned but uncompleted trilogy. Set in 1880 in Bowden, Alabama, the play revisits the Hubbard family to explore the earlier lives of the siblings and their parents. The third, unwritten play was to

have been set twenty years after *The Little Foxes* to show Regina in Europe and her daughter, an unmarried social worker. In *Another Part of the Forest* Marcus Hubbard, the family patriarch and tyrant, has amassed a fortune from war profiteering during the Civil War. His unscrupulous actions have made him a hated member of the community. The only person with whom he has a loving relationship is his daughter, Regina, who is in love with John Bagtry, Birdie's cousin and a Confederate war hero who dreams of going to Brazil to fight for the preservation of slavery. Marcus's wife, Lavinia, has been driven nearly insane by the secret she harbors of her husband's criminal past. Her only comfort is found with her maid, Coralee, and Coralee's friends in the black church. Ben is motivated by money and power, just as he is in *The Little Foxes*. His father treats him and Oscar with contempt and will not share control of the family business. Weak Oscar wants to marry Laurette, the town prostitute, and move to New Orleans.

Each member of the family fights for his or her own selfish desires, regardless of the impact these may have on others. There is no love, no loyalty in the Hubbard household. When Birdie comes to Ben for a loan, Ben sees his opportunity: he will get his father to loan Birdie $10,000, but he will pocket $5,000 for himself. Birdie wants the money for John to travel to Brazil, which would free Regina to marry money. Regina reveals Ben's trick to their father, and Ben retaliates by telling their father of Regina's affair with John.

By the end of act 2, even Oscar's plans are destroyed after Laurette verbally attacks Marcus, who then disinherits Oscar. In act 3, however, Marcus is ruined. Ben gets his mother to reveal Marcus's nasty secret by promising Lavinia she can return to her hometown to open a school for local black children. Ben learns that Marcus inadvertently caused the death of twenty-seven Confederate soldiers, and he uses this information to seize control of his father's assets. By the conclusion of the play, Ben has set into motion all the relationships that will be destroyed in *The Little Foxes*.

The play opened at the Fulton Theatre in 1946 to mixed reviews. Individual scenes were praised, but most critics complained of overwrought melodramatic contrivances used throughout. Without a socially thematic undercurrent, the play is reduced to unrelieved villainy, and although Hellman meant this work to be a satire like *The Little Foxes,* there is less humor in this play. Several critics singled out the character of Marcus as one of Hellman's most believable, well-crafted characters. *Another Part of the Forest* also marked Hellman's directorial debut, for which she received much praise. The play ran for 182 performances. Later critics have noted comparisons to the work of both

O'Neill and Tennessee Williams with respect to individual characters.

Hellman's political involvement began to cause her professional trouble during the late 1940s. By 1949 she had been informed by her friend, director William Wyler, who had wanted her to write a screenplay adaptation of Theodore Dreiser's *Sister Carrie* (1900), that she was blacklisted in Hollywood. She remained so, unofficially, until the early 1960s. Hollywood had provided Hellman a solid financial resource, and the loss of this work was significant. Hellman stated in a 1968 interview (included in *Conversations with Lillian Hellman*, 1986) that "I couldn't do movies which I had not only liked but had made a living, a steady living." Hellman did not abandon her political efforts. Instead, she seemed to become more publicly involved in political activities. She was active in Henry Wallace's presidential campaign in 1948, working on some of the Progressive Party committees and assisting in the formation of the party platform, all the while denying that communists controlled the party. That same year she accepted an assignment from the *New York Star* to travel to Yugoslavia to interview Marshal Tito; the trip resulted in a series of six articles praising his accomplishments. In 1949 she was a sponsor for the Cultural and Scientific Conference for World Peace at the Waldorf-Astoria in New York, better known as the Waldorf Conference, despite the State Department's denunciation of the conference.

While abroad, Hellman saw a production of Emmanuel Roblès's *Montserrat* and immediately acquired the American rights for an adaptation of the 1948 French play. The play is set in 1812 during the Spanish occupation of Venezuela. Montserrat, an ally of the South American liberator Simón Bolivar, is arrested by Izquierdo as a traitor for refusing to divulge where Bolivar is hiding. Izquierdo recognizes that torture will not make Montserrat talk, but he believes he can use Montserrat's compassion for others to his advantage. Izquierdo arranges for six people to be randomly chosen from those in the marketplace and then brought to the jail. The six—four men and two women—have one hour to convince Montserrat to reveal Bolivar's location. The six are told they will be released if they are successful; if they fail, they will be shot. Montserrat meets them as they individually plead for their lives. Although Montserrat is moved by their plight, he chooses not to betray Bolivar and what he believes is the greater good. Consequently, each villager is killed, as is Montserrat at the end of the play when Izquierdo learns that Bolivar has escaped. The play clearly suggests that everyone has a role to play in the overthrow of tyranny. Hellman once again directed, although

Harold Clurman took over the directing task at some point during the production.

Montserrat was not a success. Although the ideas are interesting, the play itself is not engaging. The six victims are undeveloped; the politics of the time are not explained; and Bolivar, for whom so many are killed, remains an enigma. The monotonous executions render the action of the play static. Hellman admits in her memoirs that she directed the play in "a fumbling, frightened way," at least partially because she was intimidated by the actors. The play, which opened on 29 October 1949 at the Fulton Theatre, ran for sixty-five performances.

In 1950 Hellman began work on *The Autumn Garden,* which was a departure from her earlier works in several ways, yet retained many of the Hellman trademarks. Set in 1949 at the Tuckerman summer home on the Gulf of Mexico, the play has no political overtones. Instead, it focuses on the middle-age despair of a group of people brought together on vacation at the home of Constance Tuckerman, who has opened her house as a summer resort in order to keep it. Well-bred Constance has remained unmarried after rejecting Ned Crossman, an alcoholic banker who believes he still loves Constance. Both have drifted through life without any purpose or accomplishment. In addition to Ned, retired general Ben Griggs and his wife, Rose, are also visiting. Griggs is trying to convince his wife of twenty-five years to grant him a divorce, but this conversation has been going on for years without any action. Added to this coterie are the Ellises: Carrie; her son, Frederick; and her mother-in-law, Mary. Frederick has recently become engaged to Sophie, Constance's seventeen-year-old niece from France, who desires nothing more than to return to Europe. The relationship between Sophie and Frederick lacks warmth and seems more an agreement than a romance. Frederick would rather go off to Europe with his friend, Payton, an offstage character of whom Carrie disapproves. These people, with the exception of Sophie, have been gathering here in the summer for years. This year a new guest has arrived: Nick Denery, a painter who jilted Constance long ago and is returning to the Tuckerman house for the first time in twenty-three years. Arriving with Nick is his rich wife, Nina.

The Denerys' marriage, like the Griggses', is strained, at least partially because of Nick's philandering. Nick has come, not because he wishes to renew old friendships or romances but because he needs adoration and the memories of the old days. Although charming and attractive at first, Nick soon disturbs everyone by his insinuations about everyone's lives, because of his own need to feel superior. He demands that Constance sit for a portrait, just as she did years ago, and Constance relents in order to keep him at the house, even though she is afraid of the comparison to the early work. He then tells Constance that she must return Ned's love, despite the fact that the relationship is no longer viable. Nick then turns his attention to Frederick and brings out what everyone has probably suspected privately: that Frederick's male companion is a homosexual. Finally, Nina, who has had to follow behind Nick throughout the years to clean up the messes he starts, pleads with him to stop meddling: "Have you ever tried leaving things alone? It's all around us. The flower-like odor right before it becomes troublesome and heavy. It travels ahead of you, Nick, whenever you get most helpful, most loving and most lovable . . . I smell it–and I want to leave." But despite threatening to leave without him, Nina is unable to break away.

The situation reaches a breaking point at the end of act 2, and Sophie, whose philosophy of survival has been to endure and do the best she can, sees a solution to her unhappy situation. Nick, drunk, comes into the living room, which doubles as Sophie's bedroom, and finds Sophie preparing for bed. He drunkenly tries to seduce her but passes out instead, and Sophie leaves the room. Everyone learns of Nick's behavior the next morning, and Sophie tells the Denerys that unless they pay her $5,000, she will tell the lie that Nick did succeed in his seduction attempt. Sophie, the only one who is not self-deluded, straightforwardly calls her demand extortion.

By the end of the play, everyone has come to some realization about himself or herself, but the realization does not equate to change. General Griggs gives up his dream of a divorce from Rose and a new start; Frederick, no longer engaged, consents to a European trip with his mother; Nina gives Sophie the money and decides to stay with Nick; and Constance realizes she has preserved her memory of Nick without acknowledging the kind of person he really was and is. When she acts on Nick's advice and asks Ned to marry her, she and Ned both must face some truths. Despite wanting to love her, Ned no longer harbors romantic desires for Constance; he also accepts responsibility for his own fruitless life: "I not only wasted myself, but I wanted it that way."

Many of the old influences and traits are obvious, but *The Autumn Garden* is also a departure from Hellman's earlier works. Hellman's aunts' boardinghouse, with its genteel poverty, may have suggested the setting. Blackmail, a favorite Hellman device, once again influences the outcome of the play. Hellman's judgmental views of her own characters also come through. In many other ways, however, *The Autumn Garden* shows Hellman breaking out of her mold. Part of the differ-

ence may be attributed to Hellman's stage of life. She reflected later that she wrote this play during a trouble-free period, which created the perfect working conditions: "For impatient people, calm is necessary for hard work–long days, months of fiddling is the best way of life. I wrote *The Autumn Garden* in such a period. I was at a good age." Unlike Hellman, her middle-age characters arrive at this time of life with regrets over what might have been and with the awareness that it is too late to change the patterns of life.

The most notable difference in her writing style is the obvious Chekhovian influence. Always disgruntled at having her plays labeled melodramas, she had started reading Anton Chekhov's work, considering him a non-melodramatic writer (she went on to edit Chekhov's letters in 1955). Hellman's characters are not caught in a crisis from which they must escape; instead, they are stuck in their own lives. The focus of the play is not action but reflection as the characters contemplate their lives and try to ascertain how they arrived at their present, unhappy state. In this play, her characters are similar also to O'Neill's in their confrontation of the unreality of their dreams.

The Autumn Garden is dedicated to Hammett, and his help is most obvious in the often-quoted speech by Griggs that captures the theme of the play:

> So at any given moment you're only the sum of your life up to then. There are no big moments you can reach unless you've a pile of smaller moments to stand on. That big hour of decision, the turning point of your life, the someday you've counted on when you'd suddenly wipe out your past mistakes, do the work you'd never done, think the way you'd never thought, have what you'd never had–it just doesn't come suddenly. You've trained yourself for it while you waited–or you've let it all run past you and frittered yourself away. I've frittered myself away.

Hellman had reworked that speech several times but could not write what she wanted to say; so Hammett rewrote it.

The play opened in New York on 7 March 1951 at the Coronet Theatre to mostly favorable reviews. Many noted the Chekhovian mood, the lack of villains and melodrama, and the Hellman trademark of sharp dialogue. Although a few critics complained that the play lacked focus and that Hellman tried to say too much, most agreed that *The Autumn Garden* was her most mature play to date. Her skill for creating fascinating characters that are true to life was noted by several critics. One reviewer wrote that Hellman had few peers when it came to putting meanness, loneliness, or frustration on the stage.

Mady Christians and Paul Lukas in the 1941 New York production of Watch on the Rhine

I do not like subversion or disloyalty in any form and if I had ever seen any I would have considered it my duty to have reported it to the proper authorities. But to hurt innocent people whom I knew many years ago in order to save myself is, to me, inhuman and indecent and dishonorable. I cannot and will not cut my conscience to fit this year's fashions.

She concluded the letter with an appeal to common values: "I was raised in an old-fashioned American tradition and there were certain homely things that were taught to me: to try to tell the truth, not to bear false witness, not to harm my neighbor, to be loyal to my country, and so on. In general, I respected these ideals of Christian honor and did as well with them as I knew how." She did appear before the committee and did not name names, and she refused to answer questions about her own communist associations. In a little over an hour, Hellman was dismissed. In *Scoundrel Time* (1976) Hellman recalled her pride when a man yelled from the press gallery, "Thank God somebody finally had the guts to do it." The headline for the 22 May 1952 *New York Times* read, "Hellman Balks House Unit." Hellman later wrote that she wished she had been more defiant.

Hellman survived, but not without a price. She grew increasingly disillusioned and shocked that so many people she had admired would sacrifice their convictions rather than risk suffering for them. Hellman also paid for her stand financially. The blacklisting by Hollywood deprived her of a main source of income, and perhaps more devastating, she was forced to sell her much-loved Hardscrabble Farm to pay the back taxes the government suddenly discovered she owed. A 1952 revival of *The Children's Hour,* which she directed, provided her with much-needed income until she wrote her next play. The choice of the revival was, of course, deliberate. The reviews were better than for the original, and several acknowledged with the *New York Times* reviewer (19 December 1952) that "the implications are much broader now and have new political overtones."

Hellman's next play, *The Lark* (1955), was an adaptation of *L'Alouette,* Jean Anouilh's 1953 play about Joan of Arc, the peasant girl who successfully led the French army to victory at the battle of Orleans in 1429. A year later she was captured by the British and brought to trial, accused of being a witch and a heretic. The play opens on the first day of the trial, and it is obvious that her fate has been decided before the trial begins. The play is structured around flashbacks as Joan tells her life story, interrupted only by comments from the courtroom. One of the most dramatic scenes is her recanting of her confession, which had been given under duress. Joan is tied to the stake and carried offstage against a backdrop of flames. Rather than end the

The 1950s were difficult years for Hellman politically. Her association with communist organizations and her refusal to condemn the actions of Stalin brought her unwelcome suspicion from the federal government. In 1951 Hammett was brought before a federal court and sentenced to a six-month jail term for contempt because he refused to name contributors to a Civil Rights Congress bail fund. The following year, Hellman received her subpoena to appear before the House Un-American Activities Committee. Hellman did not want to name names or go to jail, yet she also did not want to use the Fifth Amendment defense. Her initial strategy—one used unsuccessfully by other writers called before the committee who testified in private sessions—was to offer a compromise: she would speak about herself, but only herself. She offered this response in a letter to the committee (which her lawyer, Joseph Rauh, released to the press):

play with this image, Hellman concludes with the coronation of Charles VII in Reims Cathedral. The play ends with a chorus singing the Gloria of the Mass, a not-so-subtle reminder that Joan was eventually elevated to sainthood in the twentieth century.

Hellman recalled that she agreed to adapt Anouilh's play even though she disliked it. She had a sense that Joan of Arc's personality would make the play a success with American audiences. Hellman judged Joan of Arc as "history's first modern career girl," whose appeal lay "in the miraculous self-confidence that carried defeated men into battle against all sense and reason." Hellman reinterprets the French national hero as a naive, down-to-earth peasant girl who succeeds because of her invincible spirit, and Joan thus becomes a real person with universal appeal. The alterations Hellman made to Anouilh's play are substantial. Hellman believed Anouilh wrote the play as a comment on the French spirit during World War II, but she did not see the play from that perspective. Consequently, she cut much of the play, simplified the language, altered the ending and thus changed the tone, and added choral music by Leonard Bernstein that underscores the religious aspects of the play. The critics loved *The Lark,* which ran for 229 performances at the Longacre Theatre.

Hellman's professional association with Bernstein continued with her next project, a collaboration on a musical version of Voltaire's *Candide* (1759). Bernstein wrote the music; poet Richard Wilbur wrote the lyrics (with contributions from John Latouche and Dorothy Parker); and Hellman wrote the book. The operetta, set in Westphalia, opens with the impending marriage between Candide and the beautiful Cunegonde. Before they can be married, however, a Hessian army attacks, and Cunegonde is presumed dead. Candide escapes, and because of the tutelage of Dr. Pangloss, the eternal optimist, Candide remains an optimist, believing with Pangloss that there is good in everything. The remainder of the play follows Candide on his travels in search of Cunegonde, who he has learned is alive. His journey takes him to Lisbon, a brothel in Paris, a Buenos Aires slave market, a Venice gambling establishment, and back to Westphalia, which lies in ruins. Pangloss appears in each location to counteract Candide's growing disillusionment as he comes to see the worst in humans, including Cunegonde. Although Cunegonde has grown old and homely, Candide still wishes to marry her, and he has learned that he must place his hope not in philosophy but in work and in doing one's best.

The play opened on 1 December 1956 at the Martin Beck Theatre, and despite the talents of Bernstein, Wilbur, Hellman, and director Tyrone Guthrie,

the play received poor reviews and closed after only seventy-three performances. Several critics praised the ambitious idea of turning the play into a musical, and most commended the music and lyrics. Hellman was largely singled out for criticism, however. In particular, the loss of irony and satire from the original was noted, as was the loss of sexual frankness. Several also noted the heavy-handed moral tone. Hellman recounted later that *Candide* was her worst theater experience. Unfamiliar with collaboration and musical theater, Hellman said she did not fight for her script. Instead, she claims she gave in to suggestions for changes. When the Kennedy Center revived the operetta in 1972, she refused any connection with it, calling the revival "sad and wasteful." Revivals since that date, including one by Harold Prince, have abandoned Hellman's book.

Hellman recalled in her memoirs that the experience with *Candide* brought on writer's block, and only the intercession of several friends, including Hammett, helped her to write another play. Hammett suggested the idea of writing a play about a man who is pressured to make money and does so but then fails. Hellman took the suggestion, shifted the focus, borrowed from her past, and in 1960 produced *Toys in the Attic,* her last original play, for which she received her second New York Drama Critics' Circle Award. The play is set in the New Orleans home of Carrie and Anna Berniers, two unmarried sisters whose lives revolve around repetitive routines of work and concern for their brother, Julian. The sisters have saved money throughout their lives to support Julian's dreams, while their own desires, such as a trip to Europe, have always been postponed. Julian has been living in Chicago with his young, wealthy bride, Lily. Albertine Prine, Lily's mother, arrives at the Berniers house with her black "chauffeur," Henry, to inform the sisters that Julian and Lily are back home. Shortly after Albertine and Henry depart, Julian and Lily arrive laden with gifts: tickets to Europe, a piano, a new refrigerator, a paid-up mortgage on the sisters' home, and resignation letters, already sent, to their employers. For Lily, Julian has purchased an expensive diamond to replace her original cheap wedding band. Julian also has $150,000 in cash with him. The three women are wary of the sudden change in fortune. Lily, not stable to begin with, wanders around in a daze, wanting her old ring back and asking about a woman who calls Julian every night. Julian is disappointed in the lack of appreciation shown for his generosity.

Act 2 brings much of the mystery out into the open. Albertine and her daughter are reunited, and Lily reveals to her mother that Julian has become rich and seems to be seeing another woman. Since arriving home, Julian has also become impotent. Lily confesses

Leo Genn, Scott McKay, Percy Waram, Patricia Neal, and Mildred Dunnock as the Hubbard family in the 1946 New York production of Another Part of the Forest

that she has traded her diamond ring for a "knife of truth" she acquired from a group of religious fanatics she met the night before as she wandered around time in a mystical fog. Convinced her mother knows the answers, Lily demands to know if Julian married her for her money and who the mysterious woman is. Albertine convinces Lily that sometimes it is best not to seek the truth, and Henry clears up the mystery of the woman and Julian's sudden wealth. The woman who calls every night is Henry's cousin, Mrs. Warkins, an old lover of Julian's. Mrs. Warkins told Julian about some acreage that her husband wants, and Julian bought the land and sold it to Mr. Warkins for $150,000, half of which Julian gives to Mrs. Warkins so she can leave her unhappy marriage. Mrs. Warkins formed this partnership with Julian out of gratitude because Julian had a sexual relationship with her and did not care that she is mulatto, something her husband does not know.

As Henry tells this story, it becomes clear that he and Albertine have also broken the color line and are lovers. Meanwhile, Carrie has overheard all of this news. By the end of the act, the insecurities of Carrie and Lily increase. Lily deliberately hurts herself with a knife to attract Julian's attention. Carrie learns that Julian shared his secrets about Mrs. Warkins with

Anna and not her, and Carrie's irrational jealousy provokes Anna into saying that she has always suspected that Carrie harbors incestuous desires for their brother. The act ends with the bond between the sisters destroyed.

The insecure Lily and Carrie, confronted with the truth, bring about the devastation that concludes the play. Julian tells his sisters that he and Lily will leave after he concludes his business with Mrs. Warkins, and for his sake and theirs he cannot tell them where he will go. Carrie is inconsolable over the thought of losing Julian permanently to Lily. Only Anna seems to be able to respond to the changes and turmoil, as she makes plans to leave for Europe, alone. Lily's suspicion that Julian is having an affair continues to grow. Carrie convinces Lily to call Mrs. Warkins to learn the truth about Julian's relationship with her. With Carrie at her elbow, Lily makes the call but speaks to Mr. Warkins instead. She asks him to relay to his wife that she wants one more year with Julian, and then Carrie convinces Lily to tell Mr. Warkins where he can find his wife and Julian. Julian soon returns home, beaten and robbed. Recognizing her culpability, Lily prepares to confess the truth to Julian until Albertine convinces her otherwise. The play ends with the family members returned to their familiar roles. Julian and Lily will stay in New Orleans with his sisters, who will get their old jobs back and resume their roles as caretakers and providers. Although Carrie knows what Lily did, she says nothing, but the play ends with the suggestion that Carrie is not above revealing this secret if she needs to.

Like *The Autumn Garden,* Hellman's *Toys in the Attic* develops the themes of the consequences of self-deception and the folly of clinging to dreams. Nick and Carrie share the flaw of meddling in the lives of others as compensation for their own insecurities, yet there is greater compassion shown toward these unstable characters than Hellman had demonstrated in previous plays. These characters have not prepared for the future and cling to their past dreams and roles in life for comfort and security, as one might return to "toys in the attic" for solace. Like O'Neill, Hellman also cautions against pursuing truth. Although Hellman clearly believes that clinging to past dreams dooms one to unhappiness, she does not suggest that truth is always superior to illusions. The probing into Southern depravity and repressed sexuality obviously suggests a comparison to the works of Tennessee Williams, although Hellman's characters lack the psychological complexity of Williams's.

Opening at the Hudson Theatre on 25 February 1960, *Toys in the Attic* received good reviews. Most critics praised the play and, most particularly, the characters. Some objected to the melodramatic devices of the overheard conversation and the crucial telephone call, and others complained about the rigid plotting, yet Hellman was once again applauded for her crisp dialogue. A reviewer for the *New York Post* (26 February 1960) summarized the play as "stunning in its frank theatrical power, disturbing in its ugly candor, and brutally alive." The play ran for 556 performances.

Hellman did not end her playwriting career with an original play, however. Instead, she returned to adaptation for her last play, *My Mother, My Father and Me* (1963), adapted from Burt Blechman's 1961 novel, *How Much?* The play is not like any other Hellman play and seems to be her attempt to write a theater-of-the-absurd comedy. The only one of her plays to focus on Jewish characters, the play replaces Hellman's tight, methodical plotting with a string of vignettes about the Halpern family. Rather than developing characters with depth, Hellman relies on stereotypes, including the domineering Jewish mother, Rona, who is driven by her materialistic desires; her henpecked, unsuccessful husband; the senile grandmother; and the anti-establishment son, Barney. The play begins in the New York apartment of the Halperns with the arrival of the destitute grandmother and then moves to a nursing home, where the grandmother has been left for being a nuisance. The end of the play takes place on an Indian reservation, where Barney has moved to reject his family's and society's contemporary values and to get in touch with his national heritage. Barney ends the play in Native American attire, selling cheap Indian souvenirs to tourists and writing a book called "My Mother, My Father and Me."

Hellman's experimentation with form and genre was a failure. Opening at the Plymouth Theatre on 12 March 1963, the play lasted for only seventeen performances. Without a coherent plot and with too many targets for criticism, the play lacks focus. Hellman demonstrates her sharp eye for phoniness and cultural critique in the topics she satirizes, ranging from tensions between the Jewish and black communities to the treatment of the elderly and the American obsession with possessions. Critics unanimously excoriated the play. Although some found individual bits funny, all complained of the diffusesiveness. One reviewer for the *New York Daily News* (22 March 1963) called the play "flimsy whimsy," and another for the *New York Herald Tribune* (22 March 1963) condemned Hellman's attempt to "mate the extravagant satirical incoherence of the Theatre of the Absurd with the homier, milder, and more plausible nonsense of *You Can't Take It With You*."

Hellman's next work was the autobiographical *An Unfinished Woman*, published in 1969 and winner of a National Book Award that year. The book is more an assortment of recollections than a straightforward, chronological account of her life. The first seven chapters take the reader from Hellman's childhood through her 1937 trip to Moscow. In this section she recalls meeting Hemingway and F. Scott Fitzgerald in Paris and briefly mentions the trip to Moscow ("Although I have long ago lost the diary of that trip, Dash was right: I did not enjoy the Moscow Theatre Festival, except for a production of *Hamlet* with the Prince played as a fat young man in a torpor"). She then uses a diary format for a chapter on her trip to Spain and reverts to her previous style to focus on her 1944 trip to Moscow. The last three chapters are devoted to remembrances of three people who were important in her life: Dorothy Parker; Hellman's maid, Helen; and Hammett.

Hellman concludes the book with a certain nostalgia for all that has passed but states that she is "not yet old enough to like the past better than the present." Her primary regret is that she pursued "truth" or "sense" (an ironic statement, since her memoirs have been shown to be full of inaccuracies and misrepresentations) and sacrificed a further development of self because of that pursuit. The book ends with this statement: "All I mean is that I left too much of me unfinished because I wasted too much time. However." The last word, combined with the title of the book, reminds readers that her life and personality were still developing.

Pentimento: A Book of Portraits, her second volume of memoirs, published in 1973, develops her image through her recollection of others. Four of the chapters are devoted to people who were important to her at various times in her life: her cousin Bethe, her uncle Willy, her friend Julia, and eccentric attorney and suitor Arthur Cowan. There is also a chapter on theater, the only part of any of her memoirs devoted to her writing career. This chapter does not include as much about her craft as it does about the events occurring around the writing or production of the plays. She recalls the opening-night jitters and the hangover she suffered with *The Children's Hour*, and she recognizes that disaster stories make good comedy. Of the opening night of *Days to Come*, she remembers vomiting at the back of the theater, leaving to change her clothes, and returning in time to see "William Randolph Hearst lead his six guests out of the theatre, in the middle of the second act, talking very loud as they came up the aisle." She also recalls troubles with various actors and directors. She has no use for critics, saying "there are not many good critics for any art, but there have been almost none for the modern theatre. The intellectuals among them know little about an operating theatre and the middlebrows look at the plays as if they were at a race track for the morning line up."

*Maureen Stapleton, Jason Robards Jr., Irene Worth, and Anne Revere
in the 1960 New York production of* Toys in the Attic

Hellman also expresses regret over the change that came to theater after World War II: people seem not to have noticed that the theater, "like the rest of the country, became expensive, earnest, and conservative." She finally stopped writing plays because the experience ceased to be fun, and after *My Mother, My Father and Me* she wanted no further part of theater: "The playwright is almost always held accountable for failure and that is almost always a just verdict. But this time I told myself that justice doesn't have much to do with writing and that I didn't want to feel that way again. For most people in the theatre whatever happens is worth it for the fun, the excitement, the possible rewards. It was once that way for me and maybe it will be again. But I don't think so."

"Julia" has become the most famous of these chapters; it describes a mission Hellman allegedly undertook for a friend in 1937. According to Hellman's story, she was reunited with Julia, a childhood friend whom she had last seen three years earlier in a Vienna hospital, the victim of Nazi attacks on socialist workers. At this reunion Julia asked Hellman, via an intermediary, to take $50,000 across the German border (hidden in a candy box and fancy hat) to help an anti-Nazi group. The story was turned into the 1977 movie *Julia,* starring Jane Fonda, Vanessa Redgrave, and Jason Robards.

The movie brought Hellman back into the limelight—she was invited to be a presenter at the Academy Awards in 1977 and enjoyed a standing ovation—but also opened up the floodgates for attacks on her veracity. Several people, in particular journalist and fiction writer Martha Gellhorn, questioned Hellman's participation in the events she depicts because of inconsistencies with dates and others' recollections of her activities at those particular times. Hellman's preface to *Three,* the 1979 collection of her autobiographical volumes, admits that the truth is elusive: "What a word is truth. Slippery, tricky, unreliable. I tried in these books to tell the truth. I did not fool with facts. But, of course, that is a shallow definition of truth. I see now, in rereading, that I kept much from myself." The most damaging evidence to call into question the truthfulness of Hellman's recounting of Julia came in 1983 with the publication of Muriel Gardiner's memoirs, *Code Name "Mary": An American Woman in the Austrian Underground.* The book proved that there was a real Julia, but she was not a friend of Hellman's. In fact, both Gardiner and Hellman denied knowing one another.

Hellman's last volume of memoirs, *Scoundrel Time,* was published in 1976, and it was also attacked for its self-serving, inaccurate account. Unlike the previous two volumes, *Scoundrel Time* has a limited focus: her experience as an unwilling witness before the House Committee on Un-American Activities. She expresses her disappointment in others who refused to fight for their convictions and disappointment in herself for having had faith in others and for not having recognized Joseph Stalin's crimes earlier: "I feel betrayed by the ones I had believed. I had no right to think that American intellectuals were people who would fight for anything if doing so would injure them." She recalls friends and acquaintances who were called before the committee, the fright of her own ordeal, the loss of her beloved farm, and her disgust with those who cooperated, such as Clifford Odets and Elia Kazan: "But radicalism or anti-radicalism should have had nothing to do with the sly, miserable methods of McCarthy, Nixon and colleagues, as they flailed at Communists, near-Communists, and nowhere-near-Communists. Lives were being ruined and few hands were raised to help. Since when do you have to agree with people to defend them from injustice." She also argues that the Cold War politics of McCarthy led directly to Richard Nixon's crises of Vietnam and Watergate.

Hellman continued as a political activist and writer until ill health prevented her from doing so. Throughout the 1960s and 1970s she was much in demand as a visiting lecturer at some of the most prestigious universities in America, including Harvard, Yale, and the University of California at Berkeley. She was appointed to the editorial board of *The American Scholar* and received many honorary degrees, including doctorates from Wheaton College (1961), the Douglass College of Rutgers University (1963), Brandeis University (1966), Yale University (1974), Smith College (1974), New York University (1974), Franklin and Marshall College (1975), and Columbia University (1976). Yeshiva University gave Hellman an Achievement Award in 1962; Jackson College of Tufts University presented her with the Jackson Award of Distinction (1968); and in 1973 the Alumni Club of New York University gave Hellman the Woman of the Year Award. She continued to receive awards and recognition from many other organizations. Having been admitted to the National Institute for Arts and Letters in 1946, Hellman was elected vice president of the organization in 1962 and then received the Gold Medal for Drama from the Institute in 1964. She also received the MacDowell Medal and the Actors' Equity Association Paul Robeson Award in 1976.

In 1970 she and some friends founded the Committee for Public Justice, which investigated reports of First Amendment violations by the FBI and CIA. She lent her name to a fund-raising event that brought together celebrities from every field. Along with the adulation came renewed attacks on Hellman's word in her memoirs. Perhaps the most notorious was Mary McCarthy's pronouncement on *The Dick Cavett Show* in 1980 that Hellman was "terribly overrated, a bad writer and a dishonest writer." When Cavett pressed McCarthy for clarification, McCarthy said that "every word she writes is a lie, including 'and' and 'the.'" Hellman immediately filed a libel suit for more than two million dollars against McCarthy, Cavett, and the television station. The suit was still in litigation at the time of Hellman's death but was later dismissed.

Hellman's penultimate book, *Maybe* (1980), is a partially autobiographical novel. The book is written in the first person and depicts Hellman's relationships with Kober, Hammett, her father, and various other friends and relatives. The center of the book is Sarah, a person who may have been a real friend of Hellman's or a created one. Sarah is depicted as not trustworthy, and the theme of the story is the challenge in determining truth. The conflation of fiction and reality and the whimsical title underscore this emphasis.

Hellman's last published work, *Eating Together: Recipes and Recollections,* published in 1984, was a collaboration with Peter S. Feibleman, twenty-five years Hellman's junior, who had known Hellman when he was a boy in New Orleans. After Hammett's death in 1961, he seemed to fill an important void in her life

and became her close companion until her death. The book reflects Hellman's interest in gourmet cooking and is a cookbook and memoir of their relationship.

Hellman died on Martha's Vineyard on 30 June 1984 after many years of enduring emphysema and poor eyesight. Of her four-million-dollar estate, Feibleman was the primary beneficiary; he received $100,000 cash, half of the royalties from her works, and her home. Other than small cash gifts to various friends and employees, the rest of her estate was divided into two funds. The Lillian Hellman Fund provides grants to encourage the arts and sciences. The Dashiell Hammett Fund provides similar grants but requires the trustees to "be guided by the political, social, and economic beliefs which, of course, were radical, of the late Dashiell Hammett who was a believer in the doctrines of Karl Marx."

Death has not diminished interest in Hellman. In 1986 Zoe Caldwell performed in the one-woman show *Lillian,* written by William Luce, and in 1993 Elaine Stritch played Hellman in *Cakewalk,* Feibleman's play adapted from his book *Lilly: Reminiscences of Lillian Hellman* (1988). In 1999 the Arts and Entertainment network broadcast a television movie on Hammett and Hellman, *Dash and Lilly,* starring Sam Shepard and Judy Davis; there was also a PBS American Masters documentary, *The Lives of Lillian Hellman.* Books and articles continue to be written on her, and her importance in the American theater is assured.

Contemporary critics examine Hellman's plays from multiple perspectives. Hellman's politics, her interest in the power and corruption that money brings to lives, and her concern with American capitalism have spawned many studies from a Marxist perspective. Although Hellman's plays have long been categorized as Ibsenesque or Chekhovian, recent studies have been reluctant to pigeonhole her dramaturgy, and her affinity with Bertolt Brecht, Arthur Miller, Williams, and O'Neill has been noted. Her experimental plays are not considered her strongest, yet her attempts at social satire and theatricality over realism have been noted. In addition, Hellman's plays have been studied as precursors to feminism, particularly with respect to the status of her female characters. Finally, because six of her eight original plays (all except *The Children's Hour* and *Days to Come*) are set in the South, Hellman is recognized as an important playwright of the American South.

Hellman's name will be remembered in association with controversy, from the lesbian theme of *The Children's Hour* to the discussion of the truthfulness and style of her memoirs. Most of all, however, she will be remembered for her contributions to the American stage. Hellman always resented being called "the first great American female playwright," for as she said, O'Neill is not remembered as a great American male playwright. Yet, her entry into a male-dominated profession and her ability to become a force on the American stage helped the next generation of women playwrights find a place.

Interviews:

John Phillips and Anne Hollander, "Lillian Hellman," in *Writers at Work: The Paris Review Interviews, Third Series,* edited by George Plimpton (New York: Viking, 1967), pp. 116–140;

Lewis Funke, *Playwrights Talk about Writing: 12 Interviews with Lewis Funke* (Chicago: Dramatic Publishing, 1975), pp. 90–110;

Marsha Norman, "Articles of Faith: A Conversation with Lillian Hellman." *American Theatre,* 1 (May 1984): 10–15;

Jackson Bryer, ed., *Conversations with Lillian Hellman* (Jackson: University Press of Mississippi, 1986).

Bibliographies:

Manfred Triesch, *The Lillian Hellman Collection at the University of Texas* (Austin: Humanities Research Center, University of Texas at Austin, 1966);

Steven H. Bills, *Lillian Hellman: An Annotated Bibliography* (New York: Garland, 1979);

Mark Estrin, *Lillian Hellman: Plays, Films, and Memoirs: A Reference Guide* (Boston: G. K. Hall, 1980);

Mary Marguerite Riordan, *Lillian Hellman: A Bibliography, 1926–1978* (Metuchen, N.J.: Scarecrow Press, 1980);

Barbara Lee Horn, *Lillian Hellman: A Resource and Production Sourcebook* (Westport, Conn.: Greenwood Press, 1998).

Biographies:

Richard Moody, *Lillian Hellman, Playwright* (New York: Pegasus, 1972);

William Wright, *Lillian Hellman: The Image, The Woman* (New York: Simon & Schuster, 1986);

Peter Feibleman, *Lilly: Reminiscences of Lillian Hellman* (New York: Morrow, 1988);

Carl Rollyson, *Lillian Hellman: Her Legend and Her Legacy* (New York: St. Martin's Press, 1988);

Robert P. Newman, *The Cold War Romance of Lillian Hellman and John Melby* (Chapel Hill: University of North Carolina Press, 1989);

Joan Mellen, *Hellman and Hammett: The Legendary Passion of Lillian Hellman and Dashiell Hammett* (New York: HarperCollins, 1996);

Rosemary Mahoney, *A Likely Story: One Summer with Lillian Hellman* (New York: Doubleday, 1998).

References:

Jacob Adler, "Miss Hellman's Two Sisters," *Educational Theatre Journal,* 15 (May 1963): 112–117;

Adler, "The Rose and the Fox: Notes on the Southern Drama," in *South: Modern Southern Literature in its Cultural Setting,* edited by Louis Rubin Jr. and Robert Jacobs (Garden City, N.Y.: Dolphin Books, 1961), pp. 349–375;

Gayle Austin, "The Exchange of Women and Male Homosocial Desire in Arthur Miller's *Death of a Salesman* and Lillian Hellman's *Another Part of the Forest,*" in *Feminist Rereadings of Modern American Drama,* edited by June Schleuter (Rutherford, N.J.: Fairleigh Dickinson University Press, 1989), pp. 54–66;

Judith Barlow, "Into the Foxhole: Feminism, Realism, and Lillian Hellman," in *Realism and the American Dramatic Tradition,* edited by William W. Demastes (Tuscaloosa: University of Alabama Press, 1996), pp. 156–171;

C. W. E. Bigsby, *A Critical Introduction to Twentieth-Century American Drama, 1900–1940* (Cambridge: Cambridge University Press, 1982), pp. 274–297;

Will Brantley, *Feminine Sense in Southern Memoir: Smith, Glasgow, Welty, Hellman, Porter, and Hurston* (Jackson: University Press of Mississippi, 1993);

Mary Lynn Broe, "Bohemia Bumps into Calvin: The Deception of Passivity in Lillian Hellman's Drama," *Southern Quarterly,* 19 (May 1981): 26–41;

Linda Ginter Brown, "A Place at the Table: Hunger as Metaphor in Lillian Hellman's *Days to Come* and Marsha Norman's *'night, Mother,*" in *Marsha Norman: A Casebook,* edited by Brown (New York: Garland, 1996), pp. 197–220;

Barrett H. Clark, "Lillian Hellman," *College English,* 6 (December 1944): 19–24;

Harold Clurman, *On Directing* (New York: Macmillan, 1972), pp. 47–50, 83, 197–205;

Bernard F. Dick, *Hellman in Hollywood* (Rutherford, N.J.: Fairleigh Dickinson University Press, 1982);

Bernard F. Dukore, *American Dramatists 1918–1945* (New York: Grove, 1984), pp. 142–155;

Mark Estrin, ed., *Critical Essays on Lillian Hellman* (Boston: G. K. Hall, 1989);

Doris Falk, *Lillian Hellman* (New York: Ungar, 1978);

Anne Fleche, "The Lesbian Rule: Lillian Hellman and the Measures of Realism," *Modern Drama,* 39, no. 1 (Spring 1996): 16–30;

John Gassner, "Ebb Tide; Lillian Hellman; *The Autumn Garden,*" in his *Theatre at the Crossroads* (New York: Holt, 1960), pp. 132–139;

Gassner, "Lillian Hellman's *Toys in the Attic*," in his *Dramatic Soundings* (New York: Crown, 1968), pp. 481–484;

Charlotte Goodman, "The Fox's Cubs: Lillian Hellman, Arthur Miller, and Tennessee Williams," in *Modern American Drama: The Female Canon*, edited by June Schleuter (Rutherford, N.J.: Fairleigh Dickinson University Press, 1990), pp. 130–142;

Margaret Case Harriman, "Miss Lily of New Orleans," *New Yorker*, 17 (8 November 1941): 22–31;

Lynda Hart, "Canonizing Lesbians?" in *Modern American Drama: The Female Canon*, edited by June Schleuter (Rutherford, N.J.: Fairleigh Dickinson University Press, 1990), pp. 275–292;

W. Kenneth Holditch, "Another Part of the Country: Lillian Hellman as Southern Playwright," *Southern Quarterly*, 15 (Spring 1987): 11–35;

Edith J. R. Isaacs, "Lillian Hellman, A Playwright on the March," *Theatre Arts*, 18 (January 1944): 19–24;

Alfred Kazin, "The Legend of Lillian Hellman," *Esquire*, 99 (August 1977): 28, 30, 34;

Katherine Lederer, *Lillian Hellman* (Boston: Twayne, 1979);

Lagretta Tallent Lenker, "The Foxes in Hellman's Family Forest," in *The Aching Hearth: Family Violence in Life and Literature*, edited by Sara Munson Deats (New York: Plenum, 1991), pp. 241–253;

William Luce, *Lillian: A One-Woman Play Based on the Autobiographical Works of Lillian Hellman* (New York: Dramatists Play Service, 1986);

Bonnie Lyons, "Lillian Hellman: The First Jewish Nun on Prytania Street," in *From Hester Street to Hollywood: The Jewish-American State and Screen*, edited by Sarah Blacher Cohen (Bloomington: Indiana University Press, 1983), pp. 106–122;

Ralph Melnick, *The Stolen Legacy of Anne Frank: Meyer Levin, Lillian Hellman, and the Staging of the Diary* (New Haven: Yale University Press, 1997);

Vivian M. Patraka, "Lillian Hellman's Watch on the Rhine: Realism, Gender, and Historical Crisis," *Modern Drama*, 32 (March 1989): 128–145;

Yvonne Shafer, *American Women Playwrights, 1900–1950* (New York: Peter Lang, 1995), pp. 121–147;

Mary Titus, "Murdering the Lesbian: Lillian Hellman's *The Children's Hour*," *Tulsa Studies in Women's Literature*, 10 (1991): 215–232;

Carol Stongin Tufts, "Who's Lying? The Issue of Lesbianism in Lillian Hellman's *The Children's Hour*," *Minnesota Review*, 53 (1989): 63–78;

Linda Wagner-Martin, "Lillian Hellman: Autobiography and Truth," *Southern Review*, 19 (April 1983): 275–288.

Papers:

The major archive of Lillian Hellman's papers is at the Harry Ransom Humanities Research Center, University of Texas at Austin. Other materials are housed at the Butler Library, Columbia University, and in the Billy Rose Theatre Collection of the Library and Museum of the Performing Arts at Lincoln Center.

Langston Hughes

(1 February 1902 – 22 May 1967)

Deborah Martinson
Occidental College

See also the Hughes entries in *DLB 4: American Writers in Paris, 1920–1939; DLB 7: Twentieth-Century American Dramatists; DLB 48: American Poets, 1880–1945, Second Series; DLB 51: Afro-American Writers from the Harlem Renaissance to 1940;* and *DLB 86: American Short-Story Writers, 1910–1945, First Series.*

PLAY PRODUCTIONS: *Scottsboro Limited,* Los Angeles, 8 May 1932;

Mulatto, revised version, New York, Vanderbilt Theatre, 24 October 1935; original version, Cleveland, Karamu House, 1939;

Little Ham, Cleveland, Karamu House, 24 March 1936;

When the Jack Hollers, by Hughes and Arna Bontemps, Cleveland, Karamu House, 28 April 1936;

Troubled Island, Cleveland, Karamu House, 18 November 1936; opera version, libretto by Hughes, music by William Grant Still, New York, New York City Center, 31 March 1949;

Joy to My Soul, Cleveland, Karamu House, 1 April 1937;

Soul Gone Home, Cleveland, Cleveland Federal Theatre, 1937;

Don't You Want To Be Free?, New York, Harlem I.W.O. Community Center, 24 April 1938;

Front Porch, Cleveland, Karamu House, 16 November 1938;

The Organizer, libretto by Hughes, music by James P. Johnson, New York, Harlem Suitcase Theatre, March 1939;

Cavalcade of the Negro Theater, by Hughes and Bontemps, Chicago, American Negro Exposition, 4 July 1940;

Tropics after Dark, Chicago, American Negro Exposition, 4 July 1940;

That Eagle, New York, Stage Door Canteen, 1942;

The Sun Do Move, Chicago, Good Shepherd Community Center, 30 April 1942;

For This We Fight, New York, Madison Square Garden, 7 June 1943;

Langston Hughes (from Langston Hughes and Milton Meltzer, Black Magic, *1967)*

Street Scene, by Elmer Rice, music by Kurt Weill, lyrics by Hughes, New York, Adelphi Theatre, 9 January 1947;

The Barrier, libretto by Hughes, music by Jan Meyerowitz, New York, Columbia University, January 1950; New York, Broadhurst Theatre, 2 November 1950;

Just Around the Corner, by Amy Mann and Bernard Drew, lyrics by Hughes, Ogunguit, Maine, Ogunguit Playhouse, Summer 1951;

Esther, libretto by Hughes, music by Jan Meyerowitz, Urbana, University of Illinois, March 1957;

Simply Heavenly, New York, Eighty-fifth Street Playhouse, 21 May 1957; New York, Playhouse Theatre, 20 August 1957 (transferred 8 November 1957 to Renata Theatre);

The Ballad of the Brown King, libretto by Hughes, music by Margaret Bonds, New York, Clark Auditorium, New York City YMCA, 11 December 1960;

Black Nativity, New York, Forty-first Street Theatre, 11 December 1961;

Gospel Glow, Brooklyn, New York, Washington Temple, October 1962;

Tambourines to Glory, music by Jobe Huntley, New York, Little Theatre, 2 November 1963;

Let Us Remember Him, libretto by Hughes, music by David Amram, San Francisco, War Memorial Opera House, 15 November 1963;

Jerico-Jim Crow, New York, The Sanctuary (Greenwich Mews), 12 January 1964;

The Prodigal Son, New York, Greenwich Mews Theatre, 20 May 1965;

Mule Bone, by Hughes and Zora Neale Hurston, music by Taj Mahal, New York, Lincoln Center, Ethel Barrymore Theater, February 1991.

BOOKS: *The Weary Blues* (New York: Knopf, 1926; London: Knopf, 1926);

Fine Clothes to the Jew (New York: Knopf, 1927; London: Knopf, 1927);

Not Without Laughter (New York & London: Knopf, 1930; London: Allen & Unwin, 1930);

Dear Lovely Death (Amenia, N.Y.: Privately printed at Troutbect Press, 1931);

The Negro Mother and Other Dramatic Recitations (New York: Golden Stair Press, 1931);

The Dream Keeper and Other Poems (New York: Knopf, 1932);

Scottsboro Limited: Four Poems and a Play in Verse (New York: Golden Stair Press, 1932); *Popo and Fifina: Children of Haiti,* by Hughes and Arna Bontemps (New York: Macmillan, 1932);

A Negro Looks at Soviet Central Asia (Moscow & Leningrad: Co-operative Publishing Society of Foreign Workers in the U.S.S.R., 1934);

The Ways of White Folks (New York: Knopf, 1934; London: Allen & Unwin, 1934);

A New Song (New York: International Workers Order, 1938);

The Big Sea: An Autobiography (New York & London: Knopf, 1940; London: Hutchinson, 1940);

Shakespeare in Harlem (New York: Knopf, 1942);

Freedom's Plow (New York: Musette, 1943);

Jim Crow's Last Stand (Atlanta: Negro Publication Society of America, 1943);

Lament for Dark Peoples and Other Poems (N.p., 1944);

Fields of Wonder (New York: Knopf, 1947);

One-Way Ticket (New York: Knopf, 1949);

Troubled Island, libretto by Hughes, music by William Grant Still (New York: Leeds Music, 1949);

Simple Speaks His Mind (New York: Simon & Schuster, 1950; London: Gollancz, 1951);

Montage of a Dream Deferred (New York: Holt, 1951);

Laughing to Keep from Crying (New York: Holt, 1952);

The First Book of Negroes (New York: Franklin Watts, 1952; London: Bailey & Swinfen, 1956);

Simple Takes A Wife (New York: Simon & Schuster, 1953; London: Gollancz, 1954);

The Glory Round His Head, libretto by Hughes, music by Jan Meyerowitz (New York: Broude Brothers, 1953);

Famous American Negroes (New York: Dodd, Mead, 1954);

The First Book of Rhythms (New York: Franklin Watts, 1954; London: Bailey & Swinfen, 1956);

The First Book of Jazz (New York: Franklin Watts, 1955; London: Bailey & Swinfen, 1957);

Famous Negro Music Makers (New York: Dodd, Mead, 1955);

The Sweet Flypaper of Life, text by Hughes, photographs by Roy DeCarava (New York: Simon & Schuster, 1955);

The First Book of the West Indies (New York: Franklin Watts, 1956; London: Bailey & Swinfen, 1956); republished as *The First Book of the Caribbean* (London: Edmund Ward, 1965);

I Wonder As I Wander: An Autobiographical Journey (New York & Toronto: Rinehart, 1956);

A Pictorial History of the Negro in America, by Hughes and Milton Meltzer (New York: Crown, 1956; revised, 1963; revised again, 1968); revised again as *A Pictorial History of Black Americans,* by Hughes, Meltzer, and C. Eric Lincoln (New York: Crown, 1973);

Simple Stakes a Claim (New York & Toronto: Rinehart, 1957; London: Gollancz, 1958);

The Langston Hughes Reader (New York: Braziller, 1958);

Famous Negro Heroes of America (New York: Dodd, Mead, 1958);

Tambourines to Glory (New York: John Day, 1958; London: Gollancz, 1959);

Selected Poems of Langston Hughes (New York: Knopf, 1959);

Simply Heavenly, book and lyrics by Hughes, music by David Martin (New York: Dramatists Play Service, 1959);

The First Book of Africa (New York: Franklin Watts, 1960; London: Mayflower, 1961; revised, New York: Franklin Watts, 1964);

The Best of Simple (New York: Hill & Wang, 1961);

Ask Your Mama: 12 Moods for Jazz (New York: Knopf, 1961);

The Ballad of the Brown King, libretto by Hughes, music by Margaret Bonds (New York: Sam Fox, 1961);

Fight for Freedom: The Story of the NAACP (New York: Norton, 1962);

Something in Common and Other Stories (New York: Hill & Wang, 1963);

Five Plays by Langston Hughes, edited by Webster Smalley (Bloomington: Indiana University Press, 1963)—comprises *Mulatto, Little Ham, Soul Gone Home, Simply Heavenly,* and *Tambourines to Glory;*

Simple's Uncle Sam (New York: Hill & Wang, 1965);

The Panther and the Lash: Poems of Our Times (New York: Knopf, 1967);

Black Magic: A Pictorial History of the Negro in American Entertainment, by Hughes and Meltzer (Englewood Cliffs, N.J.: Prentice-Hall, 1967);

Black Misery (New York: Knopf, 1969);

Don't You Turn Back: Poems, edited by Lee Bennett Hopkins (New York: Knopf, 1969);

Good Morning Revolution: Uncollected Social Protest Writings by Langston Hughes, edited by Faith Berry (New York & Westport, Conn.: Lawrence Hill, 1973);

Mule Bone: A Comedy of Negro Life, by Hughes and Zora Neale Hurston, edited by George Houston Bass and Henry Louis Gates Jr. (New York: HarperPerennial, 1991).

SELECTED PERIODICAL PUBLICATIONS–UNCOLLECTED: *The Gold Piece, Brownies' Book,* 2 (July 1921): 191–194;

Angelo Herndon Jones: A One-Act Play, New Theatre (January 1936);

Don't You Want to be Free?, One-Act Play Magazine (October 1938): 359–393;

"Private Jim Crow," *Negro Story,* 1 (May–June 1945): 3–9.

PRODUCED SCRIPTS: *Way Down South,* motion picture, by Hughes and Clarence Muse, RKO, 1939;

Jubilee: A Cavalcade of the Negro Theater, radio, by Hughes and Arna Bontemps, CBS Showcase, 1941;

Strollin Twenties, television, 1966.

Langston Hughes's reputation as one of the most innovative American poets may be one reason he has largely been ignored as a significant playwright. He did not primarily identify himself as a playwright, writing in a variety of literary genres. Other forces also contributed to the relative lack of recognition for Hughes's talents in the dramatic genre, such as his emphasis on writing for and about African Americans as distinct historically and culturally. White dramatic circles of American cities were anything but color-blind throughout the period of the 1930s to the 1960s, when his plays were first written and produced. Political events influenced play production a great deal during these decades: the Depression and the attendant leftist movements of the 1930s, the war years of the 1940s, the McCarthy hearings targeting entertainment personalities in the 1950s, and the political divisions of the 1960s. Yet, throughout this time, talented playwrights such as Hughes were

Hughes with his mother, Carrie, 1902

contributing much to the vitality of Broadway and the cultural innovations Americans take for granted. Additionally, Hughes's collaborations with other playwrights and his efforts to establish African American theaters throughout the United States strengthened American drama in immeasurable ways. Though he was not widely acknowledged as a dramatist, Hughes's talent in the dramatic genre and his influence as a playwright are remarkable; his staging brought the artistry, vitality, and humanity of African Americans to increasingly wide audiences.

James Langston Hughes—named after his father, James, and his maternal grandfather, Charles Langston—was born in Joplin, Missouri, on 1 February 1902. His family soon moved, and Langston, as he was called from the beginning, grew up in Lawrence, Kansas. He was raised primarily by his maternal grandmother, Mary Sampson Patterson Leary Langston, and his upbringing was characterized by frequent moves and familial upheaval and also by a prevailing familial expectation of his success. His father, a professional man prevented from

Playbill for the 1935 New York production of Hughes's play about miscegenation in the South

taking the bar exam because he was black, abandoned the family when Hughes was five years old, immigrating to Mexico to better his lot in a society less bound by racial restrictions. Hughes's mother, Carrie, refusing her husband's half-hearted attempts to bring the family to live in Mexico, traveled from city to city finding jobs as a journalist and stenographer. Carrie, educated and ambitious, needed mobility to escape the plight of many young black women who were relegated to domestic service. She sometimes sent for Hughes, but most often she left him with his grandmother. The family nevertheless had high hopes for him partly because his ancestors were

well-respected, and also because they recognized his intelligence was exceptional.

Hughes discovered at an early age that reading was an antidote to loneliness. His interest in drama likewise began during his childhood as his mother, who had a "taste for musicals, plays, novels, and plain fun," often took Hughes to the theater. She also challenged the segregated school system in Topeka and enrolled Hughes in a "white" first grade. After his grandmother's death Hughes moved to Cleveland, where he attended Central High, possibly the best public school in the city. A top student, Hughes was popular and respected, chosen as the yearbook editor and class poet.

After graduation he traveled to Mexico to convince his father—from whom he was often estranged—to send him to Columbia University. During the year he spent with his father Hughes taught English and became a published writer, with work appearing in two periodicals of the National Association for the Advancement of Colored People (NAACP): the *Brownie's Book* and *Crisis*. His "The Negro Speaks of Rivers" (1921) is still one of the most anthologized poems in American letters.

Despite his success, Hughes's year in Mexico convinced him that he must go to a college in the United States. At Columbia University, however, he became disenchanted with his separation from what he considered "real life," and he dropped out to spend more time in Harlem with other urban blacks. The Harlem Renaissance, in full swing by the mid 1920s, fueled his artistic desires and talents. During this period Hughes established lifelong relationships with African American intellectuals and artists. After a few years of travel in the United States and Europe he returned to college in 1926 with a scholarship funded by Amy Spingarn of the NAACP. He graduated in 1929 from Lincoln College, an all-black institution in Pennsylvania. Though he received his formal education at Lincoln, he acquired much of his dramatic education during that influential first year at Columbia University: "college, (horrible place but I wanted to go), Broadway and the theatres—delightful memories, Riverside Drive in the mist and Harlem. A whirling year in New York."

Hughes's love for the theater flourished in Harlem and was manifested in his participation in urban theatrical projects from the late 1920s onward. He ultimately wrote more than twenty plays, at least a dozen of which were theatrical collaborations with others. Additionally, the segregationist practices of mainstream theaters and the necessity for playwrights, actors, and producers in particular to have ties to established theater networks in order to find opportunities for work led Hughes to become involved in production. He established three theatrical groups: the Suitcase Theatre in Harlem, the New Negro Theatre in Los Angeles, and the Skyloft Players of the Good Shepherd Community House in Chicago. Hughes, a frequent traveler, also worked with many drama companies worldwide, even becoming an honorary member of the Tsukuji-za Theater in Tokyo in 1933. The theaters of other countries offered Hughes opportunities to learn about alternate dramatic staging. Many foreign theaters also were quite receptive to translations of work published in America, sometimes producing Hughes's work before it found a venue in the United States.

Hughes's intended audience was narrow in his early career: he wrote primarily for a black urban audience. At times he aimed his work at middle-class blacks, who, he felt, "needed a legitimate literary artist to sanction the folk materials for them"; at other times he was more interested in the men and women in the Harlem neighborhoods. Later, as he became part of the radical left in the 1930s, he wrote for the "black masses." As he became better known, he targeted Broadway, thus including whites as well as blacks in his concept of audience. For the largest part of his career, however, his strong ties to the black urban community led him to write plays that appealed to small playhouses in Harlem and other American cities such as Cleveland, Chicago, and Los Angeles rather than theaters on Broadway in New York City. In all of his theatrical productions and writings he attempted to present, in various black idioms, the humanity and authenticity of urban blacks.

Influenced by Alain Locke's 1925 anthology *The New Negro,* Hughes responded by reinterpreting black experience to promote positive identity for the African American and to subvert white stereotypes of "Negroes." He also experimented in order to embrace those the black elite would rather obscure. The criticism each Hughes production brought from one group or another even within the African American population shows the difficulty of writing for the stage during this era. African Americans could not agree on what an authentic black production should be, and because of racism prevalent in American culture, they were especially sensitive to what audiences made of black representations. This critical judgment from all sides did not diminish Hughes's efforts to portray the African American spirit and culture in various ways. Many of Hughes's dramas remain unproduced—and unpublished in some cases. Increasing critical recognition of his contributions may, however, lead to production and publication of some of these works.

Hughes's first published play was *The Gold Piece* (1921), written when he was nineteen, during his year-long stint with his father in Mexico. Its publication in the *Brownies' Book,* a children's magazine established by W. E. B. Du Bois, fueled his efforts to return to the United States for college. The play, only a few pages long, is a moral tale of a peasant couple who acquire a gold piece. At first the couple, Pablo and Rosa, talk of all they could buy and all they could do with such wealth. But on meeting a poor woman who could cure her son's blindness if she had the money for a doctor, the couple give the gold piece to her. Though Hughes had earlier written rather bleak short stories and poems, this short play demonstrates his more characteristic optimism.

Hughes began work on his best-known play, *Mulatto,* in 1930, shortly after his graduation from Lincoln. Bert Lewis is one of four children born to Colonel Norwood and his black mistress, Cora Lewis. The racial codes of the South render Bert fatherless and powerless to change his relationship to the household, a relationship that makes him furious with frustration. Forced to enter the house by the servants' door and to pretend a humility he does not feel, Bert gets into an argument with his arrogant white father. Much alike in temperament, the two battle furiously, with Bert ultimately killing the colonel. Bert commits suicide to avoid a lynch mob that wants to hang him as an example to others as "uppity" as he; Bert's mother, Cora, is driven mad by the horror of the events. While the plot is melodramatic, as some critics complained, its wrenching themes are neither trite nor exaggerated. The colonel, too, is deprived of a life of emotional satisfaction. His white privilege and his subsequent ambivalence toward blacks rob him of his pride in his mistress and his children. Thus, racism separates him also from sympathetic human interaction. Cora seems most tragic of all the characters, as her life—over which she has had little control—comes tumbling down on her because of societal insistence on racial division and hierarchies.

Hughes's themes include the problems of racism: African Americans' lack of identity, property, visibility, and the right to speak and act. But the play also elicits the human sympathy necessary to mitigate more universal problems: relationships between fathers and sons, the sanctity of the body, hatred and love, and violence. Mulatto, the mixture of black and white races, signifies the beauty of brotherhood as much as it symbolizes the problems of an individual neither black nor white. A line in *Mulatto* illustrates this theme: "Them de ways o' de South—mixtries, mixtries."

The Broadway production of *Mulatto* in 1935 served neither Hughes nor his play, however. Criticized as "sensational," "melodramatic," and "propaganda," the production was not as Hughes had intended; producer Martin Jones rewrote large parts of it, added a gratuitous rape scene, and emphasized sexual aspects to draw a Broadway audience. Hughes was in Europe during the rehearsal and much of the production of *Mulatto* and failed to influence Jones to remedy the excesses. Still, *Mulatto* ran for 373 performances, second only to Lorraine Hansberry's *A Raisin in the Sun* (1959) for longest Broadway run by an African American playwright. After its close in New York, it ran eight months in other American cities. *Mulatto* was translated into several languages and published in other countries, but it was not published in English until 1963, in *Five Plays by Langston Hughes*, edited by Webster Smalley. This production of *Mulatto* established Hughes's reputation as a successful but not a serious nor particularly talented playwright.

Hughes's next foray in writing for the theater, a folk comedy called *Mule Bone* (1991), is still mired in controversy. The play was written jointly with Zora

Poster for the 1938 Harlem Suitcase Theatre production of the one-act play in which Hughes traces the history of African Americans from the early days of slavery to the Great Depression (Beinecke Rare Book and Manuscript Library, Yale University)

Neale Hurston, whom Hughes much admired, in 1930. Hughes was to do a plot outline and structure the dialogue, while Hurston was to give the dialogue its "Southern flavor and many of the wise-cracks," as he wrote to his friend Carl Van Vechten on 16 January 1931. The plot, which came from a folk story Hurston had collected, is simple. In the story, two hunters quarrel over who shot a wild turkey, and one of the hunters finally wields a hockbone and knocks out the other. The guilty hunter is tried for assault and battery and is exiled by the town. The court sees the incident as an example of the biblical parable of Samson and the ass's jawbone. In the play, the cause of the quarrel is changed to jealousy over a fickle woman.

Arnold Rampersad, Hughes's biographer, admits that much of *Mule Bone* must have been Hurston's, as it exemplifies her "farcical style." Nevertheless, Rampersad asserts that Hughes's work on the play was considerable. After a break in Hughes and Hurston's relationship that seemed more personal than professional, Hughes discovered that Hurston had finished the play and sold it to the Gilpin Players of Cleveland without Hughes's name on it as joint author. The break in their relationship was never mended, and Hurston withdrew the play. It was not produced until the 1991 New York City Lincoln Center production, where it was billed as *Mule Bone: A Comedy of Negro Life,* by Hughes and Hurston.

In the winter of 1930 Hughes broke not only with Hurston but also with his literary patron, Charlotte Mason. Shortly after the *Mule Bone* debacle, Hughes's creative fervor and leftist politics were ignited by the Scottsboro controversy. In March 1931, nine young black men were pulled off a train in Paint Rock, Alabama, and taken to jail in Scottsboro. Two white women on the train who had disguised themselves as men accused the nine of raping them. In the resulting trial, surrounded by a mob of ten thousand, the court sentenced one of the men to life imprisonment but condemned the other eight to death in the electric chair. Aligning himself with the radical International Labor Defense Association (ILDA), which took a strong opposing position, Hughes wrote his protest in the subsequent drama, *Scottsboro Limited.* Published in *New Masses* in November 1931, it was first performed–with Hughes participating in its production–in May 1932 at a mass meeting called to protest the Scottsboro verdicts.

The one-act play "in verse" includes choral sections that represent the voices of the people raised in protest. Hughes's innovations in the play exemplify his exploration of a black rhetoric: incantatory rhythms, patterned repetitions, and audience response. Hughes also uses a bare stage to emphasize the travesty of the trial, and a single white man to represent all the roles of the oppressive system. The play ends melodramatically, with the black characters smashing the electric chair while an audience yells "Fight, Fight, Fight." Hughes ends the act with "the red flag raised above the heads of the black and white workers together." While the play obviously was written as a protest piece and became communist propaganda under the influence of the ILDA, Hughes never joined the Communist Party, nor did he again write stage scenes with this kind of overt violence. The Scottsboro incident did, however, begin Hughes's lifelong affinity with leftist politics.

Hughes, surrounded by personal and political controversy, decided in 1932 to leave the United States and go to Russia with a group of moviemakers to put together a movie called "Black and White." While nothing came of the project, Hughes traveled throughout the world viewing dramatic productions and

immersing himself in the literary cultures of Russia, Korea, Japan, China, and Europe. He traveled much of the time with the reporter and writer Arthur Koestler. During this trip Hughes fell in love with dancer Sylvia Chen; this relationship, which ended in 1934, is one of the few love affairs of his that can be documented, because Hughes was reserved about his private life. Hughes wrote many essays during this trip; some for *Izvestia* were published in Moscow as *A Negro Looks at Soviet Central Asia* (1934). He also completed translations of some of Boris Pasternak's and Vladimir Mayakovsky's poems, as well as writing several of his own. The fourteen-month trip did not inspire Hughes to write any new dramas, but he did credit his fascination with and later use of theater in the round to his seeing it used so effectively in Russia.

Hughes returned to San Francisco, immersing himself in writing and leftist politics. During this period he wrote a one-act militant play, *Angelo Herndon Jones* (1936), for which he won a $50 prize from the *New Theatre* magazine. When no money arrived, and the producer of *Mulatto* also failed to pay him, Hughes wrote on 20 January 1936 to literary agent Maxim Lieber: "What is it about the theatre, right, left, or otherwise that makes it so loath to give up its cash?" For *Angelo Herndon Jones* he was inspired by the actual story of a young black communist from Ohio who supposedly incited an insurrection while leading a political march for relief of the black plight. As he did in *Scottsboro Limited,* Hughes calls for a stark, plain set. The plot, too, is simple, involving a protest planned by Buddy, a youth ultimately condemned by a racist society for his wanting to help others of his race who are about to be evicted. Hughes's failure to gain financially from this protest play and other radical writings shifted his emphasis in subsequent plays. He always felt the need for radical changes in society's treatment of his race; but he needed financial gain if he were to continue to write. His talent transcended writing propaganda and protest, and his spirit of hope and optimism in his people also could not easily be quenched. He thus turned to comedy and writing about blacks for blacks.

Little Ham (1936), Hughes's first foray into writing comedy for the theater, was soon followed by *When the Jack Hollers* (1936), a collaboration with Arna Bontemps, and *Joy to My Soul* (1937). *Little Ham,* set in the Harlem Renaissance of the 1920s, and Hughes's other social comedies were produced by the Gilpin Players in the Karamu House in Cleveland. In these plays Hughes saw his opportunity to express "in one of its most distinctive forms, laughter and the rich language and styles that make laughter culturally significant." While the comedies were generally well received by audiences, black critics vary considerably in assessing their worth,

Advertisement for the 1957 New York production of Hughes's dramatic adaptation of his humorous sketches about the character Jesse B. Simple (James Weldon Johnson Collection, Beinecke Rare Book and Manuscript Library, Yale University)

seeing problems in Hughes's choice of farce rather than "some more elegant version of comedy." Commentary on *Little Ham* is representative of the division of critical opinion about what an African American play should portray. Darwin T. Turner calls *Little Ham* a "slow-moving and frequently dull attempt to present within a single play all of the exotic elements which distinguish life in Harlem from the rest of America." Smalley, on the other hand, noted in his introduction to *Five Plays by Langston Hughes* the liveliness of *Little Ham:* "it is a high-spirited revel and should be accepted as just that."

Little Ham has a large cast of urban types, from Madam Lucille Bell, proprietress of a shoe-shining parlor turned numbers shop, to Little Hamlet Jones, a shoe shiner and ladies' man. Hughes builds in much high and low humor, almost in a classical sense. Little Ham's small stature contrasts with his girlfriend Tiny Lee's large size, creating a love story of absurd images. The entire plot consists of a myriad of characters breaking love promises while several women compete for Little Ham's affection. The couples participate in a Charleston contest, which the jealousy of Tiny's former lover threatens to ruin, but Ham and Tiny win the contest in an unlikely ending. Interspersed in all this satiric love-play are numbers gangsters and cons, what Turner called "shadows of a troubled world." The economic woes of the characters cannot be ignored, nor can the intrusion of the white world of law and corruption. Despite elements of a harsh reality, *Little Ham* is primarily an affectionate and exuberant social satire; the emphasis is not on character, but on humor and language. Hughes uses Harlem dialects and wordplay to heighten the humor and draws on religious and economic allusions to render the specificity of the Harlem culture.

In *When the Jack Hollers,* set in the Mississippi Delta, Hughes and Bontemps capture another richly complex black culture, that of a sharecropping community. In doing so, they depict as well the problems of poverty and racism. In all of these comedies Hughes uses the rhythms and themes of the blues to express the joy and melancholy of being black. Though his plots are simple, he draws their major component from both economic and love blues.

Hughes's short play *Soul Gone Home* (1937) is a far darker representation of Hughes's turn to social satire. Rowena Jelliffe, founder of the Karamu Theater, considered *Soul Gone Home* far superior to Hughes's more raucous comedies. The play opens with a mother mourning her son, who has died from malnutrition and neglect. Lazarus-like, he comes alive briefly to charge her with never caring for him. The comedy that arises from her worry that his accusations defy the decorum of death is harsh rather than maudlin. When a white ambulance driver comes to take the son away, the mother paints her face white and leaves for another night on the street as a prostitute, struggling to survive as her son could not. Her despair and her use of "white" cosmetics to sell herself show Hughes's bitter irony concerning the black family's economic plight and subsequent efforts to maintain dignity.

Similarly, the exaggerated and grotesque *Joy to My Soul* crudely satirizes mainstream stereotypes about blacks, but white audiences seemed to miss the satire, while black audiences were not pleased with the depictions, however much they enjoyed the dark humor. The main character, from Shadow Gut, Texas, is wealthy but rather stupid, and bumbles his way through Harlem culture.

Front Porch (1938) also shows Hughes's examination of the bleaker world brought about by the Depression. It is a dark, unfocused play intended by Hughes to satirize the black bourgeois, but its bleak plot of middle-class snobs and their snubbing of poorer brethren is overdrawn, and the Harper family seems more melodramatic than satiric. Though neither *Joy to My Soul* nor *Front Porch* had much success in Cleveland, they show Hughes's attempt to depict tragic circumstances within which the characters use comedy as a means to cope. Hughes often used this method to show the African American art of balancing mere survival with the ability to maintain some joy in living.

Even as Hughes decided to turn to comedy, he also chose during this period to try to produce a play he had been writing and revising for nearly ten years: *Troubled Island* (1936), first called "Drums of Haiti." This "singing play" was epic in proportion, with at least sixty-five actors and dancers. The play was soon reworked by Hughes as the libretto of an opera scored by William Grant Still. *Troubled Island* addresses the Haitian revolution and Jean Jacques Dessalines, a Haitian leader of the slave rebellion, who became emperor. In Hughes's play, later revised as *Emperor of Haiti* (1963), Dessalines falls because of his failure to stand by his black, uneducated wife, foolishly turning to another woman who has been appropriated by the mulattoes who seek to overthrow him. This play has both artistic and historical flaws, but nevertheless some critics call it one of Hughes's best plays.

A personal issue for Hughes while producing this play was his involvement with the ambitious and light-skinned actress Elsie Roxborough. Though she pressed for marriage, Roxborough could not convince the cool Hughes, who insisted in a 27 March 1937 article in the *Baltimore Afro-American* that there was "little compatibility between poetry and marriage." Although he never exhibited much passion for her, he claimed he cared for her a great deal. When she left for California and later New York, "passing" as white to further her career, Hughes was greatly disappointed and disturbed. The fact that Hughes never married, and his guarded response to questions about his personal life, have led many to speculate that Hughes was homosexual. Because of his colossal reserve about these matters, nothing is certain except his passion for his people and his writing.

Hughes continued to experiment with various kinds of historical and comic drama in the hopes of gaining both commercial and artistic success. Disappointed with the reception of his plays and out of sorts personally and politically, Hughes left for Paris in 1937 and then went to Spain to show his support for the International Brigade's war with Francisco Franco. The three-month trip revived his creative spirit and his political sensibilities.

Hughes had become aware that black playwrights could not depend on Broadway for success. His primary venue, the Gilpin Players at the Karamu Theater in Cleveland, was far removed from the urban landscapes of many blacks. The Federal Theater launched by Franklin Delano Roosevelt's "New Deal" had become the only serious theater venue for black performers. Hughes had been an important influence in its establishment, but its influence was limited: the Harlem unit had recently changed producers and emphasized protest plays at the expense of those providing entertainment. This shift limited its popularity and its accessibility to black playwrights. Thus, in 1938 Hughes launched his own theater: the Harlem Suitcase Theater.

Desiring to keep his political edge and in need of money, Hughes finished a one-act play, *Don't You Want to Be Free?* (1938), drawn from the poems in his 1938 volume, *A New Song.* Calling this play a poetic drama, Hughes connects the history of African Americans from their earliest beginnings in America as slaves to their less institutionalized enslavement in the Depression. The drama poetically narrates empowering scenes from black history, recounts the strengths of heroes such as Nat Turner and Sojourner Truth, and makes use of the black artistry of spirituals, blues, and idiomatic speech. Hughes's description of the play, which appears before the dialogue begins, is: "From Slavery / Through the Blues / To Now—and then some! With Singing, Music, and Dancing." The play continues Hughes's themes of economic blues, and he incorporates the "call and response" of black rhetoric, using musical history to address symbolic episodes of historic atrocity: lynchings, rapes, discrimination, and Jim Crow laws. Hughes used the blues in this play to define African American experience: "The blues is songs folks make up when their heart hurts . . . . Colored folks made the Blues! / Now everybody sings 'em. We made 'em out of being

poor and lonely. And homes busted up, and desperate and broke." The artistry of this play, which was staged by the Harlem Suitcase Theatre group at the Harlem I.W.O. Community Center, restored Hughes's sense of dramatic innovation. The unprecedented run of 1,935 performances led to other little theater projects such as the New Negro Theater in Los Angeles and the Skyloft Players of the Good Shepherd Community House in Chicago. This period, from 1939 through the early 1940s, was extremely busy for Hughes. He involved himself in many of the Federal Theater projects, tried to manage the Harlem Suitcase Theater, and traveled extensively from Cleveland to California to Illinois to New York—wherever black producers and playwrights needed him. Hughes's contribution to the theater clearly was not confined to his role of playwright.

Following the themes and methods of *Don't You Want To Be Free?*, Hughes's later *The Sun Do Move* (1942) continues his use of the dramatic musical format, which seemed best suited to his talents. Two Negro porters strip to assert their racial identity, and then the play shifts to the slave auction of Rock and Mary. Rock is sold before he is able to see the birth of his child and endures not only separation from his family but also the dysfunctions of slave life imposed by white masters as he makes failed escape attempts. Finally, Rock and Mary reunite, and Quakers help them achieve freedom. More focused than Hughes's earlier pageant, *The Sun Do Move* dramatizes the struggle of individuals caught in history.

During the World War II years, as his radical leftist politics waned, Hughes began increasing his collaboration on theatrical productions. His fame for the excellence of his poetry and for his promotion and innovation in musical theater had spread. This aspect of Hughes's career is often neglected in assessing his talents, but is one that commends him to theatrical history perhaps even more than his own original dramas. With Arna Bontemps, Hughes wrote *Cavalcade of the Negro Theater* in 1940 for the American Negro Exposition in Chicago. Bontemps and Hughes adapted this script for radio, calling it *Jubilee: A Cavalcade of the Negro Theater.* Hughes's revue *Tropics After Dark* was also produced for the exposition, though it was later stripped of his lyrics and had the setting changed to a beer hall. Hughes also wrote many radio scripts for the war effort in 1940, and in 1942 he wrote *That Eagle,* a patriotic play with music, to be performed at the Stage Door Canteen in New York. His creativity and expanding repertory, however, were not confined to either the war effort or exposition showcases.

The traditional stage still had much appeal for Hughes, and his collaborations gained him better access to theaters and audiences. For Elmer Rice's

Street Scene (1947), Hughes wrote the lyrics to Kurt Weill's music. This production, with an integrated cast, gave rise to many other productions of *Street Scene* in New York City. Hughes wrote the libretto for *The Barrier* (1950), adapted from his poem "Cross" and his play *Mulatto,* with music by Jan Meyerowitz. *The Barrier* was produced twice in 1950, by the Columbia University Opera Workshop and subsequently on Broadway. Lesser known is a 1951 production in Ogunquit Playhouse in Maine of Amy Mann and Bernard Drew's *Just Around the Corner,* with lyrics by Hughes. He also found others eager to add their own talents to his in the interest of theatrical success. The poems collected in his *Shakespeare in Harlem* (1942) were adapted for the stage by Robert Glenn in 1956, a production criticized as showing Hughes's lack of global awareness, but one that has played throughout the world. (This criticism of Hughes as too parochial actually came at the same time as the House Un-American Activities Committee was accusing him of sending political books to leftist groups in other countries. He denied the charges and was exonerated.)

An unlikely project for Hughes, but one that expressed his respect for Jews, was his 1957 libretto *Esther,* again with music by Meyerowitz. It was a great success—perhaps because, as Hughes himself said, it had a "Jewish theme, Gentile cast, cullud lyrics! American! By a Hebrew Catholic." Hughes called himself a "literary sharecropper," but he was much more than that. As further scholarly inquiry is done on Hughes's dramatic career, new evidence of his extensive collaborative efforts, particularly in writing lyrics for others, continues to surface. He began to make use of collaborators for his own scripts as well, to enhance the range and appeal of the productions. Music by David Martin, for example, accompanied his play *Simply Heavenly* (1957), which he adapted from the collections of his Jesse B. Semple ("Simple") sketches that first appeared in the *Chicago Defender.*

Hughes's Simple sketches gave him a venue for presenting the humanity and warmth of the black population to a wider audience. Through Simple's adventures, Hughes presents the cultural distinctiveness of African Americans in a humorous, affectionate way. Simple is no buffoon, despite his human frailties. He is a philosopher of sorts, pondering the difficulties of being black in a white society, of men loving women, of finding joy in sorry circumstances. The Simple sketches drew considerable acclaim, and reviews of *Simply Heavenly* were positive, praising Hughes's humor and his love for the Harlem culture so vividly depicted. Some black critics, however, argued that Simple on stage did not exhibit the philosophical intelligence and complexity evident in the written texts. They objected to the

Hilda Simms in the 1963 New York production of Tambourines to Glory *(from Langston Hughes and Milton Meltzer,* Black Magic, *1967)*

black characters as stereotypical and not accurately reflecting the lives of African Americans. Still, the play survived the closing of the playhouse and was produced again at the Forty-eighth Street Playhouse.

Despite increasing racial unrest and radicalism in the early 1960s, Hughes continued his quest to present culturally rich black theater to America. In the context of increasing civil rights activity, Hughes found that neither black nor white audiences could agree on appropriate staged depictions of race. Critics decried his characters as too stereotypical or lacking complexity. Nevertheless, Hughes's gospel plays, written during this period, are among his most successful, drawing again from the history, culture, and music of urban blacks. *Tambourines to Glory* (1963) brings together the strands of Hughes's dramatic methods and themes. The play, adapted from Hughes's 1958 novel of the same name, with music by Jobe Huntley, brings gospel singing to the stage. For three years after completing the play, Hughes endeavored unsuccessfully to get a producer for it. Hughes had just finished writing *Jerico-Jim Crow* (1964), an entertaining but serious play about the civil rights movement, when he heard that Louis Hexter, a Texas millionaire, had agreed to put up the money for the production of *Tambourines to Glory* in November 1963.

The play depicts a black neighborhood church where spirituality and the power of the gospel singing bring a message of hope. But Hughes also develops a less sanguine depiction of storefront religion. Essie Johnson's goodness and self-sacrifice serve as a model of Christian faith and generosity. Her partner, Laura Reed, however, uses the church for economic gain, shamelessly exploiting its members by selling fake holy water and using her sermons to sell "numbers." Buddy Lomax, a personification of the devil, shows his skepticism and the ease of corrupting sinners in a church setting. Good does prevail, however, and although Laura murders Buddy in fear and jealousy, she turns herself in to save Essie. Despite Hughes's melodramatic last act, the characters and the church are realistically drawn.

Other productions combining gospel music with a story show Hughes's great interest in the gospel as more about people, music, and hope than about any doctrinaire religion. Many of these gospel plays are still performed: *The Ballad of the Brown King,* first produced in 1960; *Black Nativity* (1961); *Gospel Glow* (1962); *Let Us Remember Him* (1963); and finally *The Prodigal Son* (1965), a "swinging dance pantomime," as Hughes once called it.

Hughes won acclaim in his lifetime as the poet of his people because he used his talent to celebrate his race and its achievement. But to call Hughes a good black playwright is to understate his theatrical contributions. Hughes contributed greatly to the history of drama and theater in America, for a much wider audience than he had ever envisioned early in his career. Hughes died in Harlem on 22 May 1967, leaving an important theatrical legacy to the American stage.

Letters:

Arna Bontemps–Langston Hughes Letters, 1925–1967, edited by Charles H. Nichols (New York: Dodd, Mead, 1980).

Bibliographies:

Ernest Kaiser, "Selected Bibliography of the Published Writings of Langston Hughes," *Freedomways,* 8 (Spring 1968): 185–191;

R. Baxter Miller, *Langston Hughes and Gwendolyn Brooks: A Reference Guide* (Boston: G. K. Hall, 1978);

Thomas A. Mikolyzk, *Langston Hughes: A Bio-Bibliography* (New York: Greenwood Press, 1990);

Granger Babcock, "Langston Hughes," in *American Playwrights 1880–1945: A Research and Production Sourcebook,* edited by William W. Demastes (Westport, Conn.: Greenwood Press, 1995), pp. 196–205.

Biographies:

Milton Metzer, *Langston Hughes: A Biography* (New York: Crowell, 1968);

Arnold Rampersad, *The Life of Langston Hughes,* 2 volumes (New York: Oxford University Press, 1986, 1988).

References:

Tish Dace, ed., *Langston Hughes: The Contemporary Reviews* (Cambridge & New York: Cambridge University Press, 1997);

James A. Emanuel, *Langston Hughes* (New York: Twayne, 1967);

Rena Fraden, *Blueprints for a Black Federal Theatre, 1935–1939* (Cambridge: Cambridge University Press, 1994);

Henry Louis Gates Jr. and K. A. Appiah, eds., *Langston Hughes: Critical Perspectives Past and Present* (New York: Amistad Press, 1993);

Joseph McLaren, "From Protest to Soul Fest: Langston Hughes' Gospel Plays," *Langston Hughes Review,* 15 (Spring 1998): 49–61;

McLaren, *Langston Hughes: Folk Dramatist in the Protest Tradition, 1921–1943* (Westport, Conn.: Greenwood Press, 1997);

Winston Napier, "Affirming Critical Conceptualism: Harlem Renaissance Aesthetics and the Formation of Alain Locke's Social Philosophy," *Massachusetts Review,* 39 (Spring 1998): 92–112;

Therman B. O'Daniel, ed., *Langston Hughes: Black Genius: A Critical Evaluation* (New York: Morrow, 1971);

Jay Plum, "Accounting for the Audience in Historical Reconstruction: Martin Jones's Production of Langston Hughes's *Mulatto,*" *Theatre Survey,* 36 (May 1995): 5–19;

Leslie Sanders, "Interesting Ways of Staging Plays: Hughes and Russian Theatre," *Langston Hughes Review,* 15 (Spring 1997): 4–12;

Michael Thurston, "Black Christ, Red Flag: Langston Hughes on Scottsboro," *College Literature,* 22 (October 1995): 30–49;

Steven C. Tracy, *Langston Hughes & the Blues* (Urbana: University of Illinois Press, 1988);

Darwin T. Turner, "Langston Hughes as Playwright," *CLA Journal* (June 1968): 297–309.

Papers:

Yale University houses the largest collection of Langston Hughes's papers in the James Weldon Johnson Memorial Collection. The New York Public Library Schomburg Collection in Harlem also has a large Hughes archive.

David Henry Hwang

(11 August 1957 –)

Felicia S. Pattison
Sterling College

See also the Hwang entry in *DLB 212: Twentieth-Century American Western Writers, Second Series.*

PLAY PRODUCTIONS: *FOB,* Stanford, California, Okada House dormitory, Stanford University, 2 March 1979; New York, Public Theater, Martinson Hall, 8 June 1980;

The Dance and the Railroad, New York, New Federal Theatre, 25 March 1981; New York, Anspacher Theatre, 16 July 1981;

Family Devotions, New York, Newman Theatre, 18 October 1981;

Sound and Beauty, New York, LuEsther Hall, 6 November 1983–comprised *The House of Sleeping Beauties* and *The Sound of a Voice;*

As the Crow Flies, Los Angeles, Los Angeles Theatre Center, 1986;

Rich Relations, New York, Second Stage, 21 April 1986;

Broken Promises, London, Soho Poly, 1987–comprised *The Dance and the Railroad* and *The House of Sleeping Beauties;*

M. Butterfly, Washington, D.C., National Theatre, 10 February 1988; New York, Eugene O'Neill Theatre, 20 March 1988;

Bondage, Louisville, Kentucky, Actors Theatre of Louisville, 1 March 1992;

Face Value, Boston, Colonial Theatre, February 1993;

Trying to Find Chinatown, Louisville, Kentucky, Actors Theatre of Louisville, 29 March 1996;

Golden Child, New York, Joseph Papp Public Theater, Newman Theatre, 17 November 1996; revised, New York, Longacre Theatre, 2 April 1998;

After Eros: An Exploration of the Psychic Development of the Feminine, by Hwang and Maureen Fleming, New York, The Kitchen, 5 April 1997;

Peer Gynt, adapted from Henrik Ibsen's play, Providence, Rhode Island, Trinity Repertory Company, 30 January 1998;

Aida, adapted from Giuseppe Verdi's opera by Hwang, Linda Woolverton, and Robert Falls, music by Elton John, lyrics by Tim Rice, Chicago, Cadillac

David Henry Hwang (Writers and Artists Agency)

Palace Theatre, 9 December 1999; New York, Palace Theatre, 23 March 2000.

BOOKS: *FOB* (New York: Theatre Communications Group, 1979);

The Dance and the Railroad; and Family Devotions (New York: Dramatists Play Service, 1983);

FOB; and, The House of Sleeping Beauties (New York: Dramatists Play Service, 1983);

The Sound of a Voice (New York: Dramatists Play Service, 1984);

M. Butterfly (New York: Dramatists Play Service, 1988; Harmondsworth, U.K.: Penguin, 1989); republished with an afterword by Hwang (New York: New American Library, 1989);

1000 Airplanes on the Roof: A Science Fiction Music-Drama, libretto by Hwang for a music drama scored by Philip Glass (Salt Lake City: Gibbs-Smith, 1989);

Trying to Find Chinatown; and, Bondage (New York: Dramatists Play Service, 1996);

Golden Child (New York: Theatre Communications Group, 1998).

Editions and Collections: *Broken Promises: Four Plays* (New York: Avon, 1983)–comprises *Family Devotions, The Dance and the Railroad, FOB,* and *The House of Sleeping Beauties;*

FOB and Other Plays (New York: New American Library, 1990)–comprises *FOB, The Dance and the Railroad, Family Devotions, The House of Sleeping Beauties, The Sound of a Voice, Rich Relations,* and *1000 Airplanes on the Roof;*

Trying to Find Chinatown: The Selected Plays of David Henry Hwang (New York: Theatre Communications Group, 1999)–comprises *Bondage, The Dance and the Railroad, Family Devotions, FOB, The House of Sleeping Beauties, The Sound of a Voice, Trying to Find Chinatown,* and *The Voyage.*

PRODUCED SCRIPTS: *The Dance and the Railroad,* television, Arts Cable Network, ABC, 1982;

Blind Alleys, by Hwang and Frederick Kimball, television, Metromedia Playhouse, WCVB, Boston, September 1985;

M. Butterfly, motion picture, Geffen Pictures, 1993;

Golden Gate, motion picture, Samuel Goldwyn Pictures, 1994;

The Monkey King, television, NBC, 2000.

OTHER: *1000 Airplanes on the Roof: A Science Fiction Music-Drama,* music drama with libretto by Hwang, music by Philip Glass, Vienna, Austria, Vienna International Airport Hangar #3, 15 July 1988;

The Voyage, opera with libretto by Hwang, music by Glass, New York, Metropolitan Opera, October 1992;

The Silver River, opera with libretto by Hwang, music by Bright Sheng, Santa Fe, New Mexico, Santa Fe Chamber Music Festival, 27 July 1997;

Ji-Li Jiang, *Red Scarf Girl: A Memoir of the Cultural Revolution,* foreword by Hwang (New York: HarperCollins, 1997).

SELECTED PERIODICAL PUBLICATIONS–UNCOLLECTED: "Evolving a Multicultural Tradition," *MELUS,* 16 (Fall 1989–Winter 1990): 16–19;

"(*Death of a Salesman*)," *Michigan Quarterly Review,* 37 (Fall 1998): 605–606.

David Henry Hwang is one of the most successful and prolific American dramatists at the end of the twentieth century. He challenges his audiences' notions of gender, race, and ethnicity and suggests the political implications of stereotypes and prejudice, integrating myth and history into his plays as a way to bridge differences and build understanding among audience members of all races. Hwang is the recipient of many honors, including the Tony, Drama Desk, and Outer Critics Circle Awards for *M. Butterfly* (1988); two Obie Awards, for *FOB* (1979) and *Golden Child* (1996), which was also nominated for a Tony in 1998; and fellowships from the New York State Council on the Arts, the National Endowment for the Arts, and the Guggenheim Foundation.

Hwang's major themes and concerns are influenced by his biography. He is interested in the assimilation of the Asian American, whether recent immigrant or second generation, into American culture and the retention or recapture of the Asian cultural myths and traditions along with an awareness of their limitations. In many of his plays, Hwang suggests that reconciliation with and acceptance of family is necessary for individual identity; he portrays the destruction and chaos that ensues when a family lacks integrity and an adequate means of legitimate communication. He often employs surrealistic techniques and Asian ritual dance, which is sometimes rendered as ritualistic dialogue and gesture, to investigate a character's psychological dimension or motivation. Politically, Hwang asserts that race and gender are primarily social constructions, so he deconstructs Western gender, racial, and political stereotypes of Asians. He is critical of all forms of fundamentalism, especially Christian fundamentalism.

Hwang was born on 11 August 1957 in San Gabriel, California, a Los Angeles suburb, to Henry Yuan and Dorothy Yu Huang Hwang. In 1948 Hwang's father had emigrated from Shanghai via Taiwan to California and graduated with a degree in business from the University of Southern California, where he met Hwang's mother, who was studying piano. Dorothy Hwang, born in southern China but raised in the Philippines, had been sent to the University of Southern California in 1952 by her parents to complete her training as a classical pianist. She also graduated from the university, and when Hwang and his two younger sisters, Margery and Grace, were older, she became a piano instructor. Henry Hwang became a Certified Public Accountant and successful businessman, owning his own accounting firm, managing an Asian restaurant, and eventually founding and running a bank. Because one of Hwang's maternal ancestors had become a Christian, Hwang told Gerard Raymond in a 1997 profile, "My personal family history was an odd mix of fundamentalist Christianity and Chinese culture." Hwang attended the exclusive Harvard Boys School, graduating in 1975. He earned a degree in English from Stanford University in 1979 and has done graduate work in playwriting at Yale University.

Stanford was a pivotal experience for Hwang in many ways. Hwang explained to interviewer Marty Moss-Coane that he and his sisters

> were raised pretty much as white European Americans in terms of the things we celebrated. There's an odd confluence in my family between a father who decided to turn away from things Chinese and a mother whose family had been converted to Christianity in China several generations back. Consequently between the two of them there was no particular desire for us to speak Chinese or celebrate Chinese holidays at all. I dated a Chinese girl when I was a senior in high school, and that was the first time I figured out when the Chinese New Year actually was! . . . It wasn't really until I was in college that I began to question some of this and think about roots.

Living in an Asian student dorm, Hwang began to repudiate his assimilationist upbringing; he explained to Raymond, "In order to claim my own independence or identity, it was necessary for me to demonize the very strong influences I grew up with." Without having much experience in viewing or reading plays, Hwang decided in his freshman year after seeing a play in San Francisco that he wanted to write plays. He enrolled in an introduction to drama class taught by John L'Heureux, who was then the director of the creative-writing program at Stanford, and began writing plays. He showed them to L'Heureux, who frankly told Hwang that they were horrible because Hwang did not know anything about drama. Hwang recalled to interviewer Deborah Frockt that L'Heureux told him "my problem was that I was trying to write in a vacuum, that I had the desire to write plays but that I didn't actually know anything about the theatre." Hwang began reading and attending as many plays as he could. He was able to see the premieres of many of the plays of Sam Shepard, with whom he was also able to study during a Western playwrights workshop in 1978. Out of that workshop came the ideas for *FOB,* which Hwang wrote and produced at his dorm, Okada House, during a student festival of plays and musicals.

FOB, the abbreviation for "fresh off the boat," introduces many of the themes and technical devices Hwang continues to use and develop; the play also exhibits Shepard's influence. The structure of *FOB* was modeled on Shepard's *Angel City* (1976), which Hwang explained to interviewer Chris Haines "juxtaposes scenes with monologues that seem to come out of a different place." One of Hwang's early thematic concerns is the assimilation of the Asian immigrant into American culture. In his introduction to *FOB and Other Plays* (1990), Hwang discusses this process of assimilation:

> In attempting to define my place in America, I have evolved through several different phases. . . . Initially, we tend to be motivated by that most childlike of needs: to be accepted, to belong. This leads to an assimilationist phase, the desire to "out-white the whites." The Asian child sees America defined as predominantly of one color. Wanting to be part of this land, he attempts to become the same. The difficulty is, of course, that this is not possible; our inability to become white at will can produce terrible self-loathing.

FOB elucidates the difficulty and destructiveness of assimilation through the experiences and interaction of three characters: Dale, a second-generation Chinese American; Grace, Dale's cousin, a first-generation Chinese American; and Steve, Grace's friend and a recent immigrant, the FOB. In the prologue Dale, donning the persona of an academic, lectures on the definition of the FOB. Ignoring the fact that his parents, as well as Grace, were once FOBs, Dale defines FOBs disparagingly, betraying his prejudice against the newly arrived Chinese and relying on ethnic stereotypes: "Clumsy, ugly, greasy FOB. Loud, stupid, four-eyed FOB. . . . High-water pants. . . . someone you wouldn't want your sister to marry." Hwang explains in his introduction that Dale hates Steve, the FOB, "because the latter represents all the identifications Dale has spent a lifetime attempting to avoid."

In order to heighten the contrast between the Asian and American cultures and to illustrate Dale's alienation from the former, Hwang incorporates the Chinese myths of Fa Mu Lan and Gwan Gung. (In his introduction, Hwang describes Fa Mu Lan and Gwan Gung as "two figures from American literature" because he encountered them through American literary works: Fa Mu Lan figures in Maxine Hong Kingston's *The Woman Warrior: Memoirs of a Girlhood among Ghosts,* 1976, and Gwan Gung in Frank Chin's *Gee, Pop! . . . A Real Cartoon,* 1974.) In Dale's presence Steve adopts the persona of the stereotypical FOB; however, he appears to Grace as "Gwan Gung! God of warriors, writers, and prostitutes" and the "adopted God of Chinese America." As Gwan Gung, Steve speaks flawless

Cover for Hwang's 1983 collection of plays, including his "trilogy on Chinese America"

English, but to disguise his mythic identity, as the FOB his English is accented and broken.

The premise of Steve's character and his modulation from FOB Steve to Gwan Gung Steve is that Gwan Gung aids each Chinese immigrant, including Dale's parents and Grace. Through the image of Gwan Gung, Hwang surveys the various experiences of Chinese immigrants, from the initial promise of the "beautiful country" and the disappointing labor conditions and treatment to their reception by first and second generation immigrants in the 1970s.

Even though Dale and Grace are not new immigrants—Dale having been born in America and Grace having come over when she was ten years old—they are still not fully assimilated or accepted into American culture. Dale has overestimated his acceptance; in his one soliloquy, Dale argues unconvincingly that he is "making it in America." He refers to his parents as "yellow

ghosts" who have encouraged "Chinese-ness." In contrast to his parents, he has attempted to define himself in more American ways, such as his sports car: "So, I've had to work real hard—real hard—to be myself. To not be a Chinese, a yellow, a slant, a gook. To be just a human being, like everyone else." As a former FOB, Grace has a more realistic assessment of her position in American society and recounts her loneliness as a child. Second-generation Chinese, such as Dale, shunned her, and her white peers did not accept her. She is in a better position than Dale because she was eventually willing to accept her loneliness instead of drowning it in materialism as Dale does. In her soliloquies, she implicitly contrasts her memories of adolescent loneliness with the experiences of Fa Mu Lan, the woman warrior, who recounts Gwan Gung's brutal murders of her family and waits for an opportunity to avenge her family's death.

Ultimately the struggle of the characters evolves into a ritualized encounter between Fa Mu Lan (Grace) and Gwan Gung (Steve) in which Fa Mu Lan confronts Gwan Gung with the devastation he capriciously wreaked upon her and her family. Fa Mu Lan and Gwan Gung battle, with the victory going to Fa Mu Lan. Steve interprets the ritual: "There are no gods that travel. Only warriors travel." Even though Dale participates in the ritual slaying of Gwan Gung, he never fully understands its significance because he has cut himself off from his cultural past. He is left mumbling about FOBs while Steve and Grace go out dancing.

Hwang's parents attended the performance of *FOB* at Stanford and had decided that they would encourage or discourage Hwang in his playwriting based on the strengths or weaknesses of *FOB*. Hwang's father was brought to tears by the performance, and his parents have supported him ever since. *FOB* was produced again at the 1979 O'Neill National Playwrights Conference, where Joseph Papp saw it, and in June 1980 Papp brought it to the Public Theater, where it ran for forty-two performances. The play was a critical and popular success, winning Hwang an Obie Award.

In the fall of 1980 Hwang entered the Yale graduate program and began writing his second play, *The Dance and the Railroad* (1981), an historical treatment of Asian immigration set during the 1867 railroad strike. Lone, representing the cultural tradition of the East, does not participate in the strike, choosing instead to practice opera roles. Ma, representing the idealism of the new immigrant, has been in America for four weeks and still believes the myths he hears about America. For Lone, who has been in America for two years, the myths are dispelled. Trained in the opera, kidnapped by his parents, and sent to America to make money for his family, Lone has returned to the ritual of the opera for meaning and order. Ma wishes to learn the steps of the opera and to play Gwan Gung, but first Lone must show him the discipline and dedication necessary. Ma develops the discipline; the strike is resolved; and Lone consents to let Ma play Gwan Gung. But Ma no longer sees Gwan Gung as heroic; rather, he wishes to enact his own life in the ritualistic form of the opera. For Lone, at first, the idea is nearly blasphemous, but as Ma begins the opera of his own life story, a kind of "everyman" tale, Lone joins in.

Ma's opera is a summary of the threats his parents used in sending him to America, the horrors of the passage, the virtual slavery involved in struggling with the mountain for the completion of the railroad, the rhetoric of the strike, and the resolution of the strike, which signals the end of the ritual of the dance and the return to hard labor. Through his experience with the ritual dance, Ma has a more realistic perspective of America. He vows to "toughen up" and gives up the dance.

Like Hwang's first play, *The Dance and the Railroad* both dismantles and confirms the validity of Asian myth. In both plays, Gwan Gung is insufficient for the needs of the Asian immigrant in America. Yet, the ritual through which the myth of Gwan Gung is traditionally conveyed proves to be an adequate means of dealing with the dehumanizing experiences of America. Through the ritual, Ma finds the strength to return to the labor. His return is hardly a victory, however; he makes it clear that he will not return to the ritual of the opera. He has gleaned from it what use it has to offer him but does not see any other purpose to it. The play ends as it begins, with Lone practicing the steps and movement of the drama, but his reason for the ritual has changed from what it was at the beginning. It has renewed his spirit; he tells Ma that "Today, I am dancing for no reason at all."

The Dance and the Railroad ran for 181 performances, and Hwang withdrew from Yale and began living in New York City. Hwang's relationship with Papp proved fruitful. Within four months of his production of *The Dance and the Railroad,* Papp produced *Family Devotions* (1981) at the Public Theater and saw that Hwang received the Rockefeller Grant in 1983 for being the playwright in residence at the Public Theater.

Family Devotions, dedicated to Hwang's grandparents and to Shepard, is a more ambitious effort and depicts more-complicated relationships than either of the first two plays. The ambiguity of the title focuses attention on the theme of the play: the destructive influence of Christianity on Asian cultural traditions. Although in 1996 Hwang described himself as "dead-again," he was raised as a born-again Christian. As he explained in his introduction to *FOB and Other Plays,* at Stanford, Hwang began to reject his fundamentalist upbringing, seeing "the rejection of this Western mythology" as "a casting off of the brainwashing white missionaries have consistently attempted to impose on 'heathen' Asian cultures." The play investigates the characters' devotion to family and to heritage, and the climax of the play occurs during "family devotions." Hwang told Moss-Coane that his third play is autobiographical:

At family functions we usually do this thing called family devotions. . . . We all kind of get up and witness. My grandmother tells the story of her grandfather, who was kidnaped by pirates and sold to a Chinese family that happened to be Christian. They bought him and dedicated him to God. So there is supposed to be this legacy, that we're all descended from someone who was dedicated to God, and that we're also dedicated to God. This is a really clear example of the meshing of the Christian ethic with the Confucian ancestor worship ethic. We are responsible for carrying out what my great-grandfather did, which is a Confucian idea. The specifics of what he did, however, had to do with the Christian religion and are therefore Western.

The play opens as Ama's and Popo's families are waiting for the arrival of Di-gou, the younger brother with whom Ama and Popo want to share their Christian faith and to recount the family story of when Christianity entered their lives through their deceased elder sister, See-goh-poh. The audience knows, but the family remains unaware, that Di-gou has already arrived and is wandering nearby. Hwang depicts the family as completely immersed in American culture and values and consumed with the accumulation of wealth, possessions, technological gadgets, and accolades. Ama's and Popo's grandchildren have no interest in meeting Di-gou, just "another goon" from China.

Hwang's debt to Shepard is most evident in this comically absurd play. Hwang depicts the dysfunctional nature of Ama's and Popo's families: characters spend most of their time wandering on and off the set yelling for each other or looking for someone or something. There is usually little substantive communication; everyone is so consumed with his or her own self-interest that he or she has little time to spend listening to anyone else. Chester—Popo's grandson and presumably the Hwang character—and Di-gou have the only meaningful conversation about the importance of family. Chester has given up on his family and their ridiculous behavior, but Di-gou tries to encourage him to appreciate his family and the generations that have come before. He tells Chester, "You must become one with your family before you can hope to live away from it."

Ama and Popo want Di-gou to confirm their Christian heritage, but instead, he admits that he "never did believe in God" and explains that the family myth of See-goh-poh was false and that there is no ancestral foundation for their Christian beliefs. The eventual family devotion time degrades to a squabble about who is more successful. Wilbur, Ama's son-in-law, determines his success by his possessions: the Cuisinart, the microwave, the barbeque grill, the fancy house, a tennis court with tennis ball machine, and a Ferrari. For Robert, Chester's father, who is modeled after Hwang's father, the proof of his success is that he is wealthy enough to have been kidnapped for ransom. His experience exemplifies the American Dream: "From rags to kidnap victim." The squabbling turns malicious when Ama and Popo attempt more direct means of converting Di-gou. They decide that they must rid him of the "communist demon," so they tie him to a table. The sisters demand that he repent of his communist ways and

give testimony of See-goh-poh's alleged ministry. Di-gou refuses, and so they whip him with an electrical cord. When he still refuses, Ama attempts to strangle her brother with the cord. Finally, Chester returns to stop Ama, and Di-gou stands up on the table just as the barbeque bursts into flames.

In a parody of the Pentecostal visit of the Holy Spirit, Di-gou babbles incoherently as Chester interprets, revealing the true story of See-goh-poh. Once the story is corrected, Di-gou speaks to his sisters again in English. The truth is that See-goh-poh assumed the persona of an evangelist for her family in order to have an excuse to travel so that she could visit her illegitimate child. Her family forced her to make up stories, the details of which they filled out with their own imaginations. Di-gou reveals his true purpose in coming to America:

> I come to bring you back to China. Come, sisters. To the soil you've forsaken with ways born of memories, of stories that never happened. Come, sisters. The stories written on your face are the ones you must believe.

But Ama and Popo are so overwhelmed by Di-gou's story that they both collapse and die. The family sinks into further disintegration and insignificance as Di-gou and Chester leave separately.

Hwang's family plays are grounded in his autobiography more than his other plays, which may account for their poor reception (the Tony-nominated *Golden Child* being an exception). Hwang admitted to Robert Cooperman in 1993 that *Family Devotions* and *Rich Relations* (1986), two of his most Shepardesque plays, "represent an attempt to deal with a lot of psychological issues from my past which may or may not be interesting to the general public." Hwang also believes that his unsuccessful plays share a similar problem that *Family Devotions* illustrates well. The play is meant to be a "spiritual farce, this thing that's funny in the first act and then turns dark and gets ritualistic in the second act," but the audience does not know how to take it. Up until Ama and Popo tie up and torture their brother, the play is clearly funny, and most critics have thought it absurdly so, although Hwang objects to the play being labeled absurdist. The ending—the extreme violence they go to in order to protect their mythic heritage, and their sudden, unexplainable deaths—is unsettling and horrifying. The sisters seem harmless enough in the first act, incapable of such abhorrent behavior. The audience is not prepared well enough for the drastic turn in tone. Produced just a few months after *The Dance and the Railroad*, *Family Devotions* was performed only seventy-six times at the Public Theater.

Hwang suggests that his first three plays form a kind of "trilogy on Chinese America." In *FOB, The Dance and the Railroad,* and *Family Devotions* he investigates various experiences of Chinese immigrants in America and the decisions those immigrants face in trying to maintain their cultural heritage or to assimilate to American culture. In his next two plays, *The House of Sleeping Beauties* and *The Sound of a Voice,* produced together by Papp in November 1983 at the Public Theater under the title *Sound and Beauty,* Hwang abandons the American scene and turns to Japanese material. *The House of Sleeping Beauties* is loosely based on a short story by Yasunari Kawabata and is Hwang's speculation on how Kawabata's story may have come to be written. In Hwang's play, an elderly woman runs a brothel of sorts that caters only to older "gentlemen" who may sleep with the naked, young, and beautiful girls but may not have sexual relations with them. The protagonist Kawabata, also in his seventies, comes to the house of beauties searching for a story that will enable him to write again, but the woman tries to convince him that he endangers the house if he writes about it.

Kawabata quickly comes under the spell of the house and, after five months of visits, is addicted to the girls; however, his visits are not as enjoyable as at first. Forgotten memories, increasingly unpleasant, haunt him. Kawabata requests a stronger sleeping potion to drown the flood of memories, but the woman promises him two girls instead. While she is away making the arrangements, Kawabata sneaks into the woman's potion cabinet and drinks three doses. When he goes to his room, he finds one of the girls has died from drinking too much sleeping potion. Kawabata is horrified and threatens to leave, but his own overdose overpowers him and, with the help of the woman, he returns to the remaining beauty. The mysterious death of the girl releases Kawabata's block, and he writes his story. A week later he shows a copy of the submitted manuscript to the woman, and she points out the fiction in it, the details Kawabata has changed as well as the important details that remained unchanged–such as the location of the house. She fears reprisal from the authorities.

Throughout Kawabata's months of visits to the house, he and the woman have grown closer. He confides in her about his writing problems, and she shares with him the story of her sister's death. Forced to marry when secretly in love with another, the sister committed suicide on her wedding day along with her lover, the woman's betrothed. Both Kawabata and the woman have had long lives with little pleasure or happiness. Now that the story is written, Kawabata has no objective reason for visiting the house. He returns only to show her the manuscript and to have her help him commit suicide. He has purchased poison, which she adds to his tea, and a bridal kimono, which her sister's suicide with her fiancé prohibited her from ever wearing. She dons the kimono and paints her face like a bride while he drinks the tea, and they talk, in veiled language, about their love and admiration for each other. She sings and strokes his hair until he dies, and although he has left her money and intends for her to live without him, she finishes his tea.

The idea for *The Sound of a Voice* is original to Hwang, but it is inspired by Japanese ghost stories and has the character of a myth or a fairy tale. With "only minor alteration," Hwang suggests in his introduction to *FOB and Other Plays,* "it could be set in a mysterious forest on any continent." A Japanese woman in her forties or fifties lives alone in a secluded forest. Her only joys are her flowers, her *shakuhatchi* (an end-blown bamboo flute), and the occasional visitors she receives. The play opens with the woman receiving a fifty-year-old male visitor. Throughout the early scenes of the play, the couple exchange polite conversation, but when the woman leaves the room, the man investigates the room and its contents, takes a flower from a bouquet in a vase, and listens at the screens, but resumes a restful posture when the woman returns. When they retire for the evening, the woman takes the vase of flowers with her to her room, and the man sits on his mat with a sword at his side. The man prepares to leave in the morning, but the woman convinces him to stay.

Underneath the polite chatter that continues between the two of them runs a counter dialogue of gesture. As the play progresses, the woman continues to wait on the man, guard her flowers, and play the *shakuhatchi* while the man helps the woman with the household chores, ponders his stolen flower, and practices his swordplay. The couple seemingly never sleep; the woman plays her *shakuhatchi* while the man dozes with his sword at his side, jumping awake at the slightest provocation.

The man and woman continue in this torturous dance until, when the woman surprises the man with her skill with the sword, they confess their true situation. The woman is aware of the stories about her that circulate among the surrounding villages: that she is a beautiful witch who enchants, seduces, and imprisons her would-be killers. Having heard the stories, the man has come to prove his manhood by surviving her wiles, killing her, and returning to the villages with his story. The woman challenges the man to kill her, but he is unable and promises never to leave her. Then, after a scene in which the man is unable to kill either her or himself, the man is shamed and decides to leave the woman. While she will not force him to stay, she begs him either to stay or to kill her, not to leave her alone:

B. D. Wong and David Dukes in the 1989 Broadway production of M. Butterfly (photograph by Peter Cunningham)

I won't force you to do anything. (*Pause*) All I wanted was an escape–for both of us. The sound of a human voice–the simplest thing to find, and the hardest to hold on to. This house–my loneliness is etched into the walls. Kill me, but don't leave. Even in death, my spirit would rest here and be comforted by your presence.

The woman neither confirms nor denies the gossip about her but only chides the man for his cruelty in believing it. The woman thinks the man is leaving, so she goes to her room; but the man changes his mind, returns to the front room, moves everything off his mat, including the ever-present sword, and takes up the woman's *shakuhatchi*. As he unsuccessfully attempts to play it, the lights come up behind the screen to reveal that the woman has hung herself. The man obliviously continues his futile task.

One of the main themes of the play is expressed on the first morning of the man's sojourn at the woman's house, as the woman explains that words "are too inefficient. It takes hundreds of words to describe a single act of caring. With hundreds of acts, words become irrelevant." Although she craves "the sound of

a voice," the two of them convey the most significant meaning through gesture and action, not dialogue. Scene 3 comically illustrates the contrast between voice and gesture. The man, stripped to the waist, enters the room with a load of chopped wood. Noticing the woman's eyeing of his mid-life paunch, he pats it and begins to joke about his physique. She tries to convince him that he should love his body the way it is, but he continues to hit it as an instrument, talk to it as a companion, and generally belittle its appearance. The scene culminates with the man telling his belly that at least it will be faithful and "never leave me for another man." The woman responds, "No," acknowledging that she will be faithful, even though she was not directly addressed. The man then asks her, "What do you want me to say?" She responds to his request in gesture, leaning over to him and touching his belly with her hand. Like the older woman in *The House of Sleeping Beauties*, she "bewitches" the man, not with enchantment, but with kindness and caring expressed through her actions and gestures. Referring to *The House of Sleeping Beauties*, Hwang told Cooperman that "there is the notion of stillness representing a certain amount of passion, a certain amount of need. The emotions that can't really be expressed in an explicit form or can't be understood but only act upon the individual."

From March 1979, when *FOB* was first produced at Stanford, to November 1983, when Papp produced *Sound and Beauty*, Hwang had written five plays. At twenty-six, he had established himself as a major force in American theater. In her foreword to *FOB and Other Plays*, Maxine Hong Kingston argues for the important role Hwang plays in Chinese American theater:

Chinese American actors are given too few dignified parts to play. If no playwrights like David Hwang came along, a generation of actors who speak our accents would be lost. A novelist can only invent an approximate orthography. For voices, the play's the thing. Chinese American theater, which started out with a bang – firecrackers, drums – keeps dying out. David Henry Hwang gives it life once again.

After *Sound and Beauty* Hwang spent time traveling in Europe, Asia, and Canada, where he met Ophelia Chong, a Chinese Canadian graphic artist, whom he married in Los Angeles in 1985; they divorced four years later. Living in Los Angeles gave Hwang an opportunity to experiment with television and film. In 1986 he wrote a companion piece for a Los Angeles production of *The Sound of a Voice;* this play, called *As the Crow Flies,* features an African American woman and her employer, a dying Chinese woman. The African American woman transforms from domestic helper to spiritual guide as the Chinese woman slips from life to death.

As the Crow Flies was Hwang's first attempt to draw a non-Asian character, and the play also illustrates Hwang's contemplation of his earlier "isolationist-nationalist model." While acknowledging the importance of such a phase, he concluded that the model had lost its usefulness for him. He did not want to limit himself to writing only about Asian themes and Asian characters; he wanted to develop the freedom to write about anything. In his introduction to *FOB and Other Plays* he explains this new direction in his thinking and production:

> I am quick to stress here that the freedom to write on *any* subject must certainly extend as well to those who *choose* to address only, say, Asian Americans. These fall within a great American tradition of writers such as Tennessee Williams or F. Scott Fitzgerald who concentrated primarily on one group of people. America, however, must not restrict its "ethnic" writers to "ethnic" material, while assuming that white males can master any topic they so desire.

Hwang's work after 1983 reflects the realignment of his thinking. The ethnicity of the characters in *Rich Relations,* produced in New York at Second Stage in April 1986, is not specified. The play bears many similarities to *Family Devotions:* the setting is near Los Angeles, and some of the characters are consumed by the accumulation of possessions, wealth, and a vacuous fundamentalist Christianity. Furthermore, as with the earlier play, Shepard's influence is evident in the dysfunctional familial relationships, the psychological surrealism, and the comic absurdity of the tragedy.

Hinson, the "rich relation" of the title, lives alone in a large home among the hills overlooking Los Angeles and has accumulated great wealth and possessions. Hinson had contracted tuberculosis in 1948 and was dying; but at the urging of his sister, Barbara, who converted to Christianity, he "prayed to God, 'Save my life and I will be a shining light for thee.'" He recovered, went to the University of Southern California, spent a short time as a minister, and then became successful in business. Like Wilbur, his counterpart in *Family Devotions,* Hinson interprets his wealth as a sign of God's approval. Much of the comedy of the play involves Hinson's infatuation with gadgets and blind devotion to technology; he prefers a technological gadget even when it does not function efficiently, because it is "a modern convenience." Hinson's son, Keith, accompanied by Jill, a student of his with whom he is having an affair, has returned home in disgrace from his employment as a forensic teacher at an East Coast high school.

Barbara is as absurd as her brother. She remains committed to her understanding of Christianity, but she sleeps with her husband and his mistress, Bonnie; is envious of her brother's wealth because she holds herself responsible for his "resurrection"; and wants Keith to marry her daughter—even though they are first cousins—because she does not see any other way to get her brother's money. Marilyn, Barbara's daughter, does not want to marry Keith because she is in love with a rock star with whom she had a brief affair, and spends her time watching music videos. When Keith refuses to marry Marilyn, Barbara, who has attempted suicide many times in the past, climbs up onto the railing of Hinson's balcony and threatens to jump. For the remainder of the play at least one person, either Barbara, Marilyn, or Jill, sits on the rail and threatens to commit suicide.

Jill, merely a teenage runaway facing her own crisis, is ill-equipped to handle the emotional tangle of Keith's family, but her character provides a lens of objectivity for the audience. The remaining four characters pair together in various relationships: brother-sister, father-son, mother-daughter, cousin-cousin, aunt-nephew, and uncle-niece. In the greatest ironic understatement of the play, Hinson announces: "Your family is just a chaos, Barbara." When Jill accidentally falls off the balcony to the rocks below, the focus of the play tightens on the unresolved tensions in the parent-child relationships between Barbara and Marilyn and Hinson and Keith. Hinson and Keith attempt to resolve their frustrations with violence, smashing the various electronic gadgets in the room. Barbara and Marilyn resolve theirs by ritually enacting Barbara's response to Hinson's impending death from tuberculosis. The culmination of the two struggles is Barbara's pushing Marilyn off the railing. Marilyn stops falling at a forty-five-degree angle from the rail, and the lights blacken, leaving the room illuminated only by the stars. Marilyn meditates on death and the power of resurrection, and the room is cast into complete darkness.

When the lights come up, Jill has replaced Marilyn on the railing, and Marilyn enters the room from the outside and announces that she is ready to leave because "All the TV's here are broken." Jill exits with Barbara and Marilyn, leaving Hinson and Keith alone. Hinson tries to puff himself back up with talk of his wealth and masculinity, but Keith hushes him. The play ends with the two of them kneeling with an ear to the ground, listening for the dead to return.

Hwang states that the resurrection theme of the play reflects his own experience as an artist. In some ways, he explains in the introduction to *FOB and Other Plays,* the play marked the resurrection of his writing. But Hwang admitted to Frockt that the play does not work as well as some of his earlier plays because he approached the ethnic/racial question in the wrong way. The family was modeled after Hwang's own family, yet it lacks ethnic and cultural specificity; he told Cooperman, "it's essentially my family I just made them all white." The contrast between the success of *Sound and Beauty* and the failure of *Rich Relations* underscores the importance of specific cultural details. "Ultimately," Hwang told Frockt, "it's the careful attention to the specifics of the cultural situation that allows the work to be universal."

In his article "Evolving a Multicultural Tradition" (1989) Hwang admits that he is "tempted to wonder whether there was also anger on their [critics'] part that I was attempting to break out of their literary segregation" by writing for a non-Asian cast. But the play has some weaknesses that are unrelated to the ethnic makeup of the cast. Theatrically, *Rich Relations* is loud and confusing: lights flashing; people shouting, banging on doors, and breaking things; and televisions blaring. Furthermore, the resolution to the conflict, like Shepard's *Buried Child* (1978) and Hwang's *Family Devotions,* is merely acceptance and resignation. Resurrections usually connote hope and new life, but in *Rich Relations* the characters are resurrected to a hellish existence. Nevertheless, *Rich Relations* helped to confirm Hwang's vocation for him. He told Haines that the failure of *Rich Relations* "was a wonderful experience because it was my first failure and therefore it taught me that I was always going to be a writer. Up until that point . . . I never really had my dedication to my craft tested." The experience with *Rich Relations* prepared Hwang to write his greatest critical success, *M. Butterfly.*

In 1989 Hwang explained to Moss-Coane how pivotal *M. Butterfly* is to his purpose and development as an artist:

> For instance, in terms of international issues, I felt certain attitudes from the mainstream society as an Asian American, and thought – is it reasonable to think that those values also influence our policy makers as they consider the world? And in the case of the play the answer is yes. I also think I learned from writing the play the interconnectedness of the "isms." Like racism, sexism and imperialism all being manifestations of an attempt to degrade "the other," to make "the other" less than oneself.

With the exception of *As the Crow Flies,* which had a limited production run, *M. Butterfly,* which ran on Broadway for 777 performances, is the first of Hwang's plays to feature a multiethnic cast and marks the beginning of what Hwang calls his "intercultural/internationalist" phase, which contrasts directly with his earlier "isolationist/nationalist" phase. In this later phase, Hwang is concerned with "trying to find connections between different groups in our society, rather than separating them," and with "talking about how all of us have a number of different identities" that are "not particularly static."

The seed of Hwang's idea for *M. Butterfly* came from the news story of a 1986 French espionage incident: Bernard Bouriscot, a French diplomat, had fallen in love with a Chinese opera singer, Shi Pei Pu, whom he believed to be a woman. The two engaged in a twenty-year affair, during which time Bouriscot passed government information to Shi. Following his and Shi's arrest for spying for China, Bouriscot discovered that Shi was a man. The world was fascinated with the details of the event: How was it possible for Bouriscot to remain unaware of the gender of his lover for twenty years? When asked why he did not think it odd that he had never seen Shi naked, Bouriscot replied, "I thought she was very modest. I thought it was a Chinese custom." In an afterword to a 1989 edition of the play, Hwang comments:

> Bouriscot's assumption [of his lover's modesty as a cultural custom] was consistent with a certain stereotyped view of Asians as bowing, blushing, flowers. I therefore concluded that the diplomat must have fallen in love, not with a person, but with a fantasy stereotype. I also inferred that, to the extent the Chinese spy encouraged these misperceptions, he must have played up to and exploited this image of the Oriental woman as demure and submissive.

As he further reflected on the incident, Hwang decided that Shi was playing Bouriscot's "butterfly." Hwang had not yet seen or heard Giacomo Puccini's famous opera *Madama Butterfly* (1904), but in the Asian community the term *butterfly* refers to the Asian woman who plays "the submissive Oriental number." After listening to Puccini, Hwang was convinced that he could use the opera to investigate the misconceptions Bouriscot had about the East. Hwang had discovered the "arc" of his play:

> the Frenchman fantasizes that he is Pinkerton and his lover is Butterfly. By the end of the piece, he realizes that it is he who has been Butterfly, in that the Frenchman has been duped by love; the Chinese spy, who exploited that love, is therefore the real Pinkerton.

Hwang's initial title, "Monsieur Butterfly," underscores the deconstruction of the butterfly as a cultural and gender stereotype. The final title, *M. Butterfly,* suggested by Hwang's wife, Ophelia, underscores the gender ambiguity of the characters.

In addition to what the Bouriscot-Shi incident reveals about gender/sexual stereotypes, Hwang saw in the incident a metaphor for East-West political relations. The West's sexual/gender and racial/ethnic stereotypes of the East–and the idea that the East willingly submits to the West because it is fragile and needs protection and leadership–influence and direct its political engagements. Yet, Hwang does not consider his criticism anti-American: "Quite to the contrary. I consider it a plea to all sides to cut through our respective layers of cultural and sexual misperception, to deal with one another truthfully for our mutual good, from the common and equal ground we share as human beings." *M. Butterfly* is replete with such "layers of cultural and sexual misperception," most clearly embodied in the character of Song Liling, who, when protagonist Rene Gallimard first meets him, is a Chinese man playing a Japanese woman who sings in Italian, in an American play.

M. Butterfly unfolds as a series of Gallimard's memories and psychological musings, layered upon each other in Gallimard's attempt to find "a new ending to my story." In the play, Gallimard speaks directly to the audience from his prison cell in the "present," directing his memories, the retelling of his story, for the audience to evaluate and understand. Gallimard introduces his story with a summary reenactment of Puccini's opera up to the death scene. Gallimard's retelling of the opera is broken up by adolescent memories that reveal his sexual insecurity–his refusal to go to the mountains with his friend Marc for what promises to be an orgy, and his inability to become aroused by looking at pictures of a pinup girl. As the play progresses, Gallimard confesses his preoccupation during his first sexual experience, arranged by Marc, that his legs would fall off; admits that he married his wife, Helga, older than he, for professional rather than romantic or sexual reasons; reveals that he and his wife are infertile; and divulges his discomfort with the "masculine" sexual candor of Renee, a Danish student with whom he had a brief affair. Hwang creates a character who, if not latently homosexual, has an ambivalent relationship with his own sexuality and needs validation of his sexual prowess. When Gallimard sees Song perform the death scene from *Madama Butterfly,* he is overcome with her fragile femininity. Gallimard explains to the audience:

> Here . . . here was a Butterfly with little or no voice – but she had the grace, the delicacy. . . . I believed this girl. I believed her suffering. I wanted to take her in my arms – so delicate, even I could protect her, take her home, pamper her until she smiled.

Gallimard believes that Song's "femininity" confirms his masculinity.

Gallimard's first conversation with Song reveals that she does not fulfill his ideal image of the submissive Oriental woman. She cuts him off midsentence, expresses her opinions, and derides him for his. Furthermore, Song shows surprise at Gallimard's assessment of her performance. "Convincing?" she asks Gallimard, "As a Japanese woman?" After Song exits, Gallimard concedes to the audience, "So much for protecting her in my big Western arms." Their early relationship continues in this vein. Song controls the time, place, and duration of their meetings, yet Gallimard interprets her actions and voice in terms of his image of the "Oriental woman." Even when her behavior is contrary to the image, he reasons that "She is outwardly bold and outspoken, yet her heart is shy and afraid. It is the Oriental in her at war with her Western education." Much later in the play, before Song transforms herself from female to male, Gallimard orders her to embrace him one last time as his Butterfly, but she refuses: "Rene, I've never done what you've said. Why should it be any different in your mind?"

Nevertheless, throughout the relationship Gallimard reads Song's behavior in terms of the stereotypes he holds of East and West. He believes that Song feels "inferior" to Western women: "She does – she feels inferior to them – and to me." Early in the relationship, overestimating his power, Gallimard refrains from calling or visiting Song for five weeks, refusing to answer or acknowledge her weekly letters. He wants to be cruel, to be the Western devil that he believes Oriental women are most attracted to. In his newfound cruelty, he feels "for the first time that rush of power – the absolute power of a man"; he knows that he has her "turning on my needle." Just as he begins to regret his cruelty, the ambassador promotes him to vice-counsel, responsible for the coordination of the revamped intelligence division, because he has "become this new aggressive confident . . . thing." After his promotion, Gallimard goes to Song. Reluctant at first, she confirms that she is his "butterfly," then demurely sets the ground rules for their relationship: she keeps her clothes on, and the lights must be off.

Thus begins the first six years of Gallimard and Song's affair, during which Gallimard innocently transmits information to Song about American operations in Vietnam, which Song passes on to Chin, her Maoist contact. Only once, on the heels of his unsatisfying relationship with Renee, does Gallimard demand to see Song naked. She protests, then invites him to strip her; but as he comes toward her, he realizes his mistake: "Did I not undress her because I knew, somewhere deep down, what I would find? Perhaps. Happiness is so rare that our mind can turn somersaults to protect it." Song rewards his faithfulness with the announcement that she is pregnant, further endorsement of Gallimard's masculinity. Gallimard proposes marriage, which Song graciously declines. Seven months later, after demanding a blond-haired Chinese baby boy from Chin, Song reappears with a baby whom, in spite of Gallimard's objections, she has named "Peepee."

With his masculinity confirmed, Gallimard forwards his story three years, to 1966, when he is sent back to France, disgraced because of his poor political advice regarding China and Vietnam. The Chinese opera is shut down. Song is beaten by Maoists; forced to renounce her art, her privileges as an actor, and her homosexual crimes; and sent to work at a commune in the Hunan province. After four years Chin retrieves Song and orders her to go to France, continue her relationship with Gallimard, and resume transmitting political secrets to the party in China. Meanwhile, Gallimard has been miserable in France and has already divorced his wife when Song returns. Between acts 2 and 3, during a five-minute intermission, Song makes her onstage transformation from female to male. Even though Song invites the audience "to stretch your legs, enjoy a drink, or listen to the musicians," scholar Robert Skloot observes that viewers have rarely left their seats.

When the third act opens, Song removes his wig and kimono, revealing the suit he wears, and tells the audience that he and Gallimard lived together for fifteen years until, in 1986, Song's spying was discovered and he and Gallimard were brought to trial. In a courtroom, Song explains to the judge that he was able to fool Gallimard because "men always believe what they want to hear" and because the West has an "international rape mentality": "You expect Oriental countries to submit to your guns, and you expect Oriental women to be submissive to your men." In Song, Gallimard had "finally met his fantasy woman," and "he wanted more than anything that she was, in fact, a woman." Interrupting his testimony, Song addresses Gallimard and deconstructs Gallimard's Butterfly myth by treating him "cruelly," calling him "my little one," stripping, and turning the "rape mentality" back onto Gallimard. Song claims to desire Gallimard and suggests that Gallimard also wants him. After Gallimard denies his desire for the male Song, Song tells Gallimard, "You know something, Rene? Your mouth says no, but your eyes say yes." Gallimard chides Song for revealing his true nature and casts him out, retaining the Butterfly wig and kimono.

Unable to alter his gender and racial stereotypes, Rene transforms himself into an Oriental woman, making up his face and donning the kimono and wig. While Gallimard explains his vision of the Orient to the audi-

ence, the "Love Duet" from Puccini's opera plays. Before he thrusts a knife into his body, Rene declares, "My name is Rene Gallimard – also known as Madame Butterfly." Song "stands as a man" and repeats the words that Rene spoke to begin the play: "Butterfly? Butterfly?" The deconstruction of the Butterfly myth is complete.

With the donning and stripping of gender costumes in *M. Butterfly*–suit and kimono–Hwang suggests that gender and race are social constructs. His next plays, *Bondage* (1992), *Face Value* (1993), and *Trying to Find Chinatown* (1996) further investigate the social constructions of race and gender. Hwang explained to Frockt:

> Our cultures are essentially the personal histories that we have, and those elements of that personal history that we can share with other people and form a group become a culture. Consequently, the whole idea of skin color doesn't seem to me to be that useful anymore.... We have these mythologies that skin color should mean certain things, that we can gain information about the essence of a person by observing certain things in their exterior. I don't know that that's necessarily true, because a lot of times what would be information that you infer from looking at someone's outward features may be completely at odds with what their interior actually holds.

Hwang is not suggesting that cultural differences do not exist, but that those differences may not be tied directly to racial differences. Furthermore, he believes that "the essential universal humanity is ultimately something you can get to from having acknowledged these differences."

Hwang confounds the audience's attempts to rely on skin color as an indicator of character and culture in *Bondage*, commissioned by and performed as part of the 16th Annual Humana Festival of New American Plays in Louisville, Kentucky, on 1 March 1992. Two characters in an S&M parlor–Terri, a dominatrix, and Mark, her client–wear "full face masks and hoods to disguise their identities," assuming different racial roles as part of Mark's fantasy: a Chinese man and a blonde woman, or a white man and a black woman. In the adoption of various racial personas, Mark and Terri humiliate each other by enacting many of the stereotypes each race holds toward another. Terri assails Mark with verbal insults as swiftly as she literally whips him. Mark feigns a fight but always assumes the submissive position in the battle. Eventually Terri, like Song in *M. Butterfly*, challenges Mark's dependence on disguise and strips off her leather body costume under severe protest from Mark. She invites Mark to remove her mask and hood, but instead of removing Terri's,

Jeff Weiss, Dennis Dun, Jane Krakowski, and Mark Linn-Baker in the 1993 Boston production of Face Value *(photograph by Joan Marcus)*

Mark removes his own and reveals himself to be an Asian man. Terri removes her mask and hood to reveal that she is a Caucasian woman. After working through the racial and gender stereotypes, they are both prepared to love each other without pretense. This happy ending is possible because Mark and Terri have acted out the possible racial obstacles in their relationship and have reached a plateau of understanding. They have discovered the mutability of race.

During the early 1990s Hwang was living primarily in Los Angeles and commuting, when necessary, to New York City. He used his time in Los Angeles to work at screenplay writing. Two motion pictures were produced from his screenplays in 1993—*M. Butterfly,* starring Jeremy Irons and John Lone, and *Golden Gate,* starring Matt Dillon and Joan Chen—but neither met with much critical success. The movie adaptation of *M. Butterfly* did not adequately treat Gallimard's sexual insecurities or the complicated political undertones.

In New York, Hwang was not having any greater success. His next full-length play, *Face Value,* which closed after a short run in Boston and eight preview performances on Broadway, was inspired by the casting controversy surrounding the production of *Miss Saigon* (1989): a Caucasian actor, Jonathan Pryce, was cast as the lead, an Asian character. Hwang joined many in voicing his objection to the casting decision. On the sur-

face, Hwang's objection to the cross-racial casting may seem a contradiction to his expressed racial/cultural positions. But Hwang explains that while the theater should reach the point where anyone should be able to play any character regardless of the race of the character or the actor, color-blind casting is still not possible when 90 percent of the staging companies in the United States have all-white casts. To Frockt, Hwang argued that it is "useful now to say that when a role comes along for a minority we should cast it with a minority, because otherwise these people aren't getting employed. But ultimately you do want to get to a place where you suspend your disbelief. It is theatre; it is metaphor." Hwang also suggests that greater "cultural understanding" is necessary so that a cross-racial portrayal does not degenerate into racial stereotyping.

In *Face Value* a white actor, Bernard Sugarmann, paints his face to play Fu-Manchu in "The Real Manchu." An Asian actor, Randall Lee, protesting the casting decision, paints his face white and jumps onto the stage. Two white supremacists threaten to kill Sugarmann onstage because they believe he is an Asian actor who has taken a job from a white actor. The other characters in *Face Value*—three whites, one black, and two Asians—at various times appear in painted Fu-Manchu faces to frustrate the white supremacists. In various situations where racial identity is hidden, the characters of the play each eventually find love with a member of a different race.

Hwang described the play to Cooperman as "a 'what the butler saw' farce about mistaken racial identity," but in their criticism of the play, William H. Sun and Faye C. Fei suggest that *Face Value* deconstructs itself. It aims to show the "absurdity" of casting a white in an Asian role, yet concludes that race should not be an issue. Sun and Fei also note a contrast in tone from the beginning of the play, which is satirical, to the ending, which is didactic. They further argue that Hwang does not distinguish clearly enough between "racial distinctions" and "cultural differences."

Hwang clarifies the contrast between race and culture in *Trying to Find Chinatown,* commissioned and performed as part of the 20th Annual Humana Festival of New American Plays in Louisville, Kentucky, on 29 March 1996. A white man, Benjamin, adopted as an infant by Asian parents, seeks to connect himself more intimately to his adopted father, recently deceased, by visiting his father's childhood home in Chinatown in New York City. He asks directions from Ronnie, an Asian street violinist who proceeds to harangue Benjamin for assuming that because he is Asian, he must live in Chinatown. The violinist delivers a diatribe on racial stereotyping that reveals how culturally "white" he is and includes several stereotypes of Benjamin as a Midwestern hick. Benjamin patiently listens, then reveals his own Asian cultural heritage. Throughout their brief conversation, both characters are guilty of forming prejudices about the other based on skin color.

Trying to Find Chinatown illustrates Hwang's belief that racial appearance is not always an accurate indication of the cultural makeup of a person. Race is largely an accident of genetics and geography; cultural heritage develops in one's interaction with others. As always, Hwang plays with his audience's racial and cultural preconceptions and assumes that most people will not initially make a distinction between racial and cultural differences, seeing them as two parts of the same thing.

Hwang's next play, *Golden Child,* returns to earlier themes. *Golden Child* was commissioned by the South Coast Repertory of Costa Mesa, California, with which Hwang shared a 1996 Kennedy Center Fund for New American Plays production grant. The play was first performed at the Public Theater, then in Costa Mesa, in Singapore, at the American Conservatory Theatre in San Francisco, and at the Eisenhower Theater at the Kennedy Center, Washington, D.C. Between these early performances and the Broadway premiere, Hwang reworked the narrative frame of the story to include a more prominent position for the character of Eng Ahn. *Golden Child* premiered on Broadway at the Longacre Theatre and ran from 2 April to 31 May

1998, for a total of sixty-nine performances. In contrast to the ill-fated *Face Value,* this play was a critical success; Hwang received Tony and Outer Critics Circle Award nominations for *Golden Child* in 1998.

Golden Child examines the direct confrontation of Eastern and Western cultures and ideologies, looking specifically at the effects, both positive and negative, of the introduction of Christianity into Chinese society. The idea for the play comes from Hwang's own family's experience. When Hwang was ten, his grandmother became seriously ill. Fearing she would die, Hwang recorded the stories she told of her and her family's life in China. His grandmother recovered from her illness, but her sickness contributed to Hwang's writing a ninety-page historical novel chronicling the experiences of his ancestors. As with his other autobiographical plays, *Family Devotions* and *Rich Relations,* Hwang wrote *Golden Child* as a means of investigating family questions; he told Haines:

In this case, I'm trying to understand the motivations of my great grandfather, who made this choice to convert to Christianity, which – for most of my life – I felt very alienated and disconnected from. What motivates filling in the blanks in this case is a desire to articulate the motivation that will make sense of it, so I can identify it and feel an empathy and connection with my ancestors.

As in his other domestic dramas, Hwang incorporates surrealistic techniques into *Golden Child.* The play opens in the present as the ghost of Ahn, Andrew Kwong's mother, awakens him with "Andrew—you must be born again." Andrew, sleeping next to his pregnant wife, is not a Christian and does not want to be a father. As Ahn continues to nag, encourage, and reminisce, above Andrew's protests that dead Christians are not supposed to haunt people, she transforms from an elderly woman to a young girl of ten or eleven. Simultaneously, the set changes from present-day New York to 1918 China and the three living quarters of the wives of Andrew's grandfather, Eng Tieng-Bin (played by the same actor who plays Andrew; the same actress plays Elizabeth, Andrew's wife, and Eling, Tieng-Bin's third wife). The conflict of the story Eng Ahn tells her son, Andrew, revolves around Eng Tieng-Bin's return home from an extended business trip. He comes back with an assortment of gifts: a cuckoo clock for his first wife, Eng Siu-Yong, Ahn's mother, the traditionalist; a waffle iron for his second wife, Eng Luon, the industrious schemer; and a gramophone and recordings of Italian opera for his third wife, Eng Eling, Tieng-Bin's beloved. More significantly for the family, Tieng-Bin is accompanied by Reverend Baines, an English-speaking Christian missionary. Tieng-Bin's decision to convert to Christianity and the corresponding Western values and ideologies turns the Eng household upside down, pitting the wives against each other as they negotiate their positions in the new order; they all understand that they cannot all stay if the family converts to Christianity. The beneficiary of her father's decision, Ahn is the "golden child" of the title, the one for whom everything is possible because she is "unbound."

Hwang investigates the benefits and detriments of the Christian influence on the Eng family, and by analogy, his own family. Traditional values and practices, such as foot-binding, are questioned. When Tieng-Bin orders that Ahn's feet be unbound, Ahn is overjoyed at her liberation. But her mother, the traditionalist, warns her that the unbinding will be painful, not only physically, as the foot regains its shape, but culturally, as traditions are supplanted by modern practices. In retrospect, Ahn explains to Andrew: "But when change come, come like fire. No one know—who will live, and who will be lost." Hwang explained to Raymond that Christianity is merely the first step in the process of this complete decentering of the traditions of the Eng family:

> For Tieng-Bin, Christianity is much more complex than representing some kind of assimilation of the white God. . . . It becomes an ideology (just like Marxism, which was also imported from the West) that allows him to find a framework for going forward in social history.

Tieng-Ben's motivations for conversion are complicated. He wants to modernize, but his primary reason for converting is the freedom of monogamy that Christianity provides; Tieng-Bin wants to have Eling, his pregnant third wife, as his only wife. Upon the suicide of his respected first wife and the death of his beloved Eling in childbirth, Tieng-Bin is left with the monogamous companionship of the manipulative second wife. Tieng-Ben is devastated by the unexpected results of his conversion and loses his joy and reason for living. Ahn saves her father from committing suicide, but he has clearly lost faith. Ahn, however, retains faith and attempts to exhort her father with the comfort of New Testament scripture and with the assurance that she will always remember and relate "how you made us all born again."

Ahn's story only confirms Andrew's fear of parenting. Andrew explains to his mother, "You see? Why I don't want to became a parent? Your father tried so hard, but he only brought tragedy to himself and everyone around him." But Ahn disagrees. She is thankful for what her father did, despite the tragic consequences of his conversion: "My father, Tieng-Bin—this one thing I will never forget: you see, he is the one . . . who take the

binding from my feet." Infused with the spirit of what his grandfather did for his family, Andrew has the strength to welcome the future of his own "golden child."

Having moved from Los Angeles to New York City with his second wife, Kathryn Layng, an actress, and their son, Noah (born in May 1996), Hwang continues to be active in the theater. While *Golden Child* was being groomed for its Broadway premiere, in January 1998 Hwang's adaptation of Henrik Ibsen's *Peer Gynt* (1867) was produced by the Trinity Repertory Company in Rhode Island, where Hwang was the current artist in residence. Hwang was also enlisted to assist Linda Woolverton and Robert Falls with the rewriting of the libretto for Giuseppe Verdi's *Aida* (1871) for a Disney musical theatrical presentation with music by Elton John and lyrics by Tim Rice. *Aida* previewed in Chicago in November 1999 and opened on Broadway on 23 March 2000. In addition, Hwang's rewriting of Richard Rodgers and Oscar Hammerstein's *Flower Drum Song* (1958) is in workshop production. These projects illustrate well the range of his artistic work. While Hwang has found the greatest success in his plays that deal directly with Asian American experiences, he does not limit himself to specifically Asian American contexts; most of his works make use of surrealistic and ritualistic devices and concern universal themes of displacement and identity.

Interviews:

John Louis DiGaetani, "An Interview with David Henry Hwang," *Drama Review,* 33 (Fall 1989): 141–153;

Deborah Frockt, "David Henry Hwang," in *The Playwright's Art: Conversations with Contemporary American Dramatists,* edited by Jackson R. Bryer (New Brunswick, N.J.: Rutgers University Press, 1995), pp. 123–146;

Robert Cooperman, "Across the Boundaries of Cultural Identity: An Interview with David Henry Hwang," in *Staging Difference: Cultural Pluralism in American Theatre and Drama,* edited by Marc Maufort (New York: Peter Lang, 1995), pp. 365–373;

Marty Moss-Coane, "David Henry Hwang," in *Speaking on Stage: Interviews with Contemporary American Playwrights,* edited by Philip C. Kolin and Colby H. Kullman (Tuscaloosa: University of Alabama Press, 1996), pp. 277–290;

Chris Haines, "Golden Man: An Interview with David Henry Hwang," *Tony Awards Online* [online magazine], March 1998.

References:

Hsiao-hung Chang, "Cultural/Sexual/Theatrical Ambivalence in *M. Butterfly,*" *Tamkang Review,* 23 (Fall 1992–1993): 735–755;

Gabrielle Cody, "David Hwang's *M. Butterfly:* Perpetuating the Misogynist Myth," *Theater,* 20 (Spring 1989): 24–27;

Robert Cooperman, "New Theatrical Statements: Asian Western Mergers in the Plays of David Henry Hwang," in *Staging Difference: Cultural Pluralism in American Theatre and Drama,* edited by Marc Maufort (New York: Peter Lang, 1995), pp. 201–213;

Jerry R. Dickey, "'Myths of the East, Myths of the West': Shattering Racial and Gender Stereotypes in the Plays of David Henry Hwang," in *Old West–New West: Centennial Essays,* edited by Barbara Howard Meldrum (Moscow, Idaho: University of Idaho Press, 1993), pp. 272–280;

David L. Eng, "In the Shadows of a Diva: Committing Homosexuality in David Henry Hwang's *M. Butterfly,*" *Amerasia Journal,* 20 (1994): 93–116;

Janet V. Haedicke, "David Henry Hwang's *M. Butterfly:* The Eye on the Wing," *Journal of Dramatic Theory and Criticism,* 7 (Fall 1992): 27–44;

Melanie C. Hawthorne, "Du Du That Voodoo: *M. Venus* and *M. Butterfly,*" *Esprit Createur,* 37 (Winter 1997): 58–66;

Suzanne Kehde, "Engendering the Imperial Subject: The (De)Construction of (Western) Masculinity in David Henry Hwang's *M. Butterfly* and Graham Greene's *The Quiet American,*" in *Fictions of Masculinity: Crossing Cultures, Crossing Sexualities,* edited by Peter F. Murphy (New York: New York University Press, 1994), pp. 241–254;

Douglas Kerr, "David Henry Hwang and the Revenge of Madame Butterfly," in *Asian Voices in English,* edited by Mimi Chan and Roy Harris (Hong Kong: Hong Kong University Press, 1991), pp. 119–130;

Foong Ling Kong, "Pulling the Wings off Butterfly," *Southern Review,* 27 (December 1994): 418–431;

Colleen Lye, "*M. Butterfly* and the Rhetoric of Antiessentialism: Minority Discourse in an International Frame," in *The Ethnic Canon: Histories, Institutions, and Interventions,* edited by David Palumbo-Lin (Minneapolis: University of Minneapolis Press, 1995), pp. 260–289;

Kent Neely, "Intimacy or Cruel Love: Displacing the Other by Self Assertion," *Journal of Dramatic Theory and Criticism,* 5 (Spring 1991): 167–173;

Gerard Raymond, "Good as Gold," *Stagebill* [online magazine], March 1997;

Kathryn Remen, "The Theatre of Punishment: David Henry Hwang's *M. Butterfly* and Michel Foucault's *Discipline and Punish,*" *Modern Drama,* 37 (Fall 1994): 391–400;

Karen Shimakawa, "'Who's to Say?': Or, Making Space for Gender and Ethnicity in *M. Butterfly,*" *Theatre Journal,* 45 (October 1993): 349–361;

Robert Skloot, "Breaking the Butterfly: The Politics of David Henry Hwang," *Modern Drama,* 33 (March 1990): 59–66;

Douglas Street, *David Henry Hwang,* Western Writers Series, no. 90 (Boise: Boise State University, 1989);

William H. Sun and Faye C. Fei, "Masks or Faces Re-Visited: A Study of Four Theatrical Works Concerning Cultural Identity," *Drama Review,* 38 (Winter 1994): 120–132.

Papers:

David Henry Hwang's papers, including working and final drafts of plays and screenplays, production records, reviews, and correspondence, are in the American Literary Studies Collection of the Department of Special Collections, Green Library, Stanford University.

Tony Kushner
(16 July 1956 –)

James Fisher
Wabash College

PLAY PRODUCTIONS: *The Age of Assassins,* New York, Newfoundland Theatre, 1982;

La Fin de la Baleine: An Opera for the Apocalypse, New York, Ohio Theatre, 1983;

The Umbrella Oracle, Martha's Vineyard, The Yard, Inc.;

Last Gasp at the Cataract, Martha's Vineyard, The Yard, Inc., 1984;

A Bright Room Called Day, New York, Theatre 22, 22 April 1985; San Francisco, Eureka Theatre, October 1987; London, Bush Theatre, 1988;

Yes Yes No No: The Solace-of-Solstice, Apogee/Perigee, Bestial/Celestial Holiday Show, St. Louis, Missouri, Imaginary Theatre Company, Repertory Theatre of St. Louis, 1985;

The Heavenly Theatre, New York University, Tisch School of the Arts, 1986;

In Great Eliza's Golden Time, St. Louis, Missouri, Imaginary Theatre Company, Repertory Theatre of St. Louis, 1986;

Stella, adapted from Johann Wolfgang von Goethe's play, New York, New York Theatre Workshop, 1987;

Hydriotaphia, or The Death of Dr. Browne, New York, Home for Contemporary Theatre and Art, 1987;

The Illusion, adapted from Pierre Corneille's play *L'illusion comique,* New York, New York Theatre Workshop, October 1988; revised, Hartford, Connecticut, Hartford Stage Company, December 1989; revised, Los Angeles, Los Angeles Theatre Center, April 1990;

In That Day (Lives of the Prophets), New York University, Tisch School of the Arts, 1989;

Widows, by Kushner and Ariel Dorfman, adapted from Dorfman's book, Los Angeles, 1991;

Angels in America: A Gay Fantasia on National Themes, Part One: Millennium Approaches, Los Angeles: Center Theatre Group/Mark Taper Forum, 1990; San Francisco, Eureka Theatre, May 1991; London, National Theatre, and Los Angeles, Mark Taper Forum, 23 January 1992; New York, Walter Kerr Theatre, 4 May 1993;

Tony Kushner (The Joyce Ketay Agency)

Angels in America: A Gay Fantasia on National Themes, Part Two: Perestroika, San Francisco, Eureka Theatre, 1991; London, Royal National Theatre, 20 November 1993; New York, Walter Kerr Theatre, 23 November 1993;

Slavs! Thinking About the Longstanding Problems of Virtue and Happiness, Louisville, Kentucky, Humana Festival of New American Plays, Actors Theatre of Louisville, 8 March 1994; New York, New York Theatre Workshop, November 1994; London, Hampstead Theatre, December 1994;

The Good Person of Setzuan, La Jolla, California, La Jolla Playhouse, July 1994;

A Dybbuk, or Between Two Worlds, adapted from Solomon Ansky's play *Der Dybbuk,* New Haven, Connecticut, Hartford Stage Company, February 1995; New York, Joseph Papp Public Theater, November 1997;

Reverse Transcription: Six Playwrights Bury a Seventh, A Ten-Minute Play That's Nearly Twenty Minutes Long, Louisville, Humana Festival of New American Plays, Actors Theatre of Louisville, March 1996;

Henry Box Brown, or The Mirror of Slavery, London, Royal National Theatre, 1998;

Terminating, or Lass Meine Schmerzen Nicht Verloren Sein, or Ambivalence, in *Love's Fire,* Minneapolis, Guthrie Theater Lab, 7 January 1998; New York: Joseph Papp Public Theater, 19 June 1998;

Home Body/Kabul: A Monologue for Kika Markham, London, Chelsea Theatre Centre, July 1999.

BOOKS: *Angels in America, Part I: Millennium Approaches* (London: National Theatre/Nick Hern, 1992; New York: Theatre Communications Group, 1993);

Plays by Tony Kushner (New York: Broadway Play Publishing, 1992)—comprises *A Bright Room Called Day* and *The Illusion;*

Angels in America, Part II: Perestroika (London: National Theatre/Nick Hern, 1994; New York: Theatre Communications Group, 1994);

Thinking About the Longstanding Problems of Virtue and Happiness: Essays, A Play, Two Poems, and a Prayer (New York: Theatre Communications Group, 1995; London: Nick Hern, 1995);

A Dybbuk; and, The Dybbuk Melody and Other Themes and Variations, adapted from Solomon Ansky's play and translated by Joachim Neugroschel (New York: Theatre Communications Group, 1998);

Death and Taxes: Hydriotaphia and Other Plays (New York: Theatre Communications Group, 2000)—comprises *Hydriotaphia, or The Death of Dr. Browne; Reverse Transcription; Terminating, or, Sonnet LXXV, or, Lass Meine Schmerzen Nicht Verloren Sein, or, Ambivalence; East Coast Ode to Howard Jarvis;* and *David Schine in Hell.*

Edition: *Plays by Tony Kushner* (New York: Broadway Play Publishing, 1999)—comprises *A Bright Room called Day, The Illusion,* and *Slavs! Thinking About the Longstanding Problems of Virtue and Happiness.*

OTHER: *Yes Yes No No,* in *Three Plays for Young Audiences* (New York: Theatre Communications Group, 1987);

Howard Cruse, *Stuck Rubber Baby,* introduction by Kushner (New York: Paradox Press, 1995);

David B. Feinberg, *Queer and Loathing: Rants and Raves of a Raging AIDS Clone,* introduction by Kushner (New York: Penguin, 1995);

David Wojnarowicz, *The Waterfront Journals,* edited by Amy Scholder, introduction by Kushner (New York: Grove, 1996);

"Three Screeds from Key West: For Larry Kramer," in *We Must Love One Another or Die: The Life and Legacies of Larry Kramer,* edited by Lawrence D. Mass (New York: St. Martin's Press, 1997), pp. 191–199;

Moises Kaufman, *Gross Indecency,* afterword by Kushner (New York: Vintage, 1997), pp. 135–143.

SELECTED PERIODICAL PUBLICATIONS–UNCOLLECTED: "The Secrets of *Angels,*" *New York Times,* 27 March 1994, p. H5;

"The State of the Theatre," *Times Literary Supplement,* 28 April 1995, p. 14;

"The Theater of Utopia," *Theater,* 26 (1995): 9–11;

"The Art of the Difficult," *Civilization,* 4 (August/September 1997): 62–67;

"Notes About Political Theater," *Kenyon Review,* 19 (Summer/Fall 1997): 19–34;

"Wings of Desire," *Premiere* (October 1997): 70;

"Fo's Last Laugh–I," *Nation* (3 November 1997): 4–5;

"A Modest Proposal," *American Theatre* (January 1998): 20–22, 77–89.

Tony Kushner burst onto the international stage in the early 1990s with the critical success of his two-part *Angels in America.* Already established as a director, adaptor, and playwright working in regional theaters prior to *Angels in America,* Kushner found himself thrust into the forefront of American drama. He has also emerged as a national spokesman for several social causes as a result of both the international acclaim and controversy that has accompanied *Angels in America.* Consisting of two long plays, *Millennium Approaches* (performed in 1990) and *Perestroika* (1991), *Angels in America* is a complex portrait of life in the United States during Ronald Reagan's presidency. It presents that era as a critical transitional period in the history of the nation–a time that raised complicated questions about the future of American society, particularly in the areas of morality, politics, and sexuality. In *Angels in America,* as in many of his other plays, Kushner questions the American brand of morality in a nation of diverse and often conflicted views and values. Kushner explores these issues through a blend of the hilarious and the tragic, examining a few individuals in the intimacy of their private lives at moments of significant personal crisis influenced, to a great extent, by societal conditions and the specters of the past and the future.

Kushner was born in Manhattan on 16 July 1956, the son of William and Sylvia (Deutscher) Kushner, both classically trained musicians who encouraged his budding interest in the arts and literature. Kushner spent most of his childhood in Lake Charles, Louisiana. His mother, an amateur actress, performed in local plays, and Kushner became entranced by the emotional power of the theater and the arts in general. As he recalled in a 1996 interview with David Savran, "I have very strong memories of her power and the effect she had on people. . . . And then there were other obvious things. I grew up very, very closeted, and I'm sure that the disguise of theatre, the doubleness, and all that slightly tawdry stuff interested me."

Kushner moved to New York in 1974 to begin his undergraduate college education at Columbia University, where he completed a B.A. in English literature in 1978. While in college, he also immersed himself in the New York theater scene. Following the completion of his degree at Columbia, Kushner worked as a switchboard operator at the United Nations Plaza Hotel from 1979 to 1985, during which time he also enrolled at the Tisch School of the Arts, New York University. Trained as a director under the guidance of Bertolt Brecht specialist Carl Weber, Kushner wrote plays and directed them with his fellow students prior to completing his M.F.A. in directing in 1984. Some of these plays were also staged by the Imaginary Theatre Company at the Repertory Theatre of St. Louis.

Kushner's plays in this period, beginning around 1982, demonstrate the breadth of his playwriting. These works include an opera, *La Fin de la Baleine: An Opera for the Apocalypse* (1983); an adaptation of Johann Wolfgang von Goethe's 1776 play *Stella* (1987); some children's plays, including *Yes Yes No No: The Solace-of-Solstice, Apogee/Perigee, Bestial/Celestial Holiday Show* (1985) and "The Protozoa Review" (written in 1985); and one-act and full-length plays, including *The Heavenly Theatre* (1986), *In Great Eliza's Golden Time* (1986), and *Hydriotaphia, or The Death of Dr. Browne* (1987). Even in his earliest works, Kushner explored themes and techniques that were still evident in his drama at the end of the 1990s. From the mid 1980s, Kushner's work as both a director and a playwright brought him awards and the support of several grants, including the Seidman Award in Directing from the Tisch School of the Arts in 1983–1984, a directing fellowship from the National Endowment for the Arts in 1985, the Princess Grace Award in 1986, a playwriting fellowship from the New York State Council for the Arts in 1987, and a fellowship from the National Endowment for the Arts in 1988.

J. Grant Albrecht in the 1989–1990 Hartford production of The Illusion *(photograph by T. Charles Erickson)*

As an overtly sociopolitical dramatist, Kushner is a comparative rarity in the American theater. Earlier American dramatists with political aims, such as Clifford Odets and Arthur Miller, seem to have had little direct influence on Kushner, although he directed a production of Odets's *Golden Boy* (1937) in 1986 at the Repertory Theatre of St. Louis. Kushner seems instead to be more influenced by Henrik Ibsen, George Bernard Shaw, and especially Brecht, whom he greatly admires. Kushner told Savran he believes that all theater is political and that he "cannot be a playwright without having some temptation to let audiences know what I think when I read the newspaper in the morning. What I find is that the things that make you the most uncomfortable are the best things to write plays about." Kushner's political awakening had begun during his college days, and his politics permeate his work as a dramatist. After he read Ernst Fischer's *Von der Notwendigkeit der Kunst* (translated as *The Necessity of Art: A Marxist Approach,* 1963), Kushner's commitment to the social responsibility of artists grew. However, whereas most dramatists of American political theater worked in the realistic vein, Kushner turned for inspiration to Brecht and to lyrical American plays such as those of Tennessee Williams or John Guare.

Kushner came of age in an era of major changes in the American cultural landscape. Having come to terms in his late teens with his homosexuality, following some abortive efforts to find a "cure" for his sexual orientation, Kushner became inspired, in part, by the writers and artists emerging from the Stonewall generation and after. He was especially drawn to such organizations as ACT UP and Queer Nation, whose chant, "We're here, we're queer, we're fabulous," pervades his two *Angels in America* plays. As a gay man, Kushner also acknowledges some debt to gay dramatists Larry Kramer and Harvey Fierstein, but more directly significant to his development as a dramatist is his deep admiration for Williams, the American dramatist who brought sexuality out of the theatrical closet. He told Savran, "The first time I read *Streetcar,* I was annihilated. I read as much Williams as I could get my hands on until the late plays started getting embarrassingly bad. . . . I'm really influenced by Williams." Critics have also noted Kushner's descent from Williams. John Lahr writes of Kushner that "Not since Williams has a playwright announced his poetic vision with such authority on the Broadway stage. Kushner is the heir apparent to Williams' romantic theatrical heritage: he, too, has tricks in his pocket and things up his sleeve, and he gives the audience 'truth in the pleasant disguise of illusion.' And, also like Williams, Kushner has forged an original, impressionistic theatrical vocabulary to show us the heart of a new age."

One important point is that Kushner is both unmistakably American and, at the same time, strongly connected to his Eastern European roots. As a Jew, Kushner is part of an ethnic heritage that has survived harrowing losses. He recognizes parallels between the Jewish experience and what gays contend with in American society. In attempting to deal with his conflicted feelings about his Jewishness, Kushner finds "a deep ambivalence, because there is a fantastically powerful homophobic tradition within Judaism." However, for Kushner, the connections between Judaism and homosexuality are important. Both groups have a shared history of "oppression and persecution" that offers "a sort of false possibility of a kind of an assimilation," but, Kushner insists that "as Hannah Arendt says, it's better to be a pariah than a parvenu. If you're hated by a social order, don't try and make friends with it. Identify yourself as other, and identify your determining characteristics as those characteristics which make you other and unliked and despised."

It is of central significance that Kushner identifies himself as a gay dramatist. He began his career in ear-

nest as the devastation of the AIDS pandemic in the early 1980s became all too clear. He became assistant director of the St. Louis Repertory Theatre from 1985 to 1986, and from 1987 to 1988 he was artistic director of the New York Theatre Workshop. Kushner also worked as Director of Literary Services for the Theatre Communications Group in 1989 and regularly taught courses and seminars for several universities before joining the permanent faculty of the Tisch School of the Arts in 1996. However, Kushner's work as a director and teacher was superseded by his writing and adapting.

As an adapter, Kushner has frequently turned to neglected works by great writers, including Goethe and, most successfully, Pierre Corneille. Avoiding the constraints of the naturalistic approach, Kushner found in these plays a way to present his themes in a theatrical and imaginative way. Kushner's adaptation of Corneille's comedy *L'illusion comique* (1636), which he completed in 1988, is the most frequently produced of his adaptations and the most instructive in its relation to Kushner's style and typical themes. During the late 1980s and early 1990s, it was staged by several regional and repertory theaters hungry for classics that could garner the popular appeal that Kushner's adaptation attained.

Kushner's adaptation, *The Illusion,* begins with Pridamant, a cantankerous old man, searching for a magician in a dark cave. He stumbles across a speechless amanuensis, who leads Pridamant to Alcandre, the magician. Some years before, Pridament had bitterly quarreled with his son and thrown the boy out of his house, severing all family ties. Now the regretful old man feels his life ebbing away and he misses his son, despite a stubborn unwillingness to admit it. He wants Alcandre to conjure up visions of his son's life, which the magician does in a series of scenes that depict the young man at various points under different names: Calisto, Clindor, and Theogenes. Most of these scenes focus on romantic misadventures, with the changes in name and other disjunctures confusing the impatient Pridamant. Most of Alcandre's visions depict various manifestations of love in both comic and tragic strains. In a Kushner addition to the text, Alcandre insists that "My visions are concocted through a violent synthesis, a forced conflation of light and shadow, matter and gossamer, blood and air. The magic's born of this uneasy marriage; it costs, you see, it hurts, it's dragged unwillingly from the darkest pools."

Pridamant remains confused, and his anger rises when he sees his son behaving foolishly in Alcandre's visions. Alcandre invites Pridamant to give in to "the strange, pulsing warmth; the flow of blood, the flood of time, immediate, urgent, like bathing water in a warm ocean, rocked by currents of disappointment, joy. . . . The heart chases memory through the cavern of dreams." As the visions continue, Pridamant's regrets and longing for his son overwhelm him. When Alcandre realizes that Pridamant has reached the appropriate level of vulnerability, he reveals that the images of his son are actually scenes from various plays—the son, it turns out, is an actor. "I don't know that I like that," Pridamant grumbles, complaining that the theater is "a make-believe world" consisting "of angel hair and fancy talk, no more substantial than a soap bubble. You are moved at the sight of a foul murder—then the murderer and the murdered are holding hands, taking bows together. It's sinister." Alcandre retorts in another Kushner addition to Corneille, "What in this world is not evanescent? What in this world is real and not seeming?" As Alcandre explains, the theatrical depictions of love show

> Love is a sea of desire stretched between shores—only the shores are real, but how much more compelling is the sea. Love is the world's infinite mutability; lies, hatred, murder even are knit up in it; it is the inevitable blossoming of its opposites, a magnificent rose smelling faintly of blood. A dream which makes the world seem . . . an illusion. The art of illusion is the art of love, and the art of love is the blood-red heart of the world.

Pridamant, moved to unexpected tears, wanders off to find his son as Alcandre and his amanuensis bring the play to its bittersweet conclusion.

Critics applauded Kushner's vivid revitalization of a forgotten classic, and *The Illusion* has had a healthy stage life. Audiences undoubtedly assume that much of the effectiveness of the play springs from Corneille, but as one reviewer for *The New York Times* (20 January 1994) noted, the "cosmic touch springs from Mr. Kushner's fecund imagination, not Corneille's." The multi-layered fantasy of the play respects the original source while avoiding the pitfalls of literary reverence (with much humor satirizing both theatrical and literary traditions) and the heaviness of the realistic tradition.

Other Kushner adaptations include his early version of Goethe's *Stella,* which he continues to revise, and *The Good Person of Setzuan,* his version of Brecht's *Der gute Mensch von Sezuan* (1943), produced at La Jolla Playhouse in the summer of 1994. Kushner adapted this play from a literal translation and insists that "I've taken almost no liberties with the Brecht at all, so I'm nervous about people thinking of it as an adaptation—it's not me; it's Brecht. I thought the most important function was to be true to Brecht and also playable by American actors." Brecht's play is a parable about three gods coming to earth in search of one good and decent person. Kushner's updating sets the play in contempo-

rary Southern California, where Latinos, Native Americans, and African Americans struggle for survival and where goodness is seen as a liability or a sucker's game. For Kushner, Brecht's "characters have a certain universality and fit very easily" into this updated setting. Under the direction of Lisa Peterson, the La Jolla production featured ethnically diverse cast members, and Kushner stressed the significance of a multicultural approach in which "everybody in the play is economically marginal, which I think reflects another reality; where people who are white have money and people who aren't white are frequently struggling economically." Kushner's Brecht thus presents culture clashes as a way of life. Other Kushner adaptations include *Widows*—from Ariel Dorfman's 1981 novel, *Viudas*—and Kushner's rendering of Solomon Ansky's 1920 Yiddish theater classic, *Der Dybbuk*. Written in 1994 for production at the Hartford Stage Company in Connecticut in February 1995, Kushner's adaptation, titled *A Dybbuk, or Between Two Worlds,* was well-received at Hartford as well as in a subsequent 1997 production at the Public Theater in New York.

A Dybbuk seems a logical choice for Kushner since its theatricality and emotionalism bear similarities to Kushner's own plays. Its examination of past Jewish life and beliefs provides Kushner with an opportunity to experiment with linking images of the past with those of the present and the future. Something of a forerunner to this adaptation is one of Kushner's one-act experiments, "'It's an Undoing World,' or Why Should It Be Easy When It Can Be Hard? Notes on My Grandma for Actors, Dancers and a Band" (written in 1995), in which Kushner also explores the world of fantasy. In this one-act, spirits reside in teapots ("Oooooyyyyyyyy . . . It's an undoing world, I'm telling you," wails one); daughters sleep on their fathers' graves; and knowledge is passed between the hands of men and women as they dance.

A Dybbuk recounts the tragic romance of a young rabbinical student, Chonen, who is in love with Leah, the daughter of a well-to-do merchant, Sender, who had made a pact with Chonen's long-dead father that their children would one day wed. Sender's greed leads him to break the pact, and Leah is promised in marriage to another young man whose family will bring an important financial advantage to Sender. Chonen dies in despair over this betrayal, and his spirit—a dybbuk—possesses Leah. Rabbi Azriel, an exorcist, is sent for in hopes that he can free Leah from the dybbuk's hold. He finally does, but Leah dies, and she and Chonen are ultimately united in another world.

There are parallels between the lives and dramatic styles of author and adapter. Ambivalent about

Ellen McLaughlin and Stephen Spinella in the 1993 New York production of Angels in America: A Gay Fantasia on National Themes, Part One: Millennium Approaches *(photograph © by Joan Marcus)*

his Jewish heritage, Kushner recognizes in Ansky a kindred spirit. Both writers are driven by deep religious doubts, but both express the power of the spiritual realm and the individual's eternal struggle with and search for spiritual understanding. Ansky's internal struggle with his religious skepticism and political activism are, for Kushner, central to the strengths of the play. He states that Ansky "went toward Judaism by his political convictions" and that his "sense of himself as a political revolutionary was very much at odds with this sort of emotional tie that he had with Judaism," which Ansky himself described as the sole motif of his drama: "spiritual struggle." Kushner's view of spirituality is certainly more ambiguous and complex than Ansky's, but there are striking connections.

These connections are important to understanding why Kushner was drawn to this problematic play and are essential to appreciating his treatment. Like his earlier plays, *A Dybbuk* presents intense intellectual debates on social and spiritual issues. However, in Kushner's play these questions are merged with feverish dreams and flights of fantasy as his characters grapple with their mixed feelings about their social circumstances, their heritage, and their search for love and faith. Working from a literal translation of the play by Joachim Neugroschel, Kushner substantially restructures Ansky's text and makes use of the Brechtian episodic style that he also demonstrates in his original plays.

Kushner's optimism, tempered by an unblinking view of the dark corners of life, emerges in his adaptation of *A Dybbuk*. Hope can spring from loss, Kushner stresses—Chonen cannot survive the loss of Leah in this world, but he wins her in the next. Wrongs can be righted, the universe can be put in order. The significance of the subtitle, *Between Two Worlds,* is, in part, that the play works on dual levels. As Alisa Solomon writes, "death resides in life, male in female, the spiritual in the carnal, religious doubt in devotion, evil in goodness, social well-being in private acts, Hasidism in modernity, the holy in the profane. And, in each instance, vice versa." To that list should be added real life in fantasy. Kushner uses these dualities to explore his fascination with Judaic traditions—both religious and secular—and to reflect on the impact of the spiritual and the natural worlds on the individual. Above all, he is fascinated with the suggestion of the possibility of communing with the dead, of ongoing relationships past the grave, and of the ultimate, often hard justice of the universe.

Solomon identifies the "intensely homosocial world" of *A Dybbuk,* which "vibrates with erotic implication," and it is clear that these undercurrents supply the play with considerable sensuality. For example, rabbinical students indulge in an orgiastic dance in the synagogue, and Chonen delivers a passionate recitation of the "Song of Songs" for his beloved Leah. More potently, as the dybbuk, Chonen penetrates Leah's body in ways that are simultaneously spiritual and sexual.

Kushner freely adapts Ansky's original play, adding and eliminating dialogue and abandoning antiquated theatrical and literary devices. His changes are less technical than they are a result of a deeply personal exploration of the themes of the play with the goal of drawing out its universal significances, its aesthetic power, and its emotional force. Kushner's adaptation maintains much of Ansky's emphasis on the central characters, while placing significantly greater attention on theological skepticism. For example, Kushner adds a speech that permits Rabbi Azriel to express his doubts more pointedly than Ansky does, as when at the end of act 3, alone with his Scribe, Azriel cries out to his deceased grandfather:

You have been dead sixty-seven years; in that time I only grow weaker, and the world grows wickeder. But you in Paradise have grown stronger, and I ask you to accompany me now. In Lublin, in Zlotchov, pogroms. The people talk idly of traveling and scientific marvels and don't pray. I'm older than my years, I don't sleep at night. Under my robe, my knees knock together in fear sometimes. (Softly) And sometimes, Grandfather, I do not entirely trust God. (To the Scribe) Don't write that down.

Kushner also manages to foreshadow the horrors of the coming Holocaust, most obviously in the onstage arrival of Azriel in a railroad boxcar, which visually reminds the audience of the transportation of Jews to concentration camps before and during World War II. Kushner makes this connection frequently in a variety of ways, for example by adding the line: "In a world of electric light, even Jews can ride the trains." Holocaust imagery can also be found in act 4 when during the exorcism of the dybbuk from Leah's body, the Scribe, documenting the procedure in a record book, is stunned that an unseen hand has filled a blank page with a description of the horrors Jews will face in the twentieth century:

At some not-very-distant date
the martyred dead accumulate;
books of history will contain
mountain-piles of the slain.

While the time period and ethnic specificity of the play matter to Kushner, especially in the social, historical, and sexual connotations of the dybbuk folklore, his contemporary awareness is critically important, as it is in all of his major works. Kushner's highly atmospheric orthodox Jewish world is predominantly and authoritatively male in its structure, but one that is challenged by a breaking down of expected norms and, in fact, a feminist perspective. This perspective can be seen in the comedy he produces in the first act from the layabout Talmudic scholars who debate women's exclusion from the synagogue floor and by having Leah's awkward, unwanted groom declare, "when we thank God in the morning he didn't make us women, no one's more grateful than I am." Sender's avaricious use of his daughter to better himself financially allows Kushner to emphasize the treatment of women as chattel in the world of the play. Other traditional views of this world are challenged, in part, by a mixture of spiritual longing and earthly passion that takes on a dark eroticism.

Kushner stretches the stylistic boundaries of the play, maintaining its qualities as a supernatural folktale of crossed worlds, hearts, and historical ages, while also reckoning with its religious ritual and, most importantly, its depiction of the sensuality of unformed and unutterable longings that may be beyond human governance. The claims of the dead on the living, the merging of the worlds of both, and the relationship of Jews to each other and to God shatter narrow definitions of gender and history. In the final scene of *A Dybbuk,* Azriel sends The Messenger off with a pointed message for God: "Though His love become only abrasion, derision, excoriation, tell Him, I cling. We cling. He made us, He can never shake us off. We will always find Him out. Promise Him that. We will always find Him, no matter how few there are, tell Him we will find Him. To deliver our complaint."

Critical reaction to *A Dybbuk* has been generally positive. Of the Hartford production, a critic for *The New York Times* (20 February 1995) wrote that most of Kushner's "interpolations enhance the play's inherent imagery and themes already implicit: sexual division, racial self-awareness, and (since this is Tony Kushner, after all) a glimmer of apocalyptic apprehension." A reviewer for *InTheatre* magazine (5 December 1997)found Kushner's adaptation "vital," stressing that it "is both more lyrical and more suffused with the kind of folk humor that Ansky prized."

Kushner's interest in East European Judaic traditions continues in his work. He has been grappling with another great Jewish myth that he sees as a counterpoint project, titled "The Golem." In preparation, he is studying Yiddish, "a moral imperative," he believes, stressing that it took a thousand years to make the language and "It'd be a shame to let it die." "The Golem" deals with the old myth that the golem was created as a "protector of the Jews," and it is a distinctly urban play, as opposed to the rural setting of *A Dybbuk.* Kushner stresses the historical oppression of the Jews in his approach to "The Golem" and focuses on the question of how to "confront anti-Semitism? How do you confront the genocidal intent of the world without yourself becoming a murderer, and without usurping certain things which are proscribed by God."

Kushner's combination of the political and the emotional, his episodic Brechtian style, a bold theatricality, and his love of language, all evident in his adaptations and short plays, are most effectively demonstrated in his full-length works. In April 1998 one of Kushner's earliest full-length plays, *Hydriotaphia, or The Death of Dr. Browne,* written a decade earlier, was successfully produced by the Alley Theatre in Houston. A subsequent production at the Berkeley Repertory Theatre later that year was directed by Kushner after the original director withdrew. "The moments in history that interest me the most are of transition," Kushner explains, and in *Hydriotaphia* he mixes realistic and phantasmagoric effects in a theatrical and intellectual fantasy. The play depicts the last day in the life of Sir

Thomas Browne, noted seventeenth-century scientist, writer, and in Kushner's invention, seminal capitalist.

"Hydriotaphia," meaning "urne-burial," is taken from the title of a 1658 Browne essay in which he proposes that God does not necessarily promise immortality to human beings. This notion provides Kushner with the starting point for his irreverently whimsical drama. Lying miserably on his deathbed, Browne is depicted as a grasping, emotionally barren conservative. He has become business partners with his stuttering pastor, Dogwater, whose motto, "accumulate, accumulate," is shared by Browne. They have seized some Norfolk common lands, forced the residing peasants off, and created a profitable quarry. Pounding engines are heard constantly in the distance. "God hates idle money as much as he hates idle men," insists Dogwater, as Browne, detecting "a distinctly mercenary scent in the air," falls victim to friends and family vying for his riches. These include Babbo, Browne's "imponderably old and faithful retainer" whose "charming peasant patois" provides her master some measure of comfort; Maccabbee, Browne's lecherous amanuensis, who wears a tin nose in place of the real one he has lost to venereal disease; Doña Estrelita, Browne's former lover, who is equal parts Carmen Miranda and Eva Peron (with a little Charo thrown in); Leonard Pumpkin, Browne's "spade and shovel man" (gravedigger), who sees his way out of poverty through the sexual favors of Browne's wife, Dorothy; Dr. Emil Schadenfreude, Browne's "Hessian physician" and resident fop, who expresses Kushner's fascination with "life in death"; Magdelina Vindicta, the Abbess of X, Browne's sister and a militantly subversive nun ("I'm not at liberty to say," she imperiously intones when asked for details about her particular order); three Ranters representing the "homeless and afflicted"; Browne's Soul; and Death, walking the earth in the guise of Browne's long-deceased father. This image provides a powerful death scene for Browne, a shocking and frightening moment that interrupts the frequently ludicrous action.

"I seem to have lost center stage," Browne laments, as the others battle over forged versions of his will. Despite the riotous comic drive of the plot, the play is actually a deeply disturbing meditation on death that explores Kushner's belief that "there's something vital and electric in morbidity." About to become "worm food," Browne discovers that "my later is gone," and observing the hypocritical maneuverings around him, he notes that "God moves in mysterious—and somewhat malicious—ways."

Kushner's 1998 revision of the play strengthened the image of the central character. "You who must live through this, I pity you," Browne cries from his deathbed as he is besieged by the living and the dead, all of whom provide the "phantasm in the pocket of my grief." Browne egocentrically imagines his death as the sailing of a great ship, but his wife, Dorothy, who "can't bear the accumulation" of Browne's life, sees things differently. Believing her whole generation to be "cursed by our gold," she realizes that although Browne "never meant to harm," he "did not live well upon this earth." Compounding Browne's dilemma, his Soul (who is played by a woman) is angry that he struggles to grasp the fading shreds of his life. Prevented from being celestially freed from Browne's body, Soul becomes increasingly human "meat" who believes that Browne is "murdering the song" of her delayed ascension. She declares that by his very nature, he "will die of constipation." This statement turns out to be literally the case for Browne, who suffers from an onion-sized blockage that distends his stomach to the point of explosion.

In a scientific attempt to prove the weightlessness of the soul, Browne orders three chickens weighed. Slaughtered and weighed again, two of the chickens weigh the same amount while the third becomes inexplicably heavier. It continues to gain weight as it mirrors Browne's physical and financial bloat. When the chicken finally explodes, it is discovered to be filled with maggots. After death, Browne returns to the stage to wish he were alive again "to eat, to greedily gorge" on the world itself. But his world has collapsed with his death as the sounds of his quarry machines, which match his final desperate heartbeats, grow quiet and fall into a great abyss. Soul enjoys a postmortem cigarette, but Dorothy, who longs for "a thick skin" that "won't grow," resolves to make the crossing to a New (and perhaps better) World.

A primer for appreciating the style and substance of Kushner's more mature works, *Hydriotaphia* establishes his lofty ambitions for a revitalized epic theater which, as he explains, explores possibilities that "range from a vastly improved world to no world at all." Critics disagreed on the balance of farce and seriousness in the play.

A darker vision of the perils of life prevails in Kushner's 1985 play, *A Bright Room Called Day,* which also presents his distinctive style and recurrent themes. *A Bright Room Called Day* combines an intimate and realistic portrait of the lives of German-Jewish moviemakers during the rise of the Nazis with a larger scope that addresses not only the Holocaust but also contemporary issues. These issues are introduced and placed into context by the presence of Zillah, a present-day (mid 1980s) Jewish political activist and ardent feminist. *A Bright Room Called Day* invokes Judaic imagery—sometimes to provide a mysterious sense of the past, sometimes for humor, and most importantly, sometimes to raise the troubling questions of what may

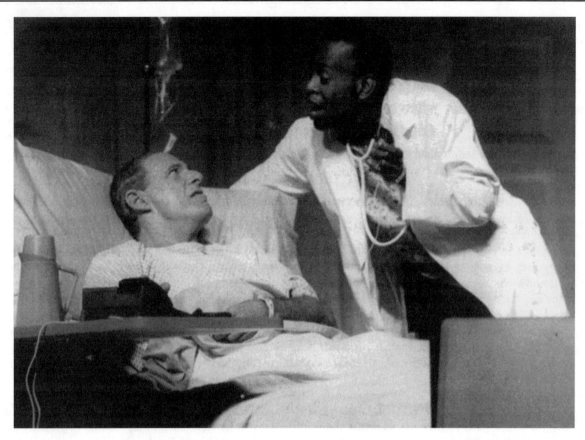

Ron Liebman and K. Todd Freeman in a scene from the 1992 Los Angeles production of Kushner's Angels in America:
A Gay Fantasia on National Themes, Part Two: Perestroika *(photograph by Jay Thompson)*

be lost to all as one world, one culture, and one faith die.

A Bright Room Called Day begins in January 1932, as the political and social conditions that paved the way for Adolf Hitler's rise to power in Germany coalesce. Kushner's central character is Agnes Eggling, a moderately successful character actress in the German movie industry who, along with her close circle of colleagues and friends, struggles to survive in their industry and, ultimately, in their country. This tightly knit group includes Baz, a gay man who works for the Berlin Institute for Human Sexuality; Paulinka, a featured player and budding star in commercial motion pictures; Annabella, a Communist who works as a graphic designer; and Husz, a Hungarian exile and cinematographer. Each character offers a different viewpoint about the ways to respond, personally and politically, to the rising evil of Nazism. Agnes is also haunted by Die Alte, an old woman presumably dead for more than twenty years, whose mysteriously poetic statements reflect on Agnes's situation. Zillah, in her own apartment, imagines the lives of Agnes and Die Alte from an old photograph of an unsmiling woman who is the only one not saluting in a crowd of Nazi supporters.

With the characters and their circumstances firmly established, Kushner sets the individual stories into a contemporary perspective with Zillah's bitter rants against Reagan's presidency, which she daringly equates with the era of Hitler. Haunted by both the past (as represented by Agnes's world—just as Agnes is haunted by the earlier world of Die Alte) and her own present, Zillah warns that understanding the late twentieth century requires "not caution or circumspection but moral exuberance. Overstatement is your friend: use it." Her comparisons of Reagan to Hitler are perhaps part of this overstatement, but she also offers observations and advice for the audience: "Don't put too much stock in a good night's sleep. During times of reactionary backlash, the only people sleeping soundly are the guys who are giving the rest of us bad dreams. So eat something indigestible before you go to bed, and listen to your nightmares."

Agnes's life and small circle of friends diminish as she can only try in vain to survive, watching her friends flee, die, or, like herself, become immobilized by fear. Alone in a dark corner of her apartment, Agnes is like a trapped animal. Zillah, aware of the restless fear that connects her to Agnes's circumstances, points out that "She still can't sleep. Restless, like me. I'm calling to her: across a long dead time: to touch a dark place, to scare myself a little, to make contact with what moves in the night, fifty years after, with what's driven, every night, by the panic and the pain."

Some critics decried the equating of Nazism with Reaganism and the grim tone of the play; a reviewer for *The New York Times* (13 January 1991) called *A Bright Room Called Day* "an ambitious, disturbing mess of a play." One critic for *The Nation* (18 March 1991) described Kushner's work as "a gay, American equivalent of David Hare's," while another for the *Village Voice* (15 January 1991) joined the chorus of disapproval over the messiness of the play, though admitted that Kushner is "infallible as a word-slinger." A review in *Newsday* (8 January 1991)more approvingly described *A Bright Room Called Day* as "a big, dense play of ideas—a welcome rarity after an era of apolitical American isolationist theatre."

In 1990, following the New York production of *A Bright Room Called Day,* Kushner received the Whiting Foundation Writers Award and playwriting fellowships from the New York State Council on the Arts and the National Endowment for the Arts. He was also given a commission from the Eureka Theatre in San Francisco, where *A Bright Room Called Day* had been staged in its earliest version. The Eureka commission, plus a special project grant from the National Endowment for the Arts, led to the completion of both parts of *Angels in America,* the drama that catapulted Kushner to international prominence.

In 1991 the first of the two *Angels in America* plays, *Millennium Approaches,* was produced at the Eureka Theatre under the direction of Oscar Eustis. The play moved to Mark Taper Forum in Los Angeles, receiving two Fund for New American Plays/American Express Awards, the 1991 Joseph Kesselring Award from the National Arts Club, and the Bay Area Drama Critics Award for the Best Play of 1991. *Millennium Approaches* was produced at the National Theatre of Great Britain in 1992, garnering significant critical acclaim and winning the London Evening Standard Award, the London Drama Critics Award, and the Olivier Award as Best Play. When *Millennium Approaches* finally made it to Broadway in 1993, under the direction of George C. Wolfe, Kushner was awarded the Pulitzer Prize in drama. *Millennium Approaches* also received the Tony Award as Best Play, as well as awards for cast members and a host of critical awards. Approximately six months after *Millennium Approaches* opened on Broadway, *Perestroika* (which had been performed in repertory with *Millennium Approaches* in San Francisco, Los Angeles, and London) was per-

formed with *Millennium Approaches* by the same cast and it, too, won a Tony Award as Best Play and several other critical accolades.

There is a sense of Greek fatality in both parts of *Angels in America,* and Kushner's blending of past, present, and future works more seamlessly here than in *A Bright Room Called Day.* The *Angels in America* plays are feverish historical dramas about immediate and current American history. Despite the socialist predilections of its author, *Angels in America* attempts to allow both sides to be seen and heard at their best and worst. Its most lovable character is dying of AIDS, but so is its most detestable, while both conservative and liberal characters have admirable moments and reprehensible ones.

Both parts of *Angels in America* are set in the same political environment that Zillah protests in *A Bright Room Called Day,* and most of its key characters are Jewish. Alisa Solomon points out the "complicated, contradictory Jewish types—reactionary Roy Cohn, liberal Louis Ironson, dead radical Ethel Rosenberg" whom Kushner uses to examine the trajectory of the Jew through American politics and popular imagery. As such, "the image of the Jew tends to become the image of everyone. . . . the metaphorical Jew." This tendency is most effectively demonstrated in *Millennium Approaches,* which begins at the funeral of an elderly Jewish woman, Sarah Ironson, whom the presiding rabbi depicts as an exemplar of Old World values and struggles. He claims that she is a representative of those who left the shtetls for the American melting pot ("where nothing melted"), bringing to America the values of nineteenth-century Eastern European culture. He lectures the subsequent generations assembled that "You can never make that crossing that she made, for such Great Voyages in this world do not any more exist. . . . She was the last of the Mohicans, this one was. Pretty soon . . . all the old will be dead." As in other Kushner plays, "the metaphorical Jew" is used to explore the profound, often contradictory issues of assimilation, otherness, and oppression.

The rabbi harangues the congregation about their lack of understanding of the past, as represented by Sarah (a woman he never knew). Having created the ominous tone of the death of the past, Kushner focuses on a married couple, Joe and Harper Pitt, and a gay couple, Prior Walter and Louis Ironson, the grandson of the deceased woman. These two relationships are both at points of profound crisis when they intersect with the life of McCarthy-era hatchet man and shark lawyer Cohn. Joe is a Mormon lawyer whose conservative politics lead him to Cohn, who would like to place Joe in the Justice Department as his man in Washington. Joe, however, is caught up in a personal struggle with his long-repressed homosexuality. He has lived according to the rules by which he was raised–to be a family man, to be devoutly religious, and to be a political conservative. However, Joe is also miserable. In an agonized plea to Harper, who demands that Joe tell her whether or not he is in fact a homosexual, Joe exclaims:

> Does it make any difference? That I might be one thing deep within, no matter how wrong or ugly that thing is, so long as I have fought, with everything I have, to kill it. What do you want from me, Harper? More than that? For God's sake, there's nothing left, I'm a shell. There's nothing left to kill. As long as my behavior is what I know it has to be. Decent. Correct. That alone in the eyes of God.

When Joe finally acknowledges his homosexuality, he phones his mother, Hannah, in the middle of the night. He painfully reveals his secret in a scene that mirrors the experiences of many homosexuals; Kushner has said that this scene is taken directly from his own coming out. After some preliminary fumbling conversation, during which Joe admits he has been drinking, he blurts out his confession: "Mom. Momma. I'm a homosexual, Momma. Boy, did that come out awkward." The devastated Hannah is unable to reply directly or even acknowledge what Joe has said, but ends the call with a burst of sudden anger, shouting "Drinking is a sin! A sin! I raised you better than that."

Later, Joe encounters Louis, who is in a desperate flight of fear from his longtime lover, Prior, who is suffering from the initial stages of full-blown AIDS. Racked with guilt at his faithlessness, the liberal Louis reflects on the era, which he sees as a metaphor for his cowardly behavior. He describes himself, and Joe, as "Children of the new morning, criminal minds. Selfish and greedy and loveless and blind. Reagan's children." Louis has a brutal, punishing sexual encounter with a stranger in Central Park. The stranger provocatively asks, "You been a bad boy?" Louis can only sardonically reply, "Very bad. Very bad."

Meanwhile, Harper, addicted to Valium, and Prior, often delirious as he becomes sicker, meet in each other's hallucinations. As a character, Prior combines both wonderment and cynicism, hope and despair in his personality; and he is also, at times, outrageously campy. Instead of shying away from Prior's stereotypical qualities, Kushner insists that there is something empowering for gays in drag and a camp sensibility. Kushner's use of various forms of humor with all of his characters, but most particularly with Prior, breaks the tension of his most unsettling scenes

Lou Diamond Phillips and Charlayne Woodward in the 1994 La Jolla production of The Good Person of Setzuan *(photograph by Ken Howard)*

to show the absurd and grotesque sides of a character's circumstances.

Kushner employs a quite different brand of humor with the character of Cohn, whose gleefully bitter corruption is both comic and frightening. One of the most effective aspects of *Angels in America* is the way in which Kushner achieves sympathetic moments for even his most monstrous and transgressing characters. Cohn is a rapacious predator who is first discovered in his command module juggling phone calls and wishing he had eight arms like an octopus. Roy's self-loathing is his most unsettling quality, vividly shown in his scathing denial of his homosexuality: "Like all labels they tell you one thing and one thing only: where does an individual so identified fit in the food chain, in the pecking order? Not ideology, or sexual taste, but something much simpler: clout." Suggesting that he could not be a homosexual because he is powerful, Cohn sneeringly adds that "Homosexuals are not men who sleep with other men. Homosexuals are men who in fifteen years of trying cannot get a pissant antidiscrimination bill through City Council. Homosexuals are men who know nobody and who nobody knows. Who have zero clout." Cohn represents a kind of trickle-down morality in *Angels in America;* he is a symbol of Kushner's notion that if there is corruption, hypocrisy, and bad faith at the top, it will ultimately seep down to each individual in the society. As Robert Brustein writes, there are "no angels in America, only angles," and *Angels in America* presents a moral combat represented at various points by the opposing poles of conservative and liberal, gay and straight, transgressor and victim.

Kushner's scathing view of Cohn as an exemplar of conservatism is paralleled by his equally harsh view of traditional liberal politics, which are seen in Louis as self-righteousness and impotence. Belize, a gay African American and close friend of Prior, becomes Cohn's nurse in *Perestroika.* Belize is angry at the horrors of AIDS and the bigotry he sees on both sides of the political spectrum. He tells Louis: "I hate this country. It's just big ideas, and stories, and people dying, and people like you. The white cracker who wrote the national anthem knew what he was doing. He set the word 'free' to a note so high nobody can reach it." And of the faithless Louis specifically, Belize remarks that his liberalism has him "Up in the air, just like that angel, too far off the earth to pick out the details. Louis and his Big Ideas. Big Ideas are all you love." Despite Kushner's left-wing politics, his sympathies lie with Prior's more human and personal politics.

Prior grapples with the politics of existence with a humane and compassionate viewpoint. He recounts a story of one of his ancestors who was forced to escape in a lifeboat with seventy other passengers when a ship foundered. Whenever the lifeboat sat too low in the water or seemed about to capsize, crew members aboard would hurl the nearest passenger into the sea. Dying of AIDS, Prior says, "I think about that story a lot now. People in a boat, waiting, terrified, while implacable, unsmiling men, irresistibly strong, seize . . . maybe the person next to you, maybe you, and with no warning at all, with time only for a quick intake of air you are pitched into freezing, turbulent water and salt and darkness to drown." Unlike Agnes's fearful paralysis in *A Bright Room Called Day,* Prior's fears are faced and overcome. At the end of *Millennium Approaches* an angel appears to a delirious Prior, who is frightened, but with courage resists his fears: "I can handle pressure, I am a gay man and I am used to pressure, to trouble, I am tough and strong and. . . ." Overwhelmed by an intense sexual response as the angel crashes through the ceiling of his room,

Prior can only react to this orgasmic spectacle with an awestruck, "God almighty . . . *Very* Steven Spielberg." The angel, calling Prior a prophet, announces that "The Great Work begins."

The convergence of past, present, and future in the play is essential to fully appreciate *Angels in America.* The past is symbolized by the death of Sarah Ironson. The present is depicted through the betrayals of the Reagan era, by Cohn, and in a general loss of faith and loyalty, as demonstrated by the behavior of Joe and Louis. The future is represented by a choice between destruction and change best exemplified at the end of *Millennium Approaches* by the angel who may be bringing news of either salvation or apocalypse.

Kushner's characters are caught between two worlds—one that is dying and one that is being born—and they are tormented by fear of the future, moral uncertainty, and a sense of inexplicable loss. In one scene a nameless, homeless woman predicts that "In the new century, I think we will all be insane." This insanity might result from the frightening questions that cannot be answered easily, such as what lies ahead as old values die, and how people will find their way without the familiar social, moral, and religious signposts of the immediate past. Louis ruefully realizes that there is no safety net under these questions and little guidance in the American experience, for "There are no angels in America, no spiritual past, no racial past, there's only the political."

To Cohn, politics is raw power—he revels in his "clout," and there is no room for compassion in his world. When Joe confides in Cohn his feelings of guilt about his abandonment of Harper, Cohn advises Joe to "Learn at least this: What you are capable of. Let nothing stand in your way." Near the end of *Millennium Approaches* Cohn is haunted by a vision of Ethel Rosenberg, whom he had been instrumental in sending to the electric chair for treason years earlier. This encounter prompts him to boast that "I have *forced* my way into history. I ain't never gonna die." Rosenberg warns, however, that "History is about to crack wide open. Millennium approaches."

Rosenberg's prediction comes true in *Perestroika,* the more intellectually and thematically complex of the *Angels in America* plays. Kushner's characters continue their difficult journeys of survival, reassessing their lives and struggling toward the fearful future. Kushner darkens the mood significantly, but he also demonstrates the necessity of forgiveness if the world is to progress. At one point Louis is appalled to find himself at the bedside of Cohn, who, despite denials of his sexuality, is dying of AIDS. Rosenberg, whose image haunts Cohn, joins Louis to chant the Kaddish over Cohn's corpse. Sinning can and must be forgiven, Kushner insists, and faith in a brighter future is essential, despite the fear and doubt that undermine the survival of hope. This idea is comedically played out near the end of *Perestroika* when Cohn, dead and now residing in hell, is seen talking on the phone with God. The Supreme Being apparently wants Cohn to represent Him for the crime of His abandonment of humanity at the time of the 1906 San Francisco earthquake. Cohn says to God, "you're guilty as hell, no question, you have nothing to plead but not to worry, darling, I will make something up."

Kushner says that when he listens to *Perestroika,* he realizes "it has so much about loss–how to deal with it and how not to be deformed by losing." Where *Millennium Approaches* depicts faithlessness and selfishness with compassion, while offering a glimpse of the retreating conscience of American society, *Perestroika* finds Kushner's indomitable characters moving tentatively toward the feared changes. Despite the overall grimness of much of *Perestroika,* the play finally brings several of the characters to some measure of forgiveness and a settling of accounts. Most shattering of all may be the scenes in which Belize reluctantly but compassionately nurses the delirious and dying Cohn, despite hateful taunts and threats from his patient. For example, Belize offers Cohn advice about getting AZT, an AIDS drug then in its experimental phase, and the mistrusting Cohn nastily says, "You're a butterfingers spook faggot nurse. I think . . . you have little reason to want to help me." Belize wryly replies, "Consider it solidarity. One faggot to another." Cohn uses his political clout to get the AZT, but it is too late to help him. As he gets sicker and is transformed, at least in his own mind, into one of the disenfranchised, he vents his fury at his recurring vision of Ethel Rosenberg:

> The worst thing about being sick in America, Ethel, is you are booted out of the parade. Americans have no use for sick. Look at Reagan: He's so healthy he's hardly human, he's a hundred if he's a day, he takes a slug in his chest and two days later he's out west riding ponies in his PJ's. I mean who does that? That's America. It's just no country for the infirm.

Through weakness and infirmity, however, compassion is possible. Hannah, Joe's mother, cares for the abandoned and increasingly disturbed Harper. While working at her volunteer job at the Mormon Welcome Center in New York, Hannah leaves Harper alone with a life-size diorama of a nineteenth-century Mormon pioneer family. Harper thinks she sees her errant spouse in the image of the "Mormon Father," while pleading for guidance from the "Mormon Mother." When the figure comes to life and grimly leads Harper toward the next stage of her personal journey, Kushner achieves a transcendent meeting of past and present.

Some of the living characters come to life, too. Hannah has lost her son as a result of her rigidity, but visiting Prior in the hospital teaches her tolerance for the "otherness" of homosexuality. She asks Prior if she should come see him again, and Prior, borrowing one of Tennessee Williams's most famous lines, says, "Please do. I have always depended on the kindness of strangers." Hannah, unfamiliar with the reference, can only reply, "Well that's a stupid thing to do." Hannah does return, no longer a stranger either to Prior or herself, for she has been visited by Prior's angel and experienced a transforming orgasmic liberation similar to Prior's.

The final scene of *Perestroika* is set at the Bethesda fountain in Central Park, which has a statue of an angel in its center. A newly created family made up of Prior, Hannah, Belize, and a repentant Louis meet there. A stronger, wiser Hannah asserts Kushner's view of the interconnectedness of all humanity–regardless of race or sexual preference–and the primacy of loyalty and commitment to others. Prior points out the angel of the fountain, his personal favorite because it is a figure commemorating death but suggesting "a world without dying." Louis proceeds to recount the story of the angel Bethesda, who "descended and just her foot touched earth. And where it did, a fountain shot up from the ground." Belize explains that if "anyone who was suffering, in the body or the spirit, walked through the waters of the fountain of Bethesda, they would be healed, washed clean of pain." Prior, the prophet, whose AIDS symptoms have stabilized, notes that the healing waters of the fountain are not flowing now, but that he hopes to be around to see the day they flow again. In a final statement made directly to the audience, Prior speaks for those who have come before: "This disease will be the end of many of us, but not nearly all, and the dead will be commemorated and will struggle on with the living, and we are not going away. We won't die secret deaths anymore. The world only spins forward. We will be citizens. The time has come."

Critics have described *Angels in America* as the best drama in decades, a masterpiece comparable only to such plays as Eugene O'Neill's *Long Day's Journey Into Night* (1956), Williams's *A Streetcar Named Desire* (1947), and Edward Albee's *Who's Afraid of Virginia Woolf?* (1962). Writer Anna Quindlen calls *Angels in America* "a brilliant, brilliant play about love and the human condition at a time when our understanding of what it means to be human and loving has, thankfully, expanded." Besides the many awards for the plays, Kushner himself received several honors, including the Los Angeles GLAAD Award for Theatre, *The Advocate* Man of the

Michael Hayden in the 1995 Hartford production of A Dybbuk, or Between Two Worlds
(photograph by T. Charles Erickson)

Year award, the *Chicago Tribune* Artist of the Year award, and the New York Public Library Literary Lion Award, all in 1993; the American Academy of Arts and Letters Award, the LAMBDA Literary Award for Drama, the New York GLAAD Theatre Award, the New York University Distinguished Alumnus Award, the Columbia University John Jay Award, an honorary doctorate from McNeese State University, a New York City Comptroller's Citation, the Princess Grace Foundation Princess Grace Statue, and the LOTOS Club Medal for Distinction, all in 1994; the Humana Award from the Humana Foundation in Louisville in 1996; and an honorary doctorate from Denison University in 1997. *Angels in America* has been performed throughout the world (Australia, New Zealand, Ireland, Germany, Canada, Denmark, Brazil, Hungary, France, Japan, Austria, Argentina, Uruguay, Sweden, and Israel) to

acclaim and controversy equal to that of the original performances in England and America.

Kushner followed the *Angels in America* plays with *Slavs! Thinking About the Longstanding Problems of Virtue and Happiness,* a 1994 drama featuring some elements Kushner had originally intended to include in *Perestroika.* He has noted that *Slavs!* is something of a coda to *Angels in America.* It was suggested by the 1986 Soviet nuclear disaster at Chernobyl and features characters and situations Kushner had originally intended to use in *Perestroika.* In fact, *Slavs!* features one holdover character from *Perestroika,* Aleksii Antedilluvianovich Prelapsarianov, the World's Oldest Living Bolshevik, who in *Slavs!* demands to know from his successors what "Beautiful Theory" they have to replace the one they are rejecting as the Soviet Union collapses. He insists that a snake that casts off its old skin must have a new one to replace it: "Have you, my little serpents, a new skin? Then we dare not, we cannot move ahead," he warns. As the debate rages on the floor of the Politburo, two babushkas debate the politics of the day while various apparatchiks worry about preserving their faltering positions. When Prelapsarianov collapses after completing his speech, his death symbolizes the end of the Soviet experiment. Once again, Kushner establishes a collision of old and new, past and present.

The focus then shifts to those left to face the future without the Beautiful Theory, most particularly Katherina Serafina Gleb, a security guard at the Pan-Soviet Archives for the Study of Cerebro-Cephalognomical Historico-Biological Materialism. At this mysterious laboratory, Katherina stands guard over the pickled brains of the great thinkers of the Russian past. Bored and directionless, she is pursued by a bureaucrat, Popolitipov, or "Poppy" as she calls him, who brings her cigarettes and sings sad songs to her while attempting unsuccessfully to seduce her. His hopes of a little romance are dashed when Dr. Bonfila Bezhukhovna Bonch-Bruevich arrives; Katherina runs to her arms, and Poppy politely withdraws, leaving Katherina and Bonfila to get drunk and fear what Poppy may do.

Their concern is justified. In the next act, set a few years later, Bonfila has been transferred to a Siberian medical facility that treats victims of the Chernobyl catastrophe. Bonfila battles for institutional support with a petty bureaucrat, Rodent, who keeps an oppressive eye on the operation of the facility. He can offer no assistance for the unmanageable disasters that Bonfila must deal with, as represented by Vodya, a mute eight-year-old girl who is suffering the devastating effects of the nuclear nightmare. Rodent—whom Kushner describes as "timorous and deferential," a disappointed Soviet who has "gotten nasty"—faces Vodya's bitter mother, Mrs. Domik, who demands to know what Rodent, as the representative of the state, intends to do about her terminally ill daughter. Rodent can only supply empty platitudes and excuses, and he attempts to hide behind a pose of Russian patriotism. His unctuous response causes Mrs. Domik to explode in fury that she is not, in fact, a Russian, but a transplanted Lithuanian. She roundly curses him, governments, the state, the motherland, and the century. Her emotional outburst leaves Rodent shaken, but he departs with no solutions, despite Bonfila's insistence on why she stays and keeps trying: "Because I thought I could do some good here. In the face of all of this impossibility, twenty thousand years, that little girl who won't live five more years, I still believe that good can be done, that there's work to be done. Good hard work." As Rodent departs, Katherina, who at Bonfila's request has followed her to Siberia, shows up to take Bonfila home, mumbling that "Siberia sucks."

The epilogue of *Slavs!* finds Vodya wandering in Heaven. She encounters Prelapsarianov and another old Bolshevik, who welcome her, but they cannot offer much wisdom in response when she asks, "And what sense are we to make of the wreckage? Perhaps the principles were always wrong. Perhaps it is true that social justice, economic justice, equality, community, an end to master and slave, the withering away of the state: These are desirable but not realizable on the Earth." All are left wondering "What is to be done?"

Slavs! is similar to *A Bright Room Called Day* and *Angels in America* in the centrality of Kushner's moral and political lessons about the immediate past and present on both the personal and the historical level. Although some critics seemed disappointed that *Slavs!* is a smaller play than *Angels in America,* most were generally approving. A critic for *The New York Times* (18 December 1994) called *Slavs!* the work of a "brilliant and restless imagination. Mr. Kushner's words dazzle, sting and prompt belly laughs." A reviewer for *The New Yorker* (9 January 1995) stresses that even in a small play Kushner "is capable of cajoling us out of our received opinions through the power of his heart and mind." *Slavs!* received an Obie Award for Best Play in 1995.

Despite the success of his original full-length plays, Kushner continues his efforts as an adapter, while also working in the often neglected form of the one-act play. In 1996 Kushner contributed a "ten-minute play," *Reverse Transcription: Six Playwrights Bury a Seventh, A Ten-Minute Play That's Nearly Twenty Minutes Long,* to the Humana New Play Festival at the Actors Theatre of Louisville. Finding the "ten-minute" form "preposterous," Kushner crafted an amusing depiction of fictional playwrights based on writers Kushner knew. Set late at night on Martha's Vineyard, *Reverse Transcription* begins with the playwrights carting the bandage-wrapped body of an old writer, Ding, to an ancient cemetery to bury him in secret. While digging Ding's grave, the playwrights unearth some home truths about the dangers and follies of the life of a dramatist. Although some critics thought the play depends too much on a theatrical "in-joke," Kushner provides an interesting discussion of the variant motivations that drive the creative impulse.

Kushner also contributed a one-act play, *Terminating, or Lass Meine Schmerzen Nicht Verloren Sein, or Ambivalence,* based on William Shakespeare's Sonnet 75, to *Love's Fire,* a bill of one-acts by several contemporary American playwrights (including Eric Bogosian, John Guare, Marsha Norman, Ntozske Shange, Wendy Wasserstein, and William Finn). It was staged by The Acting Company and toured the United States. The successful tour culminated in a monthlong run in New York at the Public Theater in the summer of 1998. *Terminating,* which is set in a psychiatrist's office, focuses on Hendryk, a disturbed and loquacious intellectual who believes he is in love with his shrink. She insists this feeling is just transference, but he replies that all love is transference. More significantly, the ambivalent Hendryk talks incessantly in a torrent of literary references, a stream of hilarious contradictions and bizarre juxtapositions, underscoring Kushner's central exploration of the powers and failures of language. Critics found this play "deliciously convoluted" and "hilarious."

Kushner has written in other forms besides drama. He worked on a screenplay for *Angels in America,* which was originally scheduled to be directed by Robert Altman as two movies. Altman later withdrew from the project and P. J. Roarke was expected to direct. The movies have not commenced production. Earlier, Kushner had worked on a planned movie of Harvey Milk's life, a project that has been shelved. Essays and articles by Kushner have also appeared in *The New York Times, Newsweek, The Nation, OUT Magazine, The Los Angeles Times, Threepenny Review, American Theater, Theater Times,* and *Mother Jones.* He is also a regular columnist for *The Advocate.*

Kushner's dramatic work continues with a projected trilogy on economic history. The first play of the trilogy, *Henry Box Brown, or The Mirror of Slavery,* has received a staged reading at the Royal National Theatre in London in 1998. He is also completing "St. Cecilia, or The Power of Music," an opera libretto based on Heinrich von Kleist's eighteenth-century story "Die heilige Cäcilie oder Die Gewalt der Musik, Eine Legende," which will feature music by Bobby McFerrin. Other Kushner works include "Caroline, or Change," *Home Body/Kabul,* and "Grim(m)," the last of which is inspired by "The Two Journeymen" by the Brothers Grimm.

Kushner's ambitious, theatrical, and political style has been a revitalizing factor in American drama in the last decade of the twentieth century. While contemporaries such as Sam Shepard and David Mamet present increasingly minimalistic and fundamentally realistic dramas, Kushner provides a model for an American drama that boldly mixes fantasy and reality—as well as tragedy and comedy—while blending elements of the past, present, and future. As Lahr proclaims, Kushner guides his audience to "that most beautiful, divided, and unexplored country—the human heart."

Interviews:

Gerard Raymond, "Q & A With Tony Kushner," *Theatre Week* (20–26 December 1993): 14–20;

Mark Marvel, "A Conversation with Tony Kushner," *Interview,* 24 (February 1994): 84;

David Savran, "Tony Kushner," in *Speaking on Stage: Interviews with Contemporary American Playwrights,* edited by Philip C. Kolin and Colby H. Kullman (Tuscaloosa: University of Alabama Press, 1996), pp. 291–313;

Robert Vorlicky, ed., *Tony Kushner in Conversation* (Ann Arbor: University of Michigan Press, 1998).

References:

Bob Blanchard, "Playwright of Pain and Hope," *Progressive,* 58 (October 1994): 42–44;

Stephen J. Bottoms, "Re-staging Roy: Citizen Cohn and the Search for Xanadu," *Theatre Journal,* 48 (1996): 157–184;

Per Brask, ed., *Essays on Kushner's Angels* (Winnipeg, Canada: Blizzard Publishing, 1995);

Robert Brustein, "Angles in America," *New Republic* (24 May 1993): 29–31;

Susan Cheever, "An Angel Sat Down At His Table," *New York Times,* 13 September 1992, section 2, p. 7;

John M. Clum, *Acting Gay: Male Homosexuality in Modern Drama,* revised edition (New York: Columbia University Press, 1994);

William W. Demastes, *Theatre of Chaos: Beyond Absurdism, Into Orderly Disorder* (Cambridge: Cambridge University Press, 1998);

Jyl Lynn Felman, "Lost Jewish (Male) Souls. A Midrash on *Angels in America,*" *Tikkun,* 10 (May/June 1995): 27–30;

James Fisher, "'The Angels of Fructification': Tennessee Williams, Tony Kushner, and Images of Homosexuality on the American Stage," *Mississippi Quarterly,* 49, no. 1 (Winter 1995–1996): 13–32;

Fisher, "Between Two Worlds: Ansky's *The Dybbuk* and Kushner's *A Dybbuk,*" *Soviet and East European Performance,* 18, no. 2 (Summer 1998): 20–32;

Fisher, "Troubling the Waters: Visions of Apocalypse in Wilder's *The Skin of Our Teeth* and Kushner's *Angels in America,*" in *Thornton Wilder: New Essays,* edited by Martin Blank, Dalma Hunyadi Brunauer, and David Garrett Izzo (West Cornwall, Conn.: Locust Hill Press, 1999), pp. 391–407;

Jonathan Freedman, "Angels, Monsters, and Jews: Intersections of Queer and Jewish Identity in Kushner's *Angels in America*," *PMLA* (January 1999): 90–102;

Deborah R. Geis and Steven F. Kruger, eds., *Approaching the Millennium: Essays on Angels in America* (Ann Arbor: University of Michigan Press, 1997);

Christopher Hitchens, "*Angels* Over Broadway," *Vanity Fair* (March 1993): 72–76;

Edward R. Isser, *Stages of Annihilation. Theatrical Representations of the Holocaust* (Madison, N.J.: Fairleigh Dickinson University Press, 1997);

Daniel Kiefer, "*Angels in America* and the Failure of Revelation," *American Drama,* 4, no. 1 (1994): 21–38;

Yale Kramer, "Angels on Broadway," *American Spectator,* 26 (July 1993): 18–25;

John Lahr, "Beyond Nelly," *New Yorker,* 68 (23 November 1992): 126–130;

Arthur Lubow, "Tony Kushner's Paradise Lost," *New Yorker,* 68 (30 November 1992): 59–61;

Carla J. McDonough, *Staging Masculinity: Male Identity in Contemporary American Drama* (Jefferson, N.C.: McFarland, 1997);

Charles McNulty, "*Angels in America:* Tony Kushner's Theses on the Philosophy of History," *Modern Drama,* 39 (1996): 84–96;

Robert McRuer, *The Queer Renaissance: Contemporary American Literature and the Reinvention of Lesbian and Gay Identities* (New York: New York University Press, 1997);

Benilde Montgomery, "*Angels in America* as Medieval Mystery," *Modern Drama,* 41 (1998): 596–606;

Edward Norden, "From Schnitzler to Kushner," *Commentary,* 99 (January 1995): 51–58;

Ross Posnock, "Roy Cohn in America," *Raritan,* 13 (Winter 1994): 64–77;

Anna Quindlen, "Happy and Gay," *New York Times,* 6 April 1994, p. A21;

John R. Quinn, "Corpus Juris Tertium: Redemptive Jurisprudence in *Angels in America*," *Theatre Journal,* 48 (1996): 79–90;

Frank Rich, "The Reaganite Ethos, With Roy Cohn As a Dark Metaphor," *New York Times,* 5 March 1992, pp. C15, C21;

Gordon Rogoff, "Angels in America, Devils in the Wings," *Theatre,* 24, no. 2 (1993): 21–29;

David Román, *Acts of Intervention: Performance, Gay Culture, and AIDS* (Bloomington: Indiana University Press, 1998);

Eric Samuelsen, "Whither Mormon Drama? Look First to a Theatre," *Brigham Young University Studies,* 34 (1995): 81–103;

David Savran, "Ambivalence, Utopia, and a Queer Sort of Materialism: How *Angels in America* Reconstructs the Nation," *Theatre Journal,* 47 (May 1995): 207–227;

Alisa Solomon, *Re-Dressing the Canon: Essays on Theater and Gender* (London & New York: Routledge, 1997);

Michele Sordi, "Angels, Critics, and the Rhetoric of AIDS in America," in *Reconceptualizing American Literary/Cultural Studies: Rhetoric, History, and Politics in the Humanities,* edited by William E. Cain (New York: Garland, 1996), pp. 185–196;

Richard Stayton, "An Epic Look at Reagan-Era Morality," *Los Angeles Times,* 13 May 1990, Calendar section, pp. 1, 45–48;

Tom Szentgyorgyi, "Look Back–and Forward–In Anger," *Theatre Week* (14–20 January 1991): 15–19;

Scott Tucker, "Our Queer World. A Storm Blowing from Paradise," *Humanist* (November/December 1993): 32–35;

Alex J. Tuss, "Resurrecting Masculine Spirituality in Tony Kushner's *Angels in America*," *Journal of Men's Studies,* 5 (August 1996): 49–63;

Hilary de Vries, "A Playwright Spreads His Wings," *Los Angeles Times,* 24 October 1992, Calendar section, pp. 3, 74, 76;

Bruce Weber, "*Angels'* Angels," *New York Times Magazine,* 25 April 1993, pp. 28–31.

Jerome Lawrence
(14 July 1915 –)

and

Robert E. Lee
(15 October 1918 – 8 July 1994)

Alan Woods
Ohio State University

PLAY PRODUCTIONS (BY LAWRENCE AND LEE): *Look, Ma, I'm Dancin'!,* with music and lyrics by Hugh Martin, New York, Adelphi Theatre, 29 January 1948;

The Laugh Maker, Hollywood, The Players Ring, 20 August 1952; revised as *Turn on the Night,* Philadelphia, Playhouse-in-the-Park, 7 August 1961; revised as *The Crocodile Smile,* Flat Rock, State Theatre of North Carolina, 15 August 1970;

Inherit the Wind, Dallas, Theatre '55, 10 January 1955; New York, National Theatre, 21 April 1955;

Shangri-La, adapted from James Hilton's novel *Lost Horizon,* with music by Harry Warren, New York, Winter Garden Theatre, 13 June 1956;

Auntie Mame, adapted from Patrick Dennis's novel, New York, Broadhurst Theatre, 31 October 1956; revised as *Mame,* with music and lyrics by Jerry Herman, New York, Winter Garden Theatre, 24 May 1966;

The Gang's All Here, New York, Ambassador Theatre, 1 October 1959;

Only in America, adapted from Harry Golden's work, New York, Cort Theatre, 19 November 1959;

A Call on Kuprin, adapted from Maurice Edelman's novel, New York, Broadhurst Theatre, 25 May 1961;

Diamond Orchid, New York, Henry Miller's Theatre, 10 February 1965; revised as *Sparks Fly Upward,* Dallas, McFarlin Auditorium, 3 December 1967;

Dear World, based on Jean Giraudoux's play *La Folle de Chaillot,* with music and lyrics by Herman, New York, Mark Hellinger Theatre, 6 February 1969;

The Night Thoreau Spent in Jail, Columbus, Ohio Historical Museum Theatre, Ohio State University, 21 April 1970; Chicago, Goodman Theatre, 1971;

Jerome Lawrence and Robert E. Lee (courtesy of Janet Lee)

The Incomparable Max, New York, Royale Theatre, 19 October 1971;

Jabberwock: Improbabilities Lived and Imagined by James Thurber in the Fictional City of Columbus, Ohio, Columbus, Thurber Theatre, Ohio State University, 18 November 1972;

First Monday in October, Cleveland, Francis E. Drury Theatre, 17 October 1975; revised, New York, Majestic Theatre, 3 October 1978;

Whisper in the Mind, Tempe, Arizona, Paul V. Galvin Playhouse, Arizona State University, 4 October 1990; revised, Kansas City, Missouri, Helen Spencer Theatre, Missouri Repertory Theatre, 2 May 1994.

PLAY PRODUCTION (BY LAWRENCE): *Live Spelled Backwards,* Beverly Hills, Beverly Hills Playhouse, 14 January 1966.

PLAY PRODUCTIONS (BY LEE): *Ten Days That Shook the World,* based on John Reed's work, Los Angeles, Freud Playhouse, 31 May 1973; *Sounding Brass,* Bronxville, New York, Reformed Church, 13 November 1975; *The Lost Letters of General Robert E. Lee,* Hollywood, 1996.

BOOKS (BY LAWRENCE AND LEE): *Annie Laurie, a Story of Robert Burns* (New York: Harms, 1954); *Roaring Camp,* based on Bret Hart's story (New York: Harms, 1955); *Inherit the Wind* (New York: Random House, 1955; London: Four Square, 1960); *Auntie Mame,* adapted from the novel by Patrick Dennis (New York: Vanguard, 1957; revised edition, New York: Dramatists Play Service, 1960); revised as *Mame* (New York: Random House, 1967); *The Gang's All Here* (Cleveland: World, 1960); *Only in America,* adapted from Harry Golden's work (New York: French, 1960); *A Call on Kuprin* (New York: French, 1962); *Sparks Fly Upward* (New York: Dramatists Play Service, 1967); *Dear World,* based on Jean Giraudoux's *The Madwoman of Chaillot,* with music and lyrics by Jerry Herman (New York: Tams-Witmark, 1970); *The Night Thoreau Spent in Jail* (New York: Hill & Wang, 1971); *The Crocodile Smile* (New York: Dramatists Play Service, 1972); *The Incomparable Max* (New York: Hill & Wang, 1972); *Jabberwock: Improbabilities Lived and Imagined by James Thurber in the Fictional City of Columbus, Ohio* (New York: French, 1974); *First Monday in October* (New York: French, 1979).

Collection: *Selected Plays of Jerome Lawrence and Robert E. Lee,* edited by Alan Woods (Columbus: Ohio State University Press, 1995).

BOOKS (BY LAWRENCE): *Oscar, the Ostrich,* as Jerome Schwartz (New York: Random House, 1940); *Live Spelled Backwards: A Moral Immorality Play* (New York: Dramatists Play Service, 1970);

Actor: The Life and Times of Paul Muni (New York: Putnam, 1974; London: W. H. Allen, 1975); *The Golden Circle: A Tale of the Stage and the Screen and Music of Yesterday and Now and Tomorrow and Maybe the Day after Tomorrow* (Los Angeles: Sun and Moon Press, 1993).

BOOKS (BY LEE): *Television: The Revolution* (New York: Essential Books, 1944); *Sounding Brass: A New Play about the 13th Apostle* (New York: S. French, 1976).

OTHER: *Off-Mike: Radio Writing by the Nation's Top Radio Writers,* edited by Lawrence (New York: Essential Books, 1944).

Jerome Lawrence and Robert E. Lee are best known for two plays, *Inherit the Wind* (performed in 1955) and *The Night Thoreau Spent in Jail* (1970), which together had more than three million copies in print by the end of the 1990s. Although their writing partnership, spanning more than a half century, produced significant work in radio, television, and cinema, the stage plays and musicals of Lawrence and Lee seem likely to remain most enduring. *Inherit the Wind* and *The Night Thoreau Spent in Jail,* along with Lawrence and Lee's comedy *Auntie Mame* (1956) and its musical version, *Mame* (1966), have remained in constant production worldwide since first appearing on North American stages. Both *Inherit the Wind* and *The Night Thoreau Spent in Jail* signaled new modes of production in the American commercial theater.

Born three years apart, the two playwrights did not make contact until they were in their mid twenties, although their lives (and careers) were on parallel tracks. Both writers were Ohio natives: Lawrence was born Jerome Lawrence Schwartz on 14 July 1915 in Cleveland, the son of Samuel Schwartz and Sarah (Rogen) Schwartz, while Robert Edwin Lee, born on 15 October 1918, was a native of Elyria, a Cleveland suburb, and the son of C. Melvin and Elvira (Taft) Lee. Both attended Ohio universities. Lawrence earned a B.A. from Ohio State University in Columbus in 1937, and Lee attended Ohio Wesleyan University in Delaware, just north of Columbus, from 1935 to 1937. Both began their professional careers as writers and directors in commercial radio and worked for KMPC in Beverly Hills, California, although at different times. Still, their paths did not cross until January 1942 in New York when, at the instigation of friends, they met and immediately formed a writing partnership. Their first collaboration was "Inside a Kid's Head," produced for the radio program *Columbia Workshop* (and later widely anthologized). By the spring of 1942 the two writers were successful enough that they established an office in Los Angeles, Lee having completed assignments as a writer/director for the Young and Rubicam advertising agency while Lawrence finished his work on the CBS series *They Live Forever*.

Both men went into the armed forces in the summer of 1942, spending most of the World War II years creating and producing programs for the Armed Forces Radio Service. With the war over, both returned to civilian life and continued their partnership as radio writers and directors, creating scripts for such programs as *Favorite Story* (starring Ronald Colman), *The Frank Sinatra Show,* and *Hallmark Playhouse*. In 1948 Lee married Janet Waldo, a radio actress then best known for playing the title role in the popular comedy series *Meet Corliss Archer*. They had two children, Jonathan and Lucy Lee. Lawrence and Lee also landed a contract for their first Broadway show, writing the book for Hugh Martin's musical *Look, Ma, I'm Dancin'!* (1948), a vehicle for comedienne Nancy Walker, choreographed by Jerome Robbins and directed by George S. Abbott. Despite the involvement of three theatrical legends–Walker and Robbins at the beginnings of their careers, Abbott already famous–the musical had only a modest success with 188 performances.

From 1948 through 1954 Lawrence and Lee maintained their focus on radio. As producers, directors, and writers, they were responsible for 299 broadcasts of the weekly series *The Railroad Hour,* while continuing work on *The Halls of Ivy, Favorite Story* (later a television series, 1952–1953), and many other radio and television programs. A complete listing is available in a 1992 bibliography by Mark Winchester.

Lawrence and Lee turned to the stage in the early 1950s, as the advent of commercial network television caused the comedy and serial programming of commercial radio to disappear; radio was beginning its transformation to music and news formats. Their first produced play, which proved to be their greatest success (806 performances), was *Inherit the Wind*. With it they established several patterns that recurred in much of their later work. *Inherit the Wind* is based on an historical event: the Scopes trial of 1925, the prosecution of a Tennessee high-school biology teacher for teaching the theory of evolution. Lawrence and Lee's play fictionalizes the events, however. They wrote in their foreword to the published edition of the text that while the characters of the play are modeled on the figures from that trial, "they have life and language of their own–and, therefore, names of their own. . . . *Inherit the Wind* does not pretend to be journalism. It is theatre."

Lawrence and Lee added several characters to the historic record, conflated several more, and sharply condensed the action. In searching for a way to dramatize the religious fundamentalism opposed to the teaching of Darwinism, the playwrights invented the character of Reverend Brown and created the revival meeting that opens act 2 to demonstrate vividly the fervor of the townspeople.

By far their most arresting invention, however, was the courtroom confrontation between Henry Drummond–the teacher's defense attorney, loosely based on Clarence Darrow–and Matthew Harrison Brady, the prosecutor derived from William Jennings Bryan. The climax of the play, with Brady on the witness stand as an expert on the Bible, and Drummond examining him, succinctly and effectively contrasts scientific progress with rigidly literal religiosity. Rationality wins out over irrationality, with Brady ineffectually thumping the witness-stand rail as the curtain falls. Although the historic Darrow did cross-examine the historic Bryan, he did so as part of a team of defense attorneys; virtually all of the dialogue in the play is invented.

While this dramatic climax occurs structurally in the second scene of the second act, the intellectual centerpiece of the play is Drummond's speech in the first scene of the third act, as he waits for the jury's decision. Remembering a flashy rocking horse he coveted as a child, but which proved rotten under the spangles and paint, Drummond articulates his motivating force: "whenever you see something bright, shining, perfect-seeming . . . look behind the paint! And if it's a lie–show it up for what it really is!" This message is reiterated in the final scene by Rachel Brown, the Reverend Brown's daughter, who has finally learned to welcome all ideas, not repressing those that challenge and thus create discomfort. Both Drummond's rocking-horse speech and Rachel's discovery help to widen the underlying themes of the play.

For Lawrence and Lee, it was clear that evolution and Darwinism represented progress and the growth of the human spirit, in opposition to the repressive censorship of Brady and Reverend Brown and their efforts to block rational development. The conflict of the play is not between evolution and creationism (a term not in common usage when it was written), therefore, but between freedom of thought and repression of free inquiry. By giving the play that focus, and also by avoiding close reproduction of the historic events in Tennessee, the playwrights were able to emphasize the broader and more-universal aspects of the conflict. The invented figure of Rachel Brown, who at first glance might be mistaken for the schoolteacher's stereotypical romantic interest, becomes–from this perspective–the fulcrum of the play. Rachel's journey from unthinking acceptance of her father's literal interpretation of Genesis to understanding that she bears the responsibility

Walter Klavun, Rosalind Russell, and Dorothy Blackburn in the 1956 New York production of Auntie Mame *(photograph by Arthur Cantor; Jerome Lawrence and Robert E. Lee Collection, Lawrence and Lee Research Institute, Ohio State University)*

for developing her own opinions is the voyage to self-consciousness that is only possible with freedom of thought.

Inherit the Wind has been translated into more than thirty languages and appeared once as a major Hollywood movie (1960) and in three television adaptations (1965, 1988, 1999), in addition to constant stage production. Its enduring appeal certainly stems, at least in part, from its focus on themes suggested by the Scopes trial rather than on a re-creation of the trial itself as an historical docudrama.

Lawrence and Lee intended *Inherit the Wind* as a comment on Senator Joseph McCarthy's campaigns against communism, which the playwrights regarded as a thinly veiled attack on the freedoms of speech and thought. Many of their later plays also use historical events and characters as springboards to explore contemporary issues, often fictionalizing real people and their actions in order to avoid the limitations of documentary.

The playwrights' first major success also shares with virtually all of the later work a sharp awareness of dramatic effectiveness: finding visual images, patterns of movement and sound, or other essentially nonliter-

ary means of conveying meaning. The closing moment of *Inherit the Wind,* as Drummond weighs and then claps together the Bible and Charles Darwin's *On the Origin of Species* (1859), is one such image. Another, more extended, comes in the revival meeting that opens the second act, with its rising emotional frenzy. Similar theatrical images exist throughout the playwrights' work.

Inherit the Wind also signaled the growing importance of professional regional theaters distant from the commercial theater center of New York City. First produced at Margo Jones's pioneering theater in Dallas, Theatre '55 (the name changed with the year), and only then given a commercial production, *Inherit the Wind* was among the first major American plays to be produced regionally before, rather than after, its Broadway premiere. The standard production process, as it existed in the early 1950s, was to have plays produced directly for the New York stage, with out-of-town tryouts for four to six weeks prior to the New York opening. Frantic rewrites were the norm out of town, and it was not uncommon for the writer's original concept and tone to vanish completely in the effort to make a piece commercially viable. Plays that failed in their initial New York productions generally disappeared without a trace; lacking the distinction conferred by success in New York, they rarely were produced by theaters (whether professional or amateur) elsewhere.

Lawrence and Lee consistently sought alternatives to that commercial production process, having experienced the less frantic and more effective tryout pattern with *Inherit the Wind*. This intent led to their creation of the American Playwrights Theatre (APT) in 1965. The APT sought unproduced plays from established playwrights, then distributed plays approved by an evaluative committee to member theaters. If enough theaters optioned APT selections for production, the organization guaranteed exclusive performance rights for a period of two years. At its height, the APT included more than 160 theaters as members, ranging from professional regional theaters to academic and amateur community organizations.

The signal APT success was Lawrence and Lee's own *The Night Thoreau Spent in Jail,* produced entirely outside commercial venues. With 155 productions under APT auspices from 1970 through 1973, *The Night Thoreau Spent in Jail* has never been produced in New York; yet it, along with *Inherit the Wind,* remains in the worldwide repertory.

The Night Thoreau Spent in Jail dramatizes the historical incident in which Henry David Thoreau, protesting the Mexican-American War of 1846–1848, went to jail for refusing to pay his taxes. Lawrence and Lee's text utilizes a fluid structure, with characters and events swirling in expressionistic patterns around the central figure of Thoreau, in jail throughout the play. Each of the flashback scenes, and those set in the jail itself, reveal aspects of Thoreau's character and philosophy, constructing, by the end of the play, a composite portrait explaining his actions. The structure of the play is reminiscent of the epic drama championed by Bertolt Brecht: short scenes connected thematically rather than by the logical causality of the well-made play of realism. The opening exchange of dialogue between Ralph Waldo Emerson and his wife, Lydian, about their confusion over Thoreau's given name sounds the theme of Thoreau's self-creation, reinforced immediately by Thoreau's renaming of himself and his rejection of conformity.

Thoreau also rejects conventional education and the rigid rules of Deacon Ball. Thoreau's resignation as a teacher after flogging students at Ball's insistence is paralleled with Emerson's resignation as a pastor because of ethical doubts. Thoreau effortlessly teaches an illiterate jailmate to spell, and his own school provides the opportunity to explain Transcendentalism. Later scenes demonstrate further facets of Thoreau's beliefs and unwillingness to conform to the social order of Concord, Massachusetts.

The first act ends with Emerson demanding of Thoreau, "What are you doing in jail?" and Thoreau responding, "Waldo! What are you doing *out* of jail?" Thoreau's nonconformity and his faithfulness to his own high moral principles have been clearly established. The second act moves Thoreau from personal to public ethics, sharply contrasting his active response to what he regards as an illegal war with Emerson's more measured, and intellectually ineffective, lack of action. Again, the act is structured thematically: personal responsibility and the need for effective action, explained to Emerson's small son in a huckleberry picking scene, is demonstrated by Thoreau's aiding an escaped slave. That scene is followed immediately by Thoreau's confrontation with Emerson over the need to publicly condemn the American involvement in the war. Emerson's failure to speak triggers the disillusioned Thoreau's nightmare of endless war, in a phantasmagoric theatrical sequence. The conclusion turns from public ethics back to the personal, as Thoreau negotiates speedy justice for Bailey, his cellmate, still awaiting trial after three months in jail.

Throughout, Thoreau remains an idealist—a logical product, the play suggests, of the high-minded idealism of Emersonian Transcendentalism. Driven by a fierce devotion to the discovery of truth, Thoreau is oblivious to the implications of his teachings when confronted by the apoplectic Deacon Ball, who rightly sees revolution in Thoreau's approach, or the gentler Ellen Sewall, whose search for enlightenment has more-

romantic overtones. Only the sudden death of Thoreau's beloved brother, John, forces personal events to intrude on Thoreau's intellectual life. As was the case in *Inherit the Wind,* Lawrence and Lee utilize some conventional theatrical devices—potential romance, personal tragedy—to connect with the central idea driving the action of the play. Moving beyond traditional convention, however, Thoreau's nightmare sequence is vividly theatrical in performance, while the conclusion, in which the stage light grows brighter rather than dimmer as Thoreau strides through the audience to confront the future, is another example of Lawrence and Lee's manipulation of stage convention to reinforce their message.

While its structure reflects the kind of theatrical experimentation particularly prominent in the latter half of the 1960s, *The Night Thoreau Spent in Jail* also comments as clearly on contemporary social and political events as did *Inherit the Wind.* Thoreau's rejection of his government's involvement in the Mexican-American War mirrors in direct ways the public's growing rejection of the U. S. military involvement in South Vietnam; indeed, the first production of the play in 1970 was abruptly closed when campuses across the country erupted after shootings at Kent State University in Ohio during war protests. The continuous-production history of the play suggests, however, that it is no more tied to the immediate issues that inspired it than was *Inherit the Wind.*

While reaction against the Vietnam War was the impetus for *The Night Thoreau Spent in Jail,* using Thoreau's antiwar protest provided distance from the events of the late 1960s. Audiences drew their own parallels between Mexico and Vietnam, between Thoreau's refusal to accept the authority of a government whose policies he rejects and contemporaneous draft resisters. Because the playwrights did not make those parallels explicit, the celebration of an individual's right to question authority has survived the war that sparked the play. *The Night Thoreau Spent in Jail* includes scenes in which Thoreau (or his brother) question the rigid authoritarianism of educational systems, organized religion, and local as well as national officials. The individualism is therefore systemic, not tied to the single issue of war (however unjust or just the specific war might be). The play assumes that questioning conformity is praiseworthy and that the established social order is necessarily and rigidly confining, making Thoreau's rejection of his neighbors' (and family's) codes heroic. That *The Night Thoreau Spent in Jail* is not bound to protests over a specific war was demonstrated in 1989, when it was performed in Hong Kong as a memorial to students who died in protests in Tiananmen Square in Beijing earlier that year.

A similar challenge to conventional authority is the mainspring of Lawrence and Lee's third enduring success, *Auntie Mame* (1956), adapted from the 1955 best-selling comic novel by Patrick Dennis. Opening in New York while *Inherit the Wind* continued its initial run, *Auntie Mame* ran for 639 performances in New York and had a similar international success. Lawrence and Lee's script was transferred with only minor changes to the screen in 1958 (with Rosalind Russell, the original star). The partners further adapted their script with a score by Jerry Herman for the smash hit musical version, *Mame,* in 1966; it ran for 1,508 performances and was filmed in 1974 from a screenplay by Paul Zindel (with Lucille Ball in the title role). Both the play and the musical are frequently produced.

Patrick Dennis's novel of the adventures of a madcap free spirit and the nephew she inherits became, in Lawrence and Lee's hands, an episodic comedy with serious undertones. The Depression of the 1930s figures largely in the comedy, as do satiric thrusts at ethnic prejudices, trendy education, hidebound conformism, pretentious intellectualism, and social snobbery. The constant redecoration of Mame's Beekman Place apartment in New York provides its own running satire of fashion, and the guests present at the cocktail party in the first scene of the play are a satiric portrait of fashionable society.

Auntie Mame is more than clever satire, however, as well as being more than a star vehicle for the performer cast in the title role, although some reviewers initially dismissed the piece as being one or the other. (The episodic structure of the comedy also misled a few reviewers, who criticized it as a musical without songs.) The play celebrates freedom of thought (and speech), particularly in Mame's defiance of the anti-Semitism of the Upsons in act 2, and also emphasizes individualism. That it does so comically rather than in a serious dramatic context may have obscured the degree to which *Auntie Mame* shares concerns with *Inherit the Wind* and *The Night Thoreau Spent in Jail.* The episodic structure, treated as a weakness by reviewers of the first production, in fact permitted the playwrights to convey important plot elements through action rather than the narrative of the novel.

In the first act, for example, Lawrence and Lee compress events from several different seasons of several years in Dennis's novel into successive Novembers and Decembers. It is accordingly always holiday season in the play, with the holidays clearly meant to contrast with the darker actions of the play. The newly orphaned Patrick arrives at Beekman Place on 1 December; Mame's disastrous attempt to earn a living in the theater ends on Thanksgiving; and Mame goes to work at Macy's during the Christmas season immedi-

ately following the 1929 Stock Market crash. The first scene not set in a New York or New England fall is in the warm South at New Year's, as Mame falls in love with Beau and begins a new life. The episodic structure, especially in the first eleven scenes, creates a rapidly paced montage, mirroring the whirlwind pace of the life Mame opens to young Patrick.

The rapid pace continues in the second act, as does the montage. As Mame and Beau's honeymoon extends to several years, short scenes allow the young Patrick of act 1 to become the adult Patrick of act 2. The remainder of the play reflects, and in some ways reverses, the action of the first act. In act 2, Mame rescues the adult Patrick from the snobbish conformity of his potential in-laws, the Upsons, and his father's banker Mr. Babcock, saving Patrick from marriage to the mindless Gloria, herself a rich parody of decoratively brainless debutantes. While this action in many ways parallels Mame's opening up an exciting world for the young Patrick in act 1, it can also be argued that the Mame of the first act is herself rescued by Patrick, as her responsibility for him separates her from the social whirl in which she is first found, a world arguably as empty as the sterility of the Upson suburbia that threatens to swallow Patrick in the second act.

Unlike *Inherit the Wind* and *The Night Thoreau Spent in Jail, Auntie Mame* is not based on an historical event (however fictionalized), nor does it comment on contemporaneous controversies. Its presentation of the dangers of conformity, however, does reflect a concern of the mid 1950s, typified in such works as Sloan Wilson's *The Man in the Gray Flannel Suit* (1955) and William H. Whyte's 1956 study, *The Organization Man.* Babcock and Upson might well have stepped from the pages of either of those two popular books; significantly, both characters are vastly expanded from their counterparts in the Dennis novel and present a far stronger threat of conformity than in the source material. Lawrence and Lee's comedy shares the concerns for individualism and freedom of ideas present in their two more-serious plays.

Having been based on a popular novel, *Auntie Mame* also was typical of another aspect of Lawrence and Lee's work: the commissioned adaptation. As radio writers, Lawrence and Lee had adapted hundreds of works of fiction for *Favorite Story* and had also done a long series of musical adaptations for *The Railroad Hour* from 1948 through 1954. As theater writers they continued the practice, frequently alternating original works with adaptations. Thus, their book for *Shangri-La* (1956), the musical version of James Hilton's novel *Lost Horizon* (1933), followed *Inherit the Wind* (and was closely followed by *Auntie Mame*). Their original play *The Gang's All Here* (1959) opened shortly

Lee with Christopher Walken and Lu Ann Post during rehearsals for the 1971 Chicago production of The Night Thoreau Spent in Jail *(photograph by David H. Fishman, Jerome Lawrence and Robert E. Lee Collection, Lawrence and Lee Research Institute, Ohio State University)*

before their 1959 adaptation of Harry Golden's *Only in America* (1958).

Many of the plays employ Lawrence and Lee's fascination with historic incidents and figures, usually fictionalized to greater or lesser degrees. *The Gang's All Here* uses many of the character traits of President Warren G. Harding for its President Griffith P. Hastings. The play is set in the early 1920s and embroils President Hastings in a series of scandals that suggest the Teapot Dome. By making Hastings fictional, the playwrights are again free from the need to be entirely faithful to fact and so can suggest that Hastings, learning finally the depth of the corruption he has permitted to blossom, commits suicide at the conclusion of the play. The cheerful corruption of President Hastings's aides is more obvious—and hence less ominous—than the corruption American audiences have discovered in presidential politics since the play was first produced, at the end of the Eisenhower presidency.

In many of Lawrence and Lee's less-successful plays, the familiar theme of the individual's rights for self-realization, often in opposition to a repressive or monocultural society, shapes a central action. Their adaptation of Golden's best-selling *Only in America,* for example, weaves the short essays of Golden's autobiographical work, drawn from his writings for his one-man newspaper, *The Carolina Israelite,* into a gentle drama about the writer's relocation to South Carolina from New York. In the process Golden confronts racism, anti-Semitism, and prejudice against convicts. He triumphs over all, even over his comically conceived landlady, dubious from the outset about renting to a newspaperman who is both Jewish and from the North.

The program for *Only in America* (and the printed text of the play) bears the warning, "The character of Harry Golden is based on Harry Golden. All the other people of the play are fictional and unrelated to any persons, living or dead, integrated or segregated." Another adaptation that was a biographical celebration not intended as literal biography was *Jabberwock: Improbabilities Lived and Imagined by James Thurber in the Fictional City of Columbus, Ohio* (1972). Both plays are essentially character studies, occasionally arbitrary in their efforts to provide excuses for including familiar stories or incidents. Both include inventive theatrical touches: Golden playacting with small African American children, teaching them how to refuse to sit at the back of the bus, for example, or the use of several Thurber aunts, taking their turns in a large portrait frame, to comment upon and move the action in *Jabberwock* forward.

Only in America had only a short run in New York (twenty-eight performances), although it did achieve popular and financial success in a yearlong Los Angeles run in 1961. *Jabberwock* never appeared in New York, being part of the same American Playwrights Theatre experimentation as *The Night Thoreau Spent in Jail* two years earlier, although without reproducing the wide acceptance and production of the earlier play.

A Call on Kuprin (1961, twelve performances), adapted from Maurice Edelman's 1959 novel, centers on a Russian rocket scientist torn between the freedom he knows he will find in the United States he left after World War II and the repression of the Soviet system in his beloved homeland. Centering on the successful launch of a Soviet cosmonaut, the play was badly timed: the real Soviets launched cosmonaut Yuri Gagarin, the first human sent into space, during the out-of-town tryout for *A Call on Kuprin*. A play that posited the future occurrence of a manned launch thus seemed dated by the time it reached New York several weeks later.

Felicia Brazo and her ruthless rise to power in *Diamond Orchid* (1965) clearly suggest another twentieth-century political phenomenon, Eva Peron. Lawrence found himself in Buenos Aires during the official week of mourning for Peron in 1952 and was fascinated by the implications of her story. The title of the play stems from Peron's symbol, a brooch the playwrights describe as "a gaudy orchid five inches across and seven inches long, made of pure white diamonds." As they had in adapting historical events previously, the playwrights fictionalized the exploits of the real Evita, and the events of her short life, in order to focus on the theme of the corrupting effects of power. They were also interested in exploring the ways in which deprivation shaped later actions, finding in Felicia's grinding poverty and defiance of a rigid class system the source for her grandiose charitable activities as well as the glittering jewels and elaborate wardrobe that help bankrupt her country. The play ran for only five performances; rewritten and later produced as *Sparks Fly Upward* (1969), *Diamond Orchid* is now only a footnote to the later treatment of Eva Peron's life, the 1978 musical *Evita* by composer Andrew Lloyd Webber and lyricist Tim Rice.

The theme of individualism reappears in two plays with theatrical themes. *The Crocodile Smile* (1970) explores the tension between theatrical performance and real life, the expectations of an adoring public in conflict with the desire of a great comedian to have a normal life. A famous story about the legendary English clown, Joseph Grimaldi (1778–1837), sparked *The Crocodile Smile*. Grimaldi, suffering from depression, was said to have been told by a doctor to cheer himself by going to see Grimaldi perform, and responded, "But doctor, I am Grimaldi." Lawrence and Lee used that as the opening for their play but transposed the setting to late-nineteenth-century Paris, retaining only the idea of the depressed comedian. Having gone through two earlier versions, titled *The Laugh Maker* (1952) and *Turn on the Night* (1961), *The Crocodile Smile* received a single regional, nonprofit production and has never been commercially produced.

The theater also provides the setting for *The Incomparable Max* (1971, twenty-three performances), an episodic comedy adapted from Max Beerbohm's stories, depicting two hapless efforts by nondescript men to reshape the social world around them. In a framing device, critic Beerbohm presents the stories to the audience in the theater. The playwrights' fascination with the medium of theater also figures, of course, in both *Auntie Mame* and *Mame,* as Mame tries performance in order to earn money, with disastrously comic results.

The playwrights' final success was also their last new play performed on Broadway: *First Monday in October* (1975) was originally presented for a limited New York engagement in 1978. Although the play was a financial success—its initial engagement was extended; it had a successful tour following its Broadway run; and it was adapted into a commercially successful motion picture in 1981—*First Monday in October* has not entered the repertory. *First Monday in October,* like *A Call on Kuprin,* became tied directly to actual events, even though it is entirely fictional. Positing the appointment of a female judge to the United States Supreme Court, Lawrence and Lee used the new justice's gender as a way of exploring the familiar issues of individuality, social responsibility, and especially freedom of speech. By making the new justice a conservative activist, and by contrasting her social conservatism with a crusty, staunchly liberal older justice—loosely modeled on Justice William O. Douglas—the playwrights created a situation that allowed them to develop moral and social debates.

As had been the case with *A Call On Kuprin,* however, Lawrence and Lee did not succeed in creating sufficient distance for *First Monday in October* to survive actual events; once President Ronald Reagan appointed Sandra Day O'Connor to the United States Supreme

Court in 1981, the central novelty of the play became less timely. The real Justice O'Connor proved as conservative as the fictional Ruth Loomis; further, as the United States became markedly more conservative during the Reagan presidency, the contrasts Lawrence and Lee established between the liberal Justice Dan Snow and the conservative Loomis became far less sharp.

First Monday in October centers around two ideologically charged debates between Snow and Loomis. In the first act the two spar over the case of an adult movie, ruled pornographic by lower courts. In the second act the public's right to know the workings of a monopolistic international conglomerate spark the debate. As mutual respect between the two grows, Snow's marriage collapses, mirroring his own physical collapse at the end of the second debate. Both arguments focus on individual rights as opposed to the rights of the majority. In the adult-movie case Snow argues that the theater owner has the right to show whatever he chooses—those who object to content are under no obligation to purchase tickets. Loomis takes the position that it is the government's right to protect the majority from objectionable and exploitative content that by its presence taints its community. Although Snow is given the stronger argument by the playwrights, Loomis is given the last word in the argument, topping Snow rhetorically as she exits. Snow is reduced to pleading with his clerk and the chief justice for male solidarity against female interlopers as the act ends.

The debate in the second act has the justices seemingly switching sides. While Snow argued in the first act for the right of the businessman to make money through whatever legal means, unsavory as they might be to most observers, in the second act Loomis is the one who argues for the right of the corporation to make profits by whatever means, again as long as they are legal. Snow, by contrast, argues for the public's right to explore the business of the powerful international conglomerate, particularly if that monopoly has squashed potentially useful inventions in order to maintain profits with technology that might otherwise become outmoded. The debate is ended not rhetorically but by Snow's apparent stroke. After his recovery the conglomerate argument takes a new twist: Loomis discovers a connection between her late husband and a principal in the legal case but is convinced by Snow that she need not resign from the Court as a result.

First Monday in October became dated when Justice O'Connor took the bench. It was also dated in several other aspects as well. Much of the humor in the first scenes derives from the response by the Supreme Court justices, conservative and liberal alike, to a woman being named to the Court. There is much discussion about equality and about the gender of Loomis's secretary and law clerk. While pointed in the mid 1970s, much of this material no longer seems current. The scene depicting Loomis's confirmation hearings, while certainly historically accurate in its treatment of an all-male Senate Judiciary Committee, seems particularly dated, as the senators sit in befuddled amazement at the sight of a woman expressing ideas about the role of law in a democracy.

More significantly, the central antagonists in *First Monday in October* do not change. They grow to respect each other and share collegial affection, but they are not influenced intellectually. Nor do they change others around them. Drummond and Brady do not convince each other in *Inherit the Wind,* but Drummond's position changes Rachel Brown. Thoreau's defiance impacts Williams, the escaped slave, and Bailey, Thoreau's cellmate, while Auntie Mame has clearly changed Patrick for the better. Both Thoreau and Mame learn from their experiences, reaching new levels of understanding as their plays end. But there are no changes among the characters of *First Monday in October*. The opposing positions remain just that, equally persuasive—which may be why neither debate is won by either side but simply is ended by the playwrights, somewhat arbitrarily. While *First Monday in October* provides the platform for the debate of important issues, both legally and socially, these issues are neither resolved nor transcended by the conclusion of the play. And that conclusion, with Snow and Loomis listing the cases they will argue over, is not really an ending but an abrupt stop.

First Monday in October was successful commercially, produced on Broadway as a vehicle for Henry Fonda (who played Snow) and Jane Alexander (nominated for a Tony Award as Loomis). Its limited engagement was extended to seventy-nine performances, and Fonda toured it with Eva Marie Saint replacing Alexander, although the tour was cut short by Fonda's illness. The play has only been produced sporadically since. Although the characters' debate on pornography presaged the rancorous debate over federal funding to the arts through the National Endowment for the Arts (then chaired by Alexander) that erupted with the Robert Mapplethorpe controversy in 1989, the issue itself remained timely. The discussion over international monopolies also took on fresh meaning with events involving international chemical and software companies, not to mention the creation of enormous conglomerates through increasingly larger corporate mergers in the latter part of the 1990s. The issues debated in *First Monday in October* did not become dated, although the context for the play itself did, thus limiting its performance history.

Several of the Lawrence and Lee plays show an individual corrupted by the larger society. In *The Gang's*

All Here a jovially mediocre senator becomes a dangerously mediocre president, led into corruption by the mendacity of his rapacious advisers and confidants, while in *Diamond Orchid* a thoroughly amoral young woman sleeps her way to power and enormous riches as her lover/husband becomes a military dictator in a South American country, only to discover the emptiness of her soul when faced with incurable cancer. In the playwrights' final play, *Whisper in the Mind* (1990), the historic figure of Anton Mesmer misinterprets his abilities to treat patients, bringing his passionate belief in the power of the mind in conflict with rational science, made concrete by the figure of Benjamin Franklin.

Mesmer was in fact investigated in late-eighteenth-century Paris by a commission chaired by Franklin, then the U. S. ambassador to France. Lawrence and Lee were brought to the story by writer Norman Cousins, who had explored the idea of the ability of the mind to transform pain in his best-selling *Anatomy of an Illness as Perceived by the Patient: Reflections on Healing and Regeneration* (1979). As the historic incident was obscure, and the figure of Mesmer little known to the general public, the playwrights felt secure in expanding the facts, linking Mesmer and Franklin through the ailing daughter of one of Franklin's Parisian romances and locating the young girl's mental instability in the context of the instabilities of France itself a few years prior to the French Revolution.

The conflict between observable phenomena and the nonobservable workings of the mind was a logical choice for the playwrights, particularly when the conflict could be personalized in two major figures of individualism: Mesmer, regarded historically as a charlatan, and Franklin, a symbol of the rights of the individual, placed in the position of evaluating those rights against the demands of the larger society. In many ways *Whisper in the Mind* was a fitting final work for the playwrights, bringing together the concerns explored over a half century of writing as partners; their first produced work, "Inside a Kid's Head," had explored how the mind worked (albeit comically), while their last play examined efforts to understand, and harness, the mind's power.

In many respects Lawrence and Lee were among the last of the professional commercial playwrights in the United States, a tradition continued only by their younger contemporary, Neil Simon. Lawrence and Lee were constant presences in the commercial New York stage, from their dramatic debut in 1955 with *Inherit the Wind* through the production of *First Monday in October* a little more than two decades later. During those twenty-three years, they were represented by eleven plays in New York, along with three premiered elsewhere. Although it may seem contradictory to hail them as commercial playwrights, given their efforts (through the American Playwrights Theatre and other ventures) to undercut the New York dominance of the American stage, Lawrence and Lee regularly wrote for the commercial stage. They accepted commissions and created adaptations and musicalizations; in short, they were professional writers. Although their stage careers could not match the sheer volume of their work for commercial radio, their theatrical dramas, comedies, and musicals share a common sensibility: the responsibility and privilege of the individual to develop and promulgate ideas, freely and without restraint, whether from a government or from a dominant social order. That ideal animates most of the plays, in varying ways. The works Lawrence and Lee adapted and the plays that originated with them are remarkably consistent.

Lee's death in 1994 brought the partnership to a close. Although both Lee and Lawrence produced dramas, nonfiction, and fiction individually, their most enduring work was created as partners. Lee died shortly after the revised version of *Whisper in the Mind* ended its premiere run at the Missouri Repertory Theatre in Kansas City; whether this last play will have a future life is not yet clear. It is certain, however, that with *Inherit the Wind, Auntie Mame,* and *The Night Thoreau Spent in Jail,* Jerome Lawrence and Robert E. Lee crafted major contributions to the world dramatic repertory while creating a body of significant work that is frequently challenging and always dealing with important social, political, and ethical issues.

Bibliography:

Mark Winchester, "Jerome Lawrence and Robert E. Lee: A Classified Bibliography," *Studies in American Drama, 1945–Present,* 7 (1992): 88–160.

Papers:

The major archives of Jerome Lawrence and Robert E. Lee's papers are at the Jerome Lawrence and Robert E. Lee Theatre Research Institute, Ohio State University, Columbus, Ohio; the Billy Rose Theatre Collection, Library and Museum of the Performing Arts, New York Public Library; and Kent State University, Ohio.

John Howard Lawson

(25 September 1894 – 17 August 1977)

Michael M. O'Hara
Ball State University

PLAY PRODUCTIONS: *Standards,* Syracuse and Albany, 23–30 November 1915;

Servant-Master-Lover, Los Angeles, Morosco Theatre, 16 July 1916;

Roger Bloomer, New York, Forty-eighth Street Theatre, 1 March 1923;

Processional, New York, Garrick Theatre, 12 January 1925; revised, New York, Maxine Elliott's Theatre, 13 October 1937;

Nirvana, New York, Greenwich Village Theatre, 3 March 1926;

Loudspeaker, New York, Fifty-second Street Theatre, 7 March 1927;

The International, New York, Cherry Lane Theatre, 12 January 1928;

Success Story, New York, Maxine Elliott's Theatre, 26 September 1932;

The Pure in Heart, New York, Longacre Theatre, 20 March 1934;

Gentlewoman, New York, Cort Theatre, 22 March 1934;

Marching Song, New York, Nora Bayes Theatre, 17 February 1937.

BOOKS: *Roger Bloomer: A Play in Three Acts* (New York: Seltzer, 1923);

Processional: A Jazz Symphony of American Life, in Four Acts (New York: Seltzer, 1925);

The International (New York: Macaulay, 1927);

Loud Speaker: A Farce (New York: Macaulay, 1927);

Success Story: A Play (New York: Farrar & Rinehart, 1932);

With a Reckless Preface: Two Plays (New York: Farrar & Rinehart, 1934);

Theory and Technique of Playwriting (New York: Putnam, 1936); revised and enlarged as *Theory and Technique of Playwriting and Screenwriting* (New York: Putnam, 1949);

Marching Song: A Play (New York: Dramatists Play Service, 1937);

John Howard Lawson

The Hidden Heritage: A Rediscovery of the Ideas and Forces that Link the Thought of Our Time with the Culture of the Past (New York: Citadel, 1950; revised, 1968);

Film in the Battle of Ideas (New York: Masses & Mainstream, 1953);

Film: *The Creative Process; The Search for an Audio-Visual Language and Structure* (New York: Hill & Wang, 1964).

PRODUCED SCRIPTS: *The Pagan,* motion picture, titles by Lawson, M-G-M, 1929;

Dynamite, motion picture, M-G-M, 1930;

Bachelor Apartment, motion picture, screen story by Lawson, RKO, 1931;

Good-bye Love, motion picture, additional dialogue by Lawson, RKO, 1933;

Success at Any Price, motion picture, RKO, 1934;

Party Wire, motion picture, adaptation by Lawson and Ethel Hill, Columbia, 1935;

Blockade, story and screenplay by Lawson, United Artists, 1938;

Algiers, motion picture, United Artists, 1938;

They Shall Have Music, motion picture, screenplay by Lawson and Irmgard Von Cube, United Artists, 1939;

Earthbound, motion picture, adaptation by Lawson and Samuel Engel, 20th Century-Fox, 1940;

Four Sons, motion picture, 20th Century-Fox, 1940;

Action in the North Atlantic, motion picture, Warner Bros., 1943;

Sahara, motion picture, Columbia, 1943;

Counter-attack, motion picture, Columbia, 1945;

Smash-up, The Story of a Woman, motion picture, Universal-International, 1947.

OTHER: John Reed, *Ten Days that Shook the World,* introduction by Lawson (New York: International Publishers, 1967);

Karen M. Taylor, *People's Theatre in Amerika,* introduction by Lawson (New York: Drama Books, 1972).

SELECTED PERIODICAL PUBLICATIONS–UNCOLLECTED: "'Inner Conflict' and Proletarian Art," *New Masses,* 11 (17 April 1934): 29–30;

"Towards a Revolutionary Theatre," *New Theatre* (1 June 1934): 6–7;

Lawson and Lester Cole, "Two Views on O'Neill," *Masses and Mainstream,* 7 (June 1954): 56–63;

"The One Hundred Days," *ICarbS,* 3 (Summer–Fall 1976): 11–24.

John Howard Lawson is better known as one of the Hollywood Ten screenwriters blacklisted in the 1950s for alleged ties to the Communist Party than as a playwright or screenwriter. Critical discussions of his works have most often focused on his politics. Lawson's best plays, however, are not just vehicles for Marxist views. They blend political analysis with dramatic innovation. Plays such as *Processional* (1925), *Loud-speaker* (1927), *Success Story* (1932), and *Marching Song* (1937) dramatize the ills of everyday life and suggest, rather than demand, leftist solutions for them. By combining dramatic techniques and ideas from German expressionism, Russian constructivism, American jazz, psychological realism, and Hollywood script writing, Lawson created new forms of dramatic expression.

Lawson was born to wealthy Jewish American parents in New York City on 25 September 1894. His father, Simeon Levy Lawson, had changed the family name from Levy to Lawson before John Howard Lawson was born. As Lawson wrote in an unpublished autobiography, his father explained he had done it primarily so that he could "obtain reservations at expensive resort hotels," many of which refused to accommodate Jews.

Lawson's mother, Belle Hart Lawson, died when he was five years old. His only memory of her was as an invalid "lying in a darkened room, aloof and resigned, waiting release from a burden that her frail body could not bear." She named her three children after people she admired. Lawson's elder brother, Wendell Holmes Lawson, was named after Supreme Court Justice Oliver Wendell Holmes Jr.; his sister, Adelaide Jaffery Lawson, was named for a friend who shared Belle Lawson's social activism; and the youngest child, John Howard Lawson, was named for an advocate of prison reform in eighteenth-century England. Interested in helping slum dwellers, immigrants, and other underprivileged people, Belle Lawson chose for her children's teacher a woman who supported economic reformer Henry George and women's suffrage.

After his wife's death in 1899, Simeon Lawson took charge of his children's education. John Howard Lawson had several governesses, who–he later wrote–were chosen for their "cultural attainments, which meant that they were not too young and had an academic manner." He attended the Halstead School in Yonkers, New York, and the Cutler School in New Rochelle, New York. In 1906 his father sent the three children on a grand tour of Europe. Visits to the theater were part of their itinerary, and from that time forward Lawson filled his notebooks and diaries with his reactions to set designs, actors, and plays. In 1909 their father sent the three children on a tour of the United States and Canada. Often critical of his father for giving his children expensive gifts more often than his attention, Lawson later tended to conceal his affluent background from his fellow leftists.

Lawson later described childhood situations in which his Jewish heritage caused him difficulties. He wrote that during a visit to the home of a Christian schoolmate he let slip that his father's real name was Simeon Levy and was never invited back. For the sake

Poster by John Dos Passos for Lawson's expressionistic play about striking coal miners in West Virginia (Collection of Lucy Dos Passos Coggin)

of appearances, said Lawson, his father decided that the whole family should join a Christian church, the First Church at 96th Street and Central Park West, but he continued strict observation of Jewish dietary laws.

Lawson also wrote about the prejudice he experienced after enrolling at Williams College in 1910. During his sophomore year, he was denied election to the editorial board of *The Williams College Monthly* when some students raised questions about his Jewish background. Later he said the experience was a good one because it forced him to begin his struggle to come to terms with his Jewish identity. Afterward Lawson stopped writing self-absorbed, lyrical poetry, and in November 1912 he began contributing articles on international affairs to the school magazine.

While at Williams, Lawson was introduced to the writings of Karl Marx by his older brother, who had been sent to live in Germany to study music and art. The works of German Marxist theoretician Karl Kautsky sharpened Lawson's political sensibilities and gave him a vocabulary to describe his sense of alienation. Despite his feelings of isolation, Lawson was involved in several campus activities at Williams. An editor of the senior-class book and a member of the varsity debating team, he was known to other students as a good-natured iconoclast and a frequent speaker at undergraduate meetings. He graduated from Williams with a B.A. in 1914 and worked as a cable editor for Reuters in New York (1914–1915) while attempting to launch his career as a playwright.

Lawson's first dramatic effort, *A Hindoo Love Drama,* was written at college and is untouched by Marxist ideas. Mary Kirkpatrick, head of the Williams College Drama Club, was impressed with this effort, giving Lawson the confidence to attempt three more plays in 1915 and 1916: *Standards, The Spice of Life,* and *Servant-Master-Lover. Standards,* which was sold to Sam Harris and George M. Cohan and given a tryout in Albany and Syracuse in 1915, is about the failure of two friends to achieve success in New York City. The play never made it to Broadway. Produced by Oliver Morosco in Los Angeles to uniformly bad reviews, *Servant-Master-Lover* (1916) dramatizes the story of a young Irish woman who is mysteriously whisked away from the slums to a rich man's home where her ideal "servant-master-lover" mate awaits her. The play had a brief run. *The Spice of Life* was never performed.

Lawson's start in theater was interrupted by the entrance of the United States into World War I, which he opposed. His father helped to secure him a position with the Norton-Harjes Volunteer Ambulance Corps, and in June 1917 he left for France. Aboard ship he met John Dos Passos, who became a close friend with whom Lawson often discussed writing and politics. Dos Passos was working on his first book, the autobiographical *One Man's Initiation: 1917* (1920), while Lawson started a new play, *Roger Bloomer* (1923). In November, when Norton-Harjes was folded into the American Red Cross Ambulance Service, Lawson and Dos Passos signed up to drive Red Cross ambulances in Italy. Before leaving, they and several other men spent about two months in Paris. Lawson attended a wide range of traditional and avant-garde theatrical events, including performances of the Comedie-Française and Sergey Diaghilev's ballet company. In January 1918, after they arrived in Italy, a letter in which Dos Passos criticized the ambulance service was turned over to Red Cross officials, and Dos Passos was forced to resign. Lawson also came under suspicion, but he managed to stay in Italy, doing public-relations work for the Red Cross.

In spring 1919 Lawson left Italy for Paris, where he married Katharine (Kate) Drain, who had been a volunteer nurse's aide during the war and later became an actress. They had one son, Alan, before they were divorced in 1923. On 25 September 1925 Lawson married Susan Edmond with whom he had two children, Jeffrey and Susan.

In Paris during 1920–1921 Lawson finished *Roger Bloomer,* the play he had begun during the war, and started *Processional.* He returned to the United States determined to be a full-time playwright. As he later wrote, his experiences in Europe forever changed his views. He had come into contact with a wide variety of people, cultures, and circumstances that forced open the doors of his sheltered, bourgeois life. He had also discovered that serious commitment to any goal or cause required action rather than words, and he returned to playwriting with a fervid commitment.

Lawson's first play to reach Broadway, *Roger Bloomer* (1923) embodies all the feelings of frustration, social alienation, and lack of direction that Lawson had felt as a youth. Staged by the Equity Players, the play opened on 1 March 1923 and ran for fifty performances, despite poor reviews. A sprawling work of thirty scenes in three acts, *Roger Bloomer* is infused with an earnest, but overwrought, expressionism. Lawson's father was the inspiration for Everett Bloomer, a materialistic owner of a large department store in Excelsior, Iowa. His son, Roger Bloomer, is an unhappy dreamer and idealist.

Fleeing from his father and the way of life he represents, Roger follows Louise, a kindred soul, to New York City. They cannot think of one another romantically without feeling that sex is dirty. After her unscrupulous boss makes sexual advances, Louise commits suicide to preserve her virtue. Roger eats rat poison but survives and is arrested for her murder. The play ends with a scene that Lawson called a "Freudian dream-ballet" like the Diaghilev ballets he saw in Paris. Though the reviewers did not like the play, Dos Passos was impressed, and influenced, by the experimental techniques in *Roger Bloomer* and wrote the foreword for the published version.

Lawson was dismayed by the reviews for *Roger Bloomer* but not cowed. His next effort, *Processional,* evoked similar responses from critics but drew larger audiences than *Roger Bloomer.* Staged by the Theatre Guild, *Processional* opened on 12 January 1925 and closed after ninety-six performances. Like *Roger Bloomer, Processional* is expressionistic, but it is more political than its predecessor. Lawson combined the structure and pace of vaudeville, the vitality and rhythms of jazz, and the swirling energy of expressionist staging to create a violent, colorful parade of American character types in the early 1920s. Set in a West Virginia coal-mining town during a strike, *Processional* features thwarted lovers, heroic striking miners, singing minstrels, evil vigilantes, greedy capitalists, yellow journalists, foreign-born radicals, and ridiculous Klansman—all clashing in what Lawson called "a jazz symphony" of American life. In 1937 he revised the play for a revival by the Federal Theatre Project, which was critically and popularly acclaimed. The 1925 production, however, failed financially, and the Theatre Guild told Lawson that they would not stage any more expressionistic plays.

Lawson's interest in theatrical and political experimentation was further strengthened in 1926 by the

George Abbott as Dynamite Jim in the 1925 Theatre Guild production of Processional *(photograph by Vandamm; Theatre Collection, New York Public Library, Astor, Lenox and Tilden Foundations)*

New York International Theatrical Exposition, which included experimental European cubist, futurist, and constructivist plays. Immediately after the exposition closed, Lawson, Dos Passos, and Michael Gold, editor of *The New Masses,* formed the Workers Drama League, with the plan of producing revolutionary plays. Only a few weeks and a single production later, the three men disbanded the group and joined with Em Jo Basshe and Francis Faragoh to create the New Playwrights Theatre. This new venture survived until 1929, largely through the generosity of millionaire Otto Kahn.

Lawson's *Nirvana* opened on 3 March 1926 at the Greenwich Village Theatre and ran for only six performances. The play calls for a new religion that can help people survive the swirling cyclone of jazz, new machinery, great buildings, science fiction, tabloids, and radio. A mad scientist, bored housewives, mordant lovers,

eccentric millionaires, and characters with names such as "Giggling Girl" talk about life, the cosmos, and love. Cardboard characters, expressionistic format and design, and a dense and incoherent plot resulted in a dull drama. The play was allowed to run as long as it did because of the excellent stage design by Mordecai Gorelik and the reputation Lawson had established with *Processional.*

Despite the expressionism that links it to his previous plays, *Loudspeaker* marked a change in direction for Lawson, as he began to attack American capitalism directly. The first play produced by the New Playwrights Theatre, *Loudspeaker* opened on 7 March 1927 at the Fifty-second Street Theatre and ran for forty-two performances. Lawson got the idea for the play while attending the ceremonial laying of the cornerstone at the new Theatre Guild playhouse in 1924. Governor Alfred E. Smith and Otto Kahn were in attendance, and Lawson wondered if Kahn would make a more interesting governor than Smith.

Employing a variety of techniques—including constructivism, jazz, expressionism, and realism—*Loudspeaker* follows Harry U. Collins's attempt to be elected governor. The play strips away the masks that politicians wear and reveals the manipulation and exploitation of American political campaigns. The humor is broad, the satire explicit, and the plot predictable. Though highly theatrical and topical, *Loudspeaker* lacks the sharp edge of other significant leftist plays.

Lawson had not yet joined the Communist Party, but in late 1926, along with Dos Passos, Gold, and others, he was on the "National Executive Committee" that attempted to found the Proletarian Artists and Writers League with backing from a similar Soviet organization. In August 1927 Lawson joined fellow committee members Dos Passos and Gold in Boston to demonstrate against the execution of Italian-born anarchists Nicola Sacco and Bartolomeo Vanzetti, who had been convicted of murder and armed robbery. The case had become a cause célèbre for left-leaning American intellectuals, who believed that the two men had been convicted because of their politics and ethnic origin. During the protest the police charged the crowd of demonstrators and beat some of them. After this experience, Lawson wrote in his autobiography, he found that he could neither ignore the flaws in American politics and economics nor bring himself to become more deeply involved in the struggle. He wanted to be a playwright, but fulfilling that goal was hampered by the financial insecurity that burdened all New Playwrights Theatre efforts. He accepted an offer from M-G-M to write for the movies and left New York for Hollywood.

Soon after his departure, New Playwrights Theatre produced the last of Lawson's expressionistic plays, *The International,* with a set designed by Dos Passos. The play opened on 12 January 1928 and ran for twenty-seven performances. Widely panned by the critics, the play follows the launching of a world revolution that sputters to a halt on Wall Street. The play combines multiple locations—Tibet, China, Russia, France, England, and New York City—many scenes, and several plots for a huge, but empty, spectacle. Whereas *Processional* is novel and theatrical, *The International* is overwhelming and overbearing. The poor reception of *The International* strengthened Lawson's resolve to succeed in Hollywood.

Lawson's resignation from New Playwrights Theatre was also prompted by his financial troubles. He had dabbled in real estate and lost money. Money was not his only motivation, however; he was also lured by the challenge of a new medium—the motion picture. Lawson prospered in Hollywood, and with his earnings he bought a large house on Long Island, living the sort of life he had satirized in his plays.

As the Depression deepened during the winter of 1930–1931, Lawson wrote *Success Story*. The script was rejected by the Theatre Guild, but Harold Clurman, a reader for the group, had just helped to found the Group Theatre and needed new scripts. Clurman and Lawson reworked the play during the summer of 1932, and *Success Story* opened on 26 September 1932 for a run of 121 performances.

Lawson's autobiographical response to his three years in Hollywood, *Success Story* follows the financial rise and moral decline of Sol Ginsberg, an employee of an advertising agency. Lawson mixed elements of expressionism and psychological realism, creating humanized characters rather than the stereotypes of his earlier works. Sol starts out as an awkward, hot-tempered clerk, filled with hatred born of his outsider status as a Jewish liberal. He resolves to make as much money as possible from the complacent establishment, while he waits for social revolution. In his single-minded focus on material success, Sol brings misery to everyone around him during his climb to the top. When he finally becomes president of his company, he looks back at the wake of broken hearts and broken promises and finds that money has not brought him happiness. The woman who once was his sweetheart and the reinforcer of his Marxist conscience, ends his misery by shooting him. The power and passion that Lawson infused in his characters nearly overcame the obvious plot. Some critics felt that it was "almost" a good play. Lawson wrote the screenplay for the movie version, *Success at Any Price* (1934), in which the original anticapitalist message nearly disappeared.

In 1933 Lawson helped to organize and became first president of the Screen Writers Guild. He was fired from his position at M-G-M and worked in Washington, D.C., to have the group recognized by the National Labor Board as a bargaining unit for screenwriters. While he was there, in 1934, two of his plays were produced in New York: *The Pure in Heart* and *Gentlewoman*.

Lawson wrote *The Pure in Heart* while he was working on *Success Story*. The Theatre Guild agreed to produce the play but closed it when the out-of-town tryout in Baltimore failed to impress audiences or critics. After the Group Theatre also rejected the play, it was produced by Richard Aldrich and Alfred De Liagre. *The Pure in Heart* opened on 20 March and ran for only seven performances.

The Pure in Heart is Lawson's attempt to explain the relationship of art and entertainment in American culture. He combined expressionism with motion-picture techniques he learned in Hollywood, and the result was less than satisfactory. The play follows the rise and fall of small-town girl Annabel Sparks, who leaves her Depression-ravaged home with dreams of success on stage and screen. Propelled by the empty images of Hollywood in popular magazines, Annabel will stop at nothing to achieve success, getting her first job because she is willing to accommodate the sexual demands of the directors. She ends up having an affair with a mobster, and the two are gunned down in one another's arms. Annabel, the play suggests, has been driven to her meaningless end by the false but compelling images of capitalist culture. Lawson's use of Hollywood clichés, however, overshadows his social criticism, and the play was roundly criticized.

Gentlewoman, produced by the Group Theatre in association with D. A. Doran Jr., opened on 22 March 1934 and ran for only twelve performances. The title character is Gwyn Ballantine, a New York socialite whose husband kills himself in a fit of capitalist angst. After his death she falls in love with a younger man, radical writer Rudy Flannigan, a Communist who lacks personal integrity. He extols the concept of the common laborer but lacks compassion for individuals. Leaving Gwen, who is pregnant with his child, he goes to Iowa to join a farmers' strike, while she mutters about the coming Communist revolution that will destroy them all.

During the 1930s leftists criticized Lawson for his lack of ideological and political commitment. Mike Gold, with whom Lawson had worked in the New Playwrights Theatre, attacked him in *The New Masses,* calling Lawson "A Bourgeois Hamlet of Our Time" (10 April 1934) who wrote adolescent works that lacked moral fiber or clear ideas. Lawson was stung by these criticisms, and in his response, "'Inner Conflict' and Proletarian Art" (*The New Masses,* 17 April 1934), he candidly acknowledged his middle-class childhood was partly to blame for his incomplete understanding of the lower classes. Lawson also recognized that his Hollywood connections and his financial prosperity made him suspect in the fight for workers' rights. As a result of the criticisms leveled at him, Lawson joined the Communist Party and began a program of educating himself about the proletarian cause. He traveled throughout the poverty-stricken South to study bloody labor conflicts in Alabama and Georgia.

During his southern tours Lawson was arrested several times on a variety of charges that were apparently linked to the frequent and outspoken anticapitalist reports he wrote for the Communist newspaper *Daily Worker.* His experiences inspired *Marching Song,* his last produced play. Performed by the radical Theatre Union, it opened on 17 February 1937 and ran for sixty-one performances.

Lawson on the witness stand before the House Un-American Activities Committee, where he refused to testify about his ties to the Communist Party, 1947 (photograph © Bettmann/CORBIS)

Set in Brimmerton, a thinly disguised version of Birmingham, Alabama, *Marching Song* depicts a bloody class struggle. Lawson used techniques that were closer to classic Greek tragedy than to the expressionism of his previous plays. The play focuses on Pete Russell, a worker who has been blacklisted after an unsuccessful strike against a local automobile plant, as unemployed workers and their families, who have been evicted from their homes, join with union members to stage a sit-down strike to demand their jobs back. Race relations, exploitation of workers by the capitalist upper class, Depression economics, and police brutality are among the themes of the diffuse and far-ranging play. Despite clear political and economic insights and lively dialogue, *Marching Song* falls short of greatness. It is, however, one of Lawson's best efforts.

Marching Song was staged not long after Lawson had addressed the problem of writing ideological drama in *Theory and Technique of Playwriting* (1936). The first part of the book, an historical overview, is a treatise advocating radical dramaturgy, while the second part is an elementary approach to how to write a play, useful to any would-be playwright in its analysis of problems and pitfalls. The book has been used as a textbook in college courses since its publication. Lawson revised the text to include screenwriting in 1949.

After *Marching Song,* Lawson was again invited to Hollywood, where he wrote the screenplay for one of the few movies that he considered truly his own work, *Blockade* (1938), starring Henry Fonda. He continued to work in Hollywood with increasing success until 1947, when he was one of the nineteen Hollywood writers called before the House Un-American Activities Committee for questioning about their ties to the Communist Party. He refused to testify and was among the Hollywood Ten cited for contempt of Congress. In 1948 he was sentenced to one year in prison, which he began serving in 1950. After his release, he was blacklisted and could no longer find work as a screenwriter. He contributed to a few motion pictures pseudonymously as Edward Lewis or without credit. During his later years, Lawson taught at several colleges and universities, including Stanford University, Loyola Marymount College, and Los Angeles University of Judaism.

Assessment of Lawson's works and career has been divided. Some critics have praised his dynamic agitprop technique and his incisive analysis of the contradictions and injustices of Western society after World War I. Others have called his plays formulaic presentations of stereotypical characters representing his vision of a dysfunctional capitalist society and a productive Soviet system. Lawson is remembered not for his plays or screenplays, or even for his radical political ideology, but as a writer who sacrificed his career to a cause.

References:

Daniel Aaron, *Writers on the Left: Episodes in American Literary Communism* (New York: Octagon, 1974);

John Baxter, *Hollywood in the Thirties* (New York: Paperback Library, 1970);

Eric Bentley, *Are You Now or Have You Ever Been: The Investigation of Show Business by the Un-American Activities Committee, 1947–1958* (New York: Harper & Row, 1972);

Michael Blankfort, "Reckless but Feckless," *New Republic,* 80 (12 September 1934): 136;

Beverle Bloch, "John Howard Lawson's 'Processional': Modernism in American Theatre in the Twenties," *Journal of American History,* 76 (December 1989): 1036–1071;

Ben Brown, *Theatre at the Left* (Providence, R.I.: Bear Press, 1938);

Richard Brown, "John Howard Lawson as an Activist Playwright," dissertation, Tulane University, 1964;

Garry Carr, "John Howard Lawson: Hollywood Craftsmanship and Censorship in the 1930s," *ICarbS,* 3 (Fall–Winter 1976): 37–48;

Carr, *The Left Side of Paradise: the Screenwriting of John Howard Lawson* (Ann Arbor, Mich.: UMI Research Press, 1984);

John Dos Passos, *The Fourteenth Chronicle: Letters and Diaries of John Dos Passos,* edited by Townsend Ludington (Boston: Gambit, 1973);

Robert Gardner, "International Rag: The Theatrical Career of John Howard Lawson," dissertation, University of California, Berkeley, 1978;

James Gilbert, *Writers and Partisans: A History of Literary Radicalism* (New York: Wiley, 1968);

Malcolm Goldstein, *Political Stage: American Drama and Theatre of the Great Depression* (New York: Oxford University Press, 1974);

Morgan Himelstein, *Drama Was a Weapon: Left-Wing Theatre in New York 1929–1941* (New Brunswick, N.J.: Rutgers University Press, 1963);

George Knox and Herbert Stahl, *Dos Passos and "The Revolting Playwrights"* (Copenhagen: Munksgaard, 1964);

Lee Lowenfish, "John Howard Lawson's 'A Calendar of Commitment,'" *ICarbS,* 3 (Summer–Fall 1976): 23–36;

Harrison McCreath, "A Rhetorical Analysis of the Plays of John Howard Lawson," dissertation, Stanford University, 1965;

Michael Mendelsohn, "The Social Critic on Stage," *Modern Drama,* 6 (1963): 277–285;

Kshamanidhi Mishra, *American Leftist Playwrights of the 1930's: a Study of Ideology and Technique in the Plays of Odets, Lawson, and Sherwood* (New Delhi: Classical Publishing, 1991);

Gerald Rabkin, *Drama and Commitment* (Bloomington: Indiana University Press, 1964);

Liliane Randrianarivony-Koziol, "Techniques of Commitment in the Thirties: A Study of the Selected Plays of John Howard Lawson," dissertation, Indiana University, 1982;

Nancy Schwartz, *The Hollywood Writers' Wars* (New York: Knopf, 1982);

Sam Smiley, *The Drama of Attack* (Columbia: University of Missouri Press, 1972);

Darwin Turner, "Jazz Vaudeville Drama in the Twenties," *Educational Theatre Journal,* 11 (May 1959): 110–116;

Mardi Valfemae, "Civil War Among the Expressionists: John Howard Lawson and the *Pinwheel* Controversy," *Educational Theatre Journal,* 20 (March 1968): 8–14;

Jay Williams, *Stage Left* (New York: Scribners, 1974).

Papers:

There is an extensive collection of John Howard Lawson's papers, including his unpublished autobiography, at Southern Illinois University, Carbondale.

Anita Loos

(26 April 1888 – 18 August 1981)

Leah Lowe
Florida State University

See also the Loos entries in *DLB 11: American Humorists, 1800–1950; DLB 26: American Screenwriters;* and *DLB Yearbook 1981.*

PLAY PRODUCTIONS: *The Whole Town's Talking,* by Loos and John Emerson, New York, Bijou Theatre, 29 August 1923;

The Fall of Eve, by Loos and Emerson, New York, Booth Theatre, 31 August 1925;

"Gentlemen Prefer Blondes," by Loos and Emerson, New York, Times Square Theatre, 28 September 1926;

The Social Register, by Loos and Emerson, New York, Fulton Theatre, 9 November 1931;

Happy Birthday, New York, Broadhurst Theatre, 31 October 1946;

Gentlemen Prefer Blondes [musical], book by Loos and Joseph Fields, New York, Ziegfeld Theatre, 8 December 1949;

Gigi, adapted from Colette's novel, New York, Fulton Theatre, 24 November 1951;

The Amazing Adele, based on Pierre Barillet and Jean-Pierre Gredy's play, Philadelphia, Shubert Theatre, 26 December 1955;

Chéri, adapted from Colette's *Chéri* and *The End of Chéri,* New York, Morosco Theatre, 12 October 1959;

The King's Mare, adapted from Jean Canolle's *La Jument du roi,* Bristol, Old Vic Theatre, October 1961; London, West End, November 1966;

Gogo Loves You, New York, Theatre de Lys, 9 October 1964.

BOOKS: *How to Write Photoplays,* by Loos and John Emerson (New York: McCann, 1920);

Breaking into the Movies, by Loos and Emerson (New York: McCann, 1921);

The Whole Town's Talking: A Farce in Three Acts, by Loos and Emerson (New York: Longmans, Green, 1925);

"Gentlemen Prefer Blondes": The Illuminating Diary of a Professional Lady (New York: Boni & Liveright, 1925; London: Brentano's, 1926);

Anita Loos in 1914 (Lester Glassner Collection)

"But Gentlemen Marry Brunettes" (New York: Boni & Liveright, 1928; London: Brentano's, 1928);

"The Struggle," by Loos and Emerson (New York: Griffith, 1931);

Happy Birthday: A Play in Two Acts (New York: French, 1947);

A Mouse Is Born (Garden City, N.Y.: Doubleday, 1951; London: Cape, 1951);

Gigi, dramatized by Loos from Colette's novel (New York: Random House, 1952; acting edition, New York: French, 1953);

179

No Mother to Guide Her (New York: McGraw-Hill, 1961; London: Barker, 1961);

A Girl Like I (New York: Viking, 1966; London: Hamilton, 1967);

The King's Mare: A Play in Three Acts, adapted from Jean Canolle's *Le Jument du roi* (London: Evans, 1967);

Twice Over Lightly: New York Then and Now, by Loos and Helen Hayes (New York: Harcourt Brace Jovanovich, 1972);

Kiss Hollywood Good-by (New York: Viking, 1974; London: W. H. Allen, 1974);

Cast of Thousands (New York: Grosset & Dunlap, 1977);

The Talmadge Girls: A Memoir (New York: Viking, 1978);

San Francisco: A Screenplay, edited by Matthew J. Bruccoli (Carbondale: Southern Illinois University Press, 1979);

Fate Keeps On Happening: Adventures of Lorelei Lee and Other Writings, edited by Ray Pierre Corsini (New York: Dodd, Mead, 1984).

PRODUCED SCRIPTS (SELECTED): *The New York Hat,* motion picture, American Biograph, 1912;

Learning to Love, motion picture, scenario by Loos and John Emerson, First National Pictures, 1925;

Gentlemen Prefer Blondes, motion picture, adapted by Loos and Emerson from their play, Paramount Famous-Lasky, 1928;

The Fall of Eve, motion picture, script by Loos and Emerson, Columbia, 1929;

The Struggle, motion picture, script by Loos and Emerson, United Artists, 1931;

Red-Headed Woman, motion picture, M-G-M, 1932;

Blondie of the Follies, motion picture, M-G-M, 1932;

The Barbarian, motion picture, M-G-M, 1932;

Down to Earth, motion picture, 20th Century-Fox, 1932;

Hold Your Man, motion picture, script by Loos and Howard Emmett Rogers, M-G-M, 1933;

The Girl from Missouri, motion picture, script by Loos and Emerson, M-G-M, 1934;

Biography of a Bachelor Girl, motion picture, adapted from S. N. Behrman's *Biography,* M-G-M, 1934;

Riffraff, motion picture, script by Loos, Frances Marion, and H. W. Haneman, M-G-M, 1935;

San Francisco, motion picture, M-G-M, 1936;

Mama Steps Out, motion picture, adapted from John Kirkpatrick's *Ada Beats the Drum,* M-G-M, 1937;

Saratoga, motion picture, script by Loos and Robert Hopkins, M-G-M, 1937;

The Women, motion picture, adapted by Loos and Jane Murfin from Clare Booth Luce's play, M-G-M, 1939;

Susan and God, motion picture, adapted from Rachel Crothers's play, M-G-M, 1940;

They Met in Bombay, motion picture, script by Loos, Edwin Justin Mayer, and Leon Gordon, M-G-M, 1941;

When Ladies Meet, motion picture, adapted by Loos and S. K. Lauren from Crothers's play, M-G-M, 1941;

Blossoms in the Dust, motion picture, M-G-M, 1941;

I Married an Angel, motion picture, adapted from Richard Rodgers and Lorenz Hart's adaptation of Vaszary Janos's play, M-G-M, 1942.

While Anita Loos is best known for her comic novel *"Gentlemen Prefer Blondes": The Illuminating Diary of a Professional Lady* (1925), her work includes many stage plays, screenplays, and memoirs of her years in the entertainment industry. Her fiction and plays, mostly in a comic vein, are notable for their heroines who, while subject to the restrictions placed on women at the time, enjoy a great deal of autonomy and power. Significantly, these heroines derive their power through their femininity rather than in spite of it. Loos's best heroines, typified by the irrepressible Lorelei Lee of *"Gentlemen Prefer Blondes,"* are sexual creatures who deploy their femininity to achieve their own ends without paying a social price for their sexuality. Rather than attacking or debunking stereotypes of women, Loos created comic characters who gleefully set their worlds upside down and expose the limitations and hypocrisy of conventional morality.

Corinne Anita Loos was born in Sissons (now Mount Shasta), California, on 26 April 1888 to Minnie Ellen Smith Loos and R. Beers Loos, a flamboyant newspaperman with a penchant for the theatrical. That same year, her father moved the family to San Francisco, where he published an entertainment weekly titled *The Dramatic Event.* Anita, along with her younger sister, Gladys, became a child actress in a local stock company playing such roles as Little Lord Fauntleroy, Willie in a stage adaptation of Mrs. Henry Wood's 1861 *East Lynne,* and one of the Helmer children in Henrik Ibsen's *A Doll's House* (1879). Her father was, in Loos's words, "a scamp." After he lost his paper and held other short-lived jobs, including managing a carnival, Loos's acting supported the family. Loos never thought of herself as an actress, however, and explained why in *A Girl Like I* (1966) as she recalled taking dance classes years later with ballet master Adolph Bohm:

one day Bohm blew up and shouted at me, "Mother of heaven, will you never stop *thinking*!" Had it been a few years later, I might have thought my little head off at the Actors Studio and been a success. But those were the good old days when playwrights did the thinking and the actor never interfered.

Loos with her collaborator and second husband, John Emerson, in a film-editing room in Hollywood

Though Loos abandoned acting for writing as soon as she was able, her early exposure to the theater undoubtedly shaped her sensibility as an author.

In 1911 the Loos family settled in San Diego, where R. Beers Loos managed a stock company that Anita acted in. In response to the growing popularity of silent movies, a typical program mixed two short plays with one silent movie. Loos avidly watched the silent pictures; realizing that they required stories, she began to write movie scenarios. She sent her stories to the Biograph Company under the name of "A. Loos," fearing that if they were known to be by a woman they would be rejected. The third scenario she sent to Biograph and the first accepted, *The New York Hat* (1912), was directed by D. W. Griffith and starred the then-unknown Mary Pickford, Lionel Barrymore, and Lillian and Dorothy Gish. All told, Loos wrote scenarios for more than one hundred silent movies, listed in her *Cast of Thousands* (1977). She is credited with introducing dialogue in subtitles of silent movies.

Loos's early writing was not restricted to the movies. She also wrote short pieces for local papers. A vaudeville skit (now lost), *The Ink Well,* written for a fellow actress who lost her job when one of R. Beers Loos's stock companies failed, was one of her first pieces written for the theater. *The Ink Well* tells the story of an attractive young woman who hires a lawyer to handle her divorce. Initially smitten with the young woman, the lawyer sympathizes with her until she becomes shrewish and shows her true colors. The lawyer eventually hurls his ink well at her and throws her out of his office. The skit, and Loos's actress friend, were booked on the Orpheum circuit for three years.

In 1915 Loos married Frank Pallma; the union lasted only six months. Later that year Loos moved to Hollywood and began to work for Griffith in the Fine Arts-Triangle script department. There, in addition to other assignments, she wrote scripts for Douglas Fairbanks that developed his comic-heroic screen persona and propelled him to stardom. Loos later wrote in *A Girl Like I* that most of her work on these movies consisted of finding "a variety of spots from which Doug could jump." John Emerson, a New York actor who starred in the 1912 Broadway hit *The Conspiracy,* directed the movies that Loos wrote for Fairbanks. Loos and Emerson successfully collaborated on nine movies with Fairbanks, and in 1918, when Fairbanks parted company with them, they continued to work on screenplays together. Loos and Emerson were married in 1920.

The marriage was a troubled one from the beginning. In *A Girl Like I* Loos wrote, "having started with the resolution to steer clear of exhibitionists of all kinds, actors in particular, I went out of my way to marry the most ardent example I've ever known. The results, quite naturally, were both tragic and comic, together with a thousand combinations of the two." Emerson was a hypochondriac, chronically unfaithful, and demanded joint-authorship credit for stage and screen projects to which, Loos later revealed, his contributions were minimal. As Loos's success and celebrity increased, her relationship with Emerson became more difficult. Frequently, when Loos took jobs at Hollywood studios, she was forced to ask them to create positions for Emerson. Through most of their marriage, Loos made the money, while Emerson mismanaged their financial affairs. In 1937 Emerson was diagnosed as a schizophrenic and confined to a sanatorium. Although they remained married until Emerson's death in 1956, they never lived together for any substantial period of time again.

In 1923 Emerson decided that he and Loos should switch from writing for the screen to writing for the stage. Though Loos never abandoned her more lucrative movie career, she broadened her scope to include the theater. Her first play, *The Whole Town's Talking,* was directed by Emerson and opened on Broadway in August 1923, running for a successful 173 performances. The play, typical of the Loos-Emerson stage collaborations of the 1920s, is a frothy comedy, reminiscent of French farce. It takes place in Sandusky, Ohio, where successful manufacturer Henry Simmons wants his daughter, Ethel, to marry his business partner, Chester Binney. Ethel, however, is infatuated with a wild young man from Chicago and finds Chester extremely dull in comparison. Simmons persuades Chester to claim that he once had an affair with glamorous Hollywood movie star Letty Lythe. As news of Chester's romantic exploits travels, all the young women of Sandusky, including Ethel, look at him in a new and far more appreciative light. Inevitably, Letty Lythe arrives in town to promote her new movie, accompanied by her extremely jealous fiancé. The play concludes with a knockabout fight between Chester, the fiancé, and Ethel's Chicago beau, from which Chester emerges the victor, winning Ethel's heart and hand.

During this period Loos also wrote *The Fall of Eve* (1925), which starred Ruth Gordon. Although it ran for only forty-eight performances, it received fairly good reviews. However, neither of these early plays is memorable or significant. Both rely on formulaic farcical situations for comic effect, and the characters, while interesting, are hardly remarkable. Loos herself seemed to think little of her early theatrical efforts; in her memoirs, she hardly mentions them. It is likely that she wrote these plays at Emerson's urging, but did not really involve herself in them.

Loos was catapulted to fame in 1925 when *"Gentlemen Prefer Blondes"* was published. Loos credited a young woman, "the dumbest blonde of all," with whom her friend H. L. Mencken was briefly infatuated, as the inspiration for the novel. She wrote a brief sketch about the woman while traveling by train to California to work on a screenplay, and then sent it to Mencken to amuse him. Mencken urged her to publish it. *"Gentlemen Prefer Blondes"* was first serialized in *Harper's Bazaar;* when it was published as a book, it sold out on its first day in the stores. *"Gentlemen Prefer Blondes"* was a critical success as well as a popular one. Edith Wharton was quoted on the dust jacket, calling it "the great American novel," and Loos was told that it was one of the few books that James Joyce, whose sight was then failing, chose to read.

"Gentlemen Prefer Blondes" tells the story of a distinctively American opportunist, Lorelei Lee, a gold-digging flapper from Little Rock, Arkansas. The novel follows Lorelei's adventures as she and Dorothy Shaw, her brunette friend and wisecracking companion, cut a wide swath through New York and European society. Lorelei's attitude toward men is encapsulated in her maxim, "Kissing your hand may make you feel very good but a diamond bracelet lasts forever." She relies on a series of wealthy and gullible men to finance her education and adventures. Lorelei is quick to take a man for all he is worth, but does so with a wide-eyed and infectious innocence and a wholly practical instinct for self-preservation. Throughout the novel, the joke is on the men who woo Lorelei. Loos skillfully satirizes the moralistic and self-satisfied pretensions of moneyed, upper-class society and the men who control it.

Loos and Emerson adapted *"Gentlemen Prefer Blondes"* for the stage in 1926. Originally Emerson was slated to direct, but persistent health problems forced him to turn the direction over to Edgar Selwyn, who produced and staged the production. Several actresses, including Helen Hayes, auditioned for the coveted role of Lorelei Lee, which was given to a promising young comedienne named June Walker. Tallulah Bankhead reportedly described the choice of Walker as a case of "perfect casting." Though critics praised Walker, she apparently did not give the charismatic performance the role demanded. In addition, Loos's picaresque novel, which ranges in setting from New York to London and Paris and back again, was not suited for a straight stage adaptation. While initially praised as a faithful reproduction of the wildly popular novel, the play did not achieve the same sort of appeal as its fictional predecessor. It opened on Broadway in September 1926 after an initial run of several months in Chicago and closed in April 1927 after around two hundred performances.

"*Gentlemen Prefer Blondes*" found a more successful theatrical afterlife as a musical. Florenz Ziegfield had first suggested the idea of a musical shortly after the publication of the novel, but Loos had already contracted with Selwyn to write a regular play. After it closed, she moved on to other projects, including the sequel to "*Gentlemen Prefer Blondes,*" "*But Gentlemen Marry Brunettes*" (1928), and its stage adaptation, *The Social Register,* which ran on Broadway for ninety-seven performances in 1931–1932. In 1948 producers Herman Levin and Oliver Smith approached Loos about writing a musical, and she embraced the project. Loos collaborated with Joseph Fields on the libretto, while Jules Styne and Leo Robin contributed music and lyrics. Billy Rose produced the musical; John Wilson directed; and Agnes de Mille choreographed.

One of the central problems encountered in the planning stages of the project was finding the right actress to play Lorelei Lee. Ethel Merman turned the project down, and though many actresses auditioned for the role, none of them won the production team over. As Loos biographer Gary Carey relates, producer Levin pinpointed the problem when he recalled, "We were looking for a gorgeous blond seductress when what we really wanted, though we didn't know it till we spotted it, was a girl who could make fun of a gorgeous blond seductress." After seeing Carol Channing perform in an obscure musical review, Loos and producer Smith persuaded the rest of the team to take a chance on her, though Channing, a tall, statuesque woman, was not physically suited for the role. Loos was determined to turn Channing's size to a comic advantage: "She can play Lorelei like a Great Dane under the delusion that it's a Pekinese," she argued. The musical, with Channing in the lead, opened on Broadway in December 1949, where it ran for more than ninety weeks. Channing's performance captivated the critics and contributed much to the success of the production.

As a result of the crosscurrents that ran between the Broadway stage and the motion-picture industry, the musical *Gentlemen Prefer Blondes* was adapted for the screen by Charles Lederer in 1953, directed by Howard Hawks and featuring performances by Marilyn Monroe and Jane Russell. Although Loos did not contribute to the classic Hollywood movie as she had to the 1928 movie version, she was pleased by Lederer's work on the book and Monroe's performance. The movie, along with the novel and stage musical, contributed to Lorelei Lee's status as a comic feminine archetype.

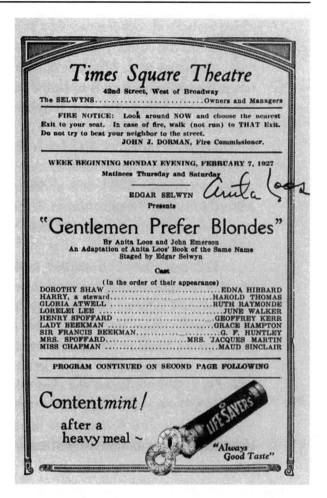

Autographed copy of the program for the play Loos and Emerson adapted from Loos's 1925 novel (from Gary Carey, Anita Loos: A Biography, 1988)

In the 1940s Loos developed a close friendship with actress Helen Hayes. The actress had started her career in light comedy but had played sentimental and dramatic characters for years and wanted to find a role that gave her an opportunity to have some fun. Loos suggested Hayes consider a new play, a cocktail bar comedy she had been contemplating. When Hayes expressed an interest, Loos began work on it. *Happy Birthday,* directed by Joshua Logan and produced by Richard Rodgers and Oscar Hammerstein II, went into rehearsals in the fall of 1946. The production, particularly Hayes's performance, was well received and was performed 564 times between October 1946 and the spring of 1948. While *Happy Birthday* is essentially a light comedy, Loos's treatment of the leading character reiterates her distaste for social convention, particularly with regard to feminine behavior.

Happy Birthday revolves around Addie Beamis (played by Hayes). The play opens as Addie, a dowdy,

Helen Hayes and Jack Binder in a scene from Loos's 1946 play,
Happy Birthday *(photograph by Anita Loos)*

self-righteous librarian, arrives at the Jersey Mecca Cocktail Bar to warn Paul Bishop, a dashing young bank teller, that her volatile father suspects that she and Paul are seeing each other. Addie finds Paul drinking at the Mecca with Maude, an attractive but manipulative young woman. From the beginning of the play, it is obvious that Addie is attracted to Paul and resents Maude's presence, but is too shy to take any action to get his attention. Though Addie begins the evening timidly sipping water, the other bar patrons persuade her to switch to Pink Ladies. She then progresses on to bourbon and eventually buys round after round of champagne for the entire bar. As she drinks, Addie displays a newfound audacity. She impulsively gets rid of Maude by placing a phone call to Maude's other boyfriend, and she is soon dancing with Paul, quoting poetry, and confessing her feelings for him. The climax of the play occurs when Homer Beamis, Addie's father, interrupts the party and threatens Paul. He is poised to hit Paul over the head with a bottle, when Addie grabs it and hits Homer, knocking him out instead. By the end of the play, Addie has not only won her man but also discovered a new and powerful aspect of herself.

Addie's self-discovery is underscored by the scenic effects. As she becomes progressively intoxicated,

the set (designed by Jo Mielziner) reflects her state of mind. The bottles on the bar begin to glow with colored light; bubbles rise up from them; and a table rises up to provide Addie and Paul with a hiding place in which they can have a private conversation. The prosaic Mecca is transformed into a place of beauty and unexpected surprises as Addie sheds her inhibitions and pursues Paul. Though Addie is nothing like Lorelei Lee, her transformation suggests that there is something limiting about her former strict adherence to social convention, a theme Loos previously explored in *"Gentlemen Prefer Blondes."* Only through rejecting her stuffy propriety and acknowledging an untamed and sexual side of her nature can Addie achieve happiness. Though *Happy Birthday* does nothing to challenge the conventions of light romantic comedy, it does establish Addie as a heroine who gets what she wants by bucking the rules rather than conforming to them.

After finishing work on the musical version of *"Gentlemen Prefer Blondes,"* Loos began to adapt Colette's 1944 novella, *Gigi,* for the stage in 1950. Loos had long been an admirer of Colette. Though superficially worlds apart, their work was informed by similar attitudes. Loos wrote in "The Creator of *Gigi*," included in *Fate Keeps On Happening: Adventures of Lorelei Lee and Other Writings* (1984): "The basis of Colette's power as a novelist was that she wrote straight from the emotions. . . . In matters of sex she followed the human heart as few writers ever have done. Most novelists, when dealing with the subject, allow a moral, or at least an editorial viewpoint to creep in. But not Colette." The admiration was mutual. Colette referred to Loos as "the most subtle and friendly of collaborators," and she gave her blessing to Loos's adaptation of *Gigi.*

In "The Creator of *Gigi*" Loos describes the heroine as a Cinderella character, "even though her story is told in terms of sex." The play takes place in Paris around 1900. Gigi, a naive and beguiling sixteen-year-old, has been raised by her grandmother and aunt, who in their younger days won fame and fortune as courtesans to the rich and powerful. They plan a similar career for Gigi, who has developed a friendship with a wealthy young man, Gaston Lachaille. Since Gigi and her family are poor, and Gaston is rich, her aunt and grandmother groom Gigi for the role of Gaston's mistress, a position in which she will be provided for, but only at Gaston's whim. Gigi, who sincerely values Gaston's friendship, refuses to go along with the plan. In the end, all is righted when Gaston and Gigi discover that they have fallen in love with each other, and he proposes to her. The play, like *Happy Birthday,* adheres to standard romantic comedy formulas—romantic love and the promise of marriage ultimately make Gigi and Gaston's relationship legitimate—but it also frankly links women's financial security to their sexual relationships with men.

When *Gigi* opened on Broadway in November 1951, the critical response was cool, partly because of the implied connection between sex and economic stability and the threat of Gigi's transformation from innocent girl to knowing courtesan. However, the young actress Audrey Hepburn received glowing notices in her first New York appearance. The relatively inexperienced Hepburn was billed as a star, and the publicity campaign for the production focused on her performance. *Gigi* ran for 219 performances until May 1952, when Hepburn, under contract to Paramount Pictures, departed to make *Roman Holiday* (1953). In 1958 a musical movie adaptation of *Gigi* was released, with Leslie Caron in the title role. Loos did not participate in this movie version, and while she supported the project publicly, privately she told friends that it was "too MGM" for her taste.

Loos's later plays were not as successful as her earlier theatrical works, and several stage projects she began were abandoned because of casting difficulties and production problems. *The Amazing Adele* (1955), a musical adaptation of *Le Don d'Adele* (1953), by Pierre Barillet and Jean-Pierre Gredy, was written with Channing in mind. Channing was not impressed by the script, and the role of Adele fell to Tammy Grimes. The reviews were disappointing, and the play closed on its initial run before ever opening in New York. Loos's last Broadway play, *Chéri,* based on two of Colette's novels, closed after only six weeks and fifty-six performances in 1959. *The King's Mare,* Loos's adaptation of Jean Canolle's *La Jument du roi* (1960), an historical comedy about the misalliance between Henry VIII and Anne of Cleves, was first produced at the Old Vic in 1961. In 1966 it had a moderately successful West End run but never transferred to Broadway. A small-scale musical, *Gogo Loves You,* produced Off-Broadway in 1964, closed after one night. In 1974 Channing and her husband, Charles Lowe, staged a musical, *Lorelei; or Gentlemen Still Prefer Blondes,* with songs by Betty Comden and Adolph Green. Though Loos did not write any new material for *Lorelei,* some of her previous work from the musical version of "*Gentlemen Prefer Blondes*" was retained.

In the mid 1960s Loos turned away from stage and screen projects and began work on a series of critically acclaimed memoirs. The first, *A Girl Like I,* tells her story from childhood to the publication of "*Gentlemen Prefer Blondes.*" Two later memoirs, *Kiss Hollywood Good-by* (1974) and *Cast of Thousands,* deal more specifically with her prolific movie career. A working writer until the end of her life, Anita Loos died of a heart attack on 18 August 1981.

Anita Loos's compositions for the popular American stage, while often overshadowed by the success of her novels, screenplays, and memoirs, constitute a significant aspect of her work. Loos's plays and their heroines demontrate her unique comic sensibility, and, like her work in other literary and entertainment genres, lightly undermine conventional precepts and principles governing social behavior.

Interview:

Matthew J. Bruccoli, "Anita Loos," in *Conversations with Writers, II* (Detroit: Gale Research, 1977), pp. 125–140.

Biography:

Gary Carey, *Anita Loos: A Biography* (New York: Knopf, 1988).

References:

Regina Barreca, introduction to *Gentlemen Prefer Blondes and But Gentlemen Marry Brunettes* by Anita Loos (New York: Penguin, 1998), pp. vii–xxvii;

T. E. Blom, "Anita Loos and Sexual Economics: *Gentlemen Prefer Blondes,*" *Canadian Review of American Studies* (Spring 1976): 39–47;

Susan Hegeman, "Taking Blondes Seriously," *American Literary History,* 7, no. 3 (1995): 525–554;

Richard J. Schrader, "*But Gentlemen Marry Brunettes:* Anita Loos and H. L. Mencken," *Menckeniana: A Quarterly Review,* 98 (1986): 1–7.

Clare Boothe Luce

(10 March 1903 – 9 October 1987)

Shannon Steen
Stanford University

PLAY PRODUCTIONS: *Abide with Me,* New York, Ritz Theatre, 21 November 1935;

The Women, New York, Ethel Barrymore Theatre, 26 December 1936;

Kiss the Boys Good-bye, New York: Henry Miller's Theatre, 28 September 1938;

Margin for Error, New York, Plymouth Theatre, 3 November 1939;

Love Is a Verb, adapted from Alexander King's "The Yohimbe Tree," Abingdon, Virginia, Barter Theatre, 20 August 1942;

Child of the Morning, Boston, Shubert Theatre, 19 November 1951.

BOOKS: *Stuffed Shirts,* as Clare Boothe Brokaw (New York: Liveright, 1931);

The Women (New York: Random House, 1937; revised, New York: Dramatists Play Service, 1966);

Kiss the Boys Good-bye (New York: Random House, 1939);

Europe in the Spring (New York: Knopf, 1940); republished as *European Spring* (London: Hamilton, 1941);

Margin for Error: A Satirical Melodrama (New York: Random House, 1940);

Slam the Door Softly (New York: Dramatists Play Service, 1971).

OTHER: "The Valor of Homer Lea," in *The Day of the Saxon,* by Homer Lea (New York: Harper, 1942), pp. 1–31;

Saints for Now, edited by Luce (London & New York: Sheed & Ward, 1952).

Clare Boothe Luce is probably better known for her publishing and political career than for her series of Depression-era comic hits. A master of the art of self-invention, she not only wrote three of the most commercially successful plays of the 1930s (as well as many other stage plays and screenplays over the course of her life that were never produced), but also at various times held the post of managing editor for *Vanity*

Clare Boothe Luce

Fair, was a war correspondent for *Life,* held a seat in the House of Representatives, became the first woman ambassador from the United States to a major foreign power, was a close friend of eight American presidents (for most of whom she had vigorously campaigned), and was the wealthiest woman in the United States for much of her life. She was also known for the conservative politics that characterized her later beliefs: she was ardently pro-military, pro–Cold War efforts, and anti-communist. Luce also supported the rights of women in the public realm.

Luce was born Ann Clare Boothe on 10 March 1903 to William (Billy) Boothe, a would-be concert violinist, and Anna Clara (Ann) Schneider, a chorus-line dancer known for her Teutonic beauty. Luce's early life was marked by the instability of her father's attempts to become a professional musician and both parents' estrangement from their respective families. Both families had been opposed to the match on the basis of differing faiths–Schneider's family were ardent Catholics, and Boothe's father was a Baptist minister. After Luce's birth, between Boothe's work with various symphonies and the business interests in which he engaged to make ends meet, the Boothe family lived in locales as diverse as New York, Nashville, Chicago, Memphis, and Des Moines in the space of a few years. Her father's musical pretensions cost the family some considerable psychological and material comfort, for which Luce was always a little rueful.

Billy Boothe abandoned the family in 1913, and Luce then fell on truly hard times. From that time onward, Luce, her older brother, David, and her mother lived in a succession of boardinghouses in New York, and Clare and David were often sent to boarding schools that left her mother with little or no money to spare. Although Ann Boothe worked in various sales positions to bring in money, she decided to set up the ten-year-old Luce with an acting career to generate extra income for the family. One of her many gentleman friends gave her an introduction to Mary Pickford's management, and Boothe brought Luce to the theater during rehearsals for David Belasco's 1913 production of *A Good Little Devil* with the child's hair done up in an imitation of Pickford's trademark corkscrew curls. Belasco hired her as Pickford's understudy, with the stage name Joyce Fair. Although Luce never performed in Belasco's production (Pickford never missed a performance), she did land a bit role that same year in *The Dummy* with Ernest Truex, in which she spent the play tied up in a chair and gagged. Luce later remarked of her acting debut, "perhaps that influenced my later character."

Ann Boothe became more ambitious for Luce, and managed to have her signed up for a screen test. Luce froze for the test but was given a walk-on part as an orphan in *The Heart of a Wolf* (1915). The event marked her final professional appearance as an actor, although after completing high school she briefly attended the drama school run by Clare Tree Major and appeared in an excoriated amateur performance of George Bernard Shaw's *Candida* (1897) in 1945.

In the meantime, Ann Boothe made a little money on a stock tip given to her by an admirer. She enrolled Luce's brother, David, in a military academy in Wisconsin and took Luce on an extended trip to Europe. They stayed in Paris for about six months and returned to the United States at the outbreak of World War I. After their return to New York, Luce moved through a series of boarding schools. She eventually graduated from the Castle School of Tarrytown, New York, and tried different types of work that she uniformly hated, from secretarial school to department store salesgirl and factory hand. After an emergency appendectomy in 1920, she returned home to live with her mother, who married Luce's surgeon, Dr. Albert Austin. With her mother's new marriage, the family's fortunes improved tremendously, and Luce began to associate with people in fairly high circles.

The Austins took Luce on another trip to Europe in 1922, where she became interested in the best and most exciting work the avant-garde art scene had to offer and developed a lifelong love of modern art. On her return passage to New York, Luce met Mrs. Alva Belmont, leader of the National Women's Party, who with Dr. Alice Paul was working to pass an early version of the Equal Rights Amendment in Congress. Belmont, recognizing the young woman's intelligence, sent Luce to work for "the cause" in Washington, D.C., where Luce lobbied, lunched with fellow devotees of women's rights, attended fund-raising functions, and distributed leaflets (from an airplane–a rare luxury at the time). However, she lacked the single-minded determination of Belmont, Paul, and the other leaders of the party, and after ten days of working for them, she quit.

In the rarefied atmosphere in which she now traveled, Luce met her first husband, George Brokaw–a wealthy bachelor considered one of the most eligible men in New York. Luce and Brokaw married on 10 August 1923. Despite the luxuries of Brokaw's money and the birth of a daughter (Ann Clare Brokaw) in August 1924, the marriage was not a happy one. Luce could not abide the pretensions of her "stuffed shirt" society companions and used the time spent with these people as fodder for her caustic wit early in her literary career. Brokaw's alcoholism, veiled before the marriage, made the relationship impossible, and in February 1929 Luce departed for Reno to obtain a divorce.

The terms of her divorce were quite favorable to Luce, but she was bored in her Manhattan penthouse and decided to pursue a career in journalism, an ambition she had fostered for some time. Luce appeared at the offices of *Vogue* and interviewed with the editor, Edna Woolman Chase, who set her up writing captions for the illustrations, with no word about continuing the work. Luce behaved as though she really had been given a full-time post with *Vogue* and continued to work without pay until she was working so much that she was indispensable. While Luce worked at *Vogue,* she set her sights on joining the staff of *Vanity Fair*. The flagship publication of the Condé Nast empire, *Vanity Fair* was known for its articles on the literati and the haut monde artistic set, and the ambitious Luce wanted to add her name to its masthead. She managed to land a job writ-

Clare Boothe as a young girl

ing for *Vanity Fair* and eventually became the managing editor in 1933.

As managing editor, she slowly shifted the emphasis of the magazine from society cocktail-lounge gossip to economics and politics, and she began to report on more serious material herself. In 1931 she had covered the Democratic National Convention in Chicago. By 1933 she was well known enough on the national political scene to be appointed to the National Recovery Administration advisory board. Within a year, however, she resigned from the panel in bitter frustration and satirized it and the New Deal (of which she had formerly been a proponent) in a play, "O, Pyramids!" which was never produced.

Her stint with satire became a more serious preoccupation, and in 1934 she decided to take a leave of absence from her position at *Vanity Fair* in order to devote herself full-time to playwriting. Over the course of that year, she wrote, collaborated on, or made notes for three unpublished plays: "The Sacred Cow" (a newspaper comedy she wrote with the sports reporter Paul Gallico), the divorce comedy "The Gaiety of Nations," and notes for a musical about New York politician Alfred Smith titled "The High Office." Despite her prolific output during the year, Luce remained unproduced, and not until almost the end of 1935 did one of her plays make it to the stage. In November of that year her play *Abide with Me,* a thinly disguised,

melodramatic treatment of her marriage to Brokaw, opened on Broadway. Despite praise for the performance of Moscow Art Theatre actress Maria Ouspenskaya, the play was flatly panned by critics. Most reviewers found the plot and dialogue to be contrived and obvious and were unimpressed by the faltering steps of the new playwright. As a reviewer for the *New York American* (22 November 1935) put it, the play was "dedicated to the somewhat inarguable proposition that drunken sadists make poor mates in the home." Many critics also guessed at (or perhaps, given the public status of Brokaw's life, had previous knowledge of) the autobiographical nature of the piece, and as her future collaborator Alexander King put it, they attacked Luce more for the public attempt to exorcise her demons than for her failure as a playwright. Luce was further humiliated after her appearance on the stage at the end of the curtain call on the first night: she had been standing in the wings and was horrified when the audience's applause transformed to booing at her entrance. She never again attended one of her opening nights, preferring instead to be in another part of the city altogether when one of her plays premiered.

Lacking financial support beyond the money raised by Luce and her then husband-to-be Henry Robinson Luce for the opening, *Abide with Me* closed after only thirty-six performances. She ended the year on a better note than her first opening promised, however: two days after the opening of *Abide with Me* she married Henry Luce, the founder of *Time, Life,* and *Fortune* magazines.

Despite her inauspicious beginning as a playwright, Luce went on to have three more plays produced during the 1930s, all far more successful than *Abide with Me.* Her comedy *The Women,* Luce's most successful and frequently revived play, opened on 26 December 1936 and went on for 657 performances, grossing almost $900,000. Set in New York in the 1930s, *The Women* follows the romantic tribulations of a set of society women headed toward middle age as they gossip, cheat on their husbands, deal with their husbands' infidelities, and spend money on hairdressing, clothing, and exercise regimes at the Elizabeth Arden salon. Luce focuses on the problems of Mary Haines, a married mother who discovers from her manicurist's gossip that her husband is having an affair. Though warned by her mother to let the matter rest, she takes the advice of her rather poisonous and ill-intending "friend" Sylvia, has a confrontation with her husband over the affair, and divorces him. She moves to Reno to "renovate" in the wake of the divorce, and her new, worldly divorcée friends convince her that in her pride, she has lost her husband by forcing him to divorce her, by not allowing him to apologize to her. She returns to

New York and, with the help of her friends, sets a trap for her former husband's new wife to expose the latter's infidelity and to get her husband back.

Despite the satirical nature of the play (or perhaps as a result of it), Luce came under heavy criticism for her portrayal of women as vicious, unfaithful, opportunistic gossips. The reviewer for *The New York Times* (28 December 1936) deemed the play "a multi-scened portrait of the modern New York wife on the loose, spraying poison over the immediate landscape." In the preface to the published edition of the play (1937), Luce defended the work not as a description of all women, but of certain types of women. She argued that there had been women in her life that did seem like the character of Sylvia Fowler: "I did not like these women. I liked them so little that I put them into this small Doomsday Book, in order to rid myself once and for all of their hauntingly ungracious images." When the play was revived in the 1970s, several feminist writers attacked Luce on similar grounds to those of the male reviewers in the 1930s. One writer for *The New York Times* (6 May 1973) asked, with plays such as *The Women,* "does feminism need an enemy?"

Luce went on to write two other comic hits. *Kiss the Boys Good-bye* opened on 28 September 1938 for a run of 286 performances. A romping parody of the search to suitably cast the role of Scarlett O'Hara in the 1939 movie version of *Gone With the Wind* (1936), Luce's second hit depicted the farcical weekend bumblings of the smart set at a holiday cottage. The young, dynamic Hollywood producer Herbert Z. Harner has decided to cast an unknown Southern woman to play the role of Velvet O'Toole in his upcoming film *Kiss the Boys Good-bye.* His talent scout, Lloyd Lloyd, has unearthed the classic belle Cindy Lou Bethany, a woman that he tells Harner is perfect for the role but in reality is Lloyd's stooge for a plan to get his lover (and fading Hollywood star) Myra Stanhope into the role. The four meet at the weekend cottage of Horace and Leslie Rand, a pair of attractive, wealthy socialites with journalism connections. The play follows a classic farcical structure: the seemingly naive Cindy Lou is at once the butt of everyone's jokes, but she ends up outsmarting everyone, winning the role of Velvet O'Toole, and then turning it down in favor of marrying a young, attractive polo player named Top Rumson, who is also staying at the cottage.

Again, Luce was criticized for her use of farce; critics deemed the work immoral, malicious, pessimistic, and destructive. Again, Luce responded by writing a defensive preface to the play when it was published in 1939, claiming it to be not merely a satire of the American intelligentsia but also a dark warning of the rise of fascism in the South. However, if Luce intended this

Clare Boothe Luce and Paul McGrath in a 1945 summer stock production of George Bernard Shaw's Candida
(AP/Wide World Photos)

message, she hid it too deep beneath the surface of the play for reviewers or audiences to notice.

Luce's last major commercial success was *Margin for Error,* which opened on 3 November 1939 and ran for 264 performances. This time, Luce brought her usual satirical style to a detective story about a German consulate who is the possible murder victim of several suspects whom he has double-crossed in the past. In keeping with Luce's simultaneously growing involvement in politics, the play reflects her public condemnation of President Franklin D. Roosevelt's promise to keep the United States out of the conflict in Europe that was developing into World War II, and it clearly depicts the Germans as ruthless, corrupt, and officious. This time, the mixture of styles provided many reviewers with ammunition, and several repeated critic George Jean Nathan's opinion in *Newsweek* (20 November 1939) that the play was "one of the most unblenching tournaments in box-office hokum that has come to this notice in some time." Meanwhile, the movie version of *The Women,* adapted by Anita Loos and Jane Murfin and directed by George Cukor, was released by M-G-M. Starring Rosalind Russell as Sylvia Fowler, the picture was extremely successful and insured the future success of the movie versions of *Kiss the Boys Good-bye* in 1941 and *Margin for Error* in 1943.

But Luce was not satisfied by her literary career. Her interest in foreign affairs led her to convince her husband to send her to Europe as a war correspondent for *Life* magazine; in 1940 she toured Britain and France (where she was one of the few journalists and the first woman allowed to view the ill-fated Maginot Line), and was in Belgium when the Germans invaded in early May. While there, she was amazed by the sangfroid with which the Europeans viewed Hitler and surprised by their refusal to take Germany's power seriously. She returned to the United States that fall and published her observations on the situation of early World War II under the title *Europe in the Spring*.

On her return, she also entered into her first sustained period of political activity, campaigning for Wendell Wilkie for president. The following spring, again bored in the United States, she departed overseas, this time to cover the war in China. She traveled to Chungking, where she interviewed Chiang Kai-shek and his wife and witnessed the brutality of the Eastern war theater as she sat in trenches in Burma. According to a 1982 *Saturday Review* sketch of her by John Kenneth Galbraith, the liberal economist with whom she often debated later in her life, Luce's experience during the war led to her shift to more conservative politics, because of the development of "a disastrous case of occupational commitment to generals, the military mystique, and the apocalyptic view."

Whatever the reason for her shift to conservative politics, by 1942 Luce had been asked by the Republican Party to run for a Connecticut seat in the House of Representatives (the same seat held earlier by her stepfather, Dr. Albert Austin). While campaigning, she stopped in Abingdon, Virginia to work on rewrites for her play *Love is a Verb,* adapted from her friend Alexander King's short story "The Yohimbe Tree." The play, produced under the pseudonym Karl Weidenbach, was a light comedy about a couple who, under the influence of contact with the exotic, discover their true love for one another. Although the producers in Virginia extended the run of the play from three to eleven performances, the play was never produced anywhere else. She narrowly won the election. Her term in office was characterized by an infamous public spat in the press with Dorothy Parker (one embarrassing enough for both Parker and Luce that Luce vowed never again to disparage another woman in public), and by frustrations with being a woman in politics as a result of the ambivalent response she drew from her colleagues as an able and quick-minded speaker on the House floor.

Luce's term in office was also marked by personal loss. On 10 January 1944 her daughter, Ann, was killed in an automobile accident on her way back to college at Stanford University. Because of Luce's busy schedule, Ann had been brought up by her grandmother and sent to boarding schools for the majority of her life; but in the few months before Ann's death, Luce had made a genuine attempt to be closer to her daughter. At Ann's death, Luce experienced a nervous breakdown and severe spiritual crisis. Although she had never actively participated in religion, she turned to Catholicism in 1945 seeking solace. She had been re-elected to office in 1944 but decided not to run again in 1946 and withdrew from elected public office forever, despite possibilities for advancement in the Republican ranks.

Luce's conversion became the focus of her writing: in 1947 she wrote a passionate account of it in *McCall's* and went to Hollywood to write a screen adaptation of C. S. Lewis's comic depiction of Satan, *The Screwtape Letters* (1942). She abandoned the project when it became clear that the movie producers were less interested in the intricacies of faith than in transforming Lewis's religious tale into a "boy meets girl" story. From this point on, she abandoned the acidly comic style of her early plays and focused on pieces that dealt with issues of faith and love; however, she never again wrote anything that brought her the success of *The Women* or her other Broadway hits.

Despite her frustrations over *The Screwtape Letters,* Luce worked on and off in Hollywood for the next five years, proposing and working on several projects, most of which were initially pursued by the studios but never filmed. In 1949, 20th Century-Fox released *Come to the Stable,* starring Loretta Young and Celeste Holm and based on a short story by Luce (although the screenplay was written by Oscar Millard and Sally Benson) about the comic attempts of two nuns to raise money for an orphanage. She pursued a project that was to star Bob Hope and Irene Dunne and was hired by Howard Hughes to write an original screenplay for RKO titled "Pilate's Wife" (about the woman's fictional post-crucifixion conversion), but neither project was ever completed by the studios.

During this time she also wrote the play *Child of the Morning* (1951), a kind of melodramatic saint-play following the short life of a young woman who is murdered as she is about to take religious vows. The play was produced initially in Boston but closed after a little more than a week. It was revived in New York in 1958 but received quite negative notices. One reviewer for *The New York Times* (22 April 1958) found the play to be "ingeniously constructed" but stated that the theme was superior to its execution: "a primer on Roman Catholicism on the one hand, and a melodrama about juvenile delinquency on the other." The failure of the play in New York marked Luce's last dramatic premiere.

In the summer of 1952 she abandoned her writing in order to campaign for Dwight D. Eisenhower.

She and Henry Luce had campaigned for Thomas Dewey's election in 1948, throwing the full weight of Henry Luce's publishing empire into the effort, and were stung when Harry S Truman defeated Dewey. When Eisenhower was successfully elected, he rewarded Luce with the position of ambassador to Italy. She ran the embassy with efficiency until she resigned from the post in 1956.

Luce and her husband relaxed for a time at a villa in Phoenix, where Henry Luce suffered a heart attack in 1959. He recovered just as Luce's name was being circulated as a possibility as the ambassador to Brazil. She was nominated and confirmed, despite some controversy in Congress (led by Senator Wayne Morse of Oregon, who had been disparaged in the pages of *Time* after his change of party affiliations from Republican to Democrat). When she began to research her assignment in Brazil, which was basically to enforce Eisenhower and John Foster Dulles's plan to withhold economic aid from the country as it attempted to move from an agrarian to an industrial economy, she began to withdraw from the failure that she felt she was sure to face. Henry Luce issued a statement that he had asked her to resign as a result of the Congressional controversy surrounding her appointment.

Although Luce went on to campaign for several Republican nominees for president and to sit on some of their advisory panels (most notably the Foreign Intelligence Advisory Board under Ronald Reagan), she never again held a major office. The last twenty-five years of her life were marked by her position as a kind of shadowy, behind-the-scenes influence on the national political scene, and by her withdrawal to her home in Hawaii. In 1973 she unsuccessfully attempted to intervene in the editorial policy of *Time* (even though Henry Luce had died in 1967 and the periodical was now run by his son Hank) in order to support Richard Nixon during the Watergate crisis. She made appearances frequently enough to be in the public eye, and in 1975 was a guest on *Firing Line*. She continued to be remotely involved in public affairs, obtaining a home in Washington, D.C. In 1983 she became the first female recipient of the Presidential Medal of Freedom, and she lived long enough to see yet another revival of *The Women* (which she claimed had been steadily bringing in royalties of $7000–8000 every year since its premiere in 1936) at the Old Vic in London in 1986.

During the last quarter of her life, she published one more play. Written in 1970, the play picks up at the end of Henrik Ibsen's *A Doll House* (1879), with Nora, now armed with the writings of Simone de Beauvoir, leaving her husband and charging him back pay for her years of housework. *Slam the Door Softly* was published in *Life* but never produced. In 1987 Luce was diagnosed

Henry and Clare Boothe Luce (AP/Wide World Photos)

with a malignant brain tumor and died in Washington on 9 October of that year.

Perhaps as a result of the largely commercial nature of Luce's theatrical writing, there has not been much secondary treatment of her plays outside of reviews. The writing regarding *The Women* forms an exception to this statement: after its New York revival in 1973 the play provoked feminist commentary on Luce's presumed "self-hatred" as a woman by scholars in both academic and popular publications well into the next decade (commentary that did not resurface at the time of the next American revival of the play, by experimental director Anne Bogart in 1992). But some of her biographers have wondered at the narrow output of Luce's theatrical writing, given the prolific nature of her journalism and the fact that she always claimed George Bernard Shaw as one of her literary models and personal heroes. Several of her biographers, following Wilfrid Sheed, have claimed that her conversion to Catholicism meant that she could never again indulge in the sharp wit that characterized her early, successful style. Luce's most enduring literary legacy, then, may be to have her plays disliked on the basis of their biting observation of feminine behavior.

Interviews:

"Feminism," *Firing Line,* 6 April 1975;

"The Gift of the Imagination: An Interview with Clare Boothe Luce," in *Fabian Feminist: Bernard Shaw and Woman,* edited by Rodelle Weintraub (University Park: Pennsylvania State University Press, 1977), pp. 207–213.

Bibliography:

Mark Fearnow, *Clare Boothe Luce: A Research and Production Sourcebook* (Westport, Conn.: Greenwood Press, 1995).

Biographies:

Faye Henle, *Au Clare du Luce* (New York: Stephen Daye, 1943);

Alden Hatch, *Ambassador Extraordinary: Clare Boothe Luce* (New York: Holt, 1955);

Stephen Shadegg, *Clare Boothe Luce* (New York: Simon & Schuster, 1970);

John Kenneth Galbraith, "An Affectionate Portrait of Clare Boothe Luce," *Saturday Review* (February 1982): 56–58;

Wilfrid Sheed, *Clare Boothe Luce* (New York: Dutton, 1982);

Joseph Lyons, *Clare Boothe Luce: Author and Diplomat* (New York: Chelsea House Publishers, 1989);

Ralph G. Martin, *Henry and Clare: An Intimate Portrait of the Luces* (New York: Putnam, 1991);

Sylvia Jukes Morris, *Rage for Fame: The Ascent of Clare Boothe Luce* (New York: Random House, 1997).

References:

Susan L. Carlson, "Comic Textures and Female Communities, 1937 and 1977: Clare Booth Luce and Wendy Wasserstein," *Modern Drama* (December 1984): 565–573;

Sylvia Jukes Morris, "In Search of Clare Boothe Luce," *New York Times Magazine* (31 January 1988): 23–27, 33.

Papers:

Clare Boothe Luce's extensive collection of papers, including material related to her dramatic works, is located in the Manuscript Division of the Library of Congress. The most complete set of production photographs, programs, and publicity clippings is in the Billy Rose Theatre Collection at the New York Public Library, Lincoln Center.

Donald Margulies

(2 September 1954 -   )

William C. Boles
Rollins College

PLAY PRODUCTIONS: *Luna Park,* New York, Jewish Repertory Theatre, 5 February 1982;

Resting Place, New York, Theatre for the New City, 22 April 1982;

Gifted Children, New York, Jewish Repertory Theatre, 22 December 1983;

Found a Peanut, New York, New York Shakespeare Festival, 17 June 1984;

What's Wrong with this Picture?, New York, Manhattan Theatre Club, 29 January 1985;

Zimmer, New York, Jewish Repertory Theatre, 24 February 1988;

The Model Apartment, Los Angeles, Los Angeles Theatre Center, 11 November 1988;

The Loman Family Picnic, New York, Manhattan Theatre Club Stage II, 21 June 1989;

Pitching to the Star, New York, West Bank Cafe Downstairs Theatre Bar, 20 March 1990;

Women in Motion, Jamestown, New York, Lucille Ball Festival, 24 May 1991;

Sight Unseen, Costa Mesa, California, South Coast Repertory, 20 September 1991; New York: Manhattan Theatre Club, January 1992;

July 7, 1994, Louisville, Actors Theatre, Humana Festival, 26 March 1995;

Collected Stories, Costa Mesa, California, South Coast Repertory, 29 October 1996; London, Theatre Royal, Haymarket, 15 November 1999;

Broken Sleep: Three Plays, Williamstown, Massachusetts, Williamstown Theater Festival, 16 July 1997—comprised *Nocturne, Broken Sleep* (music by Michael-John La Chiusa), and *July 7, 1994;*

Dinner with Friends, Louisville, Actors Theatre, Humana Festival, 4 March 1998;

God of Vengeance, adapted from the Yiddish classic by Sholem Asch, Seattle, A Contemporary Theatre, 13 April 2000.

BOOKS: *Found a Peanut* (New York: Dramatists Play Service, 1984);

Donald Margulies (photograph by Harold Shapiro)

What's Wrong with this Picture? (New York: Broadway Play Publishing, 1988);

The Loman Family Picnic (New York: Theatre Communications Group, 1989);

The Model Apartment (New York: Dramatists Play Service, 1990);

Sight Unseen (New York: Dramatists Play Service, 1992);

Pitching to the Star and Other Short Plays (New York: Dramatists Play Service, 1993);

Sight Unseen and Other Plays (New York: Theatre Communications Group, 1995);

July 7, 1994: Short Plays and Monologues (New York: Dramatists Play Service, 1997);

Collected Stories: A Play (New York: Theatre Communications Group, 1998);

Dinner with Friends (New York: Dramatists Play Service, 2000; New York: Theatre Communications Group, 2000).

PRODUCED SCRIPTS: *Divorced Kids' Blues,* television, ABC, 1986;

Baby Boom, television, NBC, 1988;

Once and Again, television, ABC, 1999.

OTHER: *Kibbutz,* in *Conjunctions 25: The New American Theater,* edited by John Guare (Avondale-on-Hudson, N.Y.: Bard College, 1995), pp. 144–149;

Dinner with Friends, in *Humana Festival '98: The Complete Plays,* edited by Michael Bigelow Dixon and Amy Wegener (Lyme, N.H.: Smith & Kraus, 1998), pp. 51–127.

SELECTED PERIODICAL PUBLICATION– UNCOLLECTED: "A Playwright's Search for the Spiritual Father," *New York Times,* 21 June 1992, sec. 2, p. 5.

Between 1982 and 1991 Donald Margulies wrote several innovative, emotionally challenging, and funny theatrical pieces. *What's Wrong with this Picture?* (1985) comically asks what happens if a dead family member comes back to life. *The Model Apartment* (1988) presents the lasting repercussions of the Holocaust on survivors and their children. And *The Loman Family Picnic* (1989) imaginatively interweaves Margulies's own Brooklyn childhood with Arthur Miller's *Death of A Salesman* (1949). In these early plays Margulies prominently explores the identity struggles and familial problems of Jews in New York City. However, the most powerful aspect of his writing that developed during this period was his ability to use little details and small moments to suggest the hollowness of life, especially in regard to personal failures, loneliness, economic struggles, familial conflicts, the numbing repetition of daily existence, and the elusive nature of love. Despite the talent displayed in these works, Margulies, for the most part, was not then considered a major theatrical voice. Not until 1992, when *Sight Unseen* (1991) won the Obie for Best Play and received a Pulitzer Prize nomination, did Margulies garner national accolades and recognition for his talent.

The play that received the most attention was slightly different from the plays he had been writing in the 1980s, however. Rather than taking place in New York City, *Sight Unseen* is set in England; and rather than depicting the domestic turmoil of a Jewish family, the play focuses on the art boom of the 1980s. Yet, despite the international context, the elements that had

been the cornerstone of Margulies's early work remained vital to the success of *Sight Unseen:* family, Jewish identity, and love are integral psychological battle points for the protagonist. Margulies had finally made his theatrical imprint, and the plays that followed *Sight Unseen* only solidified his reputation.

Donald Margulies was born in Brooklyn on 2 September 1954, the second son of Bob and Charlene Margulies. Stephen J. Dubner quotes Margulies in a 1992 *New York* magazine article as saying that he grew up in what he termed a "high rise ghetto" in Coney Island. His mother worked in offices while also raising her two children, while his father was a wallpaper salesman who left for work at six in the morning and did not return home until eleven at night. Despite the long hours he put in, he constantly feared losing his job, even though he worked for the same employers for forty years. Charlene Margulies's optimism and drive for the education and success of her two boys as well as Bob Margulies's pessimism were influential components in the playwright's development.

During his childhood Margulies's family took two separate and memorable weeklong vacations to New York City specifically to see Broadway musicals and plays. Howard Margulies, the playwright's older brother, told Dubner "We were not wealthy, but our relatives thought we were because we had style." Part of that style may have been attributed to their father's passion for Broadway musicals. On his few days off from work and on Sunday mornings he would play his Broadway cast albums the entire day. In the article "A Playwright's Search for the Spiritual Father" (1992), Margulies remembers: "I was the only kid in the sixth grade who knew by heart the entire score of *Happy Hunting,* an obscure Ethel Merman musical I heard countless times."

When he was a senior at John Dewey High School in 1972, the school literary magazine published a short story written by him. The principal found it obscene and confiscated all copies of the journal. Margulies appealed the act of censorship all the way to the United States District Court in Brooklyn, which not only overturned the principal's decision but also praised the future playwright's literary ability.

Margulies's mother encouraged both of her sons to read extensively, and Margulies was drawn to the writings of Herb Gardner, Arthur Miller, J. D. Salinger, and Philip Roth. In college he discovered the work of Harold Pinter and William Faulkner. Margulies's interests were not limited to writing and reading, however. He is also a gifted artist and received an art scholarship to the Pratt Institute; he continues to make collages, and the cover of *Collected Stories: A Play* (1998) features one of his works. Margulies stayed at Pratt for only one and a half years before transferring to the State University of New York at Purchase, a liberal arts college, where he continued studying art and literature. He later became a lecturer at the prestigious Yale School of Drama. At SUNY-Purchase, Margulies encountered his literary mentor, Julius Novick, a professor of literature and drama, who thought highly of the young writer's potential. Novick told Dubner: "He wrote this astonishing one-act play. You could just see from the way the dialogue lived and how he created the people who spoke it that the guy had a sense of dramatic shape."

One of the major themes of Margulies's early plays is the relationship between parents and their children, driven by his own troubled relationship with his father. Bob Margulies was a quiet man who had difficulty communicating with his artistically talented son. During one of the family vacations to New York, Margulies saw Herb Gardner's *A Thousand Clowns* (1962). It was at that point, as he says in "A Playwright's Search for the Spiritual Father," that he realized how drama could reflect and explain his own familial situation:

> For a boy like me, whose father worked all the time, it must have been invigorating to see a play about a man who preferred being home to toiling at a demoralizing job. In retrospect, it seems fitting that my first exposure to drama was a play about a complex father figure and his surrogate son, for the theme of fathers and sons has long figured in my plays and in my life.

While valuable to Margulies's development as a writer, the reading that his mother encouraged Margulies and his brother to do only strained their relationship with their father, who did not read and saw their voracious devouring of books as proof that his sons were growing away from him. His father only fell back further into his silences. Because of the increasing disconnectedness with his father, Margulies says in "A Playwright's Search for the Spiritual Father," he began looking for paternal connections outside his home:

> Unconsciously, I began to search for spiritual fathers, creative men with whom I could commune intellectually, older men who could help me make sense of the world. My father's silence created in me a hunger for words that drew me to surrogate fathers, men I knew only through what they wrote. Herb Gardner may have been my earliest spiritual father, but Arthur Miller came into my life not long after.

His quest for his father has provided some of the most effective and memorable moments of Margulies's work.

After graduating from SUNY-Purchase, Margulies worked steadily as a graphic artist while continuing to write. From 1977 until 1988 he was a member of the New York Writers Bloc. During the initial years of his membership he wrote several short scenes and monologues. One of the first plays he wrote, in 1978, was an unproduced work called "Pals." It was his first full-length attempt to confront his relationship with his father. In 1982 the Jewish Repertory Theatre, which produced many of his works, staged *Luna Park,* based on Delmore Schwartz's short story "In Dreams Begin Responsibilities" (1937). Theatre for the New City produced *Resting Place* (1982), comprised of two one-act plays sharing the same characters. The first act details the breakup of a marriage, while the second focuses on the husband's search for a surrogate father with a homeless African American. What makes *Resting Place* especially notable was that Margulies experimented with free verse, something he has not done since. *Tuna on Rye and Other Short Pieces* (1983) had a staged reading at Ensemble Studio Theatre and included several monologues and sketches Margulies wrote while a member of the New York Writers Bloc.

Margulies's first full-length production was *Gifted Children* (1983) at the Jewish Repertory Theatre. The main plot concerns a pregnant artist returning home to try to reconcile her strained relationship with her mother while at the same time trying to decide whether or not to have an abortion. Margulies admits to the theatrical problems in *Gifted Children,* telling Dubner that it was "a very misshapen production and a rather young play." Critic Frank Rich agreed in his review for *The New York Times* (23 December 1983), calling the play "amateur" and filled with "lumpy monologues." Rich continued: "Everything else is contrived, unstructured and unfunny comic banter that doesn't so much reveal credible characters as kill time." Rich did say that a particular monologue suggested that the author "might have certain gifts himself."

Despite the public drubbing *Gifted Children* received, Margulies had caught the attention of important New York producer Joseph Papp, who produced Margulies's next play, a full-length one-act called *Found a Peanut* (1984), at the New York Shakespeare Festival. *Found a Peanut* transpires on the last summer day before a new school year begins. It focuses on eight children, ranging in age from four to fourteen, as they play in the courtyard of a Brooklyn apartment building (adult actors play the characters). What at first appears to be a typical day turns out, during the course of the play, to be an important moment in their lives as they face an early loss of their childhood innocence.

The title is taken from a childhood song (sung in the play) in which the singer bewails the results of having found a rotten peanut and consumed it. The song highlights serious and previously unconsidered repercussions connected with a seemingly minor act (the singer dies from the resulting stomachache and goes to heaven). Margulies structures the play similarly. Within the first few minutes of the play Mike and Jeffrey, the two main characters, find a dead bird and decide to bury it next to Mike's pet turtle. Upon digging, they discover a bag containing sixty-eight dollars. The discovery of the loot disrupts friendships, provokes greediness and lies, and finally causes a violent and bloody melee. Ultimately, their seemingly simple discovery not only affects the rest of the afternoon but also awakens the children to the inherent difficulties of growing up.

Beyond the structural device suggested by the song, the play is also about the act of finding. The youngest children play a variation of hide and seek. The neighborhood bullies, Ernie and Shane, search for Jay, the leader of the group, who is absent from the action of the play, and later for Mike, who tries to hide the money from them. Jeffrey looks for the ball that the bullies take from him, and Melody, Mike's eight-year-old sister, hunts, throughout the play, for her house key. However, there are also acts of finding that have greater ramifications, including the discovery of the money and, more importantly, the discovery the night before of the dead body of Mr. Schuster, Mike's next door neighbor.

The children's innocence begins slipping away as death becomes a topic of discussion and as they faintly begin to understand their own mortality. While the bird and the pet turtle are deaths that directly affect them, they merely play at being adults by mimicking the ritual of burial. However, Mr. Schuster's death changes their perspective of the world, especially as they hear stories about rigor mortis and the difficulty of removing the body from its sitting position at the kitchen table. They first begin by discussing dead pets, but shortly thereafter Joanie shares a secret about her grandmother's open-casket funeral: "When nobody was looking I touched her hand. . . . In her coffin. On her veins. . . . It felt like chicken roll." It is a powerful moment that reflects not only the children's innocence—they all excitedly ask Joanie questions—but also their own confusion about the mysterious and final power of death in relation to themselves.

Structurally, the play becomes formulaic with the discovery of the money, as the action dissolves into stereotypical squabbles, several betrayals, and the climactic fight with the terrorizing bullies. The fight ends, though, with Jeffrey's cries of "You can't *do* this! We *live* here!" His cry has greater ramifications than just against the petty, thug-like quality of the bullies. There are hints that Margulies also intends Jeffrey's cries to comment on the inherent brutalism throughout the world, tearing neighbors and countries apart. While the concept does not quite achieve the intended impact, it is a notable first step toward Margulies's interest in connecting his characters and the action of his plays to the post-Holocaust world.

Once again, Rich, writing in *The New York Times* (18 June 1984), was critical of Margulies's playwriting (he especially thought the material was too thin for a seventy-minute production), but his criticism was not as caustic as before. In fact, he complimented Margulies's subtle ability to capture the loss of childhood. Other reviewers, including Clive Barnes and Howard Kissel, were enthusiastic in their praise for the work.

What's Wrong with this Picture? was Margulies's next major play to be produced. In interviews he has said that *What's Wrong with this Picture?* was his first serious attempt to confront his relationship with his father written since his mother's death in 1978. The play details a day or so in the life of Mort and Artie, father and son, after the death of Shirley, their wife and mother, who choked on a piece of pork at the grand opening of a Chinese restaurant. The play opens as the family finishes sitting shivah, and Mort's mother, father, and sister are helping to clean up and prepare the household to return to its everyday functions. Mort, despondent over the loss of his wife, moans: "My life is over, Ma. This is it, this is the end." His grief is one of the main elements of the play as Mort and Artie learn to overcome the death of Shirley in order to go on with their lives.

After Shirley's death, Mort refuses to deal with household problems. For example, the apartment is cluttered with their old furniture as well as new furniture Shirley ordered before dying. Mort also has nothing in common with his smart-aleck son. Once Mort's parents and sister leave, the two men unsuccessfully attempt to communicate with one another, until Mort finds the dress Shirley wore at Artie's bar mitzvah. From this point on, the play moves from being grounded in realism into something slightly more absurd. Mort convinces Artie to wear his mother's dress and dance with him. It is a comic, if slightly odd, scene; but the roleplaying by Artie improves their relationship. Mort once again believes he is with his wife, and he compassionately talks to Artie as if his son were Shirley. It is a comical premise, but is not pursued further because the play then heads in an even more absurd direction with a knock at the door. It is Shirley, caked in dirt, covered with grass, and a bit tired. After all, she has walked all the way back to their apartment on "The B.Q.E., the L.I.E., the Belt, the van Wyck." The first act then ends as Shirley blows out her own memorial candle.

The second act details the happiness Mort and Artie feel with Shirley's return, but there is some discomfort. Even though Shirley is back, she is not the same. She feels cold all the time, and when Mort feels amorous, she rebuffs his advances. Artie also learns that

Dennis Boutsikaris and Deborah Hedsall in the 1992 New York production of Sight Unseen *(photograph by Gerry Goodstein)*

his mother was not a happy woman and engaged in affairs during her marriage. More strikingly, though, Mort becomes dependent and obsessed with her return. He refuses to go to work so that he can spend all of his time with his wife. In effect, he invests too much of himself in Shirley, when he really needs to start investing in himself, his son, and his life. Mort's family comes to visit and is shocked to discover Shirley back in the house. Bella, Mort's mother, expresses her outrage: "This is not how it's supposed to be . . . . You don't get to keep a foot in the door. You're either in or you're out. And you, my dear Shirley, you are not in. . . . You think this is helping him? You think this is helping either one of them?" Ultimately, Shirley decides to return to the cemetery—Mort drives her back—so that her son and husband can continue with their lives.

What's Wrong with this Picture? is an imaginative, quirky play with a second act that does not live up to the potential of the first. Part of the problem resides in the character of Shirley and her return. If she was so discontented with her family life, then why would she return? Perhaps she comes back out of an obligation to her son or husband. It is also possible that Artie's donning of her bar mitzvah dress has some kind of talismanic conjuring power. Maybe she returns because she

feels guilty or because she is a dutiful Jewish mother and wife. Any or all of these aspects are possible, but the text never provides enough information about Shirley to come up with an answer. Despite this problem, the play highlights Margulies's inventiveness, which continued to strengthen and became, in some plays, even more outrageous. Finally, while the play posits the importance of moving on after grieving for a family member's death, it also depicts the tragedy of Mort and Artie's misunderstanding of Shirley, suggesting the miscommunication that exists in all households.

The reviews of *Gifted Children* and *Found a Peanut* still stung Margulies, and since he was not pleased with aspects of the Manhattan Theatre Club production of *What's Wrong with this Picture?* he decided not to invite New York critics to the initial run of the play. Three years passed before *What's Wrong with this Picture?* premiered before the critics at a 1988 production by the Back Alley Theatre in Los Angeles. The play did eventually return to New York and premiered Off-Broadway in 1990 at the Jewish Repertory Theatre to positive reviews. Finally, on the strength of Margulies's reputation after *Sight Unseen,* the play made it to Broadway in 1994. In an unpublished communication in 1998 Margulies called it "a long, tedious, ultimately devastating (for the play) journey," in part because the Broadway production was "egregiously misdirected."

Between *What's Wrong with this Picture?* and *The Model Apartment* (1988), Margulies married Lynn Street, a physician, in 1987. He also had a short one-act, *Zimmer,* produced by the Jewish Repertory Theatre in 1988. It is told in the manner of a docudrama, with one actor playing all the characters. The play surveys the 1960s and its music and politics by focusing on Ira Zimmer, who floats through life, or as he says, "zims." He never amounts to much, eventually becoming a manager at a record store. It is a quiet piece, showing Margulies's experimentation with voice, character, and a sense of time and place.

The Model Apartment is a full-length one-act that has been called a black comedy. The title refers to the loaner apartment that Lola and Max find themselves in when their new retirement condominium in Florida is not yet ready for occupation. Instead, they are placed in a studio apartment seemingly filled with the latest newfangled home accessories. At first glance, the set suggests that this Jewish New York couple is moving into the perfect retirement community. However, Margulies quickly begins to strip away the facade of the apartment as well as the seemingly perfect life of the married couple to reveal the disturbing present and horrific past that they want so desperately to escape from, but cannot.

Lola and Max quickly discover that the refrigerator and television are fake, exhibited only for looks and not for practicality. After they discover the sham appliances, their mentally challenged daughter, Debby, arrives, having followed them to Florida in a stolen car procured by her fifteen-year-old black lover. The plot description may sound as though the play is intended as farce, but Margulies eschews the humor of the scenario to emphasize the poignancy and pain of the couple confronting their immediate and distant past. They relocated to Florida because Debby embarrasses them; they left New York in the middle of the night without telling her. The reason for their embarrassment is that Debby continually mocks their stories of the Holocaust: "You got to watch out at Howard Johnson's. Ask Connie Francis. It's a front for the Nazis. *Lola sighs deeply.* She got raped by a Nazi dressed like a bellboy. I had a close call myself. This Nazi? . . . He was gonna sterilize me. I saw shiny tools in his jeep." Debby's continual scurrilous remarks pain her parents, both of whom survived the Holocaust. Lola was in a concentration camp, where she purports to have befriended Anne Frank and helped her keep a journal that the Nazis destroyed. Max hid in the woods during the war, losing his first wife and daughter to the Nazis.

Margulies's play documents the power of the past and its effect on those unable to escape their memories of the horror. Lola still awakens terrified at the slightest noise. Max, who so much wants to deny his past and present while awake, covets the relationship he never had with Deborah, his deceased daughter. While he sleeps, she comes to him in idealized form and they talk as if the Holocaust, his marriage to Lola, and the birth of Debby had never happened. However, the suffering is just as intense for Debby. As the daughter of Holocaust survivors, she has heard her mother's stories and acknowledged the burden of her ancestors. Equally, she knows that she is named after her dead half sister, whose image she will never replace in her father's eyes. Unable to handle the pressure of her parents' and religion's past, Debby rebels against it all. She ravenously eats, while making comments about the lack of food for concentration camp victims. She equates dressing rooms with gas chambers, and she runs screaming and naked out into the store. In effect, the onus of the Holocaust is a devastating and oppressive cloud that damages and consumes them all.

By the end of the play, the history of this family has taken its emotional, physical, and psychological toll on Debby. She attacks Max, trying to choke him. He manages to tie her up and then has her taken away in the hopes that this act will finally banish her from his life. And yet, Lola and Max's final dialogue suggests that the difficulty and inhumanity of their past will not be solved with Debby's internment in a mental institution. The memories of their survival as well as the history with their daughter can never be erased, as much as Max might want them to be. As the play ends, Max once again is in a dream state with Deborah; however, with Debby's banishment from the family, Deborah too fades away from his dreams. By expelling his real daughter, Max has expelled the fantasy creation of his dead daughter. For all of his attempts to escape into his dream with Deborah, Max's actions only doom his dreams to the same silence he has tried so hard to foster in real life. The strength of the play prompted Alisa Solomon in the *Village Voice* (7 November 1995) to call the 1995 production of *The Model Apartment* at Primary Stages "one of the most complex and harrowing Holocaust plays I've seen." Interviewer Stephanie Coen agreed, calling Margulies "a preeminent chronicler of the Holocaust-shadowed lives of American Jews."

In 1988 Margulies was drawn to Hollywood for economic reasons as well as his own sense of curiosity. He was a writer and producer on *Baby Boom,* a short-lived television series that starred Kate Jackson and was based on the motion picture of the same name. Margulies only stayed with the production for six days, but he received writing credit for three shows and supervising producer credit on one episode. While his experiment with television was not successful, he did manage to use his experience to good effect in his short one-act *Pitching to the Star* (1990), which depicts a New York playwright's eye-awakening foray into the hypocritical world of pitching a script idea to a famous actress. It is a devastating and funny look at the double dealing so prevalent in the West Coast world of television and movies.

With *The Loman Family Picnic* Margulies continues his exploration of the effect of the past on a Jewish family, but this play is a far more personal journey for Margulies as he finally captures the voice and life of his father through Herbie, the lighting fixture salesman of the play. In the afterword to *Sight Unseen and Other Plays* Margulies recalls the influence of Miller's *Death of a Salesman:* "As a boy growing up in Trump Village (the Coney Island housing project built by Donald Trump's father), I imagined that our high-rise was one of the buildings that overshadowed the Loman's modest house." While Margulies thought he grew up in one of the apartments of "bricks and windows, windows and bricks" that looked down on the doomed Willy Loman, the specter of Miller's powerful play equally hung over Margulies as he worked on *The Loman Family Picnic.* As he told Coen, however, "Once I decided to embrace the fact that I was not the first to write a play about a downtrodden salesman in Brooklyn with two sons, but rather that what Miller did contributed to the culture in which my family grew—that was tremendously liberating and artistically very exciting to me."

The Loman Family Picnic shares some similarities with *Death of a Salesman,* including a tired salesman father, two competitive sons (although considerably younger than Happy and Biff), a spectral visit from a dead relative, and imagined escapes from stressful situations. However, Margulies distinctly makes the play his own. In this case, the tragic figure is not the salesman, Herbie, but rather the long-suffering wife and mother, Doris, who is given a wonderfully comic as well as ardent voice so noticeably absent from Linda Loman. Through her monologues the audience discovers just how unhappy with her life she is, especially in regard to her husband, who never talks to her at dinner. Instead, in one scene in which Herbie eats his dinner in silence, she imagines the two of them talking about how each of them died. Like the visits from Ben that continually mock Willy Loman's failures, Doris has visits from her Aunt Marsha, who committed suicide at twenty-three and therefore still retains her youthful looks while the envious Doris continues to age.

Doris is not the only character experiencing difficulties with her life. The first act introduces the rest of the family members, who are equally struggling. Stewie, whose approaching bar mitzvah is the main action of the play, has spent his afternoons learning to recite Hebrew. After months of doing so, he wants to know the meaning behind the sentences he continually regurgitates. The aging rabbi tells him not to concern himself with the meaning. Stewie, feeling betrayed and a victim of brainwashing, decides never to go to temple again after the bar mitzvah ceremony is over. Mitchell, the younger, smarter, but neglected son, like Happy in *Death of a Salesman,* receives citywide recognition for his artwork, but his father barely registers a response to his son's accomplishment. Herbie, trapped selling lighting fixtures, hopes for a big break at work, while at home he feels neglected because his family does not seem excited to see him when he comes home at eleven at night. The significance of the title becomes apparent in the first act as well. Mitchell reveals that he is writing a musical version of *Death of a Salesman* to be called *Willy!* ("With an exclamation point. You know, like *Fiorello!? Oklahoma!? Oliver!?*"). Mitchell, though, has added a scene not present in the Miller play or in his own home life: one in which the happy, talkative, and non-combative family goes on a picnic during a glorious, sunshiny day.

The second act takes place on the day and night of the bar mitzvah, and in this section of the play Margulies demonstrates the maturity of his playwriting. At the end of the bar mitzvah, Stewie and Mitchell excitedly and in telethon-like fashion tally up all the gift money. When they are finished, Herbie takes all of the money away from Stewie in order to pay for the bar mitzvah. "Look at this bill," he tells his shocked son, "We're talking four grand here. Four grand! You think your father has four thousand dollars? Where have you been? This is what I been trying to tell you! The gifts are only gonna cover half! I'm two grand in the hole!" The family then erupts into an angry, explosive, and emotional fracas as they finally say to one another what they have kept inside for so long. This emotional section of the play not only succeeds dramatically but also was essential in Margulies finally articulating his father's long-silent voice: "The cultural, economic and social pretensions surrounding that event lead to the beleaguered father's terrifying explosion. Giving voice to that inarticulate rage helped me find my father."

Like Doris, who speaks to her dead aunt to escape her dull life, Mitchell, in order to escape the fighting, slips into the imaginary world of his musical as his arguing family members, ironically, become the Lomans on a picnic. Margulies's blending of his own characters with Miller's allows him to move beyond the ubiquitous family argument scene so prevalent in American drama. Instead, he depicts a scene much more devastating and powerful because of its irony. For all of his attempts to create a happy situation, Mitchell's musical still does not erase the conflicts, suffering, and pains of his family members (or the Lomans for that matter). Their individual problems still manage to worm their way into the song that he writes. For Mitchell, even in his imagination, there is no escape from his family.

The play, though, does not end with the musical number. Unlike *Death of a Salesman,* there is no coda to the audience. Instead, Margulies leaves the ending ambiguous by offering four different concluding scenes. In each one Herbie returns home from work to varying familial responses. In this first one, Doris leaves him. In the second scenario, Doris jumps out the window of their ten-story apartment. The third one shows Herbie being greeted like a father from a 1950s sitcom, with all forgiving him. Finally, in what is probably the true ending, Herbie comes home; Doris gives him dinner; and they sit in silence, just as they have done their entire married life. Nothing has changed.

The Loman Family Picnic premiered in 1989 at Manhattan Theatre Club Stage II. It was revived in New York in 1993 and received a Drama Desk Award nomination for Best Revival of a Play. About the 1993 production, *Time* magazine (29 November 1993) stated that Margulies was, as usual, "fearless in going for the offbeat," while Coen remarked that it was Margulies's "most audacious play." However, more important than the positive reviews was Margulies's success at finding his father's voice. Once he had done so, he was free to expand his dramatic focus, prompting the creation of some of his best plays.

One of his most successful and nationally recognized plays was the follow-up to *The Loman Family Picnic:* his award-winning play *Sight Unseen.* The play originated from a 1988 piece called "Heartbreaker," an autobiographical play, which Margulies now calls "The Donald Chronicles." Commissioned by South Coast Repertory, "Heartbreaker" was workshopped in 1989 and eventually shelved (two fragments, "Kibbutz" and "New Year's Eve," are published in *July 7, 1994: Short Plays and Monologues,* 1997). While all of the material of "Heartbreaker" was drastically rewritten or discarded, he retained the main character of Jonathan Waxman. Margulies told Dubner, "Once I decided that Waxman was not just an artist but a superstar artist; it galvanized the play. Even if the origins of a character are autobiographical, I

always raise the stakes to create situations more fraught than reality."

One of the most immediate differences about *Sight Unseen* is the scope of the play. To this point, all of Margulies's major plays had been set in New York, except for *The Model Apartment,* and even those characters were only a few hours removed from the city. *Sight Unseen,* though, takes place for the most part in England, except for two short flashbacks to Jonathan's past in the United States.

Jonathan is a successful, media-seeking artist. He has come to England for a retrospective, even though he is only in his late thirties. Most of the action and four of the eight scenes take place at a farmhouse in the English countryside, where Jonathan visits his former girlfriend, Patricia, now married to Nick, an English archaeologist. While the uncomfortable conversations dodge around their past relationship and her marriage of convenience to Nick, the underlying levels of the discussion are about Jonathan's past and, more specifically, the discrepancies between Jonathan's character as a young artist in comparison to the celebrity persona he now embraces. The other four scenes jump forward and backward in order to provide another glimpse of Jonathan's personality. The two flashbacks show the first meeting between Jonathan and Patricia (after she had posed nude for his class) and their breakup (on the day of his mother's funeral). In both of these scenes Margulies shows the discomfort Jonathan feels with his Jewish identity and the candid, extroverted, and Christian Patricia, who represents everything he is not. Unable to handle the emotional and religious conflict he feels, he breaks up with her, blaming her for the failure of their relationship rather than facing his own inadequacies and failings. The two flash-forwards take place at the gallery as Waxman is interviewed by Grete, an attractive and rather cagey German journalist. She has studied his career diligently—too diligently for Jonathan's comfort—and she critically questions not only the nature of his art but also his own image-manipulated career. She notes that he hired a public relations firm two years before he was discovered.

Unlike earlier plays that focused on the breakdowns and struggles of familial relationships, *Sight Unseen* is far more localized in its presentation of a man who sheds the values of his family and his heritage in order to embrace the commercialism and the vapidness of the 1980s art scene. Jonathan, in many ways, is a bankrupt, bereft figure who no longer has a real sense of self but instead exists more on his artificially created celebrity image. The triggering effect for the journey through Jonathan's changed character is a portrait of Patricia that he painted after their first meeting. Patricia kept it, while Jonathan destroyed most of his early canvases, eradicating evidence of the Jonathan Waxman he no longer desired to be. However, recognizing the beneficial publicity inherent in displaying a previously unseen Waxman painting, Jonathan wants it for the retrospective. The two characters' perception of the painting is central to understanding the change in Jonathan. For Patricia, the portrait represents their past together and, in turn, a part of herself. Jonathan, though, only sees the material, career, and media benefits of the painting. In fact, Jonathan no longer paints for himself. Instead, he paints for his buyers who purchase his paintings sight unseen, meaning they buy his work before it has even been painted or conceptualized. In the middle of the night, Jonathan attempts to spirit the painting away, but Nick catches him. Nick, feeling oppressed by the effect the painting has on his marriage and by his own inability to replace Jonathan in Patricia's life, sells the painting to Jonathan.

While his time with Patricia and Nick awakens Jonathan to his personality change, the interview with Grete only solidifies his resolve to continue to embrace the celebrity of Jonathan Waxman rather than the more idealistic Jonathan of his past. When Grete presses him on who modeled for the portrait and where the woman is now, he professes not to know what has happened to her; and later, fed up with Grete's probing questions, he accuses her of being anti-Semitic, indicating his own refusal to confront his past as he deflects her questions and misinterprets them as part of an ugly political agenda. Grete, though, is not innocent of trying to provoke Waxman. Part of the skill of Margulies's writing is that both the interviewer and interviewee are self-serving throughout their entire exchange, and the audience wonders after the scene is over who actually is correct in their reproaches. Jonathan's outburst, however, is the last chronological scene of the play, and it is extremely revealing that he embraces his previously discarded Jewish heritage only when it conveniently can be used as a method of attack against Grete. Margulies has created a damning but absorbing portrait of a man who sacrifices his identity and those he loves for the sake of celebrity, acclaim, and monetary comfort.

Sight Unseen generated the greatest amount of praise for his work. Reviewers drew comparisons to Harold Pinter's *Betrayal* (1978) and David Hare's *Plenty* (1978). However, a few suggested that Margulies's use of temporal shifts for the purpose of dramatic irony was not as successful as that of the two British playwrights. Margulies, though, uses time differently from Pinter and Hare. In a 1991 interview

with Jan Herman he noted, "The jumbled chronology seemed to suit the sort of memory play that I think this is. I frankly thought it should be ambiguous; it should be mysterious. Pieces should fall into place the way they would if you're analyzing a painting. You scrutinize it and something makes sense in relation to something else, but not immediately. The juxtapositions give it resonance." As other critics have observed, the structure of many of Margulies's plays is collage-like. The analogy is especially apt in regard to *Sight Unseen,* which samples and examines bits and pieces of Waxman's past, present, and future. Each section alone, like a piece of collage, is fragmentary, but fused together they create the pattern of the man.

After its initial run at South Coast Repertory Theatre in Costa Mesa, California, the play moved to New York, where it was staged at the Manhattan Theatre Club before moving to the Orpheum Theater, where it had an extended run. It also had successful productions in Germany, Canada, and Australia. *Sight Unseen* won the 1992 Obie Award for Best New American Play, the Dramatists Guild/ Hull-Warriner Award, and a Burns Mantle "Best Play" designation. It also received Best Play nominations for the Pulitzer Prize, the New York Drama Critics's Circle Awards, the Outer Critics Circle Awards, and the Drama Desk Awards.

In April 1992 Margulies's wife gave birth to a baby boy named Miles. A two-year-old boy, who never appears on stage, plays an important part in his next play. *July 7, 1994,* a one-act presented at the 1995 Humana Festival, explored new dramatic material for Margulies. The context of the play is one day in the life of a general internist named Kate. While the play begins and ends in her apartment, which she shares with Mark, her academic husband, and their two-year-old son, the majority of the action takes place in her examination room. She has consultations with four different patients: a Spanish-speaking woman whose pain is generated by family problems rather than anything medical; a randy male patient who harasses her; a battered wife who does not see the connection between her own violent marriage and the infamous celebrity case of O. J. and Nicole Simpson; and a woman dying of AIDS who refuses to acknowledge her impending death and make plans for someone to care for her children. Throughout, Kate finds herself helpless to aid any of the patients, as their suffering cannot be alleviated with anything she was taught in medical school. Lingering behind all the consultations is O. J. Simpson and the national obsession with his murder trial, as each conversation Kate has with her patients relates to the impending decision on whether the evidence found at Simpson's estate would be admitted into the trial.

The direction and purpose of the play are reminiscent of W. H. Auden's "Musée des Beaux Arts" (1940), which remarks on the great suffering that befell Icarus as he fell from the sky, and the tragedy that no one noticed his fall. In contrast to Auden, Margulies suggests that in the late twentieth century the suffering does not go unnoticed, just unaided. Equally, the play suggests that too much suffering occurs. No longer do people live restful lives. Just as the tragedy of Nicole Simpson and Ronald Goldman is played out on television, everyone experiences his or her own tragic dilemmas. Margulies embodies that concept in the last moments of the play as Kate returns home and hears about the day her husband and son had while she was at work. Mark reveals that their son fell asleep while Mark recited *Goodnight Moon*. Kate has him recite it again, and as he does so, she breaks down crying as she is struck by the contrast between the simple, organized world of the children's story, bereft of strife, and her own helpless attempts at comforting her patients' anguish. *July 7, 1994*, along with *The Model Apartment*, is one of Margulies's most powerful plays about human suffering.

Following *July 7, 1994* Margulies wrote *Collected Stories*, a two-character play that visits the world of writers, rather than artists. Of his major plays, *Collected Stories* relies on the most conventional theatrical format since *Found a Peanut*: no juxtaposed time scenes, no mothers coming back to life, no musical numbers, no dead child communicating through dreams. Instead, *Collected Stories* is about the relationship between a teacher and student. Certainly, the story is not new, but Margulies effectively tweaks the basic plot of the older, wiser teacher becoming eclipsed by her younger, extremely talented student. In the process, he explores the topics of art, friendship, and the obligation a student owes to her teacher. "Part of the inspiration was the David Leavitt/Stephen Spender controversy," Margulies remarked in a 1997 interview with Margot Ebling: "Leavitt published a novel that drew on a chapter from Spender's autobiography. Spender fought it in England and successfully suppressed it. This particular story captivated me, but I wanted distance from it. I wanted to dramatize the theme of the betrayal of the artistic endeavor."

In this play Margulies tracks the relationship between Ruth Steiner and Lisa Morrison over a six-year period, from its initial strained roots to its blossoming period of mutual self-respect to its eventual break-up. Ruth is the embattled, hard-to-please writing teacher with an extremely well established reputation, and at first she appreciates Lisa's raw talent.

Lisa, meanwhile, changes from a completely awed and intimidated fan and student of Ruth's to her overeager personal assistant to an established, confident writer in her own right. Lisa's first collection of short stories is heralded as the work of an important young voice. However, feeling the pressure to write a successful first novel, Lisa fictionalizes Ruth's life, drawing heavily from a story Ruth told her about a love affair with Delmore Schwartz.

The publication of the novel brings to the foreground the various conflicts of opinions they have had throughout their relationship. Each one views the world differently, including the roles of mentor and pupil. Margulies begins to hint at the discrepancy between the two women as they discuss the relationship between Woody Allen and Soon-Yi Previn, Mia Farrow's adopted daughter. Ruth sees no problem in Allen's action, having herself fallen for an older man when she was young, and she argues that celebrities should be allowed to have their own private lives. Lisa, though, is offended and outraged at Allen's actions and disavowal of his paternal obligation to his stepdaughter. She feels betrayed that his screen image does not correspond to the real man. It is precisely this same divergence of opinion about the motive behind Lisa's book that leads to the break-up of their relationship. Lisa sees her book as a tribute to Ruth: "I thought you'd feel. . . . Pride. Satisfaction. . . . For having been a good teacher." Ruth sees it as a betrayal of her friendship and an invasion of her privacy: "Our trust is broken. I feel like I've been bugged. My dear young friend turned out to be a spy. A spy who sold my secrets." Neither woman backs down from her position, and the play ends with the friendship in shambles.

The play also ends ambiguously, because questions still remain about the decisions that Ruth and Lisa make. Ultimately, the play questions the nature of literature that relies upon the fictionalization of real-life situations (a prevalent genre in the 1990s), but it also depicts the irreconcilable differences between these two powerful and talented women in how they define their lives, their values, and their own philosophies of the vital components of the artistic process.

Collected Stories opened in Costa Mesa in 1996, but like all of Margulies's other works it moved to New York, where the Manhattan Theatre Club production received, for the most part, favorable reviews. The play received nominations for the Pulitzer, Drama Desk Award and Dramatists Guild/Hull-Warriner Award. The play was revived Off-Broadway in 1998 with Uta Hagen (the original Martha in Edward Albee's *Who's Afraid of Virginia*

Woolf?, 1962) in a successful run. Unlike *Sight Unseen,* which received several productions across the United States but only a few international productions, *Collected Stories* has been not only a domestic success with its extended run in New York but also has received several productions around the world, including France, Austria, England, New Zealand, Australia, and Japan, with more productions scheduled in Mexico, Italy, Germany, and Finland. *Collected Stories* has thus become Margulies's most successful and internationally recognized play.

Margulies's next work, *Dinner with Friends,* premiered at the 1998 Humana Festival. With this work, he moves back into the domestic realm as he looks at the disruptive impact of a divorce on two married couples. The play explores the complex interweaving of marriage, love, friendship, and survival at the end of the twentieth century. It is perhaps, next to *The Model Apartment,* one of Margulies's darkest domestic works.

In Dubner's article John Simon, a reviewer for *New York,* aptly sums up Margulies's importance as a playwright: "Margulies is remarkable because he's not simplistic. The trend now is to couch a very simplistic point of view in a sort of symbolic, absurdist, fantastical garb. Margulies cloaks things in nothing. He gives them to you as he sees them, but as he sees them very carefully and conscientiously and thought-fully observed, from all sides." While Margulies's career began rockily in the 1980s, in the 1990s he has established himself as a preeminent chronicler of not only the Jewish experience, but also the American experience, and of the inherent joys and pains of everyday living.

Interviews:

Janice Arkatov, "Playwright Explores Emotional Legacies," *Los Angeles Times,* 11 November 1988, sect. 6, p. 22;

Jan Herman, "Drawing on Familiar Obsessions," *Los Angeles Times,* 17 September 1991, sect. 7, p. 2;

Randall Beach, "When Life is Going 'Ominously Well,'" *New York Times,* 21 November 1993, sect. 13CN, p. 27;

Stephanie Coen, "Donald Margulies," *American Theatre* (July/August 1994): 46–47;

Margot Ebling, "Something Else," *Village Voice,* 20 May 1997, p. 87.

References:

Stephen J. Dubner, "In the Paint: Donald Margulies Scores with a Play about the Art Hustle," *New York* (9 March 1992): 48–52;

June Schlueter, "Ways of Seeing in Donald Margulies's *Sight Unseen,*" *Studies in American Drama, 1945–Present,* 8, no. 1 (1993): 3–11.

Carson McCullers

(19 February 1917 – 29 September 1967)

Amy Verner
Louisiana State University

See also the McCullers entries in *DLB 2: American Novelists Since World War II* [First Series]; *DLB 7: Twentieth-Century American Dramatists;* and *DLB 173: American Novelists Since World War II: Fifth Series.*

PLAY PRODUCTIONS: *The Member of the Wedding,* New York, Empire Theatre, 5 January 1950;
The Square Root of Wonderful, New York, National Theatre, 30 October 1957.

BOOKS: *The Heart Is a Lonely Hunter* (Boston: Houghton Mifflin, 1940; London: Cresset, 1943);
Reflections in a Golden Eye (Boston: Houghton Mifflin, 1941; London: Cresset, 1942);
The Member of the Wedding (Boston: Houghton Mifflin, 1946; London: Cresset, 1947);
The Member of the Wedding: A Play (New York: New Directions, 1951);
The Ballad of the Sad Café: The Novels and Short Stories of Carson McCullers (Boston: Houghton Mifflin, 1951); republished as *The Ballad of the Sad Café: The Shorter Novels and Stories of Carson McCullers* (London: Cresset, 1952);
The Square Root of Wonderful (Boston: Houghton Mifflin, 1958; London: Cresset, 1958);
Clock Without Hands (Boston: Houghton Mifflin, 1961; London: Cresset, 1961);
Collected Short Stories and The Ballad of the Sad Café (Boston: Houghton Mifflin, 1961);
Sweet as a Pickle and Clean as a Pig (Boston: Houghton Mifflin, 1964; London: Cape, 1965);
The Mortgaged Heart, edited by Margarita G. Smith (Boston: Houghton Mifflin, 1971; London: Barrie & Jenkins, 1972);
Collected Stories of Carson McCullers, Including The Member of the Wedding and The Ballad of the Sad Café, edited by Virginia Spencer Carr (Boston: Houghton Mifflin, 1987);
Illumination and Night Glare: The Unfinished Autobiography of Carson McCullers, edited by Carlos L. Dews (Madison: University of Wisconsin Press, 1999).

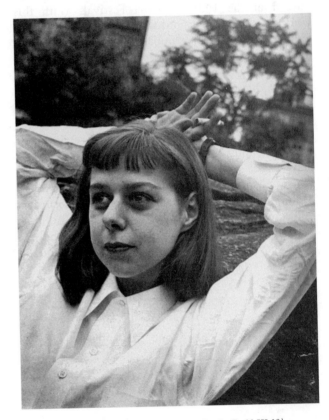

Carson McCullers (photograph by Louise Dahl-Wolfe)

PRODUCED SCRIPTS: *The Invisible Wall,* television play, adapted by McCullers from her short story "The Sojourner," *Omnibus,* CBS, 1953;
The Sojourner, television play, adapted by McCullers from her short story, NBC, 1964.

Carson McCullers has generally been viewed as a novelist who produced a small but important body of work in the Southern gothic genre. Recent critics have focused on a variety of subtle themes in her works, ranging from examinations of gender, identity, and race to psychological sketches. This new approach and a continuing interest in adapting her works for motion pictures has brought McCullers's plays back into the literary spotlight. *The Member of the Wedding: A Play* (1950) is her major dramatic success both in terms of its Broadway run and its critical reception, while her second play, *The Square Root of Wonderful* (1957), is notable not for its dramatic value but because of the insights it offers about McCullers's personal life. Her style of playwriting was innovative, and McCullers has ultimately been recognized as an important American playwright.

Lula Carson Smith was born on 19 February 1917, the oldest of Lamar and Marguerite Waters Smith's three children. She grew up in their secure and modest household in Columbus, Georgia, where her father was a jeweler. The Smiths considered their daughter an artistic genius and attempted to nurture her talents. When she showed interest in and a gift for playing the piano, they paid for lessons with accomplished teachers, first Mrs. Kendrick Kierce and then Mary Tucker. As with Mick Kelly, the twelve-year-old girl in her novel *The Heart Is a Lonely Hunter* (1940), music for a time was Lula Carson Smith's life ambition. Like another of her characters, Frankie in *The Member of the Wedding,* she renamed herself, dropping the "Lula" from her name at the age of thirteen.

Carson Smith's battle with rheumatic fever in 1932 started the pattern of poor health and debilitating illness that continued the rest of her life. She recovered sufficiently to go on with her music and graduated from high school in 1933, at age sixteen. At fifteen she had begun writing plays and short stories to entertain her family and had secretly decided to become a writer rather than a concert pianist. Though he did not know his daughter's change of career goals, Lamar Smith supported her literary efforts by buying her a typewriter.

At seventeen, with about $500 that her family had scraped together, Carson Smith went to New York City to attend the Juilliard School of Music, planning to take creative-writing classes at Columbia University as well. Her money was stolen soon after she arrived in New York. Abandoning plans to enroll at Juilliard, she worked and saved that fall, attending night classes at Columbia in the spring. She took writing courses at New York University during the following academic year, and in summer 1936 she studied with Whit Burnett at Columbia.

When she had returned home for the summer of 1935, Carson Smith had met Reeves McCullers, a young soldier who shared her aspirations to write as well as her desire to leave the South permanently. They were married on 20 September 1937 and lived in Charlotte and Fayetteville, North Carolina, while Carson McCullers wrote *The Heart Is a Lonely Hunter,* the novel that launched her career. In June 1940—with the publi-

Reeves and Carson McCullers in Fayetteville, North Carolina, winter 1939–1940

cation of this first novel and with a second novel, *Reflections in a Golden Eye* (1941), nearly complete—the McCullerses moved to New York, vowing never to live in the South again. They were divorced in late 1941, but remarried on 19 March 1945.

Though she kept her vow not to live in the South, all McCullers's works are set there—a place in which her characters struggle painfully to free themselves from being outsiders, often with limited success. To become part of a group, they must have close relationships with other people; but for a McCullers character loving someone is not easy, and lack of reciprocation results in unsettling compromises. This difficulty of belonging is one of McCullers's central themes, frequently overshadowing her concerns with identity, gender, and race.

In summer 1946 Tennessee Williams invited McCullers, whom he had not met, to visit him for a week at his home on Nantucket. The two writers

Dust jacket for McCullers's dramatic version of her 1946 novel, the story of a lonely young girl growing up in the South

have made plans to get married, Frankie becomes acutely aware that she is alone: "The trouble with me is that for a long time I have been just an 'I' person." As she watches the young couple, she realizes that most "people have a 'we.'" Seeing her role as a member of the wedding party as the perfect solution to her solitude, she begins to imagine that she will leave her old life behind and start a new one with the newlyweds, going with them to "whatever place that they will ever go."

Like the novel on which it is based, the play focuses on the inner workings of Frankie's mind as she searches for her true identity. McCullers exposes and develops Frankie's inner conflict through dialogue rather than action as Frankie progresses from a lonely young girl to a teenager, who by the end of the play has found a friend in a neighborhood girl her own age. Some of the initial reviewers were unprepared for a play that includes so little action, and their responses were mixed. Howard Barnes wrote in *The New York Herald Tribune* (6 January 1950) that the play moved "at a snail's pace through two acts in which the literary origin is all too apparent to a final burst of hysterics and melodrama." This negative opinion of McCullers's dramatic sense was shared by John Chapman of *The New York Daily News* (6 January 1950), who commented that "as a piece of playmaking it is not ideal, for it reiterates one theme for two acts with scarcely any story or character development." Many critics, however, admired the depth of the characters and the emotional reach of McCullers's writing. Brooks Atkinson of *The New York Times* (6 January 1950) exclaimed, "it may not be a play, . . . [but] it is art." The reviewer for *The New York Post* (6 January 1950), Richard Watts Jr., called *The Member of the Wedding* "an unusual play of genuine individuality" and stated that its faults as theater are "more than atoned for by its sensitivity of feeling, its delicacy of treatment, and its understanding warmth of human sympathy." One of the most interesting reviews came a few weeks after the premiere, when John Mason Brown described *The Member of the Wedding* as "no ordinary play" (*Saturday Review,* 28 January 1950). Agreeing with his contemporaries that the play lacked the action and change that traditionally move a play along to its conclusion, Brown concluded that this absence of dramatic action was a trend in modern playwriting influenced by Anton Chekhov and that "a well-made play . . . [was] completely out of fashion." The director of *The Member of the Wedding,* Harold Clurman, was an ardent believer in McCullers's dramatic ability and wrote articles for *The New York Herald Tribune* (29 January 1950) and *The New Republic* (30 January 1950) defending the adaptation and production. The popularity of *The Member of the Wedding* prompted Columbia Pictures to film a

became good friends, and Williams suggested that McCullers adapt her third novel, *The Member of the Wedding* (1946), for the stage. Relishing the opportunity to disprove critic Edmund Wilson's claim in his *New Yorker* review of the novel (30 March 1946) that she could not write dramatically, she began work at once. Her one-week stay ended up lasting the entire summer as McCullers wrote the play at Williams's kitchen table. *The Member of the Wedding* opened on Broadway on 5 January 1950 and continued for 501 performances. The New York Drama Critics' Circle named it the best play of the 1949–1950 season, and the Theatre Club, Inc., gave McCullers its gold medal for best playwright of 1950. The success of the play brought her financial security for the first time in her adult life. Despite her mercurial relationship with her husband, when *The Member of the Wedding: A Play* was published in 1951, it was dedicated to Reeves McCullers.

Frankie Addams, the main character in *The Member of the Wedding,* is a twelve-year-old girl trying to deal with the sort of isolation and loneliness that all McCullers's characters confront. When she finds out that her older brother, Jarvis, and his girlfriend, Janice,

McCullers and Tennessee Williams in Havana, Cuba, 1955

screen version of the play in 1952 with the Broadway cast and a screenplay by Edna and Edward Anhalt.

Since the mid 1950s critics have taken a variety of approaches to McCullers's first play. In 1955 W. David Sievers called *The Member of the Wedding* "one of the most notable modern American psychological plays," as he took a Freudian approach to Frankie's adolescent naiveté and limited knowledge of sex, and in 1960 Winifred L. Dusenbury argued that so-called weaknesses of the play were intentional. According to Dusenbury, the inaction of the play, the haphazard dialogue that refused to tell a story, and the superficial interactions among characters who do not successfully express or share their thoughts and feelings all emphasize the theme of loneliness and isolation. In 1962 Gerald Weales, a member of the theater community, praised *The Member of the Wedding* as the "most obvious innovation in recent American theatre" precisely because it lacked plot or dramatic unfolding. Neva Evonne Burdison's 1987 dissertation is the first full-length psychological analysis of the novel, play, and movie versions of *The Member of the Wedding*. She has argued that both the stage and screen adaptations of the novel were successful, but "As an artistic, psychological portrait of an adolescent girl, the novel stands far above its adaptations" because McCul-

lers substantially pared it down for dramatic production.

Writing in 1995, Brooke Horvath and Lisa Logan asserted that McCullers was playing "with the gender fictions underpinning our culture," calling on audiences to "acknowledge and examine the costly cultural myths that construct gender and difference." They suggest McCullers's drama has not been properly appreciated in the past because it includes provocative and often harsh social criticisms that were ahead of its time. In an essay published in *Critical Essays on Carson McCullers* (1996), Thadious M. Davis has examined the question of race relations in the novel and play versions of *The Member of the Wedding* and concluded that the novel includes a greater and more positive construction of its three African American characters than the play, which uses almost stock stereotypes of African American characters for the sake of dramatic convenience and the comfort of McCullers's predominantly white audiences.

McCullers worked on her second play, *The Square Root of Wonderful,* during 1952–1956, a particularly difficult period of her life. Reeves McCullers committed suicide on 19 November 1953, and Marguerite Smith, a lifelong support to her daughter, died suddenly on 10 June 1955.

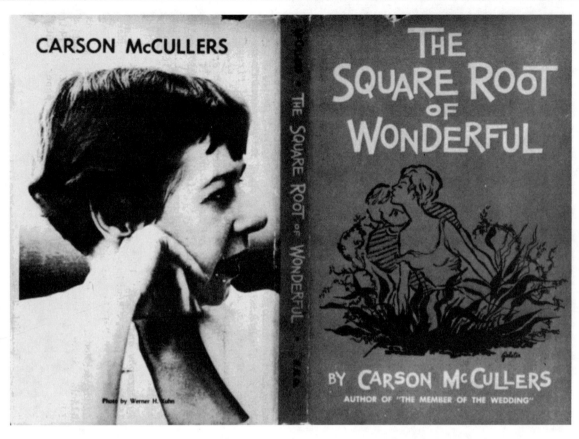

Dust jacket for McCullers's second play, in which the two main characters are based on her husband and her mother

The Square Root of Wonderful is based on McCullers's relationships with her husband and mother, and, like *The Member of the Wedding*, it is a character-driven play. McCullers's second play centers on Mollie Lovejoy as she tries to choose between her former husband, Phillip Lovejoy, to whom she has been married twice, and her new lover, John Tucker. An unstable, selfish, and petulant writer, Phillip is terrified that he will never write again while John is a mature but rather boring architect. The realization that her relationship with Phillip is based on a powerful physical need and is void of spiritual or emotional fulfillment leads Mollie to a new understanding of love. When Phillip commits suicide, she breaks free from her past to begin a new life with John.

McCullers worked with a series of producers and directors, including Arnold Saint Subber and José Quintero, and as the script progressed through many revisions, the play lost original focus and direction. The play opened on Broadway on 30 October 1957 and closed on 7 December after forty-five performances.

Even critics who had liked *The Member of the Wedding* were harsh in their assessments of *The Square Root of Wonderful*. Harold Clurman, who saw a pre-Broadway tryout of the play in Princeton, New Jersey, criticized Quintero's stage direction for reducing McCullers's "lyric writing . . . and wonderfully intuitive character sense . . . into semi-caricature" (*The Nation*, 23 November 1957). George Keathley replaced Quintero. After revision, the version of the play that opened on Broadway was still disjointed. Brooks Atkinson of *The New York Times* (31 October 1957) called the characters dull and lifeless and said that overall the play lacked the "other-worldliness of her best writing."

The published version of *The Square Root of Wonderful* (1958), which includes a preface acknowledging McCullers's mistakes and attempting to explain her intentions, is the last one McCullers wrote before the play went into production and went through revisions by producers and directors. The published version, wrote McCullers, "is the most nearly the truth of what I wanted to say."

Since the late 1950s critics have concentrated mainly on what the play says about McCullers's personal life, comparing Phillip Lovejoy to Reeves McCullers and Mollie Lovejoy to Marguerite Smith. The critics also point to similarities between both characters and McCullers herself.

After the failure of *The Square Root of Wonderful,* McCullers wrote no more full-length plays, though she allowed Edward Albee to adapt her short novel *The Ballad of the Sad Café* (1951) for the stage in 1963. She wrote a second adaptation of her short story "The Sojourner" for television broadcast in 1964. (Her first televised version of "The Sojourner" was aired as *The Invisible Wall* in 1953.)

Beginning in the winter of 1940–1941 McCullers had suffered a series of strokes that left her increasingly debilitated. On 15 August 1967 she suffered a massive brain hemorrhage and died on 29 September, at the age of fifty, after remaining in a coma for forty-six days.

In the year of McCullers's death Warner Bros.–Seven Arts released movie versions of two of McCullers's novels: *The Heart Is a Lonely Hunter,* with a screenplay by Thomas C. Ryan, and *Reflections in a Golden Eye,* with a script by Chapman Mortimer and Gladys Hill. NBC broadcast a live stage production of *The Member of the Wedding* nationwide in 1982, and in 1991 Delbert Mann adapted and directed a motion picture version of *The Ballad of the Sad Café,* for Merchant Ivory Productions. These versions of McCullers's works have helped to ensure continuing interest in her life and writing while renewed scholarly attention has enhanced her stature as an important American writer.

Bibliographies:

Robert F. Kiernan, *Katherine Anne Porter and Carson McCullers: A Reference Guide* (Boston: G. K. Hall, 1976);

Adrian M. Shapiro, Jackson R. Bryer, and Kathleen Field, *Carson McCullers: A Descriptive Listing and Annotated Bibliography of Criticism* (New York: Garland, 1980);

Virginia Spencer Carr, "Carson McCullers," in *Contemporary Authors Bibliographical Series: American Novelists,* edited by James J. Martine (Detroit: Gale Research, 1986), pp. 293–345;

Carr and Laurie Scott, "Carson McCullers," in *Bibliography of American Fiction, 1919–1988,* 2 volumes, edited by Matthew J. Bruccoli and Judith S. Baughman (New York: Facts On File, 1991), II: 338–341.

Biographies:

Oliver Evans, *Carson McCullers: Her Life and Work* (London: Owen, 1965), republished as *The Ballad of* *Carson McCullers: A Biography* (New York: Coward-McCann, 1966);

Virginia Spencer Carr, *The Lonely Hunter: A Biography of Carson McCullers* (Garden City, N.Y.: Doubleday, 1975).

References:

Eric Bentley, "The American Drama, 1944–1954," in *American Drama and Its Critics: A Collection of Critical Essays,* edited by Alan Downer (Chicago: University of Chicago Press, 1965), pp. 108–202;

Harold Bloom, ed., *Carson McCullers* (New York: Chelsea House, 1986);

Neva Evonne Burdison, "The Making of 'The Member of the Wedding,' Novel, Play and Film," dissertation, University of Mississippi, 1987;

Virginia Spencer Carr, "Carson McCullers: Novelist Turned Playwright," *Southern Quarterly,* 25 (Spring 1987): 37–51;

Beverly Lyon Clark and Melvin J. Friedman, ed., *Critical Essays on Carson McCullers* (New York: G. K. Hall, 1996);

Winifred L. Dusenbury, "An Unhappy Family," in her *The Theme of Loneliness in Modern American Drama* (Gainesville: University of Florida Press, 1960), pp. 57–85;

Brooke Horvath and Lisa Logan, "Nobody Knows Best: Carson McCullers's Plays as Social Criticism," *Southern Quarterly,* 33 (Winter–Spring 1995): 23–33;

Judith Giblin James, *Wunderkind: The Reputation of Carson McCullers, 1940–1990* (Columbia, S.C.: Camden House, 1995);

W. David Sievers, *Freud on Broadway: A History of Psychoanalysis and the American Drama* (New York: Hermitage House, 1955);

Gerald Weales, *American Drama Since World War II* (New York: Harcourt, Brace &World, 1962).

Papers:

Carson McCullers's papers, including manuscripts, photographs, letters, and publishing documents are housed at the Harry Ransom Humanities Research Center, University of Texas at Austin. The Robert Flower Collection at Duke University also has an important gathering of McCullers's correspondence, especially letters to Mary Tucker, Edward Albee, and Tennessee Williams.

David Rabe

(10 March 1940 –)

Carla J. McDonough
Eastern Illinois University

See also the Rabe entry in *DLB 7: Twentieth-Century American Dramatists*.

PLAY PRODUCTIONS: *Chameleon,* Dubuque, Iowa, Holy Trinity Auditorium, 12 April 1959;

Bridges, Villanova, Pennsylvania, Villanova University, 1963;

The Crossings, Villanova, Pennsylvania, Villanova University, 1963;

The Bones of Birds, Philadelphia, Vasey Theatre, 1968; revised as *The Orphan, or Orestes and the E=MC²,* Philadelphia, Vasey Theatre, 14 October 1970; revised as *The Orphan,* New York, Anspacher Theatre, 18 April 1973; revised, Winston-Salem, North Carolina School of the Arts, 12 November 1973; Philadelphia, Manning Street Actors Theater, 13 March 1974;

Bones, Philadelphia, Vasey Theatre, 7 February 1969; revised as *Sticks and Bones,* New York, Anspacher Theatre, 7 November 1971;

The Basic Training of Pavlo Hummel, New York, Newman Theatre, 20 May 1971;

Boom Boom Room, Philadelphia, Vasey Theatre, 1972; revised, New York, Vivian Beaumont Theatre, 8 November 1973; revised as *In the Boom Boom Room,* New York, Anspacher Theatre, 4 December 1974; London, American Repertory Company's Square One, December 1976;

Streamers, New Haven, Long Wharf Theatre, 30 January 1976; New York, Mitzi Newhouse Theatre, 21 April 1976;

Burnings, New York, Public Theatre, 1976;

Goose and Tomtom, New York, Public Theatre, 6 May 1982; revised, New York, Mitzi Newhouse Theatre, 1986; New York, Lincoln Center, August 1986;

Hurlyburly, Chicago, Goodman Theatre, 2 April 1984; New York, Promenade Theatre, 21 June 1984; New York, Ethel Barrymore Theatre, 7 August 1984; revised, Providence, Rhode Island, Trinity

David Rabe (photograph © Frederic Ohringer)

Rep, 12 December 1986; Los Angeles, Westwood Playhouse, 16 November 1988;

Those the River Keeps, Princeton, McCarter Theater, 1991; Cambridge, Massachusetts, American Repertory Company, 1992; New York, Promenade Theatre, 31 January 1994;

A Question of Mercy, New York, Theatre Workshop, 7 February 1997.

BOOKS: *The Basic Training of Pavlo Hummel* (New York: French, 1969; New York: Viking, 1973);

Sticks and Bones (New York: French, 1972; revised, 1979);

In the Boom Boom Room (New York: Knopf, 1975; revised edition, New York: Grove, 1986;

The Orphan (New York & London: French, 1975);

Streamers (New York: Knopf, 1975);

Hurlyburly (New York: Grove, 1985);

Goose and Tomtom (New York & London: French, 1986; New York: Grove, 1987);

Recital of the Dog (New York: Grove, 1993);

Those the River Keeps (New York & London: French, 1994);

The Crossing Guard, based on the motion picture by Sean Penn (New York: Miramax Books/Hyperion Press, 1995);

A Question of Mercy, based on an essay by Richard Selzer (New York: Grove, 1998).

Editions and Collections: *The Basic Training of Pavlo Hummel and Sticks and Bones: Two Plays by David Rabe* (New York: Viking, 1973);

The Vietnam Plays, 2 volumes (New York: Grove, 1993)— comprises volume 1: *The Basic Training of Pavlo Hummel* and *Sticks and Bones;* volume 2: *Streamers* and *The Orphan;*

Hurlyburly and Those the River Keeps (New York: Grove, 1995).

PRODUCED SCRIPTS: *I'm Dancing as Fast as I Can,* adapted from Barbara Gordon's book, motion picture, Paramount, 1982;

Streamers, motion picture, Rank Films, 1983;

Casualties of War, adapted from Daniel Lang's book, motion picture, Columbia, 1989;

The Firm, adapted from John Grisham's novel by Rabe, David Rayfiel, and Robert Towne, motion picture, Paramount, 1993;

Hurlyburly, motion picture, Storm Entertainment/Fine Line Features, 1998.

David Rabe is often referred to as a Vietnam playwright, largely because his reputation was established on the basis of work he wrote in the years immediately following his tour of duty in Vietnam. While the war certainly provided a catalyst for his writing and has shaped much of his subject matter, the Vietnam War and even war in general is not his only concern, even in the works that critics have termed the Vietnam Trilogy (*The Basic Training of Pavlo Hummel,* performed in 1971; *Sticks and Bones,* 1969; and *Streamers,* 1976) or that Rabe gathered in 1993 as *The Vietnam Plays* (adding *The Orphan,* 1973, to the previous three). The cultural images and expectations thrown upon individuals from their family, their religion, their country, and the media—images that corrupt, shape, limit, define, and elude them—seem to be his deepest concern. His charac-

ters tend to be confused about how to define themselves and how to make contact with others in a world punctuated by violence and cruelty. They search for answers, employing usually inept and fruitless methods drawn from the guideposts of religion, popular psychology, the media, or the military, but they ultimately find few truths that do more than entrap or damage them.

David William Rabe was born in Dubuque, Iowa, on 10 March 1940, with roots clearly in middle-class, middle America. His father, William Rabe, was a history teacher and football coach at a local preparatory school, Loras Academy, and later worked at a packing company. His mother, Ruth McCormick Rabe, worked in a department store. Rabe's sister, Marsha, was born in 1948. Rabe was raised Catholic, an upbringing common to many of his characters and most tellingly critiqued through the character of Father Donald of *Sticks and Bones.* He attended high school at Loras Academy, where he was involved in sports and band and where he also began writing short stories and poems. Upon graduation from high school, Rabe was offered a football scholarship to Loras College. Although he attended the college, he did not play football there. Instead, he majored in English and got involved with a theater company that he helped to found on campus and for which he wrote his first play, *Chameleon,* which was performed on campus in 1959. During his college days, he also contributed to the literary magazine on campus, winning several writing prizes for poetry and short stories. He graduated from Loras College in 1962.

From Loras, he went to Villanova University for an M.A. in theater, which he did not complete immediately. Dropping out of graduate school, he was drafted into the army in 1965, an event that he initially treated as simply an adventure to be experienced. After training at Fort Jackson, South Carolina, in 1966 he was sent to Vietnam, where he never participated in combat but performed a host of "support group" duties for a hospital unit. In a 1992 interview with Eric James Schroeder, Rabe recalled briefly trying to get transferred to a combat unit until he was fully hit by the reality of the killing. Although he entered the war as a fledgling writer, Rabe comments that he could not write while he was there:

> While in Vietnam, I felt I should keep some sort of journal. . . . But all my efforts brought me nothing, or very little, and the reasons were many, of course, but essentially two. . . . I was aware acutely, and in a way that makes writing impossible, of the existence of language as a mere symbol. In no way could I effect the cannon, the shuddering tent flaps. In an utterly visceral way, I detested any lesser endeavor. . . . In addition, writing requires a kind of double focus that I could not quite handle then. If you encounter an auto accident

and then go home to write of it seriously, you must bring your full sensibility to bear upon all elements of that accident. To do this in Vietnam (though there are men who have done it) was a task I didn't try. Not only to see the dead and crippled, the bodies, beggars, lepers, but to replay in your skull their desperation and the implications of their pain . . . seemed a lunatic journey.

Discharged at the end of his two-year tour of duty and flown home in January 1967, Rabe discovered that "double focus" in regard to his war experiences and entered into the most productive writing period of his life, writing the draft of a still-unpublished novel and drafts of what became *Sticks and Bones, The Basic Training of Pavlo Hummel, The Orphan,* and *Streamers* in the span of little more than a year. By 1968 he was back at Villanova, where he was offered a Rockefeller Playwriting Fellowship that had been given up by another student. During his time at Villanova he was quite influenced by professors in the M.A. program and gained much needed encouragement regarding his writing, making Villanova a place he returned to for early productions of many of his plays, including a 1969 production of *Sticks and Bones.* Rabe has commented in more than one interview about the nurturing environment he encountered in theater there, and even dedicates the 1993 publication of *The Orphan* (in volume 2 of *The Vietnam Plays*) to "the teachers and students of Villanova Theatre, 1967–1972."

In 1968 he was awarded his M.A. from Villanova. The following year he married Elizabeth Pan, with whom he had one child, a son named Jason. Moving to New Haven, Connecticut, he found work as a writer for the *New Haven Register* from May 1969 to August 1970, where he uncomfortably wrote a few theater reviews but mainly provided a series of articles on such subjects as conscientious objectors and drug rehabilitation programs. In his comprehensive stage history of Rabe's work, Philip C. Kolin posits that Rabe's stories for the *Sunday Pictorial* of that paper "are the journalistic counterparts to his plays" in their attention to the gritty moral morass of modern America. During this time he was working on revisions of his first plays and was sending out scripts in hopes of arranging professional productions.

Rabe's first professionally produced play was *The Basic Training of Pavlo Hummel.* In his introduction to the 1973 Viking edition of the play, Rabe describes how he sent copies of *The Basic Training of Pavlo Hummel* to several directors and theater agencies, including one to Joseph Papp at the Public Theatre, where it was set aside until the enthusiasm of director Mel Shapiro got Papp to read it again and decide to produce it. Eventually, because of scheduling conflicts for Shapiro, Jeff Bleckner became the director of the premiere staging.

With great enthusiasm, Papp arranged for the play to initially open at the small Open Theatre, but then moved it for its actual premiere to a larger theater within the Public, the Newman Theatre, where it opened on 20 May 1971. It was an immediate success, running for 363 performances and garnering several awards, including both an Obie Award from the *Village Voice* and a Drama Desk Award in 1971, and the Elizabeth Hull-Kate Warriner Award for the 1970–1971 season. Although initial New York critics were bothered by the somewhat incoherent development of the play, the overall tenor of their response was positive, usually hailing the play as important and extraordinary despite its inconsistencies in style and tone.

This incoherence in development no doubt has something to do with the structure of the play, which is told in flashbacks, thus incorporating both realistic and surrealistic techniques. Although Rabe has said that during rehearsals of the initial production he fought to keep the play realistic, *The Basic Training of Pavlo Hummel* does not adhere to the tenets of realism. Opening with the death of the title character, who is killed by a grenade thrown by a fellow soldier, the play traces Pavlo's life in the army up to that point. Joining Pavlo immediately after his death is a character named Ardell, who will accompany him throughout the play as something of a choral figure. Ardell is seen only by Pavlo, and his first exchange with Pavlo is to inform the latter that he is now dead. Rabe then moves Pavlo back to his days in basic training in the army, where the majority of the first act takes place.

It is clear from his first actions as a trainee that Pavlo is different from the rest of the soldiers: he has a naive, almost childish image of the army and soldiers. He tries to imitate and gain the approval of his drill sergeant, Sergeant Tower, by pushing himself physically and memorizing the rules of conduct. He also makes up stories about his supposed tough-guy past in order to impress his fellow trainees. They, however, know he is lying and already distrust him because he has stolen money from one of the other recruits. Thus, he remains unable to relate to the other trainees despite his desire to do so. Instead he inspires actual hatred from several of them. As Rabe's introduction to the 1973 Viking edition of the play notes, the "basic training" represents more than the specific military event; it is supposed to represent "essential" training regarding how a man should behave in the world. The play thus establishes a theme that continued to interest Rabe throughout his playwriting career: cultural inculcation of individuals into the concepts and values that institutions such as the military espouse.

Pavlo is certainly a person who seems to need help in the development of his self-image, in large part because of the scarcity of role models in his life, represented by his absent father. When Pavlo returns home briefly before being shipped to Vietnam, he confronts his half brother and his mother in an attempt to prove his manliness and to gain respect. After making up a story of a bonding experience with his fellow trainees in order to impress his brother, Mickey, Pavlo tells him, "I don't need you anymore, Mickey. I got real brothers now." His desire to belong and to find acceptance is clearly a crisis that stems from his inadequate family bonds, especially with the father he never knew. Pavlo's mother continually denies him the recognition he seeks, and she refuses to answer his evidently often-asked question about the identity of his father. Pavlo's confusion about his father's identity has led to confusion about his own.

His concept of how he should act and how men behave toward one another has been shaped not by real experience but by the movies his mother took him to see. She even tells him, "you had many fathers, many men, movie men, filmdom's greats–all those grand old men of yesteryear, they were your father," referring specifically to the war movies they had seen together. But this belief in the heroic or manly image of the soldier is overturned in the course of the play as Pavlo discovers his uniform does not make him attractive to women as he had hoped. Soldiering is further critiqued as Pavlo, shipped to Vietnam as part of a hospital unit, is at first gung ho about combat, trying to get himself transferred from the hospital unit to actual combat duty, but after being wounded three times as he does his job of transporting wounded and dead soldiers from the battlefield to the hospital, he just wants to go home.

While war does not ultimately help Pavlo prove his worth to himself, there is some indication that his sexual involvement with a Vietnamese prostitute, Yen, does give him a sense of his manhood, as indicated by the phallic symbol of his rifle, with which he proudly enacts a rifle drill while in Yen's bed. Pavlo's attachment to Yen is part of his newly found sense of self, but it also is clearly a misplaced attachment, given the circumstances. He believes that Yen is somehow his, and so ends up angering another soldier in an argument over her. In response, the soldier leaves the bar, only to toss back in a grenade. Pavlo instinctively grabs the grenade, perhaps trying to enact a scene from a movie that his mother had earlier described, and is killed. Thus, the play circles back to the opening death scene. After re-examining his life with the help of Ardell, Pavlo decides at his moment of death and the closing of the play that "it all shit"–the vagueness of the pronoun allowing the comment to resonate a broad critique of all the ideals that have betrayed Pavlo. *The Basic Training of Pavlo Hummel* continues to be regarded as one of Rabe's best works, and the play was given a high-profile New York revival in 1977, initiated by Al Pacino, who re-created the title role.

Pavlo's confusion as to how to live his life, what role models and values to embrace, is an issue that Rabe explores again in *Sticks and Bones,* although this time the focus is not on the soldier son but on the father. When this play opened at the Anspacher Theatre in New York on 7 November 1971, again under the auspices of Papp's Public Theatre, *The Basic Training of Pavlo Hummel* was still playing. *Sticks and Bones* opens with a series of slides of family photographs projected on the back wall of the stage, with voice-overs by a man, woman, and two children commenting on the pictures. Thus, the opening sequence conjures up images of a traditional family sharing a bonding experience over the family history and memories that have been captured by the photographs. This ideal of the family, though, is soon called into question by events in the play.

Although named after the idealized Nelson television family–Ozzie, Harriet, David, and Ricky–this family is far from happy. The action of the play begins when the eldest son, David, is delivered to their door by an army sergeant who is returning him from the Vietnam War. Ozzie is asked to sign for him as if David is some kind of package–a damaged one, however, since David is now blind. The reintegration of the returned soldier into the family unit is the focus and conflict of the play, in many ways echoing Rabe's own experience of returning from the war to find that although people wanted to debate the idea of it, no one wanted to talk about the real experience of the war.

David is the catalyst for conflict in the play, and with the immediate backdrop of the Vietnam War when the play was first produced, it is tempting to read the play as an antiwar statement with David as its moral voice. But Rabe does not offer a simplistic "war is bad" statement in this play. In fact, he manages to make the returned soldier ultimately unsympathetic in his hatred of everything now that he has had his illusions and former beliefs shattered. David has come to a greater understanding of the falsity and shallowness of his family's way of life not simply because he fought in a "bad" war that society supported, but because he chose to abandon Zung, a Vietnamese woman he loved, rather than go against his ingrained belief that a relationship between an Asian woman and a Caucasian man was wrong. He clearly blames his parents for his abandonment of Zung, and the audience recognizes how deeply set these racial prejudices are when Harriet actually vomits at the thought of her son being with an Asian woman. David is haunted by his betrayal of Zung, who appears on stage as a ghost that only David can sense until the end of the play, when Ozzie decides to protect his

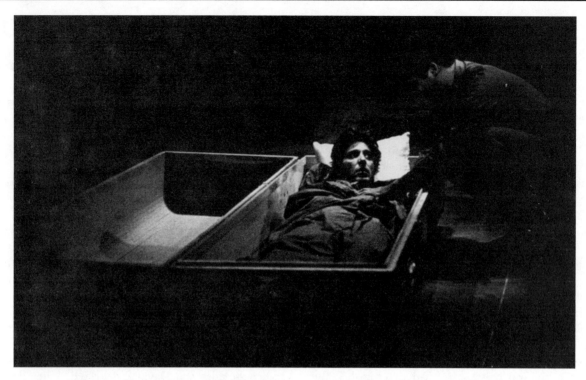

Al Pacino in the 1977 revival of The Basic Training of Pavlo Hummel *(photograph by Bert Andrews)*

household and reassert the status quo by strangling her. However fitting David's critique of the corrupt prejudices he has inherited from his parents is, he seems intent on merely destroying his family's complacency without replacing it with anything other than hatred, and thus remains a static character throughout the play.

Rabe has noted, as have later critics, that Ozzie is the real center of this play, and through Ozzie, the patriarch, Rabe's play questions the idealized image of the "perfect" family as presented in television sitcoms of the 1950s and 1960s. His soldier son's return has led Ozzie to question himself, his own role in the family, and his validity within society, initially because Ozzie has never been a "real" soldier—having only worked as a mechanic during World War II—and thus has not had the epitome of manly experience that war represents. Ozzie expresses his sense of entrapment in the role of family breadwinner, even though he fulfills all traditional expectations of men as husbands and fathers. These roles, however, ultimately do not give meaning to his life but instead make him feel that he has lost himself. So he longs for a time earlier in his life when "I was nobody's goddamn father and nobody's goddamn husband. I was myself." In the wake of his examining his life, he discovers that he has made no mark: "my life has closed behind me like water." Ozzie's solution is not to re-create himself, but finally to retreat more fully into a self-definition based on monetary worth, perhaps

serving as a critique of a capitalist way of thought. He makes an inventory of everything he owns and what each item is worth, and insists that Harriet and his sons carry this inventory around as a way to define who Ozzie really is.

While David's arrival causes Ozzie to re-evaluate the purpose or the success of his life, David proves to be simply an unwelcome disruption for Harriet and Ricky. Harriet at first tries, like a good mother, to re-inculcate her son into fitting behavior—calling upon the family priest to counsel David (quite ineffectively) and trying to get David to be interested in "normal" things again such as eating breakfast, all to no avail. David, instead, expresses even more anger and resentment, causing Harriet to flee more determinedly into her role as housekeeper and cook. Ricky, when he finally registers the problem of David, is simply upset that his brother's behavior is disrupting things for his parents, and thus distracting Ricky from his music and his girlfriends. Ricky, in his glib "Hi Mom, Hi Dad" rituals, comes to embody the desire for physical gratification (food, sex, clothes, music) that the media culture, the television culture, encourages.

Ultimately the family decides it is easier to destroy David and the critique of their world that he implies than to question the shallow lives they have been leading. David's enforced suicide is thought up and cheerfully presented by the fun-loving Ricky, whose recognition that David has disturbed the pursuits of his life leads to his idea that the simple solution is for David to go away again. Harriet's quick embrace of this idea leads to her offering the housewifely and motherly advice that he should use towels and a bowl to catch the blood. The horror of the calculated civility with which this suicide/murder takes place serves to demonstrate the power that traditional roles of behavior have over this normal, middle-class American family. By the close of the play, it is evident that Rabe is not critiquing the Vietnam War per se, or even American reactions to it. He has devastatingly captured the violence that American society will use to protect its complacent image of itself and its way of life—whether that be the assisted suicide of a troublesome son, or the larger-scale violence of military conflict.

Sticks and Bones has gone through several revisions, which seems typical of Rabe's writing process. He continues to revise after initial productions of a play reveal certain weaknesses or issues that need further development. The initial version of Sticks and Bones was titled simply Bones and was first performed on campus at Villanova in February 1969. According to an article by the director of this version (published in David Rabe: A Casebook, 1991), the basics of the final play were there, although the characters were named Andy, Ginger, David, and Ricky in order to avoid potential legal problems with using the Nelson family names. By its 1971 professional debut at the Public Theater, it had become Sticks and Bones with character names shifted to Ozzie, Harriet, David, and Ricky. Also of import in this production, the text of which was published in 1973 by Viking along with The Basic Training of Pavlo Hummel, was the character of Hank Grenweller. Mentioned often by the characters, though never seen, Hank serves as a representative of certain ideals that Ozzie has absorbed as to how to live his life, and that David now questions. There are some similarities in this version of the play between Hank and the character of Ben in Arthur Miller's Death of a Salesman (1949), the shadowy figure that Willy Loman turns to for advice and meaning. Since Rabe has commented in several interviews that he sees Miller as an influence on his work, it is not surprising that there might be echoes of the classic Death of a Salesman in early Rabe plays. However, by 1993 (the only print version available and sanctioned by Rabe), he revised Sticks and Bones and cut out almost all references to Hank, thus placing Ozzie in perhaps an even more tenuous position regarding his search for answers as to how he should live his life, as well as placing responsibility for his choices solely on Ozzie's head.

The initial production of Sticks and Bones ran to critical acclaim, winning the Tony Award for Best Play as well as the New York Drama Critics Circle Special Citation and the John Gassner Medallion for playwright from the Outer Drama Circle, all in 1972. After its initial Off-Broadway opening, it was soon moved to Broadway, where it ran for 366 performances, helping to cement Rabe's reputation as an important new American playwright. It was also turned into a television movie directed by Robert Downey that was scheduled to air in March 1973; but CBS pulled it at the last minute because of its controversial topic at a time when so many POWs were returning from the Vietnam War. It eventually did air in August 1973, but only a handful of CBS affiliate stations carried it. In the interview with Schroeder, Rabe described watching its telecast, which included a disclaimer at each commercial break but no commercial sponsors.

After starting his playwriting career with two major New York productions of his plays running simultaneously to great critical regard, Rabe discovered the true difficulties of a playwright's life in the theater with The Orphan (which opened in New York in April 1973 after previous versions had appeared at Villanova). Chronicling this experience in the afterword to the second volume of The Vietnam Plays, in which The Orphan appears, Rabe indicates that the play lived up to its title because it and its author were abandoned, in Rabe's vision, by his former mentor Papp. The assessment that Rabe gives of his falling out with Papp reveals the complexities of the business of theater that the young Rabe had yet to learn—mainly that a producer's concern is ultimately the business end of theater, not the nurturing of great art. This clash with Papp (to whom Rabe admits he owes his initial successes in theater) foreshadows Rabe's later clash with director Mike Nichols over the original staging of Hurlyburly (1984), further illustrating the powerless position to which the playwright is all too often relegated once a play is actually into rehearsal and production. The experience might also explain why in later years Rabe directed his own work.

The Orphan is a reworking of the Oresteia myth. The issues of fate and destiny as part of one's family heritage that pervade the original myth clearly fascinate Rabe, but he was specifically motivated by the question of why the words of Calchas, the seer who tells Agamemnon that he must sacrifice his daughter Iphigenia, are taken as truth and never questioned. This play is a rather jolting mix of contemporary and classical characters, dress, speech, and events. While Agamemnon, Clytemnestra, and Orestes play out the events of their story, other characters give testimony about their experiences with the Manson family and the Vietnam War. Connections between the classical myth and current events are supposedly implied by this mix, and are emphasized by the character of The

Speaker, whose speeches, infused with scientific lingo, repeatedly address the relativity of time. This spanning of time is further emphasized by the splitting of Clytemnestra into two characters—the young Clytemnestra One, and Clytemnestra Two, who is ten years older. This relativity of time is also linked to the sense that one's interpretation of events is relative, or subjective. While Agamemnon believes he is justified in killing Iphigenia, Clytemnestra believes that she too is justified in killing Agamemnon. And Orestes's dilemma is presented as a task of weighing contrasting subjective judgments as to whether or not his mother deserves death for having murdered Agamemnon in revenge for Iphigenia's murder.

Act 1 of the play focuses on the sacrifice of Iphigenia by Agamemnon as it is protested by Clytemnestra One and the murder of Agamemnon by Clytemnestra Two. The simultaneity of the action further connects the violence of the two murders. The act turns on the climactic argument between Clytemnestra and Agamemnon as the mother insists that Agamemnon's faith in Calchas is misplaced. Calchas of course claims that the bird bones he consulted clearly call for Iphigenia's death as desired by the gods. Clytemnestra asks how he knows he has read the bones accurately, basically questioning why men's goals seem always to require the sacrifice of women. Agamemnon's murder of his daughter rests on his complete faith in the reading of the gods' will that Calchas offers, and he never really wavers from this belief.

Act 2 deals with Orestes's dilemma of trying to find out what happened at and before his birth, and to decide whether his loyalty should be given to his mother or his father. The constant references to his "good mother" and his "good father"—neither of whom he actually knows—indicate value judgments that Orestes is having to make as he weighs different versions of events against each other. The character of The Figure, who stands for Apollo at times, encourages Orestes to believe that his only allegiance is to his father: "All that you are is your father's. Only your body is hers [the mother's]." Eventually, of course, Orestes agrees that his ultimate loyalty is to the father rather than the mother. In this regard, the play follows the original themes set forth by Aeschylus. The questioning of the patriarchal order that Clytemnestra One offers is much more modern in tone, although it is basically overcome by the close of the play.

Interspersed with the story of the ill-fated children of Tantalus from the Orestia myth are characters who describe the murders committed by the Manson family, perhaps as a way to further indicate the illogic of the violence in the classic myth or to update the story itself. Orestes is encouraged to take hallucinogenic mush-

rooms by The Figure throughout the second act, and he at times seems to be part of the Manson family as portrayed by the characters of The Girl and Pylades. Another level of violence is introduced by Pylades's speeches that describe killing Vietnamese people. Several times in the play, the comment is made that some people seem meant to die, and when Orestes finally kills Clytemnestra's consort, Aegisthus, he tells Aegisthus, "think of yourself as a Vietnamese." These references to both the Vietnam War and to the Manson family murders are rather oblique, increasingly so as audiences become further removed from the immediacy of those events.

In comparison to the more controlled and sophisticated *The Basic Training of Pavlo Hummel* and *Sticks and Bones*, *The Orphan* comes across as a bit sophomoric—striving for wide vision, grand scale, and uniqueness of staging, but ultimately falling into the category of bad experimental theater that was sometimes the result of Off- and Off-Off-Broadway experiments in the 1960s. Although Rabe has commented (in his 1993 afterword) that he was working with the idea of the mythologizing of violence, the play never quite forms a coherent whole. Its Off-Broadway run closed after only fifty-three performances.

Following the unsuccessful *The Orphan*, *In the Boom Boom Room* met with marginally better success. *In the Boom Boom Room* premiered (as *The Boom Boom Room*) on 8 November 1973 at the Vivian Beaumont Theatre directed by Papp for a run of only thirty-seven performances, then was directed by Robert Hedley for an Off-Broadway run that opened 4 December 1974 for thirty-one performances. Like *The Orphan* it was not as well received as his first two plays but did manage to garner some favorable reviews. The play marks a change for Rabe because the main character is a woman. However, like Pavlo and Ozzie, Chrissy of *In the Boom Boom Room* is inept at figuring out her life and how best to live it. Set in the world of go-go dancers, the play follows Chrissy through relationships with various men and women, all of them ultimately painful and degrading. She desires to be a dancer because of its fun and beauty and grace, but her dancing in a nightclub and later a topless bar is far from capturing those aspects of dance. The violence of the dancing is demonstrated when Susan, who is the emcee of Big Tom's Boom Boom Room, teaches Chrissy how to do the Jerk correctly—a dance in which the woman reaches up high and then collapses over as if she has been punched in the stomach. Susan hits Chrissy in the stomach each time to get the proper effect. Chrissy gamely tries to figure out the dance, but the scene serves quite obviously as a metaphor for Chrissy's life: she reaches for something beyond the sordid or exploitative or mean, but is constantly punched back down by circumstances, especially her choices and her fate regarding the people in her life.

Again, as was apparent in the earlier plays, the parents play a key role in creating the confusion that Chrissy feels as to how to live her life. She was evidently abused physically and sexually as a child, memories she struggles to reach and that her parents deny; her current life is but a continuation of that cycle. She falls into a relationship with a former convict who follows her home from the bar one night and seems to assume he has a right to force himself upon her, a right that she too simply accepts. When their relationship finally, inevitably results in his beating her up, she is last seen dancing at a topless bar, her bruised face covered by a mask. Throughout the play, Chrissy has looked for answers to her questions about love and relationships from various characters who are each ultimately too wrapped up in their own perceptions to offer much help. Chrissy ends up turning to the lyrics of the songs she dances to in order to explain her life, thus reducing herself to a series of clichés. The play itself offers many metaphors that might impart a message, from the names of the dances (the Jerk, the Pony) to the idea of the dance of life, but ultimately it seems to have no strong focus other than the message that without love, a person's life is hellacious.

The New York critics were generally in agreement that the play falls far short of Rabe's earlier work, and it has not been reprinted since the 1975 publication. However, later critical work on the play suggests that its critique of the patriarchy that crushes Chrissy is worthy of more attention than the predominantly male reviewers originally gave it credit for. In some ways, it should be compared to Rabe's screenplay for the 1982 movie *I'm Dancing as Fast as I Can* (based on the book by Barbara Gordon), which also chronicles the problems of a woman's struggles with drugs, her work, and the men in her life, but which is a much more successful and engaging work, even though it was not critically or popularly acclaimed. While certain aspects of *In the Boom Boom Room* definitely mark it as part of the Rabe canon (the way that the main character's ignorance finally entraps her, the inarticulate manner in which characters speak, the violence and meanness of characters in their treatment of others, and the characters' reliance on images and ideas from popular culture or psychobabble to define or explain themselves), it is ultimately a work that never fully captivates.

Rabe's 1976 play, *Streamers,* won the New York Drama Critics Circle Award for best American play of 1976 and was later turned into a 1983 motion picture directed by Robert Altman. Written initially as a one-act play about the same time that Rabe wrote first drafts of *Sticks and Bones* and *The Basic Training of Pavlo Hummel* (and thus a product of his experiences in Vietnam), the play was later expanded into a two-act form in a manner that Rabe described in a 1988 interview with David Savran as being near to having it write itself. Set in a cadre room where soldiers who have completed their basic training are waiting to see when they will be shipped to Vietnam, the play captures not only the fear of impending death in a war that none of them really understands or cares about but also the tensions, confusions, hopes, and fears of men whose need for intimacy is fraught with danger.

The play opens in the immediate aftermath of the attempted suicide by one of four soldiers who share the cadre room. Martin has been found by Richie, an upper-class kid from Manhattan, who attempts to cover up the incident and pass it off as nothing. Richie assures Martin that he is "just scared" and that nothing is seriously wrong. Both Martin and Richie enlisted in the army, initially chose to be there, though both are now miserable compared to their cadre-mates who were drafted. While Martin is soon taken offstage and not heard from again, except for the news that he has been discharged, the opening image of bloody violence as the result of personal confusion captures the essence of the world of the play. The tension of the play, while fed by the characters' real fear of being sent to war, revolves around their confusion as to how to be with one another and how to behave and identify themselves. The desire for intimacy, emotional or physical, drives much of their behavior.

These men want to connect with each other, to be accepted and understood. But as Rabe's stage directions note, "the war—the threat of it—is the one thing they share." Real understanding and intimacy does not go much beyond this shared fear, although some similarities of perspective provide connections at times. Roger and Billy, who are clean-cut, physically strong, orderly, and rule-bound, evidently share a forthright view of the military as defining the proper behavior for a man, even though they come from quite different cultural backgrounds (Roger is black and from the streets, while Billy is a Midwesterner and white). The two also share a fear and suspicion of homosexuality, manifested in their concern with Richie's "fey" behavior as he flirts with Billy, and their desire to believe that Richie is just playing a game. Carlyle, a recent arrival, enters their cadre room searching for Roger, who he has heard is one of the only other blacks in the platoon. He identifies with Roger because of their race, but he also connects with Richie because of his bisexuality. The bond between the two middle-aged sergeants, Cokes and Rooney, is also apparent from the moment they first show up drunk and singing the song "Beautiful Stream-

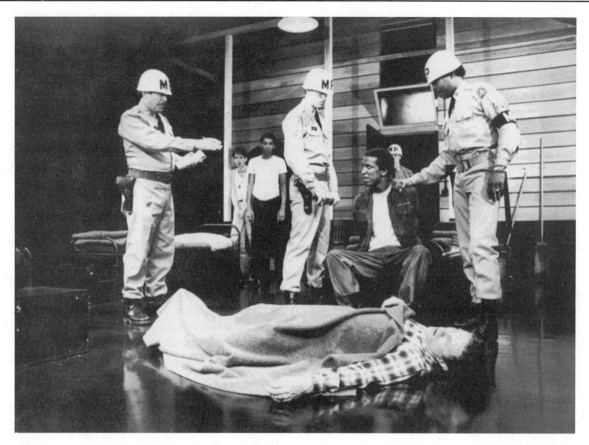

Dorian Harewood (seated) and Paul Rudd (foreground) in the 1976 New York production of Streamers *(photograph by Martha Swope)*

ers" (about a parachute that does not open), from which the play derives its title. Their morbid humor sets the tone for the play as the two are obviously presenting a facade of toughness to cover up a real sense of pain and vulnerability. They are connected by their generation and by their experiences in war–specifically World War II and Korea–but their drunken camaraderie, even their boastfulness that they are real men because they are regular army, is ultimately imbued with pathos.

The struggle for camaraderie among the four young soldiers in the cadre room leads ultimately to competition. When Roger, Billy, and Carlyle return to the room after a night spent at a "cathouse," an activity from which they have excluded Richie, the dynamics of their alliances shift. As they each share stories of their past, Carlyle and Richie are drawn together, and their growing intimacy threatens Billy, who refuses to give up the cadre room to the two men. In response, Carlyle draws a knife and mortally wounds Billy. Driven by internal fears and pressures, Carlyle erupts in violence that seems out of proportion to the events (the argument over the room) that led to his actions. Yet, this violence takes place against the impending violence of war,

stories of which have been told to the recruits (and the audience) by Cokes and Rooney. This violence is then carried over to Rooney when he wanders into the aftermath of the stabbing and is also killed by Carlyle.

Rabe has commented that in initial rehearsals there was great debate over whether the death of Rooney was necessary or just gratuitous. But he states in his afterword to the second volume of *The Vietnam Plays* that this character's death is integral to the examination of violence in the play: "Violence, I had come to believe, is almost never conceptually or formally contained and limited to its appropriate, designated targets. In other words, it is not rational." He goes on to compare events in this play to being "more like nuclear fission in which the explosion of something minuscule unlooses catastrophic, ungovernable devastation." This image of a small act setting off a domino effect is further captured in the play by Cokes's story of a car wreck in which one thing kept following another until the end result seemed hardly connected to the original action, and it all appeared rather ludicrous in the end. The pointlessness of the deaths of both Billy and Rooney seems to be the point of the play and is integrally connected to the military's treatment of its soldiers. The attitude the army has toward these men is indicated by the M.P.'s comment when he arrives to find the bodies of Billy and Rooney: "Two perfectly trained and primed strong pieces of U.S. Army property got cut to shit up here. We are going to find out how and why." This reference to men as property of the army/government further emphasizes how much the characters have to fear not just in war, but in the institution that has housed and trained them.

Streamers is generally regarded as the most effective of the Vietnam plays, running for 478 performances after its move from the Long Acre Theater in New Haven to the Newhouse Theatre in New York on 6 April 1976. It also won the Drama Desk Award and the Los Angeles Drama Critics' Circle Award in 1977. The motion picture version, released in 1983, has given the play even wider exposure. Altman's movie stays generally faithful to the original script and focused on the cadre room, but he does add some scenes. Most notable are shots of Martin, who passes through or by the cadre room twice more after his initial attempted suicide scene. Rabe, however, felt that the movie did not capture the essence of the play, and has voiced dissatisfaction even though he helped with the final editing.

The movie version of *Streamers* is one of several screenplays Rabe worked on in the late 1970s and early 1980s, many of which were never produced. *I'm Dancing as Fast as I Can* was his first produced screenplay that was not related to his plays, and his work on it was primarily because of his second wife, actress Jill Clayburgh, who starred in the movie. Rabe had divorced Elizabeth Pan in 1975 and married Clayburgh in 1979. The couple has a daughter, Lily, born in 1981. This experience of writing for Hollywood was evidently quite unsatisfactory, as Rabe has offered basically nothing but negative comments about what Hollywood directors have usually done with his work. He was dissatisfied with the 1989 movie *Casualties of War,* directed by Brian DePalma, for example, because DePalma took a rather complex script about a soldier's guilt and responsibility for an atrocity committed during the Vietnam War and turned it into a rather simplistic good-guy versus bad-guy story. This work in Hollywood, however, provided him quite a bit of material for later plays and also established his friendship with actor Sean Penn, who starred in *Casualties of War* and whom Rabe later cast in a 1986 closed Newhouse Theatre production of *Goose and Tomtom* (1982), and in the revised version of *Hurlyburly*. In turn, Penn later asked Rabe to write the novelization of the movie *The Crossing Guard* (1995), which Penn wrote and directed.

Written in the late 1970s, *Goose and Tomtom* has had a rocky production history, which is perhaps why it has long been one of Rabe's admitted favorites. Rabe worked with Papp at the Public Theatre on what Rabe thought would be a closed production of the play. Rabe evidently was looking for a production that would allow him to work on the final revision process that he so often relies on after a staging, only to find that Papp went ahead and opened the play on 6 May 1982 for a short, negatively reviewed run of fifty-nine performances. After this debacle, Rabe mounted two more closed productions (one notably with Penn, Madonna, and Harvey Keitel in the cast) trying to bring the play into more satisfactory shape.

While Rabe's plays in general move beyond or outside of strict realism (he boasted in a 1990 interview with Toby Silverman Zinman, included in *David Rabe: A Casebook,* that he has never written a realistic play), *Goose and Tomtom* is the most strikingly outside that realm, primarily because of the cartoon quality of the main characters. From this standpoint, it has much in common with *Sticks and Bones,* which derives much of its black humor from the cartoonish quality of its characters as they struggle to keep themselves as shallow as figures in television commercials. The characters in *Goose and Tomtom,* however, seem to have little depth to escape from. They are simple and even childish figures whose flatness is never questioned. Instead, they seem to serve as ciphers for an exploration of machismo that is fueled by fear and insecurity. Creation myths are also a factor in this play, as the title characters wonder about the origin of events that determine their lives and ultimately experience an apocalypse of sorts in the final moments of the play when masked figures break through the walls of the set and leave them surrounded only by dark skies punctuated by stars.

Goose and Tomtom is set in "an apartment in the underworld," in which the title characters live. The term "underworld" evokes the world of organized crime inhabited by powerful crime moguls, tough-guy detectives, and their entourages. Goose and Tomtom are evidently jewel thieves who seem mainly concerned with proving their toughness and keeping Lorraine, their woman, in diamonds. They have barricaded themselves in the apartment out of paranoia that someone or something (never clearly defined) is trying to get them. During the course of the play they have apparently kidnapped Lulu, the sister of their associate, Bingo. Believing that Bingo has stolen their jewels, they end up killing him. When the masked figures enter at the end of the play and carry off Lorraine, the two men turn to Lulu as their replacement for Lorraine, clutching the diamonds they have left.

The opening action of the play is Goose's entrance, which prompts Tomtom to pull his gun for fear that the intruder may be an enemy. After exchanging a hug, which is also a pat-down, the two men settle into inane conversation, sprinkled with Pinter-esque-style paranoia that seems to be based on their dreams (or nightmares) of victimization. Each recounts a dreamlike encounter with ghosts or witches in which each was tied up or manipulated. When Lorraine enters, it becomes apparent how easily these men are manipulated. She gets them to stick pins in their arms to prove how tough they are. Ultimately, the paranoia that the characters exhibit is not only related to their insecurities about their manliness but also is oddly existential. Each is troubled by the fear that he does not exist outside of his own perceptions, and each needs reassurance that the other characters acknowledge his existence. As a result of these fears, the two men must constantly catalogue their actions and their surroundings, clutching onto objective reality and ultimately looking to each other for assurance. "Do you see Goose, Tomtom?" Goose asks anxiously. And later, to reinstate his existence in relation to objective reality, Goose declares, "I am Goose and this is a chair!"

On one level, this play could best be described as Rabe's exploration of the power of language to create reality. Rabe commented in the interview with Zinman that this play explores language, specifically how "language can cast a spell on you." The magical power of language is apparent in this play in which speaking a fear or desire or fantasy makes it real and makes other characters immediately act upon that new reality. However, neither Goose nor Tomtom ever figures out this connection and so are unable to control their reality. For instance, Goose suggests that they kidnap Bingo's sister as not only revenge on Bingo but also as a convenient sex object for them. When Lulu suddenly enters from the bedroom, bound and gagged, evidently the victim of Goose's earlier plan, the two men are confused and even frightened by seeing their fantasy come to life; yet, they realize that they must accept Lulu's presence as if they had kidnapped her in order to pretend to have some control over their environment. They clearly believe the women in their lives have the real control, especially Lorraine, whom they believe has the power to make them disappear, to hear everything they say, and to predict the future.

This fear of women's power reflects a key issue in this play: the male characters' insecure sense of their own masculinity. It is not by chance that many of the objects they cling to for a sense of self are iconic images of masculinity, such as their guns and their cowboy hats. Goose and Tomtom's dilemmas are in many ways an intense exploration of what Jennifer McMillion, in an essay in *David Rabe: A Casebook,* has aptly termed "the cult of male identity." Given the cartoonish quality of the characters, mixed with dialogue that reaches for philosophical stances but remains simplistically inarticu-

late, it is not hard to see why this play has never been produced successfully.

After these difficulties with *Goose and Tomtom,* the 1984 Broadway premiere of *Hurlyburly* (moved from its origin at the Goodman Theatre in Chicago), directed by Nichols, opened with quite a fanfare because of its high-powered cast of well-known actors, including William Hurt, Sigourney Weaver, Keitel, and Christopher Walken. Set in the Hollywood Hills, this play chronicles the lives of four men—Eddie, Phil, Mickey, and Artie—who are separated or divorced from their wives and seem drawn together by their mutual confusion about women and their careers in the Hollywood movie and television industry. The action is mainly focused around the friendship of Eddie and Phil. Eddie shares a house with Mickey, the two of them evidently working together in their jobs as casting directors. Artie, another suit in the industry, and Phil, a would-be actor, are frequent visitors. At the opening of the play, Phil has retreated to Eddie and Mickey's house from arguments with his wife, Susie, an offstage character whose desire to have a baby has caused Phil's current crisis. His subsequent return to her, because he cannot live without her, results in a baby, followed in short order by a divorce that leads Phil to commit suicide by crashing his car. Phil's conflict—that he cannot live without Susie but is terrified of getting her pregnant—is the driving force of much of the play. However, by the end, it seems that the real focus of the play is Eddie's confusion about relationships, and the effect that Phil's death has.

In the course of the play the men's confusion and sense of displacement are evident as they try to figure out how to cope with their relationships, turning often and heavily to the escapes of drugs, alcohol, and television. In regard to the latter, this play falls in line with much of Rabe's earlier critique of television, hinted at in *Sticks and Bones* as a controlling and disillusioning drug. The working title of this play, "Guy's Play," further emphasized the actual focus—the dynamics of male friendships in light of changing gender dynamics in America. In Rabe's afterword to the 1985 printed version, he speaks of the impetus of the play:

> I remember beginning *Hurlyburly* with an impulse that took its shape, at least partly, in a mix of feelings spawned in my own experiences and also from my observations of the prices some men were paying from within their varied armored and defended stances—the current disorientation and accompanying anger many feel at having been flung out from the haven of their sexual and marital contexts and preconceptions.

As Rabe indicates, the play explores the confused and disoriented lives of these men (confusion heightened by their drug-induced stupors) in regard to their relationships both to women and to men. The three women who appear onstage constitute a triumvirate of male fantasies about women: Donna is the young, pliable thing they treat as a sex-pet; Bonnie is the sexually experienced older woman (an "artistic" nude dancer); and Darlene is the sophisticated trophy-girlfriend whom none of them can really obtain. The two offstage women–Phil's wife, Susie, and Eddie's former wife, Agnes–help to round out the stereotypes by providing images of the aggressive earth-mother and the harpy, respectively. Although it would seem that the women should be the source of conflict for the men, especially since Phil's separation from Susie and the mutual attraction that both Eddie and Mickey have for Darlene provide much of the fodder for dialogue, the focus of the play is actually the relationships among the men. Rabe's account of rehearsals for the original production demonstrate how the focus naturally shifted:

> as rehearsal progressed, what we found was that the women came in and did their work rather simply and directly. . . . Meanwhile, the men were bickering and struggling with feelings of competitiveness and resentment, shifting alliances, hurt feelings. . . . In other words, the difficulty in the play was in what the men wanted from and dreaded in one another: who was boss and could anybody be trusted?

Having abandoned their roles as husbands and fathers, these characters are left only with their friendships, which are anything but secure and reassuring. It becomes clear as the play progresses that these men are able to retain their level of friendship only because their relationships are of the most superficial and self-serving kind, or as Mickey says, they are merely "adequate." Even Eddie's seeming devotion to Phil is self-interested, as Mickey points out. He uses Phil as something of an experiment in order to keep himself relatively in control. Phil gives Eddie perspective, or as Mickey says, "Phil is very safe because no matter how far you manage to fall, Phil will be lower. You end up crawling along the sidewalk, Phil's gonna be on his belly in the gutter looking up in wide-eyed admiration."

Eddie's and Phil's characters were a source of controversy between Rabe and Nichols, the original director. Nichols's staging placed the focus squarely on Eddie and also made both Eddie and Phil unsympathetic characters in the way they exploited everyone around them. Rabe's dissatisfaction with Nichols's direction led to his including a lengthy afterword to the 1985 edition and, eventually, to rewrites and a new staging in 1988 that Rabe directed before publishing the 1991 revised version. This production is also notable because Rabe cast Penn as Eddie, evidently turning again to Penn in order to work out a problem with staging. Rabe's afterword to the revised version of *Hurlyburly* indicates that he intended Eddie to be a sympathetic character whose meanness, particularly toward the women in his life, comes from his frustration and pain. As Rabe described his intentions in the interview with Zinman, "I felt that by the end you would be with him completely, and that the play would fall into the tradition of *Look Back in Anger*."

In the revised version, the chief change is the introduction of a gun, carried by Phil, who pulls it out of his pocket to assure Eddie that he has not shot Susie. Phil leaves the gun in his coat at Eddie's house, and in the closing moments of the play, after Phil's death, Eddie finds and puts on Phil's coat, discovering the gun in the pocket. In his final monologue, Eddie rants and raves with gun in hand, clearly getting ready to shoot himself. Rabe's intention is to show that Eddie is on the brink of suicide and is saved only by Donna's unexpected entrance. Eddie's behavior in this last scene as rewritten by Rabe is perhaps more of a regression into childishness than the earlier version indicated, especially as Rabe directed it. Rabe tells of directing this scene as a reenactment of the 1960 children's book *Are You My Mother?*: "As Eddie pursued Donna through that last scene, asking her questions, I told Sean who was playing Eddie to play that idea, Are you my mother?" Regression into childhood becomes suddenly salvation and resolution, and in this way *Hurlyburly* does follow the tradition of John Osborne's *Look Back in Anger* (1956), in which men and women can find peace only in acting out childish fantasies–though whether or not the women of Rabe's play participate, ultimately, in these men's fantasies is debatable.

The title, which Rabe settled upon late in his writing of the play, captures the essence of the off-kilter and chaotic world of the play. Its allusion to William Shakespeare's *Macbeth* (1606) connects it to the ideas of destiny, fate, and personal ambition in that play. However, the heartlessness, solipsism, and ultimate despair that is exhibited by the male characters in *Hurlyburly* is best summed up by Eddie's use of the term as he tries to explain to Bonnie why he has no real sympathy for her having been thrown out of her own car by Phil: "we're all just background in one another's life. Cardboard cutouts bumping around in this vague, you know, hurlyburly, this spin-off of what was once prime time life." The callousness and solipsism that Eddie voices defines the values of the world of this play.

No doubt fueled in part by its all-star cast, *Hurlyburly* ran for 343 performances on Broadway. Critical reactions to the Broadway production were mixed. It was viewed as having moments of brilliance but being generally confused and even laborsome. Its nearly

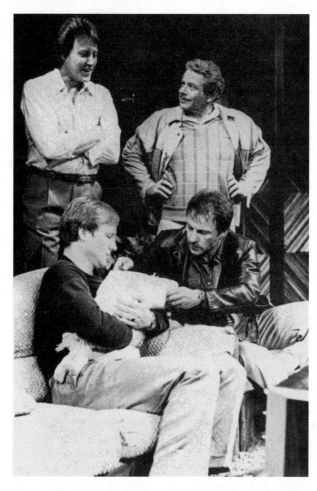

*Christopher Walken and Jerry Stiller (standing) with William Hurt and Harvey Keitel (seated) in the
1984 New York production of* Hurlyburly *(photograph by Martha Swope)*

three-hour length was part of the reason for complaint, as well as its sense of sound and fury signifying nothing in the end—much like Phil's garbled suicide note that Eddie wants to believe holds great truths. However, it was given a new life with a 1998 movie version, again starring Penn and other noted actors, including Kevin Spacey and Meg Ryan.

Rabe's fondness for the characters of *Hurlyburly* not only manifested itself in a revised version that he directed and later a movie but also led to his writing a second play that further developed the characters of Phil and Susie. *Those the River Keeps,* produced initially in Princeton in 1991 and opening Off-Broadway in 1994, is a prequel that follows Phil and his conflicts with Susie over her desire to have a baby and his fear of fatherhood. The events of act 1 lead to the argument that immediately preceded Phil's appearance in act 1 of *Hurlyburly*. The audience also learns more about Phil himself, especially his criminal background, mentioned briefly in *Hurlyburly* through the appearance of Sal, a figure from Phil's days in organized crime. Sal's ominous

presence forces Phil to admit to the secret he has been keeping: that he killed in the past. Phil's and Susie's complete unfitness for parenthood could hardly be more apparent and is something that Rabe was intending to explore, as his preface to the 1995 published version indicates.

The play opens with Susie putting a pair of diapers on a teddy bear, and then hiding the bear from Phil once he comes home. She is desperate to get pregnant, and Phil is more than a little reluctant to produce another child when he is "already a shit father to three kids" from his first marriage. Their inability to come to terms on this issue escalates into an argument that results in Phil's hitting Susie and her throwing him out of the house. By act 2 he is reduced to leaving long messages on the answering machine, hoping Susie will pick up the phone to talk with him, and then sneaking back to the house to get some of his things when she is gone.

The difficulty this couple have in resolving their differences is heightened by the advice of their friends.

Susie's friend Janice has evidently been against her marriage to Phil from the beginning, but it becomes clear in their lengthy conversations that Janice views Susie only in terms of how Susie's life affects her own. Sal, who shows up unexpectedly, expresses his disappointment in how Phil could let a woman lead him around and turn him into a "muke," evidently a derogatory term for someone outside of the mob who does not know how to hold his own with other people. Sal is also self-interested: he wants Phil to come back to the underworld and team up with him as they used to do before Phil went to prison and had what he describes as "a change of heart." Phil's conversations with Sal help to illuminate the violence of his past and the actual simplicity of what he wanted in contrast to that world—a normal life of wife and kids, a family. Yet, as his relationship with Susie demonstrates, such a life is not a simple thing that just happens. References to his first wife and kids indicate that he has already failed once at this task. What he seems to really want in his relationship with Susie is her love. Thus, when she threatens to leave him over his not wanting a baby, he cannot accept her going. Susie, too, wants a baby to have something of her own. And she also ultimately finds herself "in love" with Phil—wanting him physically as much as she wants a baby. The play closes with them in each other's arms, trying to fill the emptiness each has, even as they assert that they are not empty, but ultimately acting out what Phil had described earlier to Sal: "I am lookin' for love in her, and she is lookin' for it in me, and do you know what that means? Neither one of us got any is what it means, and so there ain't any—there ain't any love."

The title of the play is derived from the underworld of Phil's past, and the practice of slicing open the guts of murder victims before dumping them in a river so that they will sink and not rise. The river keeps, then, those who have been sliced open—and it seems that Phil and perhaps Susie have metaphorically had their guts ripped out by the emotional pain they cause one another. The New York production received scathing reviews that noted the heavy-handedness of Rabe's direction and of the dialogue. It closed after only a short run.

Before the unsuccessful production of *Those the River Keeps,* Rabe published a novel, *Recital of the Dog* (1993), which also met with unfavorable reviews. Telling the tale of a man's descent into madness, the novel itself seems to spiral out of control, offering no real sense of purpose or meaning to the work as a whole.

After these two failures, Rabe seems to have redeemed his reputation with *A Question of Mercy,* which opened on 7 February 1997 at the New York Theater Workshop to favorable reviews. Rabe based his play on a 1991 essay published in *The New York Times Magazine* by Richard Selzer, who records his struggle to decide whether or not to help a terminally ill patient commit suicide. The play opens with the character of Dr. Chapman receiving a phone call from a man who requests Chapman's help in the suicide of his lover Anthony, who is suffering horribly from AIDS and wants an easy death as release from his pain. The play explores the moral and emotional dilemmas without preaching, a trap that Rabe has fallen into in the past. Ben Brantley, in his *New York Times* review (26 February 1997), notes that the writing demonstrates "elegance, discipline, restraint, not traits habitually associated with the author."

While Rabe has many champions in the theater, his theatrical works have on the whole been rather uneven. His most powerful work remains the plays of the Vietnam Trilogy. More than twenty years after the premiere of *Streamers,* that play is still considered his best and is his most frequently staged play. The growing body of critical work written about Rabe's plays in general attests to their endurance. His connections with the motion picture industry will probably further enhance his career, since even poorly attended movies tend to draw a much larger audience than even the most successful plays. It seems, however, that his future does remain with the theater, despite forays into movies and novel writing. As the author of *The Basic Training of Pavlo Hummel, Sticks and Bones,* and *Streamers,* Rabe has secured his place as an important playwright of the American theater.

Interviews:
David Savran, "David Rabe," in his *In Their Own Words: Contemporary American Playwrights* (New York: Theatre Communications Group, 1988), pp. 193–206;
Philip C. Kolin, "An Interview with David Rabe," *Journal of Dramatic Theory and Criticism,* 3 (1989): 135–156;
Eric James Schroeder, "David Rabe: 'A Harrowing Audience Experience,'" in his *Vietnam, We've All Been There: Interviews with American Writers* (Westport, Conn. & London: Praeger, 1992), pp. 196–213;
Stephanie Coen, "When Reason Fails," *American Theatre,* 14, no. 6 (1997): 22.

Bibliography:
Philip C. Kolin, *David Rabe: A Stage History and a Primary and Secondary Bibliography* (New York: Garland, 1988).

References:
Jack Barbera, "The Emotion of Multitude and David Rabe's *Streamers,*" *American Drama,* 7, no. 1 (1997): 50–66;

Philip Biedler, *American Literature and the Experience of Vietnam* (Athens: University Press of Georgia, 1982);

Janet Brown, *Taking Center Stage: Feminism in Contemporary U.S. Drama* (Metuchen, N.J.: Scarecrow Press, 1991);

N. Bradley Christie, "David Rabe's Theater of War and Remembering," in *Search and Clear: Critical Responses to Selected Literature and Films of the Vietnam War,* edited by William J. Searle (Bowling Green, Ohio: Bowling Green State University Popular Press, 1988), pp. 105–115;

Marianthe Colakis, "The House of Atreus Myth in the Seventies and Eighties: David Rabe's *The Orphan* and Joyce Carol Oates's *Angel of Light*," *Classical and Modern Literature,* 9, no. 2 (1989): 125–130;

Pamela Cooper, "David Rabe's *Sticks and Bones:* The Adventures of Ozzie and Harriet," *Modern Drama,* 29 (1986): 613–625;

Janet S. Hertzbach, "The Plays of David Rabe: A World of Streamers," in *Essays on Contemporary American Drama,* edited by Hedwig Bock and Albert Wertheim (Munich: Hueber, 1981), pp. 173–186;

Richard L. Homan, "American Playwrights in the 1970s: Rabe and Shepard," *Critical Quarterly,* 24, no. 1 (1982): 73–82;

Catherine Hughes, *Plays, Politics, and Polemics* (New York: Drama Book Specialists, 1973);

Philip C. Kolin, "David Rabe," in *American Playwrights Since 1945,* edited by Kolin (New York: Greenwood Press, 1988), pp. 349–368;

Kolin, "Staging *Hurlyburly:* David Rabe's Parable for the 1980s," *Theatre Annual,* 41 (1986): 63–78;

Carla J. McDonough, *Staging Masculinity: Male Identity in Contemporary American Drama* (Jefferson, N.C.: McFarland, 1997);

David Radavich, "Collapsing Male Myths: Rabe's Tragicomic *Hurlyburly*," *American Drama,* 3, no. 1 (1993): 1–16;

Carol Rosen, *Plays of Impasse: Contemporary Drama Set in Confining Institutions* (Princeton: Princeton University Press, 1979);

Rodney Simard, *Postmodern Drama: Contemporary Playwrights in America and Britain* (New York: University Press of America, 1984);

Robert Vorlicky, *Act Like a Man: Challenging Masculinities in American Drama* (Ann Arbor: University of Michigan Press, 1995);

Toby Silverman Zinman, ed. *David Rabe: A Casebook* (New York & London: Garland, 1991).

Papers:

Mugar Memorial Library at Boston University has a collection of David Rabe's papers.

Mary Shaw

(25 January 1854 – 18 May 1929)

Maria Papanikolaou
Texas A&M University

PLAY PRODUCTIONS: *The Woman of It; or, Our Friends the Anti-Suffragists,* New York, Hotel Astor, January 1912;
The Parrot Cage, New York, Gamut Club, 1913.

BOOKS: *The Parrot Cage* (Chicago: Dramatic Publishing Company, 1914);
The Woman of It; or, Our Friends the Anti-Suffragists (Chicago: Dramatic Publishing Company, 1914).

SELECTED PERIODICAL PUBLICATIONS–UNCOLLECTED: "A Defense of Ibsen and Ibsenism," *New York Dramatic News* (25 December 1905): 41;
"The Psychology of an Audience," *Saturday Evening Post* (8 February 1911): 6–7, 25;
"The Boston Museum and Daly's Theater," *Saturday Evening Post* (20 May 1911): 14–15, 34–35;
"Producing a Play on a Shoestring," *Saturday Evening Post* (8 July 1911): 10–11, 40;
"The Actress on the Road," *McClure's* (July 1911): 263–272;
"The Cheap Theater," *Smith Magazine* (January 1912): 11, 638–642;
"The Box-office Value of Tears," *Saturday Evening Post* (24 February 1912): 14–15, 28;
"The Box-office Value of Laughter," *Saturday Evening Post* (9 March 1912): 10–11, 48;
"The Stage Wisdom of Joseph Jefferson," *Century* (March 1912): 731–737;
"My 'Immoral' Story," *McClure's* (April 1912): 684–694;
"The Human Side of Joseph Jefferson," *Century* (January 1913): 378–385.

Mary Shaw

Mary Shaw was not only one of the leading actresses of her day but also a feminist, suffrage activist, and, at times, a writer. Her literary credits include magazine articles on acting and producing plays, and others in which she spoke out about the controversial plays in which she acted, including those in the genre of New Drama by Henrik Ibsen and George Bernard Shaw. Mary Shaw also wrote two prosuffrage one-act plays, produced locally. Despite her fame and literary activity, Shaw's name has been all but forgotten by scholars, and her contribution to the American stage is only slowly being recognized and discussed. When she is mentioned at all, it is in connection to starring roles in ground-breaking productions of radical plays brought to the American stage. But Shaw devoted her life, public and private, to improving the plight of women throughout the country and serving as an example of an independent woman.

Born on 25 January 1854, the eldest daughter of socially prominent Levi W. and Margaret Keating Shaw, Mary Shaw was an exception to the norm of actresses being working women from the lower classes. Many young girls sought careers on the stage because they lacked education and therefore had few options for legal employment. But Shaw's father, who worked for the Boston fire department and eventually joined the public buildings department, and her mother, who emigrated from Ireland, both encouraged their daughter to continue her schooling. Shaw graduated from the Girls' Highland Normal School in 1871 and taught for five years at the Minot School in the West End of Boston. In 1879 she married Henry Leach, with whom she had a son, Arthur. Shortly after their marriage, Shaw opted for a career on the stage, claiming that she found teaching too constricting. Undocumented legend says that Shaw's interest in the stage increased after a series of elocution lessons she took to improve her voice control, having strained her voicebox so much in the classroom. Regardless of why she decided to choose this career path, she made her debut at the age of twenty-six, when she joined the Boston Museum stock company. During her first season, Shaw learned a wide range of roles. The nature of stock companies during the latter part of the nineteenth century made the Boston Museum company a valuable training ground for her. The limited cast in such a company meant that all of the actors played a variety of parts, and during this period, playwrights attempted to influence the production of a play by including detailed character descriptions and stage directions dealing with dramatic interaction. Shaw was thus able to learn from her fellow actors, the stage manager, and careful study of the script.

Two years later her career was going well, but her personal life faltered as she lost her husband to illness and was left to raise her son on her own. In 1885 she married the Duc de Brissac, a French actor-manager in Helena Modjeska's company, which Shaw had joined in 1883, but the relationship soon failed. Some scholars, including her biographer John D. Irving, argue that this incident might have been beneficial to Shaw: "emancipated . . . from the dependency upon a husband and enjoying the independence which comes with a successful career, she devoted her energies to urging her fellow women to take a more responsible attitude toward their own lives and the lives of their families and children."

It is important to understand Shaw's political background and the context that shaped her plays and periodical articles, for they follow the trend of actress activists on both sides of the Atlantic during this time period. Shaw's activism, like that of many of her contemporaries, began early in her career; her choice of profession radically broke from the norm of her social class. Throughout her life as an actress, Shaw continued to couple her feminist roles with an equally active political agenda off the stage. People advised her that speaking out on controversial political topics might be detrimental to her career, but Shaw discounted such advice and even made it a point to speak in cities in which she toured with various productions across the country.

In 1899 her political activism took her abroad when she accepted an invitation to be one of several American delegates to the International Woman's Congress in London. Such leadership roles in women's activities continued throughout her career. She was elected as one of the five vice presidents of the Professional Women's League of New York, an organization consisting primarily of actresses, in 1907. In addition to working on various philanthropic projects, the members also taught their younger counterparts valuable skills in dressmaking (so that they could make their own costumes). Older members also donated parts of their wardrobes to the club collection, and all members could participate in classes in "languages, art, music, business, law, and debates and discussions," as scholar Albert Auster described. Their all-female minstrel shows and performances of William Shakespeare plays were hits, and by 1910 the club grew to six hundred members.

Shaw also played an instrumental role in the creation in the fall of 1913 of the Gamut Club, a more relaxed group than the League that soon had a membership of two hundred women from all professions. A year after its founding, the group led a protest of more than fifteen thousand women opposed to World War I. Shaw took her experience as an actress to the university circuit as well; she frequented Columbia University, where toward the end of her life she lectured twice a week in a course on modern drama.

Shaw's experience in modern drama began in 1899 when she came in contact with the work of Henrik Ibsen, who altered her philosophies and her acting style forever. Under the direction of Emanuel Reicher, known as the "father of American acting," Shaw played Mrs. Alving in an 1899 New York production of Ibsen's *Ghosts* (1881). Six years later she was writing "A Defense of Ibsen and Ibsenism" for the *New York Dramatic News*.

In 1905 Shaw became involved in one of the most controversial productions of her career, playing the title role in George Bernard Shaw's *Mrs. Warren's Profession* (1898) under the direction of August Daly at the Garrick Theatre in New York. In speaking of her interpretation of former prostitute Kitty Warren, Shaw claimed that her primary interest centered on the relationship of Kitty with her daughter, Vivie. She called the play one "written for women about women," and she praised what she considered its two primary ideas: "a bad woman can be a good mother," and "a daughter should not sacrifice herself." Nonetheless, the production created controversy in the city of New York because of the frank discussion of Kitty's profession. Tickets were going for as much as $30 each, and reporters from the *New York Sun* passed out ballots for the audience to vote on whether the play was fit to be seen. Of the approximately 900 people who attended, more than half cast ballots, with 304 voting for the play and 272 against it. The police commissioner ignored the vote, closing the play the next day and arresting everyone in connection with the performance. This censure did not stop Shaw, who later obtained the rights and took the production on tour in 1907 and 1908. When the play was performed in Los Angeles, Shaw delivered a talk titled "Modern Drama and Its Relation to Women," in which she told her (mostly female) audience that it was their job to go to the theater. Women alone, she said, could understand and appreciate these plays, and then go on to influence men (who could not feel or understand them) to mobilize for a better society.

Shaw also acted in suffrage plays, including the American debut of Elizabeth Robins's 1907 play, *Votes for Women,* in March 1909. While it closed after only six performances, some scholars claim that this play acted as a catalyst for Shaw's own playwriting. Her writing career seemed to be a natural extension of her public speaking experiences. She began by doing a series of journal articles: in 1911 she wrote a piece titled "The Psychology of the Audience" for the *Saturday Evening Post.* Its popularity garnered Shaw a contract to write "a number of articles dealing with theatrical life . . . sparks from a seething crucible of experience and activity," according to Irving. While the articles were meant to be primarily entertaining, Shaw depicted decent women able to earn their livings through careers on the stage and showed women that in the theater they could gain respectable employment that was also profitable.

Shaw also contributed two one-act plays, both of which dealt with suffrage. The first, *The Woman of It; or, Our Friends the Anti-Suffragists,* was first performed at the Hotel Astor in New York in 1912. Suffrage plays were normally written to be staged easily and inexpensively, and usually followed one of three major trends: charwoman plays (to highlight the range of classes affected by the lack of voting rights); celebrations of women's accomplishments (Cicely Hamilton's 1910 play, *A Pageant of Great Women,* is one example); or farces that worked to blast holes in the logic of antisuffragist arguments. *The Woman of It* followed this last trend. Set in an Anti-Suffrage Club, the action centers around the antisuffragists rehearsing the speeches they will deliver at the Hearing of the Legislative Committee. The women decide to invite two guests, Miss Berry and Miss Foster, to observe, hoping to sway these women to their cause.

After Mrs. Allright calls the meeting to attention, the members repeat their pledge:

> to remember each day and remind other women every hour that there are only two great moments in a woman's life. One, when she gives her first kiss to her lover, the other when she gives her first kiss to her own little baby. And, no matter what else she may have, what else she may gain, the woman who misses these two great moments is still a failure.

From this pledge stems a great discussion of the "failures" who did not meet these criteria, including Queen Elizabeth I and Susan B. Anthony. Mrs. Grundy explains to the guests that these women may get praise, but are not revered. After a brief discussion, the speeches begin. Mrs. Allright opens with the common antisuffragist proclamation that the woman's place is in the home. True to the suffragist-play formula, Miss Moore immediately raises protest, wondering if the men on the legislative committee might find it odd that these women do not practice what they preach. Mrs. Allright brushes her aside and introduces Mrs. Sweet, who comes to inform the men in her mock audience that she knows nothing about suffrage, does not want to know, and that she and other women ought to be protected by their husbands. Miss Berry wonders what, exactly, she needs protecting from. Mrs. Sweet, of course, cannot answer.

Again, Shaw and other suffragists depict these common antisuffrage arguments as silly old tropes about woman's role and woman's place that have lost all meaning and must be reexamined. Mrs. Sweet continues with a story about a suffragist who did not recognize her baby, upon which all of the members begin to weep. Miss Noodle, the single member of the group, then gets up and makes a speech about wanting to marry, stating that if she were thought of as part of the suffragist New Woman group, she might be deemed unattractive and uninterested in marriage. Her speech concludes with a plea to the gentlemen to "fix it so the girl of the future will have a show." Mrs. Pure-Drivel follows, introduced by one of the most interesting explanatory authors' notes in suffrage one-acts. Shaw explains that Mrs. Pure-Drivel in her speech ought to "keep . . . the Circe tone and manner of luring men through sex attraction. The manner sexual, the matter she speaks supposedly intellectual, is what brings out the humor of her role." For Shaw to confront not only the logic of the antisuffragist arguments but the manners in which they speak is unusual and perhaps reflective of Shaw's awareness of body language and image through her training as an actress.

*Shaw (seated) as Kitty Warren and Catherine Countess as her daughter, Vivie, in a scene from act
4 of a 1907 production of George Bernard Shaw's* Mrs. Warren's Profession

Holes in the arguments abound, and Misses Moore, Foster, and Berry do exactly what the playwright strives for among those riding the political fence. The antisuffragists' silliness makes the young women realize that fighting for suffrage might be the most respectable thing to do for all women. Or, as Miss Berry says, the antisuffragists "guy the 'utterly womanly' so successfully that the most indifferent woman flies to suffrage as a haven of dignity and self respect." While the format is simple so that it is easy to stage, and the style is more political than poetic, the play reveals Shaw as a woman dedicated to and well-versed in the theatrical activity connected to the suffrage cause. The play is also a chief synopsis of arguments for and against the right to vote.

It is difficult to find even a mention of *The Woman of It* in discussions of Shaw or suffragist theater, however. Anyone who mentions Shaw as playwright at all discusses *The Parrot Cage,* first performed by the Gamut Club in 1913 and (as was usual for a work of its kind) played at other suffrage meetings according to the needs of the organizers. *The Parrot Cage* is distinctive among suffrage plays for its structure, more symbolic in nature than overtly political. The symbols are easily translat-

able for any audience member, however. Sitting in a parrots' cage are six birds: Philistine, Free-Souled, Reasoning, Rationalist, Idealistic, and Theological Parrots. The other character in the cast is a disembodied "Man's Voice." Much like the antisuffragists repeating men's empty tropes in the earlier play, the parrots begin by repeating the Man's "Pretty Polly." Free-Souled then continues her repetition of "I want to be free!" while the other parrots admonish her. Philistine warns her that she must play by the rules so that she can be let out of the cage and fly in the big room. Reasoning explains that because parrots are always in cages, it proves that they belong in cages. Idealistic asks the other parrots to stop arguing and explains that all parrots must subscribe to a higher mission of "happiness of a private family, by whistling and saying 'Pretty Polly'!"

The discussions are reminiscent of those made in Shaw's earlier play. Idealist represents all of the antisuffragists, and there are arguments that sound twice as illogical when put into the mouths and the world of the domesticated parrots. But somehow, the cry of the Free-Souled Parrot sounds more sad, more pathetic, more trapped and frustrated in this play. However humorous most suffragist plays try to be at some point, there is nothing funny in *The Parrot Cage*. Free-Souled is frustrated by the boundaries of the closed big room and the even smaller one of the cage she shares with the others. If Shaw can be seen as using this parrot as her mouthpiece, she seems to be almost embittered in her struggle.

Free-Souled begs her sisters to help the younger parrots that still have unclipped wings and claims that her cage-mates hold her back only because they themselves are clipped and have no power to move forward. But her anger, and perhaps Shaw's frustration, ceases when she breaks her chains. Free-Souled begs her older sisters to follow her, claiming that "even if you fall and perish, at least you will die free parrots." This suggestion is unusual in a suffrage play. Playwrights informing and entertaining suffrage audiences rarely mentioned, let alone promulgated, the risk of death to achieve freedom. Women such as the protagonist in Robins and Florence Bell's *Alan's Wife* (1893) had died in plays for crimes, of course. But it is unusual to have a character overtly pronounce that attempting to live a life in freedom, defying the social order, might invite a death better than continuing in the usual ways. The play ends with the fading voice of Free-Souled crying, "Follow me!" as the Man's Voice overlaps, repeating, "Polly's place is in the cage." There is no happy ending in this play. Shaw's final note describes the remaining parrots "huddled together in the center of the perch, listening to the distant voice of the Free-Soul Parrot, oblivious of all else till the curtain falls." Shaw, who had been making speeches on suffrage and women's rights for more than a decade by the time she wrote this play, made brasher arguments in *The Parrot Cage* than in any of her previous work.

Throughout her life Shaw, who died of heart disease on 19 May 1929, worked to encourage other women to advance the cause of women everywhere. As Irving explains, "Mary Shaw was only one of many women who dedicated their lives to the proposition that women and men are not only equal, but also have to assume fully their respective responsibilities, shared or individual, in the ordering of their society so that we all might be free."

Biography:

John D. Irving, *Mary Shaw: Actress, Suffragist, Activist (1854–1929)* (New York: Arno Press, 1982).

References:

Albert Auster, *Actresses and Suffragists: Women in the American Theater, 1890–1920* (New York: Praeger, 1984);

Bettina Friedl, ed., *On To Victory: Propaganda Plays of the Woman Suffrage Movement* (Boston: Northeastern University Press, 1987);

Robert A. Schanke, "Mary Shaw: A Fighting Champion," in *Women in American Theatre: Careers, Images, Movements,* edited by Helen Krich Chinoy and Linda Walsh Jenkins (New York: Crown, 1981), pp. 98–107.

Papers:

The Robinson Locke Collection of the Library and Museum of the Performing Arts at Lincoln Center has the largest single holding of material on Mary Shaw. The library also houses a separate Mary Shaw clipping file.

Martin Sherman

(22 December 1938 –   )

William C. Boles
Rollins College

PLAY PRODUCTIONS: *A Solitary Thing,* with music by Stanley Silverman, Oakland, California, Mills College, 9 September 1963;

Fat Tuesday, New York, Herbert Berghof Playwrights Foundation, 1966;

Next Year in Jerusalem, New York, Herbert Berghof Playwrights Foundation, 8 June 1968;

Change, libretto by Sherman, lyrics by Ed Kresley, music by Drey Shepperd, New York, BMI Music Theatre Workshop, 1969;

The Night Before Paris, New York, Actors Studio, 1969; Edinburgh, Traverse Theatre, 1970;

Things Went Badly in Westphalia, Storrs, University of Connecticut, 1971;

Passing By, New York, Playwrights Horizons, 5 March 1974; London, Almost Free Theatre, 9 June 1975;

New York! New York!, contributor, New York, Playwrights Horizons, 26 April 1975;

Cracks, Waterford, Connecticut, Eugene O'Neill Theatre Center/National Playwrights Conference, 31 July 1975; Oldham, Coliseum Theatre, 10 October 1981;

Rio Grande, New York, Playwrights Horizons, 11 November 1976;

Blackout, New York, Ensemble Studio Theatre, 1978;

Bent, Waterford, Conn., O'Neill Theatre Center, 1978; London, Royal Court Theatre, 3 May 1979; New York, New Amsterdam Theatre, 2 December 1979;

Messiah, London, Hampstead Theatre, 9 December 1982; New York, Manhattan Theatre Club, 11 December 1984;

When She Danced, Guildford, U.K., Yvonne Arnaud Theatre, 27 November 1985; New York, Playwrights Horizon, 19 February 1990;

A Madhouse in Goa, London, Lyric Theatre, Hammersmith, 28 April 1989; New York, Second Stage, 18 November 1997—comprises *A Tale for a King* and *Keeps Rainin' All the Time;*

Some Sunny Day, London, Hampstead Theatre, 11 April 1996;

Martin Sherman (photograph by John Haynes)

Rose, London, Cottesloe Theatre (National Theatre), 24 June 1999.

BOOKS: *Bent* (Ashover, U.K.: Amber Lane, 1979; New York & London: S. French, 1979);

Messiah (Oxford: Amber Lane, 1982);

Cracks (London: S. French, 1986);

When She Danced (Oxford: Amber Lane, 1988; New York: S. French, 1988);

A Madhouse in Goa (Oxford: Amber Lane, 1989; New York & London: S. French, 1998);

Some Sunny Day (Oxford: Amber Lane, 1996);

Rose (London: Methuen, 1999).

PRODUCED SCRIPTS: *Don't Call Me Mama Anymore,* contributor, television, CBS, 1972;

Clothes in the Wardrobe, adapted from Alice Thomas Ellis's novel, television, BBC Films, 1992;

released in the United States as *The Summer House,* motion picture, 1993;

Alive and Kicking, motion picture, Channel Four Films, 1997;

Bent, motion picture, Bent Productions, Sarah Radclyffe Productions, Channel Four Films, Nippon Film Development and Finance, 1997.

OTHER: *Things Went Badly in Westphalia,* in *The Best Short Plays of 1970,* edited by Stanley Richards (Philadelphia: Chilton, 1970), pp. 371–408;

Passing By, in *Gay Plays, Volume 1,* edited by Michael Wilcox (London: Methuen, 1984), pp. 99–120.

Martin Sherman is the author of *Bent* (1979), one of the significant American plays of the twentieth century because of its historical reexamination of the Holocaust and realistic depiction of homosexuals. Yet, he is one of the most underappreciated and unknown American playwrights, because he and his plays defy easy compartmentalization or classification. Sherman, descended from immigrant roots, is a gay, Jewish American artist. He repeatedly refuses to be characterized by only one aspect of his personality. In a 1980 interview with Terry Helbing, Sherman argued that gay persons should not be typified as just gay; instead he would "like to see everybody who's gay living very openly as gay within broad society and being who they are very freely. Being gay wouldn't be just who they are; all aspects of who they are would shine forth."

The same philosophy of diversification is present in his plays, which document the complexity of Sherman's varied interests. His work defies the common domestic focus of American drama—parental and sibling angst, marital strife, and middle-class tensions. Instead, his plays are almost British in nature, as they foreground political, historical, and sexual issues over domestic concerns (which may explain why many people think Sherman is British). He has written about Jewish Poles in 1665, homosexual persecution by the Nazis, dystopian chaos in America, Isadora Duncan during her final years, a spy-obsessed Egypt during World War II, and a homosexual couple who contract hepatitis. While his plays cover a variety of topics, a common theme does predominate. Sherman explained to an interviewer in 1995,

My father was born in Russia and my roots are in the Yiddish culture, which has a built-in sense of exile and rootlessness. The characters in my plays exist outside conventional society. They're generally members of an oppressed minority, whether they're gay, Jewish or artists. Because I belong to all those groups, perhaps that gives me some understanding, a sense of shared compassion.

Sherman also became an exile from the United States when he moved to London in 1980.

Martin Sherman was born in Philadelphia on 22 December 1938 to two Russian immigrants: Joseph, a lawyer, and Julia Sherman. He was an only child and grew up in Camden, New Jersey. His first introduction to the theater came at age six, and seeing a pre-Broadway version of *Guys and Dolls* (1950) starring Alfred Lunt and Lynn Fontanne was an early prompt for Sherman's interest in the theater. Talking to Sheridan Morley in 1983, Sherman recalled, "At 12 I joined the Mae Desmond Children's Players and went all around Pennsylvania being a tall dwarf in *Snow White.*" When he was old enough, Sherman would regularly take the bus into Philadelphia to attend performances. As he told Matt Wolf in 1997: "I was the only kid in junior high school to have seen *Camino Real.*" Augmenting his trips into Philadelphia, once a year he would also visit an aunt who lived in New York City. He hated school and has said that these annual trips made the school year palatable. In 1956 he enrolled at Boston University, where he earned a B.F.A. in 1960. In college he continued performing, but quickly realized that acting was not his forte. He then turned to writing plays as well as librettos for musicals. After graduation, he joined the Actors Studio to study under Harold Clurman. Sherman told Morley that he credits his tutelage there as the reason "why all my plays are written for actors rather than the directors or critics that my contemporaries seem to write for." Sherman was appointed playwright in residence at Mills College in Oakland, California, where *A Solitary Thing* (1963), a rock musical, premiered.

In the late 1960s Sherman had two plays performed in the New York area—*Next Year in Jerusalem* (1968) and *The Night Before Paris* (1969). *Things Went Badly in Westphalia,* the title of which comes from Voltaire's *Candide* (1759), became Sherman's first published play in 1970, when it was included in *The Best Short Plays of 1970.* In it Sherman continued his interest in creating a dramatic rock musical. In fact, *Things Went Badly in Westphalia* is similar to Sam Shepard's *The Tooth of Crime* (1972). Both playwrights depict a United States in which the rules of society, or "the game" in the case of Shepard's play, are ravaged. However, while Shepard's play is localized in its focus on the duel for supremacy between Hoss and Crow, Sherman's play spans the entire dystopian United States. Building on the student protests, political assassinations, and riots of 1968, Sherman extrapolates them to create a theatrical world rocked with killings, brutality, and seceding cities governed by hate groups.

The play features an idealistic protagonist named Joshua, a popular folk singer who at the beginning of

ВОТ ЭТО И КРАСОТА

WHEN SHE DANCED
MARTIN SHERMAN

Cover for Sherman's play about dancer Isadora Duncan

he discovers all the inhabitants have been crucified, including his former lover, Joanne. The play ends as Joshua sings a song of hope while the military forces come increasingly closer.

Joshua remains optimistic throughout his journey. He tells Lisa, "I keep on loving. Somehow, I always feel that something good is going to happen. It's around the corner. You just got to get there." Each time Joshua professes the desire to survive, an even worse fate awaits him. After each assault, Joshua's situation worsens as his clothes are torn, his body mangled, his magazine-cover handsome face irreparably damaged. He is raped, dragged behind a motorcycle, handcuffed, flogged, and made a party to the deaths of many individuals. However, Sherman's most cynical depiction of Joshua's optimism occurs in the final monologue, in which Joshua debates whether to commit suicide. Failing to recognize the gravity of his situation, he is more concerned with the taste and size of the pills. He decides to remain alive because a suicide attempt would be inconvenient. As he plays his guitar and sings while the war noises surround him, he still embraces his philosophy that "something good may happen."

Even though *Things Went Badly in Westphalia* is structurally problematic and the characters are simplistic, the play starkly comments on an arduous time in United States history. It is also a dark tale about the inability of the artist to provoke a change in the society around him, and in that respect the play is an early example of Sherman's interest in an outsider's relationship with the rest of the world.

While *Things Went Badly in Westphalia* displays a chaotic world of violence and hatred, *Passing By* (1974) presents a world of compassion, tenderness, and friendship. In his introduction to *Passing By* in *Gay Plays, Volume 1* (1984), Sherman wrote that he was hoping "to create a gentle, romantic and loving encounter between two men, in which their gayness was simply a fact—completely easy and open and never a problem." Despite the strides made in homosexual activism after the Stonewall riots in 1969, Sherman faced difficulties finding actors who would play homosexual characters openly and honestly. Instead, in the Playwrights Horizons production the actors camped up their roles through limp-wristed stereotypes. Upset with the initial production, Sherman sent the script to the powerful British literary agent Peggy Ramsey, who forwarded it to the Gay Sweatshop, who produced it at the Almost Free Theatre in the summer of 1975.

Except for a short opening scene in a movie theater, where Toby and Simon exchange first glances, the play takes place entirely in the studio apartment of Toby, an artist intent on leaving New York and moving to Paris for the betterment of his art. The first act

the play has finally decided to get involved in politics. Then, the presidential candidate he supports is assassinated. Joshua and his lover, Joanne, demoralized by the violence, debate escaping from their walled-in city; but before they can decide, a bomb blows up their apartment. A wounded Joshua, thinking Joanne has been killed, proceeds on a cross-country journey to find a safe haven from the chaos. Sherman uses an episodic structure to show Joshua's interaction with several factions of fractured America, including the Knights of Ganymede, a homosexual group, who capture Joshua and use him as their concubine; the Governor of New Orleans, who has Joshua publicly flogged; and the Hell Riders, who gang-rape Lisa, Joshua's young female companion. Trying to rescue Lisa, Joshua pledges to take her to Flower City, an oasis of love in the midst of the violence. However, before they can escape, Lisa is killed in an Indian attack. The Indians are, in turn, slaughtered by the police. After escaping from a police chain gang, Joshua finally reaches Flower City, where traces the two men's relationship from its one-night-stand roots to their eventual friendship. Simon, recently moved to New York, is a former Olympic medal winner in diving. He tells Toby that he moved to New York to break into sports broadcasting. However, he later reveals that he relocated to New York to escape the stultifying situation in Miami, where no one appreciated him except for his perfectly tanned body. In New York he hopes to discover who he really is.

Sherman's interest in presenting a realistic homosexual relationship becomes clear in the second scene of the play, the morning after Toby and Simon picked each other up at the movie theater. Sherman deftly uses dialogue to produce a scene of poignancy and respect. Their relationship is not based on sex; in fact, sex never plays an integral part in the play, unlike Sherman's later work. Sherman presents their homosexual one-night stand as far more respectable and compassionate than the stereotypical depictions of heterosexual one-night stands fraught with uncomfortable realizations and hasty departures. The rest of the first act develops the relationship between the two men while they, in turn, try to establish identities separate from their past lovers. Throughout, Toby prepares for Paris, but his trip is delayed with the revelation that he has hepatitis. When Simon visits his bedridden friend, he discovers that he has hepatitis too.

The second act details their five-week incubation period in Toby's apartment. It is a challenging task for Sherman's playwriting skills because the action revolves around two bedridden characters, but Sherman relies upon the odd-couple qualities of the two men—the artist versus the athlete—as the two squabble with one another about subjects ranging from characters on a soap opera to apple juice. Through their discussions, Toby and Simon learn more about one another while also beginning to show their own sense of individuality. Toby utters the most important thematic lines in the play when he explains why he has to go to Paris without Simon: "I want you to come with me so badly . . . But you're right. You can't. If I stopped you from doing what you wanted, I'd kill you. If you kept me in this awful city, you'd kill me. . . . if you're true to yourself, whatever that is, you're immortal." Once cured, Toby goes off to Paris to paint, while Simon sublets the apartment.

As Sherman intended, *Passing By* successfully presents homosexual characters as real people. The play was well received by the London theater critics, and more importantly, by Sherman himself. He remarked in his introduction that the London production

was a revelation and a turning point for me. Writing for the theatre had, until then, filled me with despair; I

was penniless, I was usually unproduced, and when I *was* produced, it was improperly so. For the first time my work came truly alive on a stage. . . . It no longer seemed quite so foolhardy to go on writing.

In 1983, the success of *Bent* and a greater comfort level among producers and actors with realistic theatrical depictions of homosexuality led to a revival of *Passing By* in New York. However, by this time AIDS had appeared, and the public was erroneously labeling it a gay disease. Because of the negative publicity linking AIDS and homosexual intercourse, Sherman decided to stop the production: "I cancelled it for fear that the tragic AIDS epidemic raging through New York would throw the story of two men who happen to contract hepatitis into a completely misleading light and fan some of the misconceived and prejudiced linkage of homosexuality and physical illness that was then popular in the American press."

A year prior to the New York premiere of *Passing By,* Sherman received a grant from the Harriet Wurlitzer Foundation. In the autumn of 1973, Taos, New Mexico, became Sherman's home, and there he wrote *Cracks* (1975). With a cast featuring Meryl Streep, Christopher Lloyd, and Jill Eikenberry, *Cracks* opened at the Eugene O'Neill Theatre Center in the same year as the Gay Sweatshop's production of *Passing By*.

Critics have compared *Cracks* to the plays of Joe Orton and to an Agatha Christie play on drugs. The play takes place in the California home of Rick, a musician, who is murdered in the first scene. As in most mystery plays in which a murderer roams free, the ability of the victims to escape or contact the outside world is conveniently hindered by some natural occurrence. In this case, an earthquake hits the area, causing a tree to fall across the driveway in front of the garage, knocking out the phones and propelling the house into occasionally convenient (for the murderer) blackouts.

Cracks shows Sherman's maturing ability to handle dialogue and character. Sherman displays a talent for comedy and strident social satire as he skewers drug usage, psychotherapy, multiple personalities, pornography, actresses, sex-change operations, and the art world. The play is filled with 1970s stereotypes tweaked by Sherman's imagination: Jade, a seventeen-year-old girl who seduced Rick and lives only for sex; Clay, Rick's lawyer, actually a former attorney turned pornographer because of his disenchantment with the law; Gideon, the envious guitar player from Rick's band; Maggie, Rick's current lover and an actress who is a "star"; Roberta, Rick's bodyguard and a recipient of a sex-change operation; Irene, Rick's persistent cousin, who actively tries to determine the killer's identity; Sammy, a Jew who is about to enter the monkhood at a Benedictine parish; and Nadine, who admits that while she would not kill Rick, her alternate personality, Cynthia, would.

Cracks not only parodies mysteries but also effectively works as a sex farce. Sherman, though, is not interested in playing by the rules of the murder-mystery genre, since he is not concerned with revealing the killer's identity. In fact, he subverts the entire structure by killing everyone. Instead, *Cracks* is a light, amusing romp that pokes fun at Hollywood, vanity, and the crass prevalence of commercialism. *Cracks* is the Sherman play closest to the vein of mainstream theater, and the positive response from the Eugene O'Neill Center production reflected that fact.

Based on the strength of the out-of-town production, New York producers wanted to move the play to the city. Sherman remarked on his newfound celebrity in his introduction to *Cracks* in *Gay Plays. Volume 2* (1984), "For someone whose work had been totally ignored until then, . . . I did suddenly have many new friends. And dinner invitations. Back in New York strangers smiled at me on the street." Shortly thereafter, the play was put into production. However, because of the misguided interference of its producer, the play was stripped of its most compelling attributes: its originality and humor. The producer found the audience's laughter offensive to the real meaning of the play, although she never told Sherman what she thought that meaning was. The rehearsal period became torturous for him. "The highpoint" of his frustration, Sherman wrote in his introduction, "occurred when the producer presented a twelve year old student who was 'interested in theatre' and had ideas for rewrites. . . . Opening night. I lay in a back aisle, coiled in a foetal ball, listening to the stunning, spectacular sound of silence."

Despite the lackluster production and the stony silence of the New York critics, *Cracks* was revived in 1977 at Playwrights Horizons. It later played in Oldham, England in 1981, and was then anthologized in a collection of gay plays. In 1993 it was revived at King's Head Theatre in London. Despite the bad experience, Sherman wrote in his introduction to the play that he acquired a philosophy of how to deal with critical response: "The experience proved profitable when years later I had a 'success' in the same city. By then I knew that it mattered not if they were throwing confetti or tomatoes—the best thing to do was to duck and get on with it."

The "later" success was *Bent,* Sherman's best-known and Pulitzer Prize–nominated play about the treatment of homosexuals by the Nazis, an aspect of the Holocaust that had never really been addressed. In a 1987 interview with David Galligan Sherman revealed, "What's been so gratifying is that *Bent* has changed the

perception of history. Today, when the topic of Nazi prison camps is discussed, gays are always included. They absolutely were *not* before *Bent.*" Sherman stumbled upon the idea for the play while assisting at a Gay Sweatshop rehearsal of Drew Griffiths and Noel Greig's *As Time Goes By* (1977), which details three important time periods for homosexuals: 1896 and the trial of Oscar Wilde; Germany in the early 1930s during the Nazi oppression and eventual incarceration of homosexuals; and Stonewall. In the section on Germany, he heard mention of the pink triangles that the Nazis made homosexuals wear. In *Bent* the character of Horst explains the significance of the pink triangles and other color-coded symbols used by the Nazis to designate their various prisoners: "If you're queer, that's what you wear. If you're a Jew, a yellow star. Political—a red triangle. Criminal—green. Pink's the lowest." After seeing the rehearsals for *As Time Goes By,* Sherman later admitted to Galligan: "It hit me like *that* and I knew I wanted to write a play about the subject." Sherman was also inspired by an article on the same topic in *Christopher Street Magazine.* Impressed with the Gay Sweatshop production of *Passing By,* Sherman offered *Bent* to them, but the group passed, stating that the play deserved a production and audience beyond the scope of Gay Sweatshop's capabilities.

Bent is a powerful and shocking play told through short episodes tracing the experiences of Max, a gay, deal-making, self-serving conniver, from the "Night of the Long Knives"—when Ernst Roehm, an openly homosexual member of Adolf Hitler's government, was murdered along with three hundred other homosexuals—through two years of hiding until his internment in Dachau. The episodic structure and the chaotic world depicted is faintly reminiscent of *Things Went Badly in Westphalia,* but the solemn subject as well as the strength of Sherman's writing demonstrate the artistic progress he has made during the ten-year period between the two plays.

The first act of *Bent* begins the morning after the "Night of the Long Knives," as the SS come into Max's apartment and kill the soldier he had picked up at a gay club the night before. Max and Rudy, his lover, flee their apartment and find themselves on the run. Max's family offers him an opportunity to leave the country, but in an indication that his character may be changing, Max refuses to go without Rudy. Both are captured and put on a train to Dachau. During the ride, Rudy is tortured by the Nazis. Max meets Horst, a Jewish prisoner, and learns from him the rules of survival under the Nazis: "You can do nothing for your friend. Nothing. If you try to help him, they will kill you. If you try to care for his wounds, they will kill you. If you even *see*—see what they do to him, *hear*—hear what they do to him—they will kill you. If you want to stay alive, he cannot exist." Max follows Horst's advice, and in order to save himself he participates in the fatal beating of Rudy. Fearing the stigma associated with the pink triangle, Max denies his homosexuality by claiming he is Jewish. The Nazis make him prove that he is not "bent" by watching him have sex with a dead thirteen-year-old girl.

The entire second act, suggestive of Samuel Beckett's apocalyptic theatrical vision, takes place in the concentration camp at a rock pile, where Horst and Max continually move rocks back and forth. Sherman presents the developing friendship and romance between the two prisoners, who can never look at or touch one another. The only thing they can share is the power of language, which allows them to mentally survive their day. Through their reliance on and use of this medium, Sherman creates what scholar John Clum called one of the "most celebrated sex scenes in contemporary drama." During one of their three-minute breaks, when they are to stand rigidly at attention, they rebelliously make verbal love to one another. It is a scene of great power and emotional import as these two figures demonstrate that love, compassion, and tenderness can overcome any type of torturous physical impairments and oppression.

After this victorious verbal assault on their confinement, Horst becomes ill. Before the sickness can kill him, the Nazis shoot him, and Max once again has to watch the Germans kill one of his lovers. However, Max has changed during his incarceration. He no longer is merely concerned with himself. Throughout the second act Max places himself in jeopardy in order to get benefits, such as medicine, for Horst. In addition, Horst's arguments about Max's true identity as a homosexual rather than a Jew have made an impact. In the closing moments of the play Max finally revolts, claiming his true identity. Holding Horst's dead body, he removes the Jewish yellow star and replaces it with Horst's pink triangle. He then suicidally runs at the electrified fence, electrocuting himself in a blaze of white light. Ultimately, *Bent* powerfully and provocatively documents not only the oppression homosexuals faced, but also the openness and support present in homosexual relationships.

Some critics, however, including some Jews, were upset that Sherman had Max pass as Jewish. In response to this criticism Sherman told Helbing, "Some people are reluctant to share the suffering [of the Holocaust], particularly with a group that they have problems with, that they think denigrates the experience. But that's one of the reasons it was an important play to write: as a Jew, I think we have the responsibility to understand everybody's sufferings." Other reviewers

found fault with his unorthodox manner of playwriting, a criticism made about most of his works.

Despite mixed reviews, the London and New York productions (starring Ian McKellan and Richard Gere, respectively) were extremely successful, as the play received accolades for the visceral impact of the presentation. Perhaps the most representative response to the emotional power of the play can be found in reviewer Walter Kerr's description of the end of act 1: "The open sound of dismay that washed across the auditorium on the night I saw *Bent* was one I have never quite heard before—belief, disbelief, shock and half-understanding all mixed together" (*New York Times,* 3 December 1979).

Bent was Sherman's first commercial and critical success in New York, and this newfound artistic and monetary recognition allowed him to move to London. Although he had finally achieved the recognition he had been seeking for so long, Sherman left New York because he felt that in England he was treated like an adult. Sherman's frustrations with the American theater dated back to his difficulties with the New York staging of *Passing By.* His experiences in London during the Gay Sweatshop production awakened Sherman to the discontent he felt with his living situation in the States. As he told Morley, "Suddenly I realized that I'd never had any American roots anyway, both my parents having gone there from Russia, and that London was really where I wanted to make my home. In New York I then had another off-Broadway failure with . . . *Cracks,* people began crossing the street to avoid meeting me, and I thought who needs any of this?" However, Sherman's departure was not precipitated solely by his unhappiness with the artistic community of New York. He also found the gay environment of the West Village, his home for several years, to be far too stifling. He told Helbing that he found "incredible self-oppression" among the gay community in West Village, whereas London was "an easier place to develop relationships; I feel a sense of gentility that I like there."

The first play to be produced after Sherman moved to London was *Messiah* (1982), another historical play set after an era when Jews had been oppressed and slaughtered. The piece takes place in Poland in 1665 after a ten-year Cossack rebellion that killed one-third of the Jewish population of 300,000 and sent the remaining citizens, who had been prosperous merchants and representatives of the nobility, into destitution. Sherman writes in an "Afterpiece" to the play that in 1665 "The ravished Jewish community became obsessed with the visions of salvation. . . . There was an all-consuming certainty that the Messiah would finally arrive."

Cover for Sherman's one-act plays, A Tale for a King *and* Keeps Rainin' All the Time

talks about his produce. The wedding is disrupted by Asher, Ellis's nephew, who announces, before fainting, that the Messiah has come in the frame of a man called Sabbatai. After this discovery, the lives of the Jewish citizens change as the preaching of Sabbatai slowly trickles into the town: people are to give away all of their possessions; men are to ask women their opinions; and self-flagellation should take place. All of the citizens, in particular Asher, believe the announcements wholeheartedly. Rachel, though, doubts, keeping her distance from the converts. Rather than finding herself consumed by the passion of the words of the Messiah, she finds herself embarrassingly enamored with the body of her husband's young nephew. Reb, convinced of the Messiah's words, gives away all of his goods and then believes he has the ability to fly to Jerusalem. He jumps off the roof of his home and dies. Asher asks Rachel to come to Constantinople with him to wait for the Messiah, but she refuses, needing a sign of proof that Sabbatai is for real. The act ends with her mute mother finally speaking: she repeats Sabbatai's name over and over.

In the second act Asher, Rachel, and her mother camp on a hill waiting for the Messiah to pass by. Through his teachings more and more rules of Judaism are contradicted, including the eating of pork. With the contradictory pronouncements of Sabbatai, Sherman's recurring theme becomes apparent as the Messiah's arrival creates an uncertain, new world where previous rules no longer have validity. Sabbatai's wife visits their camp and speaks to Rachel's mother, who once again gains the power of speech and relates the story of her pain and suffering at the hands of the Cossacks. Meanwhile, during her mother's confession, Rachel and Asher make love. Ultimately, the Messiah makes his expected trek to the Sultan to claim his position before his people. The Sultan doubts the veracity of Sabbatai's claim and proclaims that he is to be set afire and dragged through the streets. If he truly is the Messiah, the Sultan reasons, he will be saved. Sabbatai, perhaps doubting his own truth, decides instead to convert to Islam. Devastated by Sabbatai's conversion, Asher kills himself. Having briefly found happiness with Asher, Rachel believed in the Messiah and God, but with Asher's death she no longer believes in either one. But at the end of the play, Sherman provides some ambiguity to Rachel's quest for spiritual knowledge. Despite the vociferousness of her denials, at heart she still is uncertain; and as she prays in the last scene, this feeling still shows: "Oh God. After all of this. I still don't know."

Messiah is a problematic play, and it received mixed reviews. Many of the critics appreciated Sherman's experimentation, while others were troubled that

The play is told from the perspective of Rachel, a twenty-eight-year-old unmarried, big-toothed, facially spotted, keenly intelligent Jewish woman who cares for her mute, blind mother. The main theme of the work is Rachel's continuing uncertainty over whether to believe blindly in God or trust her own self-doubt. Rachel constantly questions the power and truth of God because of the physical disfigurements and suffering she and her mother have endured. In almost every other scene Rachel is at prayer, engaging God in a dialogue about what has happened to her in the previous scene and what is to come. While the play is set in 1665, Rachel is definitely a contemporary voice not only with her constant questioning of her faith but also with the importance she places on people's appearances rather than the good inside them.

Rachel, a rather selective woman when it comes to marriage, is finally forced to marry the only single man left in town whom she has not rejected: a merchant named Reb Ellis, who markets fruit and always the play featured seventeenth-century characters with twentieth-century sensibilities. However, the play also posits a powerful question about faith. How is one to know the truth of religious faith? Does one believe blindly as all the characters do, except for Rachel? Or does one question and wait and wonder, like Rachel does? Ultimately, the answer is left to the audience to discover.

Throughout the 1980s *Bent* was produced in more than thirty countries, and Sherman assisted in many of the productions. During these experiences, he became aware of the complexity and difficulty of communication when not everyone speaks the same language. At the same time, he was also entertaining the idea of writing about another interest of his: Isadora Duncan. Sherman ended up combining these two interests with *When She Danced* (1985), at times a Chekhovian-like farce that takes place during one day in 1938 at Duncan's Paris home. Focusing on Duncan during the last years of her career, the play revolves around her wily attempts to convince an Italian embassy official to fund a school for girls that she would run in Italy. In the second act, she throws a dinner party in order to impress the official, only to discover that the man is merely a file clerk who does not even understand what Duncan does.

The title of the play refers to the other characters' strained verbal attempts to explain the impact of Duncan's artistic expression. However, each one inadequately expresses the visceral power of her performance. Sherman told Diane Solway, "I was also intrigued with the idea that Isadora's art was so transient. She had such a profound influence, yet to really understand what she did, you had to experience it. I wanted to explore this inability to explain her art, the failure to capture in language just what it is she did." The action of the play is interspersed with monologues as the characters attempt to articulate Duncan's performance. Belzer, a translator, tries to describe what she saw:

> I thought I saw children dancing, but there were no children. I thought I saw the face of my mother as she lay dying. I thought I remembered the rabbi's words. I thought I was kissing my child before they took him away from me. I thought I felt the lips, the lips of a man in a great white hat on the train to Kiev–and all she was doing on the stage was walking, just a few steps up, a few steps down.

Alexandros, a nineteen-year-old Greek piano player, relates what his mother told him whenever he asked her about seeing Duncan dance: "What do you see when she dance? What is it that happen when she dance? . . . And she say, 'O yomou'–'Oh my son'. 'Then mboro na to exiyi so.'–'I cannot explain.'" With a sense of theatrical teasing, Sherman includes a scene in which Duncan rehearses for an upcoming performance; however, she only sits in a chair and listens to Alexandros play the piano. She tells her stunned accompanist and the audience: "You want to see my feet move, don't you? . . . I do not rehearse my feet. Here– lift your long, beautiful hands, and place them on your heart. And try to hear your soul. If you can, then you will be able to dance too."

While the play stresses the inexpressible quality of Duncan's art and, in general, the entire artistic process, it also examines the isolation of the dancer's life, represented through the linguistic dilemma within her household. Few of the occupants speak the same language. Throughout the play English, French, Greek, Italian, Russian, and Swedish are spoken, but never does any one person understand everyone else; hence, Duncan mistakes the filing clerk for an Italian official. The variety of languages comically conveys one of Sherman's initial intended themes, which is the difficulty of communication. However, Sherman also shows the divisiveness that occurs when communication does take place. Belzer, hired to translate between Duncan and Sergei (Duncan's young, hot-tempered Russian lover), is reluctant to translate one of Sergei's poems that Duncan understands aesthetically but not linguistically. Belzer's translation, though, causes bitterness in the lovers' relationship as Duncan discovers that the poem compares the deaths of her two children to puppies being drowned by their own mother. Tim Luscombe, the director of the London production, remarked to Solway, "Sergei and Isadora live in the world of the imagination, not in the world of words." For precisely that reason, Duncan fires Belzer at the end of the play, because the directness and accurateness of language invades and disrupts the unexplainable aesthetics of their relationship.

When She Danced became recognized as a tour de force for actresses. Pauline Collins originated the role in 1985 at Guildford, England. Sheila Gish took over the role for the 1988 London fringe premiere at King's Head Theatre, while Vanessa Redgrave played Duncan in the West End production at the Globe Theatre in 1991. London critics and audiences praised Sherman's linguistic tour de force as well as the farcical overtones of the conclusion, in which all seven different languages are spoken in a rich cacophony of miscommunication.

Sherman followed *When She Danced* with *A Madhouse in Goa* (1989). Critics have commented on, and Sherman has acknowledged, the influence of Tennessee Williams on *A Madhouse in Goa,* especially in regard to Mrs. Honey, a talkative, opinionated, comical Southern woman on an extended tour of Europe. However, in a

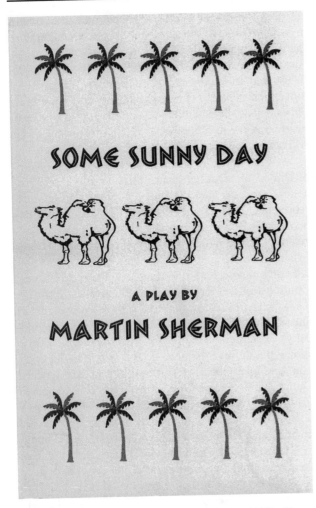

Cover for Sherman's play set in Cairo during World War II

then blackmails David to pay him for their sexual encounter. The action is sparse, as the one-act is driven more by character, but familiar Sherman themes appear again as he focuses on exiles in unfamiliar territory searching for their identity.

Keeps Rainin' All the Time, at first glance, has no connection with *A Table for a King.* It takes place in 1990 at Santorini with a completely different cast of characters. However, it soon becomes clear that *A Table for a King* is actually the fictional version of protagonist Daniel's summer travels in Europe in the 1960s (Daniel renamed himself David, while Mrs. Honey was based on a woman named Mrs. Foster). The book he wrote about the trip became a defining voice for an entire generation. In *Keeps Rainin' All the Time* Barnaby Grace, a producer, has come to Santorini to pitch to Daniel the concept of turning his book into a musical. However, Daniel, suffering from a mental breakdown, no longer has the ability to speak coherent sentences and is rarely cognizant of what occurs around him. Thrown into the scenario are Oliver, Daniel's gay handler; Heather, who is dying from cancer; Dylan, her son; and Aliki, Barnaby Grace's sexy companion. *Keeps Rainin' All the Time* recalls the manic sexual energy of *Cracks* as Dylan and Aliki's sexual antics are spied on by Oliver and Heather. Sherman's critical view of American producers continues as Barnaby explains his outrageous musical adaptation of Daniel's novel.

Despite the seeming lightness of the escapade, this one-act play is reminiscent of *Things Went Badly in Westphalia, Bent,* and *Messiah* in its depiction of a society and world in a state of collapse. Nuclear clouds travel across Europe. Acid rain dominates the weather. AIDS afflicts Oliver, while cancer consumes Heather. Food is tainted with deadly chemicals, and the ozone layer is depleting. Unlike his other plays, though, *Keeps Rainin' All the Time* offers a solution to the chaos through Mrs. Foster. She discovered that in Goa, India, people who lose their passports are placed in an asylum until they can prove their identities. In Goa, she deliberately lost her passport and found the madhouse to be the best answer to her problems, and she has remained there since. While hers is certainly an extreme reaction to a crumbling world, Heather applauds Mrs. Foster's decision as the only way to deal with the deteriorating life on earth. Although comedic at times, *Madhouse in Goa* is also a dark, pessimistic piece, especially in the coda, in which Oliver reveals that almost all of the characters have died in the four days between the scenes. Aliki turned out to be a terrorist who blew up the airplane carrying Dylan to Paris and later slashed Barnaby's throat in a hotel room. Heather died of cancer. At the close of the play, Oliver and Daniel sit on the porch while the nearby volcano erupts, suggesting that they too will be

greater sense, *Madhouse in Goa* is an amalgamation of several other Sherman plays. It comprises two one-act plays: *A Table for a King* and *Keeps Rainin' All the Time.*

A Table for a King is set on the balcony of a Corfu hotel in 1966. There are four characters: David, a young artist in search of his sexual and artistic identity; Mrs. Honey; Costos, a hotel worker; and Nikos, the hotel owner. The action has two different conflicts. The first entails the battle of wills between Mrs. Honey and Nikos over a table with a view. Specifically, Nikos wants it for the king, who is coming to visit, but Mrs. Honey refuses to give it up, having booked it for the entire length of her stay. Nikos wins their battle by discovering that she has been stealing jewelry from the guests. The other battle is David's inner struggle with his sexuality. In the most memorable moment of the play, reminiscent of the verbal lovemaking scene in *Bent,* Costos seduces David while reciting lyrics from songs of the 1960s (Costos only knows English from the songs on the radio). After consummation, Costos consumed by the explosion. Amidst the humor, Sherman has composed a sobering indictment of a world gone chaotic.

In stark contrast to the darkness of *Madhouse in Goa,* seven years later Sherman produced *Some Sunny Day* (1996), a World War II comedy. In some respects the play is extremely reminiscent of the movie *Casablanca* (1942) with its atmospheric touch of World War II exiles trapped in Cairo and desperate for a passage of transit to escape the city and Field Marshal Rommel's tanks poised in the desert. *Some Sunny Day* also offers a romantic entanglement that can never be, a murder that needs to be covered up, and questions surrounding the true identity of every character, any one of whom could be a spy.

Whereas in *Bent* Sherman exposed the unknown horrors of Nazi Germany, in *Some Sunny Day* he offers a more humorous look at one day in the life of an assortment of characters trapped in Cairo. The main character is Robin, who says he is a New Zealand reporter, but when pressed, claims to be from outer space. Robin is in love with Alec, a desk soldier who longs for desert combat. Robin, having the ability to see the future and the past, tries to persuade him not to go, since he knows Alec will die in battle. The other main character is Horatio, an embassy employee who pays city fortunetellers to say that Rommel will not attack the city. Tired of his English wife, Emily, Horatio falls in love with a belly dancer. An argument erupts between the married couple, and Horatio kills his wife in front of Robin.

In the second act Robin helps Horatio hide the body but in turn blackmails him for a passage of transit for the Duchess, one of the many exiles trapped in Cairo. Throughout the action, everyone suspects everyone else of being a spy for the Germans. Not trusting Robin, Horatio decides to kill him. At gunpoint, Robin proves he actually is an alien from outer space by melting the gun in Horatio's hand. Robin, it turns out, had answered an ad on his planet that allowed him to spend a week on earth. He then, in probably the most outrageous theatrical stunt in Sherman's canon, turns into an orange ball and flies out the window, leaving the remaining characters to muddle on with their lives.

Some Sunny Day is definitely one of Sherman's quirkier plays, and probably one of the lightest touches he has displayed onstage. However, darker elements, so prevalent in other Sherman plays, are also here, including a scene reminiscent of *Bent* in which the Duchess confesses that she betrayed her lover's identity to the Nazis so she could escape. Sherman once again depicts a world run amok as his characters struggle to survive; but the play also poignantly depicts the importance and wonders of love as well as the unhappiness

that accompanies lost love. Robin sums up the entire philosophy behind the play when he explains the struggles of being human: "The problem is, the brochures did not advertise emotions. . . . How can you people feel two things at the same time, two conflicting things? Or even more?" Through Robin, Sherman captures the joy and excitement of being human as he relishes music, food, and companionship. What Robin consumes with a passion, the rest of the characters (and the audience) take for granted. If anything, Sherman's play celebrates the mystical wonderfulness of being human, even in light of the surrounding chaos.

In the summer of 1999 Sherman's *Rose* premiered at the Royal National Theatre in the Cottesloe Theatre. *Rose* displays Sherman's ongoing interest in exploring the nature of the Jewish identity, the conflict of cultures, and the lasting repercussions of World War II, while the play also continues his experimentation with dramatic form. *Rose* is a powerful and moving one-woman show. In a 1999 interview with Jasper Rees, Sherman revealed that the character Rose is based in part on his grandmother, who worked in a hotel in Atlantic City: "For someone who only learnt English after she had gone to America, she was astonishingly articulate. I remember one day when I was about 21 she said something that was so subtly funny and so ironic that I thought, Oh, this is a humour that I don't see in the rest of the family." His grandmother's articulateness and humor is readily apparent in his engaging portrait of Rose, a strong, driven, and successful woman.

As the play begins, Rose is sitting shivah. During the ritual she describes the major events of her life. Born in the Ukraine in the midst of a civil war, Rose survived a difficult childhood and moved to the Warsaw ghettoes in the late 1930s. She escaped the Nazis' destruction of these ghettoes by hiding in the sewers of Warsaw, where she lived throughout the war. At the end of the war, she was smuggled onboard *The Exodus,* which became an international symbol of the continued persecution of the Jews as they sought to settle in Palestine. Rose eventually immigrated to the United States and settled in Atlantic City. Fulfilling the American Dream, she ended up owning a successful hotel in Miami and retiring to Arizona. Because of her son's residency in Israel, however, she still could not escape the continued persecution of Jews, which has been something she has tried to avoid all her life.

Rose once again demonstrates Sherman's flexibility as a writer. Unlike the farcical *Some Sunny Day, Rose* is incredibly simple. There is no action. Rose sits on a wooden bench throughout the play, occasionally taking a sip from her water bottle to wash down her medicine. Sherman foregrounds the power of Rose's language as she conveys not only her own story but also the story of the Jews' quest for an identity and a homeland in the twentieth century.

Rose, which featured Olympia Dukakis, was a critical and commercial success for Sherman. The play received an Olivier nomination (the British equivalent of the Tony) for best play of the year. Jeremy Kingston's review of the play for *The Times* (28 June 1999) sums up the nature of Sherman's play: "The art of storytelling needs two things to make it work: story and teller. But each must be of the highest quality. The story of Rose . . . has been woven by Martin Sherman, a master of the telling phrase and the unforgettable image."

Since the premiere of *Bent* in 1979, Sherman has written only five produced plays over a seventeen-year period. However, while his play production decreased, he became involved in screenplay production in the 1990s. He first adapted Alice Thomas Ellis's novel *The Clothes in the Wardrobe* (1987) for BBC television in 1992. It was released in the United States as a motion picture, *The Summer House,* in 1993. He then wrote the original screenplay for *Alive and Kicking* (1997), which details the relationship between a dancer with AIDS and his AIDS counselor. After the successful revival of *Bent* at the National Theatre in 1990, the play was turned into a movie in 1997, and Sherman adapted it, making major changes for the cinema.

Talking to Wolf, Sherman recalled that in the 1960s a New York astrologer "read my chart and said my life was going to be miserable for a long time and then it was going to improve radically years and years later . . . it's all true. I'm a late bloomer." Certainly for Sherman, the 1970s were an unhappy time professionally as well as personally, but since his move to London in 1980, Sherman has been much more content with his career and personal life. The 1990s were a productive and successful decade for him with his foray into the world of movies. He proudly advertises himself as not only a playwright but also a screenwriter, and he continues to explore his exiled characters in his own comedic and innovative style.

Interviews:

Terry Helbing, "Behind the Scenes at Broadway's Big Shocker–*Bent*," *Advocate,* 10 January 1980, pp. 29, 33;

Sheridan Morley, "The Gift of Big Writing," *Times,* 11 February 1983, p. 10;

David Galligan, "Martin Sherman on *Bent*," *Advocate,* 9 June 1987, pp. 64–65, 124;

Diane Solway, "As One Playwright Strikes Out for the Future . . . Another Tracks His Curiosity Into the Past," *New York Times,* 18 February 1990, II: 5;

"Out of Step," *Independent,* 29 November 1995, p. 8;

W. Stephen Gilbert, "That Sherman, He's a Funny Guy," *Independent,* 10 April 1996, pp. 8–9;

Matt Wolf, "Martin Sherman," *New York,* 30, no. 44 (17 November 1997): 60–61;

Alexandra Bandon, "Thinking Past the Barriers to Making a Movie of *Bent*," *New York Times,* 30 November 1997, II: 17;

Jasper Rees, "Telling the tale of a lifetime Martin Sherman, author of hit play *Bent*, looked no further than the inspiring story of his grandmother for his latest work," *Daily Telegraph,* 10 June 1999, p. 24.

References:

James W. Carlsen, "Images of the Gay Male in Contemporary Drama," in *Gayspeak: Gay Male and Lesbian Communication,* edited by James W. Chesebro (New York: Pilgrim, 1981), pp. 165–174;

John M. Clum, *Acting Gay: Male Homosexuality in Modern Drama* (New York: Columbia University Press, 1992);

Kai Hammermeister, "Inventing History: Toward a Gay Holocaust Literature," *German Quarterly,* 70, no. 1 (Winter 1997): 18–26.

Gertrude Stein

(3 February 1874 – 27 July 1946)

Adrienne E. Hacker Daniels
University of St. Thomas

See also the Stein entries in *DLB 4: American Writers in Paris, 1920–1939; DLB 54: American Poets, 1880–1945: Third Series; DLB 86: American Short Story Writers, 1910–1945: First Series;* and *DS 15: American Expatriate Writers: Paris in the Twenties.*

PLAY PRODUCTIONS: *Four Saints in Three Acts,* Hartford, Connecticut, Wadsworth Athenaeum, 8 February 1934; New York, Forty-fourth Street Theatre, 20 February 1934;

Identity A Poem, Detroit, Michigan, Institute of Arts, 9 July 1936;

A Wedding Bouquet, London, Sadler's Wells Ballet, 27 April 1937; New York, Metropolitan Opera House, 25 October 1948;

Yes Is for a Very Young Man, Pasadena, Pasadena Playhouse, 13 March 1946; New York, Cherry Lane Theatre, 6 June 1949;

The Mother of Us All, New York, Brander Matthews Hall, Columbia University, 7 May 1947; New York, Phoenix Theatre, 16 April 1956;

In a Garden, New York, After Dinner Opera Company, 29 December 1949; New York, Phoenix Theatre, 1 April 1957;

What Happened, Hartford, Randall Playhouse, 18 March 1950; New York, Judson Poets' Theatre, 26 September 1963;

Ladies' Voices (Curtain Raiser), New York, The Living Theatre, 15 August 1951;

Doctor Faustus Lights the Lights, New York, Cherry Lane Theatre, 2 December 1951;

Lend a Hand or Four Religions and *A Curtain Raiser,* Cedar Rapids, Coe College, March 1959;

Photograph, New York, American Theatre for Poets, 1964; New York, Open Space Theatre, 15 September 1977;

Three Sisters Who Are Not Sisters, New York, Judson Poets' Theatre, 5 June 1965;

Play I[–III], New York, Judson Poets' Theatre, December 1965;

Gertrude Stein (photograph by Carl Van Vechten)

An Exercise in Analysis, Oneonta, New York, Hartwick College Chapel, 4 May 1967;

In Circles (A Circular Play. A Play in Circles), New York, Judson Poets' Theatre, 14 October 1967;

I Like It to Be a Play, New Haven, Yale University, 20 October 1968;

Captain Walter Arnold, New Haven, Yale University, 25 April 1969;

Look and Long, New York, New York University, 4 October 1969;

Listen to Me, New York, Judson Poets' Theatre, 18 October 1974;

Leo, Gertrude, and Michael Stein in Paris, circa 1907 (courtesy of Edward M. Burns)

A Manoir. An Historical Play In Which They Are Approached More Often, New York, Judson Poets' Theatre, 22 April 1977;

For the Country Entirely, Urbana, University of Illinois, 15 December 1977;

A Lyrical Opera Made By Two, Pittsburgh, 8 March 1979; New Haven, Long Wharf Theatre, Stage II, 1 May 1979;

Am I to Go or I'll Say So, He Said It, Louis XI and Madame Giraud, Counting Her Dresses, A List, and *Every Afternoon,* Iowa City, University of Iowa, 5 May 1980.

BOOKS: *Three Lives* (New York: Grafton Press, 1909; London: John Lane, Bodley Head / New York: John Lane, 1915);

Portrait of Mabel Dodge at the Villa Curonia (Florence, Italy: Privately printed, 1912);

Tender Buttons: Objects, Food, Rooms (New York: Claire Marie, 1914);

Geography and Plays (Boston: Four Seas, 1922);

The Making of Americans (Paris: Contact Editions, 1925; New York: A. &. C. Boni, 1926; London: Owen,

1968); abridged as *The Making of Americans: The Hersland Family* (New York: Harcourt, Brace, 1934);

Descriptions of Literature (Englewood Cliffs, N.J.: George Platt Lynes & Adlai Harbeck, 1926);

Composition as Explanation (London: Leonard & Virginia Woolf at the Hogarth Press, 1926);

A Book Concluding with As A Wife Has A Cow A Love Story (Paris: Editions de la Galerie Simon, 1926; Barton, Millerton & Berlin: Something Else Press, 1973);

A Village Are You Ready Yet Not Yet A Play in Four Acts (Paris: Editions de la Galerie Simon, 1928);

Useful Knowledge (New York: Payson & Clarke, 1928; London: John Lane, Bodley Head, 1929);

An Acquaintance With Description (London: Seizin Press, 1929);

Lucy Church Amiably (Paris: Plain Edition, 1930; New York: Something Else Press, 1969);

Dix Portraits, English text with French translations by Georges Hugnet and Virgil Thomson (Paris: Librarie Gallimard, 1930);

Judith Malina and Helen Jacobs in the 1951 New York production of Ladies' Voices, *written in 1916 (photograph by Carl Van Vechten)*

Before the Flowers of Friendship Faded Friendship Faded, Written on a Poem by Georges Hugnet (Paris: Plain Edition, 1931);

How to Write (Paris: Plain Edition, 1931; Barton: Something Else Press, 1971);

Operas and Plays (Paris: Plain Edition, 1932);

Matisse Picasso and Gertrude Stein with Two Shorter Stories (Paris: Plain Edition, 1933; Barton, Berlin & Millerton: Something Else Press, 1972);

The Autobiography of Alice B. Toklas (New York: Harcourt, Brace, 1933; London: John Lane, Bodley Head, 1933);

Four Saints In Three Acts, An Opera To Be Sung (New York: Random House, 1934);

Portraits and Prayers (New York: Random House, 1934);

Lectures in America (New York: Random House, 1935);

Narration: Four Lectures (Chicago: University of Chicago Press, 1935);

The Geographical History of America; or, The Relation of Human Nature to the Human Mind (New York: Random House, 1936);

Everybody's Autobiography (New York: Random House, 1937; London & Toronto: Heinemann, 1938);

A Wedding Bouquet, Ballet Music by Lord Berners, Words by Gertrude Stein (London: J. & W. Chester, 1938)–

revised and abridged version of *They Must. Be Wedded. To Their Wife,* in *Operas and Plays* (1932);

Picasso [in French] (Paris: Librairie Floury, 1938); translated into English by Alice B. Toklas (London: Batsford, 1938; New York: Scribners / London: Batsford, 1939);

The World is Round (New York: William R. Scott, 1939; London: Batsford, 1939);

Paris France (London: Batsford, 1940; New York: Scribners / London: Batsford, 1940);

What are Masterpieces (California: Conference Press, 1940; expanded edition, New York, Toronto, London & Tel Aviv: Pitman, 1970);

Ida: A Novel (New York: Random House, 1941);

Petits Poèmes pour Un Livre de Lecture, translated into French by Madame la Baronne d'Aiguy (Charlot, France: Collection Fontaine, 1944); republished in English as *The First Reader & Three Plays* (Dublin & London: Maurice Fridberg, 1946; Boston: Houghton Mifflin, 1948);

Wars I Have Seen (New York: Random House, 1945; enlarged edition, London: Batsford, 1945);

Brewsie and Willie (New York: Random House, 1946);

Selected Writings of Gertrude Stein, edited by Carl Van Vechten (New York: Random House, 1946);

In Savoy or Yes Is for a Very Young Man (A Play of the Resistance in France) (London: Pushkin, 1946);

Four in America (New Haven: Yale University Press, 1947);

The Mother of Us All, by Stein and Thomson (New York: Music Press, 1947);

Blood on the Dining Room Floor (Pawlet, Vt.: Banyan Press, 1948);

Last Operas and Plays, edited by Van Vechten (New York & Toronto: Rinehart, 1949);

Things as They Are, A Novel in Three Parts by Gertrude Stein, Written in 1903 but Now Published for the First Time (Pawlet, Vt.: Banyan Press, 1950);

Two: Gertrude Stein and Her Brother and Other Early Portraits [1908–12], volume 1 of *Unpublished Works of Gertrude Stein* (New Haven: Yale University Press/ London: Cumberlege, Oxford University Press, 1951);

In A Garden, An Opera in One Act, libretto by Stein; music by Meyer Kupferman (New York: Mercury Music, 1951);

Mrs. Reynolds and Five Earlier Novelettes, volume 2 of *Unpublished Works of Gertrude Stein* (New Haven: Yale University Press / London: Cumberlege, Oxford University Press, 1952);

Bee Time Vine and Other Pieces 1913–1927, volume 3 of *Unpublished Works of Gertrude Stein* (New Haven: Yale University Press / London: Cumberlege, Oxford University Press, 1953);

As Fine As Melanchta (1914–1930), volume 4 of *Unpublished Works of Gertrude Stein* (New Haven: Yale University Press / London: Cumberlege, Oxford University Press, 1954);

Painted Lace and Other Pieces, 1914–1937, volume 5 of *Unpublished Works of Gertrude Stein* (New Haven: Yale University Press / London: Cumberlege, Oxford University Press, 1956);

Stanzas in Meditation and Other Poems [1929–1933], volume 6 of *Unpublished Works of Gertrude Stein* (New Haven: Yale University Press / London: Cumberlege, Oxford University Press, 1956);

Alphabets & Birthdays, volume 7 of *Unpublished Works of Gertrude Stein* (New Haven: Yale University Press/ London: Oxford University Press, 1957);

A Novel of Thank You, volume 8 of *Unpublished Works of Gertrude Stein* (New Haven: Yale University Press, 1958; London: Oxford University Press, 1959);

Gertrude Stein's America, edited by Gilbert A. Harrison (Washington, D.C.: Robert B. Luce, 1965);

Writings and Lectures 1911–1945, edited by Patricia Meyerowitz (London: Owen, 1967); republished as *Look at Me Now and Here I Am: Writings and Lectures, 1909–1945* (Harmondsworth, U.K. & Baltimore: Penguin, 1971);

Lucretia Borgia, A Play (New York: Albondocani Press, 1968);

Motor Automatism, by Stein and Leon M. Solomons (New York: Phoenix Book Shop, 1969);

Selected Operas and Plays, edited by John Malcolm Brinnin (Pittsburgh: University of Pittsburgh Press, 1970);

Gertrude Stein On Picasso, edited by Edward Burns (New York: Liveright, 1970);

Fernhurst, Q.E.D., and Other Early Writings (New York: Liveright, 1971; London: Owen, 1971);

A Primer For the Gradual Understanding of Gertrude Stein, edited by Robert Bartlett Haas (Los Angeles: Black Sparrow Press, 1971);

Reflection On the Atomic Bomb, volume 1 of *The Previously Uncollected Writings of Gertrude Stein,* edited by Haas (Los Angeles: Black Sparrow Press, 1973);

Money (Los Angeles: Black Sparrow Press, 1973);

How Writing Is Written, volume 2 of *The Previously Uncollected Writings of Gertrude Stein,* edited by Haas (Los Angeles: Black Sparrow Press, 1974);

The Yale Gertrude Stein: Selections (New Haven & London: Yale University Press, 1980);

Operas & Plays (Barrytown, N.Y.: Station Hill Press, 1987).

In his introduction to Gertrude Stein's *Four in America* (1947) Thornton Wilder observed:

> She knew that she was a difficult and an idiosyncratic author. She pursued her aims, however, with such conviction and intensity that occasionally she forgot that the results could be difficult to others. At such times the achievements she had made in writing, in "telling what she knew" (her most frequent formalization of the aim of writing) had to her the character of self-evident beauty and clarity. A friend, to whom she showed recently completed examples of her poetry, was frequently driven to reply sadly: "But you forget that I don't understand examples of your extreme styles." To this she would reply with a mixture of bewilderment, distress, and exasperation: "But what's the difficulty? Just read the words on the paper. They're in English. Just read them. Be simple and you'll understand these things."

There is no small irony in Stein's words. Her "dramatic" writings, while ostensibly simple, are paradoxically complex in their lack of signification. Stein's solipsistic and idiosyncratic use of words seems to belie the goal of communication. Her aim, however, was not to confuse audiences but to rebel against the conventional ways of engaging with them and to create an innovative rhetoric of the theater.

Stein's dramatic works have often been misunderstood and underappreciated, in part because they do

Stein and Virgil Thomson working on Four Saints in Three Acts *(Beinecke Rare Book and Manuscript Library, Yale University)*

not adhere to traditional generic constraints. Jane Pala-tini Bowers calls Stein's drama "a performed poetry, at once textual and theatrical." Stein created a language whose logic is not based on conventional modes of reasoning. Her language is bereft of the traditional context that makes ascertainable meanings accessible to readers and playgoers. As Richard Kostelanetz suggests, "instead of 'making up' plots and characters, she concentrated on inventing linguistic structures." Bowers credits Stein with devising "a new theater language and a new place for language in the theater."

Kostelanetz and Betsy Alayne Ryan consider Stein a primary influence on playwrights from Wilder to contemporary experimental playwright-directors such as Richard Foreman and Robert Wilson, performance artists such as Laurie Anderson, and theater companies such as the Wooster Group, Performance Group, and Mabou Mines. Stein's influence on postmodern playwrights such as Harold Pinter and Samuel Beckett is less demonstrable. Bowers and other scholars have noted that although language is a dominant feature in Stein's and Beckett's plays, Beckett uses language to exemplify the failure of language, while Stein

uses it with the hope of offering her audience newly discovered meanings.

Gertrude Stein was born on 3 February 1874 in Allegheny, Pennsylvania, to Daniel and Amelia (Milly) Keyser Stein—both of German-Jewish descent. She had four older siblings: Michael (born 1865), Simon (born 1867), Bertha (born 1870), and Leo (born 1872). After Bertha was born, two Stein children died in infancy. Since Stein's parents had intended to have five children—no more and no less—Gertrude and Leo Stein acknowledged that they owed their lives to the deaths of two older siblings. Stein's relationship with Leo was her most important, and yet most vexing, familial tie.

In the spring of 1875 the family moved to Europe, residing in Vienna until 1878, when they went to live in Paris. In 1880 they returned to the United States, settling in Oakland, California. Stein's mother died in 1888 and was followed by Daniel Stein in 1891. In 1893 Stein enrolled in the women's division of Harvard University, Harvard Annex, which became Radcliffe College the following year.

Stein's interest in the naming of things and her preoccupation with the present may be attributed in

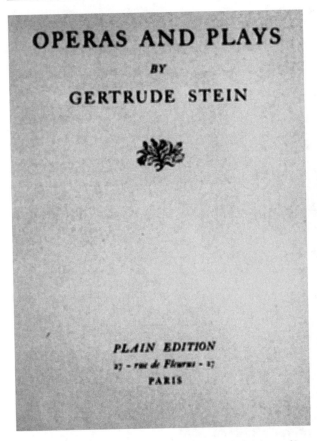

OPERAS AND PLAYS

BY

GERTRUDE STEIN

PLAIN EDITION
27 - rue de Fleurus - 27
PARIS

Title page for the 1932 book in which Stein published eighteen of her dramatic works, including Four Saints in Three Acts

part to her study of psychology and philosophy with William James, brother of novelist Henry James. Some scholars trace the roots of Stein's interest in writing and consciousness to the research on automatic writing she and Leon Solomons conducted under James's supervision. In fall 1897, before she received an A.B. from Harvard the following year, Stein enrolled in the Johns Hopkins School of Medicine, doing casework in obstetrics and gynecology. She became disenchanted and bored with her studies, failed four courses, and gave up medicine entirely in 1902.

In fall 1903 Gertrude Stein joined her brother Leo in Paris, settling with him at 27, rue de Fleurus, a residence that became a mecca for some of the most prominent writers and artists of their time. Leo Stein introduced his sister to modern art, and the two purchased paintings by Pierre-Auguste Renoir, Paul Gauguin, Paul Cézanne, Henri Matisse, and Pablo Picasso.

In 1913 Leo Stein moved out of the household on the rue de Fleurus, and the brother and sister were never on speaking terms again. Gertrude Stein wrote in her play *Accents in Alsace* (first published in *Geography & Plays,* 1922): "Brother brother go away and stay."

In addition to differences of opinion about modern art and Leo's lack of enthusiasm for Gertrude's writing, one cause of the rift was her relationship with Alice B. Toklas, who arrived in Paris in 1907 and moved in with the Steins in early 1909. Toklas became Gertrude Stein's "wife," a relationship that lasted until Stein's death from cancer on 27 July 1946. Toklas died on 7 March 1967 and is buried next to Stein in Père-Lachaise Cemetery in Paris.

Stein wrote forty-seven plays between 1913 and 1920. According to Ryan, ten plays from this period have been produced: *What Happened. A Five Act Play* (written 1913, produced 1950), *A Curtain Raiser* (written 1913, produced 1977), *He Said It. Monologue* (written 1915, produced 1980), *For the Country Entirely. A Play in Letters* (written 1916, produced 1977), *Every Afternoon. A Dialogue* (written 1916, produced 1980), *Captain Walter Arnold* (written 1916, produced 1969), *Ladies' Voices (Curtain Raiser)* (written 1916, produced 1951), *I Like It to Be a Play. A Play* (written 1916, produced 1968), *Counting Her Dresses. A Play* (written 1917, produced 1980), and *An Exercise in Analysis* (written 1917, produced 1967).

Bowers argues that Stein's plays "oppose the physicality of performance" in their preoccupation with language. Stein described the impetus for her first foray into playwriting, *What Happened. A Five Act Play,* in her lecture "Plays" (collected in *Lectures in America,* 1935): "I had just come home from a pleasant dinner party and I realized then as anybody can know that something is always happening." Stein wanted to tell a story, but not a familiar or often-told one, "So naturally what I wanted to do in my play was what everybody did not always know nor always tell." The play is divided into the traditional five acts, but, as Ulla E. Dydo has pointed out in her introduction to *A Stein Reader / Gertrude Stein* (1993), the headings "poke fun at the rigid form of five-act plays." Under each act heading is a number that may refer to the number of characters who speak the subsequent lines. As with the poems in Stein's *Tender Buttons* (1914), the ultimate goal of the play is naming things, as in the first four sentences of act 3: "A cut, a cut is not a piece, what is the occasion for representing a cut and a slice. What is the occasion for all that. A cut is a slice, a cut is the same slice. The reason that a cut is a slice is that if there is no hurry any time is just as useful." Another concerted effort to name occurs in act 4:

A birthday, what is a birthday, a birthday is a speech, it is a second time when there is tobacco, it is only one time when there is poison. It is more than one time when the occasion which shows an occasional sharp separation is unanimous. A blanket, what is a blanket, a blanket is so speedy that heat much heat is hotter and

Scene from the world premiere performance of Four Saints in Three Acts, *Hartford, Connecticut, 8 February 1934 (White Studios)*

cooler, very much cooler almost more nearly cooler than at any other time often.

Stein's license with vocabulary, syntax, and punctuation contributes to the conclusion that her language is hermetic, insofar as readers are ill equipped to "decode" it.

According to Dydo, *Ladies' Voices (Curtain Raiser)* is about women who have gathered in Mallorca, "probably at carnival time" and explores "the world of spoken words." The play had its premiere in 1951 at The Living Theatre in New York City. In this and other early plays Stein's language is archaeological. That is, she attempts to rediscover meanings that transcend superficial, conventionally agreed-on definitions, opting instead for the archetypal, which may indeed be buried and unknown. For Stein the only legitimate way of knowing the world is through language. In "Plays" Stein described her work on her early dramas: "I have of course always been struggling with this thing, to say what you nor I nor nobody knows, but what is really what you and I and everybody knows."

Stein continued her experiments with language in *A Circular Play. A Play In Circles,* written in 1920, using figures of speech, rhyme, repetition, alliteration, and homonyms, in generally convivial wordplay. In the section called "The Circle" she wrote: "The work can you work / And meat / Can you meet? And flour / Can you

flower? Calligraphy. Writing to a girl / A great many say we have wives and children to-day. / Can you be angry at women / I believe that they are pleased with us." The play was performed at the Judson Poets' Theatre in New York City in 1967. *A List,* written in 1923 and produced in 1980, emphasizes the spatial relationships of the words on the page. All the characters' names begin with M, and the names are arranged horizontally and vertically on the page to create a visual order with an inherent logic.

Stein wrote forty-three plays between 1920 and 1933. Nine of these plays have been produced: *A Circular Play. A Play in Circles* (written 1920, produced 1967), *Photograph* (written 1920, produced in 1964), *A List* (written 1923, produced 1980), *Am I to Go or I'll Say So* (1923, produced 1980), *Four Saints in Three Acts* (written 1927, produced 1934), *A Lyrical Opera Made by Two. To Be Sung* (written 1928, produced 1979), *Louis XI and Madame Giraud* (written 1930, produced 1980), *Play I [III]* (written 1930, produced 1965), *A Manoir. An Historical Play in Which They are Approached More Often* (written 1932, produced 1977). These plays are Stein's attempts at liberating words from the strictures of what she considered meaningless, stifling, and stultifying rules of composition.

The period between 1920 and 1933 is known as Stein's "landscape period," influenced by her visits to

Marquee for the first New York production of Stein's best-known dramatic work (photograph by Carl Van Vechten)

the south of France, particularly after she and Toklas began spending their summers at a farmhouse in Bilignin in 1928. In "Plays" she said,

> I felt that if a play was exactly like a landscape then there would be no difficulty about the emotion of the person looking on at the play being behind or ahead of the play because the landscape does not have to make acquaintance. You may have to make acquaintance with it, but it does not with you, it is there and so the play being written the relation between you at any time is so exactly that that it is of no importance unless you look at it. Well I did look at it and the results is in all the plays that I have printed as Operas & Plays.

Among Stein's early landscape plays are *As in Lend a Hand or Four Religions* (written 1922, performed 1959), *A*

Village Are You Ready Yet Not Yet (written 1923), and *Capital Capitals* (written 1923).

Between 1923 and 1927 Stein's dramatic writing temporarily ceased. She began again with *Four Saints in Three Acts,* a collaborative effort with composer Virgil Thomson, written in 1927. In "Plays" Stein grouped *Four Saints In Three Acts* with her landscape plays: "In Four Saints I made the Saints the landscape. All the saints that I made and I made a number of them because after all a great many pieces of things are in a landscape all these saints together made my landscape. These attendant saints were the landscape and it the play really is a landscape." Later in the essay she added, "I did write Four Saints an Opera to be Sung and I think it did almost what I wanted, it made a landscape and the movement in it was like a move-

Stein and Alice B. Toklas arriving in the United States for Stein's 1934 lecture tour
(Beinecke Rare Book and Manuscript Library, Yale University)

ment in and out with which anybody looking on can keep in time. I also wanted it to have the movement of nuns very busy and in continuous movement but placid as a landscape has to be because after all the life in a convent is the life of a landscape if it ever did go away would have to go away to stay."

Having composed scores for *Capital Capitals* and Stein's word portraits "Susie Asado," "Preciosilla," and "Portrait of F.B.," Thomson wrote the music for *Four Saints In Three Acts* because, according to Ryan, Stein's *Tender Buttons* and *Geography and Plays* had had a profound impact on him when he was a student at Harvard. In *The Autobiography of Alice B. Toklas* (1933) Stein wrote that Thomson "understood a great deal of Gertrude Stein's work, he used to dream at night that there was something there that he did not understand, but on the whole he was very well content with that which he did understand." Bowers quotes Thomson's reasons for working with Stein:

My hope in putting Gertrude Stein to music had been to break, crack open, and solve for all time anything still waiting to be solved, which was almost everything, about English musical declamation. My theory was that if a text is set correctly for the sound of it, the meaning will take care of itself. And the Stein texts, for prosodizing in this way, were manna. With meanings already abstracted, or absent, or so multiplied that choice among them was impossible, there was no temptation toward tonal illustration. You could make a setting for sound and syntax only, then add, if needed, an accompaniment equally functional.

Four Saints in Three Acts is perhaps best known for its dramatic "sound bytes"–including "pigeons on the grass alas." For Bowers, Stein "makes the writing process a part of the performance," with the words creating an "illusionary landscape where words make time stand still," a juxtaposition of movement and stasis. *Four Saints in Three Acts* may be viewed as an attempt to eradicate all temporal contexts, divesting action of any temporal references.

The first of Stein's dramatic works to be staged, *Four Saints in Three Acts* had its premiere at the Wadsworth Athenaeum in Hartford, Connecticut, on 8 February 1934, under the direction of John Houseman, with an all-black cast. It opened in New York City on 20 February for a month-long engagement at the Forty-fourth Street Theatre. According to James R. Mellow, the production "became one of the most talked-about theatrical ventures of the Depression years." He attributes the success of *Four Saints in Three Acts* to Thomson's "vital and vibrant score," as well as Maurice Grosser's scenario, Frederick Ashton's balletic choreography, and Florine Stettheimer's cellophane set design.

During the years immediately following the composition of *Four Saints in Three Acts* Stein directed her attention toward what Richard Bridgman calls "the origins and operations of language." Her ruminations are collected in *How To Write* (1931), a series of eight essays written between 1927 and 1929. Stein used the ideas expressed in these essays in her dramatic writing. She appears to have been getting back to "first principles" of language, but rather than reinforcing them she radically transformed them. According to Bowers, Stein was rebelling against the "dynamism of language itself, its linearity and continuity." Although Stein conceded that "there is no resemblance without a grammar," she ultimately asserted that "grammar is useless because there is nothing to say." She thought that the conventional arranging of words into accepted patterns destroyed the vitality of expression and promoted stagnation.

In *How to Write* Stein also stated that "a sentence is not emotional a paragraph is." That is, although it is composed of sentences, a paragraph is more than the sum of its parts because it is able to transcend the formulaic and unnatural, to be extricated from the rules. In *Painted Lace* (1956) Stein expanded on this notion: "She is my wife. That is what a paragraph is. Always at home. A paragraph hopes for houses. We have a house two houses. My wife and I are at home." In the opening section of "Plays" Stein applies her observations about sentences and paragraphs to drama, setting up the coordinates of emotionalism and time: "The thing that is fundamental about plays is that the scene as depicted on the stage is more often than not one might say it is almost always in syncopated time in relation to the emotion of anybody in the audience." That is, the audience member's

emotion concerning that play is always either behind or ahead of the play at which you are looking and to which you are listening. So your emotion as a member of the audience is never going on at the same time as the action of the play. This thing the fact that your emotional time as an audience is not the same as the emotional time of the play is what makes one endlessly troubled about a play, because not only is there a thing to know as to why this is so but also there is a thing to know why perhaps it does not need to be so.

Some of the plays of Stein's landscape period typify her syntactical and lexical struggles. Bowers suggests that in *Paisieu. A Play* (written 1928) "Stein is far more preoccupied with names than she is with the bucolic setting and the homely activities she includes in her play." The significance of names is constantly in flux. As Bowers says, "a name then has no 'meaning' beyond the one instance of its application to a particular person or place. That makes a name an exciting and perfect word because it can never grow stale like the recurring noun. Because it comes 'once in a while' a noun loses its correspondence to a particular place and time, loses its singularity and becomes a generalization, loses it concrete spatiality, as it were, and becomes abstraction." In *They Must. Be Wedded. To Their Wife* (written 1931), Bowers has observed several major patterns. First, Stein used periods between the name of the speaker and the speaker's utterance on the printed page, as in: "Josephine. Has been known by that name. Ernest. Has meant more. Than. That claim. Therese. Will be faintly neat. And they close. Julia. Name which welcomes a valley. Guy. It is a funeral. To be. Well. Paul. She says. It has. Charm. John. Will they cover. Endeavor." Second, she used punctuation and word placement "to interfere with spatial and grammatical linearity," as in the following section: "Josephine. They will announce declare. Josephine. A will wonder where. Josephine. More say more. See. Josephine. With this. And. With. Me. Josephine. As. Best. Us." Third, combining the two previous approaches, she divided among several speakers a continuous utterance that in conventional dialogue would be attributed to one speaker, as in this passage: "Julia. It is a pleasure to witness. Josephine. That they are balanced. Therese. And preserved. Julia. As more than. They mind. Josephine. As it will. Allow." Bowers refers to these dramatic forms as "schizologues," in which fragmentation is the mainstay. Stein may have derived this technique from Thomson's score for *Four Saints in Three Acts,* in which he broke up speeches and divided them among several voices.

In *An Historic Drama in Memory of Winnie Elliot; Will He Come Back Better. Second Historic Drama. In the Country;* and *Third Historic Drama*—all written in 1930—Stein employs not only schizologues but also frequent scene shifts. In another play written in 1930, *They Weighed Weighed-Layed. A Drama of Aphorisms,* Stein used the characters to differentiate acts and scenes. As in other landscape plays, says Bowers, "voices combine, separate and recombine."

In 1936 Stein wrote two plays, *Listen to Me* and *A Play Called Not and Now.* These plays came on the heels of Stein's success as a popular writer with her best-selling *The Autobiography of Alice B. Toklas* and her 1934 lecture tours in Great Britain and the United States.

Inspired by a Hollywood dinner party at which she met Dashiell Hammett, Charlie Chaplin, and Anita Loos, *A Play Called Not and Now* is about the meaning and effects of celebrity. Bridgman notes that Stein seemed particularly concerned "about the transformation she was undergoing from a private to a public self." He finds this play dull, and Bowers describes it as a void in which "no one acts; nothing happens; [and] no one speaks." Both scholars prefer *Listen to Me* (written 1936), in which Bowers finds a more successful reconciliation between language and the other components of the mise-en-scène, as in *Four Saints in Three Acts*. Bridgman calls *Listen to Me* one of Stein's greatest creations, an expression of "the difficulty of living in a world so crowded and artificial that naturalness and individuality are virtually eliminated."

Stein's dramatic writing from the late 1930s until her death in 1946 seems more conventional than her previous plays. Written in 1938, *Doctor Faustus Lights the Lights* (1938) was produced in New York at the Cherry Lane Theatre in 1951, with music by Richard Banks. Michael Hoffman sees the work as expressing Stein's "concerns to such traditional literary problems as those of moral value and human identity."

In Stein's version of the Faust legend Doctor Faustus has sold his soul to the Devil not only for eternal life but for eternal light. With the Devil's help Faustus becomes the inventor of the electric light, which serves as a metaphor for Stein's dissatisfaction with the effects of technology on personal identity. According to Bridgman, the play is about "the light cast by various sources—electricity, the moon, the sun, and candles," but "darkness overwhelms all at the end of the play."

The posthumously published *The First Reader & Three Plays* (1946) includes four dramatic works of the 1940s: *Lesson Sixteen. A Play* (written 1941), *In a Garden. A Tragedy in One Act* (written 1943, produced 1949), *Three Sisters Who Are Not Sisters. A Melodrama* (written 1943, produced 1965), and *Look and Long. A Play in Three Acts* (written 1943, produced 1969). In these plays Bridgman detects an "undercurrent of trouble and despair," but he adds, "The oppressive mood is lightened by examples of kindness, good humor, and even a measure of success." He also finds a sense of optimism in *Yes Is for a Very Young Man* (written 1944–1945), a play about the French Resistance. The first nonmusical play by Stein to be staged during her lifetime, *Yes Is for a Very Young Man* was produced in Pasadena, California, in 1946. Although Bridgman calls the play "poor, crude theater" with "ludicrously stiff" language, Hoffman finds the play "an often charming and even quite moving piece of drama," in spite of its bathos and static plot. Originally titled "In Savoy," *Yes Is for a Very Young Man* is beholden to Stein*'s Wars I Have Seen* (1945), a memoir-

Dorothy Dow in The Mother of Us All *(photograph by Carl Van Vechten)*

diary of Stein's experiences living in the French countryside during World War II. The play displays a deftness at using language to express what Hoffman calls Stein's "sense of basic social realities and of the complexity of interpersonal relationships."

Stein's last work, *The Mother of Us All* (written 1946), is another libretto for an opera by Virgil Thomson. Based on the life of nineteenth-century feminist and suffragist Susan B. Anthony, it opened in New York City in 1947. Bridgman calls the opera a "valedictory," while Hoffman says it is "Stein's finest contribution to stage literature and is also one of the major works of her late period."

As Elizabeth Fifer suggests, *The Mother of Us All* is ultimately about Stein—who, like Anthony, also struggled for reform. While Anthony was a political and social crusader, Stein was a literary crusader. Both women's ideas were ahead of their time, and both were more visionary than many of their contemporaries. According to Bowers, Anthony's speeches in Stein's work "correspond moment by moment to her thoughts and feelings. Susan listens to an inner voice, unconscious of the effect on an audience of the words that record her thoughts. Hers is the speech of the mother; it is antipatriarchal." At the end of the play Anthony says that "life is strife, I was a martyr all my life not to what I won but to what was done. Do you know because I tell you so, or do you know, do you know. My long life, my long life." She could be speaking of Stein's own long battle to overturn the stale conventions of language.

In her innovative uses of language Stein seems to have bridged the gap between conventionalism and experimentalism. A writer who strove to revitalize communication and rescue it from hackneyed clichés, she sought an instinctive use and understanding of language. For Stein language is the only tool capable of advancing social harmony and personal integrity and of negotiating the affiliation between thought and word.

Letters:
Sherwood Anderson/Gertrude Stein Correspondence and Personal Essays, edited by Ray Lewis White (Chapel Hill: University of North Carolina Press, 1972);

Dear Sammy Letters from Gertrude Stein & Alice B. Toklas, edited by Samuel M. Steward (Boston: Houghton Mifflin, 1977);

The Letters of Gertrude Stein and Carl Van Vechten, 2 volumes, edited by Edward Burns (New York: Columbia University Press, 1986);

The Letters of Gertrude Stein and Thornton Wilder, edited by Edward Burns and Ulla E. Dydo, with William Rice (New Haven & London: Yale University Press, 1996).

Interviews:
Lansing Warren, "Gertrude Stein Views Life and Politics," *New York Times,* 6 May 1934, pp. 9, 23;

Laurie Eglington, "Gertrude Stein Reveals Reactions to Home Country," *Art News* (3 November 1934): 3–4;

Isidore Schneider, "Home Girl Makes Good," *New Masses* (27 November 1934): 21–22;

Whit Burnett, "Conversations with Gertrude Stein," *Story* (May 1935): 2, 98;

Robert Bartlett Haas, "Transatlantic Interview" (5–6 January 1946), *Uclan Review,* 8 (Summer 1962): 3–11; 9 (Spring 1963): 40–48; 10 (Winter 1964): 44–48.

Bibliographies:
Robert Bartlett Haas and Donald Clifford Gallup, *A Catalogue of the Published and Unpublished Writings of Gertrude Stein* (New Haven: Yale University Press, 1941);

Robert A. Wilson, *Gertrude Stein: A Bibliography* (New York: Phoenix Bookshop, 1974);

Ray Lewis White, *Gertrude Stein and Alice B. Toklas: A Reference Guide* (Boston: G. K. Hall, 1984).

Biographies:
Elizabeth Sprigge, *Gertrude Stein: Her Life and Work* (New York: Harper, 1957);

John Malcolm Brinnin, *The Third Rose: Gertrude Stein and Her World* (Boston: Little, Brown, 1959);

Alice B. Toklas, *What is Remembered* (New York, Chicago & San Francisco: Holt, Rinehart & Winston, 1964);

W. G. Rogers, *When This You See Remember Me: Gertrude Stein in Person* (Indianapolis & New York: Bobbs-Merrill, 1964);

James R. Mellow, *Charmed Circle: Gertrude Stein & Company* (New York: Praeger, 1974);

Linda Simon, *Gertrude Stein: A Composite Portrait* (New York: Avon, 1974);

Janet Hobhouse, *Everybody Who Was Anybody: A Biography of Gertrude Stein* (New York: Putnam, 1975);

Linda Simon, *Gertrude Stein Remembered* (Lincoln & London: University of Nebraska Press, 1994);

Renate Stendhal, ed., *Gertrude Stein In Words and Pictures: A Photobiography* (Chapel Hill, N.C.: Algonquin Books of Chapel Hill, 1994);

Linda Wagner-Martin, *Favored Strangers: Gertrude Stein and Her Family* (New Brunswick, N.J.: Rutgers University Press, 1995);

Brenda Wineapple, *Sister Brother: Gertrude and Leo Stein* (New York: Putnam, 1996).

References:
Meg Albrinck, "'How can a sister see Saint Therese suitably': Difficulties in Staging Gertrude Stein's Four Saints in Three Acts," *Women's Studies,* 25 (1995): 1–22;

Shari Benstock, "Gertrude Stein and Alice B. Toklas: Rue De Fleurus," in her *Women of the Left Bank: Paris, 1900–1940* (Austin: University of Texas Press, 1986), pp. 143–193;

Jane Palatini Bowers, *"They Watch me As They Watch This": Gertrude Stein's Metadrama* (Philadelphia: University of Pennsylvania Press, 1991);

Richard Bridgman, *Gertrude Stein in Pieces* (New York: Oxford University Press, 1970);

Harriet Scott Chessman, *The Public is Invited to Dance* (Stanford, Cal.: Stanford University Press, 1989);

Marianne De Koven, *A Different Language: Gertrude Stein's Experimental Writing* (Madison: University of Wisconsin Press, 1983);

Randa Dubnick, *The Structure of Obscurity: Gertrude Stein, Language, and Cubism* (Urbana & Chicago: University of Illinois Press, 1984);

Ulla E. Dydo, Introduction to *A Stein Reader / Gertrude Stein,* edited by Dydo (Evanston, Ill.: Northwestern University Press, 1993);

Elizabeth Fifer, *Rescued Readings: A Reconstruction of Gertrude Stein's Difficult Texts* (Detroit: Wayne State University Press, 1992);

Donald Gallup, ed., *The Flowers of Friendship: Letters Written to Gertrude Stein* (New York: Knopf, 1953);

David Harris, "The Original Four Saints in Three Acts," *Drama Review,* 26 (Spring 1982): 101–130;

Michael Hoffman, *The Development of Abstractionism in the Writings of Gertrude Stein* (Philadelphia: University of Pennsylvania Press, 1965);

Hoffman, *Gertrude Stein* (Boston: Twayne, 1976);

Bruce Kellner, ed., *A Gertrude Stein Companion: Content With the Example* (New York & Westport, Conn.: Greenwood Press, 1988);

Richard Kostelanetz, Introduction to *The Yale Gertrude Stein: Selections* (New Haven & London: Yale University Press, 1980);

Marc Robinson, "Gertrude Stein, Forgotten Playwright," *South Atlantic Quarterly,* 91 (Summer 1992): 621–643;

Betsy Alayne Ryan, *Gertrude Stein's Theatre of the Absolute* (Ann Arbor: UMI Research Press, 1984);

James F. Schaeffer Jr., "An Examination of Language as Gesture in a Play by Gertrude Stein," *Literature in Performance,* 3 (November 1982): 1–14;

Catharine R. Stimpson, "Gertrice/Altrude: Stein, Toklas, and the Paradox of the Happy Marriage," in *Mothering the Mind,* edited by Ruth Perry and Martine Watson Brownley (New York & London: Holmes & Meier, 1984), pp. 122–139;

Stimpson, "Gertrude Stein and the Transposition of Gender," in *The Poetics of Gender,* edited by Nancy K. Miller (New York: Columbia University Press, 1986), pp. 1–18;

Stimpson, "The Somagrams of Gertrude Stein," *Poetics Today,* 6 (1985): 67–80;

Donald Sutherland, *Gertrude Stein: A Biography of Her Work* (New Haven: Yale University Press, 1951);

Edmund Wilson, *Axel's Castle* (New York & London: Scribners, 1931), pp. 237–256;

Wilson, *The Shores of Light: A Literary Chronicle of the Twenties and Thirties* (New York: Farrar, Straus & Cudahy, 1951), pp. 575–586;

Elizabeth Winston, "Making History in The Mother of Us All," *Mosaic,* 20 (Fall 1987): 117–129.

Papers:

The Beinecke Library at Yale University is the major repository of Gertrude Stein's manuscripts, correspondence, and unpublished notebook. There are also significant Stein collections at the Bancroft Library at the University of California at Berkeley, the Harry Ransom Humanities Research Center, University of Texas at Austin, the Butler Library at Columbia University, McKeldin Library at the University of Maryland, the Houghton Library at Harvard University, the Newberry Library in Chicago, and the Alderman Library at the University of Virginia.

Wendy Wasserstein

(18 October 1950 –   )

Nancy L. Bunge
Michigan State University

PLAY PRODUCTIONS: *Any Woman Can't,* New York, Playwrights Horizons, 1973;

Happy Birthday, Montpelier Pizz-azz, New Haven, 1974;

When Dinah Shore Ruled the Earth, by Wasserstein and Christopher Durang, New Haven, Yale Cabaret Theater, 1975;

Uncommon Women and Others, New Haven, 1975; revised and enlarged, New York, Phoenix Theater at Marymount Manhattan Theater, 21 November 1977;

Isn't It Romantic? New York, Phoenix Theater at Marymount Manhattan Theater, 13 June 1981; revised, New York, Playwrights Horizons, 15 December 1983;

Tender Offer, New York, Ensemble Studio Theater, 1983;

Miami, New York, Playwrights Horizons, January 1986;

The Man in a Case, adapted from Anton Chekhov's story, part of *Orchards, Orchards, Orchards,* New York, Lucille Lortel Theater, 22 April 1986;

The Heidi Chronicles, Seattle, Seattle Repertory Theatre, 6 April 1988; New York, Playwrights Horizons, 12 December 1988;

The Sisters Rosensweig, New York, Lincoln Center, 22 October 1992;

An American Daughter, New York, Lincoln Center, 13 April 1997;

Waiting for Philip Glass, in *Love's Fire,* Minneapolis, Guthrie Theater Lab, 7 January 1998; New York, Joseph Papp Public Theater, 19 June 1998.

BOOKS: *Any Woman Can't: A Play,* M.A. thesis, City College of New York, 1973;

Uncommon Women and Others (New York: Avon, 1978);

Isn't It Romantic (Garden City, N.Y.: Doubleday, 1984);

The Heidi Chronicles (Garden City, N.Y.: Fireside Theater, 1989);

Bachelor Girls (New York: Knopf, 1990);

The Sisters Rosensweig: A Play (New York: Harcourt Brace, 1993; London: French, 1996);

Pamela's First Musical (New York: Hyperion Books for Children, 1996);

Wendy Wasserstein (photograph by James Hamilton)

An American Daughter (New York: Harcourt Brace, 1998).

Collection: *The Heidi Chronicles and Other Plays* (New York: Harcourt Brace Jovanovich, 1990)—comprises *Uncommon Women and Others, Isn't It Romantic?,* and *The Heidi Chronicles.*

PRODUCED SCRIPTS: *Uncommon Women and Others,* television, Public Broadcasting Service, 1978;

The Sorrows of Gin: A Teleplay, adapted from John Cheever's story, television, Public Broadcasting Service, 1979;

Sketches for *Comedy Zone,* television, CBS, 1984–1985;

"*Drive,*" *She Said,* television, Public Broadcasting System, 1987;

The Object of My Affection, adapted from Stephen McCauley's novel, motion picture, 20th Century-Fox, 1998.

OTHER: *The Man in a Case,* in *Orchards, Orchards, Orchards* (New York: Broadway Play Publishing, 1987), pp. 19–31;

"The Ties that Wound," in *Between Friends,* edited by Mickey Pearlman (Boston: Houghton Mifflin, 1994), pp. 109–113;

"Workout," in *Facing Forward,* edited by Leah Frank (New York: Broadway Play Publishing, 1995), pp. 499–502;

Edith Wharton, *The Age of Innocence,* introduction by Wasserstein (New York: Bantam/Doubleday/ Dell, 1996).

SELECTED PERIODICAL PUBLICATIONS– UNCOLLECTED: "Tender Offer," *Antaeus,* 66 (1991): 452–457;

"How's He Doing?" review of *Murder at City Hall* by Edward I. Koch and Herbert Resnicow, *New York Times Book Review,* 8 October 1995, p.23;

"A Play in Nine Scenes: Jill's Adventures in Real Estate or, I Can Get It for You at 3.2," *New Yorker,* 77 (16 October 1995): 170–177;

"The Power of Beauty," *Time,* 148 (8 July 1996): 70;

"A Few Good Authors Share Their Intimate Thoughts," by Wasserstein and others, *Cosmopolitan,* 222 (1 February 1997): 98;

"Hillary Clinton's Muddled Legacy," *New York Times,* 25 August 1998, A17.

In 1989 Wendy Wasserstein became the first woman playwright to win a Tony; that same year she also collected the Pulitzer Prize and the award for best new play from New York Drama Critics Circle. These accolades for *The Heidi Chronicles* (first performed in 1988), a play that traces the confusions of a female art historian from the 1960s through the 1980s, suggest that Wasserstein has achieved her goal of writing drama that invites audiences to care about women's lives and dilemmas. Wasserstein frequently identifies herself as a member of the generation on the cusp of the women's movement; her work communicates and analyzes the confusion that has accompanied this enormous cultural transition.

Wendy Wasserstein was born on 18 October 1950 in Brooklyn, New York. Her father, Morris W. Wasserstein, was a successful textile manufacturer, who invented velveteen. Her mother, Lola (whose maiden name was Schleifer), was a dancer. Wasserstein attended the exclusive Calhoun School on the upper East Side of Manhattan and studied dancing with June Taylor, whose troupe appeared regularly on *The Jackie Gleason Show.* She also spent many Saturday afternoons at Broadway matinees. Although she has loved plays much of her life, the notion of writing them did not occur to Wasserstein until a friend convinced her to take Leonard Berkman's playwrighting course at the neighboring Smith College during her junior year at Mount Holyoke College (Wasserstein graduated from Mount Holyoke in 1971 with a B.A. in history). She enjoyed the course so much that she later studied creative writing at the City College of the City University of New York with Joseph Heller and Israel Horovitz, receiving her M.A. in creative writing in 1973. The play she wrote as her thesis, *Every Woman Can't,* was produced Off Broadway by Playwrights Horizons, a group and community Wasserstein frequently speaks of with gratitude and respect. She then moved on to the Yale Drama School, receiving her M.F.A. in 1976.

Her first acclaimed play, *Uncommon Women and Others* (1975), was initially written as a one-act play at Yale; the revised, expanded version appeared in 1977, six years after Wasserstein's graduation from Mount Holyoke. The play opens with a 1978 six-year reunion of women who had graduated from Mount Holyoke in 1972; one of the central characters, Holly Kaplan, is autobiographically based.

Shortly after the reunion begins, the play shifts back to the women's final year at Mount Holyoke, setting out their histories. This varied group includes Rita Altabel, a promiscuous rebel who repeatedly assures her friends that they will all be "amazing" in a certain number of years, moving the deadline back as they age. She had hoped to write and planned to persuade her husband to facilitate her literary career; instead, she has done essentially nothing since graduation besides getting married. In college, Samantha Stewart hoped to build her life around her fiancé, Bob, who she felt deserved this devotion because of his superiority to her; at the reunion, she seems to have succeeded in attaining her goal, but doing so has left her feeling somewhat inadequate and embarrassed by her lack of professional achievement: "Sometimes I get intimidated by all of Robert's friends who come to the house. And I think I haven't done very much of anything important." Kate Quin, the Phi Beta Kappa philosophy major who consumed romance novels during every spare moment, worried at graduation that entering law school would set her on a path to success, not happiness. Six years later, this prophecy seems fulfilled: the initial description of her reports that her "attache case alternately makes her feel like a successful grown-up, or handcuffed." When Samantha announces her pregnancy, Kate promises to babysit on Election Day, her only day off, and wonders if she'll ever have a child. Muffet Di Nicola drifts both during college and afterward, waiting for salvation. She winds up contentedly working for an insurance company.

Holly makes explicit the confusion that runs as an undercurrent through all these women's lives and prevents them from living wholeheartedly. While in college, she says she hopes she will get married, divorce, and live alone; yet, at the same time she claims to seek a solitary life, she desperately pursues a man she once met in a museum. At the reunion, when her friends tease her about roaming through multiple graduate programs, she confesses she had been reluctant to meet with them, "mostly because I haven't made any specific choices."

Throughout the play a male voiceover reassures these women of the possibilities that exist for all the uncommon women who attend Mount Holyoke, citing the achievements of the alumnae who preceded them. Toward the end of the play a woman takes over this job, announcing that "Women still encounter overwhelming obstacles to achievement and recognition despite gradual abolition of legal and political disabilities. Society has trained women from childhood to accept a limited set of options and restricted levels of aspiration." The action of the play supports her pessimistic rendition of women's opportunities. These talented women want to achieve "it all," but having options does not mean knowing how to select from them, let alone how to realize them.

But through the women's shared confusion, the play offers a kind of answer. The one thing that remains unambiguous to all of them is their love and support for one another. They care about and enjoy each other, despite the different paths they have taken. This emotional tie means that even though none of them may ever turn out to be "amazing," they will always be there for one another. Holly puts it this way: "I guess since college I've missed the comfort and acceptance I felt with all of you. And I thought you didn't need that anymore, so I didn't see you." By the end of the play these women have learned that their most crucial bond is not their shared mission to transform themselves into amazing women, but their willingness to accept each other—for by behaving generously with each other, they learn to treat themselves gently, and self-acceptance must precede self-realization.

The play seems a summation of what Wasserstein learned during the first six years after she graduated from Mount Holyoke. Uncertain about what career to pursue even after receiving her M.A. and having *Every Woman Can't* produced, she had applied to Columbia Business School and Yale Drama School and was accepted at both. She followed her heart to Yale. When a classmate complained that he could not get interested in the females populating the one-act version of *Uncommon Women and Others* she wrote as a student,

his remark helped Wasserstein realize how essential it was for her to write plays about women.

The critics generally praised *Uncommon Women and Others* for its humor and compassion. It received a *Village Voice* Off-Broadway Award as well as the Joseph Jefferson and the Boston Critics awards. A year after it appeared Off-Broadway it was telecast by PBS. It had a solid cast on both occasions: Jill Eikenberry, Ann McDonough, Alma Cuero, Ellen Parker, Swoosie Kurtz, and Anne Levine. Glenn Close also appeared in the Broadway version; Meryl Streep replaced her on PBS. When the play was revived in New York in 1994, the critics liked it less than in 1977; it often struck them as tired. For instance, one critic for *The New Yorker* (14 November 1994) wrote that she found it "impossible to avoid the conviction that in reviving and updating *Uncommon Women* the playwright has settled for being stuck in her own shtick."

Wasserstein's next play, *Isn't It Romantic?* (1984), focuses on the relationship between two women trying to make satisfying lives from the new options available to them courtesy of the women's movement. Although the play shares many characteristics with *Uncommon Women and Others,* it resolves the central issues in a radically different way. The main character, Janie Blumberg, is a young, single woman in New York City with a merchant father and a dancer mother, Simon and Tasha Blumberg, who persistently encourage their daughter to get married. The other major character, Harriet Cornwall, has an unmarried executive mother, Lillian Cornwall, who is as detached as Janie's mother is passionate. Lillian decided to leave her own marriage when it became clear that she had to choose between marriage and a career, and she sees no reason for her daughter not to make the same choice. The emotional dreariness of Lillian's life reveals itself when she encounters Tasha in the park and claims that giddy abandon has overcome her because she plans to eat a hotdog and a sundae in the same day.

Janie meets and falls in love with Martin Sterling, a doctor who calls her "Monkey" and rents an apartment in Brooklyn for the two of them. Although Janie loves him, she has just started to succeed as a freelance writer, and Marty shows signs of wanting her to put aside her ambitions to attend to his needs. He tells her, "You want to interview at 'Sesame Street,' fine. They do nice work. But don't let it take over your life. And don't let it take over our life. That's a real trap." Eventually Janie decides to leave Marty because she understands that she must live her own life fully rather than through and for someone else. As she puts it: "Marty, you're not right for me. I can't move in with you now. If I did that, I'd always be a monkey, a sweet little girl."

When Janie tells Harriet of her decision, she expects understanding, since Harriet has persistently emphasized the importance of cultivating the courage to live independently. But, instead, Janie learns that Harriet has decided to marry Joe Stine, a man she hardly knows, out of terror of being alone, like her mother: "Joe makes me feel like I have a family. I never had a family. I had you and Lillian, but I never felt I could have what other women just assumed they would get."

Janie is furious because she felt close to Harriet, but what she considered intimate, honest discussions were apparently meaningless noise: "Harriet, you never really listened to me and you never really told me about yourself. And that's sad." The only other woman friend in this play, Cynthia Peterson, exists solely through the unhappy messages she leaves on Janie's answering machine. All of them, like her concluding message asking Janie whether or not she should write to an eligible man whose picture she sees in *The New York Post,* reveal her desperate flight from accepting responsibility for her life. Female friends do not provide salvation and support in this play; they are far too busy trying frantically to meet their own needs to share genuine solace and friendship, let alone the vitality that the characters in *Uncommon Women and Others* retained even at their most anguished moments.

As Janie sits alone in her apartment, her marriage-minded parents descend on her. She points out to her mother that Tasha has not provided Janie with a stellar example of conventionality. Tasha defends herself: "I believe a person should have a little originality—a little 'you know.' Otherwise you just grow old like everybody else." Janie agrees and pleads with her mother: "All you have to do is trust me a little bit . . . . Mother, sit, relax, let me figure it out." Her mother responds, "But, honey, if I sit, who's going to dance?" Janie answers that question best by dancing alone as the play ends.

Isn't It Romantic? argues that women need to stop worrying about getting the right answer and having it all; instead, they need to focus on trusting their passions, wherever those take them. As Wasserstein put it in an interview with Kathleen Betsko and Rachel Koenig, "What's really liberating is developing from the inside out. Having the confidence to go from your gut or whatever it is you want. Janie is able to do that." Wasserstein thinks that comedy, at its best, can contribute to this spirit: "This life spirit creates a current, a buoyance, which, getting back to drama, is very important. It's important to reach the essence of that spirit in what you create. That, to me, is heroic."

Wasserstein said she got the idea for *Isn't It Romantic?* when her friends started becoming aware of their biological clocks: "When I was getting out of

Madeline Kahn, Jane Alexander, and Frances McDormand in the 1992 New York production of The Sisters Rosensweig

Mount Holyoke in 1971, there was this pressure to have a career. If you said you were getting married back then, it was embarrassing. But suddenly all my women friends were talking about getting married and having babies; things had somehow turned around. I started trying to figure it all out, and I decided it might be interesting to write a comedy about it" (*Working Woman,* August 1984). Although Wasserstein claims that her life informs all her characters and that she has as much in common with Harriet as with Janie, the ties between Wasserstein's life and Janie's seem clear. Wasserstein has frequently spoken of her mother's eccentricity and anxiety that Wasserstein marry. And when Wasserstein was twenty-eight, Janie's age, she almost married a man who asked her to choose between him and her work. Wasserstein admits that she came close to marrying: "Right about now we'd be divorced and sitting at opposite ends of the temple during the bar mitzvah. And I probably wouldn't have written most of my plays" (*Entertainment Weekly,* 13 October 1995).

Critics did not like the first version of *Isn't It Romantic?* and Wasserstein responded to their complaints about its diffusion by continuing to work on the play. But in order for the play to develop a center that would hold it together, the character of Janie had to develop. At first, Wasserstein wanted Janie to marry, but eventually she came to accept and enjoy Janie's burgeoning strength. Janie's development into a strong character gives the play vitality as well as unity and direction. In the 1983 revised production of *Isn't It Romantic?* Christine Rose played Janie, while Betty

Comedon and Stephen Pearlman played her parents, and Meryl Streep did Cynthia Peterson's voice. Critics praised the new version.

Her next play, *The Heidi Chronicles* (1988), returns to familiar Wasserstein terrain, the issue of how women deal with the new options precipitated by the women's movement. Once again, the central character must choose between pursuing her own needs and desires and having a successful relationship with a man. But this crucial choice has been made before *The Heidi Chronicles* begins. The play opens with a lecture on female artists by Dr. Heidi Holland, art historian. She concludes her talk by describing a painting by Mrs. Lily Martin Spencer as reminiscent of "One of those horrible high-school dances. And you sort of want to dance, and you sort of want to go home, and you sort of don't know what you want. So you hang around, a fading rose in an exquisitely detailed dress, waiting to see what might happen."

The next scene takes place in 1965 with the sixteen-year-old Heidi assuming just such a stance at a high-school dance with her friend Susan. By the end of the evening, Heidi has embroiled herself in her first problematic relationship, a lifelong friendship with Peter Patrone, who reveals to her ten years later that he is gay.

In the next scene, at the 1968 Eugene McCarthy campaign in New Hampshire, Heidi meets her second lifelong male problem: Scoop Rosenbaum, a Princeton dropout turned political activist who successfully propositions Heidi shortly after they meet. The third scene is set in the 1970s as Heidi attends a women's consciousness-raising group with Susan and confesses there that she submits far too easily to Scoop: "The problem is me. I could make a better choice. I have an old friend, Peter, who I know would be a much better choice. But I keep allowing this guy to account for so much of what I think of myself. I allow him to make me feel valuable. And the bottom line is, I know what's wrong."

Scoop eventually marries someone who will demand less of him than Heidi would, even though he loves Heidi. At his wedding reception, he tells her:

Let's say we married and I asked you to devote the, say, next ten years of your life to me. To making me a home and a family and a life so secure that I could with some confidence go out into the world each day and attempt to get an A. You'd say, "No." You'd say, "Why can't we be partners? Why can't we both go out into the world and get an A?" And you'd be absolutely valid and correct.

He goes on to explain that Lisa, his bride, is not "an A+" like Wendy, "But I don't want to come home to an A+. A- maybe, but not A+." As much as Scoop

admires Heidi, he predicts an unhappy life for her, because she asks too much of it: "If you aim for six and get six, everything will work out nicely. But if you aim for ten in all things and get six, you're going to be very disappointed. And, unfortunately, that's why you 'quality time' girls are going to be one generation of disappointed women. Interesting, exemplary, even sexy, but basically unhappy. The ones who open doors usually are."

Heidi winds up living an independent life and doing well at it; but she feels lonely and abandoned, not so much by men as by the women she considered her sisters. When asked to give a talk to her Alumnae Association, she loses her composure and says, "I don't blame any of us. We're all concerned, intelligent, good women. *Pauses*. It's just that I feel stranded. And I thought the whole point was that we wouldn't feel stranded. I thought the point was that we were all in this together."

Heidi's relationship with her lifelong friend Susan does not supply anything like the sustenance the characters in *Uncommon Women and Others* offered one another. Susan gets irritated with Heidi for remaining loyal to her at the high-school dance and scaring off a potential date. When consciousness raising is in, Susan drags Heidi to a group. When communes come into fashion, Susan goes to Montana to join one. But when greed comes of age, she is back in New York and then in Los Angeles, frantically chasing money. Finally, she asks Heidi to serve as a consultant on a sitcom that will explore where their generation of women went wrong, what mistakes produced their miserable lives. Heidi replies: "I don't think we made such big mistakes. And I don't want to see three gals on the town who do." Susan goes on to produce the show without Heidi's help; it is a smash hit. And Heidi does not know what to do with her unhappiness and with her envy of women who have made other choices, because she believes that she has consistently chosen the best option available to her.

At the end of the play she makes a choice that seems to make her happy. She adopts a child, names her Judy, and hopes that the girl will enjoy a world relatively free of the limits that have restrained Heidi's life. Heidi writes a history of female artists and sees herself as part of a long series of women struggling to express themselves. She hopes that through her scholarship she has contributed to giving women a chance to live more fully and that her daughter will take full advantage of it: *"The final image of the play, as the audience exits, is a slide of* HEIDI *triumphantly holding Judy in front of a museum banner for a Georgia O'Keefe retrospective."*

Wasserstein has moved her protagonist beyond Holly's reliance on her friends, and Janie's independence, into a sense of belonging to and participating in history. The structure of *The Heidi Chronicles* reflects this sense by moving rapidly from 1965 to 1989 with brief scenes that evoke telling events from the social milieu of each period. *The Heidi Chronicles* not only affirms the movement of history, it re-creates it.

The play also puts women's issues in a broader context than Wasserstein's earlier works. Heidi is one of an entire generation who, as the play reminds audiences, felt certain that they could change the world. Yet, nothing works out startlingly well for any of the characters in this play, male or female. The happiest, most confident ones, like Susan, have stopped reflecting and simply capitulated to fashion. At their last meeting Heidi brings up a paradox that she has been pondering: "Susie, do you ever think that what makes you a person is also what keeps you from being a person?" Susan responds, "I'm sorry, honey, but you're too deep for me. By now I've been so many people, I don't know who I am. And I don't care."

Once Peter begins living openly as a gay person, he seems happier; but he has the same offstage conflicts with his lovers as heterosexuals. They come and go. And in the age of AIDS, a gay person lives constantly with death. Peter tells Heidi that her trials seem trivial to him:

> Okay, Heidi, I'd say about once a month now I gather in some church, meeting house, or concert hall with handsome men all my own age, and in the front row is usually a couple my parents' age, the father's in a suit and the mother's tasteful, a pleasant face. And we listen for half an hour to testimonials, memories, amusing anecdotes about a son, a friend, a lover, also handsome, also usually my own age, whom none of us will see again. After the first, the fifth, or the fifteenth of these gatherings, a sadness like yours seems a luxury.

Even Scoop Rosenbaum shows up as the play ends to confess that his acceptance of a life that is only a six has not worked out well. There have been obvious signs of marital problems: Scoop is frequently seen in the company of young women who are not his wife and who wear fishnet stockings and short skirts. He thought the success of his magazine would satisfy him, but he tells Heidi that he has sold it because, like Heidi, he has come to see the way one leads one's personal life influences future generations: "Will my kids say, 'My dad was basically a lazy man and a philanderer, but he had a nose for Connecticut real estate, and we love him because he didn't make us weekend in the Hamptons?'"

He tells her that he, too, has decided to go for a ten after hearing about her adopting a child. Heidi replies that she hopes the world will be a healthier place for both their children:

> Scoop, there's a chance, just a milli-notion, that Pierre Rosenbaum and Judy Holland will meet on a plane over Chicago. . . . And he'll never tell her it's either/or baby. And she'll never think she's worthless unless he lets her have it all. And maybe, just maybe, things will be a little better. And, yes, that does make me happy.

By the end of the play no one expects complete bliss; all the central characters have realized their limited universe and accepted it. Reflective women continue to suffer from the limits of gender roles in this play, but so do reflective men. But Heidi, Peter, and Scoop all hope that by doing their best, they prepare the way for a better future: Heidi and Scoop raise their children, and Peter works as a pediatrician.

The critics praised *The Heidi Chronicles,* and it won several awards, most notably the Pulitzer Prize and a Tony for best play. First produced by the Seattle Repertory Theatre on 6 April 1988, it then appeared at Playwrights Horizons on 12 December 1988. It moved to Broadway on 9 March 1989. Joan Allen played Heidi Holland, and Daniel Sullivan directed.

Some critics complained that the wit in the play prevented it from saying anything large; for example, a reviewer for *Theater Journal* (March 1990) wrote that "the trouble with this play is that although it raises serious issues, Wasserstein undercuts serious consideration through facile supporting female characters, sit-com humor and a passive heroine who forms an absence at the center of the play." The reviewer ties these flaws to a judgment made by many critics that the play is not revolutionary enough: "In this way the play will become part of the system that oppresses women and so highly rewards their creative expressions when they aid in its purposes." This reaction seems to miss the fundamental point of the play: that no matter how frenzied the rush of new events, genuine social change occurs painfully slowly. *The Heidi Chronicles* does not just consider women's plight; it comments on a social period, on history, and on the damage done to men as well as women by limited gender roles.

Other critics believed that her work has too strong a political dimension. For instance, one critic for *The Hudson Review* (August 1989) argued that "*The Heidi Chronicles* is a lifeless, vulgar play, rendered all the more irritating by the many awards that this non-playwright has won simply because she is a woman writing on fashionable issues." The fact that Wasserstein writes on women's issues seems to inspire overtly political commentary from critics who bring ideological rather than aesthetic standards to judging her work.

In 1990, Wasserstein's book *Bachelor Girls* appeared; it collects essays that had first appeared in periodicals between 1984 and 1990 and that cover a range of topics, including manicures, Geraldine Ferraro, and Wasserstein's deeply disappointing rendezvous with her banker boyfriend in springtime Paris. Wasserstein admits in her preface she racked her brain to discover some commonality in these essays and then realized that "what the pieces have in common more than anything else . . . is a point of view." That perspective, she hopes, is that of a Bachelor Girl: a single woman who, unlike the spinster or old maid, enjoys a wide range of experiences. Thus, covering topics so diverse that they defy unity and organization indicates the fullness and complications of Wasserstein's or the Bachelor Girl's life and underlines the richness of her perspective.

One leitmotiv of Wasserstein's collection is the danger of women forcing themselves into molds shaped by their social milieu rather than allowing their deepest desires to propel them in distinctive directions. This theme first appears in the second essay, "The World's Worst Boyfriends," which recounts the emotional turmoil women throw themselves into trying to please impossibly demanding men. She urges women not to blame themselves for these failed relationships: "The point is, it's not our fault. It's theirs. They've been this way for centuries." Then Wasserstein proves it with a list of bad boyfriends throughout history, ranging from Arthur Dimmesdale, who let Hester carry the shame of their relationship alone in Nathaniel Hawthorne's *The Scarlet Letter* (1850), to Herman Tarnower, creator of the "Scarsdale Diet," murdered by his lover, Jean Harris, in 1980.

"Tokyo Story," an essay about attending a Tokyo production of *Isn't It Romantic?*, describes Wasserstein's pleasure at discovering an audience of primarily Japanese women who clearly appreciate her story about the life of a twenty-eight-year-old single woman, even though—or perhaps because—in Japan a woman who remains unmarried after twenty-five "is considered a Christmas cake after Christmas." The Japanese director considers presenting Wasserstein's play to a Japanese audience a revolutionary act, and the author seems to agree: "Uyama knows that his production of *Isn't It Romantic?* has made the desired impression on this audience—an audience from a world of pure Takarazuka girls and twenty-six-year-old aging Yule logs. In this matinee performance my play seems to have realized the potential of its comedy. Perhaps I had to travel this far to understand why I write."

"The Sleeping Beauty Syndrome: The New Agony of Single Men" offers a humorous account of how the relationship between the sexes would change if baby-boomer women turned to cultivating their own lives instead of trying to please men. In this alternate universe, "Bachelor Girls in their thirties, the former glut on the marriage market, after years of hearing predictions for a lifetime of desperation, depression, and empty isolation, have accepted and embraced their former plight. Baby-boomer women are now content buying condos alone at the beach, having artificial insemination, and going to Tom Cruise movies on Friday nights with their girlfriends."

Wasserstein notes the desperation of her friends to conceive after they delayed having children to build careers; she worries that deep down they suspect their fertility problems are punishment for living independently. To this generation, "Mother, who at thirty-two had blithely driven around Winnetka with four kids and a golden retriever in the backseat of a station wagon, no longer seemed a deprived person. She seemed fortunate, even blessed."

The last selection in *Bachelor Girls* is a play titled "Boy Meets Girl" that parodies the empty lives awaiting those members of the Yuppie generation, both male and female, who follow the paths laid out for them by social approval: "Apart from twenty years of couples therapy, his-and-her reconstructive surgery, one triple by-pass and four extramarital affairs—they lived happily ever after."

But, usually, when Wasserstein looks to the future in these essays, she sees hope—for both men and women. She observes in the women entering the political scene a willingness to eschew moderation and take new risks so moving that it reduces Wasserstein to tears as readily as Ferraro's nomination once did. On her way to the bar mitzvah of her cousin Rita's son Gregory, Wasserstein yearns for the illusory safety of the 1950s after she has a run-in near a welfare motel with a man who repeatedly calls her "stupid bitch." Once she arrives, she discovers Gregory's speech emphasizes the importance of facing and dealing with the kinds of social difficulties presented and represented by the welfare motel. As Gregory remarks to her: "My speech mentioned that motel. I don't think we can ignore the world around us. Stuff like that." Gregory's comment allows Wasserstein to savor the possibility that the next generation of men and women will shape a richer world with their tolerance and decency.

"My Mother, Then and NOW" indicates that Lola Wasserstein provided her daughter with a model of someone who followed her passions. Just like Janie Blumberg's mother, Wasserstein's mother repeatedly encourages her daughter to carry herself with pride: "If you carry yourself with confidence, head up, chest out, then you'll always look like you're wearing diamonds from Tiffany's." Wasserstein feels she still has more to learn from her mother; she prays that she has inherited her mother's optimism and love of life: "My mother's eyes have seen life, yet have never become bitter." And when her mother exults in producing nine grandchildren, Wasserstein "wondered if I'd ever be able to love as totally and as selflessly as she does."

The link between the issues and the perspectives presented in these essays and the plays that preceded them are obvious. In both genres Wasserstein considers the difficulties generated by gender roles, the need to learn to follow one's passions, and her hope for the future.

Her essays also make clear how seriously Wasserstein takes her art. She admits that work allows her to lose herself, but adds that "nothing is quite as gratifying as recognition for work one is truly proud of," so winning the Tony and the Pulitzer meant a great deal to her. They may even have given her the confidence to collect these essays; she confesses that writing in her own voice intimidates her: "There are no characters to hide behind in the essays. They are much tougher to write in some ways because of their directness."

Although critics seem willing to assign a particular political slant to Wasserstein's plays and then attack her because they espouse a different ideology, they have remained remarkably silent on the subject of these essays, which do present a partisan perspective. Reviews of the book focus on its wit, as though Wasserstein's use of humor somehow prevents critics from noting her political commentary. Even though the humor clearly engages their attention, they usually say that it does not measure up. A reviewer for *Time* (16 April 1990) complained that "The territory Wasserstein covers has been strip-mined by those who preceded her–Nora Ephron, Ellen Goodman and Anna Quindlen." A critic for *The Virginia Quarterly Review* (Autumn 1991) reports that "we get a somewhat amusing view of the glitzy, glamour and fashion of New York, but the humor lacks bite."

Wasserstein confesses in *Bachelor Girls* that she often uses humor to disguise and avoid pain. But she also sees it as a valuable survival mechanism as well as a defense against the pretension that invites one to claim possession of the truth: "When I speak up, it's not because I have any particular answers; rather, I have a desire to puncture the pretentiousness of those who seem certain they do." In these essays Wasserstein uses humor to disarm her readers and to soften the ideology.

According to Wasserstein's introduction to *The Sisters Rosensweig* (1992), she had to struggle to get the humor and the seriousness to coordinate in this play. At its first preview the audience's hilarity during the first act and its restlessness during the second disquieted her. On the way to the cast party, the director, Daniel Sulli-

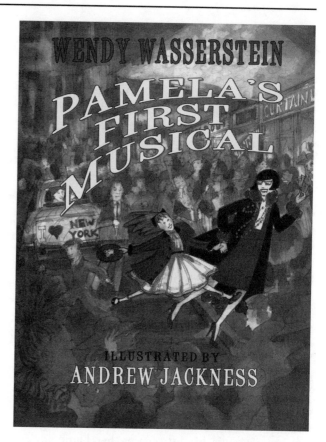

Dust jacket for Wasserstein's children's book about a young girl whose aunt takes her to a Broadway show

van, talked to her about finding a balance between laughter and tears. Wasserstein writes: "Dan has an unerring ability to put his finger always on the heart of the matter. This is neither a serious nor a comedic play. It is hopefully both. The trick writing it, playing it, or even reading it is to find the balance between the bright colors of the humor and the serious issues of identity, self-loathing and the possibility for intimacy and love when it seems no longer possible, or, sadder yet, no longer necessary." She freely admits to the influence of Anton Chekhov on all her work, but especially on this play–along with that of George S. Kaufman, Moss Hart, and Noel Coward. The intertwining of comedy and tragedy at the heart of Chekhov's work is something Wasserstein frequently comments she finds worth emulating. In writing *The Sisters Rosensweig,* she also wanted to go beyond the episodic structure central to her earlier work and write a play that observed the traditional unities, even though it meant she would have to discover new ways to get actors on and off the stage.

The setting for *The Sisters Rosensweig* is Sara Rosensweig Goode's London home. The eldest sister, Sara has worked hard to transcend her beginnings, transforming herself from a Brooklyn Jewish girl to a passionate Anglophile who will not allow her daughter to attend Harvard or Yale because she sees them as "floundering their way to being second rate." An extremely successful international banker for the Hong Kong/Shanghai Bank, she finds herself attracted to Mervyn Kant, a Jewish furrier from the States, who appropriately describes her as "an American Jewish woman living in London, working for a Chinese Hong Kong bank, and taking weekends at a Polish resort with a daughter who's running off to Lithuania!"

She capitulates to Kant's charms, surprising no one more than herself, and by the end of the play she not only admits her affection for a Jewish man who sells fake fur but also, when her daughter asks her name, describes herself as Sara Rosensweig and admits that she first sang at a Hanukkah festival. As the play ends, she accepts her ties to the Jewish background she shares with Kant, just as her eyes retain the vitality he sees in old family photographs. He tells her, "Unfortunately, most of them and their families didn't survive. But Sara, when I look into your eyes, I see those women's strength and their intelligence."

Sara's two sisters, Pfeni and Gorgeous, help her accept the reality of her life and emotions, as well as Kant. Sara and Gorgeous also help Pfeni straighten out her romantic life by offering her blunt advice. Pfeni entertains the illusion that she has a relationship and the possibility of a family with a bisexual named Geoffrey. Sara points out that Pfeni is kidding herself about a permanent relationship with him, and Gorgeous says, "Don't tell me you have Geoffrey. I know you can't judge a book by its cover, but sweetsie, you're at the wrong library altogether." Sara helps Pfeni achieve the honest self-acceptance she needs to let go of her delusion and invest herself seriously in her writing: "You . . . have a true calling, and the sad and surprisingly weak thing is you're actively trying to avoid it. I think you care too much and you're looking for excuses not to." When Geoffrey makes the predictable announcement that he wants to return to men, Pfeni goes back out into the world to do her real job as a journalist, telling Sara's daughter, Tess, as she goes through the front door that "The best advice I've ever gotten was from your mother."

Even Gorgeous, the sister who dresses up in fake designer clothes and represents herself as an exemplar of the perfect family life their mother wanted for them all, confesses that her husband has not had a job for two years, stays up all night writing detective novels, and cannot believe she is staying with him. When she receives a real Chanel suit, complete with all the accessories she contends make any outfit, Gorgeous returns it to raise money for her children's tuition.

By the conclusion of the play, Sara's daughter, Tess, also abandons a fraudulent role as an advocate for Lithuanian causes. She realizes the emptiness of her commitment while attending a rally and returns home to ask her mother, "If I've never really been Jewish, and I'm not actually American anymore, and I'm not English or European then who am I?" Sara replies that Tess resembles her "smart, . . . competent, . . . beautiful and brave" grandmother, Rita; therefore, Tess is "smart enough, and brave enough" to find her own niche. And a play that has touched repeatedly on the truism that daughters compulsively rebel against their mothers ends with Tess and her mother singing together, clearly expressing their love.

This play recalls and extends many of the themes from Wasserstein's earlier plays. The emphasis on trusting one's passions reappears here in conjunction with, rather than in opposition to, the support and encouragement women can and do provide one another. The positive sense of history moving forward functions here both individually and collectively. During two days the four women characters in this play help each other discover a clearer sense of direction. The statue representing rebirth that Pfeni brings in at the opening of the play seems an appropriate symbol for them all. But the play also alludes to positive historical movements: the East Block crumbles, while the descendants of concentration camp victims acquire power over those who destroyed their ancestors, relying on the vitality those same ancestors passed on to them. By owning one's past, one shapes a better future. To these themes Wasserstein adds another: the secret of love is honesty, with oneself and with others. These notions all emerge from an apparently quiet play about three sisters getting together to celebrate a birthday.

The Sisters Rosensweig opened on 22 October 1992 at Lincoln Center, with Frances McDormand as Pfeni, Jane Alexander as Sara, Madeline Kahn as Gorgeous, Julie Dretzin as Tess, and Robert Klein as Mervyn Kant. When the production moved to Broadway, the cast remained largely intact: only Frances McDormand was replaced by Christine Estabrook.

Critics generally admired *The Sisters Rosensweig*, seeing in it that synthesis of humor and insight Wasserstein has sought throughout her career. The critic for *New York* (2 November 1992) reported that "She is surely one of our wittiest one-liner writers, but under the bubbles and eddies of her wit are real people in deep water resolutely, resonantly trying to keep from drowning." The reviewer for *The Spectator* (6 March 1993) suggested that Wasserstein's work has achieved a new depth: "Wasserstein's art now has a settled-in feeling. It breathes." But some critics persist in measuring Wasserstein's work against their own standards for feminism, as did the critic for *The Hudson Review* (Summer 1993) who judged the play "pseudo-feminist" because the women in the play allow men control over their lives.

Wasserstein says she conceived the notion of writing a play about an American woman in London when she spent time in England on a fellowship writing *The Heidi Chronicles*. About the same time, chaperoning her niece at a chess tournament, she visited Eastern Europe, then firmly under Soviet control; later she traveled to the Polish town where her relatives once lived and saw dark evidence of the efficiency of the Holocaust in the fact that no one in the town resembled her or her sister. She vowed to keep her ancestors' stories alive. So, *The Sisters Rosensweig* reflects both Wasserstein's travels and the political, cultural, and historical questions these trips inevitably evoked.

The play is dedicated to Wasserstein's sister Sandra, an executive at American Express, whom the author admits served as a vague model for Sara. Gorgeous shares a few traits with Wasserstein's other sister, Georgette: "In the play, as in real life, she is the lighthearted sister who likes color-coordinated aerobic-wear, escapes the city and has lots of children." And Wasserstein confesses she shares traits with Pfeni, including a tendency to dash around instead of settling into the serious work she finds the most fulfilling. Wasserstein frequently comments that her characters take over their development and become virtual roommates, and she confesses that living with Pfeni sent her back to work: "Pfeni's not writing . . . may be why this play was written."

Between *The Sisters Rosensweig* and Wasserstein's next play, *An American Daughter* (1997), Wasserstein produced a children's book, *Pamela's First Musical* (1996), about a young girl whose glamorous Aunt Louise takes her to a Broadway show. Wasserstein acknowledges that the young girl is based on her niece. The book resulted from a ten-year-old plan to write a children's book with her friend, scenic designer Andrew Jackness, supplying the drawings. Wasserstein found a new challenge in writing for children: "It's a very spare kind of writing. . . . You write it all out, then strip it down to its bones" (*Publishers Weekly*, 22 April 1996). She hopes that the book will encourage children to see live performances of plays.

After this brief collaborative interlude, Wasserstein returned to handling more difficult issues in *An American Daughter*. While *The Sisters Rosensweig* shows the private and family lives of three successful, middle-aged women moving forward, *An American Daughter* argues that when accomplished women attempt to shape the world outside of their living rooms, they run into tall, thick walls, usually put there by a sexism so deeply entrenched that it resists conscious decision and good intentions.

Walter Abrahamson, the liberal professor husband of the central character, Lyssa Dent Hughes, undoubtedly sees himself and is seen by others as a man far too intelligent, aware, and successful to succumb to sexist attitudes or to resent his wife's success. Yet, when she is nominated for Surgeon General, he responds with a barrage of put-downs: she is a compromise candidate; she will not have the power to do what she hopes; she is foolish to try to change the world. When he learns that Timber Tucker, a television reporter, will come to brunch the next day, he invites a conservative friend, Morrow McCarthy, certain to cause problems. As the brunch begins, Walter dances with and kisses Quincy Quince, a former student also in attendance; and, finally, when the reporter probes for dirt about his wife, Walter offers it up: she once ignored a jury summons. Lyssa's father, conservative senator Alan Hughes, instantly senses danger and interrupts Walter's news with a reminder of his daughter's down-home values and roots: "My daughter has always been a hard worker, and, believe me, I know what hard work is. I grew up on a farm in Indiana." Then he redirects the discussion by asking the radical feminist who just kissed his son-in-law about her fascinating new book.

The senator's attempt to divert the reporter proves futile: the pro-life friend Walter insisted on inviting to brunch pulls the discussion back to Lyssa's failure to ever serve as a juror. The senator tries to divert Timber Tucker by bursting into song, but it does not work: a scandal is born, and his daughter must fight to protect her nomination.

Wasserstein frequently says that she sets characters in motion and then watches them, so fathoming Walter's behavior interests her. She thinks his wife threatens even someone with his achievements:

> Walter can sit in on a seminar about liberalism or economics and be brilliant, but his time has passed and he knows it, and he doesn't have the interior life to actually cope with it. (*American Theatre*, September 1997)

The other thing Walter can't cope with is getting older. He wants to be in, new, young; hence his interest in Quincy and Morrow.

The champions of feminist and sexual rights do not help Lyssa defend herself, nor do they conduct themselves admirably. Morrow, although vocal on gay issues in order to defend his own rights, does not hesitate to raise his voice against abortion. Quincy makes a pass at Walter after commenting that she has no sense of Lyssa's soul. As a feminist author Quincy has made a lucrative career out of reducing every other human being to a sociological type. She sees Lyssa, for instance, as an example of the harder, earlier generation of feminists. As Lyssa endures a media frenzy, Quincy makes an even larger name for herself by presenting color commentary on television.

Most American women resent Lyssa because her success persuades them she has evaded all the sexist traps that continue to imprison them. Instead of getting angry at men, or at their own passivity, they hate her for reminding them of their choices and their limits. They call her elitist because she describes her mother, who died when Lyssa was fourteen, as "the kind of ordinary Indiana housewife who took pride in her icebox cakes and cheese pimento canapes." Lyssa listens to the spin doctor her father hires, tries wearing a headband and saying what people tell her, but eventually, she lets loose in a television interview with Timber Tucker:

> A woman from good schools and a good family? That kind of woman should be perfect! And if she manages to be perfect, then there is something distorted and condescending about her. That kind of hard-working woman deserves to be hung out to dry. That's a parable the Indiana housewives can tell their daughters with pride. They can say for those of you girls who thought the Lyssa Dent Hughes generation made any impact, you're wrong. Statistically they may have made an impact, but they're still twisting in the wind just like the rest of us.

In *American Daughter,* Lyssa seems to have it all: then she moves into the political world, and the real limits of her power become crystal clear. Meanwhile, her friend Judith Abramson engages in an equally futile attempt to have a child. At the same time Lyssa withdraws her nomination, Judith gives up on fertility treatments, forced to admit that she "can't make life or stop death." Because in Judith's case the obstacles impeding her are natural, not man-made, this realization seems healthy and frees her to accept her life. On the other hand, if Lyssa just accepts her defeat, she achieves not mature wisdom but the perpetuation of the social norms that created her difficulties. Lyssa's father appears with a letter their ancestor, Ulysses S. Grant, wrote to his daughter, urging her "to rise and continue." As the play ends, Lyssa does just that: she runs to a computer so she can answer chat-room criticisms of her.

The play reasserts many of Wasserstein's themes: the importance of following one's heart, the power and value of enduring friendships between women, the strength one can draw from family history, and the importance of seeing oneself as part of an historical sequence and evaluating one's life in terms of this awareness. Once again Wasserstein's play benefited from good casting. In its first reading at Lincoln Center, Meryl Streep played Lyssa, as she did in the workshop production at the Seattle Repertory directed by Sullivan. When the play moved to Broadway the cast included Kate Nelligan, Hal Holbrook, Lynne Thigpen, Peter Riegert, Bruce Norris, and Elizabeth Marvel. Despite its cast and its ties to Wasserstein's earlier work, the play elicited mixed critical reactions and had a relatively short run. In her preface to the published play Wasserstein blames the hostility on sexual politics: "What was odd about this play was that the gender issue became so important. . . . For many women *An American Daughter* wasn't about too many things; it was, rather, about *the* thing. But to some men, and many critics, it seemed the rantings of a comedic writer trying to find something 'important' to say." She probably alludes to reviews such as that in *The New Leader,* (7 April 1997), which noted: "*An American Daughter* contains plenty of wry remarks and a few characters with resonance. . . . Wasserstein has little to say, and that little is false. The notion that a strong woman cannot survive in the male-dominated corridors of power is given the lie every day by Madeleine Albright and Janet Reno." The reviewer sidesteps the fact that Wasserstein's play was inspired by the failed nominations of the two women President William Jefferson Clinton tried to appoint Attorney General before Janet Reno.

Wasserstein reports in her preface that she had other, more personal encounters with female limits just before writing this play. Her sister Sandra developed breast cancer, which soon killed her, and Wasserstein spent years trying unsuccessfully to conceive a child:

> I spent months, years, in waiting rooms, surrounded now by women in wigs on their way to chemotherapy, now by women with cell phones and attaches waiting to hear if their blood count was still in the ballpark for bearing children. The simultaneous situations certainly redefined for me "having it all."
>
> The inevitable result of this experience was that I wanted to organize the sadness, frustration, and truth of it into play form. I have always written to find out what I'm thinking and, if not to look for answers, then at least to attempt to ask the question.

The reviews and essays she wrote between *The Sisters Rosensweig* and *An American Daughter* reflect Wasserstein's personal movement out in the world, for they cover a variety of topics and genres, from book reviews of Edward Koch's detective novel to an essay about the American obsession with weight. But a few of them center around the recurrent theme of the essential unity of women and the need for friendship between them.

For instance, her review of Nancy Friday's book *The Power of Beauty* (1996) expresses several reservations, but Wasserstein especially likes one idea: "Friday quite intelligently suggests that women who compete with other women ought to regain the admiration they felt prior to their envy of one another. It's both a useful and a sadly inventive directive."

Wasserstein's next project, the script for the 1998 movie *The Object of My Affection*, took more than ten years. She attributes the long struggle to get her rewrite of Stephen McCauley's novel produced to studio executives' reservations about a movie focusing on a relationship between a gay romantic leading man and a pregnant straight woman. Precisely the challenge of writing about this couple drew Wasserstein to the script: "What I love is to take romantic-comedy form and add something you're not supposed to show. . . . In the traditional story, it's boy meets girl, girl gets boy, and sex is the connective. But this time it's the obstacle" (*The Village Voice*, 31 March 1998).

The conventional romantic ending obviously will not work, so the movie concludes by validating a new kind of family built from friendship, with music and dancing underlining the joy of this development. As one reviewer noted in *Rolling Stone*, (30 April 1998), if one does not examine it too closely, watching the film is a pleasant experience; he praised the stars, Jennifer Aniston and Paul Rudd, for making "something memorably funny and touching out of moonshine." He also liked Wasserstein's script and thought the movie does make an important point when it "transcends its gay/straight theme to cut to the imbalance at the core of all relationships." Other reviewers regarded the happy ending less charitably. One critic wrote in *Time* (20 April 1998) that "Wasserstein turns the whole bunch into an extended family even adding a sweet-souled black policeman to the mix as Nina's consolation prize. Wasserstein can spritz New York-smart talk with the best of them, but she can't make us believe this mass conversion to sociopolitical correctness, with everybody loving and forgiving everybody despite the fact that the harms they have dealt one another remain essentially unsolved."

There are no signs Wasserstein will avoid political controversy in the future. Indeed, she all but promises in her introduction to *An American Daughter* to keep irritating audiences, for she considers the fervent reaction to that play a validation of its importance. She wrote an article for *The New York Times* (28 August 1998) expressing her dismay that Hilary Clinton's stature rises with her victimhood: "We women of her generation had hoped she would break new ground. Yet what seemed initially so positive is becoming a very unsavory parable. . . . Now, the impressive personal qualities—ideal-

Dust jacket for Wasserstein's play about the failed nomination of a woman for the post of U.S. Attorney General

ism, strength and poise under pressure—that she once directed toward influencing social policy are being used to maintain domestic tranquility."

Wasserstein freely admits that her work always has autobiographical roots and that it generally emerges from some irritant in her life. She told Leslie Jacobson: "My plays tend to be autobiographical or come out of something that's irking me, and it's got to irk me long enough for me to commit to spend all that time writing and then turn it into a play." But she has enjoyed her work more as it has taken her away from herself: "The plays become fun when they stop being autobiography." One can observe in her career a steady movement into the world, away from her own particular point of view. This development happens not only in her plays but also in the increasingly diverse essays Wasserstein writes for periodicals as well as her forays into writing a movie script and a children's book. In a brief essay for *Cosmopolitan* (1 February 1997) that sets out her common ground with the Cosmo Girl, she links the passionate response to life that her work always recommends with the act of writing well: "The best work, like the best kind of love, comes from passion. Which is not to say there aren't times when work can seem like pure drudgery, but when it's right, it clicks like the best kind of relationship."

Interviews:

Kathleen Betsko and Rachel Koenig, "Wendy Wasserstein," in *Interviews with Contemporary Women Playwrights*, edited by Betsko and Koenig (New York: Beech Tree Books, 1987), pp. 418–431;

Esther Cohen, "Uncommon Woman: An Interview with Wendy Wasserstein," *Women's Studies*, 15 (1988): 257–270;

Kent Black, "The Wendy Chronicles," *Harper's Bazaar*, 123 (March 1990): 154, 162;

Melissa Biggs, "Wendy Wasserstein," in *In the Vernacular: Interviews at Yale with Sculptors of Culture*, edited by Biggs (Jefferson, N.C.: McFarland, 1991), pp. 178–189;

Leslie Jacobson, "Wendy Wasserstein," in *The Playwright's Art: Conversations with Contemporary American Dramatists*, edited by Jackson R. Bryer (New Brunswick, N.J.: Rutgers University Press, 1995), pp. 257–276;

Jan Balakian, "Wendy Wasserstein," in *Speaking on Stage: Interviews with Contemporary American Playwrights*, edited by Philip C. Kolin and Colby H. Kullman (Tuscaloosa: University of Alabama Press, 1996), pp. 379–391;

Nancy Franklin, "The Time of Her Life," *New Yorker*, 73 (14 April 1997): 62–68, 70–71;

Laurie Winer, "Wendy Wasserstein," *Paris Review*, 142 (Spring 1997): 165–188;

Balakian, "Two Interviews with Wendy Wasserstein," *Journal of American Drama and Theatre*, 9 (Spring 1998): 58–84;

Claudia Barnett, "Interview with Wendy Wasserstein," in *Wendy Wasserstein: A Casebook*, edited by Barnett (New York: Garland, 1999), pp. 179–189.

References:

Jan Balakian, "*The Heidi Chronicles*: The Big Chill of Feminism," *South Atlantic Review*, 60 (May 1995): 93–101;

Claudia Barnett, ed., *Wendy Wasserstein: A Casebook* (New York: Garland, 1999);

Becky Becker, "The Theme of Mothering in Selected Dramas," *American Drama*, 6 (Spring 1997): 43–57;

Susan Carlson, "Comic Textures and Female Communities 1937 and 1977: Clare Boothe and Wendy Wasserstein," in *Modern American Drama: The Female Canon*, edited by June Schlueter (Rutherford, N.J.: Fairleigh Dickinson University Press, 1990), pp. 207–217;

Gail Ciociola, *Wendy Wasserstein: Dramatizing Women, Their Choices and Their Boundaries* (Jefferson, N.C.: McFarland, 1998);

Jill Dolan, "*The Heidi Chronicles*: Choking on the Rage of Postfeminism," in her *Presence and Desire: Essays on Gender, Sexuality, Performance* (Ann Arbor: University of Michigan Press, 1993), pp. 50–55;

Glenda Frank, "The Struggle to Affirm: the Image of Jewish-Americans on Stage," in *Staging Difference: Cultural Pluralism in American Theatre and Drama*, edited by Marc Maufort (New York: Peter Lang, 1995), pp. 245–257;

Helene Keyssar, "Drama and the Dialogic Imagination: *The Heidi Chronicles* and *Fefu and Her Friends*," *Modern Drama*, 34 (1991): 88–107;

Bette Mandl, "Feminism, Postfeminism, and *The Heidi Chronicles*," *Studies in the Humanities*, 17 (December 1990): 120–128;

Phyllis Rose, "An Open Letter to Dr. Holland," *American Theatre*, 6 (October 1989): 26–29, 114–117;

Daniel J. Watermeir, "The Search for Self: Attachment, Loss and Recovery in *The Heidi Chronicles*," in *Staging Difference: Cultural Pluralism in American Theatre and Drama*, edited by Maufort (New York: Peter Lang, 1995), pp. 351–362;

Stephen Whitfield, "Wendy Wasserstein and the Crisis of Jewish Identity," in *Daughters of Valor: Contemporary Jewish American Women Writers*, edited by Ben Siegel (Newark: University of Delaware Press, 1997), pp. 226–246.

Papers:

Wendy Wasserstein has donated her papers to the library at Mount Holyoke College.

Thornton Wilder

(17 April 1897 – 7 December 1975)

Lincoln Konkle
College of New Jersey

See also the Wilder entries in *DLB 4: American Writers in Paris, 1920–1939; DLB 7: Twentieth-Century American Dramatists;* and *DLB 9: American Novelists, 1910–1945.*

PLAY PRODUCTIONS: *The Trumpet Shall Sound,* New York, American Laboratory Theatre, 10 December 1926;

Lucrece, translated and adapted from André Obey's *Le Viol de Lucrèce,* New York, Belasco Theatre, 20 December 1932;

A Doll's House, translated and adapted from Henrik Ibsen's play, New York, Morosco Theatre, 27 December 1937;

Our Town, New York, Henry Miller's Theatre, 4 February 1938;

The Merchant of Yonkers, New York, Guild Theatre, 28 December 1938; revised as *The Matchmaker,* New York, Royale Theatre, 5 December 1955;

The Skin of Our Teeth, New York, Plymouth Theatre, 18 November 1942;

Our Century, New York, Century Association, 26 April 1947;

The Happy Journey to Trenton and Camden, New York, Cort Theatre, 9 February 1948;

The Alcestiad, as *A Life in the Sun,* Edinburgh, Scotland, Assembly Hall, 25 August 1955;

The Wreck of the 5:25 and *Bernice,* West Berlin, Congresshalle Theater, 20 September 1957;

Das Lange Weihnachtsmal (opera version of *The Long Christmas Dinner*), libretto by Wilder, music by Paul Hindemith, Manheim, West Germany, National Theatre, 17 December 1961;

Plays for Bleecker Street (*Infancy, Childhood,* and *Someone from Assisi*), New York, Circle in the Square, 11 January 1962;

Die Alkestiade (opera version of *A Life in the Sun*), libretto by Wilder, music by Louise Talma, Frankfurt, West Germany, Stadische Buhnen, 1 March 1962;

Pullman Car Hiawatha, New York, Circle in the Square, 3 December 1964;

Thornton Wilder

Thornton Wilder's Triple Bill (*The Long Christmas Dinner, Queens of France,* and *The Happy Journey to Trenton and Camden*), New York, Cherry Lane Theatre, 6 September 1966;

The Drunken Sisters, Brooklyn Heights, New York, Spencer Memorial Church, 28 June 1970;

A Ringing of Doorbells, Youth, In Shakespeare and the Bible, and *The Rivers Under the Earth,* Louisville, Kentucky, Actors Theatre of Louisville, 15 November 1997;

The Angel that Troubled the Waters, New York, Broadway Presbyterian Church, 23 April 1999;

Youth and *The Rivers Under the Earth,* New York, Willow Cabin Theatre Company, May 1999.

BOOKS: *The Cabala* (New York: A. & C. Boni, 1926; London: Longmans, Green, 1926);

The Bridge of San Luis Rey (New York: A. & C. Boni, 1927; London: Longmans, Green, 1927);

The Angel That Troubled the Waters and Other Plays (New York: Coward-McCann, 1928; London: Longmans, Green, 1928)–comprises *Nascunter Poetae, Prosperina and the Devil, Fanny Otcott, Brother Fire, The Penny That Beauty Spent, The Angel on the Ship, The Message and Jehanne, Childe Roland to the Dark Tower Came, Centaurs, Leviathan, And the Sea Shall Give Up Its Dead, Now the Servant's Name Was Malchus, Mozart and the Gray Steward, Hast Thou Considered My Servant Job?, The Flight into Egypt,* and *The Angel That Troubled the Waters;*

The Woman of Andros (New York: A. & C. Boni, 1930; London: Longmans, Green, 1930);

The Long Christmas Dinner and Other Plays in One Act (New York: Coward-McCann / New Haven: Yale University Press, 1931; London: Longmans, Green, 1931)–comprises *The Long Christmas Dinner, Queens of France, Pullman Car Hiawatha, Love and How to Cure It, Such Things Only Happen in Books,* and *The Happy Journey to Trenton and Camden;*

Lucrece, adapted from André Obey's *Le Viol de Lucrèce* (Boston & New York: Houghton Mifflin, 1933; London: Longmans, Green, 1933);

Heaven's My Destination (London, New York, & Toronto: Longmans, Green, 1934; New York & London: Harper, 1935);

Our Town (New York: Coward-McCann, 1938; London: Longmans, Green, 1956);

The Merchant of Yonkers (New York & London: Harper, 1939);

The Skin of Our Teeth (New York & London: Harper, 1942; London: Longmans, Green, 1958);

Our Century (New York: Century, 1947);

The Ides of March (New York & London: Harper, 1948; London: Longmans, Green, 1948);

The Drunken Sisters (New York, Hollywood, London & Toronto: S. French, 1957);

The Matchmaker (New York, Hollywood, London & Toronto: S. French, 1957);

Plays for Bleecker Street, 3 volumes (New York: S. French, 1960-1961)–comprises *Infancy, Childhood,* and *Someone from Assisi;*

The Eighth Day (New York, Evanston, Ill. & London: Harper & Row, 1967; London: Longmans, 1967);

Theophilus North (New York, Evanston, Ill., San Francisco & London: Harper & Row, 1973; London: Allen Lane, 1974);

The Alcestiad (New York, Hagerstown, Md., San Francisco & London: Harper & Row, 1977);

American Characteristics and Other Essays, edited by Donald Gallup (New York, Hagerstown, Md., San Francisco & London: Harper & Row, 1979);

The Journals of Thornton Wilder, 1939–1961, edited by Gallup (New Haven, Conn.: Yale University Press, 1985).

Collections: *Three Plays: Our Town, The Skin of Our Teeth, The Matchmaker* (New York: Harper, 1957; London: Longmans, Green, 1958);

The Collected Short Plays of Thornton Wilder, 2 volumes, edited by Donald Gallup and A. Tappan Wilder with F. J. O'Neil (New York: Theatre Communications Group, 1997, 1998).

PRODUCED SCRIPTS: *Our Town,* by Wilder, Frank Craven, and Harry Chandlee, motion picture, United Artists, 1940;

Shadow of a Doubt, by Wilder, Sally Benson, and Alma Reville, motion picture, Universal, 1943.

Thornton Wilder was a student of the human condition; in his writing he aimed for and achieved the universal. His plays in particular were concerned with both the timely and the timeless, and he most distinguished himself in the theater, although his first literary success was as a novelist. In a 1938 interview Wilder said, "Everything I have written has been a preparation for writing for the stage–my novels, my two volumes of one-act plays, my adaptations of Obey's *Lucrece* and Ibsen's *A Doll's House.* I like to think of all that as an apprenticeship. For the drama, it seems to me, is the most satisfying of all art-forms." Wilder was the first major American playwright to discard the trappings of the box set and fourth-wall realism in favor of a bare stage and presentational theatrical style. The full-length plays *Our Town* (performed in 1938) and *The Skin of Our Teeth* (1942) and the one-act plays *The Happy Journey to Trenton and Camden, The Long Christmas Dinner,* and *Pullman Car Hiawatha,* all published in 1931, influenced American playwrights from Tennessee Williams and Arthur Miller to Edward Albee and John Guare. As Wilder himself said in the preface to *Three Plays* (1957), he hoped he had played a role in preparing the way for those new dramatists to come after him.

Thornton Niven Wilder was born in Madison, Wisconsin, on 17 April 1897 to parents of New England descent, Amos Parker Wilder and Isabella Niven Wilder. His father, who had earned a doctorate in political science at Yale University, was the editor of *The*

Wisconsin State Journal during the time of the Progressive movement in Wisconsin; his mother was a daughter of a Presbyterian minister and a devotee of world literature and music. When Wilder was nine years old, his father was appointed consul general of Hong Kong under the Theodore Roosevelt administration, and the Wilder family, consisting of two girls and two boys, moved to the Orient (a third daughter was born in 1910).

Wilder's first exposure to theater occurred before he reached his teens. Isabella Wilder and the children had returned to the United States while Amos Wilder remained at the consulate in Hong Kong. Living near the University of California in Berkeley, Wilder learned of a university theater that performed classical Greek drama, which meant that they were in need of extras for the chorus. Isabella Wilder encouraged her ten-year-old son's participation by sewing costumes appropriate for his roles. Amos Wilder did not approve of such activities, but since he was thousands of miles away, Isabella's appreciation of literature and the arts had a greater influence upon Wilder's development. After a second attempt to make a home in China when Amos Wilder was named consul general at Shanghai, Isabella and the children returned to America for good. Wilder's cultural interests continued to grow, including the keeping of a journal in which he wrote poems and stories as well as his personal responses to the literature he read—a habit he maintained throughout his life, as was revealed by the posthumous publication in 1985 of *The Journals of Thornton Wilder, 1939–1961.*

Although Wilder and his older brother, Amos Niven Wilder, had wanted to attend Yale University, their father's alma mater, Amos Parker Wilder felt his sons were not ready for what he considered to be a cosmopolitan environment; thus for their first two years of college he sent them to Oberlin College in Ohio. There Wilder thrived under the tutelage of Professor Charles H. Wager, the head of the English department. Wilder's love of world literature continued to grow, and his first publication as a creative writer came when some of his pieces appeared in the college literary magazine. Several of these were later included in his third book, *The Angel That Troubled the Waters and Other Plays* (1928), a volume of short works generally regarded by scholars as Wilder's juvenilia. However, in the foreword Wilder refers to having written approximately forty of these short pieces between the time he was a high school student in Berkeley and a French teacher at the Lawrenceville School during the 1920s. Presumably, then, some of them are the product of an author who had already written two novels.

What is most significant about *The Angel That Troubled the Waters and Other Plays* is its foreshadowing of Wilder's mature drama, both in terms of a worldview informed by religious faith and of an experimentation with dramatic form. In these short pieces, which Wilder refers to in his foreword as "Three-Minute Plays for Three Persons," he first attempts to achieve a cosmic scope of time and place while simultaneously dramatizing important moments in individual lives. Nine of these short plays draw upon classical mythology, history, or literature for their subject, while six of them are concerned with characters and settings derived from the Bible or Christian doctrine. Scholar Travis Bogard compared them to the short plays making up the medieval cycles dramatizing the Bible from Genesis to Revelations, while Donald Haberman in *The Plays of Thornton Wilder: A Critical Study* (1967) put them in the exegetical tradition of the Protestant sermon that takes a biblical text and then expounds upon it, examining some of its implications for the Christian life.

For example, in *And the Sea Shall Give Up Its Dead,* the initial stage directions set the action against a macrocosmic backdrop:

> *The clangor of Judgment Day's last trumpet dies away in the remotest pockets of space, and time comes to an end like a frayed ribbon. In the nave of creation the diaphanous amphitheater is already building for the trial of all flesh. Several miles below the surface of the North Atlantic, the spirits of the drowned rise through the water like bubbles in a neglected wineglass.*

But Wilder focuses upon the microcosmic foreground of three souls who tell each other about their lives on earth: "A WOMAN," later identified as "Gertruda XXII, the empress of Newfoundland from 2638 to 2698"; "A STOUT LITTLE MAN" named Horatio Nissem, a theatrical producer who lived five hundred years before the empress; and "A TALL, THIN, DREAMY MAN," who tells the others he was a priest named Father Cosroe. In anticipation of the trial of all flesh, the three souls confess to each other the vanities of their lives, but all three realize they still cherish and fear the loss of their individuality in a union of the souls of the dead with God, which is precisely what happens as *And the Sea Shall Give Up Its Dead* concludes on the macrocosmic scale:

> *The three panic-stricken souls reach the surface of the sea. The extensive business of Domesday is over in a twinkling, and the souls divested of all identification have tumbled, like falling stars, into the blaze of unicity. Soon nothing exists in space but the great unwinking eye, meditating a new creation.*

Obviously it would be impossible to stage this cosmic action, and scholars agree that Wilder wrote these miniature plays as closet drama: meant for reading rather than playing. Indeed, many of the sixteen published

Wilder and his siblings in Madison, Wisconsin, circa 1900: (left to right) Isabel, Charlotte, Thornton, and Amos (Thornton Wilder Archive, Collection of American Literature, Beinecke Rare Book and Manuscript Library, Yale University)

three-minute plays include stage directions describing spectacles that would be virtually impossible to produce in a theater. Furthermore, their dramatic structure would not play well since their conflict is mostly conceptual rather than character-and-action based. Nevertheless, in these early literary works Wilder experimented with dramatic form in an attempt to write drama that is not bound by realistic conventions of stage production or playwriting.

Just when he had established himself as a promising student of literature and a creative writer at Oberlin College, Wilder was uprooted by his father's decision that he transfer to Yale University. At the larger and more prestigious Ivy League school Wilder again distinguished himself with his compositions on literature and with his own creative writing. He belonged to a literary group, served on the editorial board of the student literary magazine, and was a friend of Stephen Vincent Benét, who later distinguished himself as a poet and a short-story writer. Wilder's studies at Yale were briefly interrupted by his service in the U.S. Coast Artillery Corps during World War I. Like other young men, he wanted to contribute to the war effort, but the regular military branches turned him down because of his poor eyesight. After Wilder had been stationed at Newport, Rhode Island, for six months of duty, the armistice was signed, and Wilder returned to Yale. He also completed his most ambitious writing project to date: *The Trumpet Shall Sound* (1926), a four-act play for which he won the Branford Brinton Award from the university.

The Trumpet Shall Sound was published serially in the *Yale Literary Magazine* in four issues from October 1919 to January 1920; its only New York production was directed by Richard Boleslavsky in 1926 at the American Laboratory Theatre, where it was performed thirty times in repertory. Although the plot was derived from Ben Jonson's Renaissance comedy *The Alchemist*, Wilder's play is clearly meant to be an allegorical tragedy of, as its title implies, the second coming of Christ and Judgment Day. The play is set in New York City during the fall of 1871. The action follows the money-making scheme of three servants working in a mansion owned by a wealthy man who has been traveling abroad for some time but has set no definite date for his return. A maid, Flora Storey, has persuaded the other servants, Sarah and Nestor, to help her rent out rooms in the mansion to boarders who want to keep a low profile due to run-ins with the law and the like. The tenants include a captain whose ship was lost at sea, killing all the passengers; a woman wanted for shoplifting, and her son; a prostitute; and a respectable boarder, Miss Flecker, who immediately suspects that something is amiss in this mansion-turned-boardinghouse.

Despite being repeatedly warned that Peter Magnus, the rich man, may come back any day and catch them all in their plot, Flora pushes on with her plan, the real purpose of which is to find out news of Carlo, a sailor with whom she is in love, from other sailors who might take up residence there between voyages. Flora begins to think of Carlo as her savior as she becomes increasingly desperate in her attempts to divert Miss Flecker's suspicions while keeping the other boarders satisfied and maintaining the secrecy of the whole operation. Carlo arrives at the mansion, but he clearly has no particular regard for Flora. When Magnus does return, he brings the police so that he can conduct his own "trial of flesh," which was only alluded to in *And the Sea Shall Give Up the Dead;* for Magnus is, in the allegory, Christ on the Day of Judgment. Magnus forgives some of the boarders, permitting them to stay in his many-roomed mansion, but evicts other more unsavory boarders (such as the prostitute), thus not imparting the universal forgiveness that the few studies that comment on *The Trumpet Shall Sound* have ascribed to him. The harshest fate is reserved for Flora, the mastermind of the plot; after she realizes Carlo will not save her and that prison lies ahead, she goes into the drawing room and shoots herself. Reviews and scholarly studies of Wilder criticize the characters and action of *The Trumpet Shall Sound* as melodramatic and the allegory as unclear and poorly served by the realistic dramatic form. Yet, the Yale English faculty and the director of the American Laboratory Theatre production of the play believed it had literary and theatrical merit.

Despite these early literary successes as a college student, Wilder was not ready to support himself with his writing upon graduation from Yale in 1920; nor did his bachelor's degree prepare him to immediately enter any profession. The Wilder family had by this time relocated to New Haven, Connecticut, his father having taken a position as executive secretary of the Yale-in-China program. Though not poor, they were faced with the continuing educational expenses for two sons and three daughters. Fearing Wilder would become a burden, his father sent him abroad for a year at the American Academy in Rome, hoping that the study of Latin and the accompanying archaeological digs at the sites of ancient Roman ruins might make Wilder more marketable as a preparatory school teacher. In Rome, Wilder acquired the historical breadth of his worldview, as he explained in a 1957 *Paris Review* interview:

> I was sent abroad to study archaeology at the American Academy in Rome. We even took field trips in those days and in a small way took part in diggings. Once you have swung a pickax that will reveal the curve of a street four thousand years covered over which was once an active, much-traveled highway, you are never quite the same again. You look at Times Square as a place about which you imagine some day scholars saying, "There appears to have been some kind of public center here."

That telescopic view from the present to the distant past has pervaded both his drama and his fiction.

Wilder returned to America in 1921 to take a position his father had secured for him, teaching not Latin but French at the Lawrenceville School, a private preparatory academy in central New Jersey. During his time in Rome, Wilder had filled his notebooks with character sketches, which he first called "Memoirs of a Roman Student" but subsequently rewrote as his first novel, *The Cabala,* published in 1926. The book was reviewed favorably and sold well enough that he was able to take a leave of absence from Lawrenceville to earn his master's degree in French literature at Princeton University and write a second successful novel, *The Bridge of San Luis Rey* (1927). He used part of his earnings from this international best-seller to pay for the construction of a new house outside of New Haven that served as the Wilder family home for decades.

In both *The Cabala* and *The Bridge of San Luis Rey* Wilder retraces a period of time in which significant events occur—an American's year abroad in Rome, the events leading up to and proceeding from the fall of a bridge in eighteenth-century Peru—and examines the lives of characters whose significance is elevated by the workings of destiny. In *The Cabala* the narrator learns that the rich and powerful European characters he has met are the modern incarnations of the gods of antiquity and that he is the new Mercury, which is confirmed by his summoning the spirit of Virgil to speak with him on the deck of an ocean liner taking him back to America. The implication of their conversation is that the fate of the world has passed from Europe to the United States. In *The Bridge of San Luis Rey* a priest regards the deaths of five people who were on the bridge when it broke as an opportunity to prove that either humans live and die by accident or they live and die by plan. Although the narrator affects skepticism toward Brother Juniper's attempt to justify the ways of God to man, the stories of the five victims' lives dramatize that this act of God was simultaneously punishment for the wicked, reward for the good, and mercy for the suffering. For *The Bridge of San Luis Rey* Wilder won the first of three Pulitzer Prizes.

With the publication of *The Bridge of San Luis Rey* in 1927 Wilder had attained the status of a literary celebrity, as was evident in 1928 when American and European newspapers and magazines covered his walking tour of Europe with heavyweight boxing champ Gene Tunney. By this time Wilder had also met other writers and intellectuals such as F. Scott Fitzgerald, Ernest Hemingway, and the critic Edmund Wilson. He resigned his position at the Lawrenceville School, but instead of devoting himself full time to writing, he spent much of 1928 and 1929 on a tour of European theaters with his younger sister Isabel. Then he signed a contract for a cross-country lecture tour, partly to promote book sales and partly to ensure a regular income, since his father's investment in a New Haven newspaper had failed and the family was again in financial need.

His next book, *The Woman of Andros* (1930), was strongly informed by Wilder's classical background; the novel is set on an island near Greece during the pre-Christian era. But Chrysis, the title character, is clearly meant to be seen as a prefiguration of Christ, since she has followers who could be called disciples, and she teaches them by means of moral stories that could be called parables. Although the book initially received moderately favorable reviews, a later review ignited the first of two critical controversies during Wilder's career. Michael Gold, a Marxist critic who championed literature that depicted working-class characters suffering through the immediate crisis of the Great Depression, wrote a review of *The Woman of Andros* for *The New Republic* (22 October 1930) in which he accused Wilder of being out of touch with contemporary social and economic evils, of writing escapist fiction, and of daring to affirm a religious interpretation of the human condition. Subsequently *The New Republic* published many letters to the editor defending Wilder and his novel, but he never responded directly to Gold's criticism. However, most scholars agree that Gold's attack was what prompted Wilder to turn his attention to American subjects, first in drama, then in fiction.

In 1930 Wilder accepted a teaching position offered to him by the new president of the University of Chicago, Robert Maynard Hutchins, a classmate of his at Yale. Teaching courses in literary classics and creative writing for half the academic year, Wilder was able to

work on what most scholars agree was his response to Gold's demand for more socially relevant writing: *The Long Christmas Dinner and Other Plays in One Act* (1931). Five of the six one-act plays show mostly middle-class Americans who are representative types either by profession, personality, or family role. Three of the plays—*Queens of France, Love and How to Cure It,* and *Such Things Only Happen in Books*—are conventionally realistic in dramatic form and comic in tone. However, the other three plays—*The Long Christmas Dinner, Pullman Car Hiawatha,* and *The Happy Journey to Trenton and Camden*—were later praised by venerable theater critic and scholar John Gassner as a minor revolution in American drama.

Queens of France is set in 1869 New Orleans; the action takes place in the office of a lawyer, M'su Cahusac, who has duped several women into believing that they are the long lost heir to the French throne. He tells each of them that in order to be proclaimed the true heir, certain lost documents that will prove their legitimacy must be located by the Historical Society of France, which is low on funds. Cahusac deftly manipulates these women—all of whom are old, vain, and in need of something to lift their lives above the mundane—into making monetary contributions allegedly to the society. What saves the play from being an exercise in cynicism is that the stories of three of the women who visit him on this one afternoon reveal that they either deserve to be bilked or, in the case of a school teacher, need something magical in life to assuage loneliness. The play ends with yet another woman entering the office and being greeted by Cahusac as "Your Royal Highness."

In *Love and How to Cure It* Rowena Stowker, an aging but warm and compassionate comedic actress, prefigures Dolly Levi in *The Matchmaker* (1955), except that she is a benevolent match *breaker*. Rowena's beautiful but pitiless sixteen-year-old niece, Linda, complains of a young Cambridge student who has fallen in love with her after just one date and is now threatening to shoot her (or so she thinks) if she will not marry him. Linda is not eager to leave the empty theater in which they have been waiting for a rehearsal to begin because she knows the student, Arthur Warburton, is waiting for her on the street, perhaps with a gun. Wilder keeps the tone light with Joey Weston, a stage comedian, and with Rowena's charm and endearing cockney accent. The fact that the play takes place within a theater foreshadows *Our Town* and *The Skin of Our Teeth,* except that *Love and How to Cure It* never breaks the fourth wall or refers to the author of the play. Wanting to help her niece, Rowena improvises a scene for Arthur that will hopefully cure him of his love for Linda, who is cold and indifferent to him, and will allow them to unload his gun without his realizing it. They invite Arthur to

Wilder's mother, Isabella Niven Wilder, in 1907, and his father, Amos Parker Wilder, with Wilder's brother, Amos (standing left), and Wilder in 1915 (Thornton Wilder Archive, Collection of American Literature, Beinecke Rare Book and Manuscript Library, Yale University)

join them for dinner and proceed to implement the cure, which consists mostly of Joey telling about his deceased wife and the great love they shared and then contrasting that true love to those who claim to be in love but are just seeking attention. The cure works: Arthur takes out his gun and places it on the table, telling Linda she will not have to worry about him anymore because Joey was right—Arthur was just trying to attract attention by threatening to shoot not her, as she thought, but himself. Although the "scene" was meant to save Linda, it in fact saves Arthur, while Linda remains as self-absorbed and aloof as ever.

The third conventionally realistic play of the volume, *Such Things Only Happen in Books*, may appear to be another lightweight comedic piece, especially in contrast to the more philosophical and unconventionally theatrical plays in this collection; however, underneath the unsubtle farce of the play is an aesthetic reflexivity that justifies the other, bolder experiments in dramatic form. That is, as scholar Christopher Wheatley points out, in *Such Things Only Happen in Books* Wilder parodies conventional theatrical realism in order to criticize conventional realism in both fiction and drama. Almost as

if it were an inversion of Luigi Pirandello's *Six Characters in Search of an Author* (1921), *Such Things Only Happen in Books* is focused upon an author searching for a plot, believing that real life is, in effect, plotless; yet, he is surrounded by intrigue involving real persons with fervent motivations that he never perceives. His wife is having an affair with a doctor who visits them to check on their maid, who is recovering from burns on her legs. It is later revealed that the burns on her legs were caused by her getting splashed by boiling water from a pot dropped by her brother, an escaped convict whom she had been hiding in the house for months.

Furthermore, the old house has a story behind it: a brother and sister inadvertently killed their father while trying to scare him into giving them some of his fortune; they fled the country, but the money was reportedly hidden somewhere on the premises. A nurse the author had hired turns out to be the sister, and the man whom the author invited over to play chess is the brother, who wanted the opportunity to find out if his sister had taken the money from the hiding place.

By the end of the play Wilder has built up so much dramatic irony that practically every line of dialogue evokes laughter at the expense of the plotless and clueless author, who believes such things only happen in books. The ridicule notwithstanding, there are serious aesthetic implications in the author's statements about life and art.

In the three remaining plays in the volume Wilder experiments with the dramatic forms for which he became famous. *The Long Christmas Dinner* takes place over ninety years, dramatizing successive generations of the Bayard family sitting down to Christmas dinner at a dining table center stage. The rapid passage of time is signified by actors donning white wigs and adjusting their delivery of lines and movement on the stage in accordance with their characters' advancing age. During the play the audience sees baby carriages enter from a birth portal at extreme left while the elderly exit through a death portal at extreme right. The performance of the play is a continuous flow with no formal separation between the dialogue that occurs in different years; the effect is rather like watching a movie montage of time passing. *The Long Christmas Dinner* follows the Bayard family living the American dream as they grow in prosperity, but they are also shown grieving over the deaths of their children and their parents. However, the deaths are always followed by new marriages and births, suggesting that a balance between life and death is maintained.

From the first generation of Bayards, who can remember when there were Indians in the area, to the last generation, who speak of factories and sending a cable to Europe, many of the same speeches are repeated—for example, exclamations about the beauty of the icicles formed on tree branches, comments upon the sermon preached at the Christmas church service, and references to the slow passage of time when the speakers are young, or the rapid passage of time when they are older. In this way Wilder is able to dramatize one of the dominant themes of his works: that the human condition is essentially the same regardless of time or place. Although *The Long Christmas Dinner* is emotionally moving, Wilder's rejection of realistic stage conventions provides enough distance to get the audience thinking as well, perhaps applying the philosophical lesson to their own lives. Although the actors never break the fourth wall, they only pantomime eating and drinking, which, along with the jumps in time and the symbolic birth and death set pieces, prevents the audience from forgetting that they are watching a play. German playwright, director, and essayist Bertolt Brecht later promoted this technique as the alienation effect, which was central to his dramaturgy and the production style known as Epic Theatre.

Pullman Car Hiawatha is even more radical in its theatrical style than *The Long Christmas Dinner*. It takes place in the early morning hours of 21 December 1930 onboard a Pullman car traveling from New York to Chicago and carrying passengers representing a cross section of American society. As in his most famous play, *Our Town,* Wilder makes use of a character identified as the Stage Manager whose dialogue sets the stage. No scenery is used apart from chalk lines on the floor and pairs of chairs to represent the berths of a Pullman car. The Stage Manager calls characters forth, dismisses them, and even prompts them with their lines. Again as in *Our Town,* the Stage Manager performs the minor roles, and he and other characters address the audience directly about the purposes of the play.

Although the characters in *The Long Christmas Dinner* were defined primarily by age, family role, or gender, they were essentially realistic; in *Pullman Car Hiawatha* Wilder employs allegorical characters in the manner of the medieval morality play to totally destroy the illusion of reality and to suggest the universality of the human condition. In addition to characters representing the planets Saturn, Venus, Jupiter, and Earth and the hours Ten O'clock, Eleven O'clock, and Twelve O'clock (sets of figures Wilder uses again in *The Skin of Our Teeth*), *Pullman Car Hiawatha* includes the following allegorical characters: "Grovers Corners, represented by a Grinning Boy," "The Field, represented by Somebody in Shirt Sleeves," "Parkersburg, Ohio, represented by a Farmer's Wife and Three Young People," and "The Weather, represented by a Mechanic." These characters announce their identities to the audience at the Stage Manager's command, then quote poems or proverbial morality in a tongue-in-cheek didacticism. These allegorical figures and the more conventional characters, such as businessmen, married couples, and a woman going to visit relatives for the holiday, dramatize the microcosmic level of the play; the macrocosmic setting is suggested by the actors representing the planets, two archangels, and the godlike Stage Manager, who literally orchestrates the figures and actions into a universal harmony of motion and sound:

> All right. All right.—Now we'll have the whole world together, please. The whole solar system, please. *The complete cast begins to appear at the edges of the stage. He claps his hands.* The whole solar system, please. Where's the tramp? Where's the moon? *He gives two raps on the floor, like the conductor of an orchestra attracting the attention of his forces, and slowly lifts his hand. The human beings murmur their thoughts; the hours discourse; the planets chant or hum.*

Thus, although Wilder was depicting American characters concerned with matters of everyday reality, he did so in order to express the theme of universality.

The last of the nonrealistic plays from *The Long Christmas Dinner* is *The Happy Journey to Trenton and Cam-*

Wilder (right) with producer Jed Harris and actor Frank Craven, who played the Stage Manager, shortly before
Wilder's Our Town *opened on Broadway in 1938*

den, which dramatizes a physical journey from Elizabeth, New Jersey, to Camden, where Campbell's Soup—an American icon—was made. The characterizations of the Kirby family—Ma, Pa, Caroline, and Arthur—are almost photographic in their verisimilitude, and yet they are also idealized into types: mother, father, daughter, and son. But Wilder again prevents realistic theatrical illusion by the presence of a Stage Manager and by the absence of scenery apart from a platform and chairs to represent the Kirbys' car and a cot to represent a bed in the house of the last member of the Kirby family to appear onstage, their married daughter, Beulah, whose first child died immediately after being delivered. There can be no illusion of reality when the Stage Manager, played by a male actor according to the stage directions, visibly holds a script from which he reads the speeches of, in order, Mrs. Schwartz, Mrs. Hobmeyer, Mildred, Mrs. Adler, and the gas station attendant. The Stage Manager also "smokes, reads a newspaper, and eats an apple through the course of the play."

However, the majority of the action has to do with the interactions of the Kirbys, a middle-class family with whom the audience can empathize because of their universality in suffering the loss of children or affirming the small moments of daily life. Beulah also represents the progress of the Kirby family in socioeconomic terms: "It's an even nicer street than they used to live in. . . . It's better than our street. It's richer than our street. Ma, isn't Beulah richer than we are?" The progress *The Happy Journey to Trenton and Camden* most affirms is American progress. The litany of "better" and "best" in the speeches of this representative family reflects a national egotism. The father as driver, their model and make of car, their state, even their street are all said to be the best in the world. Yet, the play ends with Ma Kirby's comforting Beulah, who still grieves for her baby, with humble acceptance of God's will. Of the three significant plays in this collection, *The Happy Journey to Trenton and Camden* has been the most anthologized and performed.

Scholars have pointed out that the innovative form of these plays did not originate with Wilder, citing such sources of nonrealistic dramaturgy and theatrical style as French symbolism, German expressionism, Brecht's Epic Theatre, the medieval morality play, Chinese theater, and Japanese Noh drama. Wilder himself said of his playwriting aesthetic in the preface to *Three Plays,* "I am not an innovator but a rediscoverer of forgotten goods and I hope a remover of obtrusive bric-a-brac." He saw himself as reviving practices of classical Greek and Renaissance theater, both of which made little use of scenery; however, as John Gassner said in "The Two Worlds of Thornton Wilder" (included in *The Long Christmas Dinner and Other Plays in One Act*), "returning to tradition in the twentieth century was an innovation, and Wilder's manner of returning to it was personal and unique."

The next phase of Wilder's long preparation for the stage was a Broadway production of his translation of French playwright André Obey's *Le Viol de Lucrèce* (The Rape of Lucrece, 1931) in December 1932. *Lucrece* closed after only thirty-one performances, and although the play was published the following year, no study of Wilder discusses it in detail because of his own characterization of his work on it as a literal translation of Obey's dialogue. Curiously, several scholars cite Wilder's working on *Lucrece* as influencing the unconventional form of *The Long Christmas Dinner* plays, even though the collection had been published the year before Wilder was asked by actress Katharine Cornell to translate Obey's play for her to star in. Nevertheless, his involvement with *Lucrece* gave him more experience with unconventional dramatic forms.

Wilder returned to the novel with the publication of *Heaven's My Destination* in 1934. In this novel he continued to write about American characters from all walks of life, as he had done in the one-act plays, but he also used a conventionally realistic and traditional form, that of the picaresque novel. The narrative follows the adventures of traveling salesman and amateur evangelist George Brush over the course of a year as he rides trains around the Midwest to sell textbooks and save souls. In spite of the satirical tone, which was mostly directed at the protagonist, scholars have regarded the book as another moral allegory. Nevertheless, it could no longer be said that Wilder did not write about average working-class Americans who were struggling to just keep going during the time of the Great Depression. *Heaven's My Destination* was Wilder's fourth novel in ten years, and though critics did not embrace it in their reviews, it was a Book-of-the-Month Club selection and sold reasonably well. There was one rather significant literary person who did think highly of the book: Gertrude Stein. Wilder and Stein became friends when they met after she lectured at the University of Chicago in 1934, and they maintained a prolific correspondence upon her return to France, as documented in *The Letters of Gertrude Stein and Thornton Wilder* (1996). Scholars have characterized their relationship as her being his mentor, as did Wilder himself; some scholars go so far as to view *Our Town* as the product of her influence upon him during the 1930s. Once again, however, it should be clear to anyone who reads *The Long Christmas Dinner* plays, which had been published before

Wilder met Stein, that he had already discovered the themes and forms he later employed in *Our Town* and *The Skin of Our Teeth*.

Although biographies agree that Wilder was happy at the University of Chicago, in 1936 he resigned from a teaching position in order to concentrate more on writing. As a final warm-up for his own full-length plays, Wilder adapted Henrik Ibsen's *A Doll's House* (1879) for a Broadway production in 1937. As with *Lucrece*, scholars do not treat the script, which has never been published, as one of Wilder's own works since he only mixed and matched the best parts of several translations of Ibsen's play. Although the production had a fairly good run (142 performances), the real significance of it was that Wilder worked with producer/director Jed Harris, who had been a classmate of his at Yale and by this time was highly regarded as a director and producer. They worked together again the next season, when *Our Town* opened on Broadway.

Our Town dramatizes life in a small New England town around the turn of the century, corresponding to the time of Wilder's own childhood in Wisconsin. The audience is introduced to the town, Grover's Corners, New Hampshire, and the two families that serve to represent the townsfolk, the Webbs and the Gibbses, by the Stage Manager, who functions in much the same way as Wilder's other Stage Manager characters. He addresses the audience and the actors directly, telling the latter which scenes to play; he provides exposition with the aid of a professor from the state university and Mr. Webb, the editor of the town newspaper; he acts some of the minor roles himself (such as Mr. Morgan, the owner of the town drugstore/soda fountain, and the minister at a wedding); and he makes philosophical statements related to the events acted upon the stage. Wilder said that the Stage Manager was a "hang-over from a novelist technique"; indeed, one could say that the Stage Manager is the theatrical incarnation of an omniscient narrator, for he seems to know everything about the characters' past, present, and future, even when and how they will die.

Along with the Stage Manager's repeated breaking of the fourth wall, the absence of any set—apart from some chairs, tables, and ladders—is a constant reminder to the audience that they are watching a performance and are meant to think about the implications of what they are being told and being shown, so they might apply the insights of the play to their own lives. Although the abstract and presentational theatrical style was not new to Wilder, the unconventional dramatic form and nonrealistic theatrical style were new, for the most part, to American theatergoers in 1938.

Besides the Stage Manager, the major characters include members of two typical, middle-class American families: Doctor and Mrs. Gibbs and their children, George (age sixteen) and Rebecca (eleven), and Editor and Mrs. Webb and their children, Emily and Wally, who are also sixteen and eleven, respectively. Their houses are represented variously by two dining tables and chairs, two ladders to function as the upstairs bedroom windows of George and Emily, and two garden trellises "for those who think they have to have scenery." The Gibbses' house is to the audience's left, and the Webbs' house is to the audience's right, almost as if they were mirror images of the same place and people. In act 1, which the Stage Manager says is called "The Daily Life," the Webbs and Gibbses go through their daily routines of meals, school, chores, choir practice, and homework.

Act 2, called "Love and Marriage," initially jumps ahead three years to George and Emily's wedding day but then flashes back to their senior year in high school to show how they fell in love or, rather, realized that they had been in love all along. Act 3 is never named, but at the beginning of the second act the Stage Manager hints that it is about death. Indeed, act 3 takes place in the town cemetery, with the graves suggested by straight-back chairs upon which sit the dead, staring fixedly ahead. Among the dead are Simon Stimson, the alcoholic choir director from the first act; Mrs. Soames, one of the guests at George and Emily's wedding in the second act; Wally Webb; Mrs. Gibbs; and, finally, Emily, now a wife and mother nine years older than in act 2, but who has just died trying to give birth to her second child. The climax of the play occurs when Emily, having been allowed by the Stage Manager to go back to relive her twelfth birthday, realizes that most people go through their lives unaware of the significance, the value of being alive, not appreciating the wonders of life even in the mundane activities of daily existence. After Emily returns to her grave, the Stage Manager closes the play with a short speech and a good night to the audience.

Wilder stated that in *Our Town* he was attempting to portray "the life of a village against the life of the stars"—in other words, the microcosm and the macrocosm. Near the end of act 1, Wilder telescopes the frame of reference from the microcosmic to the macrocosmic when Rebecca Gibbs remarks on a letter sent to a friend, with the address on the envelope designating not only the town, county, and state but also the nation, continent, hemisphere, planet, solar system, universe, and, finally, "the Mind of God." This abstract expansion of setting, along with the absence of realistic scenery, enables Wilder to convey almost paradoxically both the universal and the particular or, perhaps, how the particular is universal.

Our Town provides another lesson in the universality and timelessness of the human condition when the Stage Manager refers to the similarity between the daily routine of families in the ancient Babylonian empire and in Grover's Corners, and he places a copy of the play in a time capsule to enable people a thousand years from now to know what life was like in a New England village at the turn of the century. Wilder underscores this correlation between past, present, and future by having the church choir sing "Blessed Be the Tie That Binds" immediately after the Stage Manager's speech.

While stressing the universal ties that bind the human race, *Our Town* is also imbued with American values and history. In describing the cemetery, the Stage Manager points out the oldest headstones from the seventeenth century, as well as the iron flags on the graves of Civil War veterans. The many American historical references in *Our Town* include the *Mayflower,* the Revolutionary War, the diminished population of Native Americans, the Louisiana Purchase, the Monroe Doctrine, baseball, the Ford automobile, World War I, and references to American conditions, lifestyles, and values. Nevertheless, in the preface to *Three Plays* Wilder explains his intention: "*Our Town* is not offered as a picture of life in a New Hampshire village. . . . It is an attempt to find a value above all price for the smallest events in our daily life." Emily's most moving speech is not a farewell to American culture and lifestyle at the turn of the century, but a farewell to details of daily life that are, for the most part, universal: "Mama and Papa," "clocks ticking," "sunflowers," "food and coffee," "new-ironed dresses," "hot baths," and "sleeping and waking up."

This failure to appreciate the smallest events in daily life is what *Our Town* laments. Upon arrival in the cemetery, Emily remarks that she never knew "how in the dark live persons are." With her greater awareness from the perspective of the future, she cannot bear for long reliving her twelfth birthday because of her and her parents' lack of awareness of how precious a gift life is. She asks the Stage Manager, "Do any human beings ever realize life while they live it,—every, every minute"; "No," he answers, "The saints and poets, maybe—they do some." This is the great lesson that Wilder presents his audience and readers. Earlier in the play the Stage Manager prompts one character, "A few brief notes, thank you, Professor,—unfortunately our time is limited." The line has significance beyond the performance of the play. Thus, as Arthur H. Ballet explains, the audience "learns, as Emily must, to accept the life cycle." Death is ubiquitous in the play, as it is in all of Wilder's works, yet *Our Town* has been stigmatized as dramatizing a sunny, naive view of life. Various reasons for this misperception have been offered; the most likely is that

Wilder discussing the script for his play The Merchant of Yonkers *with the director, Max Reinhardt, in 1938 (Thornton Wilder Archive, Collection of American Literature, Beinecke Rare Book and Manuscript Library, Yale University)*

Wilder's representation of the human condition, which does include bitter suffering and death, is nevertheless affirmative rather than cynical and despairing.

The most vehement of laments in *Our Town* is uttered in act 3 by Simon Stimson, the alcoholic choir director who committed suicide. However, Wilder does not permit Stimson's jeremiad against life to go unchallenged. Mrs. Gibbs, seemingly still playing the role of mother, chides him, as if he were her child: "Simon Stimson, that ain't the whole truth and you know it." The whole truth about life is more balanced, as one of the dead says earlier in act 3: "My, wasn't life awful and wonderful."

Our Town was enormously successful, running for 336 performances and winning the Pulitzer Prize for drama, and it was adapted for the screen in 1940. Initial reviews by critics were mixed, both in regard to its mundane content and abstract form, but scholarly studies of Wilder and American drama have since acknowledged the importance of *Our Town* to the development of modern American theater. The universal popularity of the play is evidenced by the many professional and amateur productions at home and abroad and by its remaining continuously in print. The original production of *Our Town* also afforded Wilder the opportunity

to study the theatrical art from the point of view of the actor when he took over the role of the Stage Manager during Frank Craven's hiatus and subsequently when Wilder played the role in summer stock productions. He also performed in productions of *The Skin of Our Teeth* as Mr. Antrobus, and even as late as 1957 in Germany he acted more than one part in performances of three of his one-act plays.

Wilder's next play, *The Merchant of Yonkers* (1938), opened while *Our Town* was in the middle of its long run; thus, for about a month Wilder had two plays running simultaneously on Broadway. However, *The Merchant of Yonkers* suffered the opposite fate of *Our Town*, closing after only thirty-nine performances to almost unanimous derision by theater critics. The production had been directed by legendary German director Max Reinhardt, which was a dream come true for Wilder, a longtime fan of Reinhardt's work in the theater. Despite the failure of the production, Wilder believed that the play could eventually succeed, implying that he knew what the problem with the initial production was, as critics and scholars have since diagnosed it: Reinhardt's direction of the play was too plodding, too heavy for what was intended as a farce about love, akin to William Shakespeare's *A Midsummer Night's Dream* (circa

1595). In August 1954 Wilder retitled the play *The Matchmaker* for the Edinburgh Festival under Tyrone Guthrie's direction; in November it moved to London, running for nearly a year, and finally had its Broadway revival in 1955, where it enjoyed the longest run of any Wilder play (486 performances). It was also the basis for the even more commercially successful musical adaptation *Hello Dolly!*, which Wilder had no part in except to collect royalties.

The explanation for the enormous success of *The Matchmaker* has been attributed mostly to Guthrie, since the play was only a slight revision from *The Merchant of Yonkers*. Although it is an adaptation of Austrian playwright Johann Nestroy's *Einen Jux will er sich Machen*, which was itself adapted in 1842 from the 1835 English farce *A Day Well Spent* by John Oxenford, *The Merchant of Yonkers/The Matchmaker*, unlike *Lucrece* and *A Doll's House*, is treated in studies of Wilder as one of his original works because he did successfully Americanize the setting, characters, and action, as explained by critic Alexander Woollcott: "He thought he was writing an adaptation from the Viennese but all unbeknownst to himself his good American ancestry took possession of him and what he really wrote was a pure Charles Hoyt farce of the 1885 vintage. If this had been given to any American stock company prior to 1900, it would have presented no problem." Furthermore, Wilder added a major character who functions as either the protagonist or antagonist of the play, as scholar Maria P. Alter says: "Wilder invented a new character, the vivacious, witty, and incomparable Dolly Levi, who thinks on her feet and gives the farce its American flavor."

The Merchant of Yonkers/The Matchmaker is set during the early 1880s, with the action taking place in Yonkers and New York City. As with any farce, the emphasis is on the frenetic action involving mostly one-dimensional characters. Act 1 takes place in the living room of Horace Vandergelder, who is the Yonkers merchant of the first title. He owns a hay and feed store, which occupies the lower story of his house while he lives in the several rooms above it. Vandergelder is a domineering, tightfisted sixty-year-old businessman in conflict with Ambrose Kemper, a young artist who wants to marry Ermengarde, Vandergelder's niece and ward. Cornelius Hackl and Barnaby Tucker, the two clerks of the store, are oppressed by the long hours and low wages Vandergelder pays them. Dolly Levi is, as the second title states, a matchmaker or "a woman who arranges things." Ostensibly, her current job is to find a wife for Vandergelder, who is a widower, but the audience soon learns that Mrs. Levi, a widow herself, intends to be the second Mrs. Vandergelder, as well as to help Ermengarde and Ambrose obtain Vandergelder's permission to marry.

Act 2 takes place in Irene Molloy's hat shop in New York City, where Vandergelder plans to propose to Mrs. Molloy, also a widow, and where coincidentally Cornelius and Barnaby have come while playing hooky from the store in order to have an adventure, which they define primarily as having kissed a girl. Dolly helps the two clerks hide from their boss and also convinces Vandergelder to meet another potential match at a restaurant later in the day. After Dolly and Vandergelder depart, Mrs. Molloy insists upon Cornelius and Barnaby taking her and her assistant Minnie Fay to dinner to make up for all the commotion they have caused, including Vandergelder's decision not to propose to her. She and Cornelius are attracted to each other, and Barnaby and Minnie become the second half of what turns out to be a double date.

Act 3 is set in the Harmonia Gardens Restaurant, where the two couples hide from Vandergelder behind a screen separating a private dining room into two areas with tables and chairs. Disaster is prevented by Dolly's improvisational genius in manipulating and, ultimately, humbling Vandergelder. Act 4 introduces a new character, Vandergelder's "spinster" sister-in-law, Flora Van Huysen, who, like Dolly, is "a friend of all young lovers." The play concludes in Flora's house, where all the characters have come, enabling Dolly to resolve all the conflicts so that, as in Shakespeare's comedies, each "Jack will have his Jill": Ermengarde and Ambrose, Cornelius and Irene, Barnaby and Minnie, and, almost miraculously, Vandergelder and Dolly.

The most striking contrast between *The Matchmaker* and *Our Town* is the conventional realism of the former. Each act takes place in front of a realistic set representing specific locations that appear as they would in the late nineteenth century. The performance time of the play also approximates the time that the events of this one day take. There is no Stage Manager outside of the action, although a few scholars have noted that Dolly Levi functions as a realistic character equivalent of the Stage Manager in the way she directs the events of the plot and comments on them. The only nonrealistic theatrical device Wilder employs in *The Matchmaker*, though sparingly, is the breaking of the fourth wall. At various times Dolly and some of the other characters speak directly to the audience about life, love, and the meaning of it all; thus, the play was a good candidate for adaptation as a musical, which conventionally mixes representational and presentational theatrical styles.

The Matchmaker is also unlike Wilder's earlier plays and novels (except for, perhaps, *Heaven's My Destination*) in tone. The play is subtitled "a farce in four acts," and Wilder published an essay, "Noting the Nature of Farce," in *The New York Times* during the brief run of the original production. The essay was perhaps meant to defend his offering such lighthearted fare for the theater, since he refers to other dramatists who have employed farce to varying degrees in their comedies—Shakespeare, Molière, William Congreve, Richard Sheridan, and Oscar Wilde—and he summarizes Henri-Louis Bergson's and Sigmund Freud's modern theories on laughter and comedy.

The fact that *The Matchmaker* was based upon an undistinguished foreign comedy and that it is Wilder's most conventional full-length play, both in terms of its story and its theatrical style, may account for why it has not received the critical attention that *Our Town* and *The Skin of Our Teeth* have. While the play is obviously not as profound or literary as *Our Town,* it does have moral implications that raise it above the level of just entertainment. When Dolly tells Barnaby to explain the moral of the play, he says, "I think it's about adventure." All of the major characters, including Vandergelder, at some point in the play express a desire for adventure. Wilder says in his preface to *Three Plays* that it was about "the aspirations of the young (and not only of the young) for a fuller, freer participation in life," a common enough theme in great literature and drama. But this theme itself is a variation upon one of the themes of Wilder's previous play, as Martin Blank interprets it: "The theme suggested by *The Merchant of Yonkers* is an extension of an idea developed in *Our Town*—the failure to fully appreciate life while we live it." Vandergelder is so much the merchant that he has a view of life based entirely on utilitarianism and commerce rather than aesthetic pleasure and love.

Although the slapstick humor of the farcical characters and plot may obscure these serious ideas in any viewing of the play, in reading it scholars have had an opportunity to trace the economic theme, which was better served by the original title. However, only a few readings of the play take this theme seriously; for example, Castronovo comments, "But for all its buoyancy, *The Merchant of Yonkers* deals with the darker side of human nature—capitalistic greed, exploitation, denial of vital possibilities, and neurosis." He further notes that "when the play was written should remind audiences that Wilder is working through the issues of the American depression." There are oblique allusions to the Great Depression in *The Matchmaker;* for example, when Malachi Stack applies to Vandergelder for a job, the merchant replies, "There's no dearth of good-for-nothing apprentices," to which Malachi responds, "That's right, Mr. Vandergelder. It's employers there's a dearth of." The economic theme is further developed by Dolly, who is the antithesis of Vandergelder when it comes to their attitudes toward money; she wants to share the wealth, though not, presumably, in a government-man-dated system, such as socialism or communism. Of Dolly, Castronovo says, "Instead of presenting a cynical or bitter character, Wilder has managed to offer Dolly as a buoyant, worldly-wise woman whose major social mission is to get the juices of the capitalist system flowing." In fact, Castronovo describes her as a "New Deal Planner."

Wilder's dramatic versatility was again apparent in his next play, *The Skin of Our Teeth,* which opened in November 1942, ran for 359 performances, and won Wilder his second Pulitzer Prize in drama and his third Pulitzer overall. This fourth full-length play combines the universal allegory and presentational theatrical style of *Our Town* with the farcical action and stock characters of *The Matchmaker.* Written at the time of the U.S. entry into World War II, *The Skin of Our Teeth* was not just Wilder's attempt to reassure his audience that although the human race is forever facing extinction, it ultimately survives each crisis, if only by the skin of its teeth; the play affirms the progress humanity has made, albeit slowly. In each of the three acts Wilder dramatizes a different threat at different times in human history: in act 1 a colossal glacier advances down the North American continent during the Ice Age; in act 2 God sends a great flood to wipe out decadent humankind, as in the Book of Genesis in the Bible; and in act 3 a modern global war lasting years saps humanity of its will to live. Thus, as he did in *The Long Christmas Dinner,* Wilder compresses long expanses of time to establish his universal theme.

The Skin of Our Teeth introduces the audience to the Antrobuses as the "typical American family," but they are meant to represent the archetypal family, the whole human race throughout the ages. "Antrobus," as pointed out in most studies of Wilder, is close to *anthropos,* the Greek word for "Man." As one character says, the play is "all about the troubles the human race has gone through," and another explains to the audience, "They're coming—the Antrobuses. Keck. Your hope. Your despair. Your selves." As in Wilder's other plays, the major characters are largely determined by their family roles: George Antrobus, husband and father, is an inventor who returns from the office each day to boast of his latest discovery; wife and mother Maggie Antrobus will "keep the home going"; the Antrobus children, Gladys and Henry, are of variable age, probably pre-teens in the first act, teenagers the second act, and young adults the third act. The final major character is Sabina, the Antrobuses' maid in act 1, a beauty-contest winner and seductress of Mr. Antrobus in act 2, and maid again in act 3.

The allegorical identities of these main characters are more complex. Mr. Antrobus represents Adam, Noah, and a modern everyman in consecutive act

The original cast of Wilder's The Skin of Our Teeth, *which opened in New York in 1942: Tallulah Bankhead, Florence Eldridge, Fredric March, Frances Heflin, and Montgomery Clift (Thornton Wilder Archive, Collection of American Literature, Beinecke Rare Book and Manuscript Library, Yale University)*

order. Mrs. Antrobus is referred to as "Eva" in act 1. Henry has a red scar in the shape of a C on his forehead because his old name is "Cain," and Mrs. Antrobus laments the loss of her other son, Abel. Sabina's name in her second-act role as temptress is changed to Lily, which scholars have identified with Lilith, Adam's first wife in noncanonical accounts of creation and the garden of Eden. Once again, Wilder is representing the microcosm against the backdrop of the macrocosm.

To assist in the impression of the multiplicity of the human race throughout history, Wilder populates *The Skin of Our Teeth* with a large cast. Minor characters in act 1 include a telegraph boy, refugees, and a pet dinosaur and mammoth, the latter two helping to establish the fantasy nature and farcical tone of the story. In act 2 the Antrobuses and Sabina interact with a broadcast official, a fortune-teller, and delegates to the six-hundred-thousandth Annual Convention of the Ancient

and Honorable Order of Mammals, subdivision Humans, of which Mr. Antrobus has been elected president. Act 3 focuses primarily on the Antrobuses again, but the audience is also introduced to employees of the theater and the acting company ostensibly putting on the play: the captain of the ushers, a dresser, a maid, and the wardrobe mistress.

These characters are part of the meta-narrative of *The Skin of Our Teeth:* the performance of a play about the Antrobuses. In other words, *The Skin of Our Teeth* is actually a play within a play. At times the action stops and the play becomes a backstage drama involving the actors playing Mr. Antrobus, Sabina, Henry, and a stage manager. This stage manager, however, is not the omniscient, omnipresent narrator and commentator of the earlier plays. Instead, he is a realistic though one-dimensional minor character named Mr. Fitzpatrick who tries to keep the performance going through disruptions most often caused by Miss Somerset, the actress playing Sabina. In fact, Sabina/Miss Somerset is the character who most functions like the Stage Manager in *Our Town,* commenting on the significance of the action, though less frequently and in a parodic manner, as when she explains to the audience, "The author hasn't made up his silly mind as to whether we're all living back in caves or in New Jersey today, and that's the way it is all the way through."

Wilder employs the action of performing a play as another metaphor for the historical progress of the human race, with the challenges to its survival occurring in the form of theatrical crises. In act 1 the actress playing Mrs. Antrobus misses her entrance cue, and Miss Somerset has to improvise dialogue but then tells the audience she can't make up lines for this play, and she continues to talk to the audience about the play throughout the act. In act 2 Miss Somerset refuses to play the seduction scene with Mr. Antrobus because it might hurt the feelings of a friend of hers in the audience. Act 3 includes two crises: The first is the actors playing the hours of the night and planets in a symbolic spectacle, which Wilder had used before in *Pullman Car Hiawatha,* have come down with food poisoning. They have to be replaced by the behind-the-scenes employees who know the speeches from listening during rehearsals, though Mr. Fitzpatrick has to run the stand-ins through an impromptu rehearsal before they can proceed with the third act. The second crisis occurs when the actors playing Mr. Antrobus and Henry get carried away in a confrontational scene and almost get into a real fight, which leads to some onstage confession and comforting by other actors.

Despite these interruptions, the action at both levels—the Antrobuses' story and the performance of that story by the actors—continues because, on those levels as well as the allegorical, as the old theatrical adage says, the show must go on. That is Wilder's message to his audience: keep going—an important message, given the economic and global situations in 1942. Early in the play Sabina alludes to the state of chaos outside the theatre: "The whole world's at sixes and sevens, and why the house hasn't fallen down about our ears long ago is a miracle to me." The fracturing of the set (pieces are flown up or lean outward in conjunction with her speech) seems to confirm that the end is near. In the second act a weather signal serves as a metaphor for the signs of the times: "One of those black disks means bad weather; two means storm; three means hurricane; and four means the end of the world." Near the end of act 2 the fourth black disk, perhaps an abstract allusion to the Four Horsemen of the Apocalypse, appears while thunder, wind, and light fill the auditorium.

Such elements in *The Skin of Our Teeth* are what a few scholars have offered as evidence that its tone is pessimistic, but there is far more textual evidence suggesting a more optimistic view of human history. For example, Sabina declares, "what the end of it will be is still very much an open question." At the end of the first act, Sabina asks the audience to bring their chairs forward to use as firewood to keep the Antrobuses from freezing to death during the Ice Age; stage directions require that the audience be able to hear the sound of chairs being broken up at the rear of the auditorium, which suggests that if everyone pitches in, the show will go on. But, of course, the human race is in trouble again in the second and third acts.

This repeated pattern of catastrophe, whether natural or man-made, is what most scholars use to interpret Wilder's view of history as cyclical—exactly what Sabina laments in act 3 after the end of the war. However, a few scholars have noted that the cycles are neither static nor stagnant; for example, Thomas P. Adler describes the play as manifesting "an optimistic philosophy of spiral progression." In fact, *The Skin of Our Teeth* is full of references and allusions to inventions and other signs of the forward movement of civilization: the wheel, the alphabet, prime numbers, the needle, the telegraph, food processing, silk, marriage, social progress in the rights of women, philosophical ideas, and great works of literature. This is not to say that Wilder ignores the negative products of technology: Henry/Cain's weapons grow more sophisticated in each act: stones, slingshots, and guns, respectively. Yet for all that goes wrong through the ages, Wilder suggests that the human race is in the process of getting it right. Antrobus tells his wife, "All I ask is the chance to build new worlds and God has always given us that. And has given us [opening a book] voices to guide us; and the memory of our mistakes to warn us. . . . We've come a long ways. We've learned. We're learning. And the steps of our journey are marked for us here."

Despite its long run and the Pulitzer Prize, *The Skin of Our Teeth* received mixed reviews, as was the case with all of Wilder's plays, and it also sparked another controversy, aired in *The Saturday Review of Literature.* In their article "The Skin of Whose Teeth?" (19 December 1942) Joseph Campbell and Henry M. Robinson implied that Wilder had plagiarized James Joyce's novel *Finnegans Wake* (1939). Critic Edmund Wilson defended Wilder, and scholars discussing the play since then have rejected the charge on several counts, one of which is that Wilder had made use of the same ideas, character types, and actions in previous works, such as the *Long Christmas Dinner* plays, which were published before Joyce's novel. Wilder did not respond to the accusation at the time, but later in his preface to *Three Plays* he acknowledged that *The Skin of Our Teeth* was "deeply indebted to James Joyce's *Finnegans Wake*," but he went on to say, "I should be very happy if, in the future, some author should feel similarly indebted to any work of mine. Literature has always more resembled a torch race than a furious dispute among heirs." Though not as frequently produced as *Our Town*, *The Skin of Our Teeth* remains in the repertory of the professional and amateur American theater.

During the 1940s Wilder responded to the world crisis not only as a playwright but also as a volunteer for military service in support of the American war effort. During 1942, between his completion of *The Skin of Our Teeth* and his induction into the military, Wilder was hired by Alfred Hitchcock, who was by then living and working in Hollywood, to write the screenplay for his latest project, *Shadow of a Doubt* (1943). Wilder scholars have only recently begun to examine the movie as part of Wilder's canon. Its focus on a serial killer hiding from the police by staying with his typical American family in a typical small town makes it a kind of evil mirror image of *Our Town*. Hitchcock thought so highly of Wilder's screenplay that he rode with him cross-country on a train to Florida, where Wilder was to begin training for active duty, so that they could work together on the script as long as possible; it was the last writing Wilder did until after the war.

Commissioned at the rank of captain, Wilder served from 1942 to 1945 in the U.S. Army Air Intelligence and was stationed variously in the United States, Africa, and Italy. His return to Rome inspired his first work about non-American subjects in almost twenty years, the novel *The Ides of March*, published in 1948. Through a series of invented letters between Julius Caesar and other historical and fictional characters, the novel retraces the events leading up to Caesar's assassination. It was a Book-of-the-Month Club main selection but did not receive accolades from the critics. Since then, studies of Wilder have praised *The Ides of March* for its nonlinear structure and its anachronistic examination of Jean-Paul Sartre's existentialism.

During the late 1940s and early 1950s Wilder worked on several dramatic pieces: a brief skit called *Our Century* (1947) for the centennial celebration of The Century Club in New York City; a full-length play called "The Emporium," which he never completed; and *The Alcestiad* (1955), an adaptation of Euripides' tragedy *Alcestis* that Wilder had begun before the war. The writing was not going well, partly because of Wilder's postwar malaise and the deaths of his mother and Gertrude Stein in 1946. Wilder briefly returned to teaching as the Charles Eliot Norton Professor at Harvard University, where he delivered a series of lectures on the American characteristics in classic American lit-

erature. Revising the lectures for publication as a book was another project he never brought to completion, although he published three of these lectures as articles in *The Atlantic*. They were posthumously reprinted in *American Characteristics and Other Essays* (1979), along with other previously published essays on theater and literature, introductions to editions of books by Stein and other authors, and three scholarly journal articles, one on *Finnegans Wake* and two on the plays of Spanish playwright Lope de Vega. The volume demonstrates Wilder's wide reading of world literature and drama and his versatility as an intellectual and writer.

After *The Merchant of Yonkers* was successfully revived as *The Matchmaker*, first at the Edinburgh Festival in 1954, Wilder completed *The Alcestiad* for its only English-language production, retitled *A Life in the Sun*, again at Edinburgh in 1955. As he had done in *The Woman of Andros*, Wilder mixed and matched characters and actions from Greek mythology to allegorize Christian doctrine and theology—in this instance, the Christian existentialism of nineteenth-century Danish theologian Søren Kierkegaard. There are parallels to Christ on several levels of the action: Zeus, the father of gods, has commanded Apollo to live upon earth for one year as a man among men, a lowly shepherd; Alcestis marries King Admetus, and then twelve years later when he is dying, she offers her own life to save his; Hercules descends to Hades and brings her back to earth. The existential theme is conveyed by the dialogue between various characters: Death, Apollo, the blind prophet Teiresias, and Alcestis, showing that whatever the intentions of the gods for humanity, there still exists the individual's free will. This theme is apparent even in the satyr play *The Drunken Sisters* (published separately in 1957), which is a comic variation of *The Alcestiad*.

Though directed by Guthrie, the same director who made *The Matchmaker* work on the stage, the first production of *The Alcestiad* was universally condemned by critics as well as by scholars commenting upon the play once it was posthumously published in English in 1977. Castronovo's succinct assessment is representative of scholarly opinion: "he failed to inform the Greek story with his own deft touch: the play was ponderous and reached the stage in Edinburgh in stillborn form." However, Wilder authorized a German translation, and a few productions were well received by the German critics. He also collaborated with composer Louise Talma on an opera version in 1962, which was his second German-language libretto; the previous year an opera version of *The Long Christmas Dinner* had premiered, with music by Paul Hindemith.

In the late 1950s and early 1960s Wilder worked on two cycles of one-act plays, "The Seven Deadly Sins" and "The Seven Ages of Man." Like other

Wilder as the Stage Manager in a production of Our Town *at The College of Wooster in Wooster, Ohio, 1950 (College of Wooster Archives)*

projects he worked on during the 1950s, the cycles were never completed; however, he did offer five of the plays for performance in two separate productions: *Bernice* (Pride) and *The Wreck of the 5:25* (Sloth) in Berlin in 1957, and *Someone from Assisi* (Lust), *Infancy,* and *Childhood,* billed together as *Plays for Bleecker Street,* in New York in 1962. The Off-Broadway production of the latter three was mounted by esteemed director Jose Quintero and enjoyed a long run (349 performances), but as always, the reviews were mixed. *Infancy, Childhood,* and *The Drunken Sisters* also appeared in *The Atlantic.* With the publication of the first volume of *The Collected Short Plays of Thornton Wilder* in 1997, six more of the cycle plays that had languished in Wilder's papers at the Beinecke Library at Yale for almost forty years became available to readers, scholars, and theater companies. Workshop productions of *Bernice* and *The Wreck of the 5:25* with Yale Drama School students were performed at a symposium celebrating the centennial of Wilder's birth in 1997. Also in the fall of that year, the Actors Theatre of Louisville staged four of the cycle plays—*A Ringing of Doorbells, Youth, In Shakespeare and the Bible,* and *The Rivers Under the Earth*—as part of the

Wilder Rediscovered conference in Louisville. *Youth* and *The Rivers Under the Earth* were produced Off-Broadway in 1999.

Taken as a whole, the eleven one-act plays differ radically from Wilder's earlier plays. After having returned to classical Rome and Greece in *The Ides of March* and *The Alcestiad,* Wilder set eight of these plays in twentieth-century America, with most of the characters belonging to middle-class families, though the poor and the rich are also represented. The stage directions do not call for elaborate or realistic scenery, but what furniture is required is meant to convey the interiors or exteriors of houses or parks. Out of all eleven cycle plays, only one, *The Drunken Sisters* (incorporated into the "Sins" cycle), breaks the fourth wall when Apollo addresses the audience directly. Yet, for Wilder to write conventionally realistic drama in the 1950s and early 1960s was unconventional, because that was the dominant period of the Theatre of the Absurd, which was characterized by nonrealistic dramaturgy and theatrical styles. However, what is most strikingly different about these plays from Wilder's earlier drama and fiction is the darker tone created by characters who are bitter, cynical, resentful, and, in some cases, even criminal.

The Drunken Sisters, representing Gluttony, is the least typical play of the two cycles. It is closer in tone and form to *The Skin of Our Teeth* than to the grimmer, more realistic characters and conflicts in the other "Sins" plays. However, its worldview is in keeping with the more pessimistic outlook of these later plays in that even a god who had come "to love all men" could not spare them from suffering. Apollo tricks the three Fates into letting King Admetus, Apollo's favorite mortal, live; however, his plot backfires when the Fates insist that someone must choose to die in Admetus's place, and Apollo realizes Queen Alcestis, whom he also holds dear, will sacrifice her life for her husband's.

Bernice takes place in 1911; the setting is a drawing room of a house in Chicago owned by George Walbeck, a wealthy man who has been away for a few years. Mr. Mallison, a lawyer, gives instructions to Bernice, the African American maid he has hired to care for Walbeck's personal needs when he takes up residence in the house again. After the lawyer exits, the rest of the play consists of Walbeck's and Bernice's conversation, which reveals that he was in prison at Joliet for swindling people out of their retirement savings and that his wife has filed for divorce and moved with their daughter to the West Coast. Bernice also spent time in prison for murder. In Wilder's morality play cycle, *Bernice* represents the deadly sin of pride, and audiences are given plenty of evidence that both characters are imbued with pride, to their and others' harm. When Walbeck is presented with the opportunity to start over–his teenage daughter is coming there to offer to live with him and take care of him–Bernice persuades Walbeck to do as she had done: to kill off his old self by pretending to have a fatal illness and to assume a new identity, thereby freeing his daughter to live her own life.

In *The Wreck of the 5:25* Wilder's microcosmic focus is upon the American middle-class family during the 1950s. Mrs. Hawkins and her daughter, Minnie, are waiting for Mr. Hawkins to return from working in the city. What sets the plot in motion is that Hawkins has telephoned them that he will not be home on the 5:25 train as usual. It turns out that one of his clients has left him a sum of money in her will because he took the time just to listen to her, to be friendly with her during their mundane business interactions. It is not the bequest of money that gives Hawkins the courage to break his daily routine; rather, it is his realization that his daily routine is the source of the alienation that caused him to stand on the street in front of his home looking through the windows watching his wife and daughter as they go about their daily routines. This third play of the "Sins" cycle depicts Sloth.

A Ringing of Doorbells, set during the Great Depression, dramatizes Envy as seen between the haves and the have-nots. A wealthy widow in her sixties and limited in her mobility by arthritis, Mrs. Beattie is paid a visit by a mother and daughter team of con artists, who are younger and healthier but transients. They envy her wealth and security; Mrs. Beattie envies their freedom and vitality. Exposing them as the swindlers they are, Mrs. Beattie nevertheless decides to write them a check, not out of compassion, but out of respect for their determination to survive.

In Shakespeare and the Bible takes place around the turn of the century in Manhattan. A wealthy older woman named Mrs. Mowbrey, who earned her wealth years ago by running a house of prostitution, has summoned John Lubbock, a lawyer who was once her customer, to her house. Before he recognizes her, she reveals that she is the aunt of his fiancée, Katy, whom she has also summoned. Katy may appear to be an innocent young woman, but she reveals she is as emotionally crippled as the other characters in this and the other plays in the cycle. From the description of the characters and their pasts one might assume that *In Shakespeare and the Bible* illustrates the sin of Lust, but instead its deadly sin is Wrath. At various points in the action all three of these characters struggle to contain their anger. The play ends with Katy unable to forgive her aunt's sordid past or to continue her engagement with Lubbock, who has accepted a bribe from Mrs. Mowbrey to handle her business affairs, the nature of which is left open.

Someone from Assisi represents Lust. A deranged old woman in the early thirteenth century describes how she is mistreated by people and laments the state of the world, and the Mother Superior of the convent to which the old woman has come concurs. When the saint alluded to in the title arrives, he expresses much the same view of people, including himself, though his humility turns to sorrow when he recognizes the old woman as his lover before he became a priest.

As with *In Shakespeare and the Bible,* the main characters of *Cement Hands* include an engaged couple and an older relative, who also is a lawyer. The action takes place in the restaurant of a distinguished Manhattan hotel. The heroine wonders if her uncle is trying to break up her engagement when he explains and then demonstrates that her wealthy fiancé has "cement hands"–avarice–in the form of never carrying money with him to leave as tips. In this play, however, the engagement is not broken, though the young woman is forced to admit her fiancé's fault and, sadly, to compensate for it herself.

The four plays of "The Seven Ages of Man" cycle are not as obviously dark as the "Seven Deadly Sins" plays, as one might expect from the different themes, but their view of human nature as the source of human suffering is no less grim. Even when the tone is comedic or nostalgic and the story fanciful, there is a fundamental pessimism that was not present in Wilder's earlier works, signaled in the last play of this cycle by an allusion to the Cold War and the potential for the end of all human progress with the invention of the atom bomb.

Infancy takes place in New York during the 1920s. In *Infancy* and *Childhood* Wilder employs a nonrealistic theatrical style: low stools are used to represent bushes in Central Park; full-grown men play the infants in baby carriages; and the actor playing the police officer enters and exits through the audience. However, the characters never address the audience or in any way acknowledge that they are part of a play. *Infancy* begins with a young nanny named Millie Wilchick bringing baby Tommy in his carriage to the park, where she hopes to run into Officer Avonzino on his beat. After a while she is joined by Mrs. Boker, who is strolling through the park with her baby, Moe. In direct contrast to the image of the contented housewife and doting mother of such 1950s television shows as *Leave It to Beaver* and *Father Knows Best,* Mrs. Boker and Millie (as a wife and mother-to-be) do not paint a joyful picture of caring for infants, and the babies perceive how the adults really feel about them. For their part, the babies also whine about what they want, and what they do not have, and what adults have. Near the end of the play, Officer Avonzino also paints a bleak portrait of human nature and the experience of growing into adulthood when he tells the babies that their best days are behind them. Far from the image of a natural state of innocence at birth and parental doting over their babies, Wilder shows human nature, young and old, as consistently selfish and unsatisfied.

Childhood, the second play of the cycle, also depicts alienation between children and adults, including their parents. The play opens with a familiar situation in Wilder's drama: the children and their mother wait in expectation of their father's return from the office. Almost immediately the conflict between the children and their parents (their father especially) is made apparent when it is revealed that their favorite game is pretending to be orphans. The mother knows about these games and is disturbed by them; her husband reminds her of one of her recurring dreams in which the children were not with them, but she responds, "Well, I didn't imagine them *dead!*" The play then dramatizes one of the children's games, in which the parents participate as strangers. The father is the bus driver on an adventure the newly orphaned children take now that their parents are no longer restricting them. Riding in a bus made of simple chairs arranged in a linear fashion,

the father tries to get the children to see things from the parents' point of view, which the children do not consider, but the children also express their perspective and adults' inability to appreciate it. After several miniadventures the bus returns to its starting point. Although there does seem to be some new awareness in the children of how difficult their parents have it in raising them, ultimately there is no reconciliation between the generations. The fantasy of the game is over, and the play returns to the real scene of the father returning home from the office, the children fleeing from him, and the mother again disturbed by the morbidity of the games her children play.

The generation gap grows even larger in *Youth,* the next play in the cycle. *Youth* is not realistic drama, although it is realistic theater. That is, the protagonist is taken from literature–Lemuel Gulliver from Jonathan Swift's *Gulliver's Travels* (1726)–but this fanciful story is staged with realistic period sets, costumes, and props. Wilder depicts Gulliver in his forties, once again shipwrecked, this time cast up on an island on which there is no one older than twenty-nine. The young men and women who meet him react in horror, seeing in Gulliver's appearance and his words–or, rather, his ideas–confirmation of their opinion of what happens to people once youth is over. The young Duke claims that the Country of the Young is free from all the ill effects of being governed by the old. Gulliver is horrified when he learns why no one over twenty-nine lives on the island: when they turn thirty, they are executed. Gulliver is even more incredulous that the youthful citizens of the island nation experience no curiosity about what lies over the horizon of the sea, or of what improvements they might make in their buildings, their lifestyle, and their society from reading books written by authors over thirty. Gulliver is able to persuade a young builder and a servant girl to free him and steal a boat to escape the island, but one of Gulliver's last lines suggests that entropy rather than evolution is the order of things.

The Rivers Under the Earth is included in the *Collected Short Plays* volume as the last of the "Seven Ages of Man" plays, seen by the editors as representing middle age, although they admit it is uncertain that Wilder wrote this as one of the plays for the cycle. This gentle, quiet piece may deceive readers or an audience into thinking Wilder is depicting a family closer to the families in the earlier, more affirmative plays; however, its portrait of human nature and life is still rather dark. In fact, the action is meant to take place literally in the dark, and the characters spend part of the play groping around the Wisconsin lake and woods where they have come for a summer vacation. The Carter family is again the perfect balance of gender: mother and father, son and daughter. But just as in *Infancy*, their relation-ships are colored by Freudian ideas about the latent sexual attraction between mother and son and father and daughter. There is also sibling rivalry between the children. Through characters remembering earlier vacations on this site, the psychological process of repressing traumatic events is also demonstrated, almost as if Wilder wrote *The Rivers Under the Earth* as an illustration of Freudian theory. He introduces an even darker note into the nostalgic mood the parents feel and the idealistic dreams of the children when the son refers to an earlier desire to become a physicist so he could invent something to neutralize all atomic bombs, which collectively could end all life on the planet.

"The Seven Deadly Sins" and "The Seven Ages of Man," which turned out to be Wilder's finale as a dramatist, portray an America that is, underneath its sunny surface, corrupted by materialism, but even more surprising is the suggestion that human nature itself is too divided, aggressive, and selfish to make lasting relationships. American playwright John Guare, in his introduction to volume 1 of *The Collected Short Plays of Thornton Wilder*, addresses the apparent contrast of Wilder's last work in the theater and what had come before: "These later plays of Thornton Wilder will only reveal the darkness in the early plays; the light in the early plays will only shine a light on the rueful later work." Perhaps, as Guare suggests elsewhere in his introduction, Wilder was merely reflecting the pessimism inherent in a time when humanity had invented the means to destroy all life on earth; perhaps even Wilder's optimism was curbed by the nuclear arms race between the United States and the Soviet Union.

In his final two literary efforts, the novels *The Eighth Day* (1967) and *Theophilus North* (1973), Wilder resurrected his faith in the gradual progress of the human race and his affirmation of America leading the way. Members of the Ashley family in the first novel, Wilder's longest, are destined for greatness in journalism, music, the women's movement, and engineering. The title character of the second novel, which is thinly disguised but also highly idealized autobiography, is nothing less than Christlike as he heals the sick, raises the dead (after a fashion), saves marriages, and uncovers counterfeiters. Both novels stayed on the best-seller lists for a long time, and *The Eighth Day* won the National Book Award. In fact, during the last two decades of his life, Wilder received several honors and awards for his long and diversified career as a playwright, novelist, teacher, lecturer, translator, essayist, literary scholar, and librettist. He was granted honorary degrees from such distinguished institutions as Yale and Harvard and three German universities. He also received the National Institute of Arts and Letters' Gold

Wilder working with the composer Louise Talma in 1956 on the score for Die Alkestiade, *the German-language operatic version of his* A Life in the Sun. *The opera premiered in Frankfurt am Main in 1962 (photograph by Matthew Wysocki).*

Medal, the German Book Sellers' Peace Prize, the Presidential Medal of Freedom, the National Book Committee's Medal for Literature, and the MacDowell Colony Medal. Also during this time his health began to fail, so he was not able to travel abroad as much as he had during the previous decades, but even at the time of his death from natural causes in 1975 Wilder was at work upon a sequel to his last novel; the manuscript at the Beinecke Library bears the title, "Theophilus North: Zen Detective."

Although Wilder's rank in the American canon of writers has fallen in the second half of the twentieth century, during the 1990s there was renewed interest in his plays and career overall, as indicated by the centennial symposium at Yale, the theater festival in Louisville, a conference at Wake Forest University, and two Wilder sessions at the 1998 Modern Language Association convention; the publication of his interviews, his letters to Gertrude Stein, one book-length study of his drama, one collection of articles and reviews of both his fiction and his drama, and a collection of new essays also attest to this renewed interest.

Letters:

The Letters of Gertrude Stein and Thornton Wilder, edited by Edward Burns and Ulla E. Dydo, with William Rice (New Haven: Yale University Press, 1996).

Interviews:

Conversations with Thornton Wilder, edited by Jackson R. Bryer (Jackson: University Press of Mississippi, 1992).

Bibliographies:

Richard H. Goldstone and Gary Anderson, *Thornton Wilder: An Annotated Bibliography of Works by and about Thornton Wilder* (New York: AMS Press, 1982);

Claudette Walsh, *Thornton Wilder: A Reference Guide, 1926–1990* (New York: G. K. Hall, 1993).

Biographies:

Richard H. Goldstone, *Thornton Wilder: An Intimate Portrait* (New York: Saturday Review Press/Dutton, 1975);

Linda Simon, *Thornton Wilder: His World* (Garden City, N.Y.: Doubleday, 1979);

Gilbert A. Harrison, *The Enthusiast: A Life of Thornton Wilder* (New Haven: Ticknor & Fields, 1983).

References:

Thomas P. Adler, *Mirror On the Stage: The Pulitzer Plays as an Approach to American Drama* (West Lafayette, Ind.: Purdue University Press, 1987);

Maria P. Alter, "The Reception of Nestroy in America as Exemplified in Thornton Wilder's Play *The Matchmaker,*" *Modern Austrian Literature,* 20, no. 3–4 (1987): 32–42;

Arthur H. Ballet, "In Our Living and In Our Dying," *English Journal,* 45 (May 1956): 243–249;

Martin Blank, "Broadway Production History," *Theatre History Studies,* 5 (1985): 57–71;

Blank, ed., *Critical Essays on Thornton Wilder* (New York: G. K. Hall, 1996);

Blank, Dalma Hunyadi Brunhauer, and David Garrett Izzo, eds. *Thornton Wilder: New Essays* (West Cornwall, Conn.: Locust Hill Press, 1999);

Travis Bogard, "The Comedy of Thornton Wilder," in *Modern Drama,* edited by Bogard and W. Oliver (New York: Oxford University Press, 1965), pp. 355–373;

Rex Burbank, *Thornton Wilder,* revised edition (New York: Twayne, 1978);

David Castronovo, *Thornton Wilder* (New York: Ungar, 1986);

Francis Fergusson, "Three Allegorists: Brecht, Wilder, and Eliot," *Sewanee Review,* 64 (1956): 544–573;

A. R. Fulton, "Expressionism Twenty Years After," *Sewanee Review,* 52 (1944): 398–413;

Donald Gallup, ed., *The Flowers of Friendship: Letters Written to Gertrude Stein* (New York: Knopf, 1953);

Malcolm Goldstein, *The Art of Thornton Wilder* (Lincoln: University of Nebraska Press, 1965);

Donald Haberman, *Our Town: An American Play,* Twayne's Masterwork Studies, 28 (Boston: Twayne, 1989);

Haberman, *The Plays of Thornton Wilder* (Middletown, Conn.: Wesleyan University Press, 1967);

Mildred Christophe Kuner, *Thornton Wilder: The Bright and the Dark* (New York: Crowell, 1972);

Paul Lifton, *Vast Encyclopedia: The Theatre of Thornton Wilder* (Westport, Conn.: Greenwood Press, 1995);

Helmut Papajewski, *Thornton Wilder,* translated by John Conway (New York: Ungar, 1968);

Gideon Shunami, "Between the Epic and the Absurd: Brecht, Wilder, Durrenmatt, and Ionesco," *Genre,* 8 (1975): 42–59;

Joel A. Smith, ed., *Wilder Rediscovered: Brown-Forman Classics in Context Festival* (Louisville: Actors Theatre of Louisville, 1997);

George D. Stephens, "*Our Town:* Great American Tragedy?" *Modern Drama,* 1 (1959): 258–264;

Hermann Stresau, *Thornton Wilder,* translated by Frieda Schutze (New York: Ungar, 1971);

Gerald Weales, "Unfashionable Optimist," *Commonweal,* 67 (1958): 486–488;

Christopher J. Wheatley, "Thornton Wilder, The Real, and Theatrical Realism," in *Realism and the American Dramatic Tradition,* edited by William W. Demastes (Tuscaloosa: University of Alabama Press, 1996), pp. 139–155;

Amos Niven Wilder, *Thornton Wilder and His Public* (Philadelphia: Fortress Press, 1980);

Douglas C. Wixson Jr., "The Dramatic Techniques of Thornton Wilder and Bertolt Brecht: A Study in Comparison," *Modern Drama,* 15 (1972): 112–124.

Papers:

The major depository of Thornton Wilder's manuscripts, letters, journals, and other papers is the Beinecke Rare Book and Manuscript Library at Yale University. Other papers are at Kent State University and the University of Virginia.

August Wilson
(27 April 1945 –   )

Jonathan Little
Alverno College

PLAY PRODUCTIONS: *Jitney,* Pittsburgh, Allegheny Repertory Theatre, 1982; St. Paul, Penumbra Theatre Company, 13 December 1984; updated version, Baltimore, Center Stage Theatre, 2000;

Ma Rainey's Black Bottom, New Haven, Yale Repertory Theatre, 6 April 1984; New York, Cort Theatre, 11 October 1984;

Fences, New Haven, Yale Repertory Theatre, 30 April 1985; New York, Forty-sixth Street Theatre, 26 March 1987;

Joe Turner's Come and Gone, New Haven, Yale Repertory Theatre, 29 April 1986; New York, Ethel Barrymore Theatre, 26 March 1988;

The Piano Lesson, New Haven, Yale Repertory Theatre, 26 November 1987; New York, Walter Kerr Theatre, 16 April 1990;

Two Trains Running, New Haven, Yale Repertory Theatre, 27 March 1990; New York, Walter Kerr Theatre, 13 April 1992;

Seven Guitars, Chicago, Goodman Theatre, 21 January 1995; New York, Walter Kerr Theatre, 28 March 1996.

BOOKS: *Ma Rainey's Black Bottom* (New York: New American Library, 1985);

Fences (New York: New American Library, 1986);

Joe Turner's Come and Gone (New York: New American Library, 1988);

The Piano Lesson (New York: Dutton/Plume, 1990);

Two Trains Running (New York: Dutton/Plume, 1993);

Seven Guitars (New York: Dutton, 1996).

Collection: *Three Plays* (Pittsburgh: University of Pittsburgh Press, 1991)—comprises *Ma Rainey's Black Bottom, Fences,* and *Joe Turner's Come and Gone.*

SELECTED PERIODICAL PUBLICATIONS–
UNCOLLECTED: "For Malcolm X and Others," *Negro Digest,* 18 (September 1969): 58;

"I Want a Black Director," *New York Times,* 26 September 1990, p. 25A;

August Wilson (photograph by Glen Frieson)

"The Legacy of Malcolm X," *Life,* 15 (December 1992): 84–94;

"The Ground on Which I Stand," *American Theatre,* 13, no. 7 (September 1996): 14–16, 71–74;

"August Wilson Responds," *American Theatre,* 13, no. 8 (October 1996): 974–989.

August Wilson is one of the leading American playwrights of the late twentieth century. He has been phenomenally successful, having won two Pulitzers, five New York Drama Critics Circle awards, and several Tonys in a long list of prestigious awards, grants, and fellowships. In a rare occurrence, in 1988 Wilson had two plays running simultaneously on Broadway–*Fences* (first performed in 1985) and *Joe Turner's Come and Gone* (1986). Dedicated to representing blacks from every decade of the century in a ten-play cycle, Wilson has completed seven of these plays. He has already expanded the range of American theater by documenting and celebrating black historical experience and by showing that embracing the African spiritual and cultural heritage can bring individual and collective healing for blacks.

In addition to his themes of the search for identity, racial exploitation and injustice, empowerment through the blues, and spiritual regeneration, his success results in part from how he has translated the specifics of black life into the conventions of realism and naturalism. While he adheres to traditional dramatic form, his plays imply no easy answers. Complex and mysterious, his plays show the poisonous effects of a bitter legacy on black individuals and their communities and include thrilling if infrequent moments of personal liberation.

Most of Wilson's plays take place in a tightly knit black neighborhood in Pittsburgh once known as the Hill, a sloping ten-block area that has now disappeared because of an "urban renewal" project. Wilson often laments the demise of the economically viable black community, an attitude informed by his experience growing up in such a community. Indeed, in a 1992 article written for *Life* magazine, "The Legacy of Malcolm X," Wilson, visiting from his home in Seattle, mourns the loss of the safe neighborhood he knew as a child when he was a newspaper carrier. Walking down streets blood-spattered by drug-related gang violence, he reminisces fondly about the former thriving community, where black-owned "stores and shops of every kind were wedged in among churches, bars and funeral homes" and where 55,000 people lived with a "zest and energy that belied their meager means."

August Wilson was born Frederick August Kittel in this Hill neighborhood on 27 April 1945, to an African American mother, Daisy Wilson Kittel, and a white German father, Frederick August Kittel, who all but abandoned them soon after August was born. August was one of six children and grew up in poverty in a two-room apartment above a grocery store. His mother supported her family with cleaning jobs and encouraged her children to read, teaching August to read at age four.

Wilson idolized his mother, who died in 1983, just a year before his first Broadway success. As an adult he changed his name to hers to reflect his allegiance to his mother and his African American heritage. Growing up in her household taught him the defining features of black culture and day-to-day life.

When Wilson was an adolescent, his mother remarried, to African American David Bedford, who moved them to Hazelwood, a mostly white suburb; there Wilson and his family were victims of racist vandalism and abuse. Wilson dropped out of high school at age fifteen after refusing to defend himself against false charges of plagiarism on a paper he had written about Napoleon Bonaparte, and after suffering from racist taunts.

After dropping out of school, Wilson spent much time in the library, preparing himself to be a writer and hoping for several months that his mother would not find out that he was not in school. He was largely self-taught, educating himself by reading all that he could by the writers in the black literature section of the library, including Richard Wright, Ralph Ellison, Langston Hughes, and Amiri Baraka, as well as books on black anthropology and sociology.

The year he was twenty, 1965, was a pivotal one for Wilson. He moved out of his mother's home into a rooming house and joined a group of young black intellectuals, poets, and playwrights. Then on 1 April 1965, Wilson bought his first typewriter and began his career as a poet. Although he recognizes his limitations as a poet, Wilson refers to his poetic work as a vocation that has deeply informed his playwrighting, especially in his expertise with metaphor. As a young poet, Wilson published in several small periodicals, including *Black World, Connections,* and *Black Lines,* and also read his work at local art houses. One of his poems, "For Malcolm X and Others," published in the *Negro Digest* in 1969, is a darkly cryptic homage to Black Power leaders he refers to as a "flock of saints."

Later in the fall of 1965, he heard Malcolm X's recorded voice for the first time. Although the media has tended to downplay this aspect of Wilson's career and life, the Black Power movement was, as he says in "The Ground on Which I Stand" (1996), "the kiln in which I was fired." He was drawn to the Black Power and Nation of Islam messages of self-sufficiency, self-defense, and self-determination, and appreciated the origin myths espoused by the controversial leader of the Nation of Islam, Elijah Muhammad. In 1969 Wilson married Brenda Burton, a Muslim, and briefly converted to Islam in an unsuccessful attempt to sustain the marriage. They had a daughter, Sakina Ansari-Wilson, and divorced in 1972.

Deeply moved by the messages of Malcolm X and the Nation of Islam, Wilson became a founder of the Black Horizon on the Hill Theater in Pittsburgh with writer and teacher Rob Penny. The theater oper-

*Steven R. Blye, Charles S. Dutton, and Robert Judd in the 1984 Yale Repertory Theatre
production of* Ma Rainey's Black Bottom *(photograph by George Slade)*

ated from 1968 to 1978. It produced Wilson's first plays and allowed him and others to celebrate the Black Aesthetic, to participate in the Black Power movement, and to discuss the influences of Baraka and Malcolm X. In addition to Baraka, the black playwrights Wilson was most influenced by include Ron Milner, Ed Bullins, Philip Hayes Dean, Richard Wesley, Lonne Elder III, Sonia Sanchez, and Barbara Ann Teer.

However, in a 1984 interview with Hilary Davies, Wilson differentiated between black theater of the late 1960s and his own less didactic dramatic vision, calling his a more "internal examination" of African American life rather than the "pushing outward" of overt political propaganda. In "August Wilson and the Four B's: Influences," included in *August Wilson: A Casebook* (1994), critic Mark William Rocha argues that while Wilson's plays, like Baraka's, center around confrontations with whites, there is the "signal difference that in Wilson's plays the confrontation occurs off-stage so that emphasis is placed not so much on the confrontation itself, but upon how the black community invests itself in that face-to-face encounter." Also, unlike the more exclusionary aesthetics held by Baraka and other Black Arts Movement proponents, Wilson often stresses the cross-cultural universals of drama and art. In his preface to *Three Plays* (1991) Wilson reflects on his first empow-

ering experiences in writing drama: "When I sat down to write I realized I was sitting in the same chair as Eugene O'Neill, Tennessee Williams, Arthur Miller, Henrik Ibsen, Amiri Baraka, and Ed Bullins." He asserts that regardless of race, all playwrights face the same problems of crafting convincing drama and characters.

Besides a typewriter, the other important purchase that Wilson made in 1965 was a used Victrola and several 78 rpm jazz and blues records for five cents each from a nearby St. Vincent de Paul's store. He often speaks of the profound impact of listening to the blues, and specifically Bessie Smith, for the first time, including her hit song "Nobody in Town Can Bake a Sweet Jellyroll Like Mine." Hearing her voice validated the complexity, nobility, and spirituality of African American folk expression for him and increased his own self-esteem and sense of himself as a member of the black community. He has called the blues the wellspring of his art, and he frequently talks about the historical value of the blues as an emotionally charged and sacred vehicle for keeping an empowering African-based oral culture alive.

Besides the blues, the other chief influences on Wilson are black artist Romare Bearden, Baraka (mostly for his black nationalist ideas rather than his plays), and Argentinean fiction writer Jorge Luis Borges. Wilson admires how Borges tells a story in nontraditional ways to create suspense. He uses Borges's postmodern method of revealing the ending at the beginning and then working backward in *Seven Guitars* (1995), which begins and ends with a central character's funeral. Bearden's collages and paintings also provided direct inspiration for at least two of Wilson's plays. Wilson has called Bearden his artistic mentor; through drama Wilson seeks to reproduce Bearden's ability to capture the richness and diversity of black culture.

Wilson relocated to St. Paul, Minnesota, in 1978 after visiting his friend Claude Purdy, who was the director of the Penumbra Theatre, and after being introduced to Judy Oliver, a social worker in St. Paul who in 1982 became his second wife. At first Wilson worked for the Science Museum of Minnesota, writing plays to enhance their exhibits. He quit this job in 1981 but continued writing plays, and for three years he was also a part-time cook for a benevolent organization, Little Brothers of the Poor. While in St. Paul, he established ties with the Playwrights' Center in Minneapolis. Despite his close attachment to Pittsburgh, it was only after he moved far away from his Pittsburgh home that he was able to hear the black voices of his past and translate them effectively into drama. One factor that stimulated his growth was learning how to write plays by listening to his characters and asking them questions rather than by asserting his authorial control and forcing them into certain situations or political positions. Wilson lived in St. Paul until 1990, when he moved to Seattle and his marriage to Oliver ended.

Wilson's first taste of success came in 1981 when one of his first plays, *Jitney*, was accepted by the Playwrights' Center in Minneapolis, where it was staged in 1982 and met with critical acclaim. *Jitney* is set in Pittsburgh in the 1970s, in a gypsy (jitney) cab station scheduled for demolition. The plot bears some resemblance to Richard Wright's *Native Son* (1940), since one of the main characters—Booster—takes his revenge on a white girl who accused him of rape, by killing her and wounding her father. Academic critics highlight the importance of *Jitney* in Wilson's development as a dramatist. Sandra G. Shannon writes that the play "marks the beginning of both a private and professional journey for Wilson," since it takes place in Pittsburgh and anticipates many of the familiar themes of Wilson's later historical-cycle plays.

Wilson frequently talks about the liberation he felt as a writer in returning to and re-creating the voices and environment he knew growing up. His second play, "Fullerton Street," which was written in 1980, has remained unpublished and unproduced. Set in the 1940s on the night of the famous Joe Louis–Billy Khan fight, it concerns the loss of values attendant with the Great Migration to the urban North. In an interview with Shannon, Wilson reflects on the experience of writing "Fullerton Street," particularly his emotions when he killed off the central character's mother.

With the encouragement of a friend, in 1981 Wilson started submitting his plays to the National Playwrights Conference of the Eugene O'Neill Theatre Center in Connecticut. After four of his early plays—including *Jitney*, "Black Bart and the Sacred Hills" (a satiric musical), and "Fullerton Street"—were rejected, *Ma Rainey's Black Bottom* was accepted. It opened at the Yale Repertory Theatre in New Haven on 6 April 1984 and ran through 21 April. The acceptance of the play marked the beginning of a long and fruitful relationship between Wilson and Lloyd Richards, Eugene O'Neill Center director and dean of the Yale School of Drama, who collaborated on most of Wilson's plays as they moved from first runs at the Yale Repertory Theatre to Broadway. Wilson frequently stresses the profound influence his collaborative work with Richards has had on his plays and on his revision process, and Richards frequently lauds Wilson's talent for creating authentic black voices for the theater.

Ma Rainey's Black Bottom opened at the Cort Theater on Broadway in October 1984 and ran for 275 performances. Wilson, relatively unprepared for the limelight and still struggling financially, was stunned by the enormous success of the play. It won the New York Drama Critics Circle Award and several Tony nominations; soon afterward, Wilson won several prestigious fellowships that allowed him to devote his attentions to full-time writing.

Unlike his other plays, *Ma Rainey's Black Bottom* is set in Chicago in 1927. The title of the play refers, on one level, to the historical Gertrude "Ma" Rainey (1886–1939), one of the first immensely popular African American blues singers. In "Speaking of Ma Rainey/Talking About the Blues," included in *May All Your Fences Have Gates: Essays on the Drama of August Wilson* (1994), Sandra Adell writes, "For the folk down home and down-home folk up North, Ma Rainey represented the epitome of black female wealth, power, and sensuality." The title of Wilson's play refers to Rainey's hit song "Ma Rainey's Black Bottom Blues" (also a black clog dance popular in the 1920s), while on another level it refers to her self-empowerment, effectively showing her white audience and record producers her "black bottom" in an act of defiance.

The play concerns a single afternoon in a studio in a disastrous recording effort. The play foregrounds the frustration and tension of racial exploitation and its explosive effects on blacks. It builds toward a stunning,

August Wilson and Lloyd Richards at the 1984 O'Neill Playwrights Conference (photograph by A. Vincent Scarano)

and somewhat unexpected, climax in which one of the central characters, Levee, the trumpeter, stabs a fellow band-member, Toledo, for accidentally stepping on his shoe. Levee's motivation seems to stem not from Toledo's action but more from the accumulated years of frustration and the bitterness of second-class citizenship. The first act ends, for instance, with Levee relating the horrific story of how his mother was raped and his father was murdered by white Southern racists. In interviews Wilson has repeatedly identified Levee as one of his characters possessing an admirable "warrior-spirit"— one who refuses to accept his oppression and lashes out against injustice in the manner of Nat Turner or Toussaint L'Ouverture. In this case Levee's revenge-inspired violence is misdirected, and perhaps stimulated by the white music producers' mistreatment of him; but the spirit is there nonetheless.

Despite the title of the play, the focus is not on Ma Rainey, but on the tensions and conflicts between the four male members of her backup band, who each represent different facets of the African American community and who chafe under the white producers' demeaning economic patronage, the artistic limitations of the outdated "jug"-band format, and Ma Rainey's control. They argue, for example, about which version

of "Ma Rainey's Black Bottom" they are going to play— the traditional version or the updated one with a new introduction by Levee.

Despite her relative absence on stage, however, Ma Rainey plays a significant role in the play. She dramatizes one of Wilson's major influences—the blues. Once Ma Rainey finally arrives at the recording session late in the play, she speaks eloquently about the significance of the blues, despite the fact that the white recording industry and her white audience treat her like a "whore" or a "dog in the alley." As the Mother of the Blues, she summarizes their significance: they make it possible for African Americans to endure and to cope with and understand a difficult life. The bluesmen in the play alleviate their sense of frustration through soaring riffs and idiosyncratic renditions of classic songs, including her signature song. Despite all its intraracial and interracial conflict, the performance is a tribute to the sustaining power of the blues and their profound visceral impact.

Critics generally embraced the play for its seriousness during what a critic for *The Washington Post* (18 November 1984) called "a shockingly bankrupt season." Reviewers praised the superb acting, especially that of Charles S. Dutton as Levee, as well as the depiction of black vernacular speech in the play and the direction of Lloyd Richards. In his 12 October 1984 review for *The New York Times* Frank Rich argued that the significance of the play is that it "sends the entire history of black America crashing down upon our heads" through its "searing inside account of what white racism does to its victims." In his "spellbinding voice," Wilson crafts a play that is "funny, salty, carnal, and lyrical." In one of the few negative reviews of the play, Clive Barnes of *The New York Post* (12 October 1984) complained that, while he admired the fine acting and the sense of characterization, not enough happened in the play.

In a 1991 article for *Black American Literature Forum* Sandra G. Shannon answers Barnes's criticism of insufficient action by arguing that the play is a "disturbing look at the consequences of waiting, especially as it relates to the precarious lot of black musicians during the pre-Depression era." She posits that the play dramatizes this waiting motif through its constant use of stalling, delay, and deferment: "Forever practicing to become but never actually 'arriving' describes each of the musicians' predicament." In "August Wilson's Burden: The Function of Neoclassical Jazz," included in *May All Your Fences Have Gates,* Craig Werner makes the opposite point that the play affirms the call-and-response jazz or blues spirit, and seeks to identify the source of the historical Ma Rainey's popularity: "the people respond to Ma's response to the call of their own burdens, their lived blues."

Fences, Wilson's second major success as a playwright, was to a certain extent written in response to the more diffuse structure of *Ma Rainey's Black Bottom.* It was written quickly on the heels of the success of the latter play. In interviews Wilson admitted to being worried about being a one-time black playwright who achieved success and then sold out to an unsuccessful career in Hollywood—the fate suffered by several of his predecessors. After warm-up runs at the Eugene O'Neill Center, the Yale Repertory Theater, Chicago, Seattle, and San Francisco, *Fences* opened on Broadway in 1987 at the Forty-sixth Street Theater and ran for more than five hundred performances. It won four Tonys, the Pulitzer Prize, and the New York Drama Circle Critics Award and garnered almost unanimous praise from critics, especially for the acting of James Earl Jones, who played the lead character, Troy Maxson.

In an interview with Richard Pettengil, included in *August Wilson: A Casebook,* Wilson stated that in writing *Fences* he wanted to create a play that featured a single central character who is in nearly every scene. *Fences* is set in the late 1950s in Pittsburgh and focuses on fifty-three-year-old Troy, a former convict and baseball player, now a sanitation worker. Like the black characters in *Ma Rainey's Black Bottom,* Troy is still angry that he was denied the opportunity for economic and professional success. While he became a star in the Negro League after learning to play baseball in prison, he was unfairly denied the chance to play in the Major Leagues because of the color line; he is only angered by the success of Jackie Robinson and others in the now desegregated Majors. He possesses a "warrior-spirit" similar to Levee's, as he continues to battle the demons of injustice. He also repeatedly battles against Death, using his baseball bat. During the play Troy builds a fence around his backyard, at the urging of his wife. As critics have noted, the figurative meanings of the fences are many: the fences between the races, between past and present, between life and death, and between Troy and his family.

When his son Cory is offered an opportunity to play football in college on a scholarship, Troy forces the past to repeat itself by ruining his son's chances at the scholarship and, therefore, a professional career. Unlike Cory, who is part of a new generation more hopeful for social change, Troy sees manual labor as the black man's only reliable means of survival in a racist society. *Fences* includes strong scenes of father-son conflicts that are not even entirely resolved at the end of the play, set in 1965 at Troy's funeral.

Samuel G. Freedman, in a 1987 article on Wilson for *The New York Times Magazine,* points out that the plot of *Fences* and the character of Troy Maxson reflect an important experience in Wilson's own life, despite Wilson's often-quoted assertion that he does not write strictly autobiographical plays. After his stepfather, David Bedford, died in 1969, Wilson discovered that Bedford had been a high school sports star of the 1930s. Since no Pittsburgh college would give a black player a scholarship, Bedford turned to crime and decided to rob a store, killing a man during the robbery. He then spent twenty-three years in prison. Like Bedford, Troy turned to crime to support his family and was convicted of assault and armed robbery, spending fifteen years in prison. But whereas Troy encouraged his son to drop out of organized sports as a way of protecting him from disappointment, Bedford had been angry with Wilson for dropping out of football in his teens.

Unlike the critical response to *Ma Rainey's Black Bottom,* the reception of *Fences* was almost unanimously positive. Barnes, who had been somewhat critical of Wilson's first Broadway play, fully embraced *Fences,* calling it in the *New York Theatre Critics Reviews* (30 March 1987) "the strongest, most passionate American writing since Tennessee Williams." A reviewer for the *Village Voice* (17 April 1987) called Wilson a mythmaker, a folk ethnologist, "collecting prototypical stories, testimonies, rituals of speech and behavior" while working with "basically naturalistic panorama plays" to create complex characters, none of whom are "unindicted or unforgiven." Another critic for the *New York Magazine* (6 April 1987) praised *Fences* for its universal qualities, calling it an "elegant play" not only because of its artful and fluid composition but also because in it "race is subsumed by humanity." The play "marks a long step forward for Wilson's dramaturgy."

Fences has not been made into a movie, perhaps in part because of controversy over a director. In "I Want a Black Director" (1990) Wilson reveals that Paramount Pictures, who purchased the movie rights in 1987, suggested white director Barry Levinson as their leading candidate. In his opinion piece Wilson gives his reasons for opposing a white director and attacks Paramount Pictures (and Hollywood in general) for not believing enough in black directors' abilities. Wilson argues that a white director does not share the same cultural specifics of black society that a black director would. He declined Levinson as a director, "not on the basis of race but on the basis of culture." Wilson ends the piece lamenting the fact that he is still waiting for Paramount Pictures to make the play into a movie. Yet, as Yvonne Shafer reports, *Fences* and *Joe Turner's Come and Gone* netted Wilson more than a million dollars in 1987–1988. The mayor of St. Paul named 27 May 1987 "August Wilson Day" to honor the fact that Wilson was the only Minnesota resident to win a Pulitzer for drama.

With his next play, *Joe Turner's Come and Gone*, Wilson achieved another notable success. Both *Joe Turner's Come and Gone* and *Fences* ran on Broadway at the same time; critics commented on how unusual this circumstance was for a black playwright. After a warm-up run at the Yale Repertory Production from 29 April to 24 May 1986, *Joe Turner's Come and Gone* ran on Broadway from 26 March 1988 at the Ethel Barrymore Theatre for 105 performances.

The play, which Wilson calls his favorite, is set in 1911 in a boardinghouse in Pittsburgh. As Wilson states in his preface to the play, the boardinghouse is a meeting place for those "sons and daughters of newly freed African slaves" who are trying to re-create their identity and to find "a song worth singing" that will make them self-sufficient. As his characters move to what is reputedly greater opportunity in the North, they necessarily become more dependent on the empowering legacies of the past and on Southern black-vernacular culture.

As Wilson has stated in several interviews, the play was initially inspired by a Bearden painting called *Mill Hand's Lunch Bucket* (1978). The painting is an eerie

and fragmentary collage depicting a boardinghouse with shadowy black figures. Fascinated especially by the mysterious man in the middle of the painting, who became a model for one of the central characters, Wilson first adopted the title of Bearden's collage as the title of his play. He changed the working title of the play after listening to the famous W. C. Handy blues song "Joe Turner's Come and Gone." Joe Turner was an historical figure who pressed Southern freedmen into servitude with impunity at the turn of the century because he was the brother of the Tennessee governor. Handy's song, thought to be one of the earliest blues songs ever recorded, is sung from the perspective of a woman who has lost her man to Joe Turner.

The most explosive character of the play, Herald Loomis, experiences firsthand the cruelty of the Reconstructed South and Joe Turner's reign of terror. He is falsely imprisoned for seven years of hard physical labor by the powerful Tennessee plantation owner. A former deacon, Loomis is a broken and angry man when he arrives at the boardinghouse after four years of searching for his wife with his daughter. He clashes with the other members of the boardinghouse, who are also looking for something that will bring them together and give them some peace. When the residents of the boardinghouse sing and dance a *juba,* an African call-and-response celebration of the spirit, Loomis cannot join in. Instead he is haunted by a horrifying vision of the Middle Passage: "I done seen bones rise up on the water."

Loomis's salvation comes only later in the play after he slashes his chest with a knife and finds the strength and the power to finally stand up on his own two feet and start afresh. He has found his own song, which Wilson calls the "song of self-sufficiency." This song helps him to attain the "warrior-spirit" and combat the racist environment in which he is forced to live. Bynum Walker, a mysterious African conjure man who "binds" people together and gives them their songs, plays an important role in Loomis's resurrection and healing. According to Bynum, Loomis becomes the spiritually charged shining man that Bynum has been looking for throughout his life.

Joe Turner's Come and Gone is a compilation of Wilson's most persistent themes. Through the play Wilson shows how embracing an African heritage—via the *juba* and Bynum's mysterious spiritual influence—can bring individual and collective healing to members of the African diaspora and the Great Migration north. Loomis's search for identity reaches a successful conclusion only when he confronts his painful past and the legacy of slavery within the framework of a communal response. Unlike previous heroes with the "warrior-spirit," such as Levee and Troy, Loomis achieves psy-

James Earl Jones and Courtney B. Vance in the 1987 New York production of Fences *(photograph by Ron Scherl/Stage Image)*

mythology in depicting Loomis's transformation to mystical "shining man": "When Wilson uses secular mythology as the source of religious conversion and overwrites Christianity with African American folkways, he merges the secular and the sacred in ways that few African American authors have attempted." Similarly, Shannon emphasizes the connections between *Joe Turner's Come and Gone* and Morrison's *Beloved* (1987): both Loomis and Beloved are mediums for "thousands of tormented slaves whose stories for centuries lay submerged beneath the currents of the Atlantic." Shannon also emphasizes Wilson's theme of reconnecting with African American heritage in the tradition of Black Nationalist writers Baraka and Larry Neal.

Another Bearden painting, *Piano Lesson,* (1983), provided the inspiration for Wilson's next play. The silkscreen painting depicts a woman looking over the shoulder of her female student seated at a large piano. *The Piano Lesson* won Wilson his second Pulitzer Prize in 1990 before it opened at the Walter Kerr Theatre on Broadway in April that year and ran for 329 performances. Previous productions included a run at the Yale Repertory Theatre from 26 November through 19 December 1987. Charles S. Dutton, who had also acted in *Ma Rainey's Black Bottom,* was highly praised for his performance in the New York production. *The Piano Lesson* was adapted as a "Hallmark Hall of Fame" television production, also featuring Dutton as Boy Willie.

The Piano Lesson further develops the familiar theme of overcoming the bitter legacy of slavery through a revitalized connection with an African heritage. Set in 1936 Pittsburgh in the home of the main characters' uncle, the play centers on a conflict between Boy Willie and his sister Berniece over the fate of their most cherished possession from their enslaved past—their family's piano. Its legs had been carved with African-styled figures by their great-grandfather in an act of mourning the loss of his missing wife and nine-year-old son, who had been traded away for the piano as an anniversary present for the slaveowner's wife.

As if this symbolic weight were not enough, Boy Willie and Berniece's sharecropper father was killed in retribution for later stealing the piano from James Sutter, a descendent of the original slaveowners. Sutter suspiciously drowns in his well, perhaps pushed by Boy Willie, who celebrates his death. However, Boy Willie recounts the legend of the Ghosts of the Yellow Dog—the boxcar in which their father was burned along with three others—and blames them for Sutter's death. Sutter's ghost inhabits their uncle's home, giving the play supernatural overtones.

In contrast to Boy Willie, Berniece wants to keep the piano and emphasizes its priceless heirloom status. She recounts how their mother polished the piano

chic unification and communal empowerment. That Loomis is able to attain his own redemption with Bynum's help is one of Wilson's strongest, most optimistic assertions of hope and possibility.

The critics were largely positive about Wilson's third Broadway showing. Writing for *The New York Times* (28 March 1988), Rich argued that *Joe Turner's Come and Gone* is Wilson's "most profound and theatrically adventurous telling of his story to date." The play "is a mixture of the well-made naturalistic boarding house drama and mystical, non-Western theater or ritual and metaphor." Writing for *Newsweek* (11 April 1988), Jack Kroll stated that *Joe Turner's Come and Gone* is Wilson's "best play to date and a profoundly American one."

Academic critics such as Trudier Harris stress Wilson's connections to such canonical African American folklorist writers as Zora Neale Hurston, Ralph Ellison, and Toni Morrison. In "August Wilson's Folk Traditions," included in *August Wilson: A Casebook,* she argues for the significance of Wilson's use of folklore and elevates Wilson's complex use of African American every day for seventeen years, until her hands bled. It is a cumulative symbol of their family's tragedy–drenched in the blood of slavery, the hypocrisy of the Fugitive Slave Law, and the horrors of Reconstruction and Jim Crow. More practical-minded Boy Willie, who arrives in Pittsburgh ostensibly to sell watermelons, is interested in selling the valuable piano so that he can buy back the plantation on which his great-grandparents were enslaved.

Before either side can resolve their dispute, however, they must confront the ghosts of the past. Boy Willie must confront Sutter's ghost, which has followed the piano from the South, and Berniece must re-establish ties to her dead ancestors. Ever since the day her mother died, she has avoided playing the piano because she did not want to wake the spirits of her dead relatives. In the end, she plays a redemptive and empowering blues song on the piano that is "both a commandment and a plea"–it serves to exorcise the ghosts and to reconnect Berniece and her brother with her ancestors. Through music, in other words, the characters have accessed the power of the African heritage. Additionally the magic counterspell in the music has driven away the demons and ghosts of the white slave-owning past. Boy Willie departs for home in Mississippi, content to let Berniece keep the piano, after both characters learn a powerful individual and cultural "lesson."

A reviewer of the Yale Repertory Theater performance (*Time,* 30 January 1989) called *The Piano Lesson* "the richest yet of dramatist August Wilson" and the piano "the most potent symbol in American drama since Laura Wingfield's glass menagerie." Barnes, writing for the *New York Post* (17 April 1990), stressed the significance and power of the piano as a living symbol of the family's past and emphasized the effective confrontations in the play between the living and the dead, between the real and the supernatural. Writing for *The New York Times* (17 April 1990), Rich called attention to the effective use of music in the play. He concluded, "That haunting music belongs to the people who have lived it, and it has once again found miraculous voice in a play that August Wilson has given to the American stage."

A review for *New York Magazine* (7 May 1990), however, was largely critical of the Broadway production for having too many confusing subplots and contradictions and for the "uncompelling" use of the supernatural. The reviewer attributes the confusing and unconvincing aspects of the play mostly to its two-year period of testing in various venues before opening on Broadway. Critic Robert Brustein's scathing attack on Wilson in his review of *The Piano Lesson* for *The New Republic* (21 May 1990) marked the beginning of a bitter relationship between the playwright and Brustein, who called the play "an overwritten exercise in a conventional style" that does not have the poetry of Wilson's previous plays. Where other critics have celebrated Wilson's treatment of African American life, Brustein sees Wilson as having "limited himself to the black experience in a relatively literalistic style." He called Wilson's acclaim among white liberal audiences the result of "a cultural equivalent of affirmative action." He also criticized the use of the supernatural as a "contrived intrusion," inappropriate in a realist drama, and concluded that "Wilson is reaching a dead end in his examination of American racism."

Some academic critics took a different, more positive view of Wilson's use of the supernatural or the mystical. In "Ghosts on the Piano: August Wilson and the Representation of Black History," included in *May All Your Fences Have Gates,* Michael Morales argues that the mystical and the historical are closely interrelated in Wilson's plays, especially *The Piano Lesson* and *Joe Turner's Come and Gone:* "In these two plays Wilson predicates the relationship of the past to the present for black Americans on an active lineage kinship bond between the living and their ancestors." In an answer to the critical controversy over the ending of *The Piano Lesson,* academic critics argue that the reliance of the play on the presence of the supernatural is a valid part of Wilson's overarching dramatic project of restoring a sense of historical-cultural connection with the past for contemporary blacks.

Two Trains Running, his next play, continues Wilson's ten-play historical cycle by examining urban black culture in the tumultuous 1960s. After a run at the Yale Repertory Theatre in New Haven from 27 March through 21 April 1990, and a year of fine tuning with the help of Richards, the play opened at the Walter Kerr Theatre on Broadway on 13 April 1992, with Laurence Fishburne playing Sterling, one of the central characters. The play won Wilson his sixth Drama Critics Circle Award. He also met his third wife, Constanza Romero, who was in charge of costume design, during the production. Together they have a daughter, Azula Carmen Wilson.

Two Trains Running is set in Pittsburgh in 1969, in a restaurant across the street from a funeral home and Lutz's, a white-owned meat market. As critics mention frequently, although the play is set in the 1960s, it does not foreground the political turmoil of that decade; instead, the race riots and heightened tensions exist in the background. Their relative insignificance highlights Wilson's belief that politics changed little for blacks. Instead of change, the play focuses on the familiar theme of overcoming the destructive effects of the pervasive economic exploitation of the black community by mainstream white society and of the trauma of the past, including slavery. As Shannon notes, Wilson's later plays, including *Two Trains Running,* feature characters who, "Instead of assailing white America's conscience . . . seem preoccupied with discovering, acknowledging, and grappling with both their collective and individual pasts in order to move their lives forward."

As in *Fences* especially, one of the central tensions exists between the older and the younger male generations. In *Two Trains Running,* Memphis Lee is the self-made man who owns the restaurant in which the play is set. Like Troy Maxson in *Fences,* Memphis rails against the younger generation. Perhaps because of the gap between himself and the younger generation, he scoffs at the Black Power rallies celebrating Malcolm X's legacy in his neighborhood, placing little hope in the power of the younger generation to change anything because of the loss of their work ethic. At the same time, however, he believes that the only way to make an impact on the white man is with a gun.

Wilson carefully balances Memphis's indignation against the younger generation with another older character, Holloway, who makes the connection between the lack of a work ethic in the younger generation and their lack of rewarding opportunity, a systemic problem that keeps the economic inequity of slavery intact. Holloway asserts a chilling logical equation: while times have changed since slavery, the basic economic policy of plenty of work for nothing and no work for pay is still in effect. Several of the other male characters in the play invest all their time and energy in playing the numbers as a seemingly viable alternative to working at a job or investing their money. Wilson's implication is that investment for the black community and the fixed, white-controlled numbers racket are essentially the same thing, since everything is set up to favor whites.

Despite their differences over how to cope with their economic disempowerment, the characters in the play seem obsessed by money and by redressing the economic exploitations of the past. For example, one of the characters, nicknamed Hambone, repeats a single line throughout the play until his death: "I want my ham." More than nine years before, the white grocery-store owner, Lutz, agreed to pay him a ham in exchange for doing a good job painting his fence. Instead of a ham, however, all Hambone gets is the offer of a chicken. Each day until his death Hambone confronts Lutz, receiving the same frustrating answer. In a symbolic act designed to redress the inequity of the past, one of the younger characters, Sterling, a former convict in his thirties, breaks the store window and steals a ham from Lutz's store to put in Hambone's coffin. Unlike Memphis, who seems paralyzed by contradictions and his own pessimism, Sterling, as a disciple of Malcolm X, takes direct action. His act underscores Wilson's admiration for those who do something to counter pervasive racial injustice by enacting the "warrior-spirit."

Memphis dreams of returning to Jackson, Mississippi, to reclaim his farm, which he was forced to leave because of attacks by white racists in 1931. He hopes to sell his restaurant, which he bought with his numbers winnings and his disabled brother's insurance money, to the city for a good price. He plans to take one of the "two trains running" south every day from the Pittsburgh train station and buy back his farm. Memphis, like Troy Maxson, is pessimistic about the future of the black community and looks forward to leaving. Most of the stores and health-care providers have already moved out in preparation for the city's "renovation" project. As Memphis grimly states, "Ain't nothing gonna be left but these niggers killing one another." By the end of the play, however, Memphis gets the money he wanted from the city, which is an unusually optimistic turn of events in Wilson's plays.

Two Trains Running features an offstage character–Aunt Esther–who, like Bynum in *Joe Turner's Come and Gone,* is the spiritual center of the play. She has the gift of prophecy, unlike the more suspect promises of the more popular, glitzy Prophet Samuel, minister of the First African Congregational Kingdom. Throughout the play different characters go to seek Aunt Esther's advice, including Memphis, who is told that he needs to take care of unfinished business–recovering his farm. Instead of boasting of the power to make people rich, as does the Prophet Samuel, the reputedly 123-year-old Aunt Esther has the "understanding" or wisdom of old age, which reinforces one of Wilson's consistent themes: that the older black generations offer empowering wisdom, experience, and spirituality. She represents the antimaterialism of true spiritual achievement, and tells several characters, including Memphis, to throw her twenty-dollar fee into the river. Aunt Esther's significance as a voice of wisdom and historical continuity cannot be overestimated; Holloway believes that she is actually 322 years old, roughly the same amount of time that Africans have lived in North America.

Critical reaction to *Two Trains Running* was less positive than to some of his earlier plays. Writing for the *New York Post* (14 April 1992), Barnes criticized the play, calling it the most diffuse play that Wilson has written. Some critics agreed with this assessment but found other aspects to praise. Chief among their criticisms was that the play lacked a strong plot and resolution, and that it was too long. Other critics, however, writing for *Time* (28 April 1992), and the *Christian Science Monitor* (27 April 1992), praised the sense of humor in

Charles S. Dutton and Ed Hall in the 1987 Seattle Repertory Theatre production of
Joe Turner's Come and Gone *(photograph by Chris Bennion)*

the play and its lyric depiction of human suffering. Also prominent in the reviews of the play was a nearly unanimous appreciation for Wilson's use of language and for the acting, especially by Fishburne.

Academic criticism counters the criticisms in the mass media. Shannon, for example, writes that "the play's lax tempo and unconventional structure imitate the often unhurried, repetitive, and sometimes amorphous form of blues music." She compares the improvisational plotlessness of *Two Trains Running* to *Ma Rainey's Black Bottom:* both plays are "best viewed as a dramatic rendering of a blues song; form and structure are secondary to catharsis." Other critics affirm Shannon's central point: in an essay included in *Three Plays,* Paul C. Harrison emphasizes the oral-history quality of *Ma Rainey's Black Bottom* and the slow accretion of tension based on a pattern of "circuitous course of parenthetical anecdotes, asides and utterances."

Wilson's next play, *Seven Guitars*, returns to the blues as an explicit controlling metaphor. The play ran first in Chicago at the Goodman Theatre from 21 January to 25 February 1995 before it opened on Broadway on 28 March 1996 at the Walter Kerr Theatre. Wilson completed it after taking a three-year break from writing; the changes in his life during this period included

his divorce from his second wife, his plans to marry Romero, and his success in giving up a heavy smoking habit.

Seven Guitars opens during a hot and humid summer in the familiar Pittsburgh Hill District in 1948. The dirt backyard set is a gathering place for the characters who occupy the apartments above and below the yard to play whist, sing the blues, dance, socialize, argue, and listen to the radio accounts of the latest Joe Louis victory over his white opponents. Despite the historical context of the country's economic boom after World War II, the Pittsburgh black community, made up largely of Southerners looking for greater economic opportunity in the North, seems completely isolated from the rest of the country and certainly does not share in its economic gains. Instead, as in many of Wilson's plays, the characters in *Seven Guitars* are fixated on money and on attaining some kind of financial retribution for past wrongs.

Seven Guitars begins and ends with musician Floyd "Schoolboy" Barton's funeral. The play creates some suspense by not answering the question of who murdered him until the final scene. The mystic and at times delusional character King Hedley dreams that someday King Buddy Bolden, a legendary blues player for whom

Hedley is named, would appear and return to him his father's money. He plans to take this money, return south, and buy a plantation, like Memphis in *Two Trains Running*. When Hedley sees Floyd in the yard with $1,200 he had stolen during a robbery from the loan offices of Metro Finance, he feels his dream has come true and kills Floyd for refusing to hand over the money. Like Levee in *Ma Rainey's Black Bottom* and Herald Loomis in *Joe Turner's Come and Gone,* Hedley embodies the "warrior-spirit." He refuses to acquiesce to white economic disenfranchisement and wants to be famous someday. Near the end of the play he calls himself a "warrior" and a "hurricane," and warns that the "black man is not a dog!" Hedley sees himself cast in a biblical drama against the Satanic whites, and he hopes to father a son who will be the new black messiah born to conquer evil. Indicative of Wilson's complex sense of irony and realism, however, is the final act: instead of realizing his dreams, Hedley kills one of his friends, and the dollar bills that he had hoped would be his ticket to a new life instead "fall to the ground like ashes" from his hands in the closing scene, similar to the tragic denouement of *Ma Rainey's Black Bottom*.

One of Wilson's most pessimistic plays, *Seven Guitars* shows the black man caught in the inexorable web of white economic oppression that exploits the black artist and fails to see his music as anything more than a means to an economic end. As in *Ma Rainey's Black Bottom,* the musicians who occupy this play have been taken advantage of and cheated by the white-controlled music industry. Despite the fact that Floyd has a hit song, ironically called "That's All Right," he is still dependent on a white agent who eventually cheats him out of his advance money (and is convicted also of insurance fraud), thereby making it impossible for Floyd to get his guitar out of hock and return to Chicago. Like all the characters in the play, Floyd is tired of having nothing and decides to "take a chance" by robbing the loan offices. With the money he is finally able to provide a headstone for his beloved mother and, before he is killed, he performs in a night of singing and fun at the local nightclub, the "Blue Goose."

Several times in the play Floyd reminisces fondly about his mother, and his music reflects her love for gospel singing. In Wilson's "A Note from the Playwright," which precedes the play Wilson admits that this play is an homage to his mother's life, her cooking, her faith, and her superstitions. These aspects come alive as well in the female characters, who spend time preparing food and talking about men and the difficulties of love. The play begins and ends with one of the women, Vera, with whom Floyd was involved, claiming to have seen angels come to take Floyd to heaven.

Critical reaction to *Seven Guitars* was mixed. Writing for the *New York Post* (29 March 1996), Barnes praised the sad anger and the poetry of the play but criticized the lack of an effective climax. The reviewer for *The New York Times* (29 March 1996) also found fault with the ending but raved about the rest of the play and its spiritual power. Several other critics were impressed by the wisdom in the play, Wilson's use of language, the acting, and the homage to the blues spirit despite the less effective second act, which could have been improved.

Shortly after *Seven Guitars* opened, Wilson gave the keynote address to the Theatre Communications Group National Conference on 26 June 1996. This address, titled "The Ground on Which I Stand" and published in *American Theatre* in September 1996, can be read as the culminating manifesto of his personal politics, his aesthetics, and his vision for the future. In the address he differentiates between two traditions, the white and the black. While he recognizes his debt to great white dramatists, including William Shakespeare and Eugene O'Neill, the ground on which he stands as an artist is firmly in the black tradition, dating back to the spiritually empowering and functional art practiced not within the white slaveowner's home for white consumption, but within the slave quarters for an exclusively black audience. This art was designed to nurture the spirit, to celebrate black life, and to pass on strategies for survival in a hostile and antagonistic environment. Strategies for maintaining control over black cultural capital include rejecting colorblind casting (the practice of placing black actors in "white" plays or vice versa, such as an all-white cast of Lorraine Hansberry's 1959 play, *A Raisin in the Sun*) as cultural appropriation. Wilson also argues for increasing the number of black regional theaters. Out of the sixty-six theaters in the League of Resident Theaters (LORT), Wilson claims, only one is dedicated to black drama. Wilson challenges theater managers to increase the number of regional black theaters and to make theater more accessible to the masses.

Wilson goes on to reject the label of being a separatist, since he believes that whites and blacks can meet on a jointly constructed "common ground" of the theater in pursuing dramatic excellence, as long as that common ground allows blacks to explore and celebrate their cultural distinctiveness. He argues that in addition to the formalist commonalities of theater, which include plot and characterization, there are such human universals as love, honor, duty, and betrayal that all audiences can appreciate, regardless of race. Theater was developed by Aristotle and other Greek, European, and Euro-American playwrights; however, Wilson avers, "We embrace the values of that theatre but reserve the right to amend, to explore, to add our African consciousness and our African aesthetic to the art we produce." Wilson ends with an appeal to work together to create a common ground and to use the universal truth-telling power of the theater to improve all lives across the lines of culture and color.

Wilson's keynote address also includes attacks on the "cultural imperialist" critics who, like Brustein, are antagonistic to a diversified theater because they see a lowering of aesthetic standards. Wilson counters by arguing that the new voices in the theater represent a raising of the standards and levels of excellence in the theater.

Wilson's address was met with a veritable firestorm of print activity, including counterattacks by Brustein. In the next issue of *American Theatre* Brustein responded to Wilson's attacks with an article titled "Subsidized Separatism," to which Wilson also replied in the same issue. In the article, Brustein seeks to defend himself and to explore "troubling general issues" raised in Wilson's speech, which he calls a "rambling jeremiad." Brustein interprets Wilson's speech as a call for separatist theater and reads Wilson's comments about artistic universals and common ground as "boilerplate rhetoric," afterthought, and pretense. He repeats his objections to Wilson's plays, made clear especially in his review of *The Piano Lesson,* and adds a further complaint that "Wilson has fallen into a monotonous tone of victimization which happens to be the leitmotif of his TCG speech." Brustein asserts that Wilson is part of the "rabid identity politics and poisonous racial consciousness that have been infecting our country in recent years."

In his response following Brustein's article, Wilson defends himself against what he calls Brustein's misinterpretations of his speech and repeats his points about the cross-cultural commonalities inherent in great art. At the end of his response he turns around Brustein's scolding that he has left Dr. Martin Luther King Jr. out of his list of black American heroes by arguing that Brustein is the one who denies the possibility of a theater capable of absorbing or assimilating different traditions and cultural values.

The dramatic and well-publicized feud between Wilson and Brustein reached its peak during a 27 January 1997 debate at New York City Town Hall, moderated by Anna Deavere Smith and titled "On Cultural Power." In a review of the two-and-a-half-hour debate for *American Theatre,* Stephen Nunns emphasizes the evening as a flashy media spectacle. Accompanying photographs depict "a diverse and celebrity-studded audience." Nunns writes that both men began by repeating their earlier positions, with Brustein attacking multiculturalism as being without intellectual content

Cover for the play inspired by Romare Bearden's 1983 painting Piano Lesson

and Wilson again emphasizing the need for more black regional theaters and his activist position that art has the power to transform society and individuals. While the two debaters were relatively civil, the 1,500-member audience had to be reprimanded several times by Smith for heckling the speakers.

Critical reaction to the debate was mixed. In *Newsweek* (10 February 1997) Kroll emphasized the significance of their debate and the need to explore issues of multiculturalism and cultural synthesis as the country becomes more diverse. An editorial in the *Boston Globe* (9 February 1997) praised the intelligence and depth of the evening. However, several critics noted that the event was not too enlightening because neither man seemed able to listen to the other or to come to any kind of reconciliation. Rich wrote in an article for *The New York Times* (1 February 1997) that both men ignored the larger crisis that serious theater is virtually dead: "Both men narcissistically fiddle (and bicker) while the world of serious culture they share burns." And a writer for the *Village Voice* (February 1997) found the evening disappointing because both men are stuck in "a monolithic modernism. Both hold faith in a capital-T Truth out there waiting to be uncovered."

In a 3 February 1997 article in *The New Yorker*, "The Chitlin Circuit," eminent literary and social critic Henry Louis Gates Jr. responded at length to Wilson's keynote address but mentioned the debate only in passing. While Gates calls Wilson the "dean of American dramatists" and "the most celebrated American playwright now writing and . . . certainly the most accomplished black playwright in this nation's history," Gates's article is largely critical of Wilson. Gates reviews the controversies around Wilson's "disturbing polemic," points out that many black actors disagree with Wilson's condemnation of colorblind casting, and quotes Baraka's support for actors crossing color lines to get parts. Gates also attacks Wilson's "divided rhetoric" in calling for a self-determining black theater and government subsidies at the same time.

As if to answer the critiques of Gates and others, Wilson has become quite active in the cause of developing and nurturing serious black theater. He was featured at the opening of the foundation-subsidized new vehicle for black theater, The African Grove Institute for the Arts in partnership with the National Black Arts Festival. According to its brochure, the African Grove Institute, which is based at Dartmouth College, is "dedicated to the advancement and preservation of black Theater as an agent for social and economic change." Its initial event, which coincided with the National Black Theatre Summit II, was held in Atlanta in July 1998. The opening featured a performance of *Jitney* and included a closing conference session titled "A Vision for the New Millenium."

Not surprisingly, given Wilson's historically minded plays, Wilson's vision for the future concerns the past. He wants to see a new black community created in the South that emulates the closely knit, more economically self-sufficient black communities of the 1940s—such as the Hill—that Wilson knew and loved as a child and young adult. Wilson's play *King Hedley II* had its premiere in Pittsburgh in December 1999 and opened in Seattle on 13 March 2000. The main character in *King Hedley II*, the eighth play in Wilson's historical cycle, is an ex-con trying to rebuild his life in 1990s Pittsburgh. As part of his retrospective vision, the play depicts the decline of the black family and the prevalence of violence and guns in contemporary inner-city neighborhoods. While some critics may call this impulse to reject the present in favor of the past "sentimental separatism" or romantic illusion, Wilson sees nothing negative in revivifying a supportive separate black community or in attempting to reverse the mistake of leaving the South for a dream that did not come true. He also continues to support the idea of a diversified American theater, built on the common, cross-cultural ground of dramatic form.

Interviews:

Hilary Davies, "August Wilson—A New Voice for Black American Theater," *Christian Science Monitor,* 16 October 1984, pp. 29–30;

Alex Poinsett, "August Wilson: Hottest New Playwright," *Ebony,* 43 (November 1987): 68, 70, 72, 74;

Bill Moyers, "August Wilson," in his *A World of Ideas: Conversations with Thoughtful Men and Women about American Life Today and the Ideas Shaping Our Future,* edited by Betty Sue Flowers (New York: Doubleday, 1989), pp. 167–180;

Michael O'Neill, "Interview," in *American Playwrights Since 1945: A Guide to Scholarship, Criticism, and Performance,* edited by Philip C. Kolin (New York: Greenwood Press, 1989), pp. 175–177;

Sandra G. Shannon, "August Wilson Explains His Dramatic Vision: An Interview," in her *The Dramatic Vision of August Wilson* (Washington, D.C.: Howard University Press, 1995), pp. 201–237.

References:

Mary L. Bogumil, *Understanding August Wilson* (Columbia: University of South Carolina Press, 1998);

Robert Brustein, "Subsidized Separatism," *American Theatre,* 13 (October 1996): 27, 100–101;

Marilyn Elkins, ed. *August Wilson: A Casebook* (New York: Garland, 1994);

Samuel Freedman, "A Voice from the Streets," *New York Times Magazine,* 15 March 1987, pp. 36–50;

Henry Louis Gates Jr., "The Chitlin Circuit," *New Yorker* (3 February 1997): 44–55;

Joan Herrington, *I Ain't Sorry for Nothin' I Done: August Wilson's Process of Playwriting* (New York: Limelight Editions, 1998);

Alan Nadel, ed. *May All Your Fences Have Gates: Essays on the Drama of August Wilson* (Iowa City: University of Iowa Press, 1994);

Stephen Nunns, "Wilson, Brustein and the Press," *American Theatre,* 14, no. 3 (March 1997): 17–19;

Kim Pereira, *August Wilson and the African-American Odyssey* (Urbana: University of Illinois Press, 1995);

Yvonne Shafer, *August Wilson: A Research and Production Sourcebook* (Westport, Conn.: Greenwood Press, 1998);

Sandra G. Shannon, *The Dramatic Vision of August Wilson* (Washington, D.C.: Howard University Press, 1995);

Peter Wolfe, *August Wilson* (New York: Twayne, 1999).

Books for Further Reading

Adler, Thomas P. *American Drama, 1940–1960: A Critical History.* New York: Twayne, 1994.

Adler. *Mirror on the Stage: The Pulitzer Play as an Approach to American Drama.* West Lafayette, Ind.: Purdue University Press, 1987.

Baker, George Pierce. *Dramatic Technique.* Boston & New York: Houghton Mifflin, 1919.

Berkowitz, Gerald M. *American Drama of the Twentieth Century.* London & New York: Longman, 1992.

Berkowitz. *New Broadways: Theatre across America, 1950–1980.* Totowa, N.J.: Rowman & Littlefield, 1982.

Bigsby, Christopher. *Confrontation and Commitment: A Study of Contemporary American Drama, 1959–1966.* London: MacGibbon & Kee, 1967.

Bigsby. *A Critical Introduction to Twentieth-Century American Drama,* 3 volumes. Cambridge: Cambridge University Press, 1982–1985.

Bigsby. *Modern American Drama, 1945–1990.* Cambridge & New York: Cambridge University Press, 1992.

Bonin, Jane F. *Prize-Winning American Drama: A Bibliographical and Descriptive Guide.* Metuchen, N.J.: Scarecrow Press, 1973.

Coven, Brenda. *American Women Dramatists of the Twentieth Century: A Bibliography.* Metuchen, N.J.: Scarecrow Press, 1982.

Coven and Christine E. King. *Joseph Papp and the New York Shakespeare Festival: An Annotated Bibliography.* New York: Garland, 1987.

Craig, Evelyn Quita. *Black Drama of the Federal Theatre Era: Beyond the Formal Horizons.* Amherst: University of Massachusetts Press, 1980.

Debusscher, Gilbert, and Henry I. Schvey, eds. *New Essays On American Drama.* Amsterdam & Atlanta: Rodopi, 1989.

Demastes, William W. *American Playwrights, 1880–1945: A Research and Production Sourcebook.* Westport, Conn.: Greenwood Press, 1995.

Demastes. *Beyond Naturalism: A New Realism in American Theatre.* Westport, Conn.: Greenwood Press, 1988.

Demastes. *Theatre of Chaos: Beyond Absurdism, into Orderly Disorder.* Cambridge & New York: Cambridge University Press, 1998.

Demastes, ed., *Realism and the American Dramatic Tradition.* Tuscaloosa: University of Alabama Press, 1996.

DiGaetani, John L. *A Search for a Postmodern Theater: Interviews with Contemporary Playwrights*. New York: Greenwood Press, 1991.

Dukore, Bernard F. *American Dramatists, 1918–1945*. New York: Grove, 1984.

Esslin, Martin. *The Theatre of the Absurd,* third edition, revised. London & New York: Penguin, 1991.

Esslin, ed. *The Encyclopedia of World Theater*. New York: Scribners, 1977.

Fearnow, Mark. *The American Stage and the Great Depression: A Cultural History of the Grotesque*. Cambridge & New York: Cambridge University Press, 1997.

Flanagan, Hallie. *Arena: The History of the Federal Theatre*. New York: Duell, Sloan & Pearce, 1940.

Gassner, John. *Directions in Modern Theatre and Drama*. New York: Holt, Rinehart & Winston, 1965.

Gassner. *Dramatic Soundings: Evaluations and Retractions Culled from 30 Years of Dramatic Criticism,* edited by Glenn Loney. New York: Crown, 1968.

Gassner. *Theatre at the Crossroads: Plays and Playwrights of the Mid-Century American Stage*. New York: Holt, Rinehart & Winston, 1960.

Gassner. *The Theatre in Our Times: A Survey of the Men, Materials, and Movements in the Modern Theatre*. New York: Crown, 1954.

Harris, Andrew B. *Broadway Theatre*. London & New York: Routledge, 1994.

Henderson, Cathy, comp. *Twentieth-Century American Playwrights: Views of a Changing Culture*. Austin: Harry Ransom Humanities Research Center, University of Texas at Austin, 1994.

Herman, William. *Understanding Contemporary American Drama*. Columbia: University of South Carolina Press, 1987.

Kolin, Philip C., ed. *American Playwrights Since 1945: A Guide to Scholarship, Criticism, and Performance*. New York: Greenwood Press, 1989.

Laufe, Abe. *Anatomy of a Hit: Long Run Plays on Broadway From 1900 to the Present Day*. New York: Hawthorn Books, 1966.

Lawson, John Howard. *Theory and Technique of Playwriting*. New York: Putnam, 1936. Revised and enlarged as *Theory and Technique of Playwriting and Screenwriting*. New York: Putnam, 1949.

Miller, Arthur. *The Theater Essays of Arthur Miller,* edited by Robert A. Martin. New York: Viking, 1978.

Miller, Jordan Yale. *American Drama Between the Wars: A Critical History*. Boston: Twayne, 1991.

Murphy, Brenda. *American Realism and American Drama, 1880–1940*. Cambridge & New York: Cambridge University Press, 1987.

Murphy, ed. *The Cambridge Companion to American Women Playwrights*. Cambridge & New York: Cambridge University Press, 1999.

Olauson, Judith. *The American Woman Playwright: A View of Criticism and Characterization*. Troy, N.Y.: Whitston, 1981.

Rice, Elmer. *The Living Theater*. New York: Harper, 1959.

Robinson, Marc. *The Other American Drama*. Cambridge & New York: Cambridge University Press, 1994.

Roudané, Matthew Charles. *American Drama Since 1960: A Critical History*. New York: Twayne, 1996.

Sarlós, Robert Károly. *Jig Cook and the Provincetown Players: Theatre in Ferment*. Amherst: University of Massachusetts Press, 1982.

Scharine, Richard G. *From Class to Caste in American Drama: Political and Social Themes Since the 1930s*. New York: Greenwood Press, 1991.

Shank, Theodore. *American Alternative Theater*. New York: Grove, 1982.

Stanton, Sarah, and Martin Banham, eds. *Cambridge Paperback Guide to Theatre*. Cambridge & New York: Cambridge University Press, 1996.

Wilder, Thornton. *American Characteristics and Other Essays,* edited by Donald Gallup. New York: Harper & Row, 1979.

Williams, Mance. *Black Theatre in the 1960s and 1970s: A Historical-Critical Analysis of the Movement*. Westport, Conn.: Greenwood Press, 1985.

Wilmeth, Don B., and Tice L. Miller. *The Cambridge Guide to American Theatre*. Cambridge & New York: Cambridge University Press, 1996.

Wilmeth and Christopher Bigsby, eds. *The Cambridge History of American Theater,* 1 volume to date. Cambridge & New York: Cambridge University Press, 1998– .

Contributors

Phaedra D. Bell . . . . *Stanford University*
William C. Boles . . . . *Rollins College*
Robert E. Brooks . . . . *Eastern Illinois University*
Nancy L. Bunge . . . . *Michigan State University*
Adrienne E. Hacker Daniels . . . . *University of St. Thomas*
Marta J. Effinger . . . . *Northwestern University*
Kurt Eisen . . . . *Tennessee Technological University*
James Fisher . . . . *Wabash College*
Glenda Frank . . . . *New York, New York*
Leslie Goddard . . . . *Northwestern University*
Kathleen M. Gough . . . . *University of Maryland, College Park*
Barbara Lee Horn . . . . *St. John's University*
Lincoln Konkle . . . . *The College of New Jersey*
Jonathan Little . . . . *Alverno College*
Leah Lowe . . . . *Florida State University*
Deborah Martinson . . . . *Occidental College*
Carla J. McDonough . . . . *Eastern Illinois University*
Jude R. Meche . . . . *Texas A&M University*
Pamela Monaco . . . . *Hampton, Virginia*
Michael M. O'Hara . . . . *Ball State University*
Maria Papanikolaou . . . . *Texas A&M University*
Mary E. Papke . . . . *University of Tennessee, Knoxville*
Felicia S. Pattison . . . . *Sterling College*
Shannon Steen . . . . *Stanford University*
Amy Verner . . . . *Louisiana State University*
Alan Woods . . . . *Ohio State University*

Cumulative Index

Dictionary of Literary Biography, Volumes 1-228
Dictionary of Literary Biography Yearbook, 1980-1999
Dictionary of Literary Biography Documentary Series, Volumes 1-19

Cumulative Index

DLB before number: *Dictionary of Literary Biography,* Volumes 1-228
Y before number: *Dictionary of Literary Biography Yearbook,* 1980-1999
DS before number: *Dictionary of Literary Biography Documentary Series,* Volumes 1-19

B

H

McCorkle, Samuel Eusebius
1746-1811 . . . . .DLB-37

McCormick, Anne O'Hare 1880-1954 . . . .DLB-29

McCormick, Robert R. 1880-1955 . . . . . . .DLB-29

McCourt, Edward 1907-1972. . . . . .DLB-88

McCoy, Horace 1897-1955 . . . . .DLB-9

McCrae, John 1872-1918 . . . . .DLB-92

McCullagh, Joseph B. 1842-1896. . . . . . . .DLB-23

McCullers, Carson
1917-1967 . . . . DLB-2, 7, 173, 228

McCulloch, Thomas 1776-1843. . . . . .DLB-99

McDonald, Forrest 1927- DLB-17

McDonald, Walter 1934- DLB-105, DS-9

McDougall, Colin 1917-1984 . . . . .DLB-68

McDowell, Obolensky. DLB-46

McEwan, Ian 1948- DLB-14, 194

McFadden, David 1940- DLB-60

McFall, Frances Elizabeth Clarke
(see Grand, Sarah)

McFarlane, Leslie 1902-1977 . . . . .DLB-88

McFee, William 1881-1966 . . . . .DLB-153

McGahern, John 1934- DLB-14

McGee, Thomas D'Arcy 1825-1868 . . . . . .DLB-99

McGeehan, W. O. 1879-1933 . . . . . . .DLB-25, 171

McGill, Ralph 1898-1969. . . . . .DLB-29

McGinley, Phyllis 1905-1978 . . . . .DLB-11, 48

McGinniss, Joe 1942- DLB-185

McGirt, James E. 1874-1930 . . . . .DLB-50

McGlashan and Gill. DLB-106

McGough, Roger 1937- DLB-40

McGraw-Hill DLB-46

McGuane, Thomas 1939- DLB-2, 212; Y-80

McGuckian, Medbh 1950- DLB-40

McGuffey, William Holmes 1800-1873 . . . .DLB-42

McHenry, James 1785-1845. . . . . .DLB-202

McIlvanney, William 1936- DLB-14, 207

McIlwraith, Jean Newton 1859-1938 . . . . .DLB-92

McIntyre, James 1827-1906 . . . . .DLB-99

McIntyre, O. O. 1884-1938 . . . . .DLB-25

McKay, Claude 1889-1948 . . . .DLB-4, 45, 51, 117

The David McKay Company DLB-49

McKean, William V. 1820-1903 . . . . .DLB-23

McKenna, Stephen 1888-1967. . . . . .DLB-197

The McKenzie Trust Y-96

McKerrow, R. B. 1872-1940 . . . . .DLB-201

McKinley, Robin 1952- DLB-52

McLachlan, Alexander 1818-1896. . . . . . .DLB-99

McLaren, Floris Clark 1904-1978 . . . . . . .DLB-68

McLaverty, Michael 1907- DLB-15

McLean, John R. 1848-1916 . . . . .DLB-23

McLean, William L. 1852-1931. . . . . .DLB-25

McLennan, William 1856-1904 . . . . .DLB-92

McLoughlin Brothers. DLB-49

McLuhan, Marshall 1911-1980 . . . . .DLB-88

McMaster, John Bach 1852-1932. . . . . . . .DLB-47

McMurtry, Larry
1936- DLB-2, 143; Y-80, Y-87

McNally, Terrence 1939- DLB-7

McNeil, Florence 1937- DLB-60

McNeile, Herman Cyril 1888-1937 . . . . . .DLB-77

McNickle, D'Arcy 1904-1977. . . . . . DLB-175, 212

McPhee, John 1931- DLB-185

McPherson, James Alan 1943- DLB-38

McPherson, Sandra 1943- Y-86

McWhirter, George 1939- DLB-60

McWilliams, Carey 1905-1980 . . . . .DLB-137

Mda, Zakes 1948- DLB-225

Mead, L. T. 1844-1914 . . . . .DLB-141

Mead, Matthew 1924- DLB-40

Mead, Taylor ?- DLB-16

Meany, Tom 1903-1964 . . . . .DLB-171

Mechthild von Magdeburg
circa 1207-circa 1282 . . . . .DLB-138

Medieval French Drama DLB-208

Medieval Travel Diaries DLB-203

Medill, Joseph 1823-1899 . . . . .DLB-43

Medoff, Mark 1940- DLB-7

Meek, Alexander Beaufort 1814-1865 . . . . .DLB-3

Meeke, Mary ?-1816? DLB-116

Meinke, Peter 1932- DLB-5

Mejia Vallejo, Manuel 1923- DLB-113

Melanchthon, Philipp 1497-1560 . . . . . . .DLB-179

Melançon, Robert 1947- DLB-60

Mell, Max 1882-1971. . . . . .DLB-81, 124

Mellow, James R. 1926-1997 . . . . .DLB-111

Meltzer, David 1937- DLB-16

Meltzer, Milton 1915- DLB-61

Melville, Elizabeth, Lady Culross
circa 1585-1640 . . . . .DLB-172

Melville, Herman 1819-1891 . . . . .DLB-3, 74

Memoirs of Life and Literature (1920),
by W. H. Mallock [excerpt] DLB-57

Mena, María Cristina 1893-1965. . . .DLB-209, 221

Menander 342-341 B.C.-circa 292-291 B.C.
. . . . .DLB-176

Menantes (see Hunold, Christian Friedrich)

Mencke, Johann Burckhard
1674-1732 .DLB-168

Mencken, H. L.
1880-1956 . . . . DLB-11, 29, 63, 137, 222

Mencken and Nietzsche: An Unpublished
Excerpt from H. L. Mencken's *My Life
as Author and Editor*. Y-93

Mendelssohn, Moses 1729-1786. . . . . . . .DLB-97

Mendes, Catulle 1841-1909 . . . . .DLB-217

Méndez M., Miguel 1930- DLB-82

Mens Rea (or Something) Y-97

The Mercantile Library of New York Y-96

Mercer, Cecil William (see Yates, Dornford)

Mercer, David 1928-1980 . . . . .DLB-13

Mercer, John 1704-1768 . . . . .DLB-31

Meredith, George
1828-1909 . . . . DLB-18, 35, 57, 159

Meredith, Louisa Anne 1812-1895 . . . . . .DLB-166

Meredith, Owen (see Lytton, Edward Robert
Bulwer)

Meredith, William 1919- DLB-5

Mergerle, Johann Ulrich
(see Abraham ä Sancta Clara)

Mérimée, Prosper 1803-1870 . . . . . . .DLB-119, 192

Merivale, John Herman 1779-1844 . . . . . . .DLB-96

Meriwether, Louise 1923- DLB-33

Merlin Press. DLB-112

Merriam, Eve 1916-1992. . . . . .DLB-61

The Merriam Company DLB-49

Merrill, James 1926-1995. . . . . DLB-5, 165; Y-85

Merrill and Baker DLB-49

The Mershon Company DLB-49

Merton, Thomas 1915-1968 . . . . . . .DLB-48; Y-81

Merwin, W. S. 1927- DLB-5, 169

Messner, Julian [publishing house] DLB-46

Metcalf, J. [publishing house]. DLB-49

Metcalf, John 1938- DLB-60

The Methodist Book Concern. DLB-49

Methuen and Company. DLB-112

Meun, Jean de (see *Roman de la Rose*)

Mew, Charlotte 1869-1928 . . . . .DLB-19, 135

Mewshaw, Michael 1943- Y-80

Meyer, Conrad Ferdinand 1825-1898 . . . .DLB-129

Meyer, E. Y. 1946- DLB-75

Meyer, Eugene 1875-1959 . . . . .DLB-29

Meyer, Michael 1921- DLB-155

Meyers, Jeffrey 1939- DLB-111

Meynell, Alice 1847-1922 . . . . .DLB-19, 98

Meynell, Viola 1885-1956 . . . . .DLB-153

Meyrink, Gustav 1868-1932 . . . . .DLB-81

Mézières, Philipe de circa 1327-1405 . . . . .DLB-208

Michael, Ib 1945- DLB-214

Michael M. Rea and the Rea Award for the
Short Story Y-97

Michaëlis, Karen 1872-1950. . . . . .DLB-214

Michaels, Leonard 1933- DLB-130

Micheaux, Oscar 1884-1951 . . . . .DLB-50

Michel of Northgate, Dan
circa 1265-circa 1340. . . . . .DLB-146

Micheline, Jack 1929-1998. . . . . .DLB-16

Michener, James A. 1907?-1997. . . . . .DLB-6

Micklejohn, George
circa 1717-1818 . . . . .DLB-31

Middle English Literature:
An Introduction DLB-146

The Middle English Lyric DLB-146

Middle Hill Press. DLB-106

Middleton, Christopher 1926- DLB-40

Middleton, Richard 1882-1911 . . . . .DLB-156

Middleton, Stanley 1919- DLB-14

Middleton, Thomas 1580-1627 . . . . .DLB-58

N

Na Prous Boneta circa 1296-1328 . . . . DLB-208

Nabl, Franz 1883-1974 . . . . DLB-81

Nabokov, Vladimir
1899-1977 . . . . DLB-2; Y-80, Y-91; DS-3

Nabokov Festival at Cornell Y-83

The Vladimir Nabokov Archive
in the Berg Collection Y-91

Nádaši, Ladislav (see Jégé)

Naden, Constance 1858-1889 . . . . DLB-199

Nadezhdin, Nikolai Ivanovich
1804-1856 . . . . DLB-198

Naevius circa 265 B.C.-201 B.C. DLB-211

Nafis and Cornish. DLB-49

Nagai, Kafū 1879-1959 . . . . DLB-180

Naipaul, Shiva 1945-1985 . . . . DLB-157; Y-85

Naipaul, V. S. 1932- . . . DLB-125, 204, 207; Y-85

Nakagami Kenji 1946-1992 . . . . DLB-182

Nakano-in Masatada no Musume (see Nijō, Lady)

Nałkowska, Zofia 1884-1954 . . . . DLB-215

Nancrede, Joseph [publishing house] DLB-49

Naranjo, Carmen 1930- DLB-145

Narezhny, Vasilii Trofimovich
1780-1825. . . . . DLB-198

Narrache, Jean 1893-1970. . . . . DLB-92

Nasby, Petroleum Vesuvius (see Locke, David Ross)

Nash, Ogden 1902-1971 . . . . DLB-11

Nash, Eveleigh [publishing house] DLB-112

Nashe, Thomas 1567-1601? DLB-167

Nast, Conde 1873-1942 . . . . DLB-91

Nast, Thomas 1840-1902 . . . . DLB-188

Nastasijević, Momčilo 1894-1938 . . . . DLB-147

Nathan, George Jean 1882-1958 . . . . DLB-137

Nathan, Robert 1894-1985 . . . . DLB-9

The National Jewish Book Awards Y-85

The National Theatre and the Royal
Shakespeare Company: The
National Companies. DLB-13

Natsume, Sōseki 1867-1916 . . . . DLB-180

Naughton, Bill 1910- DLB-13

Navarro, Joe 1953- DLB-209

Naylor, Gloria 1950- DLB-173

Nazor, Vladimir 1876-1949. . . . . DLB-147

Ndebele, Njabulo 1948- DLB-157

Neagoe, Peter 1881-1960 . . . . DLB-4

Neal, John 1793-1876 . . . . DLB-1, 59

Neal, Joseph C. 1807-1847 . . . . DLB-11

Neal, Larry 1937-1981 . . . . DLB-38

The Neale Publishing Company DLB-49

Nebel, Frederick 1903-1967 . . . . DLB-226

Neely, F. Tennyson [publishing house]. . . . DLB-49

Negoiţescu, Ion 1921-1993 . . . . DLB-220

Negri, Ada 1870-1945 . . . . DLB-114

"The Negro as a Writer," by
G. M. McClellan DLB-50

"Negro Poets and Their Poetry," by
Wallace Thurman DLB-50

Neidhart von Reuental
circa 1185-circa 1240 . . . . DLB-138

Neihardt, John G. 1881-1973 . . . . DLB-9, 54

Neledinsky-Meletsky, Iurii Aleksandrovich
1752-1828. . . . . DLB-150

Nelligan, Emile 1879-1941 . . . . DLB-92

Nelson, Alice Moore Dunbar 1875-1935 . . DLB-50

Nelson, Thomas, and Sons [U.S.] DLB-49

Nelson, Thomas, and Sons [U.K.] DLB-106

Nelson, William 1908-1978 . . . . DLB-103

Nelson, William Rockhill 1841-1915 . . . . DLB-23

Nemerov, Howard 1920-1991 . . . . DLB-5, 6; Y-83

Nepos circa 100 B.C.-post 27 B.C. DLB-211

Nėris, Salomėja 1904-1945 . . . . DLB-220

Nerval, Gerard de 1808-1855 . . . . DLB-217

Nesbit, E. 1858-1924 . . . . DLB-141, 153, 178

Ness, Evaline 1911-1986. . . . . DLB-61

Nestroy, Johann 1801-1862 . . . . DLB-133

Neukirch, Benjamin 1655-1729. . . . . DLB-168

Neugeboren, Jay 1938- DLB-28

Neumann, Alfred 1895-1952 . . . . DLB-56

Neumann, Ferenc (see Molnár, Ferenc)

Neumark, Georg 1621-1681 . . . . DLB-164

Neumeister, Erdmann 1671-1756 . . . . . . DLB-168

Nevins, Allan 1890-1971 . . . . DLB-17; DS-17

Nevinson, Henry Woodd 1856-1941 . . . . DLB-135

The New American Library DLB-46

New Approaches to Biography: Challenges
from Critical Theory, USC Conference
on Literary Studies, 1990. . . . . Y-90

New Directions Publishing
Corporation DLB-46

A New Edition of *Huck Finn* Y-85

New Forces at Work in the American Theatre:
1915-1925 . . . . DLB-7

New Literary Periodicals:
A Report for 1987 . . . . Y-87

New Literary Periodicals:
A Report for 1988 . . . . Y-88

New Literary Periodicals:
A Report for 1989 . . . . Y-89

New Literary Periodicals:
A Report for 1990 . . . . Y-90

New Literary Periodicals:
A Report for 1991 . . . . Y-91

New Literary Periodicals:
A Report for 1992 . . . . Y-92

New Literary Periodicals:
A Report for 1993 . . . . Y-93

The New Monthly Magazine
1814-1884 . . . . DLB-110

The New Ulysses Y-84

The New Variorum Shakespeare Y-85

A New Voice: The Center for the Book's First
Five Years Y-83

The New Wave [Science Fiction] DLB-8

New York City Bookshops in the 1930s and 1940s:
The Recollections of Walter Goldwater . . . Y-93

Newbery, John [publishing house] DLB-154

Newbolt, Henry 1862-1938 . . . . DLB-19

Newbound, Bernard Slade (see Slade, Bernard)

Newby, Eric 1919- DLB-204

Newby, P. H. 1918- DLB-15

Newby, Thomas Cautley
[publishing house] DLB-106

Newcomb, Charles King 1820-1894. . . DLB-1, 223

Newell, Peter 1862-1924. . . . . DLB-42

Newell, Robert Henry 1836-1901 . . . . . . DLB-11

Newhouse, Samuel I. 1895-1979. . . . . DLB-127

Newman, Cecil Earl 1903-1976 . . . . DLB-127

Newman, David (see Benton, Robert)

Newman, Frances 1883-1928 . . . . Y-80

Newman, Francis William 1805-1897 . . . . DLB-190

Newman, John Henry
1801-1890 . . . . DLB-18, 32, 55

Newman, Mark [publishing house] DLB-49

Newnes, George, Limited DLB-112

Newsome, Effie Lee 1885-1979 . . . . DLB-76

Newspaper Syndication of American
Humor DLB-11

Newton, A. Edward 1864-1940 . . . . DLB-140

Nexø, Martin Andersen 1869-1954 . . . . . DLB-214

Nezval, Vítěslav 1900-1958 . . . . DLB-215

Németh, László 1901-1975 . . . . DLB-215

Ngugi wa Thiong'o 1938- DLB-125

Niatum, Duane 1938- DLB-175

The *Nibelungenlied* and the *Klage*
circa 1200. . . . . DLB-138

Nichol, B. P. 1944- DLB-53

Nicholas of Cusa 1401-1464 . . . . DLB-115

Nichols, Beverly 1898-1983 . . . . DLB-191

Nichols, Dudley 1895-1960 . . . . DLB-26

Nichols, Grace 1950- DLB-157

Nichols, John 1940- Y-82

Nichols, Mary Sargeant (Neal) Gove
1810-1884 . . . . DLB-1

Nichols, Peter 1927- DLB-13

Nichols, Roy F. 1896-1973 . . . . DLB-17

Nichols, Ruth 1948- DLB-60

Nicholson, Edward Williams Byron
1849-1912 . . . . DLB-184

Nicholson, Norman 1914- DLB-27

Nicholson, William 1872-1949 . . . . DLB-141

Ní Chuilleanáin, Eiléan 1942- DLB-40

Nicol, Eric 1919- DLB-68

Nicolai, Friedrich 1733-1811 . . . . DLB-97

Nicolas de Clamanges circa 1363-1437 . . . DLB-208

Nicolay, John G. 1832-1901 and
Hay, John 1838-1905 . . . . DLB-47

Nicolson, Harold 1886-1968 . . . . . . DLB-100, 149

Nicolson, Nigel 1917- DLB-155

Niebuhr, Reinhold 1892-1971 . . . . . . DLB-17; DS-17

Niedecker, Lorine 1903-1970 . . . . DLB-48

Nieman, Lucius W. 1857-1935 . . . . DLB-25

Z